CHARTERED INSTITUTE FOR SECURITIES & INVESTMENT

Level 4 Qualification

Investment Management

Edition 2, August 2016

This learning manual relates to syllabus version 2.0 and will cover examinations from **21 Oct 2016 to 20 February 2022**

GW00500814

APPROVED WORKBOOK

Welcome to the Chartered Institute for Securities & Investment's Investment Management study material.

This workbook has been written to prepare you for the Chartered Institute for Securities & Investment's Investment Management examination.

Published by:
Chartered Institute for Securities & Investment
© Chartered Institute for Securities & Investment 2016
20 Fenchurch Street
London
EC3M 3BY
Tel: +44 20 7645 0600
Fax: +44 20 7645 0601

Email: customersupport@cisi.org
www.cisi.org/qualifications

Author:
Kevin Petley, MSCI

Reviewers:
Jonathan Beckett, Chartered MCSI
Alan Kinna, Chartered FCSI

A learning map, which contains the full syllabus, appears at the end of this manual. The syllabus can also be viewed on cisi.org and is also available by contacting the Customer Support Centre on +44 20 7645 0777. Please note that the examination is based upon the syllabus. Candidates are reminded to check the Candidate Update area details (cisi.org/candidateupdate) on a regular basis for updates as a result of industry change(s) that could affect their examination.

The questions contained in this manual are designed as an aid to revision of different areas of the syllabus and to help you consolidate your learning chapter by chapter.

Learning manual version: 2.2 (August 2016)

Learning and Professional Development with the CISI

The Chartered Institute for Securities & Investment is the leading professional body for those who work in, or aspire to work in, the investment sector, and we are passionately committed to enhancing knowledge, skills and integrity – the three pillars of professionalism at the heart of our Chartered body.

CISI examinations are used extensively by firms to meet the requirements of government regulators. Besides the regulators in the UK, where the CISI head office is based, CISI examinations are recognised by a wide range of governments and their regulators, from Singapore to Dubai and the US. Around 50,000 examinations are taken each year, and it is compulsory for candidates to use CISI learning manuals to prepare for CISI examinations so that they have the best chance of success. Our learning manuals are normally revised every year by experts who themselves work in the industry and also by our Accredited Training Partners who offer training and elearning to help prepare candidates for the examinations. Information for candidates is also posted on a special area of our website: cisi.org/candidateupdate.

This learning manual not only provides a thorough preparation for the examination it refers to, it is also a valuable desktop reference for practitioners, and studying from it counts towards your Continuing Professional Development (CPD). Mock examination papers, for most of our titles, will be made available on our website, as an additional revision tool.

CISI examination candidates are automatically registered, without additional charge, as student members for one year (should they not be members of the CISI already), and this enables you to use a vast range of online resources, including CISI TV, free of any additional charge. The CISI has more than 40,000 members, and nearly half of them have already completed relevant qualifications and transferred to a core membership grade. You will find more information about the next steps for this at the end of this manual.

With best wishes for your studies.

It is estimated that this manual will require approximately 140 hours of study time.

Chapter One
Economics

This syllabus area will provide approximately 5 of the 80 examination questions

An understanding of economics is essential to investment management and involves the study of how individuals, firms and countries behave in response to the scarcity of resources to meet their needs.

Scarcity refers to the natural limitations on the availability of resources to meet needs. Because of this scarcity individuals, firms and countries have to make decisions about which goods and services they can buy and which they must forgo.

So, because of scarcity, people and economies must make decisions over how to allocate their resources. Economics, in turn, aims to study why we make these decisions and how we allocate our resources most efficiently.

The study of economics can be divided into two broad categories:

- **Microeconomics** – as its name suggests, is the smaller-picture view of the economy: that is, the study of the decisions made by individuals and firms in a particular market.
- **Macroeconomics** – takes the bigger picture view, seeking to explain how, by aggregating the resulting impact of these decisions on individual markets, variables such as national income, employment and inflation are determined.

1. Microeconomic Theory

Microeconomics views the economy from the standpoint of how individuals and firms allocate their limited resources, in order to maximise an individual's financial position or the production, profitability and growth of a firm. It seeks to analyse certain aspects of human behaviour, in order to show how individuals and firms respond to changes in price and why they demand what they do at particular price levels.

The study of micro-economics is fundamental to investment management, as an evaluation of a company and its securities requires an understanding of what drives the behaviours of firms, industries and consumers and the forces at work that affect the costs and revenues of firms.

1.1 Interaction of Demand and Supply

Learning Objective

1.1.1 Understand and be able to assess how price is determined and the interaction of supply and demand: supply curve; demand curve; reasons for shifts in curves; elasticities of demand and supply; change in price; change in demand

Price and output in the free market are determined by the interaction of the demand for goods and services from individuals and the supply of production from firms.

This can be readily understood by considering that you only have limited resources available to spend and have to make choices as to where you spend those resources. For an individual these scarce resources include time, money and skills.

At a national level the same principle applies and scarce resources include natural resources, land, labour, capital and technology.

Economics seeks to understand how individuals and economies make decisions about how they allocate these resources and how they can be allocated most efficiently.

The relationship between supply and demand underlies how resources are allocated, and the economic theories of demand and supply seek to explain how these resources are allocated in the most efficient manner. This relationship provides important background to understanding how prices are determined in competitive markets.

1.1.1 The Demand Curve

Demand refers to the quantity of a product that people are prepared to buy at any given price. The relationship between price and the quantity demanded is known as the **demand relationship**.

Terminology

- **Demand**
  - Is the quantity of a good or service that consumers are willing and able to buy at a given price in a given time period.
  - Each of us has an individual demand for particular goods and services and the level of demand at each market price reflects the value that consumers place on a product and their expected satisfaction gained from purchase and consumption.
- **Market demand**
  - Market demand is the sum of the individual demand for a product from each consumer in the market.
  - If more people enter the market and they have the ability to pay for items on sale, then demand at each price level will rise.
- **Effective demand**
  - A consumer's desire to buy a product is only effective when backed up by an ability to pay for it and so they must have sufficient purchasing power to have any effect on the market and allocation of scarce resources.
  - For example, what price are you prepared to spend to watch Premiership soccer on a pay-per-view basis?
- **Latent demand**
  - Is potential demand for a product and exists when there is willingness among consumers to buy a good or service, but they lack the purchasing power to be able to afford the product.
  - Is affected by advertising where the producer is seeking to influence consumer tastes and preferences.
- **Derived demand**
  - The demand for a product might be strongly linked to the demand for a related product.
  - For example, the demand for steel is strongly linked to the demand for new vehicles and other manufactured products; that when an economy goes into a downturn or recession, the demand for steel will decline as the capacity to purchase new vehicles and other manufactured products reduces.

The law of demand states that, if all other factors remain equal, then the higher the price of a product, the less will be demanded. The rationale behind this is that people will buy less of a product as the price rises, as it will force them to forgo the consumption of something else.

The Law of Demand

Other factors remaining constant (*ceteris paribus*), there is an inverse relationship between the price of a good and demand. As prices fall, we see an expansion of demand. If price rises, there will be a contraction of demand.

The *ceteris paribus* assumption is that many factors can be said to affect demand. Economists assume most factors are held constant (ie, do not change) except one – the price of the product itself.

The diagram below shows the demand curve, which represents the quantity of a particular good that consumers will buy at a given price. Although it is referred to as a demand curve, you will see that it is depicted as a negatively sloped straight line. In practice, of course, it is rarely so but it does illustrate the economic relationship between the two.

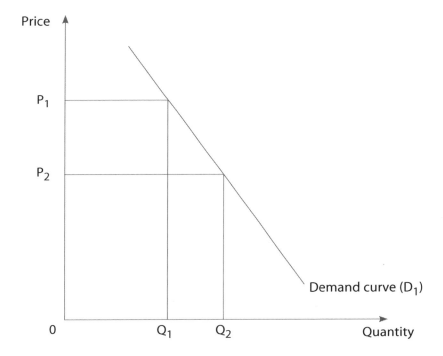

Figure 1: The Demand Curve

The demand curve depicts the inverse relationship between the price of a good and the amount demanded. The point where price (P_1) and quantity (Q_1) intersect on the curve represents the demand for the product. The point where P_2 and Q_2 intersect illustrates that more of the product will be demanded if the price is lower. The converse is also true if the price rises.

There are two reasons why more is demanded as price falls:

- **The Income Effect** – there is an income effect when the price of a good falls, because the consumer can maintain current consumption for less expenditure. Providing that the good is normal, some of the resulting increase in real income is used by consumers to buy more of this product.
- **The Substitution Effect** – there is also a substitution effect when the price of a good falls, because the product is now relatively cheaper than an alternative item and so some consumers switch their spending to this product.

A change in the price of a good, then, generates movement along the demand curve. A fall in the price of a good causes an expansion of demand; a rise in price causes a contraction of demand.

Many other factors can affect total demand and when these change, the demand curve can shift. Changes in demand curve result in a shift in the demand curve to the right or left as a greater or lesser quantity of the good is demanded.

This is shown in the diagram below.

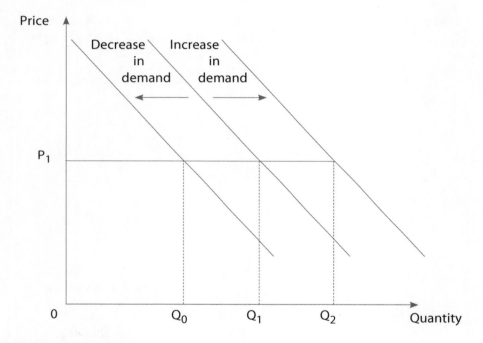

Figure 2: Shifts in the Demand Curve

Such parallel shifts can result from:

- **The price of other goods changing** – the direction of the shift depends on whether these other goods are substitutes that may be purchased instead, or complementary goods that are typically purchased in conjunction with a particular product.
- **Growth in consumers' income** – a rise in income should result in increased demand for the good at each price level, ie, in the demand curve shifting to the right, assuming the good is a normal one. This is true of all luxury goods and some day-to-day necessities. However, if the good is an inferior one, the demand curve will shift to the left, in response to consumers moving away from this product to another more desirable, or more innovative, product.

- **Changing consumer tastes** – this can also result in the demand curve shifting to either the left or right, depending on whether or not the product is currently fashionable.

Shifts in the demand curve can also occur as a result of speculative activity. Buyers of the goods are attempting to benefit from the potential rise in market price and so generate a capital profit. So, changes in the price of a good or service cause a movement along the demand curve. Change in any factor other than price causes the demand curve to shift to the left or right.

1.1.2 The Supply Curve

Supply refers to the amount of a good that producers are willing to supply when receiving a certain price. In other words, the level of production they are prepared to undertake to provide a supply of goods at any given price.

The basic law of supply is that as the price of a commodity rises, so producers expand their supply onto the market. The supply curve shows a relationship between price and the quantity a firm is willing and able to sell.

This supply relationship is demonstrated in the supply curve which is shown below.

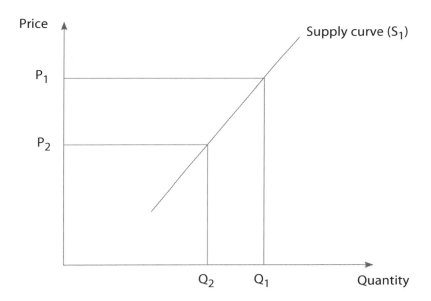

Figure 3: The Supply Curve

As before, the supply curve is drawn assuming that all factors influencing supply are being held constant except price. Movement along the supply curve results in a greater quantity being supplied, the higher the price rises.

The supply relationship shows an upward slope, reflecting that the higher the price at which the producer can sell a product, the more they will supply, as selling at a higher price will generate increased revenues.

The Law of Supply

There are three main reasons why supply curves for most products are drawn as sloping upwards from left to right, giving a positive relationship between the market price and quantity supplied:

- **The profit motive** – when the market price rises it becomes more profitable for businesses to increase their output. Higher prices send signals to firms that they can increase their profits by satisfying demand in the market.
- **Production and costs** – when output expands, a firm's production costs rise, therefore a higher price is needed to justify the extra output and cover these extra costs of production.
- **New entrants coming into the market** – higher prices may create an incentive for other businesses to enter the market, leading to an increase in supply.

However, once again, a change in anything other than the price of the good could result in the supply curve shifting to either the left or right.

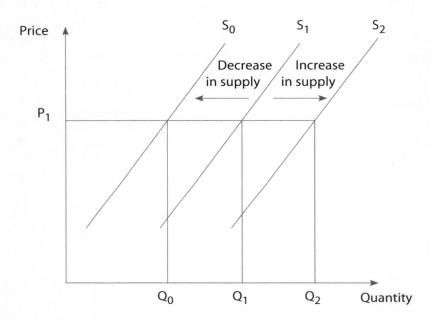

Figure 4: Shifts in the Supply Curve

Changes in supply that cause a shift in the supply curve can be due to a myriad of reasons including:

- **Production costs**
  - An increase in the cost of production resulting from, say, rising resource prices may see the supply curve shift to the left.
  - Lower costs of production resulting from, say, lower resource prices may see the supply curve shift to the right.
- **Changes in production technology**
  - A more efficient production process resulting from utilising new production technology, or increased competition from new firms entering the industry, will shift the curve to the right.
  - Production technologies can change quickly and, in industries where technological change is rapid, you can see increases in supply and lower prices for the consumer. This was seen, for example, in the response of mobile telephone manufacturers to the success of the iphone[*].

- **Exchange rates**
  - Changes in the exchange rate may make imported goods cheaper and so reduce the cost of production. For example, a manufacturer might benefit from a stronger exchange rate by a reduction in the cost of the resources it uses and pass some of these savings in lower prices in order to generate greater demand.
  - Conversely, a fall in the exchange rate will make the prices of imported raw materials, components and goods more expensive and could lead to a reduction in supply.
- **Government taxes**
  - A tax increase raises the costs of production and could see the supply curve shift to the left.
  - A tax decrease or subsidy encourages an increase in supply because the subsidy lowers the firm's costs of production.
- **Climate**
  - Climatic conditions can have a great influence on the supply of certain commodities such as fruit and vegetables. Favourable weather will produce a bumper harvest and will increase supply. Unfavourable weather conditions will lead to a poorer harvest, lower yields and therefore a decrease in supply.
- **The profitability of a substitute product**
  - If a firm has a choice of which goods it produces, a change in profitability may affect supply. For example, a farmer may choose to grow wheat rather than barley if there is a greater profit.
- **Number of producers**
  - The number of businesses in an industry affects market supply. When new businesses enter a market, supply increases cause downward pressure on price.

Unlike the demand curve, however, the supply relationship is heavily influenced by time, as producers cannot react quickly to changes in demand or price.

1.1.3   Equilibrium

When you bring the forces of demand and supply together you encounter the concept of the determination of equilibrium prices.

The market price for a good or service is set by the interaction of demand and supply which will determine the quantity of the good and the price at which it is to be supplied. This result is known as **reaching a state of equilibrium**.

The equilibrium price is the price at which the quantity demanded by consumers and the quantity that firms are willing to supply is the same.

Equilibrium is the point at which demand and supply are equal. The following diagram shows the point at which demand and supply are equal, with output Q_1 being produced at price P_1. P_1 is known as the market clearing price.

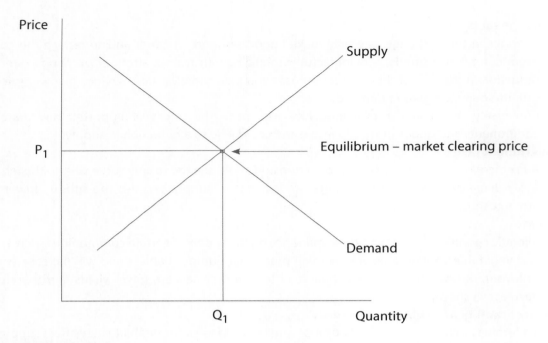

Figure 5a: Equilibrium

The demand and supply of a good can be listed in a table showing the quantities demanded in total by consumers and the amount offered for sale by producers at all possible prices.

Price per unit	Quantity demanded (thousands)	Quantity supplied (thousands)
0	500	0
10	400	100
20	300	200
25	250	250
30	200	300
40	100	400
50	0	500

From this you can see:

- The equilibrium price is 25 where demand and supply are equal at 250,000.
- At prices above 25 there is an excess amount supplied over that demanded.
- At prices below 25 the opposite is true and demand outstrips supply.

We can see the impact of this on the supply curve and the equilibrium price in the following diagram.

If, for example, output Q_2 had been produced rather than Q_1, insufficient demand for these goods at price P_2 would have resulted in the building up of surplus stocks. Production would have contracted until the price of these unsold stocks had been forced down to the market clearing price of P_1.

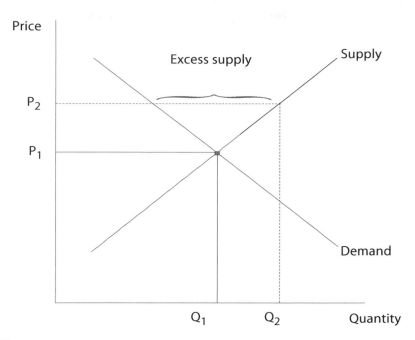

Figure 5b: Equilibrium

Changes in equilibrium prices and quantities, however, do not happen quickly. So, for example, a shift to the right in the demand curve may lead to a short-term rise in prices due to a shortage of goods. The higher price then acts as an incentive for suppliers to raise their output, causing a movement up the short term supply curve towards the new equilibrium point.

Whether the goods in question are doughnuts or derivatives, when a market is allowed to operate freely, the price mechanism always brings supply and demand back into equilibrium. This is known as **Say's Law**: supply creates its own demand. You need look no further than your local fruit and vegetable market to see the free market at its most efficient, with transparent pricing reflecting supply and demand.

1.1.4   Elasticity of Demand

The demand curve we have looked at so far suggests that demand will change in proportion to changes in the price.

In practice, this is not the case as some goods are more essential to a consumer than others and so demand can be insensitive to price changes, as consumers will still need to buy the product. Conversely, other goods are less of a necessity and an increase in price will deter consumers from buying.

Economics seeks to explain this relationship by referring to the degree with which a demand or supply curve reacts to a change in price as the curve's **elasticity**.

A product is said to be highly elastic if a slight change in price leads to a sharp change in the quantity demanded or supplied, such as with luxury goods. At the other end of the spectrum, a product is said to be inelastic if changes in price bring about only modest changes in the quantity demanded or supplied as with products that are a necessity such as food and heating.

There are three types of elasticity that we need to consider: **price**, **income** and **cross elasticity of demand**.

Price Elasticity of Demand (PED)

One of the most important factors affecting the demand for a good is price. The price elasticity of demand (PED) quantifies the extent to which the demand for a particular good changes in proportion to small changes in its price.

Price elasticity of demand is calculated as follows:
$$\frac{\% \text{ change in quantity}}{\% \text{ change in price}}$$

By knowing the PED of a product, firms are able to calculate the impact that a small price rise or price reduction will have on the total revenue generated by the product.

Example

Using simple numbers, let us assume that a gadget is priced at £2 and 1,000 units are sold. If, however, the price is reduced to £1.90 per unit, 1,200 units are sold.

A 5% reduction in price, therefore, results in a 20% increase in the volume of sales, thereby increasing total sales revenue from £2,000 (1,000 units x £2) to £2,280 (1,200 units x £1.90).

Its PED is therefore:

$$\frac{(+20\%)}{(-5\%)} = -4$$

The PED of −4 tells us that for a 5% reduction in price, the quantity demanded will increase at four times the rate.

The reason for the PED having a negative value is that, as we have seen, when price falls, so the quantity of a normal good demanded rises and vice versa.

Since changes in price and quantity nearly always move in opposite directions, economists usually do not bother to put in the minus sign. Instead, we are concerned just with the co-efficient or multiplication factor.

- **PED = 0**
  - Demand is said to be perfectly inelastic.
  - This means that demand does not change at all when the price changes and so the demand curve will be vertical.

- **PED is between 0 and 1**
  - In this case, the percentage change in demand is smaller than the percentage change in price and demand is described as inelastic.
  - Producers know that the change in demand will be proportionately smaller than the percentage change in price.

- **PED = 1**
  - In this case, the percentage change in demand is exactly the same as the percentage change in price.
  - Demand is said to be elastic as a 15% rise in price leads to a 15% contraction in demand, leaving total spending the same at each price level.

- **PED > 1**
  - Demand is elastic as it responds more than proportionately to a change in price
  - For example a 20% increase in the price of a good might lead to a 30% drop in demand. The price elasticity of demand for this price change is −1.5.

Luxury goods tend to be in relatively elastic demand, whilst necessities follow a pattern of inelastic demand.

This can be seen by looking at demand curves with different price elasticity of demand.

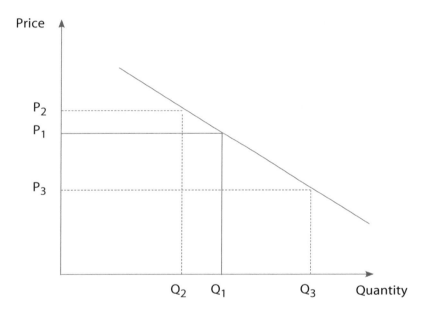

Figure 6: Relatively Elastic Demand

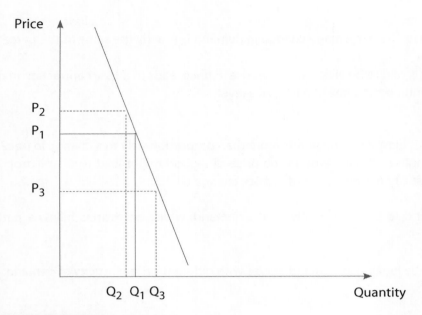

Figure 7: Relatively Inelastic Demand

Demand curves are, however, rarely elastic or inelastic across their entire length. As you move down the demand curve, successive price decreases result in a diminishing increase in sales and slow the rate at which total revenue increases. Total revenue is maximised at the point of unit elasticity, as demonstrated below.

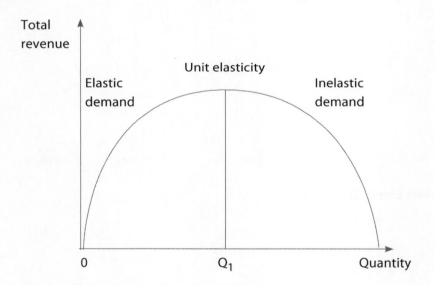

Figure 8: Price Elasticity of Demand and Total Revenue

This can be more clearly seen in the revenue pattern below.

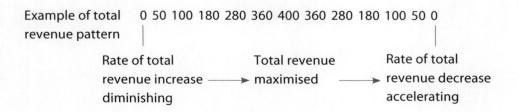

There are numerous factors that determine the PED for a good. These include:

- Substitutes – in the short run, consumers may find it difficult to adjust their behaviour or spending patterns in response to a price rise, unless there is a viable alternative. A rise in the cost of peak-time train travel faced by city commuters illustrates this. However, if over time substitutes become available, the demand for this good or service becomes increasingly price elastic. The availability of choice alters spending patterns.
- The percentage of an individual's total income, or budget, devoted to the good – goods that account for a small percentage of one's income are usually price inelastic.
- Habit-forming goods – goods that can become addictive, such as tobacco, are also price inelastic.

The relationship between price elasticity of demand and a firm's total revenue is a very important one. Firms can use price elasticity of demand (PED) estimates to predict:

- The effect of a change in price on the total revenue and expenditure on a product.
- The likely price volatility in a market following unexpected changes in supply.
- The effect of a change in an indirect tax on price and quantity demanded and also whether the business is able to pass on some or all of the tax onto the consumer.
- The extent to which the firm can use price discrimination by charging different prices for the same product at different times or in different markets. Rail companies, for instance, meet inelastic demand for peak services with higher prices than for elastic off-peak travel. Larger multi-branded motor vehicle manufacturers also operate discriminatory pricing through their various marques.

We will come back to this point when looking at profit maximisation in Section 1.2.1.

Cross Elasticity of Demand (XED)

Very often, a change in the price of one product leads to a change in the demand for another. Economists call this the cross-price effect or the cross elasticity of demand (XED).

XED measures the change in quantity demanded against the change in price of either a substitute or complementary good.

- Substitute goods are ones that can be bought instead of another as there is no perceived difference. An example is washing powder or brands of cereal.
- Complementary goods are where the demand for one product leads to an increase in the demand for another. An increase in the demand for smartphones and tablets has lead to an increased demand for protective covers.

Cross elasticity of demand is calculated as follows:

$$\frac{\% \text{ change in quantity demanded}}{\% \text{ change in price of substitute/complementary good}}$$

The stronger the relationship between two products, the higher the co-efficient of cross-price elasticity of demand:

- **Substitute goods have a positive XED**
  - ○ For example, if the price of cars rises, then the demand for alternative methods of travel will increase.
- **Complementary goods have a negative XED**
  - ○ So, for example, if the price of diesel and petrol increases then the demand for cars will fall.
  - ○ If the price of ipads® falls then the demand for protective covers rises.
  - ○ Unrelated products have a zero cross elasticity.

Income Elasticity of Demand (YED)

As consumer's real incomes change, so will the demand for certain products.

Income elasticity of demand (YED) is used to measure this and the results give an indication of how the product is perceived by consumers. It also illustrates the extent to which changes in economic growth affect the level and pattern of demand for goods and services.

YED measures the sensitivity of demand to consumers' disposable income and shows the percentage change in the quantity demanded, given a small change in income.

Income elasticity of demand is calculated by: $\dfrac{\text{\% change in quantity}}{\text{\% change in income}}$

Rising income results in increased demand for **normal goods**:

- All normal goods have a positive YED – this is represented by a parallel shift to the right in the demand curve.
- Normal necessities have an income elasticity of demand of between 0 and +1.
  - ○ Demand rises (or falls) proportionately less than income. For example, if income increases by 10% the demand for fresh fruit might increase by only 4% then the income elasticity is +0.4.
- Luxuries have an income elasticity of demand >+1.
  - ○ By definition, luxury goods have a YED of greater than one, in that, as consumers' income increases, so the proportion of total income spent on luxury items increases at a greater rate.
  - ○ Demand rises (or falls) proportionately more than a change in income. For example a 10% increase in income might lead to a 15% rise in the demand for restaurant meals, giving an income elasticity of demand in of +2.0.

Some necessities of life, however, have negative values:

- Those with negative values are inferior goods, that is, goods that account for a smaller percentage of an individual's budget as their income rises.
- Inferior goods have a negative income elasticity of demand – demand falls as income rises.
- Typically, inferior goods or services tend to be products where there are superior goods available if the consumer has the money to be able to buy it. Examples include own label foods in supermarkets.
- Product innovation often distinguishes a normal good from an inferior good.

Again, knowing the YED for a particular good or service helps firms plan for future production and assists government in deciding how to raise revenue from applying indirect (or expenditure) taxes, such as VAT, given forecasts of income growth.

1.1.5   Elasticity of Supply

Price elasticity of supply measures the relationship between the change in the quantity of a good that is supplied and a change in price.

Price elasticity of demand is calculated by: $\dfrac{\% \text{ change in quantity}}{\% \text{ change in price}}$

The value of elasticity of supply is positive because an increase in price is likely to increase the quantity supplied to the market and vice versa.

- When supply is perfectly inelastic, a shift in the demand curve has no effect on the equilibrium quantity supplied onto the market, such as the supply of tickets for sports or musical venues.
- When supply is perfectly elastic a firm can supply any amount at the same price. This occurs when the firm can supply at a constant cost per unit and has no capacity limits to its production. A change in demand alters the equilibrium quantity but not the market clearing price.
- When supply is relatively inelastic a change in demand affects the price more than the quantity supplied.
- When supply is relatively elastic, the reverse is the case. A change in demand can be met without a change in market price.

The elasticity of supply depends on the following factors:

- **Spare capacity** – if a firm has plenty of spare capacity, it should be able to increase output quite quickly without a rise in costs and therefore supply will be elastic.
- **Level of stocks or inventories** – if stocks of raw materials, components and finished products are high then the firm is able to respond to a change in demand quickly, by supplying these stocks onto the market – supply will be elastic.
- **Ease of factor substitution** – can manufacturers or producers switch their production processes quickly and easily to meet the high demand for the product?

Elasticity of supply is therefore determined by the ease with which firms can access factors of production and use them flexibly.

Over a short time period, firms may be able to increase output only slightly in response to an increase in prices. Over a longer period of time, the level of production can be adjusted greatly as production processes can be altered, additional workers can be hired and more plants can be built. Therefore, elasticity of supply is expected to be greater over longer periods of time.

Economic Bubbles

An economic bubble (also known as a market or price bubble) in an asset market involves a quickly created spike in asset prices within an asset type/class – that is often based on speculation.

A speculative bubble is usually caused by inflated expectations of future growth. Investors' attitudes and their perception of risk can have a high propensity for irrationality, with traditional economic considerations and fundamentals becoming relatively unimportant in assessing new information.

In a highly speculative environment, the level of investor optimism can drive trading volumes higher and, with a herding mentality, more and more investors succumb to the heightened expectation and thus demand and prices rise beyond what a more usual conservative, objective analysis of true value would suggest.

As the bubble starts to wane, prices and volume return to normal levels. During this relatively fast-paced period, the opposite of the bubble occurs and a period of sharp price decline is witnessed and involves a similar herding mentality: selling outweighs buying, as investors panic and dispose of their investments. Successful timing in entering and exiting a bubble scenario can yield large gains for investors, although those who enter quite late in the cycle often leave nursing large losses.

A good example is the dot-com bubble between 1997 and 2000 when equity values rose quickly, fuelled by the growth of the internet sector and related support services. The year 1995 saw a major advance in the number of internet users, resulting in a vast amount of internet-based start-up companies, later labelled as dot-coms, as com became the usual tag in US internet addresses.

1.2 Theory of the Firm

Learning Objective

1.1.2 Understand and be able to apply the theory of the firm: profit maximisation; normal, supernormal and sub-normal profits; all types of costs relating to the firm; associated cost curves; explicit and opportunity costs; increasing and diminishing returns to factors; economies and diseconomies of scale; relationship between the different types of revenue

In this section we consider the influences that affect the supply of goods and services by firms and producers.

Economics takes the view that firms make price and output decisions in order to maximise profits and will base these decisions on costs and the revenue to be earned. Note that economics views these concepts of revenue and costs differently than accountancy.

Terminology

- **Revenue** – the amount earned by a firm from selling its output over a given time period.
- **Costs** – the outgoings associated with production in the same time period.
- **Profit** – the difference between revenues and costs.
- **Marginal cost** – the addition to total cost that is brought about by an additional unit of production.
- **Marginal revenue** – the additional revenue earned from one more unit of sales.

1.2.1 Profit Maximisation

In economics, a simplifying assumption is made that firms seek to maximise profits.

Firms maximise profit by equating marginal revenue (MR) to marginal cost (MC). That is, a firm will manufacture units of a product until the extra, or marginal, revenue generated by the sale of one additional unit equals the cost of producing this one additional unit.

Example

Let us use the following table to illustrate the concept. The table shows:

- The firm incurs costs even when nothing is being produced as, even though there is no production, fixed costs for items such as rent, power, telephones and marketing are still incurred. These are fixed costs or overheads.
- As production is begun, additional costs are incurred for materials and wages. These will vary with the level of production and so are known as variable costs.
- Typically they will not rise smoothly as additional production can be added without further costs until a certain point is reached. For example, a fixed amount of raw materials may need to be bought that is enough for more than one product and there will be capacity within the workforce to produce more without incurring overtime or additional staff having to be employed.
- At some stage, costs will rise by a proportionately greater amount as additional workers will need to be recruited or new machinery purchased.
- The price per item falls as more production takes place in order to sell more.

Output	Total Cost	Marginal Cost	Price per Item	Total Revenue	Marginal Revenue	Profit
0	100					−100
1	125	25	75	75	+75	−50
2	140	15	70	140	+65	0
3	153	13	65	195	+55	42
4	165	12	60	240	+45	75
5	175	10	55	275	+35	100
6	187	12	50	300	+25	113
7	200	13	45	315	+15	115
8	215	15	40	320	+5	105
9	235	20	35	315	−5	80
10	275	40	30	300	-15	25

By examining the table, we can see that:

- Fixed costs are 100.
- The marginal cost of producing one more unit falls as more items are produced until five units have been produced, when they start to rise. This may be because, for example, overtime costs have to be incurred.
- Once production reaches ten units, the marginal cost rises significantly as, say, more workers have to be recruited.

- On the revenue side, total revenues increase with more sales and the firm breaks even with the sale of the second item.
- As sales rise, the marginal revenue generated for the sale of each additional item declines because of rising costs.
- Profit continues to grow until marginal cost is greater than marginal revenue.
- So, to maximise profits the firm would produce seven units as it is the highest output level before additions to costs are greater than marginal revenue.

So, profits are maximised where MR = MC. This is explained further in the following diagram.

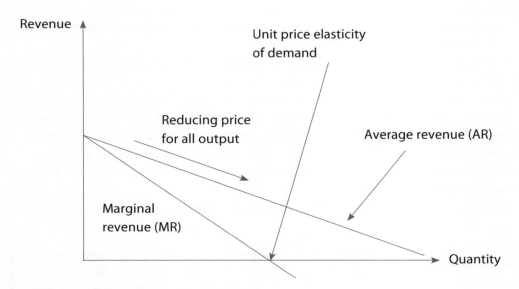

Figure 9: Total Average and Marginal Revenue

We saw earlier that the more units of a product we buy from a firm, the lower the average price per unit we expect to pay. This is depicted by the **average revenue (AR) curve**, which is also the demand curve for the product.

The progressively smaller additional amount of revenue received from the sale of each additional unit of product as we move down the AR curve is illustrated by the MR curve. You will notice that the slope of the MR curve is steeper than that of the AR curve given this progressively smaller contribution made to total revenue as the sale of units increases.

MR will always be lower than AR. This is because a downward sloping demand curve implies that the price has to fall in order to sell one more item of production.

At the point where the MR curve cuts the horizontal axis, any additional sales will detract from the firm's total revenue. By producing and selling the quantity of goods at this point, the firm maximises its revenue. You may recall that at this point on the demand, or AR, curve there is unit price elasticity of demand for the product. Below this point, the demand curve is inelastic, so any further fall in price resulting from increasing sales of the product will reduce total revenue.

1.2.2   Short and Long Run Costs

Above, we saw that the output level where profit is maximised is where MR = MC. We can now turn to the relationship between a firm's output and costs.

In economics, the treatment of costs is unique in three respects.

- Firstly, costs are defined not as financial but as opportunity costs; that is, the cost of forgoing the next best alternative course of action.
- Secondly, cost includes what is termed normal profit, or the required rate of return for the firm to remain in business.
- Finally, economics distinguishes between the short run and the long run when analysing the behaviour of costs.

This differentiation between short and long run costs arises because of the impact of time. As we saw above, certain costs are fixed, namely buildings and equipment. A firm, could, however, buy a new building or new equipment so, in that respect, there are no fixed costs. Instead, the costs are variable but it will take time to add these additional factors of production. This leads us to distinguish between long and short run costs.

Short Run Costs and Increasing and Diminishing Returns

In the short run, it is assumed that the stock of capital equipment available to each firm and its efficiency in the production process is fixed. This gives rise to what is known as **fixed cost**; fixed because the cost will be incurred regardless of production.

The only resources available in varying quantities to the firm in the short run are labour and raw materials. Both, therefore, are **variable costs**.

In the short run, the short run average total cost (SRATC) faced by the firm in its production is given by the sum of this fixed and variable cost divided by the number of units produced. It is depicted as follows.

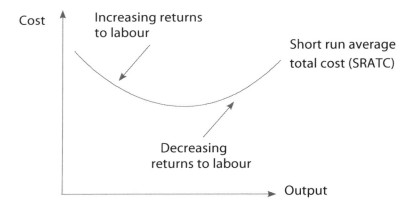

Figure 10: Short Run Average Total Cost

It is **u-shaped** because as we saw above, as more items are produced marginal cost at first falls before later rising. This is because in the short run, the law of diminishing returns states that as we add more units of variable input to fixed amounts of land and capital, the change in total output will at first rise then fall.

Diminishing returns to labour occur when productivity starts to fall which means that total output will be increasing at a decreasing rate. This might occur because although the labour force has been increased to meet demand, there is less experience or not enough equipment to go around. When this occurs, it becomes more expensive to produce an additional item of output and so marginal cost and average variable cost eventually starts to rise.

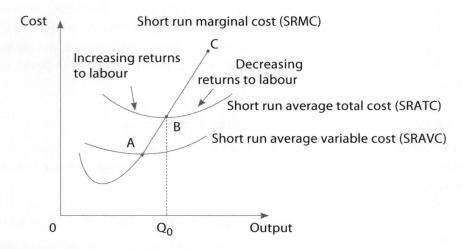

Figure 11: Short Run Average and Marginal Total Cost

The SRMC curve depicts the cost to the firm of increasing its production by one additional unit of output. Therefore, in the same way that MR is the increase in total revenue resulting from the sale of one additional item, so the SRMC is the increase in total cost resulting from the production of this additional unit.

As the amount of labour employed in the production process increases, so the SRATC of producing additional units falls, as a direct result of the fixed cost being spread over a greater number of units and increasing returns to labour, or rising productivity. At output Q_0, the optimal level of production, SRATC is minimised. This is shown as point B. At this point, the SRMC curve cuts the SRATC curve, as marginal cost and average total cost are now the same.

Beyond this level of output, however, the marginal cost of producing one additional unit is greater than the average total cost of producing Q_0 plus this one additional unit, as shown by the SRMC curve rising above the SRATC curve. This causes the SRATC curve to rise. The reason for this is that diminishing returns to labour begin to set in, as the increased use of labour becomes less productive, given that the firm's productive capacity is constrained by a fixed amount of capital equipment.

Progressively, this effect begins to far outweigh that of spreading the fixed cost across a greater amount of production, resulting in the slope of the rising SRATC curve becoming steeper.

Finally, in the short run, each firm only needs to cover its variable costs of production with the revenue generated by product sales, when deciding whether or not to produce units, as the fixed costs will be incurred regardless of any production decision. In this context, fixed costs are known as sunk costs.

Long Run Costs and Economies and Diseconomies of Scale

What differentiates the short run from the long run is the length of time necessary for adjustments to be made to each and every one of the factors of production used in the production process.

In the long run, all factors of production, or inputs to the production process, are variable. The long run average total cost (LRATC) curve shows the minimum average cost to produce different levels of output given this flexibility and is illustrated in the diagram below.

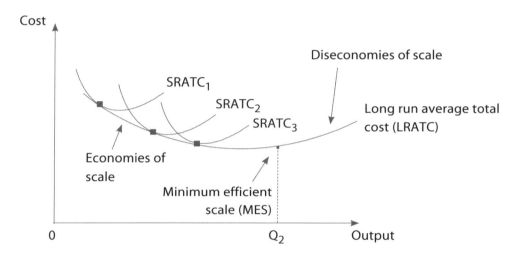

Figure 12: Long Run Average Total Cost (LRATC)

As you can see from the diagram, in effect, the long run is an amalgamation of a series of short runs, though without the capital constraints. From this you should note:

- If marginal cost is lower than average cost, then the average cost must be falling since we are adding a lower number to total cost than the current average.
- When marginal cost becomes greater than average cost, then the average cost must be rising.
- Each point on the LRATC curve will not necessarily correspond with the lowest point on each of the SRATC curves where the stock of capital equipment is fixed.

In the long run, the production process benefits from economies of scale, as the firm's productive capacity increases. Note that the term **economies of scale** rather than simply increasing returns to labour is used here given the flexibility with which all factors of production can be employed.

Production costs are minimised on the LRATC curve at Q_2, known as the minimum efficient scale (MES). Beyond this point, diseconomies of scale set in as management bureaucracy negatively impacts the production process.

Finally, in the long run, unlike in the short run, all costs of production must be covered when making the decision to produce output. Remember, so long as the revenue generated by product sales covers all costs, then the firm will be making a normal profit.

1.3   Industrial Structure

Learning Objective

1.1.3   Understand firm and industry behaviour under: perfect competition; price discrimination; perfect free market; monopoly; oligopoly

In the previous sections, we have looked at how costs influence the decisions a firm makes on the level of output in both the short and long run. We can now extend this analysis to consider how the structure of a market or industry affects the determination of price and output in that market. The following diagram provides a simplified representation of different market structures.

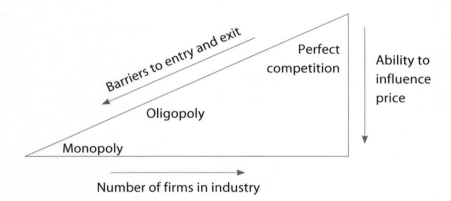

Figure 13: Industrial Structure

Although it does not necessarily follow that in all industries the greater the number of firms, the more competitive the industry, for the purposes of simplifying the analysis of firms' production decisions based on profit maximisation, it is a useful assumption to make.

In this section, we will first consider how firms operate under the two extremes of competition – perfect competition and monopoly – and then turn to how we can assess companies who are more likely to be operating in between the two.

1.3.1   Perfect Competition

Perfect competition is a theoretical representation of how a perfectly free market operates if no one buyer or seller is able to influence the price of a single homogeneous product.

No individual buyer or seller can influence the market price by actions of their own. Both, therefore, are described as being price takers.

A perfectly competitive firm is one that operates within an industry containing an infinite number of firms, each of which accepts the market price for a homogeneous product set by the interaction of consumer demand for the industry's total supply. In the long run, perfectly competitive firms only generate normal profits.

Although impossible to fully replicate in practice, the market for grain comes close to meeting the assumed characteristics of a perfectly competitive industry, as the actions of an individual grain farmer or a grain merchant are unlikely to influence the market price of grain. No individual farmer can influence the market price by selling more or less of any product as their supply has a negligible impact on the overall market supply.

The characteristics of a perfectly competitive industry are as follows:

- No one firm dominates the industry which contains an infinite number of firms.
- Firms do not face any barriers to entry or exit from the industry.
- A single homogeneous product is produced by all firms in the industry.
- There is a single market price at which all output produced by any one firm can be sold.
- There are an infinite number of consumers who all face the same market price.
- Perfect information about the product, its price and each firm's output is freely available to all.

Given these assumptions, each firm in a perfectly competitive industry faces a horizontal, or perfectly elastic, demand curve for its output. The following diagram illustrates that if the firm faces a horizontal demand curve then marginal revenue equals average revenue or price.

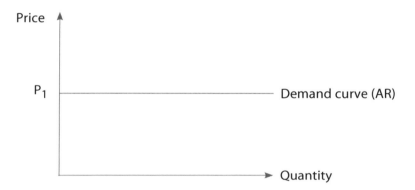

Figure 14: Demand curve for a perfectly competitive firm

This implies that:

- They can sell as much as they want at the prevailing market price but if it raises its prices, no one will buy since similar products are available from other firms at the market price.
- Equally, there is no point in cutting prices since it can sell as much as it wants at the market price.
- Clearly, this requires firms to be producing very similar products, hence the term homogenous product.

Facing this environment, what amount will a firm produce? Given that each firm's output represents a minute fraction of total industry output, their individual output decisions will not affect the industry price, so each firm can sell as much or as little of their output as they wish at this price.

To maximise profits, however, they will set output at where MR = MC. At this point they are covering all of their costs and generating normal profit. They are, therefore, in a state of equilibrium.

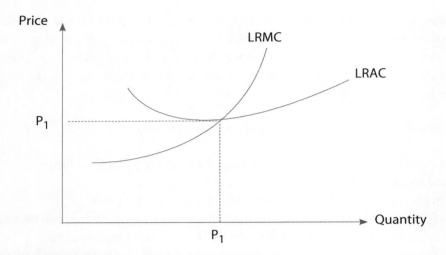

Figure 15: Cost curves for firm in perfect competition

However, if this single industry price rises for whatever reason, each firm will then produce greater output, generating supernormal profits in the process. This is illustrated in the following diagram.

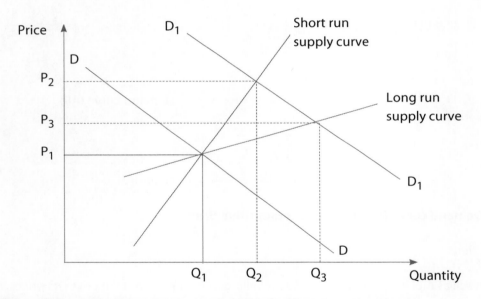

Figure 16: Effect of an increase in demand in a perfectly competitive industry

If demand rises from D to D_1 then the price will initially rise to P2 as output expands along the short run supply curve.

But, this state of disequilibrium will not last for long, as other firms learning of these supernormal profits, given freely available information, will be attracted to the market in search of these excess returns.

Inevitably, the resulting increase in supply will shift the industry supply curve to the right, eventually driving the price back down to a new equilibrium price and output of P_3 and Q_3, eliminating the supernormal profits in the process. Equilibrium will be restored once each firm is again producing at the point where MR = MC.

1.3.2 Monopoly and Oligopoly

At the other end of the spectrum from perfect competition is a pure monopoly.

In the case of perfect competition, no firm can influence industry price. The opposite is true of a pure monopoly where there is only one supplier.

- A monopoly is a market structure where there is only one producer or supplier and entry into the industry is restricted due to high costs or economic, political or social restrictions – in other words, there are barriers to entry.
- An oligopoly exists where a limited number of highly interdependent firms dominate an industry, typically through either implicit or explicit collusion on price and output.

Firms that operate in either form of market have some influence on their own output and pricing decisions and can therefore generate profits somewhere between the normal and supernormal levels. This is achieved mainly through subtle product differentiation, through defensive advertising to increase brand loyalty and so reduce the elasticity of demand for their product, and through limited price competition.

The monopolist faces a downward sloping demand curve and so it has to reduce prices to sell more goods. A monopolist firm is able, however, to set rather than accept the market price for its output.

The following diagram shows the level of output that would be chosen by a perfectly competitive firm if faced by the same demand curve and cost structure as a monopolist – Q_P.

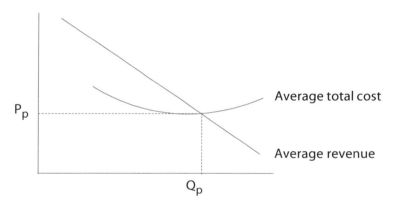

Figure 17a: Price and Output for a Monopolist

This level of output would never be chosen by the monopolist, as only normal profits would be generated at this point.

Instead, it would choose output Q_M. This is because, facing a demand curve represented by the average revenue (AR) it receives for selling successive amounts of output, the monopolist, like any other profit-maximising firm, sets its output where MR = MC.

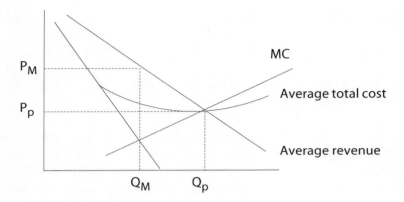

Figure 17b: Price and Output for a Monopolist

At output Q_M and price P_M the monopolist not only maximises its profits but also generates sustainable supernormal profits. You will also notice that the monopolist only operates at a single point on the elastic part of the demand curve and does not have a supply curve.

Moreover, the only time a monopolist will change its output decision and move along the elastic part of the demand curve is in response to a shift in its MC curve. A shift to the right may be as a result of falling labour costs, for instance.

Given the monopolist's ability to set price solely on the elastic part of the demand curve, it is in an ideal position to engage in **price discrimination** and, in some instances, perfect price discrimination; that is, charge each and every customer a different price for its output, so as to eliminate what is known as **consumer surplus**. Consumer surplus arises where a firm, by setting a single price for its output, forgoes the additional revenue that could have been generated by segmenting the market for its product and charging each segment a different price.

Monopolies are usually the result of industries that require large-scale capital investment to fully exploit the enormous economies of scale on offer. These natural monopolies mainly comprise utility companies that substantially invest in the nation's infrastructure. Some firms, however, gain monopoly status through being the original innovator in what proves to be a growth industry – a phenomenon known as **first mover advantage** – and retain this status by patenting the product or by creating other barriers to entry. Some may prevent new firms from entering the industry by engaging in anti-competitive behaviour, such as creating products that can only be used in conjunction with others that only they produce, or spending large sums on advertising to raise the fixed costs of entering the industry.

Recognising the deadweight loss, or inefficient allocation of resources, that monopolies create by restricting output and raising price above marginal cost, the price and output decisions of most natural monopolies are now regulated or have been introduced to limited competition.

Examples of this in the UK include the telecoms industry and the rail industry. The telecoms industry was dominated by British Telecom (BT), a nationalised industry which was privatised and floated on the stock market. The market was then opened up to competition to stimulate innovation, leading to the wide choice of providers seen today. A similar approach was adopted with the rail industry, where a nationalised industry, British Rail, was split up into regional operating companies to bring in some limited competition.

Those monopolies that operate in industries with limited economies of scale, however, can also be split up into smaller and less dominant companies by the regulatory authorities. Controls also exist on preventing monopolies being created through merger and takeover activity.

2. Macroeconomic Analysis

Having considered the allocation of resources and the determination of price and output within different industrial structures, we now look at how key economic variables are determined in the wider economy.

2.1 Determination of National Income

Learning Objective

1.2.1   Understand how national income is determined, composed and measured in both an open and closed economy: gross domestic product; gross national product

At the very simplest level an economy comprises two distinct groups or economic agents:

- Individuals or consumers.
- Firms.

Individuals supply firms with the productive resources of the economy – land, labour and capital – or the inputs to the production process, in exchange for an income. In turn, these individuals use this income to buy the entire output produced by firms employing these resources.

This gives rise to the circular flow of income as shown in the following simplified model of such an economy.

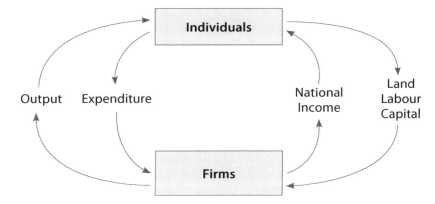

Figure 18: Simple model of the economy

This economic activity can be measured in one of three ways:

- by the total income paid by firms to individuals
- by individuals' total expenditure on firms' output, or
- by the value of total output generated by firms.

Each measure should produce the same answer in this simple economy. However, as economies develop from simple agrarian barter-based societies through to being manufacturing-based and finally services-based, or post-industrial, economies with developed monetary and financial systems, so this simple model of the economy becomes more complex.

These complexities arise from:

- Individuals save some of their income for future consumption.
- Financial markets channel these savings to firms to invest in both new and replacement capital equipment for future production.
- Government spending and taxation decisions.
- International trade becoming an integral part of the economic system.

Consequently, the circular flow becomes subject to:

- Injections in the form of business investment, government spending and firms' exports to overseas economies.
- Leakages in the form of saving, taxation and imported goods and services.

Moreover, by engaging in international trade, an economy that could once be described as closed becomes an open economy. The diagram below shows how the simple model shown above becomes more complex when these factors are taken into account.

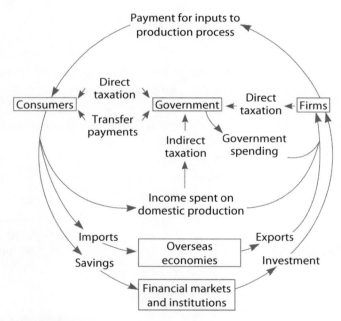

Figure 19: The Circular Flow of Income

From this, we can determine that so long as total leakages are precisely counteracted by total injections in the circular flow that the difference between the amount that individuals are saving and the amount that firms are investing is equal to the difference between what the government is spending and receiving in tax revenue, plus the difference between exports and imports. Therefore, any imbalance between what the government is spending and receiving as tax revenue, for instance, must be met by an imbalance between saving and investment and/or between exports and imports.

2.1.1   Gross Domestic Product (GDP)

At a national level, the amount of economic activity within the circular flow is measured by the National Income Accounts on either an income, expenditure or output basis and stated in terms of gross domestic product (GDP) or gross national income (GNI).

GDP measures the total market value of all final goods and services produced domestically typically during a calendar year. **Market value** is the value of output at current prices inclusive of indirect taxes, such as VAT, while **final output** is defined as that purchased by the end user of a product or service.

This latter point is particularly important as national income accounting, by:

*   distinguishing between final goods and those intermediate products or inputs used in a prior production process, and
*   employing the concept of value added, which avoids any double counting in the national accounts.

The most common method of calculating GDP is the expenditure method. GDP is calculated using the following formula:

GDP = Consumption + Investment + Government Spending + (Exports – Imports)

The formula is often abbreviated to GDP = C + I + G + (X–M) and each component is defined as follows:

*   **Consumption** – represents personal expenditure of households on goods and services such as food, rent and services.
*   **Investment** – represents expenditure by businesses and individuals for capital investment.
*   **Government spending** – is the sum of government spending on goods and public sector jobs.
*   **Exports** – captures the amount of goods produced for export to other countries.
*   **Imports** – subtracts the value of goods and services imported from other countries.

We will now briefly consider each of these components of GDP, what influences them and what their impact, both individually and collectively, is on the level of national income within a simple aggregate demand model.

The impact is based on the work of renowned economist John Maynard Keynes, whose ideas, now called Keynesian economics, had a major impact on modern economic and political theory as well as on many governments' fiscal policies.

Consumer Spending (C)

Consumption is driven by:

*   The level of national income.
*   Consumer confidence.
*   Actual and expected changes in the level of consumers' wealth, known as wealth effects.
*   Expectations of future income.
*   The availability and cost of credit.

The consumption function shows the planned level of consumer spending at each level of national income or GDP. It comprises a fixed amount of spending that is independent of the national income level, representing spending on necessities and an amount that varies directly with GDP.

This planned or fixed amount of spending at each level of GDP output is known as the **marginal propensity to consume (MPC)** and determines what proportion of consumers' post-tax, or disposable, income is spent, rather than saved, on goods and services.

Obviously, by incorporating factors that make this model dynamic, such as consumer confidence – itself determined by job security and employment prospects – changes in the level of wealth, the availability and cost of borrowing and expectations of future income levels, the relationship between consumer spending and national income becomes more complex.

Knowing that consumer spending usually accounts for about two-thirds of demand in a mature economy, its importance can never be overlooked.

Example

If consumers decide to start saving more and spending less, as a result of declining confidence for instance, this will:

* impact adversely on the demand for firms' output
* this will then lead to a reduction in the demand by firms for labour and other resources
* this results in a further decline in the demand for firms' output and so on.

This spiralling deficiency in demand may eventually require an element of government intervention to restore the economy to its potential or full employment level of output.

Business Investment (I)

Investment is the amount firms spend on capital equipment and stocks built up in anticipation of consumer demand. Investment is determined by:

* firms' ability to invest given the level of their retained profits and the cost of external finance
* business confidence and expectations of future returns from this investment spending
* the rate of technological innovation
* the rate at which the capital stock is depreciating.

In a basic aggregate demand model, investment spending is assumed to be independent of the level of national income and depicts the relationship between the level of investment spending and the rate of interest for a given expectation of future investment returns. This is known as the **marginal efficiency of investment (MEI)**.

Investment spending is, however, also sensitive to change in the demand for firms' output, to the rate of technological innovation and to the rate of depreciation of the capital stock. A change in any one of these variables will result in a shift in investment and therefore to a greater or lesser amount of business investment being undertaken at each level of the interest rate.

Government Spending (G)

An increase in government spending and/or a reduction in the level or rate of taxation can be used to stimulate the level of demand in an economy in the short term.

Government spending takes many forms. It includes infrastructure spending, spending on public services, and transfer, or benefit, payments to individuals. All but the latter are captured within the national accounts. Government spending can be financed through a combination of direct and indirect taxation and/or borrowing. Tax cuts, however, can be financed through borrowing and/or a reduction in government spending.

Terminology:

- **Fiscal policy** – collectively, government spending, taxation and borrowing are known as fiscal policy.
- **Balanced budget** – when the government spends the same as it is receiving in tax revenue, it runs a balanced budget.
- **Budget surplus and deficit** – however, if it is receiving more in tax revenue than it is spending, then it is running a budget surplus and a budget deficit if the opposite is true.
- **Public Sector Net Cash Requirement (PSNCR)** – the extent to which the government needs to borrow to finance this deficit is given by the PSNCR.
- **National debt** – the financing of successive fiscal deficits gives rise to the national debt.

Fiscal policy has been an important feature of modern-day economies, mainly being used to boost deficient demand, in an attempt to move the economy back to its potential level of output.

The Aggregate Demand Curve

Having considered three of the four components of aggregate demand – those that exist within a closed economy – we now need to examine how they collectively impact the output of the economy.

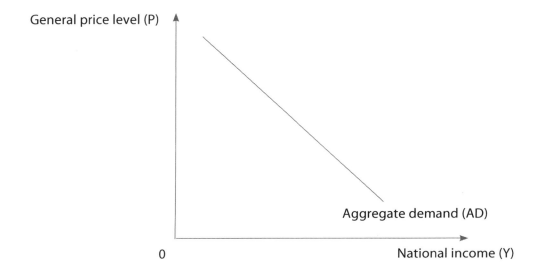

Figure 20: Aggregate Demand (AD)

The aggregate demand curve is similar to that of the demand curve in microeconomics, but differs in that it shows the aggregate, or total, demand in the economy at each general, or average, price level as you move along the AD curve.

A shift in any one of the above sources of demand or spending will shift the AD curve – to the right if demand is increased or to the left if decreased. However, this shift will increase national income disproportionately.

The reason that the shift in national income will be disproportionate is the existence of the **multiplier** (multiplier effect).

If, for example, the government increased the level of its spending by £1 billion, thereby shifting the AD curve to the right, the resulting increase in national income would be greater than £1 billion, since the recipients of this sum would then spend a proportion of it on other goods and services, whilst the recipients of that smaller sum would do the same. This process will continue until the multiplier effect has worked itself throughout the economy.

One of the key insights of Keynesian theory is that additions to the flow of income by some form of injection of income, eg, through a government stimulus package of increased expenditure on public services, will add more to national income than just the size of the injection.

This concept can be seen today in the attempts by government to stimulate the economy through the use of quantitative easing (QE) (considered later in Section 2.5.2). QE involves the government buying assets in order to inject enough funds into the economy to provide a stimulus, but not so much that it causes inflation.

Net Trade (X – M)

We now need to consider the final component of aggregate demand – net exports – that which makes a closed economy an open economy – and in particular its impact on the multiplier.

Net trade represents the difference between the value of goods and services exported (X) and those imported (M).

In simple aggregate demand models, exports are assumed to be autonomous of the level of domestic national income; they are determined instead by the level of national income within overseas economies.

Imports, however, are assumed to be directly related to the level of domestic national income: this direct relationship being given by the marginal propensity to import goods and services (MPM). As imports are a leakage from the circular flow of national income, the MPM will necessarily dampen the value of the multiplier in an open economy.

Aggregate Supply

Having considered aggregate demand, we now turn to aggregate supply.

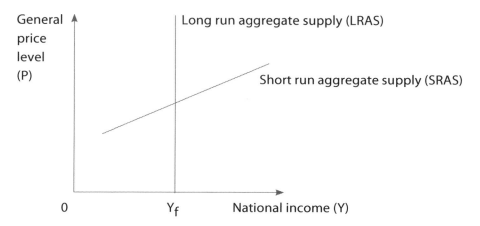

Figure 21: Aggregate Supply

Aggregate supply quantifies the amount of output firms are prepared to supply at each general price level, assuming the price of inputs to the production process is fixed.

As in microeconomics, we need to differentiate between the short and long run.

* The LRAS curve denotes the economy's potential or full employment level of output (Yf) given the amount of resources, available technology and rate of productivity it can draw upon.
* The SRAS curve is subject to diminishing returns to labour as a consequence of a fixed capital stock.

Shifts in the LRAS curve follow from changes in the amount of available resources, technological innovation and the efficiency of production techniques; whereas changes in production costs, principally the wage rate, and other factors that impact the production process in the short term – known as supply shocks – will shift the SRAS curve.

Through the interaction of the AD and LRAS curves, we arrive at the economy's full employment equilibrium level of output and general price level. However, we know that short-term fluctuations in economic activity mean that the economy can operate in disequilibrium – that is, either above or below its full employment level of output – often for significant periods of time.

The aggregate demand and supply framework can therefore be utilised to illustrate how different policy prescriptions available to governments can be used in an attempt to bring aggregate demand and supply back into equilibrium.

2.1.2   Gross National Product (GNP)

What differentiates GDP from GNP is that GNP also includes the contribution made during the calendar year to an economy's circular flow by its nationals – both firms and individuals – based overseas.

*   This contribution is known as **net property income** and comprises wages, profits, interest and dividends.
*   GNP at market prices, therefore, is simply GDP at market prices plus net property income generated from overseas economies by UK factors of production.

As so many countries have many of their nationals working abroad, GNP is becoming less used and GDP represents the most commonly used measure of economic activity.

2.1.3   Uses and Limitations of GDP Measures

By dividing GDP by the population, one obtains GDP per head or GDP per capita. GDP per capita, along with growth of GDP between calendar years, more commonly known as economic growth, are used as barometers of national prosperity.

Gross Domestic Product Index

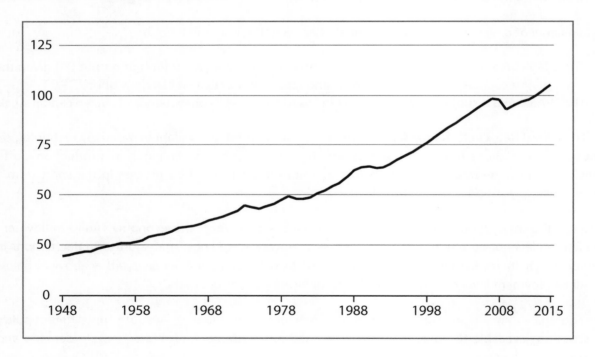

Source: Office for National Statistics

Whereas GDP and GDP per capita are calculated at market prices, or in nominal terms, economic growth is always expressed in real terms. The difference between real and nominal GDP is accounted for by a broadly based measure of inflation known as the GDP deflator.

Economic growth as a barometer of national prosperity, or standard of living does, however, have significant shortcomings:

*   The effects of economic growth may just benefit a narrow section of society rather than society as a whole, depending on the composition and distribution of GDP.
*   GDP, and therefore economic growth, only capture those aspects of economic activity that are measurable.

Therefore, both fail to account for:

*   the undesirable side effects of economic activity, such as pollution and congestion
*   non-marketable production such as DIY
*   the albeit subjective value attributed to leisure activities
*   economic activity in the so-called shadow economy, where, as a result of tax evasion, certain activities go unrecorded.

A further limitation of GDP data is simply the complexity of collecting the data and the time it takes to do so. The initial reported GDP figures are constantly revised upwards or downwards owing to the time lag in collecting data.

2.2   Economic Cycle

Learning Objective

1.2.2   Understand the stages of the economic cycle

Although there are many sources from which economic growth can emanate, in the long run the rate of sustainable or trend rate of growth ultimately depends on the:

*   growth and productivity of the labour force
*   rate at which an economy efficiently channels its domestic savings and capital attracted from overseas into new and innovative technology and replaces obsolescent capital equipment
*   extent to which an economy's infrastructure is maintained and developed to cope with growing transport, communication and energy needs.

This trend rate of growth also defines an economy's potential output level or full employment level of output.

*   An economy's potential output level is the sustainable level of output an economy can produce when all of its resources are productively employed.
*   When an economy is growing in excess of its trend growth rate, actual output will exceed potential output often with inflationary consequences.
*   When a country's output contracts – that is, when its economic growth rate turns negative for at least two consecutive calendar quarters – the economy is said to be in recession, or entering a deflationary period, resulting in spare capacity and unemployment.

Unlike in microeconomics, where the establishment of a market-clearing price in a single market brings supply and demand into equilibrium, in macroeconomics the interaction of individual markets and sectors may cause the economy to operate in a state of disequilibrium, often for significant periods of time. We consider this when we examine fiscal and monetary policy.

The fact that actual growth fluctuates and deviates from trend growth in the short term gives rise to the **economic cycle**, or business cycle.

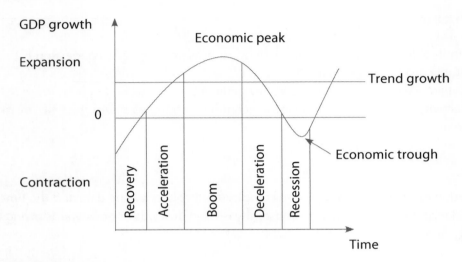

Figure 22: The Economic Cycle

Economic cycles describe the course an economy conventionally takes, usually over a seven- to ten-year period, as economic growth oscillates in a cyclical fashion. The length of a cycle is measured either between successive economic peaks or between successive economic troughs.

Although cycles typically assume a recovery, acceleration, boom, overheating, deceleration and recession pattern, in practice it is difficult to identify exactly when one stage ends and another begins and, indeed, to quantify the duration of each stage.

Where an economy is positioned in the economic cycle also has an effect on the structure of portfolios, such as whether they are growth or defensively orientated or where they are focused, domestically or internationally.

Finally, empirical evidence shows that if the short-term peaks and troughs of conventional cycles are ignored, economic cycles of 50 years or so pervade economies. These so-called Kondratieff cycles flow from the benefits of innovation and investment in new technology.

2.3   Balance of Payments and International Trade

Learning Objective

1.2.3   Understand the composition of the balance of payments and the factors behind and benefits of international trade and capital flows: current account; imports; exports; effect of low opportunity cost producers

2.3.1   The Balance of Payments

The balance of payments is a summary of all economic transactions between one country and the rest of the world, typically conducted over a calendar year.

The main components of the balance of payments are as follows:

- **The trade balance** – this comprises a visible trade balance – the difference between the value of imported and exported goods - and an invisible trade balance – the difference between the value of imported and exported services. (Visibles are items such as manufactured goods; invisibles are earnings from service areas such as finance, insurance and tourism.) Being a post-industrial economy, the UK typically runs a deficit on visible trade but an invisible trade surplus. Also, being an open economy, imports and exports combined total over 50% of UK GDP.
- **The current account** – the current account is equal to the trade balance less government transfer payments to overseas economies, plus the net flow of interest, profits and dividends derived from net UK holdings of overseas assets. This latter net flow can be substantial given that the UK is one of the world's largest owners of overseas assets.
- **The financial account** – this accounts for the net amount of long- and short-term capital that has flowed between the UK and the rest of the world over the period. Long-term capital flows are known as foreign direct investment (FDI) and include the overseas expansion plans of multinational companies, whether that results in the financing of a new plant or acquiring an existing business. Short-term capital flows, typically footloose movements of capital attracted by potentially high short-term returns, however, are termed portfolio investment.

For the balance of payments to balance, the current account must equal the financial account plus or minus a balancing item – used to rectify the many errors in compiling the balance of payments – plus or minus any change in central bank foreign currency reserves.

So a current account deficit resulting from the UK being a net importer of overseas goods and services must be met by a net inflow of capital from overseas, taking account of any measurement errors and any Bank of England intervention in the foreign currency market.

2.3.2 International Trade

International trade is the exchange of goods and services between countries. It is conducted because it confers the following benefits on those countries that participate in this exchange:

- **Specialisation**
  - Economies of scale in the production of a particular good or provision of a particular service can be fully exploited if the MES is not being achieved when producing solely for the domestic market.
  - Increased production levels can also take full advantage of and further develop any particular skill possessed by the labour force, known as the **division of labour**.
- **Competition**
  - Global competition in the provision of goods and services results in improved choice and quality of products, as well as more competitive prices and productivity improvements in the industries concerned.

This point can be taken one stage further. Even though country A may have an absolute cost advantage, ie, is more efficient in the production or provision of two particular goods or services than country B, there is still scope for A and B to benefit collectively from international trade, if each specialises solely in the provision of the good or service where they have a comparative cost advantage. So, if A specialises in the provision of the good or service where its absolute and comparative cost advantage over B is greatest, while B concentrates solely on the provision of the good or service where A's cost advantage is smallest, ie, where B's comparative advantage is greatest, by trading each other's production, both can be shown to be better off in terms of the positive impact this specialisation and trade has on their respective GNPs. This is known as the **law of comparative advantage**.

Despite the substantial benefits of conducting international trade free from any governmental interference, governments often engage in protectionism, or the erection of trade barriers, in the misguided belief that certain domestic industries, often those that are inefficiently run, should be protected against global competition. This usually results in some sort of trade retaliation. However, the General Agreement on Tariffs and Trade (GATT) of 1948, which created an international trade organisation with responsibility for liberalising international trade, a role since assumed by the World Trade Organisation (WTO), has led to a gradual reduction in these barriers to free trade.

2.3.3 International Competitiveness

In an open economy, where international trade accounts for a significant share of GDP, having the right exchange rate is imperative to its international competitiveness.

This was seen in summer 2011, in Switzerland, whose currency appreciated as investors sought safe havens from continued market volatility. The effect was to drive up the value of the Swiss franc to a level that made its exports uncompetitive and threatened deflation. The Swiss National Bank intervened in the currency markets in an attempt to drive down the value of its currency particularly against the Euro which had appreciated from CHF 1.7 against the euro in 2008 to near parity in August 2011. Its interventions are aimed at keeping the Swiss franc at a level above CHF 1.20 against the euro.

An exchange rate is the price of one currency in terms of another. The overall effect of a change in the exchange rate on the trade balance, assuming that demand is price elastic and all other factors such as productivity are held constant, is as follows:

- A rise in the nominal value of sterling will reduce a trade surplus or worsen a trade deficit as exports will be less competitive, unless UK exporters reduce their sterling prices; whereas imports will be more competitive, unless exporters to the UK raise their prices.
- A fall in the nominal value of sterling will increase a trade surplus or reduce a trade deficit as exports will be more competitive, unless UK exporters raise their sterling prices; whereas imports will be less competitive, unless exporters to the UK reduce their prices.

By taking account of whether exporters and importers alter their prices when faced with a change in the **nominal exchange rate**, we can establish whether a country's overall international competitiveness has improved or declined.

The World Economic Forum's (WEF) report on global competitiveness analyses the competitiveness landscape of 140 economies. In the 2015–16 report the WEF reported:

'Despite substantive efforts to re-ignite recovery, global economic growth remains low and unemployment persistently high. The Global Competitiveness Report 2015–16 calls for productivity-enhancing reforms to break with this pattern.

Seven years after the beginning of the financial crisis in 2008, its consequences are still being felt around the world. The recovery has been less robust, more uncertain and taken longer than many expected, suggesting a 'new normal' of subdued economic growth, lower productivity growth and high unemployment. Recent geopolitical shocks – from the crisis in Ukraine to conflicts in the Middle East, terrorism and the migrant crisis – have added to economic difficulties.

Addressing constraints to growth on the supply side could go a long way to restoring growth. Through a systematic assessment of the drivers of productivity, the Report identifies priority areas for structural reforms.

The Report shows that competitiveness – understood as higher productivity – is a key driver of growth and resilience. The historic proportions of the economic crisis and the relative performance of economies since its onset in 2008 have shed light on how structural weaknesses can exacerbate the effects of, and hinder recovery from shocks.

During the crisis, the more competitive economies systematically outperformed the least competitive in terms of economic growth: they either withstood the crisis better or recovered more quickly. This result holds true at every stage of development (see chart below).'

Average growth rates of the most and least competitveness economies, by income group, 2007–14

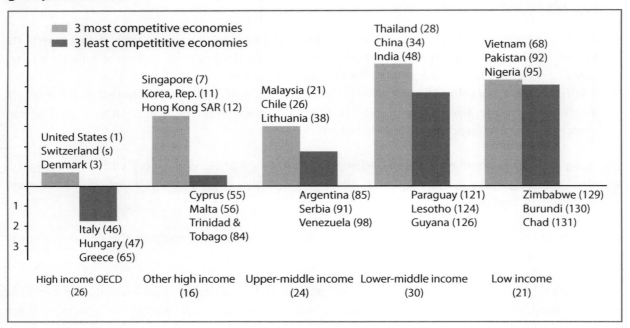

One way of establishing international competitiveness is by calculating the **real exchange rate**. The UK's real exchange rate relative to that of the US can be formally stated as:

$$\text{Real exchange rate} = \frac{\text{UK price level}}{\text{US price level}} \times \frac{\text{US\$}}{£}$$

A rising real exchange rate signifies a reduction in international competitiveness. So, if UK inflation is rising at a faster rate than in the US, without a compensating weakening of the nominal exchange rate, the UK's international competitiveness declines. The precise effect on the trade balance and the revenues of importing and exporting firms will of course also depend on factors such as the price elasticity of these internationally traded goods and services, any productivity improvements in those industries and the speed with which consumers substitute goods and services when faced with a change in price.

As consumers are typically slow to change their spending patterns when faced with changing prices, the impact of a change in the real exchange rate on the trade balance is never instantaneous. In fact, a weakening of the nominal exchange rate will immediately raise import prices, while reducing export prices, thereby worsening the trade balance. However, once consumers adjust to these new relative prices, the trade balance will improve. The trade balance, therefore, tends to experience a J-curve effect.

2.4 Money Supply

Learning Objective

1.2.4 Understand the nature, determination and measurement of the money supply and the factors that affect it: reserve requirements; discount rate; government bond issues

The money supply is the amount of money that exists in the economy at any point in time. However, before the money supply can be quantified, the term **money** must be defined.

Money is anything that is generally acceptable as a means of settling a debt. Money, therefore, must fulfil several functions.

Most importantly, it must overcome the problem of finding someone else with matching trading requirements, known as the **mutual coincidence of wants problem**, and the associated search costs encountered with exchange through a system of barter, by acting as an acceptable medium of exchange. It must also act as a store of value for future consumption, by maintaining its purchasing power, and provide a unit of account against which the price of goods and services can be compared.

To be acceptable, however, money must also be easily recognisable, divisible, portable and durable. In a developed economy, money takes the form of fiat currency – that is, currency that has no intrinsic value, but which is demanded for what it can itself purchase.

As a result of the various forms that money can take in an economy with a sophisticated financial system, it will probably come as no surprise that there is no single definition of the money supply. Since 1976, several measures of the money supply have been defined and redefined in the UK. However, only two measures remain: M0 and M4. M0, the monetary base, is the narrowest measure of the two, in that it only contains notes and coins in circulation and banks' operational deposits at the Bank of England – the UK's central bank – while M4, the broadest measure, is defined as M0 plus bank and building society deposits.

The definition of the money supply is further complicated by the existence of credit creation and the money multiplier.

As banks are only required to hold a small proportion of their deposits as reserves to meet day-to-day withdrawals – known as the **reserve ratio** – they can lend out the significant remainder, assuming that bank depositors' required ratio of cash holdings to deposits does not exceed this ratio. This is known as **fractional reserve banking**.

As a sizeable proportion of each loan made from bank deposits is redeposited and then extended as another loan, so credit is created and the money supply expands. The impact on the money supply can be quantified by multiplying the level of cash deposits in the banking system by the money multiplier, which is given by:

$$\frac{1}{\text{Reserve ratio}}$$

So, a bank with £100,000 of cash deposits subject to a 10% reserve ratio will create loans of £900,000 until a total of £100,000/0.1 = £1 million of deposits is on the bank's books with £100,000 of cash being held to satisfy the reserve ratio requirement.

The money supply is also affected by a number of other factors which are considered in Section 2.6. These include:

- **Reserve requirements** – these are the amounts that commercial banks are required to hold as deposits at the central bank and are expressed as a percentage of the commercial bank's liabilities. An increase in reserve requirements forces banks to hold greater balances at the central bank and so reduces their ability to lend and affects the amount of money in circulation.
- **Discount rate** – central banks act as bankers to the banks and as lenders of last resort to the banking system. Central banks provide lending facilities to commercial banks, which they can use to manage their cash flows and which the central bank can use to influence the cost of money. The interest rate charged is known as the discount rate and the lending facility as the discount window.
- **Government bond issues** – central banks can also influence the amount of money in circulation as a result of the issuance and repayment of bonds and treasury bills.

2.5   Central Banks and Macroeconomic Tools

Learning Objective

1.2.5   Understand the macroeconomic tools and mechanisms that the central banks and supranational organisations use and how they have been applied during recent economic cycles: quantitative easing; lenders of last resort; other mechanisms

In this section we look at how economic considerations and policy come together in practice by looking at the role of central banks and the macroeconomic tools available to them. We will consider how they have been applied during the recent economic cycle and specifically to counter the credit crisis and recession of 2007–08 and the economic conditions encountered in 2009.

2.5.1   The Role of Central Banks

Central banks operate at the very centre of a nation's financial system. Most are public bodies, though increasingly central banks operate independently of government control or political interference.

The following are some of the core responsibilities of central banks, but it is undoubtedly their role in the management of the economy and as lender of last resort to the banking system that have been most closely observed and discussed during the recent economic cycle.

- Acting as banker to the banking system by accepting deposits from and lending to commercial banks.
- Acting as banker to the government.
- Managing the national debt.
- Regulating the domestic banking system.
- Acting as lender of last resort to the banking system in financial crises to prevent its systematic collapse.

- Setting the official short-term rate of interest.
- Controlling the money supply.
- Issuing notes and coins.
- Holding the nation's gold and foreign currency reserves to defend and influence the value of a nation's currency through intervention in the currency markets.
- Providing a depositors' protection scheme for bank deposits.

Before looking at the range of macroeconomic tools available to central banks and how these were applied during the recent economic cycle, we will first consider their roles and responsibilities.

The Bank of England

The UK's central bank was founded in 1694, nationalised in 1946 and gained operational independence in setting UK monetary policy in 1997.

Sometimes known as the Old Lady of Threadneedle Street, the bank's roles and functions have changed over time, but today it has two core purposes: monetary stability and financial stability.

- Monetary stability means stable prices and confidence in the currency. Stable prices involve meeting the Government's inflation target which, since November 2003, has been a rolling two-year target of 2% for the consumer prices index (CPI). This it does by setting the base rate, the UK's administratively set short-term interest rate.
- Financial stability refers to detecting and reducing threats to the financial system as a whole. A sound and stable financial system is important in its own right, and vital to the efficient conduct of monetary policy.
- To promote the safety and soundness of individual financial firms, the Prudential Regulation Authority (PRA) of the Bank regulates and supervises roughly 1,700 banks, building societies, credit unions, insurers and major investment firms. (See Chapter 3, Section 2.2.)

The European Central Bank (ECB)

The ECB is based in Frankfurt, Germany. It assumed its central banking responsibilities upon the creation of the euro, on 1 January 1999. The euro has since been adopted by 16 of the European Union's (EU) 27 member states, which have collectively created an economic region known as the **eurozone**.

The ECB is principally responsible for setting monetary policy for the entire eurozone, with the sole objective of maintaining internal price stability. Its objective of keeping inflation, as defined by the harmonised index of consumer prices (HICP), *close to but below 2% in the medium term* is achieved by making reference to factors that may influence inflation, such as the external value of the euro and growth in the money supply.

The ECB sets its monetary policy through its president and council, the latter comprising the governors of each of the Eurozone's national central banks.

The Federal Reserve

The Federal Reserve system in the US dates back to 1913. The Fed, as it is known, comprises 12 regional Federal Reserve banks, each of which monitors the activities of and provides liquidity to the banks in their region. Although free from political interference, the Fed is governed by a seven-strong board appointed by the president of the US. This governing board, in addition to the presidents of six of the 12 Federal Reserve banks, makes up the Federal Open Market Committee (FOMC). The chairman of the FOMC, also appointed by the US president, takes responsibility for the committee's decisions, which are directed towards the FOMC's statutory duty of promoting price stability and full employment.

The FOMC meets every six weeks or so to examine the latest economic data and the many economic and financial indicators it monitors to gauge the health of the economy and determine whether the economically sensitive Fed Funds rate should be altered in response to its findings. Very occasionally it meets in emergency session, as and when circumstances dictate.

As lender of last resort to the US banking system, the Fed has, in recent years, rescued a number of US financial institutions and markets from collapse and prevented widespread panic, or systematic risk, spreading throughout the financial system, by judicious use of the Fed Funds rate.

The Bank of Japan (BOJ)

Japan's central bank has a statutory duty to maintain price stability. It is also responsible for the country's monetary policy, issuing and managing the external value of the Japanese yen, and acting as lender of last resort to the Japanese banking system.

The People's Bank of China

The People's Bank of China is the Chinese central bank. It is responsible for designing and implementing monetary policy and for ensuring financial stability, and for managing China's significant foreign reserves and gold reserves.

It has a monetary policy objective to maintain the stability of the value of the currency and thereby promote economic growth. Policy is determined by a monetary policy committee.

2.5.2 Macroeconomic Tools used during the Recession

The economic crisis of 2007–08 saw an unprecedented level of co-operation between the major central banks as they took concerted action to stave off the worst depression since the 1930s.

When the transatlantic financial crisis began in 2007–08, governments responded with emergency measures, which included direct support to the financial system, low interest rates, vastly expanded central bank balance sheets and massive fiscal stimulus.

What is involved with each policy is considered below.

Background to the Recession of 2008

The seeds of the problems encountered in 2007–08 can be traced back to the development of financial and trade imbalances among the major economies over the previous decade.

- Increased borrowing in a number of developed countries was in part financed by inflows of foreign capital, and by growing current account surpluses in oil-exporting countries and in some Asian economies.
- High savings in Asia contributed to low interest rates and a consequent rise in borrowing.
- Cheap exports from China and elsewhere in Asia contributed to falls in inflation in a number of developed countries.
- Economic conditions remained stable by historic standards and helped foster expectations of continued stability. This, along with rising asset prices and low global real interest rates, boosted the demand for and supply of credit in a number of developed economies.
- Over time, banks took on progressively more credit risk, by lending to households with high loan-to-income ratios, to leveraged buyout firms and, in the US, to the sub-prime sector.

Financial innovation led to the creation of very complex risk exposures not fully understood and assessed by both investors and the banks' own risk management systems.

More specifically, the Financial Stability Forum identified critical weaknesses that included:

- Poor underwriting standards and some fraudulent practices in the US subprime sector.
- Poor assessment and management of market, funding, liquidity, concentration and reputational risks.
- Poor investor due diligence practices, especially an excessive investor reliance on credit rating agency ratings.
- Poor performance by the credit rating agencies in evaluating the risks of structured credit.
- Distortions in relation to the regulatory capital treatment of securitised products and the structure of compensation schemes in the banking industry.

The old Basel I capital adequacy rules provided a regulatory capital incentive to the **originate and distribute** model, which resulted in a reduced incentive for banks to monitor the credit quality of the loans they pumped into collateralised loan obligations and other structured vehicles. There is little doubt that the Basel I rules failed to highlight contingent credit risk adequately, which put strain on banks' capital, once the credit risk from these instruments started to come back on to bank balance sheets.

Capital adequacy rules under Basel II were mid-implementation when the crisis happened. They attempted to ensure that the regulatory capital charge for a bank moving assets off balance sheet is roughly in line with the charge had the bank retained those assets on the balance sheet. The Basel Committee chairman stated that the subprime crisis may not have occurred – or may not have been so severe – had the new Basel II regime with its improved robustness of valuation practices and market transparency for complex and less liquid products been in place.

However it was not and when the US tried to adopt Basel II capital tests in 2006–07, by flagging sub-prime mortgages on balance sheets, it led to growing awareness of cross-border liquidity and commercial mortgage-backed security (CMBS) exposure which had a domino effect, leading to impairments of mortgage-backed securities (MBSs) and re-ratings of collateralised debt obligations (CDOs).

Market turmoil was then triggered and amplified by a resulting increase in risk aversion, falling market liquidity and de-leveraging of risky exposures, in an attempt by firms to build up liquidity positions.

While these weaknesses had been identified by central banks, few predicted that they would lead to such dislocation in the global financial system.

Financial Sector Intervention

2007–08 saw exceptional instability in the UK and the global financial system.

This instability was rooted in weaknesses within the financial system that had developed during an extended global credit boom. The problems included:

- expansion of balance sheets that far outpaced growth in the real economy
- exposure to assets whose underlying value, credit quality and liquidity were uncertain
- over-reliance on wholesale funding
- low capital levels relative to underlying balance sheet risks.

Rising defaults on US sub-prime mortgages ultimately triggered these vulnerabilities, and the losses spilled over across global financial markets, turning the previous cycle of rising asset prices into reverse. Investor appetite for risky assets collapsed, strains in the global interbank market placed financial institutions under intense pressure and a number failed, prompting national authorities to take unprecedented actions aimed at underpinning the banking system.

The package of measures implemented included:

- guarantees of bank assets and liabilities aimed at averting potential bank runs
- direct lending from central banks to allow rollover and prevent default
- capital injections to ward off insolvency
- nationalisations to allow failed institutions to continue to serve their customers
- removal of low-quality loans from bank balance sheets
- supporting the prices of assets where liquid markets had disappeared
- public certification by banking supervisors of the capital adequacy of large banks.

In the UK, this included the government taking control of Northern Rock bank, and encouraging the merger or takeover of weaker banks. It announced a financial support package aimed at supporting the recapitalisation of UK banks to remove the risk of default and to bring confidence back to the inter-bank money markets.

Government intervention stabilised the position and allowed time for money markets to return to normal and for banks to recapitalise their balance sheets.

Low Interest Rates

Central banks use interest rates to control inflation. They set an interest rate at which they will lend to financial institutions and this influences the rates that are available to savers and borrowers. The result is that movements in base rate affect spending by companies and their customers and, over time, the rate of inflation.

Changes in base rate can take up to two years to have their full impact on inflation and so the central bank has to look ahead when deciding on the appropriate monetary policy. If inflation looks set to rise above target the central bank raises rates in order to slow spending and reduce inflation. Similarly, if inflation looks set to fall below its target level, it reduces bank rates to boost spending and inflation.

The impact of using interest rates in this way can be seen by looking at what happened during the financial crisis in the UK from the beginning of 2008 to mid-2011. Spending in the UK slowed sharply in late 2008 as the global slowdown gathered pace and so the Bank of England cut the base rate substantially to reduce the risk of inflation falling well below target further ahead.

The base rate was reduced in stages, from 5.5% at the beginning of 2008 to 0.5% in March 2009; it was reduced still further to 0.25% on 4 August 2016, as a result of the UK's decision to exit the European Union (EU).

The reduction in the base rate was reflected in falling mortgage rates and many people benefited from mortgage rates that tracked the base rate. This helped to reduce the impact of falling growth.

The effect of lower interest rates also tracked through to inflation, which started in early 2008 at around 3.8% as measured by the retail prices index (RPI), peaked at 5% in September 2008 and then fell to negative levels in the second and third quarters of 2009. However, the lower interest rate eroded the returns on cash-based savings and impacted annuity rates. Subsequently, inflation started to rise again, as the economy felt the impact of rising oil and commodity prices.

There is more than one way of measuring inflation and in the UK it is now commonly shown by the consumer price index (CPI). CPI is measured from the average price of goods and services purchased by consumers. It calculates the change in price for a static market basket of goods and services from one period to the next. The RPI is a measure of the change in cost of the market basket of retail goods and services. It includes housing costs, such as mortgage interest costs and council tax; CPI does not. (See also Section 2.7 of this chapter.)

The CPI rate has fallen more or less consistently since mid-2011 but by 2016 it had stabilised at around or below 1.5%, although in April 2014 it went into negative territory at –0.2%. Lower oil prices have helped to reduce the inflation rate with oil-related transport costs falling in tandem. A fall in oil prices is akin in many ways to a cost-free tax reduction with disposable income rising. In theory, a fall in oil prices can also lead to higher spending on other goods and services, thus adding to GDP. Tumbling oil prices have also had an impact on US inflation with the measure also falling into negative territory in February 2015.

Quantitative Easing (QE)

The last economic cycle saw governments across the world follow a policy of reducing interest rates to counter the effect of a slowing global economy and the risks of depression.

As mentioned above, when a central bank is concerned about the risks of very low inflation, it cuts the base rate to reduce the cost of money and provide a stimulus to the economy.

The key difference in the last recession was that interest rates were reduced massively by central banks in developed countries. Interest rates cannot fall below zero and so, when they are close to zero, central banks need an alternative policy instrument. This involves injecting money directly into the economy in a process that has become known as **quantitative easing (QE)**.

QE involves the central bank creating money, which it then uses to buy assets such as government bonds and high-quality debt from private companies, resulting in more money in the wider economy.

According to the International Monetary Fund (IMF), the policies adopted globally by major central banks, have helped to reduce systemic risk and improve market confidence.

However, the former US Federal Reserve Chairman, Alan Greenspan has stated that in the US there was very little impact on the economy.

Many studies have been and will be conducted on the merits of QE on the domestic, European and wider global economies. The debate on its effectiveness is outside the scope of this workbook due to the large number of countries in different stages of QE, other economic factors and measures as well as opinion that would contribute to a proper assessment.

Creating more money does not involve printing more banknotes. Instead, the central bank buys assets from private sector institutions and credits the seller's bank account, so the seller has more money in their bank account, while the central bank holds assets as part of its reserves. The end result is more money out in the wider economy.

Injecting more money into the economy through the purchase of bonds can have a number of effects:

- The seller of the bonds ends up with more money and so may spend it, which will help boost growth.
- Alternatively, they may buy other assets instead and in doing so boost prices and provide liquidity to other sectors of the economy, resulting in people feeling better off and so spending more.
- Buying assets means higher asset prices and lower yields, which brings down the cost of borrowing for businesses and households, encouraging a further boost to spending.
- Banks find themselves holding more reserves, which might lead them to boost their lending to consumers and business; again, borrowing increases and so does spending.

The extra money works its way through the economy, resulting in higher spending and therefore growth, or reducing the impact of recession and preventing the onset of a depression.

Fiscal Stimulus

In conjunction with these macroeconomic policies, governments also used massive fiscal stimulus to counter the effect of the recent recession.

As an economy enters recession, governments can expect to see tax revenues fall, and they need to balance their spending plans carefully against falling receipts. In normal times, monetary rather than fiscal policy is used but against the backdrop of a deep economic downturn, however, world governments determined that additional macroeconomic stimulus was needed. Globally, governments spent trillions of dollars bolstering their economies and ran up significant public deficits in the process.

Fiscal stimulus packages need to be evaluated carefully and judged against factors such as the:

*   extent to which room for budgetary manoeuvre exists within a country's finances
*   timeliness and effectiveness of any discretionary action
*   period it will operate for.

For example, infrastructure investment will boost both supply and demand, providing that the investments are well chosen, but typically takes a long time to be brought on-stream and is difficult to wind down in line with a recovery in activity. Alternatives, such as tax cuts or transfer payments aimed at credit-constrained, poorer households, may prove more effective in boosting demand.

Stimulus packages involve governments borrowing money against future revenues. This means that once there are clear signs of a recovery taking hold, it is necessary to begin to unwind the macroeconomic stimulus promptly to prevent inflationary pressures from gaining a foothold. At the same time, it is equally important that a credible fiscal framework is in place, to ensure that government debt can be reduced back to manageable levels

High levels of public debt in the UK and other Organisation for Economic Co-operation Development (OECD) countries, combined with the spending pressures associated with population ageing, make this return to long-run public finance sustainability especially challenging.

2.5.3   Post-Recession and Macroeconomic Tools

Large cuts in base rates and quantitative easing have provided economies with a substantial boost and staved off the risk of a fall into depression as seen in the 1930s.

Macroeconomic support, however, has its limits:

*   Continuing government support of financial institutions creates a risk of delays to the vital post-crisis reforms needed for financial institutions.
*   The scale of the fiscal stimulus means high and growing government debt, which in some countries is clearly unsustainable.
*   Keeping interest rates near zero for too long, with abundant liquidity, leads to distortions and creates risks for financial and monetary stability.

We will consider each of these points below, but the key question, as countries emerge from recession, is when and how to stop the economic stimulus that has been provided. Policy decisions on this are complicated by the state of the financial sector and the macroeconomic outlook, which are fragile in many parts of the industrial world and which make policy-tightening uncertain and risky.

Post-Crisis Reforms

Addressing the causes of the financial crisis remains difficult while banking systems in some countries remain fragile and certain banks remain within government support programmes.

Global economic policy is focused on the following key areas:

- Reducing the probability of individual bank failure through measures addressing the size, composition and riskiness of bank balance sheets, requiring banks to hold capital and liquidity that better reflect their risk exposures.
- Reducing the risk of system-wide failure where the collapse of one institution causes a cascade of failures amongst other financial institutions.
- Reducing the impact of procyclicality. This refers to the relationship between the financial system and the real economy. As the economy booms, lending tends to become easier and cheaper: banks are flush with funds and capital, borrowers are more creditworthy, and collateral is more valuable.

In a downturn, these conditions are reversed: banks are forced to absorb unexpected losses which make them less well capitalised, so they cut back on lending; borrowers become less creditworthy; and collateral values fall. Addressing this may involve banks being required to build capital reserves during the good times to bolster positions during downturns.

Fiscal Consolidation

The combination of large-scale fiscal stimulus, financial rescue packages and falling tax revenues has led to historically large government budget deficits and record levels of actual and projected public debt in most industrial countries.

The crisis has left the global macroeconomic situation in a position where, in the US, Europe and Japan, public deficits are now in excess of 5% of GDP and base rates are near zero. Although private sector debt has started to decline, public debt has taken its place, with sovereign fiscal positions already at an unsustainable level in a number of countries.

These debt levels have raised serious concerns about the sustainability of fiscal policy in the industrial world, and heightened worries about sovereign risk. Sovereign risk concerns have centred on the fiscal situation in Greece, but also extended to other countries facing a toxic combination of high fiscal deficits and lack of competitiveness, such as Ireland, Portugal and Spain. The downgrading of Greek debt to junk status led to EU and International Monetary Fund (IMF) policymakers having to announce a €750 billion joint fiscal stabilisation package to support the Greek economy.

Fiscal consolidation or the reduction in public debt is now the priority for many countries. Reducing the size of the public deficit will be challenging for a number of reasons:

- **Economic recovery is expected to be slow**. During a cyclical downturn there are sharp declines in tax revenues, and expenditure on welfare benefits rises. The gap between the two will need to be continually funded and is unlikely to vanish soon, as economic recovery is expected to be slow.
- **Lower output will generate lower tax revenue**. In many countries, the large increase in tax revenues before the crisis was associated with an unsustainable boom in the construction and financial sectors. As output in these sectors is unlikely to recover to pre-crisis levels quickly, this will impact tax revenues, while at the same time higher unemployment levels will mean that unemployment benefits will remain high.

- **Structural deficits tend to be corrected only slowly**. Experience has shown that unwinding the deficits run up during an economic downturn takes time, as they require growth and unemployment to return to more acceptable levels.
- **Ageing populations present funding issues**. In many industrial countries, governments face rising costs to meet the retirement needs of an ageing population, and action to address this by containing costs and increasing retirement ages will take some years to work through.

There is also the question of the public acceptability of these measures, as the public reaction to austerity budgets in Greece and France has shown.

Interest Rate Policy

During the crisis, central banks cut base rates and adopted unconventional monetary policies to avert the risk of another depression.

With some of these monetary policies still underway, the timing for moving interest rates back up has still to be determined, and will differ across economies, depending on the relative speeds of recovery in financial markets and real activity.

Low interest rates cause distortions and may cause problems for the future. A prolonged period of exceptionally low real interest rates has the effect of:

- altering investment decisions
- postponing the recognition of losses
- increasing risk-taking in the search for yield
- encouraging high levels of borrowing.

This same combination fuelled the financial binges, the boom in asset prices and credit and the underpricing of risk in the first half of the previous decade. While the current environment is very different, ultimately it has devastating consequences, and our recent experience should make us extremely wary this time around.

Tapering

In June 2013, the US announced a tapering of some QE policies that was dependent on economic conditions, such as inflation and unemployment, being favourable.

Following this announcement, stock markets dropped by over 4%. During the QE programme a lot of the extra money had found its way into the equity markets and had previously driven up share prices. The Fed started paring purchases in early 2014 and ceased in Q4 2014. By this time, the Fed had accumulated assets with a value of $4.5 trillion. The end of QE is indicative that the US has enough confidence in the economic recovery to continue without its QE programme.

2.6 Monetary and Fiscal Policy

Learning Objective

1.2.6 Understand the role, basis and framework within which monetary and fiscal policies operate: government spending; government borrowing; private sector investment; private sector spending; taxation; interest rates; inflation; currency revaluation/exchange rates/purchasing power parity; Monetary Policy Committee

Governments can use a variety of policy instruments when attempting to reduce short-term cyclical fluctuations in economic activity, so as to maintain the economy at or near its full employment level of output. Collectively, these measures are known as **stabilisation policies** and are categorised under the broad headings of fiscal policy and monetary policy.

Fiscal policy was used as the key policy instrument by successive governments between the late 1930s and the mid-1970s, until an economic condition known as **stagflation** – a combination of rising unemployment and high rates of inflation – began to pervade the world economy, despite the implementation of fiscal policies to counter it. Governments then began to adopt **monetary policy** instead as the key instrument to influence the economy, until it too was abandoned as a sole economic tool in the late 1980s.

Most governments now adopt a pragmatic approach to controlling the level of economic activity, through a combination of fiscal and monetary policy. Governments will deploy both fiscal and monetary policy to achieve their economic objectives.

They will use monetary policy to control the supply and cost of money and fiscal policy to set their objectives on borrowing, spending and taxation. In an increasingly integrated world, however, controlling the level of activity in an open economy in isolation is difficult, as financial markets rather than individual governments and central banks tend to dictate economic policy.

2.6.1 Fiscal Policy

Fiscal policy refers to government policy that attempts to influence the direction of the economy through changes in taxes and spending.

In using fiscal policy, governments aim to influence:

*   aggregate demand and the level of economic activity
*   the pattern of resource allocation
*   the distribution of income.

Government fiscal policy can be neutral, expansionary or contractionary:

- A **neutral** stance implies the government is operating a balanced budget where spending is fully funded by tax revenues and where the overall effect of the budget is to have a neutral effect on the economy.
- An **expansionary** stance involves the government increasing government spending to stimulate economic activity, and funding this through borrowing to create a larger budget deficit.
- A **contractionary** fiscal policy is where a government seeks to reduce the level of economic activity by increasing taxes or reducing government spending.

Governments use fiscal policy to influence the level of aggregate demand in the economy in an effort to achieve their economic objectives of **price stability**, **full employment** and **economic growth**.

In times of recession they can adjust government spending and taxation to stimulate aggregate demand and provide a framework for strong economic growth and increased employment. This will be funded through increased borrowing, and the theory is that the deficits this creates can be paid for by an expanded economy.

In times of high economic growth, governments can adjust their tax and spending plans to create a budget surplus and so decrease activity in the economy by removing funds from the economy, thereby reducing the levels of aggregate demand.

Determining whether or not a government is pursuing an expansionary or a restrictive fiscal policy is not always easy. Although the existence of a budget deficit, or PSNCR, may imply that an expansionary fiscal stance is being adopted, this deficit may simply be as a result of the economy operating below its full employment level.

To establish whether a deficit has been caused by structural or cyclical factors and to determine the fiscal stance being taken, economists usually calculate whether a budget deficit, budget surplus or balanced budget would result at current government spending and tax rates if the economy were operating at full employment, rather than below this level.

There are, however, three practical problems associated with fiscal policy:

- **Time-lags** – the length of time that elapses between recognising the need for action (based on economic data that is itself time-lagged), implementing the appropriate policy and the policy impacting the economy can be considerable. So much so that these time-lags can render fiscal policy a destabilising rather than a stabilising influence, especially if fiscal policy is used excessively in an attempt to fine-tune demand, as it used to be immediately before and after general elections.
- **Crowding out** – if an expansionary fiscal policy is financed through borrowing, this borrowing will increase the market rate of interest to the detriment of that element of business investment and some consumer spending that would have been undertaken at the lower interest rate.
- **Higher future tax rates** – pursuing an expansionary fiscal policy may result in a higher future tax burden being imposed on the economy.

2.6.2 Monetary Policy

Monetary policy refers to government policy that aims to achieve growth and stability in the economy, through a set of controls designed to influence the supply of money in the economy.

Monetary policy is usually implemented by a central bank or monetary authority, and seeks to influence economic activity by controls on the:

- supply of money
- availability of money, and
- cost of money or rate of interest.

In the UK, interest rate decisions are made by the Monetary Policy Committee (MPC), which comprises nine members: five from the Bank of England, including the Bank of England governor and his deputy governors, and four independent members, drawn from both industry and finance.

The MPC's sole policy instrument is setting the base rate. At its monthly meetings it must consider all of the factors that can influence this measure of inflation over both the short and medium term. These include the level of the exchange rate, the rate at which the economy is growing, how much consumers are borrowing and spending, wage inflation, and any changes to government spending and taxation plans. When setting the base rate, however, it must also be mindful of the impact any base rate changes will have on the sustainability of economic growth and employment in the UK and the up-to-12-months' time-lag of base rate changes feeding through to the economy.

If the CPI is either below 1% or above 3% for three successive months, the governor of the Bank of England must write a letter of explanation to the Chancellor of the Exchequer.

The principle underlying monetary policy is the relationship between the price at which money can be borrowed, ie, interest rates, and the total supply of money. Monetary policy uses a range of tools to control one or both of these, including setting interest rates, adjusting the size of the monetary base and setting bank reserve requirements. These have the effect of either increasing or contracting the money supply.

Monetary policy is referred to as contractionary if it reduces the size of the money supply or raises interest rates, and as expansionary if it increases the size of the money supply or decreases the interest rates.

A central bank influences interest rates by expanding or contracting the monetary base, which is the currency in circulation and banks' short-term reserves on deposit at the central bank. It does this by open market operations, where it buys or sells government debt, depending upon whether it wishes to tighten or ease the amount of money in circulation. The short-term goal of open market operations is usually to achieve a specific interest rate target.

Alternatively, it can lower the interest rate it charges banks for loans, which can make it more attractive for commercial banks to borrow from the central bank; these banks will then use the additional liquidity to expand their balance sheet and increase the credit available in the economy.

A central bank can also influence money supply by changing the reserve requirements, which are the amount of deposits that commercial banks are required to maintain at the central bank. It can also influence long-term interest rates according to its issuance of long-dated bonds and calls.

As with fiscal policy, there are some practical problems associated with monetary policy:

- defining what constitutes the money supply
- controlling the money supply.

Although the central bank can influence the supply of money through interest rate setting, open market operations and changes to the reserve ratio, its impact can be limited as a result of securitisation, whereby firms raise finance through the issue of securities rather than bank loans.

To compound this, the **velocity of circulation of money**, or the demand for money, is not stable or predictable in the short run. This is mainly as a result of financial innovation, deregulation and structural changes in financial markets, as well as changes in the rate of inflation and rate of interest. Therefore, changes in the money supply do not directly translate into changes in the price level.

As with fiscal policy, considerable **time-lags** exist between recognising the need for action through to the implementation of policy having an effect on the economy. Time-lags of up to 12 months typically exist between the date of implementing monetary policy and its effect working through to the economy.

2.6.3   Exchange Rates

An exchange rate is the rate at which one currency trades against another on the foreign exchange market. Like most other rates in economics, the exchange rate is essentially a price: the amount you have to give up to acquire something else, in this case another currency. So an exchange rate is the price you will pay in one currency to get hold of another.

An exchange rate is determined by supply and demand, and some of the factors that will influence this are:

- **Inflation** – if inflation in the UK is lower than elsewhere, UK exports will become more competitive and there will be an increase in demand for sterling. Sterling will rise and this will make imported goods less competitive. Low inflation and low interest rates can cause a liquidity trap. For example, even if interest rates are zero, it does not necessarily deter people from saving and creates a fall in the velocity of circulation when consumer spending is depressed. This in itself can cause deflation; therefore an increase in money supply will not necessarily cause inflation.
- **Interest rates** – if interest rates rise relative to other countries, then that currency will become attractive to investors seeking higher returns and the demand for that currency, and therefore its exchange rate will rise.
- **Change in competitiveness** – if a country's exports become more attractive and competitive, this will cause the value of the exchange rate to rise.
- **Balance of payments** – if imports are greater than exports, this will create a deficit on the current account which needs to be financed by a surplus on the capital account. If a country fails to attract sufficient capital inflows, then there will be a depreciation in the value of the currency.
- **Speculation** – speculative activity in the foreign exchange markets can cause exchange rates to rise or fall.
- Relative strength of other **currencies**.

Purchasing power parity (PPP) is a theory which states that the exchange rate between one currency and another is in equilibrium when their domestic purchasing powers at that rate are equivalent. In simple terms, this means that a basket of goods should cost the same in each country once the exchange rate is taken into account. The theory tells us that price differentials between countries are not sustainable in the long run, as market forces will equalise prices between countries and change exchange rates in doing so.

Exchange rates are determined using either a fixed exchange rate system or a floating exchange rate system.

In a **fixed exchange rate system**, the exchange rate is fixed against another currency such as the dollar. To maintain a fixed exchange rate, a government needs to have a significant level of foreign currency reserves, as it will need to intervene actively in the markets to keep it at the fixed rate.

In a **floating exchange rate system**, one currency is allowed to float freely in the market and find its own level. Although most world currencies currently operate within a system of managed floating, some currencies remain formally pegged to the US dollar, whilst others are managed against a basket of currencies – known as a **crawling peg** – or operate within regional fixed exchange rate systems.

Exchange rate changes can have a significant effect on the economy.

If a currency appreciates in value, this means that it is worth more in terms of a foreign currency. The effects of a rise in the exchange rate are:

*   Exports become more expensive and so fewer goods will be demanded.
*   Imports become cheaper and so demand increases.
*   Aggregate demand falls, leading to lower growth.
*   Inflation falls because of the effect of cheaper prices for imported goods, lower aggregate demand and less demand-pull inflation.

Of course, the value of a currency can also fall in relative terms. In a floating exchange rate system this is referred to as **depreciation** and in a fixed exchange rate system as **devaluation**.

The effect in both cases is a fall in the value of a currency. The effects of a fall in the exchange rate or devaluation are:

*   More competitive exports, increasing demand for those goods.
*   More expensive imports, reducing demand for those goods.
*   Higher economic growth and rising aggregate demand.
*   Potential for rising inflation as increasing aggregate demand may cause demand-pull inflation, and imports are more expensive, causing cost-push inflation. The actual impact will depend on other factors, however, such as spare capacity in the economy and the extent to which firms pass on increased import costs.
*   An improvement in the current account balance of payments.

2.7 Inflation and Unemployment

Learning Objective

1.2.7 Understand how inflation, deflation and unemployment are determined, measured and their inter-relationship

1.2.8 Be able to apply the concept of nominal and real returns

2.7.1 Inflation and Returns

Inflation is the rate of change in the general price level or the erosion in the purchasing power of money.

Controlling inflation is the prime focus of economic policy in most countries, as the economic costs inflation imposes on society are far-reaching, for the following reasons:

- It hinders the ability of the price mechanism to clear markets.
- It reduces the spending power of those dependent on fixed incomes.
- Individuals are not rewarded for saving as borrowers gain at the expense of savers.

This occurs when the inflation rate exceeds the nominal interest rate, ie, when the real interest rate is negative.

Real interest rates are calculated as follows:

$$\text{Real interest rate} = \frac{(1 + \text{nominal interest rate})}{(1 + \text{inflation rate})} - 1$$

So the real return takes into account the inflation rate.

- It creates uncertainty, leading to deferral of firms' investment decisions and consumers' spending decisions.
- Time is spent guarding against inflation rather than being devoted to more productive means.
- Exported goods and services become less competitive internationally.

It is important, however, to distinguish between inflation that can be anticipated and that which cannot when assessing its costs. If inflation can be fully anticipated by society then its costs can be minimised.

Inflation is typically categorised as either:

- **Cost-push inflation** – if firms face increased costs and inelastic demand for their output, the likelihood is that these rising costs will be passed on to the end consumer. Consumers will in turn demand higher wages from firms, causing a wage-price spiral to develop.

or:

- **Demand-pull inflation** – when the economy is operating beyond its full employment level of output, prices are pulled up as a result of an inflationary gap emerging. This excess demand can often stem from the optimism that accompanies rising asset prices but has resulted, on innumerable occasions, from politically inspired tax cuts.

Inflation can be measured in several ways. However, the two most widely monitored are:

- retail prices, and
- producer prices.

The UK's principal measure of inflation is the **consumer prices index (CPI)**. EU countries, of which the UK is one, each calculate a CPI so that inflation rates can be compared between EU nations on a uniform basis.

The other most well-recognised measure of inflation in the UK is the **retail prices index (RPI)**. Originally launched in 1947, this measures the rate at which the prices of a representative basket of goods and services purchased by the average UK household – that is, excluding pensioners and the top 4% of income earners – have changed over the course of a month. Needless to say, the composition and weighting of the various goods and services in the basket has altered dramatically since its inception.

There are a number of different RPI measures. The three most keenly observed are the headline RPI, RPIX, which excludes mortgage interest payments, and RPIY, which further excludes VAT and council tax. The RPI indices are usually published within two weeks of the end of the month covered. The CPI differs from the RPIX both in its method of construction and in totally excluding owner-occupied housing costs.

Inflation at the **factory gate** is measured by two producer price indices (PPIs). These are usually published at about the same time as the RPI indices. The **input index** measures the rate at which the prices of raw materials and other inputs to production processes are increasing, and the **output index**, how the prices of goods leaving factories are behaving. The producer price indices are a useful indicator of inflationary pressures that may eventually feed through to RPIX.

2.7.2   Deflation

Deflation is defined as a general fall in price levels. Although not experienced as a worldwide phenomenon since the 1930s, deflation has been in evidence over the past ten years in countries such as Japan. More recently it has been seen in some of the European countries affected by the sovereign debt crisis. The tough fiscal measures implemented in Ireland following the credit crisis brought about deflation. Irish consumer prices and average wages have fallen by about 4% since 2009, allowing Ireland to regain some competitiveness.

Deflation typically results from negative demand shocks, such as the bursting of the 1990s technology bubble, and from excess capacity and production. It creates a vicious circle of reduced spending and a reluctance to borrow, as the real burden of debt in an environment of falling prices increases.

It should be noted that falling prices are not necessarily a destructive force per se and, indeed, can be beneficial if they are a result of positive supply shocks, such as rising productivity growth and greater price competition, caused by the globalisation of the world economy and increased price transparency.

Japan Inflation Rate 2015–2016

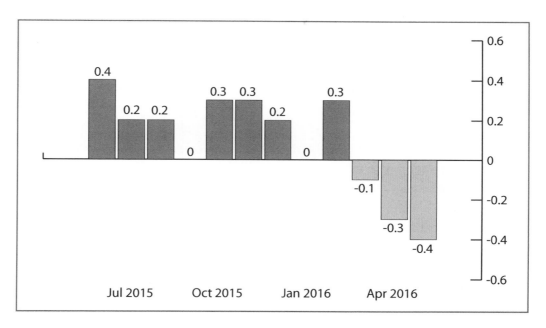

Source: http://www.tradingeconomics.com/japan/inflation-cpi

2.7.3   Unemployment

Another problem with inflation is unemployment. Unemployment can be defined as the percentage of the labour force registered as available to work at the current wage rate.

There are, of course, many other reasons why unemployment exists and they are categorised as:

- **Structural unemployment** – which arises as a result of the changing nature of the economy where certain skills in particular sectors of the economy become redundant.
- **Frictional unemployment** – which is where workers are between jobs or cannot be employed because of disabilities.
- **Keynesian unemployment** – which is structural unemployment on a national scale, as a result of a drop in aggregate demand, causing unemployment in manufacturers and service providers.
- **Classical unemployment** – which is when wages are priced too high.
- **Seasonal unemployment** – where people are employed only for certain parts of the year.

An important concept to understand is that there is a natural rate of unemployment. This is the rate of unemployment in the economy when the labour market is in equilibrium, so that all those who want a job can get one and any unemployment is purely voluntary. This natural or voluntary rate of unemployment therefore includes structural, frictional, classical and seasonal unemployment. Keynesian unemployment is regarded as involuntary.

End of Chapter Questions

Think of an answer for each question and refer to the appropriate workbook section for confirmation.

1. Explain why a linear demand curve may shift in a parallel fashion to the right.
    Answer reference: Section 1.1.1

2. Explain what income elasticity of demand describes and provide an example of what type of goods have YED greater than one.
    Answer reference: Section 1.1.4

3. Identify three factors that affect the elasticity of supply and explain why they have an impact.
    Answer reference: Section 1.1.5

4. Explain the concept of profit maximisation and how it impacts production.
    Answer reference: Section 1.2.1

5. What is marginal propensity to consume and how does it impact GDP?
    Answer reference: Section 2.1.1

6. What factors determine the sustainable or trend rate of growth in the long run?
    Answer reference: Section 2.2

7. If the exchange rate between the UK and a main trading partner strengthens or weakens, how will this affect the balance of payments?
    Answer reference: Section 2.3.3

8. Explain the essential difference between fiscal and monetary policy.
    Answer reference: Section 2.6

Chapter Two
Financial Mathematics and Statistics

This syllabus area will provide approximately 4 of the 80 examination questions

Investment decisions require analysis and interpretation of a wide range of data. As a result, this chapter firstly describes the different types of data, how it is collected and how it can be presented by market data providers, and then looks at some of the core mathematical calculations that are needed for investment management.

1. Statistics

The ability to source and interpret all kinds of information, both qualitative and quantitative, in a timely fashion is key to the portfolio management process. However, since information, or data, can be sourced from a variety of media, is presented in a wide range of formats and is not always in a readily usable form, becoming familiar with information sources and being able to assimilate data is imperative, if informed investment decisions are to be made and investment opportunities are to be capitalised upon.

1.1 Research and Reports

Learning Objective

2.1.1 Understand the different types, uses and availability of research and reports: fundamental analysis; technical analysis; fund analysis; fund rating agencies and screening software; broker and distributor reports; sector-specific reports

The data needed by an investment manager can be sourced from a wide range of sources including:

- Internet websites – these range from those that provide up-to-the-minute general and finance news to those which provide access to comprehensive and more specialist economic, social, demographic and industry information.
- Commercial quote vendors that provide real time security pricing information, as well as historic security and economic data, such as Bloomberg and Reuters.
- Company financial statements.
- Share price charts.
- Independent company analysis provided by specialist research consultancies and credit rating agencies.
- Authoritative in-depth analysis of financial, economic and social trends produced by government statistical departments, central banks, international agencies (such as the World Bank, the International Monetary Fund (IMF) and the Organisation for Economic Co-operation and Development (OECD)), business schools and other academic research organisations.
- Economic bulletins and financial reports.
- Newspapers and other journals.
- Social media.
- Professional interest forums.

1.1.1   Fundamental and Technical Analysis

Fundamental analysis involves the financial analysis of a company's published accounts, along with an analysis of its management, markets and competitive position. It is a technique that is used to determine the value of a security, by focusing on the underlying factors that affect a company's business.

Technical analysis also seeks to evaluate the value of a company, but instead of analysing a company's intrinsic value and prospects, it uses historical price and volume data to assess where the price of a security or market will move in the future. In essence, technical analysts use different quantitative and statistical tools to analyse time-series data of asset prices, behaviours and other characteristics, with a view to discerning recurrences of similar price-development patterns or chart formations.

Both topics are considered further in Chapter 9.

1.1.2   Fund Analysis

There is a dizzying array of investment funds available for equity investment, and it is important to understand the types that are available. This is covered in Chapter 4.

There are a number of independent ratings agencies that provide ratings for investment funds. The majority of these ratings are based on risk-adjusted past performance, though some place considerable weight on qualitative factors, such as how a portfolio manager runs their fund.

Although none of these ratings agencies claims to have predictive power, they seek to provide a valuable tool to filter out those funds that consistently underperform and identify consistent sucess stories by discerning skill as opposed to simple luck. With so many funds available, the ratings agencies provide a valuable way of filtering them down to a manageable number that can be reviewed to determine whether they are suitable for inclusion in a portfolio.

1.1.3   Broker Reports

All major investment banks and brokers publish research reports on numerous matters which are of interest to investors and fund managers.

These research reports may only be made available to clients of the firm, but are also sometimes placed in the public domain.

- These reports may cover macroanalysis, eg, a broker's analyst may be showing research and evidence for the prospects for growth in the US economy over the next year or they may be at the micro-level examining the prospects for specific companies.
- In addition, there are numerous other investment research firms, which provide specialised information on specific sectors of the market, as well an overview of sector performance in general.

1.2 Categorising and Presenting Data

The data that is collected can be categorised into two main types:

- Information or material that is specifically collected for a particular purpose is known as primary data and the conditions under which it was collected and any limitations will be known.
- Secondary data is collected by government agencies and other international bodies. It is then distributed in a convenient form, such as data from the Office for National Statistics (ONS) and typically requires further analysis, if each user is to maximise the value of the information contained within it.

Numerical data can be categorised into that which is continuous, where numbers in a data series can assume any value; or discrete, where the numbers in the data series are restricted to specific values, such as whole numbers.

Recent years have seen the growth of what is known as big data, which refers to large sets of data that exceed the capability of more traditional systems for processing and analysing it. Big data requires a set of techniques and technologies with new forms of integration to reveal insights from datasets that are diverse, complex and of a massive scale.

1.2.1 Populations and Samples

When dealing with data, you must be able to distinguish whether the information relates to an entire population or a sample of a population.

If a population is being considered, then every member or constituent of a particular group will be included in the analysis: all companies contained in the FTSE All Share index for instance. A sample of this population, however, as its name suggests, will only contain a selection of UK company shares from this index.

It is often the case that populations become so large and cumbersome that using and making inferences from samples is the only viable and cost-effective means of analysing the population. As with all samples, the larger this sample of UK shares is, the more representative it will be of the index.

Samples can be either:

- **Random** – that is they are selected randomly, such that each constituent has an equal chance or probability of being included, by using a table of random numbers to ensure that the selection is free from any bias.
- **Non-random** – the alternative is to employ a non-random method of selection that it is believed will select a more representative sample.

1.2.2 Data Presentation

Raw numerical data can be presented in a wide variety of tabulated and graphical formats to enhance its informational value and ease of interpretation.

Tabulated numerical data often takes the form of a frequency distribution table.

A frequency distribution table involves categorising the number of times that something has occurred in each category of investigation. The results are arranged in order of their size and value and may be grouped into subsets, so that the information can be displayed more meaningfully.

For example, you could analyse the age range of the people working in your firm as shown below.

Age Range	No. of People
50 to 60	15
40 to 50	22
30 to 40	26
25 to 30	12
20 to 25	13
Under 20	12
Total	100

As a result of grouping the data, it is possible to detect patterns in the data, such as how many people are employed by different age ranges.

By adding the number of times that something has occurred, it is possible to create cumulative frequency distribution table. It looks almost the same as a frequency distribution table, but it has added columns that give the cumulative frequency and the cumulative percentage of the results, as well.

Age Range	No. of People	Cumulative Frequency	Cumulative Percentage
50 to 60	15	15	15%
40 to 50	22	37	37%
30 to 40	26	63	63%
25 to 30	12	75	75%
20 to 25	13	88	88%
Under 20	12	100	100%
Total	100		

As a result of grouping the data, it is possible to detect further patterns in the data, such as you potentially have an experienced workforce, as over 60% of your staff is aged over 30.

The width of the band, or interval, used will necessarily impact on the usefulness of the data and should, therefore, be chosen carefully.

Knowing how to convey information graphically is important in the presentation of statistics, as is knowing what type of graph to use.

There are many different types of graphs that can be used to convey information including:

- **Bar charts** – display information as bars or columns representing each class of data according to their frequency of occurrence; they are useful for comparison of items and relationships or frequency distribution.
- **Pie charts** – a circle divided into different slices, each representing a different set of data; they are useful for describing the component parts of the data being presented.
- **Histograms** – look similar to bar graphs but it is the area and not the height of the bar that represents the frequency of occurrence; they are often used to illustrate the major features of the distribution of the data in a convenient form.
- **Time series graphs** – display data over time, such as a share price.
- **Scattergrams** – are used to determine whether there is a relationship between two variables and are often used to illustrate a correlation or pattern between different assets.
- **Semi-log graphs** – are used to show the rate of change of a variable and so are used to illustrate an accelerating rate of growth over time.

1.3   Measures of Central Tendency

Learning Objective

2.1.2   Be able to calculate the measures of central tendency: arithmetic mean; geometric mean; median; mode

When dealing mainly with raw numerical data or with ordered numerical distributions, you must be able to make inferences about the data being considered and ideally use it to make predictions. Statistics makes this possible, by drawing on what are known as measures of central tendency and measures of dispersion.

- Measures of central tendency establish a single number or value that is typical of the distribution – that is, the value for which there is a tendency for the other values in the distribution to surround.
- Measures of dispersion, however, quantify the extent to which these other values within the distribution are spread around, or deviate from, this single number.

When you have a set of data and need to summarise it, you will often wish to establish an average that converts the data into a single number that you can use more usefully. The measures of central tendency help capture a single number that is typical of the data. There are three measures of central tendency:

- **Mean** – the average value of all the data.
- **Median** – the middle item that has exactly half the data above it and half below it.
- **Mode** – the most common number that occurs.

The way in which each is calculated is shown below.

1.3.1 Mean or Arithmetic Mean

The arithmetic mean is calculated by adding together all the values in a data set and then dividing that sum by the number of observations in that set to provide the average value of all the data.

Example

If you have six investment funds in your portfolio that produce returns of:

7%; 8%; 9%; 10%; 11%; and 12%

then the average or mean return is (7% + 8% + 9% + 10% + 11% + 12%) ÷ 6 = 9.5%.

The mean is expressed as the following formula:

The average or mean $(\bar{x})$ = $\dfrac{\text{Sum of all observed values}}{\text{Number of observed values}}$ = $\dfrac{\Sigma x}{n}$

1.3.2 Median

The median is the value of the middle item in a set of data arranged in chronological order. It is established by sorting the data from lowest to highest and taking the data point in the middle of the sequence.

Example

So, for example, with a range of data, as below, the median can clearly be seen and that there is an equal series of numbers both below and above it:

2	5	8	9	12	13	15	16	18
4 numbers				Median	4 numbers			

To calculate the median, you place the values in numerical order and then use the following formula where n equals the number of values in the data set:

$$\frac{(n + 1)}{2}$$

So, as you can see in the above example, there are nine values and the median is the fifth one.

If the data has an even set of numbers then the median is equal to the average of the two middle items and the formula in this case is therefore:

$$\frac{(\text{Value below the median} + \text{Value above the median})}{2}$$

Example ——

So, extending the range of data used above we can see that the value below the median is 12 and the value above is 13.

2	5	8	9	12	13	15	16	18	19
				Median = 12.5 (12+13) 2					

1.3.3   Mode

The mode is the most frequently occurring number in a set of data.

- There can be no mode if no value appears more than any other.
- There may also be two modes (bimodal), three modes (trimodal), or four or more modes (multimodal).

Example ——

If we take the following house price values:

£100k; £125k; £115k; £135k; £95k; and £100k

then £100k is the mode.

1.3.4   Which Measure to Use

Several conclusions can be drawn from the above.

- The mean is the most commonly used measure of central tendency, but it needs to be recognised that the outlier numbers at the extremes of the data influence the result.
- The median is not influenced in the same way and is often used if there are extreme outliers or where there is skewed data that is not normally distributed.
- The mode can be problematic, as there may be no mode at all, but is useful if categorical data is used, such as if a café has ten different meals on its menu, the mode will represent the most popular.

So, while it is possible that both the mean and median may result in a number or value that isn't contained within the distribution, the mode will always be one or more of the observed values.

However, only the mean will be influenced by any extreme values within the distribution as only the mean takes every value into account; the median and mode do not.

The relationship between the mean, median and mode depends on how evenly the values are distributed within the sample or population.

- **Symmetrical relationship**.
  - Where the distribution is symmetrical – that is where the ordered data is normally distributed – the three measures of central tendency will produce the same value.
  - Each of these measures is positioned at the peak of a symmetrical, continuous, bell shaped normal curve.
- Where the data is **asymmetrical**, or skewed, however, each measure of central tendency will produce a different value.
  - Negatively skewed frequency – for a negatively skewed distribution, where a larger number of observed values are concentrated towards the higher end of the distribution, the mode, which always pinpoints where a frequency distribution peaks, will be greater than median which will be greater than the mean.
  - Positively skewed frequency – for a positively skewed distribution, where a greater number of observed values are at the lower end of the distribution, the ordering of the mean, median and mode are reversed.

Under most circumstances the mean tends to be a more stable measure of central tendency than the median. However, when moving between samples of a population, and distributions are highly skewed with extreme values, such as the distribution of annual investment returns over long time periods, or the distribution of household income, the median often provides a more representative measure of central tendency. This quality is also possessed by the geometric mean.

1.3.5 Geometric Mean

There is another method of calculating the average that we need to consider: the geometric mean.

The geometric mean is similar to the arithmetic mean except that instead of adding the set of numbers and then dividing the sum by the count of numbers in the set, the numbers are multiplied and then the nth root of the resulting product is taken.

Example

If you have a deposit of £10,000 that you expect will earn 5% pa this year, 6% next year and 5.5% in the third year, then you can use the geometric mean to calculate what the average rate of return is. The geometric mean rate of return is calculated as follows:

$$\sqrt[3]{(1.05 \times 1.06 \times 1.055)} - 1 = 0.054992101 \text{ or } 5.499\%$$

With interest reinvested, the balance of the account at the end of the three years will be:

£10,000 x 1.054992101^3 = £10,000 x 1.174215 = £11,742.15

You can prove this is correct as below:

Balance	Interest Rate	Interest	End Year Balance
10,000.00	5%	500	10,500.00
10,500.00	6%	630	11,130.00
11,130.00	5.5%	612.15	11,742.15

The geometric mean can be useful when looking at compound changes such as portfolio returns.

It will always result in a number that is less than the arithmetic mean, but despite this shortcoming it has a fundamental use in portfolio management, where geometric progressions can be used to establish the compounded value of a variable over time, with the geometric mean then being employed to determine the average compound annual growth rate implied by this cumulative growth.

1.4   Measures of Dispersion

Learning Objective

2.1.3   Be able to calculate and distinguish between the different types of measures of dispersion: variance (sample/population); standard deviation (sample/population); range

Having calculated a typical value from the data that we have available, we now need to see how widely spread out the set of data is around this average value. Understanding how widely investment returns vary is the basis of many hedging techniques, as well as being an important indicator of portfolio returns.

We can quantify this through the use of dispersion measures and can use the following measures:

- Range
- Variance
- Standard deviation
- Inter-quartile range.

Standard deviation is used to establish the distribution of values around the mean and the range and inter-quartile range are used for the median. Each of these is considered below.

1.4.1   Range

The simplest measure of dispersion is the range, which is the difference between the highest and lowest values in a set of data.

Example

Let us assume that the following numbers represent the returns from an investment fund over a ten-year period:

Year	2002	2003	2004	2005	2006	2007	2008	2009	2010	2011
Return	13	11	2	6	5	8	7	9	7	6

Using the range measure indicates that the average returns from the fund had a range of 11 (13 – 2).

The main drawback in using range as a measure of dispersion is that it is distorted by extreme values and ignores the numbers in between.

1.4.2 Variance

Variance measures the spread of data to determine the dispersion of data around the arithmetic mean.

Example

The arithmetic mean for the average fund returns used in the range example above is as follows: (13% + 11% + 2% + 6% + 5% + 8% + 7% + 9% + 7% + 6%) ÷ 10 = 7.4%.

The variance takes the difference between the return in each year from the arithmetic mean and then squares it. These are then totalled and the average of them represents the variance.

This is shown in the table below. Row 2 shows the difference in the return each year from the arithmetic mean and row 3 shows this difference squared.

	Year	2000	2001	2002	2003	2004	2005	2006	2007	2008	2009	Total
1	Return	13	11	2	6	5	8	7	9	7	6	
2	Difference from the arithmetic mean $x - \bar{x}$	5.6	3.6	–5.4	–1.4	–2.4	0.6	–0.4	1.6	–0.4	–1.4	
3	Difference squared $(x - x)^2$	31.36	12.96	29.16	1.96	5.76	0.36	0.16	2.56	0.16	1.96	86.34
4	Average (86.34 ÷ 10)											8.634

Variance is useful in that it provides a measure of dispersion and is used to calculate the beta of a stock, but it results in a value in different units than the original. It is obviously much easier to measure dispersion when it is expressed in the same units, and this is known as standard deviation.

1.4.3 Standard Deviation

The standard deviation of a set of data is simply the square root of the variance and is the most commonly used measure of dispersion. The formula for calculating it is therefore:

$$\text{Population standard variance} = \sigma = \sqrt{\frac{\sum (x - \bar{x})^2}{n}}$$

So, staying with the above example, the standard deviation of the returns from the investment fund is the square root of the average of 8.634, which is 2.94.

Although the variances and standard deviations of both ordered raw and frequency distribution data can be calculated quickly and easily by using a scientific calculator, it is useful to understand how to work through the calculation manually. In summary, the steps you should take in making these calculations manually are as follows:

- obtain the arithmetic mean
- obtain the set of deviations from the mean
- square each deviation
- divide the sum of the squared deviations by the number of observations, to obtain the population variance; and finally
- take the square root of the variance to obtain the standard deviation.

To ensure precision in the calculation of the variance and standard deviation, statistical rules require a slight change to the formula if measuring a sample.

The limitations of small data sets include the fact that they may not provide a representative picture of the population as a whole, and so sampling error may arise. As a result, a slight adjustment to the standard deviation formula is made by reducing the number of observations by one.

The formulas for calculating sample standard deviation is:

$$\text{Sample standard variance} = \sigma = \sqrt{\frac{\sum (x - \bar{x})^2}{n - 1}}$$

In effect, by taking the square root of the variance, the standard deviation represents the average amount by which the values in the distribution deviate from the mean.

With sufficiently large data, the pattern of deviations from the mean will be spread symmetrically on either side and, if the class intervals are small enough, the resultant frequency distribution curve may look like the cross-section of a bell, in other words a bell-shaped curve.

Statistical analysis shows that in a normal frequency distribution curve:

- Approximately two-thirds or 68.26% of observations will be within one standard deviation either side of the mean.
- Approximately 95.5% of all observations will be within two standard deviations either side of the mean.
- Approximately 99.75% of all observations will be within three standard deviations of the mean.

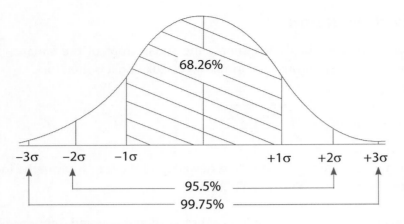

68.26%

95.5%

99.75%

−3σ   −2σ   −1σ   +1σ   +2σ   +3σ

Figure 1: Normal Frequency Distribution Curve

Data does not always conform to a normal pattern and is then referred to as skewed. If the peak of the curve is to the left of centre it is said to be positively skewed and if to the right, negatively skewed. Most long-run distributions of equity returns are positively skewed. That is, equity markets produce more extreme positive and negative returns than should statistically be the case – a phenomenon known as kurtosis – but these extreme positive values far outweigh the negative ones.

1.4.4 Inter-Quartile Range

Another measure of dispersion is the inter-quartile range. The inter-quartile range ranks data such as comparable performance returns from funds against each other, presents the data as a series of quartiles, and then measures the difference from the lowest rank quartile to the highest.

Let us assume that the following figures represent the returns from a number of comparable investment funds. The data is first ranked in order of highest to lowest, the median is identified and the set is then divided into a series of quartiles.

Fund	A	B	C	D	E	F	G	H	I	J	K	L
Return	9%	8%	7.5%	7%	6.5%	6%	5.75%	5%	5%	4.75%	4%	3.5%
Median 5.875%											
Quartiles	1st Quartile			2nd Quartile			3rd Quartile			4th Quartile		
Inter-quartile range	←								→	

A fund with a return in the second quartile will therefore rank in the top half of fund performances, whereas a fund in the fourth quartile will have delivered returns that have been exceeded by 75% of the rest of the sample.

The inter-quartile range is the difference in returns between the 25th percentile ranked fund and the 75th percentile-ranked fund. The smaller the range, the less difference there is in the funds being examined.

76

1.5 Diversification

The risk of holding securities A and B in isolation is given by their respective standard deviation of returns.

However, by combining these two assets in varying proportions to create a two-stock portfolio, the portfolio's standard deviation of return will, in all but a single case, be lower than the weighted average sum of the standard deviations of these two individual securities. The weightings are given by the proportion of the portfolio held in security A and that held in security B.

This reduction in risk for a given level of expected return is known as **diversification**.

To quantify the diversification potential of combining securities when constructing a portfolio, two concepts are used:

- correlation, and
- covariance.

This involves analysing the relationships between the movements of different assets, and so firstly we need to consider the key features of regression analysis, which is the basis of quantifying the relationship between two variables.

1.5.1 Regression Analysis

Learning Objective

2.1.5   Understand the use of regression analysis to quantify the relationship between two variables and the interpretation of the data

Regression analysis is a statistical tool for the investigation of relationships between variables.

Regression analysis is used to ascertain the effect of one variable upon another – the effect of a price increase upon demand, for example, or the effect of changes in the money supply upon the inflation rate. To explore such issues, data is gathered and regression analysis is employed to estimate the quantitative effect of the one variable upon another. The statistical significance of the estimated relationships is also assessed, that is, the degree of confidence that the true relationship is close to the estimated relationship.

A regression equation allows the relationship between two (or more) variables to be demonstrated algebraically. It indicates the nature of the relationship and the extent to which you can predict some variables by knowing others, or the extent to which some are associated with others.

A linear regression equation is usually written as follows:

$$Y = a + bX + e$$

where:

Y = dependent variable.
a = intercept.
b = slope or regression coefficient.
X = independent variable (or covariate).
e = error term.

The equation will specify the average magnitude of the expected change in Y, given a change in X.

The regression equation is often represented on a scatterplot by a regression line. A regression line is a line drawn through the points on a scatterplot to summarise the relationship between the variables being studied.

To achieve this, regression analysis employs a concept known as least squares regression, which by drawing on the data calculates the position of a unique straight line that best represents, or best fits, the collective position of all of these points. It does this by calculating how to collectively minimise the square of each of the vertical distances of these points from a single straight line.

*   When it slopes down (from top left to bottom right), this indicates a negative or inverse relationship between the variables.
*   When it slopes up (from bottom left to top right), a positive or direct relationship is indicated.

As a simple example of this, ask the question: is there a correlation between the amount of time studying for CISI exams and the number of questions answered correctly? Data could be collected and plotted as points on a graph, where the x-axis is the average number of hours of study and the y-axis represents exam scores out of 100. Together, the data points will typically scatter on the graph. The regression analysis creates the single line that best summarises the distribution of points.

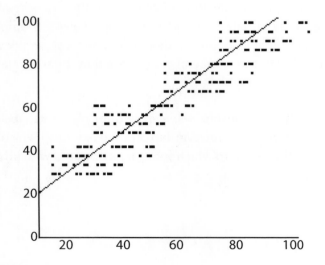

Figure 2: Regression Line

1.5.2 Correlation

Learning Objective

2.1.4   Be able to calculate the correlation and covariance between two variables and analyse the data

Diversification is achieved by combining securities whose returns ideally move in the opposite direction to one another, or if in the same direction, at least not to the same degree.

The correlation coefficient measures the strength of the relationship between two variables, such as shares.

- A positive correlation describes a relationship where an increase in the price of one share is associated with an increase in another.
- A negative correlation is a relationship where an increase in one share price is associated with a decrease in another.
- A perfect correlation is where a change in the price of one share is exactly matched by a change in another. If both increase together they have a positive correlation and the correlation coefficient is +1. If one decreases as the other increases they are said to have a perfect negative correlation and this is described by a correlation coefficient of –1.
- Where there is no predictable common movement between security returns, there is said to be zero or imperfect correlation.

Diversification and risk reduction is achieved by combining assets whose returns have not moved in perfect step, or are not perfectly positively correlated, with one another.

Only when security returns are perfectly negatively correlated, in that they move in the opposite direction to one another at all times and in the same proportion, can they be combined to produce a risk-free return providing diversification and risk reduction. Where there is zero or imperfect correlation, there are still diversification benefits from combining securities. In fact, a perfectly positive correlation, when security returns move in the same direction and in perfect step with each other, is the only instance when diversification benefits cannot be achieved.

It should be noted, however, that correlations can arise from pure chance and so the past correlation coefficients of investment returns are rarely a perfect guide to the future.

The formula for calculating the correlation coefficient is shown below.

$$r = \frac{n(\Sigma xy) - (\Sigma x) \times (\Sigma y)}{\sqrt{([n\Sigma x^2 - (\Sigma x)^2]) \times [n\Sigma y^2 - (\Sigma y)^2]}}$$

where:

n   =   number of values or elements.
X   =   first score.
Y   =   second score.
Σxy =   sum of the product of first and second scores.

Σx = sum of first scores.

Σy = sum of second scores.

Σx^2 = sum of square first scores.

Σy^2 = sum of square second scores.

To calculate the correlation coefficient let's assume that we have the following data on the returns from two assets and see how this is then used in the calculation.

Period	Asset A	Asset B
1	2.0%	3.0%
2	3.0%	5.0%
3	1.0%	2.0%
4	12.0%	8.0%
5	7.0%	4.0%

Example

The first step is to add some additional columns to the data table to enable us to calculate xy, x^2 and y^2.

Period	Asset A	Asset B	xy	x^2	y^2
1	2.0%	3.0%	2.0 x 3.0 = 6	$2.0^2 = 4$	$3.0^2 = 9$
2	3.0%	5.0%	3.0 x 5.0 = 15	$3.0^2 = 9$	$5.0^2 = 25$
3	1.0%	2.0%	1.0 x 2.0 = 2	$1.0^2 = 1$	$2.0^2 = 4$
4	12.0%	8.0%	12.0 x 8.0 = 96	$12.0^2 = 144$	$8.0^2 = 64$
5	7.0%	4.0%	7.0 x 4.0 = 28	$7.0^2 = 49$	$4.0^2 = 16$

Next we can find the sum of those.

Period	Asset A	Asset B	xy	x^2	y^2
1	2.0%	3.0%	6	4	9
2	3.0%	5.0%	15	9	25
3	1.0%	2.0%	2	1	4
4	12.0%	8.0%	96	144	64
5	7.0%	4.0%	28	49	16
Σ	25	22	147	207	118

Now we have those, we can put the numbers into the formula.

$$\frac{5 \times 147 - (25 \times 22)}{\sqrt{[5 \times 207 - (25^2)] \times [5 \times 118 - (22^2)]}} = \frac{735 - 550}{\sqrt{(1035 - 625) \times (590 - 484)}} = \frac{185}{\sqrt{410 \times 106}} = \frac{185}{\sqrt{43460}}$$

$$= \frac{185}{208.4706} = 0.887415$$

In the table above, the returns on the assets over that period show there is a strong tendency for the returns to move together in a close association. This has resulted in a coefficient of correlation between the returns for A and B of 0.89 which indicates a strongly positive correlation. There is strong correlation because there is close degree of co-movement in the returns and the relationship is one of positive correlation because not only are the magnitudes of the changes in returns similar but the sign of the changes track each other. In other words when A is going up so is B, and when A is going down so is B.

1.5.3   Covariance

Learning Objective

2.1.4   Be able to calculate the correlation and covariance between two variables and analyse the data

Covariance is a statistical measure of the relationship between two variables such as share prices.

The covariance between two shares is calculated by multiplying the standard deviation of the first share by the standard deviation of the second share and then by the correlation coefficient.

A positive covariance between the returns of A and B means they have moved in the same direction, while a negative covariance means they have moved inversely. The larger the covariance, the greater the historic joint movements of the two securities in the same direction.

1.5.4   Correlation and Covariance

Both correlation and covariance are time consuming to calculate but it is useful to remember how they are related.

Relationship Between Correlation and Covariance

$$\text{Correlation (A,B)} = \frac{\text{(Covariance (A,B)}}{\text{(Standard deviation (A) x Standard deviation (B)}}$$

As a result of the above:

Covariance (A,B) = Correlation (A,B) x Standard deviation (A) x Standard deviation (B)

It is therefore possible to calculate either, as long as other terms are provided, by remembering the relationship and substituting the terms given.

Example

The covariance between two numbers is 30 and their standard deviations are 5 and 15. What is their correlation?

$$\text{Correlation} = \frac{30}{(5 \times 15)} = 0.40$$

The correlation between two numbers is 0.40 and their standard deviations are 5 and 15. What is their covariance?

$$\text{Covariance} = 0.40 \times 5 \times 15 = 30$$

From these two equations, the following conclusions can be drawn:

- Although it is perfectly possible for two combinations of two different securities to have the same correlation coefficient as one another, each may have a different covariance, owing to the differences in the individual standard deviations of the constituent securities.
- A security with a high standard deviation in isolation does not necessarily have a high covariance with other shares. If it has a low correlation with the other shares in a portfolio then, despite its high standard deviation, its inclusion in the portfolio may reduce overall portfolio risk.
- Portfolios designed to minimise risk should contain securities as negatively correlated with each other as possible and with low standard deviations to minimise the covariance.

2.   Financial Mathematics

Money has a time value. That is, money deposited today will attract a rate of interest over the term it is invested. So, £100 invested today at an annual rate of interest of 5% becomes £105 in one year's time. The addition of this interest to the original sum invested acts as compensation to the depositor for forgoing £100 of consumption, for one year.

Some of the standard calculations based on the time value of money are:

- **Present value** – present value of an amount that will be received in the future.
- **Present value of an annuity** – present value of a stream of equally sized payments.
- **Present value of a perpetuity** – present value of a regular stream of payments that last indefinitely.
- **Future value** – the future value of an amount invested now at a given rate of interest.
- **Future value of an annuity** – the future value of a stream of interest payments at a given rate of interest.

These equations are used frequently in investment management to calculate the expected returns from investments, in bond pricing and for appraisal of investment opportunities.

2.1 Simple and Compound Interest

Learning Objective

2.2.3   Be able to calculate and interpret the data for compound interest; simple interest; net present value (NPV); internal rate of return (IRR)

Interest, whether payable or receivable, can be calculated on either a simple or compound basis. Whereas simple interest is calculated only on the original capital sum, compound interest is calculated on the original capital sum plus accumulated interest to date.

2.1.1   Simple Interest

Simple interest is calculated on the original amount only and assumes that, at the end of each interest period, the interest is withdrawn.

This is obviously the most basic of interest calculations and very straightforward, so if £100 is invested at 5% for one year then you will clearly receive £5 interest.

The variations on this straightforward calculation are where the time period that the amount is invested for is for a number of years or alternatively, for a number of days. So, for example:

- If £200 is invested at a rate of 7% for two years, the simple interest calculation is:
  £200 x 0.07 x 2 = £28.00.
- If £300 is invested at a rate of 5% for 60 days, the simple interest calculation is:
  £300 x 0.05 x 60/365 = £2.47.

It should be noted that the interest rate convention in the UK is to use a 365 day interest year even, in a leap year. Some other countries have different conventions.

In formula terms, this calculation can be expressed as:

Simple Interest = Principal x Rate x Time

or

I = p x r x t

where:

I   =   simple interest, which is the total amount of interest paid
p   =   initial sum invested or borrowed (also called the principal)
r   =   rate of interest to be expressed as a decimal fraction, ie, for 5% use 0.05 in the calculation
t   =   number of years or days expressed as a fraction of a year.

2.1.2   Compound Interest

Compound interest assumes that the interest earned is left in the account or re-invested at the same rate, so that in subsequent interest periods, you are earning interest on both the principal and the interest that has been earned to date.

So, for example, if £100 is deposited in an account at 5% per annum, which is credited to the account at the end of the year, then the balance at the end of the year will be £105. In the second year, interest at 5% will be earned on the starting balance of £105 amounting to £5.25 and the balance on which interest will be earned in the third year will be £110.25 and so on. This is shown in the table below:

Year	Balance at the start of the year	Interest rate	Interest for the year	Balance at the end of the year
1	100.00	5%	5.00	105.00
2	105.00	5%	5.25	110.25
3	110.25	5%	5.51	115.76
4	115.76	5%	5.79	121.55
5	121.55	5%	6.08	127.63

The basic formula for calculating compound interest is:

Initial sum invested x $(1 + r)^n$

where:

- $(1 + r)$ turns the rate of interest into a decimal, so 5% pa becomes 1.05.
- That decimal is then raised to the power where n equals the number of years.

You can prove this by entering the data for five years into your calculator by entering 100 x 1.05 ^ 5 which will show:

$100 x 1.05^5 = $127.62815625

2.2   Present Value

Learning Objective

2.2.1   Be able to calculate and explain the present value of: lump sums; regular payments; annuities; perpetuities

Calculating present value is used to determine how much to invest today, given a rate of interest and frequency of payment, in order to achieve a required amount.

The methods used to calculate present value are known as discounted cash flow (DCF) techniques. The rate of interest that is to be received is known as the discount rate, and the amount that is required to be achieved is known as the terminal value or future value.

2.2.1 Present Value of a Future Sum

The amount that needs to be invested today is established by discounting the amount that is required by the rate of interest. It can be calculated by rearranging the formula for compound interest to:

$$\text{Present value} = \frac{\text{Terminal value}}{(1 + r)^n}$$

We will use the data from the compound interest formula to show that this is the case.

Example

So, although we already know the answer, how much needs to be invested today a 5% per annum to generate $127.62815625 over five years? The formula is:

$$\$127.62815625 \div 1.05^5 = \$100$$

You can prove this by entering into your calculator 127.62815625 ÷ 1.05 ^ 5.

As the present value formula expresses future cash flows in today's terms, it allows a comparison to be made of competing investments of equal risk, which have the same start date but have different payment timings or amounts

2.2.2 Present Value of an Annuity

Present value of an annuity refers to a series of equal cash payments that will be received over a specified period of time.

As before, the present value of an annuity is calculated by discounting the cash flows to today's value. The same formula can be used for regular payments.

$$\text{Present value of an annuity} = £x \times \frac{1}{r} \left[1 - \frac{1}{(1 + r)^n} \right]$$

where:

£x = amount of the annuity paid each year
r = rate of interest over the life of the annuity
n = number of periods that the annuity will run for.

If we expect to receive payments of £100 each over the next three years, we can calculate their present value assuming interest rates are 5% using the above formula.

Example

Using the formula we can calculate that the present value of the cash flows is:

$$\pounds100 \times \frac{1}{0.05}\left[1 - \frac{1}{(1 + 0.05)^3}\right] = \pounds272.32$$

To enter this into a calculator, start with the figures inside the square brackets and enter $1 - 1 \div 1.05 \wedge 3$ followed by = to give 0.136162401. Then multiply this by the values outside the square bracket, in other words, 0.136162401 x 100 x 1 ÷ 0.05 followed by = which will give the answer of 272.32.

The formula enables the present value of each of the cash flows to be established, rather than having to calculate each cash flow individually. The following table shows the calculation and that the interest rate of 5% is referred to as a discount rate.

Year	Cash Flow	Discount Rate	Formula	Discount Factor	Present Value
1	100.00	5%	100.00 ÷1.05	0.9524	95.24
2	100.00	5%	100.00 ÷1.05^2	0.9070	90.70
3	100.00	5%	100.00 ÷1.05^3	0.8638	86.38
Total					272.32

So the present value of those future payments is £272.32. The table also shows how this converts into a discount factor, that is, by how much is the future value is discounted by in decimal terms.

The present value of an annuity can be used for calculating such things as an annuity or the monthly repayments on a mortgage. It can also be used in investment appraisal.

Example

An alternative version of the formula and one that can also be used to find out the present value of a bond is:

Present value of an annuity $=$ Annuity $\times \left[\dfrac{1 - (1+r)^{-n}}{r} \right]$

You should note that $(1+r)^{-n}$ is more simply calculated as $\dfrac{1}{(1+r)^n}$

So, using the same figures as above, the formula becomes:

$$\pounds 100 \times \left[\frac{1 - \left(\dfrac{1}{1.05^3} \right)}{0.05} \right] \quad \text{or} \quad \left[\frac{1 - \left(\dfrac{1}{1.157625} \right)}{0.05} \right] \quad \text{or} \quad \left[\frac{1 - 0.8638376}{0.05} \right] =$$

$$100 \times \frac{0.13616}{0.05} = 272.32$$

2.2.3 Present Value of Perpetuities

Perpetuity is a series of regular cash flows that are due to be paid or received indefinitely, which in practice is defined as a period beyond 50 years.

It is simply calculated using the following formula:

Present value of a perpetuity $=$ annuity $\times \dfrac{1}{r}$

So, for example, if £1,000 is to be received each year in perpetuity, what is its present value at an interest rate of 5%?

$\pounds 1,000 \times \dfrac{1}{0.05} = \pounds 20,000$

Although a perpetuity really exists only as a mathematical model, it can be used to approximate the value of a long-term stream of equal payments by treating it as an indefinite perpetuity.

Example

If you have a commercial property that generates £10,000 of rental income and the discount rate is 8%, then the formula can be used to calculate its present value by capitalising those future payments into its present value, which will be £125,000.

2.3　Future Value

Learning Objective

2.2.2　Be able to calculate and explain the future value of: lump sums; regular payments

Future value refers to the future value of an amount invested now at a given rate of interest.

We effectively already looked at future value when we considered compounding interest. We saw that the future value of £100 deposited today at 5% per annum for a period of years was:

Year	Balance at the start of the year	Interest for the year at 5% per annum	Balance at the end of the year
1	100.00	5.00	105.00
2	105.00	5.25	110.25
3	110.25	5.51	115.76
4	115.76	5.79	121.55
5	121.55	6.08	127.63

The formula for calculating future value is a version of the one we saw earlier.

Future value = Present value x $(1 + r)^n$

So, to calculate the value in five years' time of £100 invested today at 5% per annum, we enter this into a calculator as 100 x 1.05 ^ 5 = 127.63.

If interest is paid more frequently, the formula is adjusted, so that if interest is instead paid half-yearly it will become:

£100 x 1.025^{10} = £128.00845

In the example above, therefore, the rate of interest for the half-year has been calculated first: namely, half of 5% which is then expressed as a decimal as 1.025. The term is then converted into the number of periods on which interest will be paid, in other words, ten half-yearly interest payments.

2.3.1　Applying Compound Interest to Regular Payments

So far we have concentrated on establishing the final value of invested lump sums when compound interest is applied. We now move on to looking at how final values are established when a series of equal payments are invested either at the start or the end of each year. The former payments are known as being made in advance, while the latter are termed as being made in arrears.

The next two tables show the formula that is used when investing at the start of the year and an example of how the formula is used.

If investing at the start of each year, then the formula is:

$$FV_n = \text{regular payment} \times \left\{ \left(\frac{(1+r)^{n+1} - 1}{r} \right) - 1 \right\}$$

Example

£100 is invested at the start of each year for five years at a fixed rate of interest of 6% per annum compounded annually. What will the accumulated value of these series of payments be at the end of the five-year period?

Solution

$$£100 \times \left\{ \left(\frac{(1 + 0.06)^{5+1} - 1}{0.06} \right) - 1 \right\} = £597.53$$

The following table shows a detailed calculation to prove the formula.

Year	Opening Balance	Deposit	New Balance	Interest Rate	Interest	Balance at Year End
1	0	100	100.00	6%	6	106.00
2	106.00	100	206.00	6%	12.36	218.36
3	218.36	100	318.36	6%	19.10	337.46
4	337.46	100	437.46	6%	26.25	463.71
5	463.71	100	563.71	6%	33.82	597.53

The next two tables show the formula that is used when investing at the end of the year and an example of how the formula is used.

If investing at the end of each year, then $FV_n = \text{regular payment} \times \left(\frac{(1+r)^n - 1}{r} \right)$

Example

£100 is invested at the end of each year for five years at a fixed rate of interest of 6% per annum compounded annually. What will the accumulated value of these series of payments be at the end of the five year period?

Solution:

$$£100 \times \left(\frac{(1 + 0.06)^5 - 1}{0.06} \right) = £563.71$$

Note: The difference between this final sum and that above where each payment had been made at the start of the year = £597.53 – £563.71 = £33.82. This difference is solely accounted for by one earlier payment being invested over the entire five-year period, ie, (£100 x 1.06⁵) – £100 = £33.82.

This can be validated as shown in the following table.

Year	Opening Balance	Interest Rate	Interest	Deposit	Balance at Year End
1	0.00	6%	0.00	100.00	100.00
2	100.00	6%	6.00	100.00	206.00
3	206.00	6%	12.36	100.00	318.36
4	318.36	6%	19.10	100.00	437.46
5	437.46	6%	26.25	100.00	563.71

2.4 Investment Appraisal

Learning Objective

2.2.3 Be able to calculate and interpret the data for compound interest; simple interest; net present value (NPV); internal rate of return (IRR)

Discounted cash flow (DCF) techniques can be used as means to assess a company's investment projects, such as whether it should expand by acquiring additional capacity.

Companies are often faced with a number of alternative courses of action and must decide which of these alternatives will maximise profit or achieve some other corporate objective. Obviously it is imperative that the correct course of action is taken as, once an investment is made, the success of the business will inevitably be dependent upon on the profitable utilisation of the assets purchased and the cash flows they generate.

DCF analysis is rarely used in isolation. There are known inherent issues with earnings and cash flow forecasting and the model is reliant on the quality of assumptions being made.

2.4.1   Net Present Values

The DCF technique seeks to discount a project's expected cash outflows, in order to compare them against the present value of the expected cash inflows. In other words, it seeks to discount the costs of the investment made and then compares this to the present value of the revenue it expects to derive from the project.

The difference between the present value of the inflows and the present value of the outflows is known as the **net present value (NPV)**.

Example

A company is considering undertaking an investment project that will require it to spend £75,000 this year and which, in return, it expects to generate revenues of £20,000 in the first year and the same amount in each of years two, three, four and five. The discount rate it uses is 10%.

To calculate the net present value of the proposed expenditure, we know that the investment was made at the beginning of year one and so does not require discounting, but that we need to calculate the present value of the expected income streams as below:

Year	Cash Outflows	Cash Inflows	Formula	Discount Factor	Discounted Cash Flow	Total
1	−75,000.00			1.00	−75,000.00	−75,000.00
1		20,000	20,000.00 ÷ 1.10	90.91	18,181.82	
2		20,000	20,000.00 ÷ 1.10 ^ 2	82.64	16,528.93	
3		20,000	20,000.00 ÷ 1.10 ^ 3	75.13	15,026.30	
4		20,000	20,000.00 ÷ 1.10 ^ 4	68.30	13,660.27	
5		20,000	20,000.00 ÷ 1.10 ^ 5	62.09	12,418.43	75815.74
Net Present Value (NPV)						815.74

The difference between the cash outflow and the discounted cash inflows is £815.74, so the project has a net present value of £815.

We could, of course, have used the formula for calculating the present value of an annuity to arrive at the same answer.

Example

The discounted value of the cash inflows would be:

$$£20,000 \times \frac{1}{0.10} \left[1 - \frac{1}{(1 + 0.10)^5} \right] = £75,815.74$$

This could then have been deducted from the value of the cash outflows of £75,000 to give a net present value of £815.74.

If the NPV is positive, a company will consider undertaking the project, as a positive NPV shows that the project is expected to generate a surplus in present value terms, having taken account of the amounts invested and all costs associated with the project.

2.4.2 Internal Rate of Return (IRR)

By applying a discount rate to a project's anticipated cash flows, we can determine that if the result is a positive NPV then this implies that the project should return in excess of the discount rate over the term of the project, if the cash flow estimates prove correct.

However, the cash flows associated with any prospective project are just estimates, and the cost of capital used may not always accurately reflect the risk of the project.

Therefore it is useful to establish what the break-even rate of return is, or that discount rate which implies a NPV of zero. This rate of return is called the internal rate of return (IRR) or DCF yield.

As the only accurate way to establish this IRR is through a lengthy process of trial and error, using a range of discount rates, an approximate IRR is usually derived through a short-cut methodology known as **interpolation**. Interpolation takes a lower discount rate that produces a positive NPV and a higher discount rate that results in a negative NPV, and then finds the rate between them that produces a zero NPV.

Competing projects are usually ranked in ascending order of their respective NPVs rather than their IRRs, as the NPV provides a superior means of ranking. The IRR, instead, should only be used as a way of establishing the break-even rate of return for investment projects. The formula is:

$$\text{Approximate IRR} = r_1 + \left\{ \frac{\text{Positive NPV}}{(\text{Positive NPV} - \text{Negative NPV})} \times (r_2 - r_1) \right\} \times 100$$

The reference to r_1 and r_2 is to the discount rate used to produce a positive NPV and a negative one as explained in the following example.

Example

An example of how an IRR can be calculated is shown below but candidates should note that in the examination only a straightforward calculation would be required.

Assume that a project has the following cash flows and that we use a discount rate of 10% and 20%.

Year	Cash Flows	NPV at 10%	NPV at 20%
1	−10,000	−10,000.00	−10,000.00
2	6,500	5,371.90	4,513.89
3	6,500	4,883.55	3,761.57
NPV		255.44	−1,724.54

Note:

- The discount rates selected should ideally produce a positive NPV and a negative one.
- As you should see from the table, the first produced a positive NPV and so is referred to as r_1 and the second a negative one which is therefore r_2.
- For simplicity, it is assumed that the expenditure in year 1 (shown as a negative cash flow) takes place at the beginning of the year and does not require discounting.
- The positive cash flow in year 2 is assumed to take place at the end of year 2 so that is discounted for the full two years. The net present value of the cash flow of 6,500 at a discount rate of 10% is $6{,}500 \div (1.10^2) = 5{,}371.91$. The NPV at a discount rate of 20% is $6{,}500 \div (1.20^2) = 4{,}513.89$.
- The positive cash flow in year 3 at an NPV of 10% is $6{,}500 \div (1.10^3) = 4{,}883.55$ and the NPV at a discount rate of 20% is $6.500 \div (1.20^3)$.

We can use the formula to find out the approximate IRR as follows:

$$\left\{ 10 + \frac{255.44}{(255.44 - 1{,}724.54)} \times (10 - 20) \right\} \times 100 = \text{Approximate IRR of } 11.7\%$$

Note:

- The discount rate that produces a positive NPV (r_1) of 10% is shown simply as 10. The notation 'x 100' indicates that you should turn the result back into a percentage.
- The result is shown as an approximate IRR as this only gives the starting point for further calculations, because as you can see from the table below using the discount rate of 11.7% does not give you an NPV of zero.

Year	Cash Flows	NPV at 11.7%
1	−10,000	−10,000.00
2	6,500	5,209.63
3	6,500	4,663.95
NPV		−126.42

- Instead, further calculations are needed to find out the actual IRR. As the discount rate is producing a negative NPV, it is too high and a lower one is needed.
- You might start identifying this by picking a discount rate of, say, 11%. Using this produces a positive NPV and so indicates a figure a little higher is needed. You would then use higher rates until by a process of trial and elimination you can narrow down the band in which the actual IRR can be found.
- Using a discount rate of 11.2% produces a negative NPV of −16.26, which is only a little too high, and a discount rate of 11.1% produces a positive NPV of 5.97, indicating that the actual IRR lies between the two. Further iterative calculations show that the actual IRR is 11.125%.

Year	Cash Flows	NPV at 11.2%	NPV at 11.1%	NPV at 11.15%	NPV at 11.125%
1	–10,000	–10,000.00	–10,000.00	–10,000.00	–10,000.00
2	6,500	5,256.59	5,266.05	5,261.32	5,263.68

2.4.3   Using Discounted Cash Flow (DCF) Techniques

Further considerations that should be borne in mind when using DCF techniques include:

- **Forecasting errors** – the initial investment and any subsequent costs and/or the anticipated revenues may be incorrectly forecast.
- **Government policy** – government policy has been ignored in the above analysis. However, a change in tax policies and/or legislation may impact the project either positively or negatively.
- **Inflation** – inflation has also been ignored. However, if expected inflation is incorporated into the analysis, then the project's cash flows must be expressed in current prices, or in real terms, if they are to be discounted by a real, or inflation-adjusted, discount rate.
- **Assessing the risk of the project** – depending on its exact nature, acceptance of a project can increase or indeed reduce the risk attached to a company's existing operations. This must be taken into account when choosing the discount rate.

2.4.4   Discount Rate Used

Learning Objective

2.2.4   Understand the importance of selecting an appropriate discount rate for discounting cash flows

The rate of interest or discount rate used to calculate the net present value of a project is one of the most important factors in investment appraisal.

For a project to be viable, the return needs to be greater than its cost of capital. A company's cost of capital depends upon the sources of that capital and will typically be either equity or debt.

If it is equity, then this involves the use of share capital and reserves, and the cost of capital is equal to the return expected by shareholders. If debt is used, then the cost of capital is the interest payments on any debt less any corporation tax relief.

Most projects undertaken by companies involve financing by both debt and equity. As a result, the weighted average cost of capital (WACC) is the appropriate discount rate to use for investment appraisal. It is often known as the hurdle rate, in that it represents the minimum return that must be achieved from a project to be worthwhile.

End of Chapter Questions

Think of an answer for each question and refer to the appropriate workbook section for confirmation.

1. How does a sample differ from a population?
   Answer reference: Section 1.2.1

2. You have a choice of the following types of graph to display information – bar chart; pie chart; histogram; scatter diagram. Which would be most useful to understand the relationship between two variables?
   Answer reference: Section 1.2.2

3. What is the arithmetic mean and median for the following series of stock returns?
   7%; –7%; 3%; 9%; –2%
   Answer reference: Sections 1.3.1 and 1.3.2

4. State what the most commonly used measure of dispersion is and describe it?
   Answer reference: Section 1.4.3

5. We can summarise the relationship between two variables using bivariate linear regression. What is shown on the x and y axis?
   Answer reference: Section 1.5.1

6. £10,000 is invested in a fixed term account for three years at a fixed rate of 3% per annum payable quarterly. If interest is left in the account what will be the balance of the account at the end of the term?
   Answer reference: Section 2.1.2

7. A client needs £10,000 in five years' time. How much needs to be invested today if a return of 5% pa can be achieved over the period?
   Answer reference: Section 2.2.1

8. £100 is invested at the start of each year for five years at a fixed rate of interest of 3% per annum compounded annually. What will the accumulated value of these series of payments be at the end of the five-year period?
   Answer reference: Section 2.3.1

Chapter Three
Asset Classes and Investment Strategies

This syllabus area will provide approximately 15 of the 80 examination questions

1. Characteristics of Equities

1.1 Different Classes of Equities

Learning Objective

3.1.1   Understand the main investment characteristics, behaviours and risks of different classes of equity: ordinary, cumulative, participating, redeemable and convertible preference shares; bearer and registered shares; voting rights, voting and non-voting shares; ranking for dividends; ranking in liquidation; tax treatment of dividend income

---

A company's share capital can be broadly divided into two distinct classes of share:

- Ordinary shares.
- Preference shares.

1.1.1 Ordinary Shares

Ordinary shares represent the primary risk capital of a company.

This can be readily understood by considering that buying a company's ordinary shares confers what is known as an equity interest in the company, that is, a direct stake is taken in the company's fortunes. If the company does well, shareholders can expect to share in that success, but, if it were to go bust, the investor could lose the total value of their investment. They are only entitled to receive what is left over, once all other claims on the company's resources have been settled.

Over the longer term, ordinary shareholders have been handsomely rewarded for assuming this equity risk, though in the short term they have generally experienced a greater volatility in returns than any of the other main asset types.

Ordinary shares are usually referred to as ordinary £1 shares, ordinary 25p shares or some similar variation, with the amount – £1 or 25p – representing what is known as their nominal value.

Nominal Value of Shares

When a company is first created, individuals come together and subscribe funds to form the company. They may subscribe equal amounts or different ones but they will obviously have a share in the company. This ownership or part share in the company is represented by the number of shares they have in the business.

For example, imagine you and a friend decide to create a company to undertake business and the initial amount of capital that is subscribed by both of you is £100 but that you subscribe £60 and your friend subscribes £40. At the outset of the business, you clearly own 60% and your friend owns 40%. This ownership is reflected in the number of shares that are allocated to you.

You could decide to set the nominal value of shares in the company at £1, in which case you would have 60 ordinary £1 shares and your friend 40 ordinary £1 shares. Your respective shareholdings determine the amount of the business that you own and how profits will be shared in the future.

The nominal value of the shares in this case is £1. At the outset of the company, it was worth £100; the cash you both subscribed. As the business progresses, the value of the business will hopefully grow and let's assume that very quickly it is worth £10,000. Your shares remain as ordinary £1 shares but you own 60% of a business worth more than that. This is why they are referred to as having a nominal value of £1.

The nominal value is of no special significance, except if a company wishes to issue further shares, when it must do so at or above this price, and in the event of the company going into liquidation.

Shares of No Par Value

Some countries have ordinary shares that have no par value. The US is the most obvious example where ordinary shares are instead referred to as common shares or common stock.

Under company law, a company's shareholders have what is known as limited liability. This means that they have no personal liability for the payment of the company's debts and their liability extends only to the extent of any outstanding payment on the nominal value of the company's shares held if issued partly paid.

Partly Paid Shares

Staying with the example above, let's assume that instead of paying the full nominal value of each share when the business is incorporated, you each only pay half. In that case, you still own 60 ordinary £1 shares but they will be described as partly paid. In this example, they are 50p paid, reflecting that you only paid half of the amount due.

Should the business not go as planned and it has debts beyond what it owes, as an ordinary shareholder you have a liability for payment of those debts. Under the legal concept of limited liability, however, your liability to make further payments to the company is limited to the unpaid amount. You have a liability to subscribe a further £30 – in other words, you committed to subscribe to 60 ordinary £1 shares, but paid only half of that and so are liable to pay the remaining amount to the liquidator of the company.

Ordinary shares are typically irredeemable as there is no specified provision for their repurchase by the company.

Other types of ordinary shares include:

- **Non-voting shares** – they are often designated as either A or B shares, and rank equally alongside other ordinary shares in all other respects.
- **Deferred shares** – in order to retain an element of control, a company's original promoters may have deferred, or founders', shares that confer enhanced voting rights in exchange for their right to a dividend being deferred for a set period.
- **Redeemable shares** – companies are permitted to issue ordinary shares that can be redeemed, or bought back, by the company, so long as conventional non-redeemable ordinary shares are also in issue.

For publicly listed companies that are quoted on a main market such as the London Stock Exchange (LSE), it is rare to see non-voting shares or deferred shares. They are more regularly encountered with unlisted companies or smaller companies that only have relatively small proportion of their shares listed on a stock exchange.

Redeemable Shares

Publicly listed companies will on occasions issue redeemable shares. This is often done as a way to return capital to the ordinary shareholders in a tax efficient manner.

A company must always have conventional ordinary shares in issue and these cannot have redemption provisions, as they represent the equity capital of the company. If a company has been successful and built up funds, there may come a point where it wants to return some of that capital to the ordinary shareholders. It could do so by paying dividends or winding the company up and paying the funds to the shareholders.

The latter would be a dramatic solution but paying out as dividends may involve significant tax liabilities for some shareholders. An alternative method is to issue redeemable shares to existing shareholders who hold these in addition to their existing shares. These redeemable shares will have fixed dates on which the shares can be surrendered to the company, in return for payment of a cash sum and a final date at which the nominal value of the shares will be paid. The range of dates is intended to give shareholders flexibility over when they redeem their shares, so that they can time this to best suit their personal tax position.

These shares are often referred to as B shares or even C shares. They should not be confused with the non-voting shares referred to above.

1.1.2   Preference Shares

In addition to ordinary shares, companies can also issue preference shares. Financial institutions, such as banks, have been regular issues of preference shares.

Preference shares rank ahead of ordinary shares for the payment of dividends and for capital repayment in the event of the company going into liquidation. They are usually only entitled to a fixed rate of dividend based on the nominal value of the shares, so a 6% preference £1 share will pay a net annual dividend of 6p per share. The dividend is payable only if the company makes sufficient profits and the board of directors declare payment of the dividend.

Most preference shares in issue are cumulative, which means they are entitled to receive all dividend arrears from prior years before the company can pay its ordinary shareholders a dividend. Normally, they do not carry voting rights except when the dividend is in arrears.

Other types of preference shares include:

*   **Participating preference shares** – in addition to the right to a fixed dividend, these shares are also entitled to participate in the company's profits, if the ordinary share dividend exceeds a pre-specified level.
*   **Redeemable preference shares** – these are issued with a predetermined redemption price and date. Some redeemable preference shares are issued as convertible preference shares.

- **Convertible preference shares** – these preference shares, as well as having a right to a fixed dividend, can be converted by the preference shareholder into the company's ordinary shares at a pre-specified price or rate on pre-determined dates. If not converted, then the preference shares simply continue to entitle the shareholder to the same fixed rate of dividend until the stated redemption date.

Convertible preference shares are usually issued in the following circumstances:

- **Takeovers** – the bidding company in a takeover will issue convertible preference shares to the target company's shareholders, so as to defer the dilution of the bidder's ordinary share capital.
- **Company restructuring** – companies undergoing a capital restructuring may issue convertible preference shares to their creditors in exchange for waiving outstanding debts.

Convertible preference shares will have a specified conversion ratio, which sets out how many convertible shares can be converted into one ordinary share. As a result, a conversion premium or discount can be calculated.

If it is at a discount then the convertible is a less expensive way of buying into the ordinary shares than buying these shares directly. This happens when the price of the convertible has lagged behind the rise in the ordinary share price or offers a relatively less attractive rate of dividend. The opposite is true if the convertible stands at a premium.

The conversion premium/discount is calculated as follows:

$$\left[\frac{(\text{Conversion ratio} \times \text{market price of convertible shares})}{\text{Market price of ordinary shares}} - 1\right] \times 100$$

The conversion ratio in the formula refers to the number of convertible preference shares that have to be converted into one ordinary share.

The calculation and its use can be seen by looking at the following example.

Example

A company has issued 7% cumulative redeemable preference shares at 110p. They are currently priced at 125p per share and can be converted into the company's ordinary shares at the rate of five preference shares for one ordinary share.

If the ordinary shares are priced at 600p, the conversion premium or discount is calculated as follows:

$$\left[\frac{(5 \times 125)}{600} - 1\right] \times 100 = 4.2\%$$

The result shows that the convertible shares are at a premium to the ordinary shares and so buying the convertible preference shares is a more expensive route than buying the ordinary shares directly. However, the fixed rate of dividend currently being paid on the preference shares may be sufficiently attractive, when compared to that being paid on the ordinary shares, to justify the premium.

The fact that the shares are at a premium also indicates that it is not worth exercising the option to convert into ordinary shares. This can be seen by simply comparing the respective values of the shares as follows:

Shares	Number of Shares	Price	Market Value
Convertible Preference Shares	5	£1.25	£6.25
Ordinary Shares	1	£6.00	£6.00

When considering whether to convert the shares, an investor should also look at the effect that conversion will have on the income received.

1.1.3   Bearer and Registered Shares

An investor's share of a company is determined by the number of shares they own and these shares can be either registered or bearer.

When a company is first created, individuals come together and subscribe funds to create the company and in exchange receive shares in the company to reflect that ownership. Share ownership is usually recorded in a register of shareholders, hence the name registered shares.

A private company will typically issue a share certificate to each shareholder to show the number of shares they hold. The share certificate records the number of shares they hold and their name but it is the entry in the share register that is definitive proof of ownership.

In the past, when a shareholder wanted to sell their shares to another person this involved completing a transfer form and then sending the share certificate and the form to the company so that their ownership could be cancelled and the new owner's name entered on the share register.

This was inefficient and lead to delays and difficulties settling share transactions. As a result, today it is normal for ownership of shares to be held electronically and for transfer of ownership to take place by amending this electronic record. This process is known as book entry transfer.

All developed markets require shares to be held and settled in this way. The shares held in this way may be referred to as immobilised or dematerialised.

- **Immobilised** – refers to where share certificates are still issued but they are held in a central vault and not issued to shareholders, hence the term immobilised.
- **Dematerialised** – was a process that was developed later and involves dispensing with the certificate altogether.

In most markets, there will be one organisation responsible for holding the electronic records and settling trades, known as a central securities depository (CSD). In the UK, this is undertaken by Euroclear and in the US by the Depository Trust Corporation (DTC).

In the UK, the method used is dematerialised but it is not compulsory and so investors can still demand and hold physical share certificates. This is usually only done by private shareholders who have just a few shares however.

The alternative to registered share ownership is bearer.

Bearer Shares

This involves issuing a share certificate to represent the number of shares that an investor owns but the fundamental difference is that there is no name on the share certificate. The company therefore only keeps a record of the share certificate issued and each has a unique number to identify it.

As there is no name on the share certificate or share register, transfer of ownership takes place simply by passing the certificate on to another person. The person who holds the share certificate – the bearer – is the owner.

In practice, bearer shares are held by a central securities depository to overcome the problems that would otherwise arise of lost share certificates and the risk of them being used by criminals to launder money.

Bearer is the method often used for eurobond and other international bond issues.

Traditionally, few UK companies issued bearer shares and they were abolished, after a phasing out period, in February 2016. This was in order to improve the transparency of company ownership.

1.1.4 Voting Rights

Ordinary shareholders are entitled to a number of rights, which will be specified in the company's Articles of Association.

Rights of Ordinary Shareholders

As we saw above, ordinary shareholders own the company. Under the Companies Acts, however, day to day control of the company is undertaken by the board of directors, which is empowered to act on behalf of the company.

Imagine that you are a shareholder in a company. This means that you are a part owner in that business and the board of directors is running it on your behalf. Although they have authority to run it, as an owner you need a mechanism to ensure that they can be held accountable for the actions they undertake on behalf of the owners and that you have a say in certain key issues affecting the company. This is the reason why shareholders need rights.

The rights of ordinary shareholders include the following:

- Being notified in advance of all company meetings and attending and voting on resolutions put by the directors at these meetings.
- Receiving a copy of the company's annual and interim report and accounts.
- Sharing in the profits of the company through the payment of dividends.
- Subscribing for new ordinary shares issued to raise additional capital before they are offered to outside investors.

These are considered below.

- **Company meetings**
  - Companies need to hold the directors to account in their management of the company and they do so through formal company meetings.
  - Companies are required to hold annual general meetings and further extraordinary meetings when certain special proposals need the approval of the shareholders, the owners. (An example is a proposed takeover of the company.)
  - Shareholder must be notified in advance of all company meetings and there are formal notice periods that must be adhered to.
- **Receiving a copy of the company's annual and interim report and accounts**
  - The board of directors are required to present the annual report and accounts to shareholders at the annual general meeting (AGM).
  - The purpose is to seek shareholder endorsement of their management of the business during the period, which is achieved by asking shareholders to vote on a resolution to accept the accounts.
- **Voting**
  - The directors present resolutions to the shareholders at company meetings and ask them to vote in favour in order to obtain approval.
  - Shareholders are entitled to attend meetings and vote on the resolutions put by the directors at these meetings.
  - A shareholder typically has one vote per share and can attend and vote in person or appoint a proxy to attend and vote on their behalf.
- **Sharing in the profits of the company**
  - Shareholders are the owners of the company and participate in the profits made through the payment of dividends.
  - The board of directors is empowered to run the company and their powers include determining whether there is sufficient profit to warrant payment of a dividend.
  - It is for the directors to propose that a dividend be paid and up to the shareholders to decide whether they agree with the proposal, by voting on this at the AGM.
- **Subscribing for new ordinary shares**
  - Shareholders are the owners of the company and if the company wants to raise additional equity capital they must first seek shareholder approval.
  - This is known as a pre-emption right, as the company must seek approval from shareholders to do so and must allow existing shareholders to subscribe additional capital, before they are offered to outside investors.

1.1.5 Ranking for Dividends

A dividend is a payment, or distribution, to shareholders out of the profits of the company.

Ordinary shareholders represent the owners of a company and so are entitled to participate in the profits of a company. They typically participate in profits by payment of dividends from the profits the company has made, although there are other ways in which they may do so. As a result, they can only do so once all other obligations of the company have been met.

Preference shareholders have a prior claim on payment of their dividend, hence the use of the term 'preference' in their title. Preference shares are typically entitled to a fixed dividend of a certain percentage of the nominal value of the shares and this must be paid before any dividend can be declared and paid to ordinary shareholders. Unless the preference shares are non-cumulative, any arrears of dividends from a previous year is paid first, followed by that year's dividend and then only if there is sufficient profit remaining can an ordinary share dividend be declared.

1.1.6 Ranking in Liquidation

Equity capital is the risk capital of a company and so is the last to be paid out in the event of liquidation of a company.

On the liquidation of a company, its assets will be realised and the proceeds distributed. The order of priority for payment is governed by the Insolvency Act 1986 which is shown below.

The Insolvency Act 1986 priority list

1. Fixed charge holders.
2. Insolvency practitioner fees and expenses.
3. Preferential creditors.
4. Ring fenced fund for unsecured creditors.
5. Floating charge holders.
6. Unsecured creditors.
7. Interest on debts proved in winding up.
8. Money due to a member under a contract to redeem or repurchase shares not completed before winding up.
9. Debts due to members.
10. Repayment of residual interests to preference, and then ordinary shareholders.

The key point to note is that preference and ordinary shareholders are paid out only after all other claims are met. As with dividend payments, preference shareholders have priority over ordinary shareholders. Preference shareholders receive back the nominal value of the shares held if sufficient funds remain; ordinary shareholders are entitled to share the funds that remain, if there are any.

1.1.7 Tax Treatment of Dividend Income

The tax treatment of dividends depends upon whether they are paid on preference shares or ordinary shares:

* Preference share dividends are treated for income tax purposes as payments of interest and so are taxed in the same way as other forms of interest such as bank interest or bond interest payments.
* Ordinary share dividends are treated as dividend income.

Chapter 8 contains more detail on the tax treatment of dividends and interest.

1.2 Depository Receipts

Learning Objective

3.1.2 Understand the purpose, main investment characteristics, behaviours and risks of depositary receipts: American depositary receipts; global depositary receipts; beneficial ownership rights; structure; unsponsored and sponsored programmes; transferability

Investor demand for Depositary receipts is growing and is driven by the increasing desire of individual and institutional investors to diversify their portfolios globally, reduce risk, and invest globally in the most efficient manner. Depositary receipts provide a cost effective and simple way of investing in overseas companies, without the higher costs that are normally associated with owning foreign shares.

A depository receipt is a negotiable instrument that represents an ownership interest in securities of a foreign issuer, typically trading outside its home market. The two common types that are encountered are:

- American depositary receipts (ADRs).
- Global depositary receipts (GDRs).

1.2.1 American Depositary Receipts (ADRs)

American depositary receipts (ADRs) were introduced in 1927 and were originally designed to enable US investors to hold overseas shares, without the high dealing costs and settlement delays associated with overseas equity transactions.

An ADR is dollar-denominated and issued in bearer form, with a depository bank as the registered shareholder. They confer the same shareholder rights as if the shares had been purchased directly. The depositary bank makes arrangements for issues such as the payment of dividends, also denominated in US dollars, and voting via a proxy at shareholder meetings. The beneficial owner of the underlying shares may cancel the ADR at any time and become the registered owner of the shares.

The United States is a huge pool of potential investment and so ADRs enable non-US companies to attract US investors to raise funds. ADRs are listed and freely traded on the New York Stock Exchange (NYSE), the American Stock Exchange (AMEX) and NASDAQ. An ADR market also exists on the LSE.

Each ADR has a particular number of underlying shares, or is represented by a fraction of an underlying share.

Example

Volkswagen AG (the motor vehicle manufacturer) is listed in Frankfurt and has two classes of shares listed – ordinary shares and preference shares. There are separate ADRs in existence for the ordinary shares and preference shares. Each ADR represents 0.2 individual Volkswagen shares.

This gives investors a simple, reliable and cost-efficient way to invest in other markets and avoid high dealing and settlement costs. Other well-known companies, such as BP, Nokia, Royal Dutch Shell and Vodafone, have issued ADRs.

1.2.2   Global Depositary Receipts (GDRs)

They are not the only type of depositary receipts that may be issued. Those issued outside the US are termed global depositary receipts (GDRs). These have been issued since 1990 and are traded on many exchanges.

Depository receipts are increasingly issued by Asian and emerging market issuers. For example, more than 400 GDRs from 37 countries are quoted and traded on a section of the LSE. GDRs are also listed and traded in Luxembourg, Singapore and Dubai.

The rise of sophisticated international markets has driven a shift since 2001 toward GDRs, as global corporations increasingly seek to raise capital in the international markets. In some cases, GDRs are created not to raise capital but to establish a presence in a new market in order to increase the company's visibility and pave the way for future offerings.

1.2.3   Sponsored and Unsponsored Programmes

Issues of depositary receipts can be either sponsored or unsponsored.

- **Sponsored Programmes**
  - This is where depositary receipts are issued by one depositary appointed by the company under a deposit agreement or service contract.
  - Sponsored depositary receipts give control of the facility to the company, provide flexibility on which exchange the listing takes place and provide the ability to raise capital.
- **Unsponsored Programmes**
  - This is where depositary receipts are issued by one or more depositaries in response to market demand but without a formal agreement with the company.
  - This method is now little used by issuers, due to the lack of control and costs.

1.2.4   Structure

London is the main centre for the issue of new global depositary receipts.

Listing GDRs on the LSE involves using the formal listing process. The company will need to appoint a sponsor, decide on whether a public offer or placing is most appropriate and meet the listing requirements of the United Kingdom Listing Authority (UKLA).

Some of the key requirements that have to be met include:

- GDRs must be must be freely transferable, fully paid and free from any restrictions on transfer.
- They must be admitted to trading on a recognised investment exchange (RIE).
- The expected aggregate market value of all GDRs to be listed must be at least £700,000 unless there are shares of the same class already listed on the LSE.

- 25% of the GDRs (not total share capital) must be in public hands.
- The GDRs must not impose obligations on the depositary except to the extent necessary to protect the GDR holders' rights.

Instead of listing on the main market, the issuer may choose to list on the Professional Securities Market or at PLUS Markets where some of the obligations to be met will be different.

The percentage of shares that may be converted into depositary receipts will depend on local restrictions on foreign ownership.

As mentioned above, the issuer will appoint a depository bank and enter into a deposit agreement which defines depositary's role and allows it to issue the company's depositary receipts.

DR certificates are not issued; instead a master certificate is issued to a custodian who is also known as the common depositary. They will hold the certificate on behalf of the depository in an international CSD such as agents Clearstream and Euroclear. As DRs are issued and cancelled, the number of DRs outstanding goes up and down automatically.

The Company must announce its intention to float on the market via the exchange at least 10 business days before the start of trading of the shares or 20 business days if they are joining from a designated market. DRs listed on the LSE are traded on the international order book.

In certain circumstances, the custodian bank may issue depositary receipts before the actual deposit of the underlying shares. This is called a pre-release of the DR and so trading may take place in this pre-release form. A pre-release is closed out as soon as the underlying shares are delivered by the depository bank.

1.2.5   Beneficial Ownership Rights

Depositary receipts carry most but not all ownership rights associated with the underlying shares.

- Depositary receipts provide for dividends to be converted and the net proceeds after deduction of any fees to be paid out in the currency of the DR, which is typically US dollars.
- Good corporate governance requires an issuer to give their DR holders the right to vote in shareholder meetings. The depository bank will obtain details of meetings and provide details of voting arrangements to DR holders. They will then receive their voting instructions and provide the custodian voting instructions and any necessary paperwork for the votes to be included in the shareholders' meeting.
- Because of the structure of DRs, it is not possible for rights issues to be taken up and instead the depository bank will sell the rights and distribute proceeds to DR holders.

1.2.6   Transferability

Once the depositary receipts are listed, they are traded and settled in the same way as other equities.

The market price of a depositary receipt is equivalent to the ordinary share price times the depositary receipt ratio, multiplied by the applicable foreign exchange rate plus any transaction costs.

DRs are usually priced in dollars although it is possible for them to be established in other currencies. They can therefore trade as normal for other equities but one major difference is that they are not liable to stamp duty reserve tax (SDRT) which is charged at 0.5% on other equity purchases.

The DRs will typically be held in Europe at either Clearstream or Euroclear and in the US at the Depository Trust and Clearing Corporation (DTCC) depository bank.

A brief summary of the role of the issuer, the depository bank and the custodian is shown below.

Issuer	Depository Bank	Custodian
• Provides notices of shareholder meetings • Pays corporate distributions • Meets ongoing listing obligations	• Issues depositary receipts against deposit of local shares with the custodian • Handles investor queries • Converts and pays dividends • Provides tax withholding documentation	• Registers shares in depositary account with issuer's registrar • Notifies details of corporate actions • Remits dividends to depository

2. Issuing Equity Securities

2.1 Primary and Secondary Issues

Learning Objective

3.2.1 Understand the purpose, key features and differences between the following: primary issues; secondary issues; issuing, listing and quotation; dual listings

Recognised stock exchanges, such as the LSE in the UK and the NYSE in the US are marketplaces for issuing securities and then facilitating the trading of those securities, via the trading and market-making activities of their member firms. All stock exchanges provide both a primary and a secondary market.

2.1.1 Primary Issues

The primary market, or the new issues market, is where securities are issued for the first time.

The primary markets exist to enable issuers of securities, such as companies, to raise capital and enable the surplus funds held by potential investors to be matched with investment opportunities that the issuers offer. It is a crucial source of funding.

The terminology often used is that companies **float** on the stock exchange when they first access the primary market. The process that the companies go through when they float is often called the initial public offering (IPO). Companies can use a variety of ways to achieve flotation, such as offers for investors to subscribe for their shares, offers for sale and offers for subscription.

There are no guarantees that an IPO will succeed in selling all of the shares being offered, and, if markets are going through periods of adversity and turmoil, it is common for an IPO to be withdrawn. New issues may be sold on a **best efforts** basis by the manager of the IPO or can be underwritten by an investment bank or the shares sold in an offering.

A large IPO is usually underwritten by a **syndicate** of investment banks led by one or more major investment banks. Upon selling the shares, the underwriters keep a commission, based on a percentage of the value of the shares sold, called the **gross spread**. Usually, the lead underwriters, ie, the underwriters selling the largest proportions of the IPO, take the highest commissions – up to 8% in some cases.

When a company applies for a listing on a stock exchange, it must comply with a series of rules and, once listed, comply with a series of ongoing obligations. The competent authority for authorising the listing of shares in the UK is the UKLA which is part of the Financial Conduct Authority (FCA). It sets the rules relating to becoming listed on an exchange, including the implementation of any relevant EU directives.

The UKLA is responsible for authorising the listing of shares and bonds, but it is then up to a stock exchange to further approve them for trading on their exchange, a process known as 'admitted to trading'. The LSE is responsible for the operation of the exchange, including the trading of the securities on the secondary market, although the UKLA can suspend the listing of particular securities and remove their secondary market trading activity on the exchange.

In a similar way in the US, the Securities and Exchange Commission (SEC) requires companies seeking a listing on the US exchanges to register certain details with the SEC first. Once listed, companies are then required to file regular reports with the SEC, particularly in relation to their trading performance and financial situation.

2.1.2 Secondary Issues

The secondary market is where existing securities are traded between investors, and stock exchanges provide a variety of systems to assist in this, such as the LSE's stock exchange electronic trading service (SETS) system that is used to trade the largest companies' shares. These systems bring together liquidity giving investors the ability to sell their securities if they wish.

Secondary issuances or secondary public offerings of shares are often referred to as 'follow-on offerings' as they refer to an issuance of stock subsequent to the company's initial public offering. A follow-on offering can be either dilutive or non-dilutive or a mix of both.

In the case of a dilutive offering, such as a rights issue, a company's board of directors agrees to increase the number of shares in issue by selling more equity in the company. The proceeds from the secondary offering may be used to pay off some debt or used for business expansion. When new shares are created and then sold by the company, the number of shares outstanding increases and this causes dilution of earnings on a per share basis. Usually the gain of cash inflow from the sale is strategic and is considered positive for the longer term goals of the company and its shareholders.

The non-dilutive type of follow-on offering is when privately held shares are offered for sale by company directors or other insiders (such as venture capitalists) who may be looking to diversify their holdings. Because no new shares are created, the offering is not dilutive to existing shareholders, but the proceeds from the sale do not benefit the company in any way.

As with an IPO, the investment banks who are serving as underwriters of the follow-on offering will often be offered the use of a green shoe or over-allotment option by the selling company.

2.1.3   Issuing, Listing and Quotation

To offer shares for sale to the public via an IPO, a UK company must be a public limited company. It must then meet the listing requirements of the exchange and, once listed, fulfil the continuing obligations.

A listing on a Stock Exchange involves two applications. Responsibility for the approval of prospectuses and admission of companies to the Official List lies with the UKLA. The exchange is responsible for the admission to trading of companies to the market. Arranging a listing on an exchange consequently involves two applications: one to the UKLA and one to the exchange.

Companies seeking a listing have to meet stringent entry criteria. These criteria are known as the Listing Rules and are administered by the FCA in its capacity as the UKLA. The requirements that have to be met for a main listing on the London Stock Exchange or AIM are covered in Section 2.3.

Once companies have obtained a listing, they are subject to a strict set of rules and regulations set by the UKLA known as continuing obligations.

Among other things, these require a company to promptly make public all price-sensitive information and issue the annual and interim report and accounts to shareholders within a set timeframe.

Price-sensitive information is information which would be expected to move the company's share price in a material way once in the public domain. This includes details of any significant change to a company's current or forecast trading prospects, dividend announcements, directors' dealings and any notifiable interests in the company's shares. A notifiable interest is where a shareholder or any parties connected to the shareholder has at least a 3% interest in the nominal value of the company's voting share capital. Where that is the case, they must inform the company of their interest within two business days.

2.1.4   Dual Listings

Dual listing refers to the fact that many securities are listed on more than one exchange. A company's shares can be listed and traded internationally both on the London Stock Exchange and the New York Stock Exchange, such as in the case of BP, Vodafone and HSBC.

Dual listing can also refer to stocks trading on more than one exchange within the same jurisdiction. Many stocks are traded on the New York and other regional exchanges. For example, the common stock of General Motors is listed on the NYSE but it also enjoys a large amount of activity on regional exchanges.

Although dual listing theoretically should improve the liquidity of a stock thereby benefiting investors, most dual listed securities trade chiefly on one exchange.

Dual listing can have other consequences. For example, a UK company with a US listing is obliged to meet the requirements of the US Sarbanes Oxley Act on the accuracy of financial statements and is subject to the US Foreign Corrupt Practices Act.

2.2   Regulatory Framework for UK Financial Markets

Learning Objective

3.2.2   Understand the main regulatory, supervisory and trade body framework supporting UK financial markets: Companies Acts; the Financial Conduct Authority (FCA); Prudential Regulation Authority (PRA); UK Listing Authority (UKLA); HM Treasury; the Panel on Takeovers and Mergers (POTAM); exchange membership and rules; relevant trade associations and professional bodies

The regulatory framework that underlies the way that financial markets operate includes oversight and compliance with the following:

- Companies Acts.
- Regulations and requirements of the FCA, formerly the Financial Services Authority (FSA).
- Supervision and vigilance by HM Treasury.
- The Panel on Takeovers and Mergers (POTAM), also known as the Takeover Panel.
- Rules of membership set by exchanges, clearing houses, trade associations and professional bodies.

2.2.1   Companies Acts

The Companies Act 2006 is the longest act ever, running to 1,300 sections. It introduces many reforms and is also a consolidation of virtually all existing company legislation.

Some of the key areas it covers include:

- company names
- memorandum of association
- articles of association
- share capital and maintenance of capital
- company meetings
- communication with shareholders
- directors' duties
- company secretary and company records
- annual reports and accounts
- strategic reporting.

One of the key aims of the act is to provide a statutory statement of directors' duties. The act contains a statutory statement of directors' general duties, replacing the existing common law rules arising from decisions made by the courts.

These new duties were introduced from 1 October 2007. In codifying directors' duties, the Government's intention was, for the most part, not to change them, but to establish good business sense for companies to embrace wider social responsibilities.

As the directors of a company are empowered to undertake the day-to-day management of a company, this clearly needs to come with some legal obligations to its owners, the shareholders. Directors are therefore required to act in good faith when undertaking their legal duties and to comply with their statutory responsibilities under the Companies Act 2006.

High-level guidance has been issued as to how directors should act to ensure compliance with their duties as follows:

- Act in the company's best interests, taking everything you think relevant into account.
- Obey the company's constitution and decisions taken under it.
- Be honest, and remember that the company's property belongs to it and not to you or to its shareholders.
- Be diligent, careful and well informed about the company's affairs. If you have any special skills or experience, use them.
- Make sure the company keeps records of your decisions.
- Remember that you remain responsible for the work you give to others.
- Avoid situations where your interests conflict with those of the company. When in doubt, disclose potential conflicts quickly.
- Seek external advice where necessary, particularly if the company is in financial difficulty.

The Act also introduced the concept of enlightened shareholder value. This broadly replaced the old duty to act in the company's best interests, but requires directors to have regard to the longer term and to various corporate social responsibility factors, including the interests of employees, suppliers, consumers and the environment.

Section 172 requires each director to act in a way that he or she considers, in good faith, is most likely to promote the success of the company for the benefit of its members as a whole, and in doing so have regard to factors such as:

- The likely long-term consequences of their actions.
- The interests of employees.
- Relationships with customers and suppliers.
- The impact of the company's operations on the community and environment.
- The desirability of maintaining a reputation for high standards of business conduct.
- The need to act fairly between members of the company.

However, it is important to note that this is a single duty to work for the benefit of shareholders, rather than a separate set of duties in relation to the stakeholders, represented in the list of factors. Directors will only be liable for breach of this duty if it can be demonstrated that a loss has been suffered as a result of the breach.

In addition to these duties, directors continue to have responsibilities to ensure that:

*   The company is not wrongfully trading.
*   The company does not pay an illegal dividend.
*   They are not illegally involved with 'phoenix' companies – where the assets of a failed company are moved to another legal entity.
*   They do not act in breach of disqualification orders.
*   Accounts are prepared properly, with proper keeping of books and records

There are civil and criminal sanctions and penalties for breaches of the responsibilities and duties of a director.

2.2.2 The Financial Conduct Authority (FCA) and the United Kingdom Listing Authority (UKLA)

The FCA authorises financial services business in the UK and, more specifically in terms of financial markets, has to give its recognition before an exchange is allowed to operate in the UK.

As we have already seen, the UKLA is the body responsible for setting and administering the listing requirements and continuing obligations for public limited companies seeking and obtaining a full list on a UK stock exchange.

All listed companies are expected to abide by the UK Corporate Governance Code as a condition of their listing on the LSE, and report on how they have applied the code in their annual report and accounts.

UK Corporate Governance Code

The code is a guide to a number of key components of effective board practice. It is based on the underlying principles of all good governance: accountability, transparency, probity and focus on the sustainable success of an entity over the longer term.

The code is not a rigid set of rules but a set of main and supporting principles and provisions. The listing rules require companies to apply the main principles and report to shareholders on how they have done so.

The code recognises, however, that an alternative to following a provision may be justified in particular circumstances if good governance can be achieved by other means. A condition of doing so is that the reasons for it should be explained clearly and carefully to shareholders – the **comply or explain** principle.

Some of the key elements of the code are:

*   Principles on the composition and selection of the board, to encourage boards to be well-balanced and avoid 'group think'.

- To promote proper debate in the boardroom, there are principles on the leadership role of the chairman, the responsibility of the non-executive directors to provide constructive challenge and the time commitment expected of all directors.
- A requirement for the chairman to hold regular development reviews with each director and three yearly board evaluations.
- All directors of FTSE 350 companies should be re-elected annually.
- A requirement for the company's business model to be explained to improve risk management.
- Performance-related pay should be aligned to the long-term interests of the company and its risk policies and systems.

Public limited companies and the concept of limited liability first came about in Victorian times and a key element of this approach is to give Boards of Directors the responsibility to manage the company effectively and deliver long-term success for the benefit of its owners, the shareholders.

The UK Corporate Governance Code states that: *'The board and its committees should consist of directors with the appropriate balance of skills, experience, independence and knowledge of the company to enable it to discharge its duties and responsibilities effectively.'*

The code also states that the board should have a strong presence of both executive and non-executive directors, so that no individual or small group can dominate its decision-taking. At least half the board, not counting the chairman, should be independent, non-executive directors. This means that a board of nine, for example, needs to have at least four independent non-executives to balance four executive directors, with the chairman being the ninth director. An exception is made for a smaller company outside the FTSE 350. These are urged to have at least two independent non-executive directors.

This approach requires what is referred to as a 'unitary board' made up of a chairman, executive directors and non-executive directors to act as a single decision-making board. This can be contrasted with the German model where the non-executive directors form part of a separate supervisory body.

One of the independent non-executive directors should also be appointed as the senior independent director. Their role is to act as an alternative point of contact for major shareholders, who may have made little headway in discussions with the chairman, chief executive or finance director – or who may have concerns about the performance of such individuals. They also serve as a sounding board for the chairman and act as an intermediary for the other directors. The senior independent director also takes the lead in annual appraisals of the chairman.

The importance of sound corporate governance cannot be overstated, as public anger over remuneration in the banking sector has clearly demonstrated. The scrutiny by investors of how executive remuneration is set in banking and other sectors has meant that remuneration issues dominate the corporate governance agenda.

At one time, public shareholder anger was a rarity, but nowadays significant votes against the directors' remuneration report are increasingly common. Scrutiny of executive remuneration has never been higher. As a result, the role of the remuneration committee has increased in terms of its responsibility to its stakeholders and, because of this, its processes have become more onerous.

The code and the related guidance for remuneration committees resulting from the Greenbury and Higgs reports are designed to strengthen the effectiveness of remuneration committees, clarify and enhance their oversight roles, and enhance their accountability for the setting of an executive remuneration process.

Remuneration committees are faced with trying to balance the expectations of executives on one hand with the needs of the company and its shareholders on the other. This requires them to set remuneration at a level that provides the incentives needed for executives to strive effectively to make the business successful, but not to pay so much that it will fail an appropriateness test and be voted against by shareholders.

UK Stewardship Code

The UK Stewardship Code was published in July 2010. It aims to enhance the quality of engagement between institutional investors and companies, to help improve long-term returns to shareholders and the efficient exercise of governance responsibilities, by setting out good practice on engagement with companies.

The code is addressed at firms who manage assets on behalf of institutional shareholders, such as pension funds, insurance companies, investment trusts and other collective investment vehicles. Investment firms are expected to disclose on their websites how they have applied the code. Pension fund trustees and other owners are also actively encouraged to participate, through the mandates given to fund managers.

It was developed by the Financial Reporting Council and the FCA has begun consultation on proposals to make this a mandatory requirement for authorised asset managers.

The code states that institutional investors should:

- Publicly disclose their policy on how they will discharge their stewardship responsibilities.
- Have a robust policy on managing conflicts of interest, in relation to stewardship and this policy should be publicly disclosed.
- Monitor their investee companies.
- Establish clear guidelines on when and how they will escalate their activities as a method of protecting and enhancing shareholder value.
- Be willing to act collectively with other investors where appropriate.
- Have a clear policy on voting and disclosure of voting activity.
- Report periodically on their stewardship and voting activities.

Prudential Regulation Authorty (PRA)

The Prudential Regulation Authority (PRA) was created as a part of the Bank of England by the Financial Services Act (2012) and is responsible for the prudential regulation and supervision of around 1,700 banks, building societies, credit unions, insurers and major investment firms. The PRA's objectives are set out in the Financial Services and Markets Act (FSMA) 2000.

The PRA's approach to using regulation and supervision has three characteristics: judgment-based, forward-looking and focused. It seeks to ensure that a financial firm which fails does so in a way that avoids significant disruption to the supply of critical financial services. It is a UK public regulatory body.

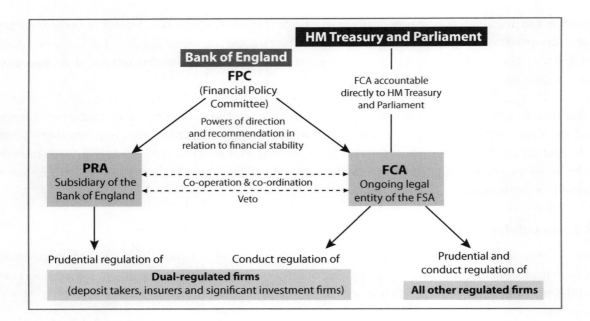

2.2.3 HM Treasury

HM Treasury is the economics and finance ministry, with overall responsibility for fiscal policy, as well as providing a supervisory role for the entire financial framework in the UK.

2.2.4 The Panel on Takeovers and Mergers (POTAM)

The UK supervisory authority that carries out the regulatory functions required under the EU Takeover Directive is the Panel on Takeovers and Mergers (the Panel or POTAM).

The Panel's requirements are set out in a code that consists of six general principles, and a number of detailed rules. The code is designed principally to ensure that shareholders are treated fairly and are not denied an opportunity to decide on the merits of a takeover. Furthermore, the code ensures that shareholders of the same class are afforded equivalent treatment by an offeror. In short, the code provides an orderly framework within which takeovers are conducted, and is designed to assist in promoting the integrity of the financial markets.

The code is not concerned with the financial or commercial advantages or disadvantages of a takeover. These are matters for the company and its shareholders. Nor is the Code concerned with competition policy, which is the responsibility of government and other bodies.

The six general principles are:

- All holders of the securities of an offeree company of the same class must be afforded equivalent treatment; moreover, if a person acquires control of a company, the other holders of securities must be protected.
- The holders of the securities of an offeree company must have sufficient time and information to enable them to reach a properly informed decision on the bid; if it advises the holders of securities, the board of the offeree company must give its views on the effects of implementation of the bid on employment, conditions of employment and the locations of the company's places of business.

- The board of an offeree company must act in the best interests of the company as a whole and must not deny the holders of securities the opportunity to decide on the merits of the bid.
- False markets must not be created in the securities of the offeree company, or the offeror company or of any other company concerned by the bid, in such a way that the rise or fall of the prices of the securities becomes artificial and the normal functioning of the markets is distorted.
- An offeror must announce a bid only after ensuring that he/she can fulfil in full any cash consideration, if such is offered, and after taking all reasonable measures to secure the implementation of any other type of consideration.
- An offeree company must not be hindered in the conduct of its affairs for longer than is reasonable by a bid for its securities.

2.2.5 Exchange Membership and Rules

The regulatory framework in the UK allows the FCA to recognise exchanges as being fit and proper to undertake their activities and clearing houses to similarly be recognised to manage their day-to-day operations.

Investment exchanges and clearing houses have to follow the requirements detailed in the FCA's Recognised Investment Exchange (RIE) and Recognised Clearing House (RCH) Sourcebook.

Orderly markets are maintained via rules, guidance and through the monitoring of trading and market activity. Stock exchange notices disseminate amendments to market rules and guidance. All LSE member firms are bound by the rules of the LSE and must ensure compliance with these rules.

2.2.6 Trade Associations and Professional Bodies

As with exchanges and clearing house, certain professional bodies are recognised as being competent authorities for the supervision of their members' activities.

There is a special section of the Financial Services and Markets Act that enables professional firms, such as law firms and accountancy practices, to conduct some types of regulated activity in certain circumstances without contravening the general prohibition. This special regime is available because professional firms are already subject to high standards of supervision by their professional body, and so an additional layer of regulation is considered unnecessary.

There are a range of other trade associations and professional bodies that supervise or represent the interest of their members.

For example, the International Capital Markets Association (ICMA) represents a broad range of capital market interests, including global investment banks and smaller regional banks, as well as asset managers, exchanges, central banks, law firms and other professional advisers. The ICMA's market conventions and standards have been the pillars of the international debt market for over 40 years.

The ICMA promotes the development and efficient functioning of the international capital market by:

- Maintaining the framework of cross-border issuing, trading and investing through development of internationally accepted standard market practices.

- Liaising closely with governments, regulators, central banks and stock exchanges, both at national and international level, to ensure that financial regulation promotes the efficiency and cost effectiveness of the international capital market.
- Providing education and training.
- Encouraging networking, flow of information and the organisation of market events.

The ICMA is both a self-regulatory organisation and a trade association. It represents members in Europe and elsewhere, with over 370 members located in 47 countries worldwide, who are active in the international capital market on a global or cross border basis. The ICMA is distinctive amongst trade associations in representing both the buy-side and the sell-side of the industry.

Dealings in the international debt market take place between ICMA members. The ICMA Primary Market Handbook (IPMA Handbook) provides standard documentation and a set of recommendations for the primary market side of the industry, whilst the ICMA's rules and recommendations provide a framework of best practice in the secondary market.

2.3 Structure of UK Stock Exchanges

Learning Objective

3.2.3 Understand the structure of the London Stock Exchange, the types of securities traded on its markets and the criteria and processes for companies seeking admission: main market; Alternative Investment Market; PLUS markets; market participants; implications for investors

2.3.1 The LSE Main Market

The LSE began life in 1773, when traders who regularly met to buy and sell the shares of joint stock companies in Jonathan's Coffee House voted to change the name of the coffee house to the London Stock Exchange.

The LSE is Europe's largest stock exchange, accounting for over 35% of European stock market capitalisation, about 10% of world stock market value and over 50% of foreign equity trading on world stock exchanges.

In the rapidly changing financial markets, the LSE has to continue evolving, to adapt to the new platforms and technologies of a very competitive global marketplace.

The LSE is a recognised investment exchange (RIE) and, as such, is responsible for:

- Providing a primary and secondary market for equities and fixed interest securities.
- Supervising its member firms.
- Regulating the markets it operates.
- Recording all transactions, or bargains, executed on the exchange.

- Disseminating price-sensitive company information received by its regulatory news service (RNS) and distributed through commercial quote vendors, also known as secondary information providers (SIPs).

The LSE operates both a primary and secondary market. The major securities which are traded daily on the LSE are:

- Shares of domestic listed public companies or PLCs which are of two main varieties: companies with a full listing and smaller UK companies admitted to the alternative investment market (AIM).
- Exchange-Traded Funds (ETFs) and other new investment products on its extraMARK exchange.
- International equities.
- Domestic corporate bonds.
- UK gilts.
- Local authority fixed interest securities.
- International bonds, including eurobonds.

Membership is available to investment firms and credit institutions authorised in the European Economic Area (EEA).

Companies seeking a full listing on the LSE have to meet stringent entry criteria. These criteria are known as the Listing Rules and are administered by the FCA in its capacity as the UKLA.

These include the following requirements:

- The market value of the company's issued share capital, or market capitalisation, must be at least £700,000, of which no less than 25% must be made freely available to the investing public to ensure an active market in the shares. This 25% is known as the free float.
- The market value of any company bond issues must be at least £200,000.
- All securities issued by the company must be freely transferable, that is, third-party approval to deal in these securities must not be required.
- Any subsequent issue of ordinary shares or of securities that can be converted into the company's ordinary shares must be made to existing shareholders first, unless the shareholders pass a special resolution to forgo their pre-emption right.
- No one shareholder can hold 30% or more of the company's ordinary voting shares.
- The company must have at least three years of audited accounts.
- The company's directors must have appropriate expertise and experience for managing the business.
- For certain types of listings such as equities, the company must appoint a sponsor which is duly authorised by the FCA.

Companies seeking a listing can choose either a premium or a standard listing.

- A premium listing means that a company must meet standards that are over and above (often described as 'super-equivalent') those set forth in the EU legislation, including the UK's corporate governance code and is only available to equity shares issued by commercial trading companies.
- With a standard listing, a company has to meet the requirements laid down by EU legislation. This means that their overall compliance burden will be lighter, both in terms of preparing for listing and on an ongoing basis. Standard Listings cover the issuance of shares and Depositary Receipts as well as a range of other securities, including fixed-income.

As stated earlier, a listing on the LSE involves two applications. Responsibility for the approval of prospectuses and admission of companies to the Official List lies with the UK Listing Authority (UKLA). The Exchange is responsible for the admission to trading of companies to the Main Market. Joining the Main Market consequently involves two applications: one to the UKLA and one to the Exchange.

These rules are relaxed for technology companies that seek a full listing but lack a three-year trading record. Technology companies often require development capital and can apply for a listing on a separate segment of the LSE known as techMARK. Companies applying for a listing on techMARK must possess a market capitalisation of at least £50 million, make £20 million or more of this ordinary share capital available to investors on flotation, and agree to provide quarterly financial reports.

The advantages to a company of obtaining a full listing include:

- raising its public profile
- increasing the liquidity and marketability of its shares so that they can be more easily traded
- gaining easier and less expensive access to new capital.

The disadvantages, however, include:

- the costs and increased accountability associated with obtaining and maintaining a full listing as a result of greater disclosure and compliance requirements
- relinquishing an element of control
- becoming a potential takeover target.

2.3.2 Alternative Investment Market (AIM)

Gaining admission to the AIM is far less demanding than obtaining a full listing, as a minimum market capitalisation, free float and past trading record are not required.

Most AIM companies tend to be those in the early stages of development, typically operating in growth industries or in niche sectors, with a view to applying for a full listing once they become more established.

The criteria to be satisfied to gain admission to AIM includes appointing:

- A nominated adviser (NOMAD) to advise the directors of their responsibilities in complying with AIM rules and the content of the prospectus that accompanies the company's application for admission to AIM.
- A nominated broker to make a market and facilitate trading in the company's shares, as well as provide ongoing information about the company to interested parties.

2.3.3 ISDX

ISDX is an independent recognised investment exchange (RIE) under the FSMA 2000.

Unlike AIM, which is part of the LSE, ISDX is an independent UK stock exchange regulated by the FCA and is a member of the ICAP Group.

The ISDX main board is a market for larger companies; the ISDX Growth Market is for newer, entrepreneurial companies and is regulated as a multilateral trading facility (MTF); while the ISDX Secondary Market allows member firms to quote prices and report trades in listed or quoted securities that are admitted to trading on other non-ISDX markets.

2.3.4 Market Participants

LSE membership consists of all major multi-national banks, as well as smaller boutique private client banks, brokers, dealers, market makers, clearing firms and other financial intermediaries.

Historically the main buyers and sellers, responsible for the bulk of trading activities on the LSE, were high net worth individual investors and corporate investors who were investing in the shares and bonds of other companies. In more recent times, the participants in the daily activities of the LSE, in common with all financial markets, is overwhelmingly conducted by institutional investors such as pension funds, index funds, exchange-traded funds, hedge funds, investor groups, banks and other miscellaneous financial institutions.

2.3.5 Implications for Investors

To operate effectively, investment exchanges need to bring together sources of liquidity and ensure that price formation process is fair and transparent. Exchanges are recognised and supervised by the FCA but they have a vital role to play in ensuring that stock market dealing takes place in an open and honest way.

3. Equity Markets and Trade Execution

3.1 Trade Execution and Reporting

Learning Objective

3.3.1   Be able to apply fundamental UK regulatory requirements with regard to trade execution and reporting: best execution; aggregation and allocation; prohibition of conflicts of interests and front running

3.1.1 Best Execution

The best execution rules are set out in the Conduct of Business rulebook (COBS) and require firms to execute orders on the terms that are most favourable to their client. Broadly, they apply where a firm owes contractual or agency obligations to its client and is acting on behalf of that client.

Specifically, they require that firms when executing orders take all reasonable steps to obtain the best possible result for their clients taking into account the **execution factors**. These factors are price, costs, speed, likelihood of execution and settlement, size, nature or any other consideration relevant to the execution of an order.

The relative importance of each factor will depend on the following criteria and characteristics:

* The client and their client categorisation.
* The client order.
* The financial instruments involved.
* The execution venues to which that order can be directed.

The requirements for best execution extend beyond just price; speed of execution, the likelihood of execution, the likelihood of settlement, the size and nature of the order, market impact and any other implicit transaction costs may be given precedence over the immediate price and cost consideration.

For retail clients, best execution is judged by total consideration. Firms must take account of the total consideration for the transaction; in other words the price of the financial instrument and the costs relating to its execution, including all expenses directly related to it such as execution venue fees, clearing and settlement fees, and any fees paid to third parties.

If a firm can execute the client's order on more than one execution venue, the firm must take into account both its own costs and the costs of the relevant venues, in assessing which will give the best outcome.

Its own commissions should not allow it to discriminate unfairly between execution venues, and a firm should not charge a different commission or spread to clients for execution in different venues, if that difference does not reflect actual differences in the cost to the firm of executing on those venues.

Firms are required to establish an order execution policy to enable them to obtain the best possible results for their clients. This must include, for each class of financial instrument in which the firm deals, information about the different execution venues where the firm executes its client orders, and the factors that will affect the choice of venue used. The policy must include those venues that would enable the firm consistently to obtain the best possible result for its clients.

Firms must give their clients appropriate information about their execution policies; this must be more detailed for retail clients. Firms must obtain their clients' prior consent to their order execution policies, although this may be tacit.

Firms must review their order execution policies whenever a material event occurs, but at least annually and notify clients of any material changes to their order execution arrangements or execution policy.

Wherever a firm receives a specific instruction from a client, it must execute the order as instructed. It will be deemed to have satisfied its obligation to obtain 'the best possible result' if it follows such specific instructions, even if an alternative means of executing the order would have given a better result.

Firms must monitor the effectiveness of their execution arrangements and policies, to identify and, if need be, correct any deficiencies.

In addition they must be able to demonstrate to their clients, on request, that they have executed their orders in accordance with their execution policy.

Portfolio managers and firms receiving and transmitting orders must also maintain order execution policies, but need not get client consent to them. Portfolio managers must act in their clients' best interests when placing orders for them, on the basis of the firm's investment decisions. Firms receiving and transmitting orders for clients must also act in their clients' best interests, when transmitting those orders to other parties such as brokers to execute. This means taking account of the execution factors listed.

3.1.2   Aggregation and Allocation

Firms are required to have procedures and arrangements which provide for the prompt, fair and expeditious execution of client orders, relative to the other orders or trading interests of the firm.

In particular, these should allow comparable client orders to be executed in the order in which they are received. Firms should ensure that:

- Comparable orders are executed sequentially and promptly, unless this is impracticable or client interests require otherwise.
- Retail clients are informed of any material difficulty in the prompt execution of their order, promptly on the firm becoming aware of this.
- Executed client orders are promptly and accurately recorded and allocated.
- If the firm is responsible for arranging settlement, that the assets or money are delivered promptly and correctly.

Firms must not misuse information relating to client orders and must also take steps to prevent its abuse, for example, in order to profit by dealing for its own account.

Firms must only aggregate their own-account deals with those of a client, or aggregate two or more clients' deals, if:

- This is unlikely to disadvantage any of the aggregated clients.
- The fact that aggregation may work to their disadvantage is disclosed to the clients.
- An order allocation policy has been established, which provides, in sufficiently precise terms, for the fair allocation of transactions. This must cover how volume and price of orders will affect allocation; it must also cover how partial allocations will be dealt with.

If an aggregated order is only partly executed, the firm must then allocate the various trades in order with this allocation policy.

If a firm has own-account deals in an aggregated order along with those of clients, it must not allocate them in a way which is detrimental to the clients. In particular, it must allocate the client orders in priority over its own, unless it can show that without the inclusion of its own order, less favourable terms would have been obtained. In these circumstances, it may allocate the deals proportionately.

The firm's order allocation policy must incorporate procedures preventing the reallocation of own-account orders aggregated with client orders, in a way detrimental to a client.

Unless the client instructs otherwise, a firm which receives a client limit order for shares listed on a regulated market and which cannot immediately execute it under the prevailing market conditions must make the limit order public immediately so that it can be executed as soon as possible.

It may do this by transmitting the order to a regulated market or MTF operating an order book trading system or ensuring the order is made public and can be easily executed as soon as market conditions allow.

It need not do so, however, for orders over normal market size.

3.1.3 Conflicts of Interests and Front Running

The rules on conflicts of interest are contained in the FCA's Senior Management Arrangements, Systems and Controls Sourcebook (SYSC).

They require that firms take all reasonable steps to identify conflicts of interest between:

*   The firm, including its managers, employees, appointed representatives/tied agents and parties connected by way of control and a client of the firm.
*   One client of the firm and another.

Firms under these obligations should:

*   Prepare, maintain and implement an effective conflicts policy.
*   Provide retail clients and potential retail clients with a description of that policy.
*   Maintain and apply effective organisational and administrative arrangements designed to prevent conflicts of interest from adversely affecting the interests of their clients.
*   If investment research is produced for external use, have appropriate information controls and barriers to stop information from these research activities from flowing to the rest of the firm's business.
*   If a specific conflict cannot be managed away, ensure that the general or specific nature of it is disclosed.
*   Keep records of those of its activities where a conflict has arisen.

Conflicts of interest rules apply if a firm owes a fiduciary duty to its clients and a conflict arises between its own interests and those of the client. From an investment management perspective, conflicts can arise in how a trade is executed, hence the best execution rules, and over how it is aggregated and allocated, hence the rules on those.

Conflicts can also arise as a result of front running. The practice of front running or pre-positioning – dealing ahead of customer orders – has long been considered wrong since it takes advantage of knowledge of the order and its likely impact on the trading price. It is a form of market abuse and is prohibited under the Code of Market Conduct.

Extract from the FSA Code of Market Conduct (predecessor to the FCA)

1.3.1   *The first type of behaviour is where an insider deals, or attempts to deal, in a qualifying investment or related investment on the basis of inside information relating to the investment in question.*

1.3.2 Description of behaviours that amount to market abuse (insider dealing)

The following behaviours are, in the opinion of the FSA, market abuse(insider dealing):

(1) dealing on the basis of inside information which is not trading information;

(2) front running/pre-positioning – that is, a transaction for a person's own benefit, on the basis of and ahead of an order which he is to carry out with or for another (in respect of which information concerning the order is inside information), which takes advantage of the anticipated impact of the order on the market price.

Other areas where conflicts of interest can arise include:

*   Investment research.
*   Dealing ahead of investment research.
*   Inducements and commissions.
*   Churning.
*   Order of priority given to customer trades.

3.2 Trading Venues

Learning Objective

3.3.2 Understand the key features of the main trading venues: regulated and designated investment exchanges; recognised overseas investment exchanges; structure and size of markets; whether quote or order driven; main types of order – limit, market, iceberg, named; liquidity and transparency

3.2.1 Recognised and Designated Investment Exchanges

The FCA recognises and supervises a number of recognised investment exchanges (RIEs) and recognised clearing houses (RCHs) under FSMA 2000.

Recognition gives an exemption from the need to be authorised to carry on regulated activities in the UK. To be recognised, RIEs and RCHs must comply with the recognition requirements laid down in the FSMA 2000 (Recognition Requirement for Investment Exchanges and Clearing Houses) Regulations 2001.

RIEs, in their capacity as market operators, may operate regulated markets and multilateral trading facilities.

Recognised Investment Exchanges and Markets	Recognised Clearing Houses
• LIFFE Administration and Management • London Stock Exchange plc • ICAP Securities & Derivatives Exchange (ISDX) • The London Metal Exchange ltd • ICE Futures Europe	• CME Clearing Europe ltd • Euroclear UK & Ireland ltd • European Central Counterparty ltd • ICE Clear Europe ltd • LCH.Clearnet ltd

A designated investment exchange (DIE) is one which does not carry on a regulated activity in the UK and is not a regulated market. It may apply to be included on the FCA's DIE list, but before adding an investment exchange to the DIE list, the FCA will look at whether the investment exchange provides an appropriate degree of protection for consumers. The FCA will also undertake a public consultation prior to adding the investment exchange to the DIE list. Designation allows firms to treat transactions effected on a DIE in the same way as they would treat transactions effected on an RIE.

Designated Investment Exchanges

- American Stock Exchange
- Australian Stock Exchange
- Bermuda Stock Exchange
- Bolsa Mexicana de Valores
- Bourse de Montreal Inc
- Channel Islands Stock Exchange
- Chicago Board of Trade
- Chicago Board Options Exchange
- Chicago Stock Exchange
- Coffee, Sugar and Cocoa Exchange, Inc.
- Euronext Amsterdam Commodities Market
- Hong Kong Exchanges and Clearing Ltd.
- International Capital Market Association.
- Johannesburg Stock Exchange
- Kansas City Board of Trade
- Korea Stock Exchange
- MidAmerica Commodity Exchange
- Minneapolis Grain Exchange
- New York Cotton Exchange
- New York Futures Exchange
- New York Stock Exchange
- New Zealand Stock Exchange
- Osaka Securities Exchange
- Pacific Exchange
- Philadelphia Stock Exchange
- Singapore Exchange
- South African Futures Exchange
- Tokyo International Financial Futures Exchange
- Tokyo Stock Exchange
- Toronto Stock Exchange

3.2.2 Recognised Overseas Investment Exchanges (ROIEs)

The FCA has recognised and supervises a number of recognised overseas investment exchanges (ROIEs), and has the power to recognise and supervise recognised overseas clearing houses (ROCHs) under FSMA 2000. In order to be recognised, ROIEs and ROCHs must satisfy the requirements of S.292(3) of FSMA.

Since 1 April 2013, a body applying for ROCH status may not be a central counterparty. The only ROCH is ICE Clear U.S., Inc.

Recognised Overseas Investment Exchanges
• Australian Securities Exchange Ltd
• Sydney Futures Exchange Limited
• Chicago Board of Trade (CBOT)
• EUREX (Zurich)
• National Association of Securities Dealers Automated Quotations (NASDAQ)
• New York Mercantile Exchange Inc (NYMEX Inc)
• SIX Swiss Exchange AG
• The Chicago Mercantile Exchange (CME)

The requirements for recognition under FSMA are that:

- Investors are afforded protection equivalent to that which they would be afforded if the body concerned were required to comply with recognition requirements.
- There are adequate procedures for dealing with a person who is unable, or likely to become unable, to meet his obligations in respect of one or more market contracts connected with the investment exchange or clearing house.
- The applicant is able and willing to co-operate with the FCA by the sharing of information and in other ways.
- Adequate arrangements exist for co-operation between the FCA and those responsible for the supervision of the applicant in the country or territory in which the applicant's head office is situated.

3.2.3 Structure and Size of Markets

According to the statistics from the World Federation of Exchanges, the total value of shares quoted on the world's stock exchanges was US$47 trillion at the end of 2011. The value of shares quoted globally had seen a steady rise from 2002 when they were valued at US$23 trillion to a peak of over US$60 trillion at the end of 2015. The credit crisis had seen values drop by nearly half to a low of US$32 trillion.

World Equity Market Capitalisation

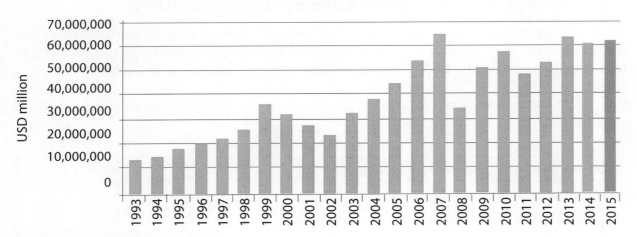

Source: World Federation of Exchanges

The largest stock exchanges in the world are in the US. The New York Stock Exchange (NYSE Euronext) is the largest exchange in the world and had a domestic market capitalisation of over US$19 trillion at the beginning of 2015 – domestic market capitalisation is the value of shares listed on an exchange. (The NYSE is part of the NYSE Euronext Group and, when the value of stock quoted on that European exchange is included, this jumps to over US$22 trillion).

The other major US market, NASDAQ, is ranked as the second largest and had a domestic market capitalisation of US$6.8 trillion, meaning that the two New York exchanges account for close to one third of all exchanges.

In Europe, the largest exchanges are the LSE, NYSE Euronext, the Deutsche Börse and the Spanish exchanges. The LSE has market capitalisations of over US$6 trillion and Euronext (Europe) over US$13 trillion.

The same report shows that Asian exchanges also have an important share of world trading. The Tokyo Stock Exchange is the world's fourth-largest market and has a domestic market capitalisation of US$4.4 trillion, whilst the Shanghai and Hong Kong exchanges are ranked fifth and sixth, with a market capitalisation of around US$3 trillion each.

The economic growth of China and India is also reflected in the domestic market capitalisation of their exchanges. The National Stock Exchange of India and the Bombay Stock Exchange have a combined domestic market capitalisation of over US$3 trillion.

Largest Domestic Equity Markets by Capitalisation	US$ billion
NYSE Euronext (US)	19,223
NASDAQ OMX	6,831
London Stock Exchange Group	6,187
Tokyo Stock Exchange Group	4,485
Shanghai Stock Exchange	3,986
Hong Kong Exchanges	3,325
Euronext (Europe)	3,321
Shenzhen Stock Exchage	2,285
TMX Group	1,939
Deutsche Börse	1,762
Bombay Stock Exchange	1,682
National Stock Exchange of India	1,642
SIX Swiss Exchange	1,516
Australian Securities Exchange	1,272
Korea Exchange	942

Source: World Federation of Exchanges (data as at January 2015)

Rivals to traditional stock exchanges have also arisen with the development of technology and communication networks known as multilateral trading facilities (MTFs). To date, MTFs have had a significant impact within the European markets. MTFs were permitted under the Markets in Financial Instruments Directive (MiFID) in 2007. MiFID describes an MTF as follows:

'A multilateral system, operated by an investment firm or a market operator, which brings together multiple third-party buying and selling interests in financial instruments – in the system and in accordance with non-discretionary rules – in a way that results in a contract.'

MiFID also imposes a number of requirements under which each MTF should operate, according to its own rule book including: pre-trade transparency; pricing must be public and consistent; there must be an application process for membership.

MTFs generally operate on a low-cost base with systems that bring together multiple parties that are interested in buying and selling financial instruments, including shares, bonds and derivatives. These systems can be crossing networks or matching engines that are operated by an investment firm or another market operator.

3.2.4   Quote- and Order-Driven Markets

The trading systems provided by exchanges around the world can be classified broadly as either quote-driven or order-driven.

Quote-driven trading systems employ market makers to provide continuous two-way, or bid and offer, prices during the trading day in particular securities regardless of market conditions. The buying price is the **bid** and the selling price is the **offer**. Market makers make a profit, or turn, through this price spread. Although outdated in many respects, many practitioners argue that quote-driven systems provide liquidity to the market when trading would otherwise dry up. The NASDAQ and the LSE's stock exchange automated quotation (SEAQ) trading systems are two of the last remaining examples of quote-driven equity trading systems.

With order-driven systems, the investors indicate how many securities they want to buy or sell and at what price. The system then simply brings together the buyers and sellers. Order-driven systems are very common in the equity markets, the NYSE, the TSE and the LSE's SETS are all examples of order-driven equity markets.

3.2.5   Main Types of Market Orders

The main types of orders that can be entered into stock exchange systems are described in Chapter 5.

3.2.6   Liquidity and Transparency

Transparency in the securities markets may be defined as the degree to which information regarding quotations for securities, the prices of transactions, and the volume of those transactions is made publicly available.

Transparency can be divided into two discrete components:

*   **Pre-trade transparency**
    *   At its broadest level, this includes information accurately indicating the size and price of prospective trading interest, such as firm quotations in representative size, and resting limit orders, both at the best firm bid and ask quotations and away from such quotations.
    *   Some markets, particularly these that have developed completely automated trading markets that display the entire contents of the limit order book for a particular security, permit total transparency.
    *   Other markets permit lower levels of transparency, such as limiting the display of quotations to only the inside prices (ie, highest bid and lowest offer).
*   **Post-trade transparency**
    *   This refers to the dissemination of trade price and volume of completed transactions from all markets trading that security.

The level or degree of transparency is an essential determinant of an effective market and regulators and exchanges work to ensure there is the greatest degree of transparency to permit the investor to make an informed investment decision.

It is critical to note that pre-trade transparency alone is not sufficient for adequate levels of investor protection. Even if firm quotes exist, a substantial number of price-sensitive transactions may take place between or outside of the spread. Although quotes may help investors decide where and when to trade, transaction reports help investors determine whether the quotes are reliable, and help them assess the quality of the markets and transaction executions.

Also, all market participants attempt to anticipate market trends. Without trade and volume information, there are few warnings of impending marked trends. Market participants cannot respond quickly to selling or buying surges because they do not see them happening.

Maximum transparency requires the dissemination of transaction reports and quotations on a prompt, real-time basis.

3.3 Trading Conventions

Learning Objective

3.3.3 Understand the concepts of trading cum, ex, special cum and special ex: the meaning of books closed, ex-div and cum div, cum, special ex, special cum, and ex rights; effect of late registration

Trading inevitably takes place around the time when dividends are to be paid or corporate actions are underway. As a result, trading conventions have developed to ensure that there is certainty as to who a dividend or corporate action benefit belongs.

The process surrounding dividend payments is discussed more fully in Section 4 so for now, we will restrict consideration to the principles surrounding entitlement to benefits.

When a dividend payment or corporate action takes place, the issuer needs to identify holders of the security in order to distribute the event to them. The issuer will therefore announce the event and state that holders of the security who are registered on its books at close of business on a given day will benefit. That date is the **books closed date** or record date.

Equity trading typically settles at T+2 which means that the trade will settle on trade date plus two business days. So, for example, if a security is traded on Monday then it will settle two business days later on Wednesday. At that date, ownership of the security will move from seller to buyer and the latter will be on the share register from that point.

If the books closed date for a corporate action is on Friday of that week (as is usual) then the buyer will be on the register and automatically receive the entitlement from the issuer. Issues can therefore arise if there is a delay or if the trade takes place close to the books closed date.

If the trade fails to settle for whatever reason, there is potentially late registration of the purchaser, but they will still be entitled to the benefit. In such cases, the broker acting for the purchaser should claim the entitlement from the seller and where necessary, instruct the seller's broker to take the desired action, under a corporate action, in order to protect the buyer's position. The UK settlement system has automated systems to identify unsettled trades and will claim benefits but the obligation is on the buyer's broker to ensure their client receives the benefits associated with their purchase.

If trading takes place close to the record date, the exchange sets an **ex-date**. For example, equities are always quoted ex-dividend on a Thursday and the books closed date or record date is the Friday. Trading that takes place before Thursday is described as cum-dividend which is market shorthand that the sale of shares is made with (cum) the benefit of the dividend. Trading on Thursday onwards is described as ex-dividend as the sale of shares is made without (ex) the dividend.

The same principle applies for rights issues and other corporate actions which will have their associated record dates and ex-dates.

During the ex-dividend period, it is possible to arrange a special cum-trade. That is where, by special arrangement between the buyer and seller, the buyer of the share during the ex-dividend period does receive the next dividend. These trades can be done up to and including the day before the dividend payment date, but not on or after the dividend payment date. In a similar manner to a special cum-trade, an investor can also arrange a special ex-trade. This is only possible in the ten business days before the ex-date.

The motivation for investors buying or selling with or without the dividend entitlement tends to be related to tax.

3.4 Factors Influencing Equity Markets

Learning Objective

3.3.4 Assess how the following factors influence equity markets and equity valuation: trading volume and liquidity of domestic and international securities markets; relationship between cash and derivatives markets, and the effect of timed events; market consensus and analyst opinion; changes to key pricing determinants such as credit ratings and economic outlook

Prices of equities, in common with most asset classes, move continually during trading hours. Investors will differ as to their valuations of security prices based on different time horizons, different economic outlooks and different vested interests.

For markets to work properly there need to be disagreements, different time horizons amongst the participants and different agendas and priorities. While some investors and traders think that an asset is worth buying at a specified price, there must be others who, for various reasons, think that it is worth selling at that same price.

The two most common frameworks for financial markets are the open outcry model, used at futures exchanges such as the New York Mercantile Exchange (NYMEX) and the electronic order book and, in both cases, for sustained trading to take place there needs to be a fragmentation of opinions.

Assuming that there are a dedicated group of traders that want to trade a particular asset, the more evenly divided opinions are regarding the suitability of the current price, the more liquid the market will be.

In very liquid markets buying and selling preferences will show a high degree of non-alignment. Trading stances will be dispersed and there will be no obvious internal coherence to them. But when the fragmentation is replaced by a near-consensus view amongst traders, the liquidity evaporates and markets are prone to behaving in erratic and sometimes dramatic price swings and crashes can result.

The same securities can be traded in both the cash and derivatives markets. Arbitrage opportunities arise if there are misalignments or discrepancies between the futures prices and the cash price. Indeed, programme trading is an arbitrage strategy, which exists to exploit these opportunities, which tend to be fairly small discrepancies and which require very fast executions to deliver profits.

The possibility of arbitrage and the fact that the futures contracts are very convenient for many speculative purposes means that there is a real sense in which the action in the futures market will (often) tend to drive the price behaviour of the cash market. While this may seem like an aberration, in the very complex and algorithmic nature of most cash market transactions today, the notion of the tail (derivative) wagging the dog (underlying) is not so hard to contemplate.

The expirations of futures contracts can sometimes provide short-term volatility in the cash markets as many large speculators and commercials (ie, investment banks) which are **rolling over** futures positions will sometimes create **whipsaw** and turbulent market conditions. This situation is described by some in the market as **witching** and when contracts on futures, options on individual stocks, and options on stock index futures occur (once each quarter) this phenomenon is referred to as **triple witching**.

For long-term investors, these kinds of activities might be considered as examples of **noise** in the equity markets. However, the impact of the derivatives markets upon the cash market is often not as unidirectional as some commentators and text books imply. Rather than the derivative deriving its value from the behaviour of the underlying cash instrument, the situation can often be better understood from the converse perspective.

Because it is unquantifiable and generally misunderstood by most traders and investors, psychology is the often overlooked intangible aspect of trading. In relation to trading and investing, we can consider two very different approaches to psychology in the markets: individual psychology and group psychology. Attempting to draw conclusions based on the actions of crowd psychology (sometimes disparagingly referred to as herd behaviour) examines how the behaviour of investors en masse exerts an effect on stock prices.

The foundations of how crowd behaviour relates to investing have a long history which includes such bubbles as the South Sea Bubble, the Dutch tulip mania and the dot-com frenzy of the 1990s.

When most investors are in consensus and are driving the market in a particular direction, it is natural to think that the consensus will continue ad infinitum and that the best trading decision is to follow the crowd. But, it has been suggested that historical examples prove this to be a paradox.

- When driven strongly by consensus, crowd behaviour is actually a contrary indicator.
- When the consensus of the majority of investors or traders is strongest, the individual trader should do exactly the opposite of what the crowd is doing.
- When the market is strongly bullish, according to the contrarian view, it is more prudent to short the market.
- When the consensus is bearish, it is time to get ready to buy.

Mass psychology may continue to drive the trend for a longer period of time. The question that is asked by investors who subscribe to the notion that the consensus is wrong at important market turning points is *'How can one expect to identify the moment when the consensus indicator is strongest and which is the best moment to make a contrary investment decision?'*

The answer is, of course, that there is no way of determining the timing or, for that matter, of empirically verifying that treating consensus as a contrarian indicator actually results in profitable investment.

Market consensus can be used as one clue that a trading/investment opportunity may be available. It may simply indicate that it is a good time to apply more detailed analyses to particular stocks or currencies. Several tools are used to help investors roughly identify the consensus of the market. Most of these tools tabulate a numerical consensus indicator on the basis of advisory opinions, signals from the press or even polling, done amongst investment managers.

Other factors can influence individual equities and the market as a whole. Examples are publication of research for individual equities or sectors, changes in credit ratings for individual companies and key economic data for the direction of the market as a whole.

3.5   Stock Market Indices

Learning Objective

3.3.5   Understand the purpose, construction, application and influence of indices on equity markets: developed and emerging market regional and country sectors; market capitalisation sub-sectors; free float and full market capitalisation indices

A stock market index is a method of measuring the movement of a stock market or a section of it. Some of the world's major providers of index information are the FTSE and the Dow Jones.

An index can be constructed to measure the performance of all shares quoted on a country's main stock exchange, for a sector of that market or for a region. There are also a wide range of other indices that track the performance of investment strategies, thematic issues such as infrastructure and environmental issues such as socially responsible investing.

Markets are classified into developed, emerging and frontier markets. Morgan Stanley Capital International (MSCI) undertakes an annual exercise to classify countries into each category. The results can be important as they can determine when the securities of a country classed as Frontier become eligible for inclusion in emerging market funds.

The MSCI market classification framework consists of three criteria: economic development, size and liquidity as well as market accessibility. The economic development criterion is only used in determining the classification of developed markets. The size and liquidity requirements are based on minimum investability requirements. Market accessibility aims to reflect international investors' experience in investing in a given market. It includes consideration of factors such as openness to foreign ownership, ease of capital flows and well-functioning market infrastructures.

Market data can also be broken down to the sector level. FTSE International Ltd maintains the industry classification benchmark (ICB) system to categorise over 70,000 companies and 75,000 securities worldwide, enabling the comparison of companies across four levels of classification and national boundaries.

It is used for the FTSE All Share Index where companies are categorised into nine sectors: oil and gas; basic materials; industrials; consumer goods; health care; consumer services; telecommunications; utilities; financials and technology.

Construction of an index usually involves the total market capitalisation of the companies, weighted by their effect on the index, so the larger stocks make more of a difference to the index as compared to a smaller market cap company.

Market capitalisation indices are usually adjusted to allow for the amount of an issuer's share that can free float. This adjusts the percentage weighting of a company in an index to reflect the actual number of shares that can be actually traded and so excludes government holdings in a company which are regarded as not for sale.

There is one major exception to this method of construction and calculation which is the Dow Jones Industrial Average (DJIA) which is price weighted. The index sums each share price in the index and then divides it by its 30 constituents. The index pre-dates the availability of technology to allow complex real time calculations but its market acceptability means there is perceived value in it continuing to be produced. It is however not a suitable benchmark against which portfolio performance is normally judged.

The different methods of index construction are considered again in Chapter 12 when portfolio performance is considered.

4.   Corporate Actions

4.1   Characteristics of Corporate Actions

Learning Objective

3.4.1   Understand the purpose and structure of corporate actions and their implications for investors: stock capitalisation or consolidation; stock and cash dividends; rights issues; open offers, offers for subscription and offers for sale; placings

A corporate action is something that affects the capital structure of a company. There are over 150 different types of corporate action and they can be classified into three types:

- **Mandatory** – a mandatory corporate action is one mandated by the company, not requiring any intervention from the shareholders or bondholders themselves. The most obvious example of a mandatory corporate action is the payment of a dividend, since all shareholders automatically receive the dividend.

- **Mandatory with options** – a mandatory corporate action with options is an action that has some sort of default option that will occur if the shareholder does not intervene. However, until the date at which the default option occurs, the individual shareholders are given the choice to go for another option. An example of a mandatory with options corporate action is a rights issue, which is considered below.
- **Voluntary** – a voluntary corporate action is an action that requires the shareholder to make a decision. An example is a takeover bid – if the company is being bid for, each individual shareholder will need to choose whether to accept the offer or not.

These classifications are the ones used by the European Central Securities Depositary Association. Other countries often use the simpler distinction of mandatory and voluntary (a mandatory with options event then becomes a voluntary event followed by a separate mandatory event) but this does not alter the corporate action event itself.

4.1.1   Dividends

Day to day management of a company is undertaken by the board of directors and their power to run the company extends to whether a dividend can be paid. The board determine whether the company is sufficiently profitable to pay a dividend and if so, how much. They then present a resolution to the ordinary shareholders, requesting approval to the proposed dividend and the ordinary shareholders then vote whether to accept or reject the resolution.

It should be noted therefore that ordinary shareholders participate in profits by way of dividends, but that they do not have any right to a dividend; it is up to the board to propose payment of dividends.

The board have to operate within a set of rules that limit their ability to pay dividends.

- To ensure that the assets of a company are not depleted at the expense of the creditors, company law restricts the type of profit which can be distributed to shareholders. Profits and losses can be divided into two types: realised and unrealised.
  - Realised profit is one which has arisen from a real transaction. For example, if a company sells an asset then it will make, or realise, a profit or a loss on the transaction.
  - Unrealised profit is one which arises simply because the asset has increased in value but has not been sold. For example a company may buy a building for £1 million and in three years the building may be worth £1.6 million. The company may recognise the increase in value in its accounts but the profit of £0.6 million is unrealised; it has not arisen from a sale. An unrealised profit is sometimes referred to as a book profit.
- Net realised profits can be distributed as a dividend but unrealised profits cannot be distributed.
- A covered dividend is a payment made from this year's profit. An uncovered dividend is a payment made by the company where an insufficient profit has been made in the current financial year to cover the dividend payment.
- The Companies Acts allows for the payment of dividends by companies from previous years' profits, which are shown on the company's balance sheet as reserves. In addition, a public company has to cover net losses, whether realised or not, from realised profits before paying a dividend.

138

The frequency with which companies pay dividends varies: some companies pay one dividend a year, some pay two dividends a year and some pay four dividends.

- If more than one dividend is paid, the earlier dividends are called interim dividends and the last dividend is called a final dividend.
- The interim dividend is paid after the results for the first six months of a company's financial year have been announced.
- Before declaring an interim dividend, the directors must satisfy themselves that the financial position of the company warrants the payment of such a dividend out of profits available for distribution.
- The final dividend is paid after the AGM has approved the accounts and the dividend for the full financial year.

Dividends are paid to shareholders whose name appears on the share register. Because shares are continually changing hands, the share register is inevitably behind the actual trading of the shares and so there is a defined process and a well-established timetable in place for the payment of dividends so that investors, both buyers and sellers, know exactly what their entitlements are and nothing is left to chance.

The LSE publishes dividend procedures annually to document the defined process that companies need to follow.

There are three key dates in the payment of dividends for registered securities:

- **Ex-dividend date**
  - The amount of the dividend is announced several days before the ex-dividend day.
  - On the ex-dividend day, the share trades without the right to the next dividend payment; they are said to be ex-dividend.
  - Prior to the ex-date the shares are said to be trading cum-dividend.
  - In theory, on the ex-date the share price should fall by the amount of the dividend.
- **Record date**
  - Record date is the day on which the company closes its share register for the purpose of the payment of dividends and is sometimes known by its alternative name of books closed date.
  - In other words, the company will pay the dividend to those persons recorded as shareholders on the register of shareholders on record day.
- **Payment date**
  - The dividend payment day is the day on which the shareholder will receive the dividend, either by cheque or bank transfer.

For purchases and sales close to the record day, there will be uncertainty as to whether the transfer will or will not be recorded on the share register in time for record day. To eliminate that uncertainty, the stock exchange will declare the shares ex-dividend some days before the record day.

The basic principle is that ex-dividend dates normally fall on Wednesdays, with the associated record date falling two business days later usually on a Friday. If a dividend is to be made ex, the dividend must be declared via a Primary Information Provider (PIP) or notified to the exchange at least six business days before the proposed record date, otherwise the ex-dividend date will be deferred until the following week unless otherwise agreed by the exchange.

Example

A company determines that it intends to pay a dividend shortly before the end of 2012. So that it can pay the dividend within the recommended 30 day deadline, it announces the dividend in late November using the following schedule:

Announcement date	Thursday, 17 November 2015
Ex-div date	Wednesday, 23 November 2015
Record date	Friday, 25 November 2015

Companies should aim to pay straightforward cash dividends within 30 business days of the record date.

A dividend timetable which follows the guidelines set by the Dividend Procedure Timetable need not be notified to the Exchange in advance, provided the dividend information is disseminated via a PIP under a correct headline. The announcement should or must include:

- the dividend amount
- whether it is paid net or gross
- the record date and pay date
- the availability of any Scrip, DRIP, Currency Election or other alternative and if available the last day to elect for the alternative.

4.1.2   Dividends with Options

Instead of paying a cash dividend, a company may choose to provide options as to how it is paid. Some of the main types encountered are:

- scrip dividends
- dividend reinvestment plans (DRIPs)

Instead of distributing dividends to shareholders as a cash payment, a company may choose to pay the dividend instead in the form of new shares in the company. Such a dividend is called a scrip or stock dividend and is offered as an alternative to receiving the cash dividend.

Example

A company has a share price of 200p and pays a dividend of 8p per share. If the company were to offer a scrip dividend to its shareholders it might offer shareholders one new share for every 25 shares that they hold.

The formula for the scrip issue of 1:25 (one new share for each 25 shares held) is calculated as:

$$\frac{\text{Share price}}{\text{Dividend per share}} = \frac{200p}{8p} = 25$$

So, if an investor holds 10,000 shares he may take a cash dividend of £800 (10,000 x 0.08) or he may take 400 new shares (10,000 ÷ 25) which at 200p per share are also worth £800.

The price of 200p is calculated by a formula that is usually based on the average closing mid-market price in the week that the shares are marked ex-dividend.

The advantage of a scrip dividend for the shareholder is that he acquires new shares without incurring dealing costs. The advantage for the company is one of cash flow; the cash which would have been used to pay the dividend is retained within the company.

The shareholder is taxed on the cash equivalent of the dividend and so there is no tax advantage. If the shareholder accepts the scrip alternative the consequences are:

- The grossed-up amount of the cash dividend still represents taxable income of the investor.
- A basic rate taxpayer will have no further liability and non-taxpayers cannot reclaim the tax credit.
- Higher rate and additional rate taxpayers will have to pay additional tax as with a cash dividend.
- Providing that the market value of the shares on the first day of trading is not more than 15% different from the cash dividend, the cash dividend is used as the acquisition price for capital gains tax (CGT) purposes. If the 15% rule is breached, then the market value on the first day of trading is used as the CGT base cost.

A scrip dividend is offered as an alternative to the cash dividend and, therefore, the company must ask shareholders if they wish to take it up. This involves sending a letter to shareholders requesting them to return it within a deadline if they want to take up the scrip dividend offer. If the letter is not returned then the shareholder will receive a cash dividend.

Dividends with options which follow the guidelines of the dividend procedure timetable need not be notified to the LSE in advance of the announcement. Those which are outside the guidelines should be cleared with the stock situation department and advance notice given of any election date which should fall at least 10 business days after the record date, or 10 business days after the despatch of an appropriate circular to shareholders, whichever is the later.

A DRIP is a variation on this theme. Under a DRIP, however, the company makes a cash payment to all shareholders and offers a scheme, whereby shareholders can instead ask the company to use the cash to buy shares on their behalf in the market.

DRIPs differ from scrip issues in the following ways:

- With a scrip dividend new shares are issued by the company and the cash which would otherwise be used for the dividend is retained within the company. With a DRIP, the company pays the full amount of the cash dividend.
- With a scrip dividend issue, the company issues newly created shares to those investors electing to receive their dividend in this way. With a DRIP, the company uses the cash dividend to buy the shares in the market and passes on the benefit of the low commission rates it can negotiate for a large bulk purchase.

- It can take up to three weeks for the shares to be added to a portfolio in the case of a DRIP and one week in the case of a scrip dividend.
- A scrip dividend dilutes existing holdings as new shares are issued. A DRIP does not as the shares required are purchased in the market.

Scrip dividends and DRIPs can be carried out in CREST. The new shares will be recorded in the member's account and the company registrar will update the register of shareholders.

4.1.3 Capitalisation and Consolidation Issues

From time to time, companies may decide to issue further shares to existing shareholders or change the nominal value of ordinary shares. The former is a bonus issue and the latter a consolidation.

Occasionally a company may issue new shares to its shareholders without raising further capital, often as a public relations exercise to accompany news of a recent success or as a means to make its shares more marketable.

The issue of new shares to existing shareholders without requiring any payment from them is usually known as a bonus issue. It can also be referred to as a capitalisation issue or scrip issue and the names are interchangeable. (Note: do not confuse the term 'scrip issue' with a scrip dividend; they are completely different actions.)

A bonus issue involves the company in issuing further units of a security to existing holders based on the holdings of each member on record date.

- This involves the company converting reserves into the form of share capital. These reserves may have arisen from the accumulation of undistributed past profit or from issuing new shares in the past at a premium to their nominal value.
- These shares rank pari passu (ie, the same in all respects) with those already in issue and are distributed to the company's ordinary shareholders in proportion to their existing shareholdings free of charge.

Once a UK company's share price starts trading well into double figures its marketability starts to suffer as investors shy away from the shares. Therefore, a reduction in a company's share price as a result of a bonus issue usually has the effect of increasing the marketability of its shares. This in turn usually results in the share price settling above its new theoretical level and the company's market capitalisation increasing slightly.

An alternative to a scrip issue as a way of reducing a share price is to have a subdivision or share split, whereby each existing share is split into a greater number of shares with a lower nominal value.

Example

A company with shares having a 25p nominal value and a £10 market price have a share split whereby each 25p share is divided into five shares, each with a nominal value of 5p. In theory, the market price of each new share should be £2 (£10/5).

It might appear as though there is little difference between a bonus issue and a subdivision, but a bonus issue does not affect the nominal value of the company's shares.

A consolidation is the reverse of a split: shares are combined or consolidated. A consolidation issue is also known as a reverse split. This is where a company decides to decrease the number of issued securities, for example, by consolidating every four shares currently existing into one share of four times the nominal amount.

Example

A company with a share price of 10p may consolidate 10 shares into one. The market price of each new share should then be 100p (10p x 10).

A company may do this if the share price has fallen to a low level and they wish to make their shares more marketable.

It may also be done when the company wants to raise more equity capital from existing shareholders. Under companies law, new shares cannot be issued at less than their nominal value and so this can present a problem when companies need to raise new capital. A rights issue will be priced at a discount to the current share price, in order to make it attractive to existing shareholders to subscribe new capital. If the share price is too low, this may make it impractical as an insufficient discount can be priced in.

A company may therefore need to announce a consolidation in conjunction with the rights issue. The consolidation issue will raise the market price of each share, so that it can then have a rights issue to raise additional capital, which it will price at a discount to that figure.

4.1.4   Rights Issues

A rights issue is where a company gives existing investors the right to subscribe for additional new shares at a discount to the market price at the time of announcement.

When a company wishes to raise further equity capital, whether to finance expansion, develop a new product or replace existing borrowings, it can make a rights issue to its existing ordinary shareholders.

The rights issue is accompanied by a prospectus, which outlines the purpose of the capital-raising exercise, but does not require an advertisement of the issue to be placed in the national press.

New shares are offered in proportion to each shareholder's existing shareholding, at a price discounted to that prevailing in the market, to ensure that the issue will be fully subscribed and often to avoid the cost of underwriting the shares.

The number of new shares issued and the price of these shares will be determined by the amount of capital to be raised. This price, however, must be above the nominal value of the shares already in issue.

The choices open to shareholders under a rights issue are:

*   Take up the rights in full by purchasing all of the shares offered.
*   Sell the rights.
*   Sell sufficient of the rights to take up the balance (an approach sometimes known as tail-swallowing).
*   Take no action and allow the rights to lapse, which means that the company will sell the rights for the investor and distribute any proceeds to the investor. For the smaller shareholder not wishing to increase their shareholding in the company, this is often the most economic way to proceed.

4.1.5   Open Offers

An open offer is a method of raising new capital that is similar to a rights issue. It is another type of secondary market offering, whereby a company seeks to raise new capital.

An open offer invites shareholders to buy new shares at a price below the current market price but, unlike a rights issue, it cannot be sold and so, if the shareholder decides not to take up the entitlement, it lapses.

Open offers are made at a discount and as this leads to dilution in value for the non-accepting shareholder the listing rules limit the discount to a maximum of 10%

For normal open offers holders cannot apply for more than their entitlement. The issue, however, can be structured so that holders may be allowed to apply for more than their pro rata entitlement, with the possibility of being scaled back in the event of the offer being over-subscribed.

It can also be structured as an open offer with compensation where any shares not taken up are sold in the market and proceeds distributed.

4.1.6   Offers for Subscription and Offers for Sale

A company applying for a listing on a stock exchange is said to be undertaking an initial public offering (IPO). It can use one of four different methods:

*   Offer for sale.
*   Offer for subscription.
*   Placing.
*   Introduction.

Offers for subscription and offers for sale are methods of issuing new shares in the primary market in order to raise new capital. They should be differentiated from secondary market capital raising issues such as rights issues and open offers.

An offer for sale involves the issuing company selling its shares to an issuing house, which then invites applications from the public at a slightly higher price and on the basis of a detailed prospectus, known as the offer document.

To satisfy the requirements of the UKLA:

- The offer document should contain comprehensive information about the company and its directors and how the proceeds from the share issue will be applied.
- It must be prepared by the company's directors and be assessed by an independent sponsor, such as a solicitor or accountant.
- The company's sponsor must confirm that the company's working capital is adequate.
- An advertisement detailing the flotation must be placed in a national newspaper.

An offer for sale can be made on either a fixed or a tender price basis.

- **Fixed price offer**
  - When a fixed-price offer is made, the price is usually fixed just below that at which it is believed the issue should be fully subscribed, so as to encourage an active secondary market in the shares.
  - Subscribers apply for the number of shares they wish to purchase at this fixed price.
  - If the offer is oversubscribed, as it nearly always is, given the favourable pricing formula, then shares are allotted either by scaling down each application or by satisfying a randomly chosen proportion of the applications in full. The precise method used will be detailed in the offer document.
- **Tender offer**
  - Under the alternative method, investors subscribe for the number of shares they wish to purchase and state the price per share they are prepared to pay.
  - Once the offer is closed, a single strike price is then determined by the issuing house to satisfy all applications tendered at or above this price.
  - As with a fixed-price offer, this single strike price is typically set at a level just below that required for the entire share issue to be taken up, again to ensure an active secondary market in the shares.
  - Although this auctioning process is the more efficient way of allocating shares and maximising the proceeds from a share issue, tender offers are also more complex to administer, and tend to be outnumbered by fixed-price offers.

An IPO that uses the offer for subscription method requires the company to offer its new shares directly to the public, by issuing a detailed prospectus and placing an advertisement in the national press. The company will also arrange for an issuing house to underwrite the share issue, in exchange for a commission so that, in the event of the issue being undersubscribed, the underwriter will take up the remaining shares.

An introduction is not really an IPO in the true sense, as no capital is raised; instead, it involves a company obtaining a stock market listing. A listing on the LSE via an introduction is potentially available to companies that are already quoted on another overseas stock exchange. These will typically be multinationals wishing to expand their shareholder base.

4.1.7 Placing

In placing its shares, a company simply markets the issue directly to a broker, an issuing house or other financial institution, which in turn places the shares to selected clients. A placing is also known as selective placing.

A placing is the least expensive IPO method as the prospectus accompanying the issue is less detailed than that required for the other two methods and no underwriting or advertising is required. If the company is seeking a full listing the issue must still be advertised in the national press.

A placing is the preferred new issue route for most AIM companies.

4.2 Calculating the Effect of Corporate Actions

Learning Objective

3.4.2 Calculate the theoretical effect on the issuer's share price of the following mandatory and optional corporate actions: bonus/scrip; consolidation; rights issues

Corporate actions are usually expressed using a securities ratio. The term **securities ratio** refers to the terms of a particular bonus issue, rights issue or other corporate action.

In European and Asian markets, the market convention is to quote the terms as 'X new shares for each existing Y shares'.

Example

If a company announced a 3:2 bonus issue, this indicates that an investor will receive three new shares for each existing two shares held. The first number therefore indicates the number of new shares that will be received and the second number refers to the existing holding. So, for example, if an investor has a holding of 10,000 shares then they will receive an additional 15,000 shares, making their total holding 25,000.

In US markets, however, the first number indicates the holding that the investor will have after the event and the second number indicates the original holding.

Example

If the terms of a US bonus issue were 3:2, this indicates that the investor would have three shares after the event in place of their original two shares. Staying with the example above of an investor holding 10,000 shares, the investor would end up with 15,000 shares.

Given that shares in an investor's portfolio are likely to cover many different markets, it is important to understand which method will be used, otherwise wrong instructions may be given.

4.2.1 Bonus Issues

Under a bonus issue, a company will issue new shares to existing shareholders in proportion to their existing shareholding. The purpose of a bonus issue is often to increase the marketability of a share by reducing the share price.

If a company's shares were trading at £16 it might announce a 3:5 bonus issue to reduce the price and improve marketability. So what is the theoretical effect on the post-bonus issue share price?

Let us assume that an investor holds 1,000 shares which are valued at £16,000. Under the terms of the issue they will receive an additional 600 shares and the effect on the share price is shown in the table below.

Shares	No of Shares	Price	Value
Before the bonus issue	1,000	£16.00	£16,000
Bonus issue	600	–	–
After the bonus issue	1,600	£10.00	£16,000

The theoretical ex-bonus share price is simply calculated by dividing the value of the shares by the increased number of shares that the investor now holds – in other words, £16,000 ÷ 1,600.

The value of the shares has not changed as no new money has been raised by the company; instead the share price reduces and is hopefully more attractive at that lower level. (Note: it is referred to as the theoretical post-bonus issue price as, in practice, investor perception and the effect of demand and supply will determine what really happens.)

A company can also reduce the market price of its shares to make them more marketable, without capitalising its reserves, by undertaking a subdivision or stock split.

A stock split simply entails the company reducing the nominal value of each of its shares in issue whilst maintaining the overall nominal value of its share capital. For instance, if the company has one million shares in issue, each with a nominal value of £1, it can simply split each share into four, each share now having a nominal value of 25p.

Assuming that an investor held 1,000 ordinary £1 shares which were priced at £4 per share, the theoretical effect on its share price can be seen in the table below.

Shares	No of Shares	Price	Value
Before the split	1,000 ordinary £1 shares	£4.00	£4,000
After the split	4,000 ordinary 25p shares	£1.00	£4,000

Although the total nominal value of the shares in issue remains unchanged, the overall market capitalisation of the company should increase as its shares become more marketable. Other things being equal, the effect of a stock split on the share price should be the same as for a bonus issue.

The reason that a company may choose a stock split, as opposed to a bonus issue, is that whilst the reduction in the share price as a result of a bonus issue may have its advantages, it also has disadvantages. If share prices are falling, it may result in the price dropping below the nominal value which will prevent a company from raising finance by issuing more shares. An alternative way of lowering the price per share but avoiding this problem is to undertake a stock split.

4.2.2 Consolidation

A consolidation is where a company increases the nominal value of each of its shares in issue while maintaining the overall nominal value of its share capital.

If a company has 1 million shares in issue each with a nominal value of 50p, it can simply increase the nominal value per share to £1 and reduce the number of shares in issue to 500,000.

Assuming an investor holds 1,000 ordinary 50p shares which are priced at £1 per share, the theoretical effect on the share price can be seen in the following table:

Shares	No of Shares	Price	Value
Before the consolidation	1,000 ordinary 50p shares	£1.00	£1,000
After the consolidation	500 ordinary £1 shares	£2.00	£1,000

4.2.3 Rights Issue

The following example shows what takes place during a rights issue, the effect on the share price and the options available to shareholders.

Example

ABC Holdings has one million shares in issue, currently trading at £4.00 each. To raise finance for expansion, it decides to offer its existing shareholders the right to buy one new share for every five previously held. This is described as a 1 for 5 rights issue. The price of the rights share is set at a discount to the prevailing market price, at only £3.50.

The new shares issued will rank equally, or pari passu, with the original shares. As a result, the share price will be adjusted once the shares are traded ex-rights, to take account of the additional capital that the company will have and the greater number of shares in issue.

The price to which the share price will fall as a result of the rights issue is called the theoretical ex-rights price. To see how this is calculated consider the following:

Shares	No of Shares	Price	Value
Before the rights	1,000,000	£4.00	4,000,000
Rights	200,000	£3.50	700,000
After the rights	1,200,000	£3.91667	£4,700,000

The table above shows the initial number of shares in issue of 1,000,000 shares which, at the current price of £4, are valued at £4 million. Under the terms of the rights issue, investors can subscribe for one new share for every five existing shares held, so the total number of shares will increase by 200,000 and the company will receive an additional £700,000 of capital.

The company is now theoretically worth £4.7 million but has more shares in issue. To work out the theoretical ex-rights price, therefore, we need to divide its value by the increased number of shares in issue. The theoretical ex-rights price will therefore be £3.91667, that is, £4,700,000 divided by 1,200,000 shares. This is the theoretical price that the shares trade at once they are ex-rights, but the actual price will be determined by demand and supply and investor sentiment towards the issue.

During the period of the rights issue, the rights are known as nil-paid rights and are separately tradeable and will have some value. This is known as the rights premium and the theoretical rights premium can be calculated using the above information.

If the theoretical ex-rights price is £3.92 and each right gives an investor the right to subscribe for one additional share at £3.50, then the theoretical rights premium is the difference between the two: £0.42 per right. Again, the actual price will be determined by demand and supply.

Each shareholder is given choices as to how to proceed following a rights issue. An individual holding 1,000 shares in ABC Holdings, could:

• take up the rights by paying the £3.50 and increasing their holding in ABC Holdings to 1,200 shares
• sell the rights on to another investor. The rights entitlement is transferable (often described as renounceable) and will have a value because it enables the purchase of a share at the discounted price of £3.50
• as an alternative, the investor could, of course, sell just part of the rights and, with the cash raised, take up the remainder
• do nothing. If the investor chooses this option, the company's advisers will sell the rights at the best available price and pass on the proceeds (after charges) to the shareholder.

4.3 The Impact of Corporate Actions

Learning Objective

3.4.3 Understand and be able to assess the following in respect of corporate actions: rationale offered by the company; the dilution effect on profitability and reported financials

When a company announces a corporate action, it will describe the rationale for the event in its communication of the event and in the corporate action documentation.

If a company is raising capital, its rationale will be examined closely. Essentially, investors are being asked to invest further funds and will therefore analyse whether committing further funds is warranted, given the company's prospects. If a company wishes to raise additional capital, therefore, it will need to provide a compelling case that investors are prepared to back.

Example

An example of this in practice was the proposal by Prudential Corporation in May 2010 to raise funds to buy the Asian arm of US insurer AIG. The company's case was that its traditional markets for insurance products are highly competitive and offered little scope for growth, whereas Asian markets are still in a growth phase as more and more consumers gain wealth.

They therefore proposed the largest ever proposed rights issue to raise £14.5bn to help the proposed $35bn acquisition. The terms were 11 new shares for each existing 2 shares at 104p which was an 80.8% discount on the 542.5p closing price on Friday 14 May.

Prudential required 75% backing from its shareholders at an extraordinary general meeting (EGM) in order for the rights issue to proceed. It failed to convince them of the merits of the acquisition, however, and the rights issue had to be cancelled. The cost of its aborted takeover was estimated at £450m.

Apart from the rationale for a corporate action and the investor's reaction to the proposal, a further key consideration is whether the issue will be earnings dilutive.

Analysts look at earnings per share (EPS) and other key ratios to determine the performance of a company and establish trends. EPS are one of the key measures of the profitability of a company and are covered further in Chapters 8 and 9. For now, it is sufficient to understand that the quality of a company's earnings and its ability to grow them in a consistent manner are probably the most important factors affecting the share price.

Any corporate action that will affect reported earnings is therefore analysed quite closely.

A capital raising event will raise further capital for the company, but analysts will want to know whether the revenue that the additional capital will generate will add positively or negatively to the company's earnings stream. If it will reduce average earnings as measured by EPS, then this negative effect is described as being earnings dilutive. The market's view on whether to support the corporate action will be determined by the results of this analysis.

5. Fixed-Income Securities

Fixed-interest securities are commonly termed bonds, loan stock and debt. A fixed-interest security can be defined as:

- A tradeable **negotiable instrument**, issued by a borrower for a fixed term, during which a regular and predetermined **fixed rate of interest** based upon a **nominal value** is paid to the **holder** until it is **redeemed** and the **principal** is repaid.

Each of the terms above is defined as follows:

- **Negotiable instrument** – bonds are negotiable instruments in that ownership of the security can pass freely from one party to another. This makes bonds tradeable.
- **Borrower** – bonds can be issued by a wide range of borrowers, including supranationals, such as the World Bank, governments, government agencies, local authorities and companies, in a variety of different forms.
- **Fixed rate of interest** – most bonds are issued with a predetermined fixed rate of interest, known as the bond's coupon. This can be expressed either in nominal terms or, in the case of index-linked bonds, in real terms, and is usually paid semi-annually. However, some bonds are issued with variable, or floating, coupons while others are issued without any coupon at all.
- **Nominal value** – also known as the par value, most bonds have a nominal value of £100. In contrast to the nominal value of equity shares, a bond's nominal value is of practical significance as it is the price at which the bond is usually issued and redeemed, though some issues are made and/or redeemed either at a discount or at a premium to par. Bonds are also traded on the basis of nominal value rather than market value. In addition, the coupon is expressed as a percentage of the nominal value. So, a bond with a nominal value of £100 and a 7% coupon paid semi-annually means the holder will receive £3.50 every six months.
- **Holder** – the holder is the owner of the bond. Title to holdings in the UK is usually in registered form and is recorded in the share register, and transfer of title takes place through CREST when a trade is settled.
- **Redeemed** – most bonds have a fixed redemption date upon which the bond matures and the underlying principal, known as the redemption payment, is returned to the holder by the issuer. Others are dual-dated in that they have two redemption dates between which the bond is redeemed by the issuer. Some bonds, however, are issued in irredeemable, or undated, form or effectively become undated by virtue of the wording of their redemption terms.
- **Principal** – the principal amount of a bond is its nominal value and represents the redemption payment made by the issuer to the holder of the bond at maturity.

Bonds are usually classified according to the issuer, their structure or defining characteristics and the market into which they are issued:

- **Issuer** –most bonds are issued by governments and supranationals (known collectively as sovereign borrowers), companies and, to a lesser extent, local authorities.
- **Structures** – bond structures can range from conventional, or straight, issues as described above, through to ones that have other unique features such as bonds:
  - with index-linked coupon payments and redemption proceeds
  - without coupon payments, which are known as zero coupon bonds and which are issued at a discount to their nominal value but are redeemed at par, thereby providing their entire return as

capital gain. (Note that although they provide their return as capital, they are treated as income for UK individual taxpayers)

○ with conversion rights. These convertible bonds may confer a right on the holder to convert into other bonds, or if issued by a company, into its ordinary shares, on pre-specified terms and on predetermined dates

○ with floating rather than fixed coupons. These are termed floating rate notes (FRNs)

○ with provisions for early redemption. A callable bond enables the issuer to call for early repayment, whereas a bond with put provision enables the holder to call for early repayment.

• **Where issued** – bonds can be issued into the issuer's own domestic bond market, internationally in one or across a range of bond, or debt, markets. Primary and secondary markets exist in the UK for the following bonds:

○ UK government bonds, or gilts

○ local authority bonds

○ eurobonds

○ domestic corporate bonds, and

○ sterling foreign bonds.

5.1 Government Debt

Learning Objective

3.5.1 Understand the main issuers of government debt and the main investment characteristics, behaviours and risks of the major government bond classes: supranationals; sovereign governments; public authorities: local government/municipalities; short-, medium- and long-dated; dual-dated; undated; floating rate; zero coupon

Governments use the bond markets to raise finance in order to meet the excess of government spending over taxation. In doing so, they issue a wide range of government bonds, offering differing maturity dates and coupons which can be used in the construction of a bond portfolio for investors.

In this section, we consider some key features that are common to all government bonds and then look in more detail at the type of government bonds issued in the UK, the US and Japan.

5.1.1 Features of Government Bonds

Government bonds are ones that are issued by a national government and which are denominated in that country's own domestic currency. Bonds issued in foreign currencies are usually referred to as sovereign bonds although the term has now come to be used to refer to all government bonds.

Typically, the government guarantees payment of interest and the redemption proceeds on predetermined due dates. As governments can raise taxes, reduce spending, or simply print more money to redeem the bond at maturity, they are often described as being risk-free.

It should be recognised, however, that they are only theoretically risk-free and that the guarantee is only as good as the government that is giving it and so instead of being **risk free** they are perhaps better thought of as having **minimal risk**. Governments do occasionally default, as Argentina did in 2001 and Russia did in 1998, which lead to the collapse of the US hedge fund Long Term Capital Management.

The recent Greek debt crisis emphasises the message that, while in the good times it is easy for commentators to say that government debt is risk-free, because they can simply print more money, the reality is significantly different. Years of unrestrained spending left Greece badly exposed when the global economic downturn struck, which revealed debt levels and deficits that exceeded limits set by the Eurozone.

Investors in sovereign bonds have the additional risk that the issuer is unable to obtain foreign currency to redeem the bonds.

The risk associated with government bonds is assessed by the ratings agencies, who regularly issue reports on the creditworthiness of various governments (the role of ratings agencies is considered later in this chapter). For example, the UK is rated AA by Standard & Poor's, having been downgraded in June 2016 from AAA. The US and Japan's sovereign debt is rated AA which indicates that they have a very strong capacity to meet financial commitments.

Some other governments, however, have less financial strength, and this translates into a lower rating.

For example, Greece's rating was downgraded to BB+ in April 2010, making it the first Eurozone country to have its debt downgraded to junk status, and in 2011 to CCC, branding it the lowest credit rating of any government in the world. Investors demanded higher returns to compensate for the increased risk and the two-year government bond yield surged to 15%, making it highly expensive for the country to borrow from the debt market. Its five-year bond yields hit 10.6%, which is higher than the yields on bonds issued by many emerging market economies.

The responsibility for the issue of government bonds is undertaken by a government agency; for example, by the Bureau of Public Debt in the US, by the Ministry of Finance in Japan and by the Debt Management Office (DMO) in the UK.

They are issued into the primary market and are usually sold by auction. They are then subsequently traded in the secondary market, either via a stock exchange or over the counter by market participants.

Most government bonds are issued as conventional-dated fixed-interest securities and typically assume the following form: Treasury 3.75% 2020. The name of the stock is simply for identification and its title will change country by country. The coupon is expressed as a percentage of nominal value, as is the usual convention, and paid gross or without deduction of tax. The redemption date signifies that the government will redeem the stock in 2020.

5.1.2 Issuers

Both government, international agencies and local authorities may issue bonds. Apart from governments, other issuers include:

- Supranational organisations such as the IMF, World Bank, European Investment Bank and Asian Development Bank issue bonds – so-called supranational bonds.
- Government-sponsored agencies issue bonds, known as 'agency bonds', for particular purposes. These are common in the US where examples include the Federal Home Loan Banks (FHLBs), the Federal National Mortgage Association ('Fannie Mae') and the Federal Home Loan Mortgage Corporation (FHLMC) – also known as 'Freddie Mac' – which was created in 1970.
- Local Government and Municipalities raise their financing through their government or by raising funds through the issue of bonds.
- Sub-sovereign, provincial, state or local authorities issue bonds. In the US, state and local government bonds are known as municipal bonds and municipalities in the US issue these bonds to finance local borrowing. These bonds are often tax efficient – particularly for investors who reside in that municipality.

5.1.3 Types of Government Bonds

Governments issue a range of different types of bonds in order to raise finances. The main types encountered are conventional fixed interest bonds, with a range of maturity dates and index linked or inflation protected bonds.

From time to time they will also issue other types of bonds such as:

- **Dual-dated bonds** – these are ones that have two maturity dates and the government has a choice of when the bond is repaid. These are less common, as they bring uncertainty as to when repayment will take place and therefore cause difficulties in valuation.
- **Floating rate notes** – these are alternatives to conventional fixed coupon bonds where the coupon payable on the bond is reset after each coupon payment and so can rise and fall in line with market rates. They are less common, as the interest rate to be received by the investor will fluctuate, making them potentially unattractive.

5.1.4 US Government Bonds

Government bonds issued by the US government are known as Treasuries and there are four main marketable types that are considered next.

- **Treasury bills**
  - Treasury bills are a money market instrument used by governments to finance their short-term borrowing needs.
  - They have maturities of less than a year and are typically issued with maturities of 28 days, 91 days and 182 days.
  - They are zero coupon bonds, so pay no interest, and instead are issued at a discount to their maturity value.
  - Once issued, they trade in the secondary market and are priced on a yield to maturity basis.

- **Treasury notes**
  - Treasury notes are conventional government bonds that have a fixed coupon and redemption date.
  - They have maturity dates ranging from two to ten years and are commonly issued with maturities of two, five and ten years.
- **Treasury bonds**
  - Treasury bonds are again conventional government bonds but with longer maturities of between ten and 30 years.
- **Treasury inflation-protected securities** (**TIPS**) – these are index-linked bonds.
  - The principal value of the bond is adjusted regularly, based on movements in the consumer prices index, to account for the impact of inflation.
  - Interest payments are paid half yearly and, unlike the UK version, the coupon remains constant but is paid on the changing principal value.

Separate trading of registered interest and principal securities (STRIPS) are also traded based on the stripped elements of Treasury notes, bonds and TIPS. As discussed above, each bond is broken down into its underlying cash flows: that is, each individual interest payment plus the single redemption payment. Each is then traded as a separate zero coupon bond.

5.1.5   UK Government Bonds

Gilt-edged securities, or gilts, are UK government securities principally issued to finance government spending. Once issued, gilts are traded on a secondary market provided by the LSE.

The main types are:

- **Conventional Gilts**
  - In the UK, conventional gilts are instruments that carry a fixed coupon and a single repayment date, for example, Treasury 3.75% 2020.
  - This type of bond represents the majority of UK government bonds in issue.
  - Conventional gilts guarantee to pay the holder of the gilt a fixed interest payment every six months until the maturity date, at which point the holder receives the final coupon payment and the return of the principal.
  - Conventional gilts are usually issued with coupon dates of 7 March and September or 7 June and December to allow them to be stripped, which converts them into a form of zero coupon bond as discussed below.
  - Issues of conventional gilts are now termed Treasury gilts and older bonds will have titles such as Treasury stocks, conversion stock and exchequer stock. This is simply a change in terminology and has no other significance.
- **Index-Linked Bonds**
  - Index-linked bonds are ones where the interest payments and the redemption amount are increased by the amount of inflation over the life of the bond.
  - As with conventional gilts, investors receive two interest payments a year and get a redemption payment based on the nominal or 'face value' of their gilt holding.
  - However, these payments are adjusted to take account of what inflation has done since the gilt was issued. The amount of inflation uplift is determined by changes in the retail prices index (RPI).
  - An example is 2.5% Treasury Index-Linked Stock 2020. When this stock was issued, it carried a coupon of 2.5%, but the amount received is uplifted by the amount of inflation at each interest payment. Similarly, the amount that will be repaid in 2020 is adjusted.

Gilts are traditionally categorised as either:

*   **Shorts** – conventional-dated gilts with up to seven years remaining to redemption.
*   **Mediums** – conventional-dated gilts with between seven and 15 years remaining to maturity.
*   **Longs** – conventional-dated gilts with more than 15 years remaining to redemption.
*   **Index-linked**.

Conventional gilts are categorised by their remaining term to maturity, while dual-dated bonds are classified according to the later of the two dates.

The above definition differs from that used by the *Financial Times*, which adopts five, rather than seven, years as the cut-off point between shorts and mediums.

5.1.6   Japanese Government Bonds

The Japanese government bond (JGB) market is one of the largest in the world. JGBs are classified into six categories:

*   short-term
*   medium-term
*   long-term bonds
*   super-long-term
*   individual investor
*   Inflation-indexed.

Short-term JGBs have maturities of six months and one year and are issued as zero coupon bonds; in other words they are issued at a discount, carry no interest and are repaid at their face value.

Medium, long and super-long JGBs are conventional bonds and so have fixed coupons that are paid semi-annually and have set redemption dates. The individual investor bonds and 15-year super-long JGBs pay floating interest rates.

Inflation-indexed bonds operate in a similar way to TIPS: that is, the principal amount is inflation-adjusted based on movements in the consumer prices index and the coupon is fixed but payable on the inflation-adjusted principal amount.

5.1.7 Index-Linked Debt

Learning Objective

3.5.3   Understand the main investment characteristics, behaviours and risks of index- linked debt: Retail Prices Index as a measure of inflation; process of index linking; indexing effects on price, interest and redemption; return during a period of zero inflation

Index-linked bonds are ones where the interest payments and the redemption amount are increased by the amount of inflation over the life of the bond. The amount of inflation uplift is determined by changes in the Retail Prices Index (RPI).

As with conventional gilts, investors receive two interest payments a year and get a redemption payment based on the nominal or 'face value' of their gilt holding. However, these payments are adjusted to take account of what inflation has done since the gilt was issued. An example is 2½% Treasury Index-Linked Stock 2020. When this stock was issued, it carried a coupon of 2½%, but the amount received is uplifted by the amount of inflation at each interest payment. Similarly, the amount that will be repaid in 2020 is adjusted.

There are two methods of calculating the inflation uplift, depending upon when the gilt was issued. Both use the inflation rate and period of months prior to the forthcoming interest payment or maturity payment, thereby allowing accrued interest to be calculated. This is known as the **indexation lag**, and is eight months for index-linked gilts, issued prior to July 2005, and three months for ones issued since.

The method of indexation for index-linked gilts with a three-month indexation lag uses an interpolated RPI figure which is converted into a daily adjustment ratio to be calculated known as the **index ratio**. The semi-annual interest payments are calculated using the index ratio as follows:

$$\text{Interest Payment} = \frac{\text{Coupon}}{2} \times \text{Index Ratio}$$

The redemption proceeds are calculated in the same way.

It should also be noted that there is no deflation 'floor', so the final redemption payment could be less than £100 per £100 nominal, if there is a general fall in the level of prices in the UK. The amount of capital that the investor will get back on redemption will depend on what inflation does up until a point three, or eight, months before the stock is redeemed.

Index-linked bonds are attractive in periods where a government's control of inflation is uncertain by providing extra protection to the investor.

They are also attractive to long-term investors such as pension funds. They need to invest their funds and know that the returns will maintain their real value after inflation so that they can meet their obligations to pay pensions.

5.2   Relationship between Interest Rates and Bond Prices

Learning Objective

3.5.2   Understand the relationship between interest rates and government bond prices: yield; interest payable; accrued interest (clean and dirty prices); effect of changes in interest rates

Gilts pay coupons half yearly and the annual interest received when expressed as a percentage of a bond's current price is referred to as its yield.

The price at which a gilt or other bond is traded will depend on the yield required by investors, taking into account interest rate expectations and risk of default. However, one factor can be calculated with precision and is independent of other factors: the time which has elapsed since the most recent coupon payment, and thus the interest which has accrued since the most recent interest payment.

Many bond markets require that bond prices are quoted excluding the accrued interest element, which is then calculated as a separate item and for which the price is adjusted. The price of a stock excluding the accrued interest is known as the clean price. Most markets quote clean prices, but a price might be quoted which includes accrued interest. A price which includes accrued interest but does not calculate it separately is known as a dirty price.

There are two features are vital for understanding the way in which bond pricing works.

*   There is an inverse relationship between bond prices and interest rates, ie, as interest rates rise, or specifically the required yield from investors rises, so the present or market value of a bond will fall (and vice versa).
*   When the coupon rate on the bond is equal to the prevailing interest rate (or desired yield), the bond will be valued at par.

In most cases, the income (coupon) from a bond remains the same through its life. However, during the life of the bond, there are many factors, especially inflation and the changes in the interest rate environment that can make the bond more or less attractive to investors.

These factors lead to the price of bonds changing.

*   If investors see interest rates rising, the prices of bonds will fall. There is thus an inverse relation between the yield of a bond and its price.
*   The reason for this can be seen if we appreciate that investors will require a particular level of return, depending upon rates of interest generally.
*   If interest rates rise, investors' required rate of return rises. That means that they will be prepared to pay less for a particular bond with a fixed coupon rate than they were prepared to pay previously.
*   If interest rates generally fall, then investors will be prepared to pay more for a fixed-rate bond than previously, and bond prices will tend to rise.

- Investors will generally require a higher return if the expected rate of inflation rises. Therefore, prices of fixed-rate bonds will tend to fall with rising expectations of inflation. However, index-linked bonds have a coupon that is linked to the inflation rate, with the result that the price of index-linked stock will tend to rise as higher inflation is expected.

6. Characteristics of Corporate Debt

6.1 Secured Debt

Learning Objective

3.6.1 Understand the main issuers of corporate debt and the main investment characteristics, behaviours and risks of secured debt: corporates; financial institutions and special purpose vehicles; fixed and floating charges; debentures; types of asset backed securities; mortgage-backed securities; securitisation process; yield to maturity; roles of participants

6.1.1 Corporate Debt

Corporate debt is simply money that is borrowed by a company that has to be repaid.

Generally, corporate debt requires servicing by making regular interest payments. Corporate debt can be subdivided into money borrowed from banks via loans and overdrafts, and directly from investors in the form of IOU instruments, typically debentures or, as they are more commonly known, bonds.

Debt finance can be less expensive than equity finance, ie, issuing shares, because investing in debt finance is less risky than investing in the equity of the same company. The interest on debt has to be paid and is paid before dividends, so there is more certainty to the investor in corporate debt than in corporate equity. Additionally, if the firm goes into liquidation, the holders of debt finance will be repaid before the shareholders receive anything.

However, raising money via debt finance does present dangers to the issuing company. The lenders are often able to claim some or all of the assets of the firm, in the event of non-compliance with the terms of the loan – for instance, a bank providing mortgage finance technically can seize the property assets of a firm if there is any default, and not necessarily an outright bankruptcy of the company.

For a corporation the power to borrow needs to be laid out in the Articles of Association and the decision about taking on new debts is taken by the board of directors and may have to be agreed at an AGM of a company's shareholders.

The development of financial engineering techniques has resulted in a large variety of corporate debt being issued and traded. Some of the main types are described below.

- **Medium-Term Notes**
  - Medium-term notes are standard corporate bonds, with maturities ranging usually from nine months to five years; though the term is also applied to instruments with maturities as long as 30 years.
  - They differ from other debt instruments in that they are offered to investors continually over a period of time by an agent of the issuer, instead of in a single tranche of one, sizeable, underwritten issue.
  - The market originated in the US to close the funding gap between commercial paper and long-term bonds.
- **Fixed-Rate Bonds**
  - The key features of fixed-rate bonds have already been described. Essentially, they have fixed coupons, which are paid either half-yearly or annually and predetermined redemption dates.
- **Floating-Rate Notes**
  - Floating-rate notes are usually referred to as FRNs and are bonds that have variable rates of interest.
  - The rate of interest will be linked to a benchmark rate such as London InterBank Offered Rate (LIBOR). This is the rate of interest at which banks will lend to one another in London, and is often used as a basis for financial instrument cash flows.
  - An FRN will usually pay interest at LIBOR plus a quoted margin or spread.
- **Convertible Bonds** – these are considered Section 6.2.4.
- **Zero Coupon Bonds**
  - A zero coupon bond (ZCB) is one that pays no interest and instead is issued at a discount to its par value and is eventually redeemed at the full par value. All of the return is provided in the form of capital growth rather than income. (Note: as mentioned earlier, although they provide their return as capital, they are treated as income for UK individual tax payers.)
- **Permanent Interest-Bearing Securities (PIBS)**
  - PIBS are irredeemable fixed-interest securities issued by mutual building societies.
  - PIBS pay relatively high semi-annual coupons, net of basic rate income tax, and potentially offer attractive returns. However, this income is non-cumulative and PIBS holders rank behind all other creditors in the event of liquidation.
  - If the building society has demutualised, its PIBS are reclassified as Perpetual Subordinated Bonds (PSBs). Both PIBS and PSBs can be traded on the LSE.
  - The liquidity of PIBS is generally not high and they currently have a wide bid-offer spread as liquidity conditions remain uncertain following the financial crisis.

6.1.2 Financial Institutions and Special Purpose Vehicles

Like other companies or corporates, financial institutions issue bonds to finance borrowing. These financial institutions also arrange borrowing for themselves and others by creating special purpose vehicles (SPVs) to enable money to be raised that does not appear within the accounts of that entity.

This type of finance is often described as off-balance sheet finance, because it does not appear in the balance sheet that forms part of the company's accounts.

6.1.3 Bond Security and Redemption Provisions

Apart from the type of bond and the issuer, other distinguishing features of bonds are the security and redemption provisions that are attached to them.

Bond Security

Although many companies are reliant upon short-term bank borrowing and retained profits to finance their operations, longer-term finance can be obtained for expansion by issuing bonds in the domestic corporate bond market.

When a company is seeking to raise new funds by way of a bond issue, it will often have to offer security to provide the investor with some guarantee for the repayment of the bond. In this context, security usually means some form of charge over the issuer's assets (eg, its property or trade assets) so that, if the issuer defaults, the bondholders have a claim on those assets before other creditors (and so can regard their borrowings as safer than if there were no security). In some cases, the security takes the form of a third-party guarantee – for example, a guarantee by a bank that, if the issuer defaults, the bank will repay the bondholders.

The greater the security offered, the lower the cost of borrowing should be.

Domestic corporate bonds are usually secured on the company's assets by way of a fixed or a floating charge. A fixed charge is a legal charge, or mortgage, specifically placed upon one or a number of the company's fixed, or permanent, assets.

A floating charge, however, places a more general charge on those assets that continually flow through the business and whose composition is constantly changing, such as the issuing company's stock-in-trade. It is important to note that a company may not be inhibited from disposing of any specific assets, if its borrowing is only subject to a floating charge. The floating charge may simply cover whatever the company has in its possession at any time and, unless itemised in an addendum to a floating charge, no sale or disposition is excluded.

In liquidations fixed charges have priority over floating charges.

The type of security provided is incorporated into a legal deed, and the company's compliance with it is overseen by an independent trustee appointed by the company. If any of these terms are breached, then the trustee has the right to appoint a receiver to realise the asset(s) subject to the charge.

Redemption Provisions

In some cases, a corporate bond will have a call provision, which gives the issuer the option to buy back all or part of the issue before maturity.

This is attractive to the issuer as it gives it the option to refinance the bond (ie, replace it with one at a lower rate of interest) when interest rates are lower than the rate currently being paid on the bond. This is a disadvantage, however, to the investor, who will probably demand a higher yield as compensation.

Call provisions can take various forms. There may be a requirement for the issuer to redeem a specified amount at regular intervals. This is known as a **sinking fund** requirement.

You may also see bonds with put provisions; these give the bondholder the right to require the issuer to redeem early, on a set date or between specific dates. This makes the bond attractive to borrowers and may increase the chances of selling a bond issue in the first instance; it does, however, increase the issuer's risk that it will have to refinance the bond at an inconvenient time.

6.1.4   Debentures

The term debenture is used differently from country to country and so it is important to understand its meanings.

In the UK, a debenture refers to a bond that is secured on specific assets. A debenture is a legal document that is used to take a charge over specific assets. It will appoint a trustee who is responsible for safeguarding the interests of the bond holders and taking action to enforce the charge if conditions are breached.

Debentures and details of their charge have to be registered under the Companies Act 2006 with Companies House. The purpose of the registration is to publicise the priority that the borrowing has in the event of default by the company. This does not extinguish the debt itself, but any advantage from priority is lost and the lender will be an unsecured creditor.

By contrast, the term 'loan stock' is used to describe stock which is not so secured.

In the US, a debenture is a type of debt instrument that is not secured by physical asset or collateral. Debentures are backed only by the general creditworthiness and reputation of the issuer. Both corporations and governments frequently issue this type of bond in order to secure capital.

6.1.5   Securitisation and Asset-Backed Securities

Securitisation involves packaging the rights to the future revenue stream from a collection of assets into a bond issue.

There is a large group of bonds that trade under the overall heading of **asset-backed securities**.

These are bundled securities, so-called because they are marketable securities that result from the bundling or packaging together of a set of non-marketable assets.

The assets in this pool or bundle range from mortgages and credit card debt to accounts receivable. The largest market is for mortgage-backed securities, whose cash flows are backed by the principal and interest payments of a set of mortgages. These have become known worldwide as a result of the sub-prime collapse in the US.

A significant advantage of asset-backed securities is that they bring together a pool of financial assets that otherwise could not easily be traded in their existing form. By pooling together a large portfolio of these illiquid assets, they can be converted into instruments that may be offered and sold freely in the capital markets.

6.1.6 Yield to Maturity (YTM)

Yield to maturity (YTM) can be defined as the annual compound return from holding a bond to maturity taking into account both the timing of interest payments and any capital gain or loss at maturity. This is also known as the internal rate of return of a bond and the gross redemption yield (GRY).

6.1.7 Roles of Participants

The principal participants with regard to corporate debt are the issuer, the underwriter which is responsible for issuing bonds in a primary market, the debenture trustee, and brokers/dealers who are involved in maintaining and making a secondary market for the bonds issued. Exchanges such as the LSE are venues for trading of corporate debt instruments, as well as a global and de-centralised electronic network of dealers.

6.2 Unsecured Debt

Learning Objective

3.6.2   Understand the main investment characteristics, behaviours and risks of the main types of unsecured debt: income bonds; subordinated; high yield; conditional convertible bonds; convertible bonds; rating

6.2.1 Income Bonds

Income bonds are the most junior of all bonds. Their payments are made only after the issuer earns a certain amount of income. The issuer is not bound to make interest payments on a timely or regular basis if the minimum income amount is not earned. The investor is aware of the risks involved and may be willing to invest in these bonds if there is an attractive coupon rate or high yield-to-maturity.

6.2.2 Subordinated Bonds

Subordinated debt is not secured and the lenders have agreed that, if the company fails, they will only be reimbursed when other creditors have been paid back, and then only if there is enough money left over.

Interest payments on subordinated borrowings will be higher than those on equivalent unsecured borrowings that are not subordinated. This is simply because of the additional default risk faced by subordinated lenders.

6.2.3 High Yield Bonds

Customarily, participants in the money markets regard all debt that does not have an investment grade as speculative and sometimes refer to this as **junk** debt. Bonds with a grade below BBB–, in the case of the S&P's rating system, are also typically known as high-yield bonds as they will require issuers to provide a high coupon to the bond issue, in order to compensate investors for the higher credit risk associated with an inferior credit rating.

In the 1980s, Michael Milken was a pioneer of the use of junk bonds, as a way of financing for new companies or companies which had a track record of credit problems. Although his demise from the world of finance was linked to an abusive mode of operation with high yielding debt, which also added some stigma to the term 'junk', there is no inherent obstacle for capital markets to issue and raise money by using high yielding debt instruments, as the market should know how to 'price in' the additional risk, in setting the terms of the issue including the amount of the coupon.

6.2.4 Convertible Bonds

Typically, a convertible bond will pay a lower coupon, though this is compensated by the option to convert into shares at the conversion date. Convertibles are often subordinated, meaning that all senior creditors must be settled in full before any payment can be made to holders in the event of insolvency.

Convertible bonds are often deployed as a form of deferred share. Issuers expect them to be converted into shares at the conversion date. Convertibles have some of the characteristics of bonds, responding to changes in interest rates, and some of the characteristics of shares, responding to share price movements.

Convertible bonds are issued by companies and give the investor holding the bond two possible choices:

- simply collect the interest payments and then the repayment of the bond on maturity, or
- convert the bond into a pre-defined number of ordinary shares in the issuing company, on a set date or dates, or between a range of set dates, prior to the bond's maturity.

The attractions to the investor are:

- If the company prospers, its share price will rise and, if it does so sufficiently, conversion may lead to capital gains.
- If the company hits problems, the investor will retain the bond – interest will be earned and, as bondholders, the investor would rank ahead of existing shareholders if the company went bust. (Of course, if the company was seriously insolvent and the bond was unsecured, the bondholder might still not be repaid, but this is a more remote possibility than that of a full loss as a shareholder.)

For the company, relatively cheap finance is acquired. Investors will pay a higher price for a bond that is convertible because of the possibility of a capital gain. However, the prospect of dilution of current shareholder interests, as convertible bondholders exercise their options, has to be borne in mind.

6.2.5 Conditional/Contingent Convertible Bonds (CoCos)

Conditional or contingent convertible bonds (also known as CoCos) are similar to traditional convertible bonds (sometimes referred to as hybrids). The key difference is that a price is set, which the underlying equity share price must reach before conversion can take place (ie, conversion is contingent on the ordinary shares attaining a certain market price over a specified period of time). They are also quite useful to the banking industry. CoCos can be issued whereby conversion happens when an uplift in the percentage of capital is required in order for the bank to remain solvent. Thus, conversion into shares is automatic if the specified capital ratio is likely to be breached.

6.2.6   Ratings

Bondholders face the risk that the issuer of the bond may default on their obligation to pay interest and the principal amount at redemption. This so-called 'credit risk' – the probability of an issuer defaulting on their payment obligations and the extent of the resulting loss – can be assessed by reference to the independent credit ratings given to most bond issues.

Unsecured debt by its nature will have a lower credit rating than more highly rated debt that offers greater security in the event of liquidation.

7.   Characteristics of Eurobonds

Learning Objective

3.7.1   Understand the main investment characteristics, behaviours and risks of Eurobonds: types of issuer: sovereign, supranational and corporate; types of eurobond: straight, FRN/ VRN, subordinated, asset-backed; convertible; international bank syndicate issuance; immobilisation in depositories; continuous pure bearer instrument: implications for interest and capital repayment; taxation of interest and capital gains; accrued interest, ex-interest date

Essentially, eurobonds are international bond issues.

They are a way for an organisation to issue debt without being restricted to their own domestic market. They are generally issued via a syndicate of international banks. Generally, eurobond issuers do not keep a record of the holders of their bonds; the certificates themselves are all that is needed to prove ownership. This is the concept of bearer documents, where the holder of the certificates (the bearer) has all the rights attached to ownership.

Eurobonds are issued internationally, outside any particular jurisdiction, and as such they are largely free of national regulation. For example, a US dollar eurobond could be issued anywhere in the world, except for the US. As such, a better name for it might be an **international bond**.

For a number of pragmatic reasons, the clearing houses in the euromarkets maintain a form of register of ownership, but this register is not normally open either to government or tax authorities. Combined with the feature of being bearer documents, an aspect of the eurobond is that, unlike most government bonds, it does not attract withholding tax.

7.1   Types of Eurobonds

The investment banks who originate eurobond issues have been innovative in their structure to accommodate the needs of issuers and investors. Accordingly there are many different flavours for eurobonds. The basic forms are as follows:

- straight or plain vanilla
- floating rate notes/variable rate notes
- subordinated
- asset backed
- convertible.

Typically, eurobonds pay coupons gross and usually annually.

Other types of eurobond include:

- Zero coupon eurobonds.
- Floating rate eurobonds are bonds where the coupon rate varies. The rate is adjusted in line with published, market interest rates such as LIBOR or Euribor plus a margin.
- Subordinated eurobonds, as with subordinated notes in general, are notes which have a junior or inferior status within the capital structure hierarchy and have greater risk than a senior or secured note.
- Asset-backed eurobonds, as the name implies, are those where a specific asset or item of collateral has been pledged by the issuer as security for the bond.
- Convertible eurobond issues are those where the issuer has granted certain rights to the holder to convert the bond into equity of the issuer according to the terms of the offering prospectus.

Most eurobonds are bought by major institutions looking for a sound long-term investment, delivering a fixed rate of return. Eurobond prices in the secondary market tend to be less sensitive than a company's shares to changes in its commercial performance or business prospects. Instead, eurobond prices are more sensitive to wider economic shifts, such as changes in interest rates and currency fluctuations.

A London listing of a eurobond consists of admission to listing by the UKLA and admission to trading on a recognised investment exchange such as the LSE.

As far as the UKLA is concerned, issuers of convertible bonds and bonds with equity warrants must also include more detailed disclosures in order to gain admission to trading on the LSE. The additional disclosures include the following:

- Profit and loss accounts, balance sheets and cash flow statements for the last three years and, where appropriate, an interim statement.
- Information on the shares into which the bonds are convertible.
- Information on the issuer's directors, including their aggregate remuneration and their total interest in the issuer's shares.

7.2   Issuance of Eurobonds

Most new eurobond issues are placed by an international securities house, appointed by the issuer to act as the lead manager to the issue. This lead manager will then form a syndicate of other securities houses through which the bonds will be marketed and sold to their respective clients.

As the eurobond market has grown, a self-regulatory organisation has been formed that oversees the market and its participants – the International Capital Market Association (ICMA).

7.3   Immobilisation

As bearer documents, it is important that eurobonds are kept safe, and this is often achieved by holding the bonds in depositaries, particularly those maintained by Euroclear and Clearstream.

Eurobonds which are deposited in these clearing house organisations are described as being immobilised. Immobilisation does not mean that the bonds cannot be transferred in secondary market transactions, it simply means that the bonds are safely held within a reputable depositary and transfers of ownership take place electronically by book entry transfer.

7.4   Dealing and Settlement

The eurobond market is, in effect, an international market in debt. Companies issuing debt in the eurobond market have their securities traded all around the world and are not limited to one domestic market place.

There is no formal market place for eurobond trading, although several exchanges will provide a listing for major issues, such as the LSE. The market is based on electronic and telephone contact between the main investment houses which are primarily based in London.

The market is regulated by the ICMA, which operates rules regulating the conduct of dealers in the market place.

Settlement is conducted for the market by two independent clearing houses, Euroclear and Clearstream. Settlement and accrued interest conventions have been established for the secondary market. Settlement is on a T+2 basis.

Accrued interest is the portion of coupon interest applicable to a eurobond, should the bond be transacted for a settlement date between two coupon dates. Accrued interest is either cum-interest or ex-interest. Unlike domestic bond issues within the UK, where accrued interest is calculated on the basis of an actual/365 basis, in the case of eurobonds the convention is that accrued interest will be calculated on the basis of 30 days per month and 360 days per year (30/360 basis).

An absence of national regulation means that eurobonds can pay interest gross, making the buyer responsible for paying their own tax and avoiding withholding tax (WHT) (tax being withheld in the country of origin). Initially, Eurobonds were aimed at wealthy individuals, but as the market has grown they have increasingly become investments held by institutional investors.

8. Separate Trading of Registred Interest and Principal (STRIPs) and Repos

Learning Objective

3.8.2 Understand and be able to explain the characteristics and uses of strips and repos: use in packaged products; which gilts strippable; resulting number of securities; coupon and redemption payments; as zero coupon bond; payment dates

A stripped gilt is one that is separated into its individual coupon payments and its redemption payment. Each of these payments can then be separately traded as a zero coupon bond (ZCB) with a known nominal redemption value. As each ZCB is purchased at a discount to this redemption value, the entire return is in the form of a capital gain.

Example

Stripping a gilt refers to breaking it down into its individual cash flows which can be traded separately as zero-coupon gilts. A three-year gilt will have seven individual cash flows: six (semi-annual) coupon payments and a principal repayment.

The strip market began in 1997 and all conventional fixed coupon gilts are strippable. There are two series of strippable gilts:

- Gilts that pay coupons on 7 June and December.
- Gilts that pay coupons on 7 March and September.

The US Treasury market also has a well-developed strip market with a wide variety of bonds of different maturities, with different coupons available for stripping and the secondary market for the zero coupon instruments resulting from the stripping process is very active.

STRIPs can be used both as a portfolio management tool and as a personal financial planning tool. The redemption proceeds from these bonds, each with their own unique redemption date, can be used to coincide with specific future liabilities or known future payments. They can also be used within structured products, where the zero coupon bond provides the capital protection and a call option the scope for growth in line with an index.

All gains and losses on gilt strips held by individuals are taxed as income on an annual basis. At the end of the tax year, individuals are deemed for tax to have disposed of and reacquired their holdings of gilt strips at their then current value; any gain (or loss) arising during the year on the holding is taxed (or relieved) as income.

Gilt strips can be held by individuals within individual savings accounts (ISAs) on the same basis as conventional and index-linked gilts.

Repos are discussed later in this chapter in Section 11.3.

9. Fixed-Income Markets and Trade Execution

9.1 Bond Trading

Learning Objective

3.9.1 Understand the role, structure and characteristics of global corporate bond markets: decentralised dealer markets and dealer provision of liquidity; impact of default risk on prices; relationship between bond and equity markets; bond pools of liquidity versus centralized equity exchanges; access considerations; regulatory/ supervisory environment; ICMA and other relevant trade associations

There is no central physical location or exchange for bond trading, as there is for publicly traded stocks. The bond market is known as an over-the-counter (OTC) market, rather than an exchange market.

There are some exceptions to this. For example, some corporate bonds are listed on the NYSE and on the LSE. The latter has also launched a retail bond platform recognising the growing interest in this segment of the market.

Investors can trade marketable bonds among themselves in principal-to-principal deals and this can be done at any time. However, most trading is done through the network of bond dealers, and more specifically, the bond trading desks of major investment dealers. The dealers occupy the pivotal position in the vast network of telephone and electronic platforms that connect the interested players.

9.1.1 Decentralised Dealer Market

Unlike the traditional centralised stock exchanges for dealing in equities, the method of dealing in corporate bonds tends to be away from the major exchanges in what is commonly described as a **decentralised dealer market**.

A decentralised dealer market structure is one that enables investors to buy and sell without a centralised location. In a decentralised market, the technical infrastructure provides traders and investors with access to various bid/ask prices and allows them to deal directly with other traders/dealers rather than through a central exchange.

Bond dealers usually **make a market** for bonds. In essence this means that the dealer employs traders who have detailed knowledge and expertise in a specific sector of the bond market, and are prepared to quote a price to buy or sell them.

9.1.2 Bond Pools of Liquidity

The primary function and role of market makers in corporate bonds is to provide liquidity to the marketplace and to act as a facilitator or agent in trades between the principals. Dealers are those that have been appointed by the corporate issuer to act as distributors on their behalf in the issuance and underwriting of bond issues. There is often a combination of such roles by large financial institutions.

Dealers provide liquidity for bond investors, thereby allowing investors to buy and sell bonds more easily (business-to-consumer (B2C)) and with a limited concession on the price. Dealers also buy and sell amongst themselves (business-to-business (B2B)) either directly or anonymously via bond brokers, an exercise which is known as proprietary trading, as the profit and loss for such trades are taken on to the dealer's books rather than those of its customers or clients.

The primary incentive for trading bonds amongst dealers is to take a spread between the buying and selling price. Dealers often have bond traders located in the major financial centres and are able to trade bonds 24 hours a day (although not usually on weekends).

Most debt instruments are traded by investment banks making markets for specific issues. If an investor wants to buy or sell a bond, he or she will need to make a request for quote (RFQ) from the issuing bank.

9.1.3   Default Risk

In the corporate bond market, unlike the government bond markets where it is assumed that no sovereign borrower will default, the determination of the likelihood that a corporate borrower may default is a vital part in the pricing mechanism for corporate bonds.

The price of a corporate bond will be influenced by the prices (and inversely to the yields) on an equivalent government bond. However, the corporate bond's price will be subject to a discount, to represent the risk that the corporate may default compared to the default risk-free nature of the government bond.

Credit rating agencies provide a rating system for corporate bonds. The highest grade corporate bonds are known as AAA or Aaa and these are bonds that these agencies have deemed the least likely to fail. Companies such as General Electric (GE) have been given this status, although there is always the possibility of a downgrade when the perceived riskiness of the borrower changes.

Lower grade corporate bonds are perceived as more likely to default, so the borrower will have to entice lenders with a higher coupon payment and higher yield to maturity. Equally, there is also a chance they may also be upgraded in the near future and, therefore, may be considered as a potentially good investment.

9.1.4   The Relationship between Bond and Equity Markets

The primary difference between the corporate bond market and the equity market relates to the nature of the security being traded.

*   A corporate bond usually has a specified income stream, in the form of coupon payments which will be paid to the holder of the bond, and a bondholder has a more senior claim against the assets of the issuer in the case of a bankruptcy or restructuring.
*   Investors in equities may receive a dividend payment from the corporation but this is less certain and can fluctuate. Indeed, less mature companies may not even pay a dividend. The equity holder also has a greater risk that, if the corporation which has issued the shares becomes insolvent or undergoes a re-structuring, there may be insufficient assets to be liquidated or reorganised and then distributed to shareholders. In such instances shareholders may find that their equity stakes in a corporation have little or no residual value.

This gives rise to the concept of the equity risk premium.

The reason behind this premium stems from the risk-return trade-off, in which a higher rate of return is required to entice investors to take on riskier investments. The risk-free rate in the market is often quoted as the rate on longer-term government bonds, which are considered risk free because of the low chance that the government will default on its loans.

Investment grade bonds are considered to be relatively low in risk and are of more appeal to a conservative investor. On the other hand, an investment in stocks is far less guaranteed, as companies regularly suffer downturns or go out of business.

If the return on a stock is 15% and the risk-free rate over the same period is 7%, the equity-risk premium is 8% for this stock over that period of time.

9.1.5   Regulatory and Supervisory Environment

All authorised dealer firms, and all of the individuals employed within them in the UK, are subject to all of the rules and regulations of the FCA.

The FCA's supervisory approach has changed dramatically as a result of the banking crisis of 2008. The risks of discipline and criminal prosecution, resulting from violation of FCA regulations by somebody who is FCA authorised, or is an **approved person** at an FCA-authorised firm, are greater now than previously.

Approved persons have a contract with the FCA which has its own code of conduct and principles to follow. They can be disciplined by the FCA for breaches of these, with penalties including a public reprimand (which has associated reputation issues) and/or a fine, or a prohibition order, which prevents the individual from acting in the financial services industry.

In addition to the de-centralised dealer network model, the trading of bonds on the LSE is subject to the rules and regulations of the exchange. The UKLA and the LSE have a statutory obligation to protect all investors on an ongoing basis and to maintain a fair and orderly market. To fulfil this obligation, the UKLA requires all issuers of bonds listed in London to meet a number of continuing obligations.

Issuers of London-listed securities have the ongoing obligation to disclose to the investor community any information deemed to be price sensitive, which must be disseminated to the market via a regulatory information service such as the LSE's regulatory news service (RNS).

OTC trading takes place between International Capital Markets Association (ICMA) dealers, rather than being conducted on a physical exchange. Dealers are subject to the standards and rules of the ICMA.

9.2 Price Quotation Methods

Learning Objective

3.8.1 Understand the main bond pricing benchmarks and how they are applied to new bond issues: spread over government bond benchmark; spread over/under LIBOR; spread over/under swap

3.9.2 Understand the differences in yield, spread and price quotation methods, and the circumstances in which they are used

Financial analysts and investment professionals pay close attention to spreads in the bond markets. A spread is simply the difference between the yield available on one instrument and the yield available elsewhere. It is usually expressed in basis points. A basis point is equal to 0.01% which means that a 100 basis point uplift or premium is equal to 1%.

- **Spread Over/Under Government Bond Benchmark**
  - Spreads are commonly expressed as spreads over government bonds.
  - For example, if a ten-year corporate bond is yielding 6% and the equivalent ten-year gilt is yielding 4.2%, the spread over the government bond is 6% – 4.2% = 1.8% or 180 basis points.
  - This spread will vary, mainly as a result of the relative risk of the corporate bond compared to the gilt, so for a more risky corporate issuer, the spread will be greater.
- **Spread Over/Under LIBOR**
  - Spreads are also calculated against other benchmarks, such as the published interest rates represented by the London Interbank Offered Rate (LIBOR).
  - Because the government is less likely to default on its borrowings than the major banks (that provide the LIBOR rates), the spread of instruments versus LIBOR will generally be less than the spread against government bonds.
  - In the earlier example, if the equivalent LIBOR rate is 4.5%, the spread over LIBOR is 6% – 4.5% = 1.5% or 150 basis points, compared to the 180 basis point spread over government bonds.
- **Spread Over/Under Swap Rates**
  - There is a very active market in exchanging floating rates for fixed rates in the so-called swaps market. Also, credit default swaps (CDS), which are a form of insurance against the risk of borrowers defaulting on their debt, are some of the most actively traded instruments each day in the capital markets.
  - The rates available on various swaps – both for corporate credits and also sovereign credits – are also used as benchmarks against which to benchmark the yield available on any specific security.
  - The swap spread is the difference between the ten-year Treasury and the swap rate, which is the fixed rate on a LIBOR-based interest rate swap.
  - Under normal market conditions, the ten-year Treasury yield is lower than the swap rate, reflecting the credit quality of the US government versus that of the participants in the interbank credit markets.
  - In general terms, the swap spread is defined as the difference between the swap rate and yield of ('on-the-run') government bonds of equal maturity. On-the-run means the most recent issuance of a US Treasury bond or UK gilt.

The specific features of a bond can mean that pricing off a benchmark security/rate becomes more difficult. For example, a ten-year corporate bond, with a put/call feature, is unlikely to price off the ten-year gilt, but rather a benchmark curve, as the estimate of the maturity of the corporate bond is unlikely to coincide with the specific maturity of the given gilt because of the put/call feature.

The term **pricing off** simply means the price/value of one thing – here a bond – being determined from the price/value of something else – here another bond.

10. Valuation of Fixed-Income Securities

10.1 Debt Seniority and Credit Ratings

Learning Objective

3.10.1 Understand the purpose, influence and limitations of global credit rating agencies, debt seniority and ranking in cases of default/ bankruptcy: senior; subordinated; mezzanine; payment in kind (PIK)

A credit rating estimates the credit worthiness of an individual, corporation or even a country.

For corporate and sovereign credits, a rating is an evaluation made by credit ratings agencies of a borrower's overall credit history and provides a classification system enabling a lender or investor to estimate the probability of the issuer of a credit, such as a bond, being able to make repayment in accordance with the terms of the borrowing, or more specifically the offering prospectus for a bond issuance.

A major factor in the credit rating given to a bond is the level of security associated with it and its ranking in the event of bankruptcy.

When there are multiple forms of debt the issuer will have to establish an order as to which debt will be serviced and the so-called seniority within the entity's capital structure in the event of financial difficulties leading to a re-structuring or liquidation. In broad terms, the seniority of debt falls into three main headings:

- Senior.
- Subordinated.
- Mezzanine and payment in kind (PIK).

10.1.1 Senior Debt

Senior debt is a class of corporate debt that has priority with respect to interest and principal over other classes of debt and over all classes of equity by the same issuer.

Senior debt is often secured by collateral on which the lender has put in place a first lien or charge. Usually this covers all the assets of a corporation and is often used for revolving credit lines. Senior debt has priority for repayment in a debt restructuring or winding up of a company.

However, in various jurisdictions and under exceptional circumstances, notwithstanding the nominal label given to senior debt, there can be special dispensations which may subordinate the claims of holders of senior debt. Holders of particular tranches of debt which may have been designated and sold as senior debt may find that other claimants have super-senior claims.

Example

In 2008, the largest savings and loan institution in the US, Washington Mutual Bank was seized by the Federal Deposit Insurance Corporation (FDIC) to prevent its collapse following losses on sub-prime mortgages. The FDIC then sold the bank to JP Morgan Chase.

All of the assets and most of its liabilities were assumed by JP Morgan. However other debt claims, including unsecured senior debt, were not. By doing this, the FDIC effectively subordinated the unsecured senior debt to depositors, thereby fully protecting depositors while also eliminating any potential deposit insurance liability to the FDIC itself.

In this and similar cases, specific regulatory and oversight powers can lead to senior lenders being subordinated in potentially unexpected ways.

Furthermore, in US Chapter 11 bankruptcies, new lenders can come in to fund the continuing operation of companies and be granted status as super-senior to other (even senior-secured) lenders. This so-called **debtor in possession** status also applies in other jurisdictions, including France.

10.1.2 Subordinated

Subordinated debt or bonds have accepted that their claim to the issuer's assets ranks below that of the senior debt in the event of a liquidation. As a result of accepting a greater risk than the senior debt, the subordinated borrowing will be entitled to a greater rate of interest than that available on the senior debt.

10.1.3 Mezzanine and Payment In Kind (PIK)

The mezzanine level of debt, if it exists at all, will be even more risky than the subordinated debt. It will rank below other forms of debt, but above the equity in a liquidation. As the most risky debt, the mezzanine debt will offer a greater rate of interest than the subordinated and senior levels of debt.

Mezzanine borrowing can be raised in a variety of ways – one example is the issue of payment in kind (PIK) notes. PIK notes are simply zero coupon bonds that are issued at a substantial discount to their face value. When they are repaid, the difference between the redemption value and the purchase cost will provide the investor's return.

It should be noted that each of the three main categories can themselves contain sub-categories such as senior secured, senior unsecured, senior subordinated and junior subordinated. In practice, the various rating agencies look at debt structures in these narrower terms. Seniority can be contractual as the result of the terms of the issue, or based on the corporate structure of the issuer.

10.2   Analysis of Credit Ratings

Learning Objective

3.10.2   Be able to analyse sovereign, government and corporate credit ratings from an investment perspective: main rating agencies; country rating factors; debt instrument rating factors; investment and sub-investment grades; use of credit enhancements; impact of grading changes

10.2.1 The Main Rating Agencies

The three most prominent global credit rating agencies that provide credit ratings – Standard & Poor's, Moody's and Fitch Ratings – carry on business across the world and all have major operations in New York, London and Tokyo.

In the case of Standard & Poor's, the rating agency is a division of the US publishing company McGraw-Hill, which trades on the NYSE under the symbol MHP. Moody's is also a publicly listed company on the NYSE, trading under the symbol MCO, and amongst its major shareholders is the renowned investor Warren Buffet. Fitch Ratings is headquartered in New York and London and is part of the Fitch Group.

Although the three rating agencies use similar methods to rate issuers and individual bond issues, essentially by assessing whether the cash flow likely to be generated by the borrower will comfortably service, and ultimately repay its debts, the rating each gives often differs, though not usually significantly so.

10.2.2 Country Rating Factors

The ratings agencies assess the creditworthiness of individual countries and assign ratings. Since the credit crisis, a number of countries have had their credit ratings downgraded and changes to these are closely watched by the market and have a direct impact on their cost of funding.

Governments have unique powers, such as the ability to raise taxes, set laws, and control the supply of money, which generally make them more creditworthy than other issuers. As a result, there is a greater proportion of sovereign ratings at the higher end of the scale compared with other sectors.

Country Ratings as at July 2016

AAA-Rated

Australia

Canada

Denmark

Germany

Hong Kong

Liechtenstein

Luxembourg

Netherlands

Norway

Singapore

Sweden

Switzerland

Source: Standard & Poor's

The rating agencies use a combination of several quantitative and qualitative variables (economic, social and political) in order to assign a credit rating to a debtor or to a debt instrument.

When assessing the creditworthiness of sovereign issuers, the ratings agencies will take into account a number of factors including both political and economic factors.

- **Political factors**
  - Since the willingness of a government to pay is a crucial factor that distinguishes sovereign debts from corporate debts, political factors play a key role in determining sovereign ratings.
- **Economic factors**
  - The main economic variables considered are: per capita income; gross domestic product (GDP) growth; inflation rate; economic development; ratio of foreign debt to GDP; real exchange rate; and default history.

The relevance of the economic factors that are considered includes the following.

Per capita income	An increase of the per capita income implies a larger potential tax base and a greater ability for a country to repay debt.
Gross domestic product (GDP) growth	An increasing rate of economic growth tends to decrease the relative debt burden. Moreover, it may help in avoiding insolvency problems
Inflation rate	A low inflation rate reveals sustainable monetary and exchange rate policies. It can also be seen as a proxy of the quality of economic management.
Economic development	Developed countries are integrated within the world economy and are less inclined to default on their foreign debt in order to avoid sanctions from lenders.
Current account	A large current account deficit implies the dependence of a country on foreign creditors. A persistent deficit affects the country's sustainability.
Foreign debt/GDP	This ratio is negatively related to default risk.
Real exchange rate	The real exchange rate assesses the trade competitiveness of the economy.
Default history	A country's default history affects its reputation.
Ratio debt/GDP	The higher this ratio is, the greater the occurrence of a liquidity crisis.
Ratio reserves/ imports	The higher this ratio is, the more reserves are available to service foreign debt.
Ratio investment/GDP	This ratio captures the future growth ability of a country and it is a decreasing function of default.
Rule of law	These provide a means of evaluating the governance of a country and affect a country's willingness to pay.

10.2.3 Debt Instrument Rating Factors

The financial obligation to which a rating refers is usually a bond or similar debt instrument. The company wishing to raise money by issuing a bond relies on an independently verified credit rating to inform potential investors regarding the relative ability of the company to meet its financial commitments. The agencies themselves make it clear that they are not in the business of recommending the purchase or sale of any security, but address only credit risk.

There are two types of issue credit ratings, dependent upon the length of time for which the financial obligation is issued. There are long-term issue credit ratings and short-term issue credit ratings, each with their own set of standards. The latter relate to obligations which were originally established with a maturity of less than 365 days (and to short-term features of longer-term bonds).

Ratings may be public or private. They provide opinions, not recommendations, and are derived from both audited and unaudited information.

It is important to appreciate that credit ratings are tailored to particular sectors. Ratings should be comparable across different sectors, but a rating may serve a very specific purpose in, say, the banking or insurance sectors; for example, the likelihood of a bank running into serious financial difficulty requiring support, and whether it will get external support in such an event. This obviously has no equivalent outside the financial sector.

The credit rating for a particular instrument is not meant to be a recommendation to an investor to buy, sell or hold onto the instrument. That is a decision for individual investors, based on their appetite for risk. The debt instruments with the lowest credit ratings will carry the highest levels of potential reward but also the highest level of risk.

10.2.4 Investment and Sub-Investment Grades

Although the three rating agencies use similar methods to rate issuers and individual bond issues, the rating each gives often differs, though not usually significantly so. The scope of this analysis has recently been widened to take account of the size of an issuer's pension scheme deficit and, following the collapse of Enron, the nature and extent of its off-balance sheet liabilities.

Bond issues subject to credit ratings can be divided into two distinct categories: those accorded an investment grade rating and those categorised as non-investment grade or speculative. The latter are also known as high-yield or junk bonds. Investment grade issues offer the greatest liquidity. The following table below shows the credit ratings available from the three companies.

Bond Credit Ratings					
Credit risk			Moody's	Standard & Poor's	Fitch Ratings
Investment Grade					
Highest quality			Aaa	AAA	AAA
High quality	Very strong		Aa	AA	AA
Upper medium grade	Strong		A	A	A
Medium grade			Baa	BBB	BBB
Non-Investment Grade					
Lower medium grade	Somewhat speculative		Ba	BB	BB
Low grade	Speculative		B	B	B
Poor quality	May default		Caa	CCC	CCC
Most speculative			C	CC	CC
No interest being paid or bankruptcy petition filed			C	D	C
In default			C	D	D

Standard & Poor's and Fitch Ratings modify their ratings by adding a plus or minus sign to show relative standing within a category, whilst Moody's do the same by the addition of a 1, 2 or 3.

The highest grade corporate bonds are known as AAA or Aaa and these are bonds that the three agencies have deemed the least likely to fail.

Bonds rated in the BBB category or higher are considered to be investment grade. Very few organisations, with the exception of supranational agencies and some western governments, are awarded a triple-A rating, though the bond issues of most large corporations boast an investment grade credit rating.

Securities with ratings in the BB category and below are considered high-yield or below investment grade. While experience has shown that a diversified portfolio of high-yield bonds will have only a modest risk of default, it is extremely important to remember that the higher interest rate that they carry is a warning of higher risk.

10.2.5 Use of Credit Enhancements

Credit enhancement refers to a process where measures are taken to ensure bonds have the required credit rating for investors by enhancing their security.

Issues such as asset-backed securities are credit enhanced in some way to gain a higher credit rating. The simplest method of achieving this is through some form of insurance scheme that will pay out should the pool of assets be insufficient to service or repay the debt.

Examples of credit enhancement include:

- Over-collateralisation.
- Pool insurance.
- Senior/junior note classes – rights of junior note class are subordinated and do not receive payments until certain agency rating requirements have been met, specifically satisfactory performance of the collateral pool over a period or until senior note classes have been redeemed.
- Margin step-up – bonds are usually structured with a call date and, to make sure the issuer did not pass on this provision for coupon to be stepped-up.
- Excess spread – difference between the return on the underlying assets and interest rate payable on bonds is used to cover expenses and losses. Any surplus is held as a reserve against future losses.
- Substitution – enables the issuer to utilise principal from redemptions, to purchase new collateral, so lengthening the effective life of the bond.

10.2.6 Impact of Grading Changes

Ratings are regularly reviewed and are often revised in the light of changed economic conditions and/or changes in the outlook for an industry or the issuer's specific circumstances. Rating agencies will signal they are considering a rating change by placing the security on CreditWatch (S&P), Under Review (Moody's) or on Rating Watch (Fitch Ratings).

Most revisions result in credit downgrades rather than upgrades. The price change resulting from a credit downgrade is usually much greater than for an upgrade, given that the price of a bond can fall all the way to zero, whereas there is a limit to how high a bond's price can rise. A downgrade will also make future finance raising more expensive for the bond issuer, as investors will demand a higher return for the higher risk.

The bond issues of many large telecom companies, as a result of taking on large amounts of additional debt to finance their acquisition of third generation (3G) telecom licences in 2000, suffered severe credit downgrades and, as a consequence, experienced an indiscriminate marking down in the prices of their bond issues.

More recently, ratings changes for Eurozone countries have seen the cost of borrowing rise over concerns that they may follow the same route as Greece. Its rating was downgraded to BB+ in April 2010, making it the first Eurozone country to have its debt downgraded to junk status, and in 2011 to CCC, branding it with the lowest credit rating of any government in the world. Investors demanded higher returns to compensate for the increased risk, making it highly expensive for the country to borrow from the debt market. The downgrading of Greek debt to junk status led to an emergency package to support the Greek economy and eventually to bondholders having to accept a writedown on the value of their bonds.

10.3   Role of Credit Rating Agencies

Learning Objective

3.10.3   Understand the role of ratings agencies; their impact on the market and the structure of their credit ratings: agencies; rating effect on the cost of raising funds; use as a risk identification tool; types of securities rated; rating securitised products; implications of the conflicts in the rating process

10.3.1 Agencies

Rating agencies assign ratings to many bonds when they are issued and monitor developments during the bond's lifetime. The three most prominent credit rating agencies that provide these ratings are Standard & Poor's, Moody's and Fitch Ratings.

Each of the agencies assigns its ratings based on in-depth analysis of the issuer's financial condition and management, economic and debt characteristics, and the specific revenue sources securing the bond.

The credit rating agencies are paid by the debt issuer and offer different types of rating services: public ratings; private ratings for internal or regulatory purposes; shadow ratings – again for private consumption – and model-based ratings. Each kind involves differing degrees of evaluation.

Public ratings are available to the public through their ratings information desks, through published reports and via the internet.

10.3.2 Rating Effect on the Cost of Raising Funds

An inferior credit rating indicates a higher risk of defaulting on a loan, and investors will want to be compensated for this additional risk by higher interest rates and other provisions, or they may simply be unwilling to purchase the bonds being offered by the issuer.

The cutting of a credit rating makes it more expensive for governments to raise money with their sovereign bond issues, as it will require higher coupon payments to attract investors who perceive more risk, for example, in an Irish government bond than in a US Treasury one.

10.3.3 Use as a Risk Identification Tool

When a bond is first issued, the issuer will provide details of its financial soundness and creditworthiness in a document known as an offering document, prospectus or official statement. But as the bond may not be due for redemption for many years, investors need a method of checking on a regular basis whether the government or company remains capable of meeting its obligations.

The **credit risk** for bonds – the probability of an issuer defaulting on their payment obligations and the extent of the resulting loss – can be assessed by reference to the independent credit ratings given to most bond issues.

The ratings grades used by the three main credit ratings agencies (CRAs) provide a guide for investors who are seeking knowledge regarding risk and as a way of assisting in determining the appropriate prices at which bonds of each category should trade in the secondary markets for such issues.

10.3.4 Types of Securities Rated

The types of securities provided with a credit rating depend on the demand for the bond and the willingness of the issuer to pay for the credit rating. All types of instruments are therefore potentially covered by a credit rating but just because some of an issuer's bonds have a credit rating does not mean that all are rated.

10.3.5 Rating Securitised Products

During the financial crisis that developed following problems that arose regarding asset-backed securities in 2007/08 the CRAs were subject to a large amount of criticism for the manner in which they failed to correctly assess the risk of certain kinds of securities that were issued.

There was alleged to be a conflict of interest on the part of the manner in which the credit ratings agencies were paid for their services by the issuer of securitised products, whereas the risk was borne by the purchaser of such securities. As a result of the deficiencies of the method of rating credits there has been increased oversight by regulators of the credit rating function.

For securitisation issues, the complex nature of the instruments means that the credit rating agencies consider the following:

- The credit quality of the securitised assets, focusing on the effect of worst case stress scenarios.
- Legal and regulatory issues and, in particular, whether the securitised assets have been appropriately isolated from the bankruptcy or insolvency risk of any entities that participate in the transaction.
- Payment structures and how cash flows from the securitised assets are dealt with.
- Operational and administrative risks associated with the company responsible for managing the securitised assets.

Counterparty risk arising from the ability of third parties to meet obligations, such as financial guarantees, bank liquidity or credit support facilities, letters of credit, and interest rate and currency swaps.

10.3.6 Conflicts in the Rating Process

The role of credit rating agencies was criticised during the aftermath of the sub-prime crisis, particularly on their rating of asset-backed bonds and other securitisation issues, especially as many were downgraded suddenly from AAA status to non-investment grade.

The ratings agencies have an unusual relationship with the principal participants in bond markets. On the one hand their ratings are used by buyers of bonds, such as pension funds and other asset management companies and regarded as independent and objectively determined, and on the other hand their instructions and appointment comes from the seller of the bonds. As was seen in cases which have been the focus of testimony before the US Congress, there are at least grounds for believing that the manner in which the agencies are commissioned by, and paid by, bond issuers, provides a reasonable question as to the reliability and independence of the assessments made.

This led to calls for change. In April 2009, the European Commission (EC) introduced new regulations for credit rating agencies which issue opinions on creditworthiness of companies, governments and sophisticated financial structures. All credit rating agencies that would like their credit ratings to be used in the EU have to apply for registration.

Registered credit rating agencies will be subject to regulatory supervision and have to comply with rules designed to ensure the following:

- Ratings are not affected by conflicts of interest.
- Credit rating agencies remain vigilant on the quality of the rating methodology and the ratings.
- They act in a transparent manner.

10.4   Factors Influencing Bond Prices

Learning Objective

3.10.4   Be able to analyse the factors that influence bond pricing: yield to maturity; credit rating; impact of interest rates; market liquidity; clean and dirty prices

10.4.1 Yield to Maturity (YTM)

The yeld to maturity (YTM) for a bond is also known as the gross redemption yield (GRY).

The YTM for a bond is a more sophisticated and precise measure of a bond's yield, than the simple flat yield, because it takes into account both the timing of coupon payments right through to maturity, as well as the discounted value, or present value, of the redemption of the principal. As such, it is more appropriate for long-term investors than the flat yield. Also, because it ignores the impact of any taxation (hence gross redemption yield), this measure of return is useful for non-taxpaying, long-term investors such as pension funds and charities.

The calculation of the YTM employs a discounted cash flow approach to arrive at the net present value of all of the cash flows thrown off by a bond during its lifetime. All of the cash flows are discounted according to the appropriate rate of interest, such as the prevailing short-term rate or base rate.

Another way of regarding the YTM is to consider it as the internal rate of return of the bond. The internal rate of return is simply the discount rate that, when applied to the future cash flows of the bond, produces the current price of that bond.

Expressed in its simplest form, the yield to maturity is the internal rate of return (IRR) of:

- The dirty price paid to buy the bond.
- The gross coupons received to redemption.
- The final redemption proceeds.

10.4.2 Credit Rating

As seen above, bondholders face the risk that the issuer of the bond may default on their obligation to pay interest and the principal amount at redemption. Credit ratings give an indication of the scale of the risk and, when comparing similar bonds, the lower the credit rating the higher the return that will be demanded by investors to compensate for the risk.

10.4.3 Impact of Interest Rates

Probably the most important risk to a bond holder is the impact of changing interest rates, because of the method of discounting future cash flows, at the prevailing rate of interest, to calculate the net present value of the bond's cash flow and thereby arrive at the current bond prices.

There is an inverse relationship between the price of a bond with a fixed coupon and the prevailing rate of interest. For example, a bond issued with a 5% coupon will be less desirable as interest rates increase and further bonds are issued with higher coupon rates, for example, with 6% coupons. In simple terms, the price of the bond obtainable in the secondary market will have to decline so that the YTM for the 5% bond becomes equal to the YTM for the 6% bond. The manner in which the lower coupon bond remains competitive in YTM is by having a lower current price.

Duration and modified duration (volatility) are the means of measuring this risk more precisely and they are covered in Section 10.6.5.

10.4.4 Market Liquidity

The ease with which an issue can be sold in the market will affect the investor's perception of the risk of holding a bond.

In certain markets, the volume of trading tends to concentrate into the benchmark stocks, or the on-the-run stocks, especially in the gilts market, thereby rendering most other issues illiquid. Other bonds become subject to seasoning, as the initial liquidity dries up and the bonds are purchased by investors who wish to hold them to maturity.

During market turmoil, difficulties can arise in the liquidity and trading conditions of bonds. In such conditions, investors have a preference for the most liquid instruments, which may force their price to be out of normal alignment with similar bonds, which have a slightly different maturity date. This can result in a breakdown in complex strategies designed to exploit the spreads or price differences across the yield spectrum.

10.4.5 Clean and Dirty Prices

The market convention concerning the quoting of clean and dirty prices is as follows:

* The price of a stock excluding the accrued interest is known as the clean price. Most markets quote clean prices but a price might be quoted which includes accrued interest.
* A price which includes accrued interest but does not calculate it separately is known as a dirty price.

Under UK tax law the accrued interest must be calculated because, for individuals, it is dealt with according to income tax rules (the accrued income scheme), whereas the capital value is subject to capital gains tax rules (which in most cases will mean that it is exempt from tax).

Under the actual/actual convention which is used for gilts, interest is calculated using the actual number of days of accrual, compared with the actual number of days in the period between coupon payments; the latter period may be between 181 and 184 days, depending on the particular months in the period.

The amount of accrued interest is calculated as follows:

$$\text{Accrued interest} = \text{Nominal value} \times \tfrac{1}{2} \text{ Annual coupon} \times \frac{\text{Days of accrual}}{\text{Days in the coupon period}}$$

The accrued interest adjustment for gilt-edged securities depends on whether the stock is traded cum-interest or ex-interest. The cum-interest adjustment is added to the clean price and the ex-interest adjustment is deducted from the clean price.

* Cum-Interest Transaction
  * The accrued interest is added to the clean price.
  * The days of accrual are the days from the day after the most recent coupon payment through to the transaction settlement date, both days inclusive.
* Ex-Interest Transaction
  * The accrued interest on an ex-interest transaction is called rebate interest.
  * The rebate interest is deducted from the clean price.
  * The days of accrual are the days from the day after the transaction settlement date through to the next coupon payment, both days inclusive.

Example

A Cum-Interest Transaction

On 25 April there is a transaction involving £100,000 of a 9% gilt with interest payable on 15 January and 15 July. The clean price is £102. What is the total price paid by the purchaser?

$$\text{Accrued interest} = \text{Nominal value} \times \tfrac{1}{2} \text{ Annual coupon} \times \frac{\text{Days of accrual}}{\text{Days in the coupon period}}$$

$$\text{Accrued interest} = £100,000 \times 4.5\% \times \frac{101}{181} = £2,511.05$$

- The coupon period runs from 16 January to 15 July = 181.
- The accrual period runs from 16 January (15+1) through to 26 April (25+1) = 101.
- Note that gilts settle at T+1 so the settlement date is 26 April.

The total price is (£100,000 x 102%) + £2,511.05 = £104,511.05.

Example

An Ex-Interest Transaction

On 3 October there is a transaction involving £60,000 of a 5½% gilt with interest payable on 8 October and 8 April. The clean price is £91. What is the total price paid by the purchaser?

$$\text{Rebate interest} = \text{Nominal value} \times \tfrac{1}{2} \text{ Annual coupon} \times \frac{\text{Days of accrual}}{\text{Days in the coupon period}}$$

$$\text{Accrued interest} = £60,000 \times 2.75\% \times \frac{4}{183} = £36.07$$

- The coupon period runs from 9 April to 8 October = 183 days.
- The accrual period runs from 5 October (3+1+1) through to 8 October both days inclusive. The trade will settle on T+1 (4 October) and the day after is 5 October.

The total price is (£60,000 x 91/100) – 36.07 = £54,563.93.

10.5 Yield Curve

Learning Objective

3.10.5   Understand the characteristics of the yield curve: normal; inverted

Interest rates differ depending upon the term of the investment and, typically, a long-dated bond will carry a higher GRY than a shorter one.

This relationship between yield and maturity is known as the term structure of interest rates and can be illustrated diagrammatically by a redemption yield curve, or yield curve, as it is more commonly known.

The following diagram demonstrates a typical yield curve:

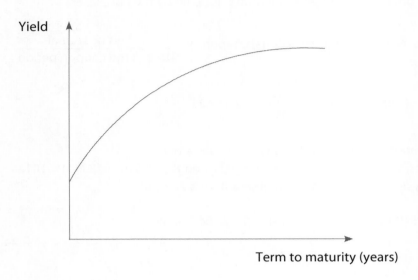

Although yield curves can assume a range of different shapes, more often than not the yield curve is described as being upward-sloping, in that it displays a positive slope. This is known as a normal yield curve as it depicts the commonly observed relationship of long-term interest rates being higher than short-term interest rates. Note, however, that the actual yield curve fluctuates along the curve from short term to long term.

If the yield curve is said to be steep, it means the yields on short-dated stocks are relatively low when compared to longer-dated stocks. This means that an investor can obtain significantly higher yields, and therefore income, by buying a stock with a longer maturity than they can with a shorter one.

Alternatively, the yield curve may be described as flat, which means that the difference between short- and long-term rates is relatively small. This means that the reward for buying longer-dated stocks is relatively small and investors may choose to stay in the short end of the maturity range.

When yields on shorter-dated stocks are higher than those on longer-dated ones, the yield curve is said to be inverted and is usually seen when the market expects interest rates to decline.

10.6 Bond Valuation Measures

Learning Objective

3.10.6 Be able to analyse fixed income securities using the following valuation measures, and understand the benefits and limitations of using them: flat yield; nominal and real return; gross redemption yield (using internal rate of return); net redemption yield; modified duration

The return from bonds comprises the income return and the capital return.

The income return represents the interest paid on a bond during its lifetime, and the capital return represents the difference between the acquisition price of the bond and the amount received at maturity.

10.6.1 Flat Yield

The simplest approach to establishing the return from a bond is to calculate its running yield, also known as the flat or interest yield.

This expresses the coupon as a percentage of the market, or clean, price of the bond. The formula for calculating the flat yield is:

$$\text{Running Yield} = \frac{\text{Coupon}}{\text{Price}} \times 100$$

So, for example, a bond with a 6% coupon that is due to be redeemed at par in five years and is currently priced at 110 will have a running yield of:

$$\frac{6}{110} \times 100 = 5.45\%$$

There are three key drawbacks for using flat yield as a robust measure in assessing bond returns.

- Since it only measures the coupon flows and ignores the redemption flows, when applicable, it is giving an incomplete perspective on the actual returns from the bond. A bond which has been purchased at a price away from redemption will be significantly under-valued when the par value is excluded from the calculation.
- The calculation completely ignores the timing of any cash flows and, because there is no discounted cash flow analysis, the time value of money is completely overlooked.
- With floating rate notes, the return in any one period will vary with interest rates. If the coupon is not a constant, then using a flat yield basis for measuring returns becomes an arbitrary matter of selecting which coupon amount, amongst many possible values, to use for the calculation.

10.6.2 Nominal and Real Return

The nominal return on a bond is simply its return, whilst the real return on a bond is the nominal return adjusted for the effect of inflation. This concept was explained in Chapter 1, Section 2.7.1.

10.6.3 Gross Redemption Yield

The flat yield ignores the difference between the current market price and the redemption value. We also need to take into account the gain or loss that an investor will make if a stock is held until redemption to determine the return that the investor is actually receiving.

To remedy this, the GRY or yield to redemption is used.

Simply put, the GRY is a combination of the running yield, plus the gain or loss that will occur if the bond is held until it is redeemed to give an average annual compound return.

In the example above, the GRY will be lower than the running yield, as the market price is higher than the bond's par value and the bond will suffer a capital loss if held to maturity. If, however, the market price is below par, then the GRY will be greater than the running yield, as a capital gain will be made if the bond is held to maturity.

The formula for yield to redemption is complex, but a simple example will show its importance.

Example

Let us assume that there is a government bond that will be repaid in exactly seven years' time. Its current price is £105 and so if an investor were to buy £10,000 nominal of the stock today it will cost £10,500 excluding brokers' costs. The annual interest payments would amount to £500 and its flat yield, using the formula above, is 4.76%.

In seven years' time, however, the investor is only going to receive £10,000 when the stock is redeemed and so will make a loss of £500 over the period. If an investor were simply to look at the flat yield then it would give a misleading indication of the true return that they were earning. The true yield needs to take account of this loss to redemption, and this is the purpose of the redemption yield.

Very simply, the investor needs to write off that loss of £500 over the seven-year period of the bond, let us say at the rate of £70 per annum, so the annual return that the investor is receiving is actually £430 – the annual interest of £500 less the £70 written off. If you recalculate the flat yield, the return reduces to 4.09%.

It can be seen that this gives a more accurate indication of the return that the investor receives and can be used to compare the yields from different bonds to identify which is offering the best return.

A simple formula for calculating the GRY is:

$$\text{GRY} = \text{Running yield} + \left(\frac{(\text{Par} - \text{Market price}) \div \text{Number of years to redemption}}{\text{Market price}} \right) \times 100$$

The way in which it is calculated in practice is more complex and the only way to get the answer is through a process of iteration to calculate the bond's internal rate of return. Calculation of an IRR was considered in Section 2.4.2 in Chapter 2 and that approach is needed to calculate a true GRY.

Its use can be seen by considering GRYs for two government stocks from late 2009.

Example

The following data gives the prices of two UK government stocks that are both due to be repaid in 2021. Consider the data and identify which is producing the best overall return, assuming that the investor will hold the stock until redemption.

Stock Name	Redemption	Price	Flat Yield	GRY
8% Treasury	2021	£150.95	5.30%	2.14%
3¾% Treasury	2021	£112.41	3.34%	2.34%

As can be clearly seen, although the first stock appears to be the most attractive on the face of it, it will in fact produce a poorer overall return to the investor. An investor concerned with maximising their overall return will clearly pick the second stock and only an investor prepared to sacrifice their capital at the expense of current income will select the second.

The GRY as a yield measure, however, has its drawbacks. Firstly, it assumes that the bond will be held to redemption. More fundamentally though, it assumes that the interest payment can be reinvested at the same rate as the bond. This inability to reinvest coupons at the same rate of interest as the GRY is known as reinvestment risk.

10.6.4 Net Redemption Yield

For a taxpayer, the GRY only tells part of the story. Any gain that is made if a bond is held until maturity is often likely to be free of tax, whereas the half-yearly or annual interest received will be subject to income tax in the investor's hands.

Redemption yields are also quoted on a net-of-tax basis so that a direct comparison can be made of the after-tax return to the investor. This can be calculated by using the same simple formula as above, but reducing the running yield to the net yield after tax at the holder's income tax rate.

The net redemption yield allows investors to review the after tax yields, to determine which will be most tax effective for their particular tax position.

10.6.5 Duration

Duration is a measure that reveals how sensitive a bond is to changes in yields. It provides an estimate of the average sensitivity of a bond's price to a 100 basis points (bps) change in a bond's yield.

There is an inverse relationship between bond prices and yields. As yields rise, the price of bonds falls and vice versa. Bond yields in turn reflect the required rate of return (and credit risk premium) which varies as interest rates move up and down.

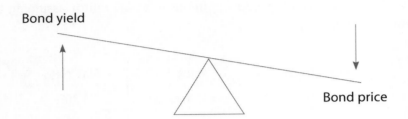

The degree to which the price moves, however, is determined by a number of other factors:

- **Coupon** – the size of the coupon on the bond will affect the degree of price movement. The smaller the coupon, the more the bond's price will move in response to an interest rate changes, so low-coupon bonds are more volatile than higher-coupon bonds.
- **The time to redemption or remaining life** – will also have an impact and is known as the pull to maturity. The closer a bond is to maturity, the less effect a change in interest rates will have as the price will move towards its par value.
- **Its yield** – the sensitivity of a bond's price will also be affected by its yield: the lower the yield, the more sensitive it will be to any changes in interest rates. So, for example, an increase in yields from 2% to 3% will have a greater proportionate effect than an increase from 5% to 6%.

Additional factors that may impact the degree a price moves include:

- The term structure and convexity of the yield curve
- Credit risk premium
- Demand and supply
- Any embedded options or early-redemption options (put/call), and
- The prevailing premium or discount to par.

In order to assess how sensitive one bond is compared to another, a measure that incorporates the coupon, the remaining life and the yield, is used. This is known as **Macaulay Duration** or, more simply, duration.

Simple duration is expressed in years; the higher the duration, the more sensitive is the bond's price to changes in interest rates. However it is more accurate to consider duration as an average indicator, at a point in time, and one that indicates the sensitivity of a bond's price to a 100 bps (1%) change in yield. Note that duration refers to the equivalent duration for a zero coupon bond.

The formula for duration is:

$$\frac{\Sigma \text{ (Net present value of the bond's cash flows x Time to cash flow being received)}}{\Sigma \text{ Net present value of the cash flows to be received}}$$

So to calculate duration we need to use the formula for calculating the present value of a future sum.

Example

Let us assume that we want to calculate the duration of a 7% coupon bond that has a GRY of 8% and a term of three years. To keep the calculation simple, we will assume that the interest is paid annually.

Firstly, we need to calculate the present value of the future cash flows on the bond as we did in earlier. You will recall that present value is established by discounting the amount to be received by the rate of interest, which in our example is the GRY of 8%.

Year	Cash Flow		Discount Rate	Formula	Present Value
1	Interest	7.00	8%	$7.00 \div 1.08$	6.48
2	Interest	7.00	8%	$7.00 \div 1.08 \wedge 2$	6.00
3	Interest	7.00	8%	$7.00 \div 1.08 \wedge 3$	5.56
3	Redemption	100.00	8%	$100.00 \div 1.08 \wedge 3$	79.38
Total		121.00			97.42

The sum of net present value of the cash flows represents the current price of the bond. We then need to multiply each discounted cash flow by the number of years before the cash flow is received.

Year	Cash Flow	Present Value	No of Years	Present Value x No of Years
1	7.00	6.48	1	6.48
2	7.00	6.00	2	12.00
3	7.00	5.56	3	16.68
3	100.00	79.38	3	238.14
Total	121.00	97.42		273.30

We can then use the formula above to calculate duration:

$$\frac{\Sigma \text{ NPV of the bond's cash flows x Time}}{\Sigma \text{ NPV of the bond's cash flows to be received}} \text{ or } \frac{273.30}{97.42} = 2.81 \text{ years}$$

As mentioned above, duration is a relative measure that allows one bond to be compared with another, to determine which is the more volatile. It does not, however, quantify how sensitive a bond is to changes in interest rates. This is done by using **modified duration**.

The modified duration of a bond estimates how much a bond's price will change if there is a change in interest rates and so yields. The formula for calculating modified duration is:

$$\frac{\text{Duration}}{(1 + \text{GRY})}$$

As with duration, the higher the modified duration, the more sensitive a bond is to changes in its yield.

Using the results of the calculation above, we can therefore calculate what the effect of a 1% rise in yields will be on the bond's price. The modified duration of the bond is:

$$\frac{2.80}{(1 + 0.08)} = 2.59$$

So, for a 1% change in yields, the price should change by 2.59%. We saw above that the price of the bond is 97.42, so if yields rise by 1%, the price of the bond should fall to:

$$97.42 - (97.42 \times 0.0259) = 94.90$$

It should be noted, however, that this is only an approximation of the impact. Macaulay and modified duration are not the most accurate forms of duration and to build an accurate picture it is better to calculate the option adjusted duration (OAD) and the effects of the bond's convexity.

10.7   Analysing Bond Features

Learning Objective

3.10.7   Be able to analyse the specific features of bonds from an investment perspective: coupon and payment date; maturity date; embedded put or call options; convertible bonds; exchangeable bonds

3.10.8   Calculate and interpret: simple interest income on corporate debt; conversion premiums on convertible bonds; flat yield; accrued interest (given details of the day count conventions)

10.7.1 Coupons

There are a range of possible options as to how a coupon on a bond is paid.

- Fixed coupon bonds are where the coupon is at a set level for the entire life of the bond.
- Stepped coupon bonds are those where the coupon increases or decreases in steps to pre-specified amounts as the bond moves through its life cycle.
- Zero coupon bonds carry no coupon and simply redeem at face value at maturity. Such bonds are purchased at a discount to the face value or redemption value.
- Coupons can be variable and include:
    ○ floating rate bonds – where the coupon varies as interest rates vary.
    ○ index-linked bonds – where the coupon and redemption proceeds, figures get scaled for the effects of inflation.

10.7.2 Maturity Dates

Initially all bonds were redeemable after a specific maturity date which determines when the principal is due for repayment. However, as bonds have become more complex, there are now a number of variations including:

*   Irredeemable bonds.
*   Double-dated bonds.
*   Callable bonds where the issuer of the bond is able to redeem the bond at an earlier date.
*   Puttable bonds which gives the holder the ability to sell the bond back to the issuer.

The vast majority of bonds are redeemed in cash at maturity. This redemption may be either:

*   At par value – redeemed at the nominal value of the bond at the redemption date.
*   At a premium – redeemed at a specified premium above the nominal value of the bond at the redemption date.

Other variations exist where instead of obliging the issuer to repay cash at the maturity date, the bond may offer the holder the choice between normal cash redemption proceeds and some other asset, such as an alternative bond of a later maturity or shares issued by a corporation.

10.7.3 Embedded Options

Embedded options are sometimes a part of a bond's characteristics. An embedded option is a part of the formal structure of the bond that gives either the bondholder or the issuer the right to take some action against the other party.

There are several types of options that can be embedded. Some common types of bonds with embedded options include callable bonds, puttable bonds, convertible bonds and exchangeable bonds.

A callable bond, which is also known as a redeemable bond, allows the issuer to retain the privilege of redeeming the bond at some point before the bond reaches the date of maturity. If the bond contains such an option, on the call date(s), the issuer has the right, but not the obligation, to buy back the bonds from the bond holders at a defined call price.

The call price will usually exceed the par or issue price. In certain cases, mainly in the high-yield debt market, there can be a substantial call premium.

Thus, the issuer has an option, for which it pays in the form of a higher coupon rate. If interest rates in the market have gone down by the time of the call date, the issuer will be able to refinance its debt at a cheaper level and so will be incentivised to call the bonds it originally issued.

With a callable bond, investors have the benefit of a higher coupon than they have with a straight, non-callable bond. On the other hand, if interest rates fall, the bonds is likely to be called, and they can only invest at the lower rate.

The price behaviour of a callable bond is the opposite of that of puttable bond. Since call options and put option are not mutually exclusive, a bond may have both options embedded.

- Price of callable bond = Price of straight bond – Price of call option.
- Price of a callable bond is always lower than the price of a straight bond, because the call option adds value to an issuer.
- Yield on a callable bond is higher than the yield on a straight bond.

A puttable bond or put bond is a combination of a straight bond and embedded put option. The holder of the puttable bond has the right, but not the obligation, to demand early repayment of the principal. The put option is usually exercisable on specified dates.

This type of bond protects investors: if interest rates rise after bond purchase, the future value of coupon payments will become less valuable. Therefore, investors sell bonds back to the issuer and may lend proceeds elsewhere at a higher rate. Bondholders are ready to pay for such protection by accepting a lower yield relative to that of a straight bond.

Of course, if an issuer has a severe liquidity crisis, it may be incapable of paying for the bonds when the investors wish. The investors also cannot sell back the bond at any time, rather on specified dates. However, they would still be ahead of holders of non-puttable bonds, who may have no more right than 'timely payment of interest and principal' (which could perhaps be many years to get all their money back).

The price behaviour of puttable bonds is the opposite of that of a callable bond. Since call option and put option are not mutually exclusive, a bond may have both options embedded.

- Price of puttable bond = Price of straight bond + Price of put option.
- Price of a puttable bond is always higher than the price of a straight bond because the put option adds value to an investor.
- Yield on a puttable bond is lower than the yield on a straight bond.

10.7.4 Convertible Bonds

A convertible bond can be converted into the shares of the issuing company at an agreed-upon price by the holder. It is a hybrid security with debt- and equity-like features.

As with convertible preference shares, given the terms on which the convertible loan stock can be converted into the issuing company's ordinary shares, a conversion premium or discount can be established.

The conversion premium/discount is calculated as follows:

$$\left[\frac{\text{Market price of convertible stock}}{(\text{Conversion ratio x Market price of ordinary shares})} - 1 \right] \times 100$$

The conversion ratio in the formula refers to the number of ordinary shares that will be received in exchange.

The calculation and its use can be seen by looking at the following example.

Example

A company has issued an 8% convertible loan stock at £100 nominal. This can be converted into the company's ordinary shares at a rate of 18 ordinary shares for every £100 nominal of the loan stock.

If the loan stock is priced at £120 and the ordinary shares are priced at £5.75, the conversion premium or discount can be calculated as follows:

$$\left[\frac{120}{(18 \times 5.75)} - 1 \right] \times 100 = 15.9\%$$

The result shows that the convertible is at a premium to the ordinary shares and so buying the convertible bond is a more expensive route than buying the ordinary shares directly. However, the 8% coupon currently being paid on the convertible bond may be sufficiently attractive, when compared to that being paid on the ordinary shares, to justify the premium.

The fact that the bonds are at a premium also indicates that it is not worth exercising the option to convert into ordinary shares. This can be seen by simply comparing the respective values of the shares as follows:

Shares	Nominal	Price	Market
Convertible bond	100	£1.20	£120.00
Ordinary shares	18	£5.75	£103.50

When considering whether to convert into shares, an investor should also look at the effect that conversion will have on the income received.

If the price of the convertible stands at a discount to the price of the ordinary shares, then it is a less expensive way of buying into the company's ordinary shares or worth converting. Staying with the above example, if the bond is priced at £110 and the shares are priced at 675p then it is worth converting as can be seen below.

Shares	Nominal	Price	Market
Convertible bond	100	£1.10	£110.00
Ordinary shares	18	£6.75	£121.50

The higher the premium, the more the convertible loan stock will behave like a conventional stock, whereas the lower the premium, the nearer the loan stock will be to conversion and therefore the closer its price movements will be to that of the company's equity.

10.7.5 Exchangeable Bonds

An exchangeable bond is a straight bond with an embedded option to exchange the bond for the stock of a company other than the issuer (usually a subsidiary or company in which the issuer owns a stake) at some future date and under prescribed conditions.

An exchangeable bond is different from a convertible bond, as the convertible only gives the holder the option to convert bonds directly into shares of the issuer.

The pricing of an exchangeable bond is similar to that of convertible bond, splitting it in to a straight debt part and an embedded option part and valuing the two separately.

Price of exchangeable bond = Price of straight bond + Price of option to exchange

* Price of an exchangeable bond is always higher than the price of a straight bond because the option to exchange adds value to an investor.
* Yield on an exchangeable bond is lower than the yield on a straight bond.

10.8   Bond Strategies

Learning Objective

3.10.9   Understand and be able to apply the main bond strategies: bond switching; riding the yield curve; immunisation; rate anticipation; horizon analysis; barbell/bullet/ladder portfolios

Bonds can be managed along active or passive lines.

10.8.1 Active Bond Strategies

Generally speaking, active-based strategies are used by those portfolio managers who believe the bond market is not perfectly efficient and, therefore, subject to mispricing. If a bond is considered mispriced, then active management strategies can be employed to capitalise upon this perceived pricing anomaly.

Bond switching, or bond swapping, is used by those portfolio managers who believe they can outperform a buy-and-hold passive policy, by actively exchanging bonds perceived to be overpriced for those perceived to be underpriced.

Bond switching takes three forms:

* **Anomaly switching** – this involves moving between two bonds similar in all respects apart from the yield and price on which each trades. This pricing anomaly is exploited by switching away from the more to the less highly priced bond.
* **Policy switching** – when an interest rate cut is expected but not implied by the yield curve, low duration bonds are sold in favour of those with high durations. By pre-empting the rate cut, the holder can subsequently benefit from the greater price volatility of the latter bonds.

- **Intermarket spread switch** – when it is believed that the difference in the yield being offered between corporate bonds and comparable gilts, for example, is excessive given the perceived risk differential between these two markets, an intermarket spread switch will be undertaken from the gilt to the corporate bond market. Conversely, if an event that lowers the risk appetite of bond investors is expected to result in a flight to quality, gilts are purchased in favour of corporate bonds.

Active management policies are also employed where it is believed the market's view on future interest rate movements, implied by the yield curve, are incorrect or have failed to be anticipated. This is known as market timing.

Riding the yield curve is an active bond strategy that does not involve seeking out price anomalies, but instead takes advantage of an upward-sloping yield curve. For example, if a portfolio manager has a two-year investment horizon, then a bond with a two-year maturity can be purchased and held until redemption. Alternatively, if the yield curve is upward-sloping, and the manager expects it to remain upward-sloping, without any intervening or anticipated interest rate rises over the next two years, a five-year bond can be purchased and sold two years later when the bond has a remaining life of three years. This rate anticipation method may use horizon analysis to project a bond portfolio's expected returns over several time frames, or investment horizons, to arrive at a more realistic expectation of performance from different bond strategies.

Assuming that the yield curve remains static over this period, the manager benefits from selling the bond at a higher price than that at which it was purchased as its GRY falls.

10.8.2 Passive Bond Strategies

Passive bond strategies are employed either when the market is believed to be efficient, in which case a buy-and-hold strategy is used, or when a bond portfolio is constructed around meeting a future liability fixed in nominal terms.

Immunisation is a passive management technique employed by those bond portfolio managers with a known future liability to meet. An immunised bond portfolio is one that is insulated from the effect of future interest rate changes. Immunisation can be performed by using either of the following techniques: cash matching or duration-based immunisation.

- **Cash matching** involves constructing a bond portfolio whose coupon and redemption payment cash flows are synchronised to match those of the liabilities to be met.
- **Duration-based immunisation** involves constructing a bond portfolio with the same initial value as the present value of the liability it is designed to meet and the same duration as this liability. A portfolio that contains bonds that are closely aligned in this way is known as a **bullet portfolio**.

Alternatively, a **barbell strategy** can be adopted. If a bullet portfolio holds bonds with durations as close as possible to ten years to match a liability with a ten-year duration, a barbell strategy may be to hold bonds with a durations of five and 15 years. Barbell portfolios necessarily require more frequent rebalancing than bullet portfolios.

Finally, a **ladder portfolio** is one constructed around equal amounts invested in bonds with different durations. So, for a liability with a ten-year duration, an appropriate ladder strategy may be to hold equal amounts in bonds with a one-year duration, two-year duration right through to 20 years.

10.9   Role of Bonds in a Portfolio

Learning Objective

3.10.10 Understand the role of fixed interest in a portfolio: stable cash flow; lower volatility; standard investment vehicles

As bonds have a predictable stream of interest payments and the repayment of principal, they can have a large role to play in constructing a portfolio to meet the needs of an investor, whether that is providing a secure home for their funds, generating a dependable level of income or providing funds for a known future expense or liability.

Their main advantages are:

* For fixed-interest bonds, a regular and certain flow of income.
* For most bonds, a fixed maturity date (but there are bonds which have no redemption date, and others which may be repaid on either of two dates or between two dates – some at the investor's option and some at the issuer's option).
* A range of income yields to suit different investment and tax situations.

Their main disadvantages are:

* The 'real' value of the income flow is eroded by the effects of inflation (except in the case of index-linked bonds).
* Default risk, namely that the issuer will not repay the capital at the maturity date.

The main risks associated with holding either government or corporate bonds are:

* **Credit risk** – the certainty of the guarantee attached to the bond being honoured.
* **Market or price risk** – the risk that movement in interest rates can have a significant impact on the value of bond holdings.
* **Unanticipated inflation risk** – the risk of inflation rising unexpectedly and its effect on the real value of the bond's coupon payments and redemption payment.
* **Liquidity risk** – some bonds are not easily or regularly traded and can, therefore, be difficult to realise at short notice or can suffer wider than average dealing spreads.
* **Exchange rate risk** – bonds denominated in a currency different to that of the investor's home currency are potentially subject to adverse exchange rate movements.

There are a number of further risks attached to holding corporate bonds, notably:

* **Early redemption risk** – the risk that the issuer may invoke a call provision if the bond is callable.
* **Seniority risk** – the seniority with which corporate debt is ranked in the event of the issuer's liquidation.

Of these risks, credit risk and market risk are of principal concern to bond investors.

Credit risk refers to the general risk that counterparties may not honour their obligations. A subset of credit risk is default risk which occurs when a debtor has not met its legal obligations which can be either when it has not made a scheduled payment or when it has violated a loan covenant.

Government bonds are sometimes described as having no default risk as government guarantees mean there is little or no risk that the government will fail to pay the interest or repay the capital on the bonds. Although government guarantees reduce the risk of holding government bonds, it is important to remember that it is not eliminated altogether.

Credit risk for other types of bonds needs to be carefully monitored, hence the reason why bonds will have security, insurance and covenants and be carefully monitored by the ratings agencies. The ongoing sovereign debt crisis in the Eurozone highlights this.

As we saw earlier, bond prices have an inverse relationship with interest rate movements and so price or market risk is of particular concern to bondholders, who are open to the effect of movement in interest rates, which can have a significant impact on the value of their holdings.

11. Cash and Money Market Instruments

Whereas bond markets are populated by issuers and investors seeking to raise and invest capital over the medium to long term, cash investments are geared to short-term liquidity management and providing a temporary safe haven for investment funds. Cash investments take two main forms: cash deposits and money market instruments.

11.1 Cash Deposit Accounts

Learning Objective

3.11.1   Be able to analyse the main investment characteristics, behaviours and risks of cash deposit accounts: deposit-taking institutions and credit risk assessment; term, notice, liquidity and access; fixed and variable rates of interest; inflation; statutory protection; foreign currency deposits

11.1.1 Deposit-Taking Institutions

Cash deposits generally comprise bank, building society and National Savings products, all of which are targeted at retail investors, though companies and financial institutions also make short-term cash deposits with banks.

Fixed-term deposits can also be made in the interbank market. The interbank market originally served the short-term deposit and borrowing needs of the commercial banks, but has since been tapped by institutional investors and large corporates, with short-term cash surpluses or borrowing needs in excess of £500,000. The term of deposits made on the interbank market can range from overnight to one year with deposit rates being paid on a simple basis at the London Interbank Bid Rate (LIBID) and short-term borrowing being charged at the London Interbank Offered Rate (LIBOR).

11.1.2 Returns

The main characteristics of cash deposits are:

- The return simply comprises interest income with no potential for capital growth.
- The amount invested is repaid in full at the end of the investment term.

The interest rate applied to the deposit is usually:

- A flat rate or an effective rate. An effective rate, also known as an annual equivalent rate (AER), is where interest is compounded more frequently than once a year.
- Fixed or variable.
- Paid net or gross of tax.
- Dependent upon its term and/or notice required by the depositor. Fixed-term deposits are usually subject to penalties if an early withdrawal is made.

11.1.3 Liquidity and Access

One of the key reasons for holding money in the form of cash deposits is liquidity, which is the ease and speed with which an investment can be turned into cash to meet spending needs.

The ease and speed of access will clearly depend upon the terms of the account. Deposits held in instant access accounts are highly liquid, as access can be gained to them immediately, so that they can be used to meet spending needs as and when they arise. Other accounts will require notice of withdrawal to be given, such as seven day or 30 day notice accounts, and so can be accessed reasonably quickly or sooner, if early withdrawal penalties are incurred.

Most investors are likely to have a need for cash at short notice and so should plan to hold some cash on deposit to meet possible needs and emergencies before considering other less liquid investments.

The other main reasons for holding cash investments are as a savings vehicle and for the interest return that can be earned on them. A cash deposit account can serve as a vehicle for reaching a savings target; for example, when saving for the cost of a major purchase such as the deposit (part payment) on a house purchase.

11.1.4 Default Risk

The collapse of a number of banks and building societies in 2008 showed that the risk that one might go bust to be a very real one. The risk associated with a particular institution therefore needs to be assessed carefully and to judge the level of risk it is important to consider:

- the creditworthiness of the bank or building society, and
- the extent to which any compensation scheme will protect the deposits made.

Assessing the creditworthiness of a bank or building society requires a judgement to be made about its capital strength. This can be assessed by looking at its:

- **Tier one capital ratio** – this is the ratio that regulatory authorities use to judge the adequacy of a bank's capital position and is expressed as a percentage; so the higher the percentage, the greater its strength.
- **Credit rating** – these are issued by credit rating agencies, such as Standard & Poors, Fitch and Moody's, principally to assess the default risk associated with bonds issued by government companies but also to give an indication of bank stability and their ability to repay debts.
- **Credit Default Swap (CDS) rates** – this is the cost of insuring a bank against default by using a CDS. Most major UK banks have CDS rates of between 100 and 300, anything higher indicates that the market considers there is a higher risk of default.

The extent of any compensation payable under bank deposit protection schemes should also be considered.

11.1.5 Inflation Risk

Inflation risk refers to the impact that inflation has on the real value of money.

The purchasing power of interest earned on cash investments is undermined by rising prices. If an investor is locked in for a considerable period, the final return may be unsatisfactory in real terms if inflation has risen unexpectedly.

Long-term investors in cash deposits face the real possibility that the final sum paid out including interest may buy less than the original sum invested would have purchased. In the 1970s and early 1980s, the rates of interest were often so much lower than the rates of inflation that even shorter-term deposit holders who reinvested all the interest received experienced substantial erosion of the real value of their deposits

11.1.6 Statutory Protection

In the UK, the FCA's Financial Services Compensation Scheme (FSCS) is the statutory fund of last resort that can be called on in the event of the failure of a bank or other financial firm. All retail cash deposits placed with licensed deposit-taking institutions in the UK are covered by the FSCS. The maximum level of compensation is £75,000 per person for claims against firms declared in default.

Under the FSCS bank deposit protection scheme, protection is limited to the first £75,000 of deposits per authorised institution. The maximum compensation that will be paid is therefore £75,000 and this limit applies to each depositor, regardless of how many accounts they hold. If a depositor holds accounts with more than one bank, then each of those accounts is protected up to the limit per institution. If accounts are held at banks which are subsidiaries of a larger group and it is only the parent company that is authorised, then the limit is simply £75,000.

11.1.7 Foreign Currency Deposits

Deposits can be held with many UK deposit takers in currencies other than sterling.

Individuals may choose to hold accounts in foreign currencies, because they need to undertake transactions in another country, such as spending on an overseas property, or they may do so for investment purposes.

An investor may choose to hold cash in foreign currency, because the interest rates earned on that currency exceed those which can be obtained on sterling. There is the risk, however, that the currency depreciates against sterling and that the additional income earned is more than outweighed by a loss in capital value when the deposit is converted back.

Alternatively, an investor may hold the foreign currency for speculative reasons in the belief that the currency is due to appreciate against the pound and that a capital gain can be made. This runs the risk, of course, that the currency depreciates against the pound instead, generating a loss.

Currency movements are notoriously difficult to predict, and the risks mentioned above are not trivial. In addition, a UK bank holding foreign currency deposits may apply higher charges, because of the greater administrative costs involved, and these may offset some of the additional returns that might otherwise be earned.

Many investors have been tempted to invest in offshore accounts to earn higher rates of interest or to invest in another currency.

Chasing higher rates of interest by investing in accounts that are based offshore and from overseas financial institutions carries additional risks, as was experienced by investors in the collapsed Icelandic banks.

If investment in such an account is appropriate for an investor, particular attention should be paid to assessing the credit risk of the institution and the arrangements that are in place in the event of default. The extent of any depositor protection scheme needs to be assessed along with the reliability of any government guarantee.

There are special rules where deposits are held with the UK branch of banks from the European Economic Area (EEA) and the FSCS scheme does not cover deposits with institutions outside of the EEA or in the Channel Islands or Isle of Man.

If cash is deposited overseas either onshore or offshore, depositors should also consider the following:

- The costs of currency conversion and the potential exchange rate risks if sterling deposits cannot be accepted.
- The creditworthiness of the banking system and the chosen deposit-taking institution and whether a depositors' protection scheme exists.
- The tax treatment of interest applied to the deposit.
- Whether the deposit will be subject to any exchange controls that may restrict access to the money and its ultimate repatriation.

11.2 Money Market Instruments

Learning Objective

3.11.2 Be able to analyse the main investment characteristics, behaviours and risks of Treasury bills and commercial paper: purpose and method of issue; minimum denomination; normal life; zero coupon and redemption at par; redemption; market access, trading and settlement; maturity; discounted security; unsecured and secured; asset backing

The money markets are the wholesale or institutional markets for cash and are characterised by the issue, trading and redemption of short-dated negotiable securities, usually with a maturity of up to one year, though typically three months or less is more common.

Money market instruments are investments with a lifespan of one year or less that can be sold at very short notice, usually within a day. Their basic characteristics and the size of the players in the market make for high levels of liquidity.

The dollar, euro and sterling money markets are particularly deep and liquid. The issuers are all top-quality names of high creditworthiness, meaning that the instruments are extremely high quality assets. The investors are mainly banks, shuffling reserves around the world and speculating on the direction of interest and exchange rates, so there are high levels of trading.

The short maturity date of money market instruments and the high issuer quality means that money market instruments carry low investment risk and, as a result, they usually offer very low returns. The returns will differ based on the level of creditworthiness of the issuer, with treasury bills at the bottom of the risk reward curve and one-year commercial paper at the top.

Due to the short-term nature of the market, most instruments are issued in bearer form and at a discount to par, to save on the administration associated with registration and the payment of interest.

Investment in money market instruments is often subject to a relatively high minimum subscription and therefore tends to be more suitable for institutional investors. Retail investors can gain access through money market funds.

The main types of money market instruments are:

- Cash instruments such as deposits and repos.
- Treasury bills.
- Certificates of deposit.
- Commercial paper.
- Bankers' acceptances.

Money market instruments are a contract between borrower and lender. The lender (the investor) pays a sum of money to the borrower (issuer) for a fixed period of time - the term to maturity. At the end of this period – at maturity – the principal is repaid to the lender. In return for lending the money, the investor will require a return to compensate for the:

- Loss of cash during the period of the loan.
- Expected erosion of the real value of the money, due to inflation.
- Risk that the borrower could default on its obligation to repay the capital at maturity.

The return on a money market instrument is either in the form of income or capital gain. As a result, there are two main classes of money market instrument:

- **Instruments quoted on a yield basis**
    - These are interest-bearing instruments.
    - Issued at their full face value and the purchaser's return is the yield or interest.
    - Types include deposits; loans; certificates of deposit; and some commercial paper.
- **Instruments quoted on a discount basis**
    - These are discount instruments or zero coupon bonds.
    - Issued at a discount to its face value and repaid at face value at maturity.
    - Investor's return is the difference between the discounted purchase price and the face value of the security.
    - Types include Treasury bills; bankers' acceptances; and most commercial paper.

The date on which the instrument starts to accrue a return is called the value date; the beginning of the term to maturity. If the instrument is negotiable the lender can sell it on in the secondary market and the principal will be paid to whoever holds the instrument at maturity.

The key features of the main types of money market instrument are shown next.

- **Cash instruments such as deposits and repos**
    - Money market deposits are fixed-term deposits of up to one year with banks and securities houses and are also known as time deposits.
    - They are not negotiable and so cannot be liquidated before maturity. The interest rate offered will be fixed by reference to the LIBOR of the same term.
    - Repos are considered in Section 11.3.
- **Treasury Bills**
    - Treasury bills are similar to commercial bills, in that they are issued at a discount to par, while being redeemed at their nominal value.
    - They are issued weekly via a Bank of England auction, usually with a term of 91 days and a £100 redemption value, and are backed by the UK government.
    - Treasury bills are highly liquid and act as the benchmark risk-free interest rate, when assessing the returns potentially available on other asset types.
    - Treasury bills are used as a monetary policy instrument to absorb excess liquidity in the money markets, so as to maintain short-term money market rates, or the price of money, as close as possible to base rate.

- **Certificates of Deposit (CDs)**
  - CDs are negotiable bearer securities issued by commercial banks in exchange for fixed-term deposits. With a fixed term and a fixed rate of interest, set marginally below that for an equivalent bank time deposit, the holder can either retain the CD until maturity or realise the security in the money market whenever access to the money is required. CDs can be issued with terms of up to five years.
  - As they are a fixed-interest security, the price will fluctuate with the competitiveness of the interest rate compared to the prevailing yields.
- **Commercial Paper**
  - Commercial paper is the term used to describe the unsecured negotiable bearer securities, or short-term promissory notes, that are issued by companies with a full stock market listing.
  - These securities are issued at a discount to par, with a maturity of between eight and 365 days. Being redeemed at par, the return on commercial paper entirely comprises capital gain.
- **Bills of Exchange**
  - Another short-term financing instrument that can be issued by companies is a bill of exchange. A bill of exchange is essentially an invoice, for goods or services supplied, which states the amount and date by which this amount is due to be paid by the recipient of the transaction.
  - Once the obligation to pay this amount by the due date is formally accepted by the party in receipt of these goods and services, the instrument becomes a negotiable bearer bill and can be traded at a discount to its face value until maturity. To minimise the credit risk associated with holding such a bill, and to narrow the discount at which it can be sold, the issuer may obtain the formal acceptance of an eligible bank to guarantee the face value of the bill at maturity.

11.3 Repos

Learning Objective

3.11.3 Be able to analyse the main investment characteristics, behaviours and risks of repurchase agreements: purpose; sale and repurchase at agreed price, rate and date; reverse repo – purchase and resale at agreed price and date; documentation

The term **repo** stands for a sale and repurchase agreement and is similar to a secured loan. Typically, a repo enables a holder of securities to obtain funding (raise cash) against the securities as collateral and for a lender of cash to obtain high-quality collateral against a loan. This puts vital liquidity into the markets.

Under a repo, one party agrees to sell securities, for example gilts, to the other and receives collateral of, say, cash to secure the loan. At the same time, the parties agree to repurchase the same or equivalent securities at a specific price in the future. At that point, the securities are returned by the borrower and the lender returns the collateral. The cost of this secured finance is given by the difference between the sale and repurchase price of these bonds and is known as the repo rate.

A reverse repo is simply the same repurchase agreement from the buyer's viewpoint, not the seller's. Hence, the seller executing the transaction describes it as a repo, while the buyer in the same transaction describes it as a **reverse repo**. So repo and reverse repo are exactly the same kind of transaction, just described from opposite viewpoints.

The parties to a repo are exposed to risk in the event that the counterparty fails to honour their obligation. To manage this risk, the loan will be subject to a legal agreement and the collateral taken will be greater than the amount loaned, so that in the event of default, the collateral can be realised and the 'lost' securities replaced. The ICMA produces standard legal agreements that can be used, titled a global master repurchase agreement.

11.4 Money Market Funds

Learning Objective

3.11.4 Be able to analyse the main characteristics, risks and returns of money market funds: cash assets only; near cash assets; pricing, liquidity and fair value; market access, trading and settlement

Money market instruments rarely feature in a private client's investment portfolio, because they are primarily used by the Treasury operations of central banks, international banks and multinational companies and are traded in a highly sophisticated market.

That does not mean, however, that they have no role to play in the investment management of a client's portfolio. Indeed, they can have a very useful and significant role to play, but they need to be accessed through specialist investment funds. Private investors can utilise money market accounts offered by banks or money market funds.

Money market deposits can be used as a temporary home for idle cash balances, rather than using a standard retail bank account. For the retail investor these accounts can offer higher returns than can be achieved on standard deposits, and money market accounts are offered by most retail banks. The disadvantage is that the higher returns can usually only be achieved with relatively large investments. With interest rates at low levels, however, the rates on offer on money market accounts compare unfavourably with what can be achieved in instant access or short notice accounts.

There is a range of money market funds available and they can offer some advantages over pure money market accounts. There is the obvious advantage that the pooling of funds with other investors gives the investor access to assets they would not otherwise be able to invest in. The returns on money market funds should also be greater than a simple money market account offered by a bank.

Placing funds in a money market account means that the investor is exposed to the risk of that bank. By contrast, a money market fund will invest in a range of instruments from many providers, and as long as they are AAA-rated they can offer high security levels. They are still exposed to risk however, as the credit crisis revealed, when a major US mutual fund 'broke the buck' and others both in the US and Europe had to seek financial support from their parent groups and impose redemption delays.

Breaking the buck is when the net asset value (NAV) of a money market fund falls below $1 – in other words, when the value of what was invested falls below what was originally deposited. Investors in money market funds typically see them as a variation on a cash deposit and so there is no expectation that the value of what was invested will fall. The term entered common usage during the credit crisis when the money-market world was rocked by the news that the Reserve Primary Fund in the US which had $64 billion in assets had seen its NAV drop to 97 cents a share, because of its holdings in Lehman Brothers. Investors pulled more than $200 billion from prime money-market funds over the next two days.

The European Fund and Asset Management Association (EFAMA) classifies money market funds into different types to reflect different investment strategies. In addition, money market funds can be differentiated by the currency of issue of their assets. The EFAMA fund classification statistics have over 220 funds from 15 different fund management groups.

The Investment Management Association (IMA), now known as the Investment Association (IA), also introduced two money market sectors with effect from 1 January 2012. These are based on the European definitions of money market funds that have been adopted by the FCA – short-term money market funds and money market funds.

- Under COLL rules, money market funds may only invest in approved money market instruments and deposits with credit institutions and meet other conditions on the structure of the underlying portfolio.
- Short term money market funds must maintain a constant NAV which means that it should have an unchanging NAV if income in the fund is accrued daily and can either be paid out to the unitholder or used to purchase more units in the scheme.
- Money market funds, by contrast, should have a fluctuating net asset value.

It should be noted that money market funds may invest in instruments where the capital is at risk and so may not be suitable for some investors.

11.5   Selecting Cash Type Assets

Learning Objective

3.11.5   Be able to analyse the factors to take into account when selecting between different types of cash deposits, accounts and money market funds

Cash deposits and money market instruments provide a low-risk way to generate an income or capital return, as appropriate, while preserving the nominal value of the amount invested. They also provide a valuable role in times of market uncertainty.

However, they are unsuitable for anything other than the short term as, historically, they have underperformed most other asset types over the medium to long term. Moreover, in the long term, the post-tax real return from cash has barely been positive.

Cash deposits and money market funds can fulfil a number of roles within a client's portfolio, including:

- Short-term home for cash balances.
- As an alternative to bonds and equities.
- As part of the asset allocation strategy.

They also offer a potentially safe haven in times of market falls. When markets have had a long bull period and economic prospects begin to worsen, an investor may want to take profits at the peak of the market cycle and invest the funds raised in the money markets, until better investment opportunities arise. The same rationale can be used where the investor does not want to commit new cash at the top of the market cycle. The nature of money market instruments means that they offer an alternative investment that does not give exposure to any appreciable market risk.

The factors that should be considered when selecting between different types of cash deposits include:

- The actual rate of interest being earned, allowing for frequency of payment and any one-off bonuses or penalties for withdrawal.
- The speed of access to the funds.
- Notice periods and any restrictions on the number of withdrawals.
- The credit rating of the deposit-taking institution.
- The extent of protection from depositor protection schemes.
- The need to diversify funds amongst providers to reduce the impact of default.
- The prevailing rate of inflation and inflation expectations.

To assess whether a money market fund is suitable for inclusion in a portfolio, you need to consider a number of other issues, including:

- The relative rate of return, compared to a money market account or other cash deposit.
- The charges that will be incurred and their effect on returns.
- Speed of access to the funds on withdrawal.
- The underlying assets that comprise the money market fund.
- How the creditworthiness of the underlying assets is assessed.
- The rate of return compared to other money market funds and how that is being generated.
- The experience of the fund management team.

End of Chapter Questions

Think of an answer for each question and refer to the appropriate workbook section for confirmation.

1.   What does the term 'cumulative' entail when applied to the preference shares of a company?
     Answer reference: Section 1.1.2

2.   What is meant by the term 'green shoe option' in regard to a public offering of securities?
     Answer reference: Section 2.1.2

3.   What does the term 'front running' mean in regard to the activities of brokers and other financial intermediaries?
     Answer reference: Section 3.1.3

4.   Explain the key characteristics of a Multilateral Trading Facility?
     Answer reference: Section 3.2.3

5.   How does the clean price of a bond differ from the dirty price?
     Answer reference: Section 5.2

6.   If the prevailing rates of interest are rising, what will be the effect on recently issued bonds and explain your answer?
     Answer reference: Section 5.2

7.   Explain the difference between a fixed and floating charge in relation to a corporate bond or debenture and indicate which would have priority in liquidation.
     Answer reference: Section 6.1.3

8.   What is the key characteristic and purpose of a gilt repo?
     Answer reference: Section 11.3

9.   What is the current level of protection provided to depositors at UK-licensed deposit taking institutions and to whom should claims be made?
     Answer reference: Section 11.1.6

Chapter Four
Collective Investments

This syllabus area will provide approximately 5 of the 80 examination questions

1. Characteristics of Collective Investment Funds and Companies

1.1 Open-Ended Funds

Learning Objectives

4.1.1 Be able to analyse the key features, accessibility, risks, tax treatment, charges, valuation and yield characteristics of open-ended investment companies (OEICs)/investment companies with variable capital (ICVCs).

4.1.2 Be able to analyse the key features, accessibility, risks, tax treatment, charges, valuation and yield characteristics of unit trusts

1.1.1 Unit Trusts

A unit trust is a collective investment scheme, which is structured as a trust in which the trustee is the legal owner of the underlying assets and the unit holders are the beneficial owners.

Unit trusts are described as an **open-ended** collective investment scheme because the trust can grow as more investors buy into the fund, or shrink as investors sell units back to the fund, and they are either cancelled or reissued to new investors.

The role of the unit **trust manager** is to decide, within the rules of the trust and the various regulations, which investments are included within the unit trust and to then market the fund to potential investors. This includes deciding what to buy, when to buy it, and what to sell and when to sell it. The unit trust manager may outsource this decision making to a separate investment manager in some cases.

The manager also provides a market for the units, by dealing with investors who want to buy or sell units. It also carries out the daily pricing of units, based on the NAV of the underlying constituents.

These prices can be either single-priced or dual-priced. Single-pricing refers to the use of the mid-market prices of the underlying assets, to produce a single price, while dual-pricing involves using the market's bid and offer prices of the underlying assets, to produce separate prices for buying and selling of units in the fund.

Traditionally, unit trusts have used dual-pricing and OEICs have used single-pricing. All funds now have a choice of which pricing methodology they use, but whichever is chosen it must be disclosed in the prospectus.

Every unit trust must also appoint a **trustee**. The trustee is the legal owner of the assets in the trust, holding the assets for the benefit of the underlying unit holders. The trustee also protects the interests of the investors by, among other things, monitoring the actions of the unit trust manager. Whenever new units are created for the trust, they are created by the trustee. The trustees are organisations that the unit holders can trust with their assets, normally large banks or insurance companies.

1.1.2 Open-Ended Investment Companies (OEICs) and Investment Companies with Variable Capital (ICVCs).

An open-ended investment company (OEIC) is another form of collective investment scheme. OEICs are referred to as investment companies with variable capital (ICVCs) by the FCA.

As their name suggests, OEICs are companies, but they differ from conventional companies, because they are established under special legislation and not the Companies Acts. They are, therefore, able to create new shares and redeem existing shares much more easily than traditional companies. This means they are open-ended in nature.

OEICs were introduced in the UK in 1997 in response to the UK unit trust industry losing considerable market share in open ended investment funds to continental and offshore fund management centres. Luxembourg is the largest fund centre outside the US and the main centre for fund management groups intending to market their investment funds across Europe and further afield. An OEIC is similar in structure to a Société d'Investissement à Capital Variable (SICAV) which is the main structure used for Luxembourg funds.

When an OEIC is set up it is a requirement that an authorised corporate director (ACD) and a depositary are appointed. The ACD is responsible for the day-to-day management of the fund, including managing the investments, valuing and pricing the fund and dealing with investors. It may undertake these activities itself or, again, delegate them to specialist third parties.

The OEIC's investments are held by an independent depositary, responsible for looking after the investments on behalf of the OEIC shareholders and overseeing the activities of the ACD. The depositary occupies a similar role to that of the trustee of a unit trust.

The depositary is the legal owner of the OEIC's investments and the OEIC itself is the beneficial owner, not the shareholders. The register of shareholders is maintained by the ACD.

OEICs are single-priced which means that their underlying investments will be valued based on their mid-market value. This method of pricing does not provide the ability to recoup dealing expenses and commissions within the spread, so large trades may be subject to a separate charge known as a dilution levy. It is important to note that the initial charge for investing in the fund will be charged separately, compared to a dual-priced unit trust where it is included in the price.

1.1.3 Unit Trust and OEIC Charging

Investment funds will clearly make charges for undertaking the management of the fund and the types of charges that arise include:

- **Initial charges**
  - Investment funds may impose an initial charge for investing in a fund and that is expressed as a percentage of the amount invested.
  - The range of charges varies widely from fund to fund and depending upon whether the investor deals direct with a fund or uses a fund supermarket or fund platform.
  - Because of investor dissatisfaction with the high level of initial charges, a number of fund groups have dispensed with these and instead moved to a basis of charging exit fees if the investor disposes of their holding within a specified period of time.

- **Ongoing charges**
  - A fund will incur costs and expenses for the running of the fund, such as dealing commissions, audit fees and custody fees.
  - The fund management group will also make a charge for the management of the fund and this is usually expressed as a percentage of the funds under management.
- **Performance charges**
  - Performance fees may also be charged in certain funds over and above the annual fee, providing that specified levels of growth over a benchmark have been achieved.

As a result of its thematic review in 2014 on the clarity of fund charges, the FCA sent out two clear messages to the industry:

1. Using the annual management charge (AMC) in some marketing material and the ongoing charges figure (OCF) in other documents may confuse investors and hinder their ability to compare charges.
2. Using the OCF consistently in all marketing material for UCITS funds is likely to help investors understand and compare charges.

Charges vary from fund to fund, but the charging structure must be detailed in the fund's prospectus. There are also various other charges made by a fund and the combined effect of these is disclosed in the total expense ratio.

The **total expense ratio (TER)** is a measure of the total annual charges for a fund.

The costs included in the TER are all the annual operating costs, principally the AMC but also administration fees, and trustee and audit fees.

The total cost of running the fund is divided by the fund's total assets and the TER is then expressed as a percentage. The size of the TER is very important to investors, because these costs come out of the fund, and affect the value of an investment in a fund.

Institutional investment in funds is clearly going to be significantly larger than any retail investment. As a result, most funds have different share classes for retail and institutional investors.

Institutional share classes will usually carry lower charges than a comparable retail fund. Institutional share classes are also used to restrict access to certain types of investment strategy to investors who can qualify as institutional or professional investors.

1.1.4   Valuation and Pricing of OEICs and Unit Trusts

The prices at which authorised unit trusts or OEICs are bought and sold are based on the value of the fund's underlying investments.

The authorised fund manager is, however, given the flexibility to quote prices which can be either single-priced or dual-priced (although this decision must be taken at the outset and the manager cannot switch between the two as and when it suits).

Traditionally, authorised unit trusts have used dual-pricing and OEICs have used single-pricing. All funds now have a choice of which pricing methodology they use; whichever is chosen must be disclosed in the prospectus.

Single-pricing refers to the use of the mid-market prices of the underlying assets to produce a single price, while dual-pricing involves using the market's bid and offer prices of the underlying assets to produce separate prices for buying and selling of shares/units in the fund.

Example

If the net asset value of each share in an OEIC is £1.00, the OEIC will both sell (create) new shares at 100p each, and buy back and cancel old shares at 100p. Since there is no spread between the buying and selling prices, this is described as being single-priced.

If a fund is single-priced, its underlying investments will be valued based on their mid-market value. This method of pricing does not provide the ability to recoup dealing expenses and commissions within the spread. Such charges can be recouped either by applying a separate charge, known as a **dilution levy**, on purchases or redemptions or by 'swinging' the daily price to a dual-priced basis, depending on the ratio of buyers and sellers on any day. It is important to note that the initial charge will be charged separately, whichever pricing method is used.

If a fund is dual-priced, the underlying investments are valued using the bid and offer prices for that investment from the market in which they are quoted. As well as taking a price that more accurately reflects what the investment might be bought or sold for, the price will also take into account dealing charges and the initial charges that the fund will make for investing in it.

Example

If the net asset value of each unit on the single-price basis is £1.00, the fund manager might quote 97p–103p on the dual-price basis. This means that the fund manager is willing to sell (create) new units at 103p each, and is willing to buy back and cancel old units for 97p. This spread of buying and selling prices is also referred to as two-way pricing.

The difference between the buying and selling prices is designed to cover dealing expenses and provide the fund manager and its sales agents with commission.

The prices that are quoted are known as bid and offer prices: the offer price is the higher of the two and is the price paid when buying units; the bid price is the lower of the two and the price received when selling units.

The maximum price at which the fund manager is able to sell new units is prescribed by the FCA.

It is known as the maximum buying price and, under dual-pricing, comprises the creation price (ie, the price the manager must pay to the trustee to create new units, which broadly consists of the value of the underlying investments and an allowance for dealing costs) plus the fund manager's initial charge.

Value of the portfolio (at offer prices) divided by the number of units	100.00p
Add allowance for dealing costs: brokerage at, say, ¼%	0.25p
Stamp duty at ½%	0.50p
Subtotal (= creation price)	100.75p
Add fund manager's initial charge at, say, 6.5%	6.55p
Maximum buying price	107.30p

The actual buying price does not have to be 107.30p and, because of the sensitivity of investors to charges, the fund manager may feel that a lower price of, say, 103p per unit is more appropriate.

The price at which the fund manager will repurchase units is calculated in a similar manner. From the investor's viewpoint, it is referred to as the selling price and the minimum selling price is also the cancellation price, ie, the price received from the fund by the manager when he cancels the units, using as its starting point the value of the portfolio at bid prices. Again, the manager has flexibility about the price that is set subject to it being no less than the minimum selling price.

The prices of most individual funds are provided in broadsheet newspapers each day. The telephone numbers and addresses of the fund managers are normally provided alongside the prices.

1.2   Closed-Ended Funds

Learning Objective

4.1.3   Be able to analyse the key features, accessibility, risks, tax treatment, charges, valuation and yield characteristics of investment trusts

Closed-ended funds originated with investment trusts but in recent years this type of structure has been used for other types of funds, where the structure can offer advantages over open ended funds.

1.2.1   Investment Trusts

Investment trusts are a form of closed-ended investment fund and were the first type of collective investment vehicle introduced in the UK in 1868.

Despite its name, an investment trust is actually a company, not a trust. However, like a unit trust, an investment trust will invest in a diversified range of investments, allowing its shareholders to diversify and lessen their risk.

They are established as companies and so trusts are commonly described as closed-ended, in contrast to unit trusts and OEICs that are described as open-ended. Therefore, the portfolio manager can take a longer-term view when implementing their investment policy than the manager of an open-ended fund that must maintain an element of liquidity to meet potential redemptions.

Investors' interests are protected by an independent board of directors, the continuing obligation requirements of the UKLA and the Companies Acts.

As companies, they are allowed to borrow money on a long-term basis by taking out bank loans and/or issuing bonds. This can enable them to invest the borrowed money in more stocks and shares and add a level of gearing to the portfolio potentially to enhance shareholder returns. As gearing can work to the advantage or to the detriment of the investor, this makes investment trusts a more risky proposition than open-ended funds.

They are quoted and traded on the LSE. Although investment trusts value their portfolios daily and publish the underlying NAV per share, they do not necessarily trade at their NAV. The price they trade at will instead be determined by demand and supply as with any other share.

- When the investment trust share price is above the NAV, it is said to be trading at a premium.
- When the investment trust share price is below the NAV, it is said to be trading at a discount.

Investment trust company shares generally trade at a discount to their NAV. A number of factors contribute to the extent of the discount, and it will vary across different investment trust companies. Most importantly, the discount is a function of the market's view of the quality of the investment trust and its choice of underlying investments. A smaller discount (or even a premium) will be displayed if investment trusts are nearing their winding-up, or about to undergo some corporate activity such as a merger/takeover.

The tax treatment of investment trusts is the same as for normal equities.

1.2.2   Other Closed-Ended Companies

Closed-ended funds can also be set up to invest in areas such as private equity or property or infrastructure.

Typically these are long-term investment strategies and so the closed-ended nature of the structure is more appropriate to their needs. It may require investors to commit their money for long periods of time so that the planned investments have time to deliver their expected returns.

This can have advantages for a fund in that it does not need to realise assets at possibly distressed prices to meet investor redemptions. Closed-ended companies may not be traded on a stock market and so periodic redemptions offer investors a way to realise all or part of their investment.

1.2.3   Offshore Investment Companies

Investment companies may be established in the UK or in other jurisdictions such as the Channel Islands.

In recent years, investment companies domiciled in the Channel Islands have had a slight tax advantage particularly when investing in alternative asset classes, so that the vast majority of new closed-ended investment vehicles listing on the LSE have been off-shore investment vehicles.

This lead the government to modernise the tax rules for investment trust companies. The intention is that a more principles-based and flexible regime together with the changes in taxation of overseas dividends will help to remove some of the barriers to setting up investment trusts in the UK.

2.   Exchange-Traded Products

Learning Objective

4.2.1   Be able to analyse the key features, accessibility, risks, tax treatment, charges, valuation and yield characteristics of the main types of exchange-traded products

Exchange traded products (ETPs) are open-ended investments that are listed on an exchange and traded and settled like shares. The main types are:

- Exchange-traded funds (ETFs).
- Exchange-traded commodities (ETCs).
- Exchange-traded notes (ETNs).

They are passive investments aiming to replicate the performance of a given market, generally by tracking an underlying benchmark index.

2.1   Exchange-Traded Funds (ETFs)

Exchange-traded funds (ETFs) are a type of open-ended investment fund that are listed and traded on a stock exchange. They typically track the performance of an index and trade very close to their net asset value (NAV).

Some of their distinguishing features include:

- They track the performance of a wide variety of fixed income and equity indices, as well as a range of sector and theme-specific indices and industry baskets. Some also now track actively managed indices.
- Some ETFs are more liquid, or more easily tradeable, than others, depending upon the index they are tracking.
- The details of the fund's holdings are transparent so that their NAV can be readily calculated.
- They have continuous real time pricing so that investors can trade at any time. They will generally have low bid-offer spreads, depending upon the market, index or sector being tracked.
- They have low expense ratios and no initial or exit charges are applied. Instead, the investor pays normal dealing commissions to his stockbroker.

ETFs can be used by retail and institutional investors for a wide range of investment strategies, including the construction of core-satellite portfolios, asset allocation and hedging.

In Europe, they are usually structured as UCITS III-compliant funds. A UCITS fund is an open-ended fund that can be sold cross-border in Europe and is the structure used by the large fund groups who want to sell their funds in multiple countries.

2.1.1 Physical or Synthetic Replication

ETFs usually track equity or fixed income market indices and, in order to achieve their investment objectives, ETF providers can either use physical or synthetic replication. The risks of the latter have been the subject of intense regulatory scrutiny by regulators around the world.

Physical replication can be achieved either through full replication or by sampling.

Physical Replication Methods

- **Full Replication** – this is an approach whereby the fund attempts to mirror the index by holding shares in exactly the same proportions as in the index itself.
- **Stratified Sampling** – this involves choosing investments that are representative of the index. The expectation is that overall the tracking error or departure from the index will be relatively low. The amount of trading of shares required should be lower than for full replication, since the fund will not need to track every single constituent of an index. This should reduce transaction costs and therefore will help to avoid such costs eroding overall performance.
- **Optimisation** – is a computer-based modelling technique which aims to approximate to the index through a complex statistical analysis based on past performance.

The optimised sampling approach is more common for indices with a large number of components, in which case the provider will only buy a basket of selected component stocks, reflecting the same risk-return characteristics as the underlying index.

The alternative is to use synthetic replication. This involves the ETF providers entering into a swap agreement with single or multiple counterparties. The provider agrees to pay the return of a pre-defined basket of securities to the swap provider in exchange for the index return.

- The ETF will enter into a swap agreement with a single counterparty or multiple counterparties.
- The first type of swap used was an unfunded swap. This is where the ETF purchases a basket of securities and undertakes to swap the return on that basket. The constituents of the basket do not necessarily have to correspond with the index that is being tracked.
- Since 2009, funded swaps have been more common where the ETF provider transfers the cash instead and receives collateral as security for the money transferred. The collateral will typically be greater than the value of the cash transferred and will consist of high-quality sovereign government bonds and equities that can be readily realised.
- In both cases, the counterparty undertakes to deliver the performance of the index that the ETF is tracking.

Synthetic replication generally reduces costs and tracking error, but increases counterparty risk. For markets not easily accessible, swap structures do have an advantage over physical replication.

The main advantage of physical replication is its simplicity. This, however, comes at a cost which brings about greater tracking error and higher TER. The main advantage of synthetic replication tends to be lower tracking error and lower costs, but with the downside of counterparty risk.

2.1.2   Reverse ETFs

ETFs can also be constructed as reverse ETFs or inverse funds, which means that they are constructed in a manner that the ETF has either outright short positions in the underlying instruments for the sector or derivatives that provide a synthetic short position for that sector.

Accordingly an investor who buys or takes a long position in such an inverse fund is effectively short the sector or index designated, and will benefit from a downward movement in that particular sector or index. This feature makes it easier for many investors to take a short position rather than having to borrow stock from a brokerage.

2.1.3   Leveraged ETFs

Leveraged ETFs are a specialised type of ETF that attempt to achieve returns that are more sensitive to market movements than non-leveraged ETFs.

To accomplish their objectives they pursue a range of investment strategies, through the use of swaps, futures contracts, and other derivative instruments. An important characteristic of these index-tracking leveraged UCITS is that they seek to achieve their stated objectives on a daily basis, and their performance over longer periods of time can differ significantly from the multiple or inverse multiple of the index performance over those longer periods of time. This effect can be magnified in volatile markets.

Leveraged index ETFs are often marketed as bull or bear funds.

- A leveraged bull ETF might for example attempt to achieve daily returns that are 2x or 3x more pronounced than an index such as the FTSE 100 or the S&P 500.
- A leveraged inverse (bear) ETF will attempt to achieve returns that are -2x or -3x the daily index return, meaning that it will gain double or triple the loss of the market.
- Leveraged ETFs require the use of financial engineering techniques, including the use of equity swaps, derivatives and rebalancing to achieve the desired return.

2.1.4   Collateral and Counterparty Risk

As well as being aware of the different types of ETFs available, it is also important to be aware of the risks that arise from stock lending and the use of swap counterparties.

Many ETFs or traditional index funds will utilise stock lending to generate fee income. This involves the fund lending its securities to other market counterparties in exchange for fees which can help reduce the operating expenses of the fund. This introduces the following risks:

- **Counterparty risk** – the party to whom the securities have been lent fails to return the securities when demanded.
- **Collateral risk** – the collateral taken as security for stock that is loaned out is insufficient if it has to be realised to replace the securities loaned.

Stock lending is a specialised function and there are established techniques for managing the risks associated with lending including:

- Enforceable legal agreements
- The taking of collateral greater in value than the securities lent, and
- The regular mark-to-market of the securities lent so that additional collateral can be called.

As for swaps, most funds in Europe are structured as UCITS funds and so have to meet certain concentration and diversification requirements which include the requirement that a fund cannot invest more than 20% of its NAV in instruments issued by the same body. The maximum exposure to any swap counterparty is limited to 10% of the fund's net asset value so that an ETF will have to have multiple counterparties and will look to hedge its exposure by requiring collateral to be posted with an independent custodian. Most providers disclose the composition of the collateral taken daily on their websites.

2011 saw a number of concerns about the risks that ETFs pose in this area. This has led the European Securities and Markets Authority (ESMA) to propose a new regulatory framework for ETFs and other UCITS investment funds that have similar investment objectives in order to increase disclosure on areas such as collateral and the counterparty risks that can arise from securities lending practices.

Their proposals which are expected to come into force from mid-2012 include requirements to disclose the following:

- **Index tracking UCIT funds**
  - Details of the tracking methodology to be used and the size of the tracking error.
- **Leveraged ETFs**
  - How leverage is achieved and the costs associated with the strategy.
- **Exchange-traded funds**
  - A common identifier is to be used to identify whether a fund is an ETF and to recognise that ETFs have unique characteristics that are different from traditional open-ended funds.
- **Actively-managed funds**
  - Make clear it is not an index tracker and explain how outperformance will be achieved.
- **Collateral and counterparty risk**
  - Participation in securities lending and a detailed description of the risks, conflicts of interest, and impact on performance.
  - Its collateral management policy and the extent to which it is able to recall any securities lent or to terminate lending agreements at any time.
  - Details of fees arising from securities lending and fee sharing arrangements with lending agents.

2.2   Exchange-Traded Commodities (ETCs)

Exchange-traded commodities (ETCs) are investment vehicles that track the performance of an underlying commodity index, including total return indices based on a single commodity. Similar to ETFs and traded and settled exactly like normal shares on their own dedicated segment, ETCs have market maker support with guaranteed liquidity, enabling investors to gain exposure to commodities, on-exchange, during market hours.

Most ETCs implement a futures trading strategy, which may produce quite different results from owning the commodity. In the case of many commodity funds, they simply roll so-called front-month futures contracts from month to month. This does give exposure to the commodity, but subjects the investor to risks involved in different prices along the term structure of futures contracts, which may include additional costs, as the expiring contracts have to be rolled forwards.

In addition to investment vehicles which track commodities there are also exchange traded currencies (ETCs) which provide exposure to foreign exchange (FX) spot rate changes and local institutional interest rates.

ETCs are not UCITS III-compliant but will be fully collateralised, meaning that counterparty risk is hedged out.

2.3   Exchange-Traded Notes (ETNs)

An exchange-traded note (ETN) is a senior, unsecured, unsubordinated debt security issued by an underwriting bank. Again, they are not UCITS III-compliant.

When an investor buys an ETN, the underwriting bank promises to pay the amount reflected in the index, minus fees upon maturity. Thus the ETN has an additional risk compared to an ETF. Upon any reduction of credit ratings or if the underwriting bank goes bankrupt, the value of the ETN will be eroded.

There are two types of ETNs; namely collateralised and uncollateralised notes. Collateralised ETNs are hedged partly or fully against counterparty risk, whereas uncollateralised ETNs are fully exposed to counterparty risk.

Though linked to the performance of a market benchmark, ETNs are not equities or index funds, but they do share several characteristics of the latter. Similar to equities, they are traded on an exchange and can be shorted. Similar to index funds, they are linked to the return of a benchmark index. But as debt securities, ETNs don't actually own anything they are tracking.

The first ETN, marketed as the iPath Exchange-Traded Note, was issued by Barclays Bank on 12 June 2006. ETNs may be liquidated before their maturity by trading them on the exchange or by redeeming a large block of securities directly to the issuing bank. The redemption is typically on a weekly basis and a redemption charge may apply, subject to the procedures described in the relevant prospectus.

Since ETNs are unsecured, unsubordinated debts, they are not rated, but are backed by the credit of underwriting banks. Like other debt securities, ETNs do not have voting rights. Unlike other debt securities, interest is not paid during the term of most ETNs.

2.4   Charges and Taxation

Many exchange-traded products are managed by large financial intermediaries, including Barclays and JP Morgan Chase. The fees and charges are very competitive and often considerably lower than those applied for more traditional managed funds.

Also, no stamp duty is applied to purchases of exchange-traded products available on UK stock exchanges, as they are typically domiciled offshore.

Their tax treatment will typically mirror that of other open-ended investment funds. It is important to establish, however, that the fund is treated as a reporting fund by Her Majesty's Revenue & Customs (HMRC) to be sure of this.

3. Structured Products

Learning Objective

4.3.1 Be able to analyse the key features, accessibility, risks, valuation and yield characteristics of the main types of retail structured products and investment notes, compared with other forms of direct and indirect investment: Structure; Income and capital growth; Investment risk and return; Counterparty risk; Expenses; Capital protection; Tax efficiency

Structured products is a term that is used to describe a series of investment products that are more commonly known as guaranteed growth bonds, stock market-linked growth bonds and a whole variety of other marketing names.

Structured products have their base in the guaranteed bonds marketed by life offices from the 1970s onwards. In recent years, the providers of these products have explored ever more innovative combinations of underlying asset mixes which have enabled them to offer a wider range of terms and guarantees.

These types of structured product have been around for some time and their features and terms differ markedly from product to product. There are ones designed for the mass retail investment market, ones that target the high net worth market only, ones that are for the customers of a single private bank and even ones designed around individuals for the ultra-wealthy.

3.1 Characteristics of Structured Products

Structured products are packaged products based on derivatives which generally feature protection of capital if held to maturity, but with a degree of participation in the return from a higher-performing, but riskier, underlying asset.

They are created to meet the specific needs of high net worth individuals and general retail investors, that cannot be met by standardised financial instruments that are available in the markets.

These products are created by combining underlying assets, such as shares, bonds, indices, currencies and commodities with derivatives. This combination can create structures that have significant risk/return and cost-saving advantages compared to what might otherwise be obtainable in the market.

3.2　Structured Products and Investment Notes

Structured products have offered a range of benefits to investors and generally have been used either to provide access to stock market growth, with capital protection, or exposure to an asset, such as gold or currencies, that is not otherwise achievable from direct investment. Their major disadvantage has been the fact that they have had to be held to maturity to secure any gains. The gain that an investor will make on, say a FTSE 100-linked bond, is only determined at maturity and few bonds offered the option of securing profits earlier.

This need for greater flexibility led to the development of listed structured products, and in May 2005 the LSE created a new market segment to accommodate both primary and secondary markets in them.

There is a wide range of listed structured products, and the terms of each are open to the discretion of the issuing bank. They are known by a variety of names including certificates and investment notes.

Despite being traded on the LSE, they are not standardised exchange products and the specification will change from issuer to issuer. One key feature they do have, however, is that they are listed, held and settled in Euroclear UK and Ireland.

They do, however, fall into some broad categories that are considered below.

3.2.1　Trackers

As the name suggests, a tracker replicates the performance of an underlying asset or index. They are usually long-dated instruments or even undated so that they have an indefinite lifespan.

As a tracker replicates the performance of the underlying asset, its price will move in proportion to it. No dividends are paid on the tracker and instead, any income stream is built into the capital value of the tracker over its lifetime.

If the underlying asset is, say, an index on an overseas market such as the Standard & Poor's 500, an investor may be exposed to currency movements. Some trackers will therefore incorporate features that ensure the tracker is constantly fully hedged for currency risk.

An investor can achieve the same performance as a tracker by buying other instruments, such as an exchange-traded fund or a unit trust tracker fund. Where they come into their own is their ability to be used to track other assets, such as commodities and currencies or an index representing the same.

Some ETFs now track the total return of an index/portfolio so they include not only the capital but also interest, dividends and any other benefits.

3.2.2　Accelerated Trackers

With an accelerated tracker, the investor will participate in the growth of the underlying index or asset providing that when it matures its value is greater than the initial value.

If the asset or index is valued at less than its initial value, then the investor will lose the same amount.

Example

An accelerated tracker might provide for the investor to participate in 200% of the growth of an index. If an investor buys £1,000 of an instrument and the index it is based on grows by 10%, then they will receive back their initial investment of £1,000 plus 200% of the growth, which amounts to £200 – that is, £100 growth x 200% = £200.

If the final value of the underlying asset is, say 10% less than the issue price, then the investor will receive back the initial price of £1,000 less the change in the underlying asset – 10% or £100 – which amounts to £900.

The investor will usually surrender any right to the underlying income stream from the asset in exchange for the right to participate in any performance.

3.2.3 Reverse Trackers

A reverse tracker is similar to a standard tracker except that, should the underlying asset fall, then the value of the tracker will rise. These trackers are also referred to as bear certificates.

3.2.4 Capital-Protected Trackers

Capital-protected trackers, as the name suggests, allow investors to gain some exposure to the growth of an underlying asset or index while providing protection for the capital invested.

The amount of participation in any growth and the protection over the capital invested will vary from product to product and is obtained by surrendering any right to income from the underlying asset.

Example

An instrument might be issued to track the performance of the FTSE 100 and provide participation of 140% of any growth but with 100% capital protection. If the FTSE 100 index is at a higher level at maturity, then the investor will receive back the initial price, plus 140% of the growth over that period. If the index is lower than at the start, then the capital protection kicks in and the investor will receive back the initial price.

3.3 Trading and Settlement

Listed structured products will usually be structured as an instrument such as a zero coupon bond and will be firstly offered in the primary market where they are made available to investors.

They are treated as derivatives for the purpose of conduct of business rules. A firm distributing these products must give a two-way risk warning, in the form of a generic warrants/derivatives warning notice and either a tailored risk warning or a copy of the listing particulars.

Once the investment date has passed, they can be traded in the secondary market. The issuers of the products are obliged to maintain continuous prices throughout the lifetime of the product and to adhere to the standard market maker obligations of minimum size and maximum spread. On any subsequent dealing in the secondary market, a contract note is issued as normal, which will specify the name of the investment, the nominal amount purchased, the price at which it has been dealt and any commission charged.

The instruments are issued in uncertificated form and are held in Euroclear UK and Ireland. Settlement takes place as normal at T+2.

At the end of the term, the investor will usually sell the investment on the last valuation day, but if it is not traded, then the instrument representing the structured product will be redeemed using settlement functionality at the Central Securities Depository (CSD).

3.4   Charges and Tax Treatment

The fees payable for these products are higher than for many simpler and direct holdings of assets, reflecting the fact that some high-margin packaging skills are required. The fee structure should be transparent and laid out clearly in the offering documentation.

Structured products are normally created so as to ensure the proceeds returned at maturity are categorised as capital gains rather than income. The products can also be held within a Self-Invested Pension Plan (SIPP) in the UK, which provides additional shelter from current taxation. Tax treatment is subject to change, however, and cannot be guaranteed to remain the same during the term of any such product.

3.5   Benefits and Risks

The benefits of structured products include:

*   Potential protection of initial capital investment.
*   Tax-efficient access to fully taxable investments.
*   Enhanced returns and reduce volatility.
*   Reduced risk.

Interest in these investments has been growing in recent years, and high net worth investors now use structured products as a way of achieving portfolio diversification.

Structured products are also available at the mass retail level, particularly in Europe, where national post offices, and even supermarkets, sell investments on to their customers.

Structured products do have drawbacks. A notable one concerns the level of principal protection that is available, which will depend upon the credit worthiness of the counterparty providing the protection guarantee. Most structured products do not have FSCS coverage and so the risk to an investor in case of default can be high.

Other drawbacks include:

- **Credit risk** – structured products are unsecured debt from investment banks and, as the case of Lehman Brothers shows, the possibility exists of a complete loss of capital either permanently or until the administration process is completed, which may take years to work out.
- **Lack of liquidity** – structured products rarely trade after issuance and someone who wants or needs to sell a structured product before maturity should expect to sell it at a significant discount.
- **No daily pricing** – structured products are priced on a matrix, not NAV. Matrix pricing is essentially a best-guess approach and the lack of pricing transparency can make it very hard for present valuation purposes.
- **Highly complex** – the complexity of the return calculations means it can be difficult to understand how the structured product will perform relative to simply owning the underlying asset.

4. Analysis of Collective Investments

Learning Objective

4.4.1   Be able to analyse the factors to take into account when selecting collective investments: quality of firm, management team, product track record and administration; investment mandate – scope, controls, restrictions and review process; investment strategy; exposure, allocation, valuation and quality of holdings; asset cover and redemption yield; track record compared with appropriate peer universe and market indices; keyman risk (KMR) and how this is managed by a firm; measures to prevent price exploitation by dominant investors; total expense and turnover ratios; liquidity, trading access and price stability

A fund manager with a good past performance record may be able to repeat the performance in the future. Some statistical surveys have, however, suggested that past performance is not an indicator of future performance. It is important therefore to be aware of the factors that will influence the future performance of the fund.

4.1   Fund Management

Some of the factors concerning the fund management firm that operates the collective investment scheme that should be considered when analysing investment funds are considered next.

4.1.1   Investment Mandate

The investment mandate of a collective investment vehicle, which is often defined in a trust deed, is a statement of its aims, the limits within which it is supposed to invest, and the investment policy it should follow.

A fund mandate will typically define the following:

- The aim of the fund (eg, to generate dividend income or long-term growth).
- The type of strategy it will follow (which will tend to follow from the above).
- What regions it will invest in (UK, Europe, emerging markets, etc).
- What sectors it will invest in.
- Maximum and minimum exposures for strategic and tactical asset allocation (eg, a fund of fund may have limits at the fund or sector level).
- What types of securities it will invest in (equities, bonds, derivatives).
- Whether the fund will short sell and whether it will be hedged.
- Whether it will be geared and to what extent.
- A benchmark index that the fund aims to beat (or match, if it is a tracker fund).
- The maximum error in tracking the benchmark.

Fund mandates are set by the fund management company, but publicised so that investors can choose a fund that suits their requirements.

4.1.2 Investment Strategy

The Investment Association (IA), based in the UK, has published a classification system for the investment strategies which are broadly followed by the major collective investment vehicles.

The groups correspond to broadly different investment objectives.

- Funds principally targeting capital protection.
- Funds principally targeting income.
- Funds principally targeting capital growth.
- Specialist sector.

The general principle for qualification within a given sector is that the fund holds at least 80% of its assets in that sector.

The following diagram shows the groupings of funds in the IA classifications.

IA Fund Sectors						
Capital Protection	Income			Growth		Specialist
	Fixed Income	Equity	Mixed Asset	Equity	Mixed Asset	
Money Market	UK Gilts	UK Equity Income	UK Equity and Bond Income	UK All Companies	Mixed Investment 0–35% Shares	Absolute Return
Short-Term Money Market	UK Index-Linked Gilts	Global Equity Income		UK Smaller Companies	Mixed Investment 20–60% Shares	Personal Pensions
Protected	£ Corporate Bond			Japan	Mixed Investment 40–85% Shares	Property
	£ Strategic Bond			Japanese Smaller Companies	Flexible Investment	Specialist
	£ High Yield			Asia Pacific incl Japan		Technology and Telecoms
	Global Bonds			Asia Pacific excl Japan		
				China/ Greater China		
				North America		
				North America Smaller Companies		
				Europe excl UK		
				Europe incl UK		
				European Smaller Companies		
				Global Growth		
				Global Emerging Markets		

The IA classifications above are based on broad criteria. Within particular categories such as UK All Companies, there will be some funds focusing on mainstream blue chip stocks, some funds investing in recovery stocks and some funds concentrating on special situations such as companies that are rich in cash relative to their share price. It is for this reason that fund analysts often sub-divide large sectors such as UK All Companies into smaller groups.

Within the specified IA categories of funds are the following types of fund, for which there is not a separate classification:

- Index-tracking funds which track a share index such as the FTSE 100 Index rather than being actively managed by fund managers.
- Ethical funds which aim to satisfy the criteria of some investors who only wish to invest in companies whom they consider to be ethical. For example, there are some investors who do not wish to invest in tobacco companies or to invest in companies who have dealings with certain foreign jurisdictions or who may employ labour in developing world countries under relatively poor working conditions.

The asset allocation of the fund will be decided by the management team and there is scope for a fair degree of discretion. However, if the mandate or trust deed for the fund is very specific then there will be fewer degrees of freedom for the class of assets and individual securities that the manager can select for the fund. The assessment of the fund by the trustees and the reporting of the list of assets to fund participants will provide a means of ascertaining whether the fund is being managed in accordance with its stated strategy and the domain of permissible assets.

NAV of a collective investment scheme is calculated by reference to the total value of the fund's portfolio (its assets) less its accrued liabilities (money owed to lending banks, fees owed to investment managers and service providers and other liabilities).

- The portfolio's assets are generally valued by objective criteria established at the outset of the fund.
- If assets are traded on a securities exchange or cleared through a clearing firm, the most common method of valuation is to use the market value of the assets in the portfolio (using, for example, the closing bid price or last traded price).
- The value of OTC derivatives may be provided by the counterparty to the derivative, which may be trading similar derivatives with other parties.
- If there is no objective method of calculating the value of an asset, the fund manager's own valuation methods, subject to a fund's directors or trustees, is usually used.

The last issue raised in the valuation techniques is very relevant to the quality of the assets under management. Some funds have made investments in assets for which there may be illiquid markets, for example complex asset-backed securities, which not only hinders the mark to market valuation methodology but can also prove to be a major problem if the fund has to liquidate holdings following client redemptions in adverse market conditions. It is certainly not fair to conclude that assets which do not trade in liquid markets suffer from inferior quality. However, the percentage of such assets should be relatively small in a fund where the shareholders or participants can exit the fund at short notice.

This is less of a problem for some hedge funds which have 'gating' provisions which allow the fund manager to suspend redemptions in adverse market conditions.

The table of fund classification illustrates that investors have the choice between funds that are primarily focused on capital growth and those which are mainly focused on income. There are also funds of a hybrid nature which attempt to provide both.

Certain objectives will be more suited to different kinds of investor profiles and will not only include the investor's needs for income on a current basis but also will depend on their appetite for risk and their investment horizons.

- As a simple rule of thumb, for those investors who have a low propensity to liquidate their holdings in a short time frame and who do not require a steady stream of income, the focus on more adventurous asset classes such as emerging markets and equity investments in technology funds may offer the highest long-term prospects for capital gains.
- For an investor that is looking for current yield or income the most appropriate kinds of collective investment vehicles are those which are focused on fixed income securities and high dividend stocks such as utility companies.

4.1.3 Key Man Risk

One important risk for investors in certain high profile funds relates to the possible loss of a key manager. The manager may be lured away by higher compensation from a competitor, may go out on his/her own to start a new fund, or may be required to leave a firm for violation of FCA rules.

Firms which rely heavily on the input of a 'star' manager can find themselves subject to large-scale redemptions if the manager leaves. This can lead to loss of capital, the possible recall of any borrowed funds and reputational damage.

Fund management companies have devoted considerable resources to reduce the impact of senior figures. Paying the key managers more, insuring against executives' departure, inventing quant systems to do away with manager decisions altogether are just some of the tactics that have been used.

From the short-term perspective, the loss of a key manager may cause a lot of disruption to a firm, although the more diversified the team of professionals within the fund as well as the more diversified the investment strategy, the less likely that reputational damage will be lasting. Perhaps the biggest risk is in hiring a top manager and paying him/her too much and finding that the manager fails to consistently deliver above-average returns.

4.1.4 Administration

The back office functions of collective investment vehicles, which refer to the administration and reporting to clients, are sometimes a major source of differentiation from the client's perspective.

With many funds to choose from, and often very little in terms of performance differentiation, the funds which have the best methods of communicating with clients and following the best procedures with respect to administration will have a competitive edge.

4.2   Fund Location

Collective investment vehicles come in many flavours with respect to their location and domicile, ie, which jurisdiction and to which tax regime the fund itself is accountable.

4.2.1   Authorised and Unauthorised Funds

In the UK, some collective investment schemes are authorised, while others are unauthorised or unregulated funds.

Authorisation is granted by the FCA. Broadly, the FCA will authorise only those schemes that are sufficiently diversified and which invest in a range of permitted assets.

Collective investment schemes that have been authorised by the FCA can be freely marketed in the UK.

Collective investment schemes that have not been authorised by the FCA cannot be marketed to the general public. These unauthorised schemes are perfectly legal but their marketing must be carried out subject to certain rules and, in some cases, only to certain types of investor such as institutional investors.

4.2.2   Undertakings for Collective Investment in Transferable Securities (UCITS)

UCITS are a series of EU regulations that were originally designed to facilitate the promotion of funds to retail investors across Europe.

A UCITS, therefore, complies with the requirements of these directives, no matter which EU country it is established in.

The directives have been issued with the intention of creating a framework for cross-border sales of investment funds throughout the EU. They allow an investment fund to be sold throughout the EU, subject to regulation by its home country regulator.

The key point to note, therefore, is that when an investment fund first seeks authorisation from its regulator, it will seek authorisation as a UCITS fund. So, for example, instead of it just being authorised by the FCA for marketing to the general public in the UK, approval as a UCITS fund means that it can be marketed across Europe.

The original directive was issued in 1985 and established a set of EU-wide rules governing collective investment schemes. Funds set up in accordance with these rules could then be sold across the EU, subject to local tax and marketing laws.

Since then, further directives have been issued which broadened the range of assets a fund can invest in – in particular allowing managers to use derivatives more freely – and introduced a common marketing document – the simplified prospectus. A fourth directive is currently being implemented.

While UCITS regulations are not directly applicable outside the EU, other jurisdictions, such as Switzerland and Hong Kong, recognise UCITS when funds are applying for registration to sell into those countries. In many countries, UCITS is seen as a brand signifying the quality of how a fund is managed, administered and supervised by regulators.

4.2.3 Onshore and Offshore Funds

Some UK collective investment schemes are established and operated in the UK and are described as being onshore, to contrast them with funds that are established and operated in other jurisdictions.

Collective investment schemes that are established outside the UK are commonly described as offshore funds. They include schemes that are established in Dublin, the Isle of Man, Luxembourg, Jersey or Guernsey.

Some (but not all) offshore vehicles are less heavily regulated than their UK equivalents, perhaps enabling funds to pursue a more risky strategy. In addition, offshore funds are likely to be subject to different tax treatment from their onshore equivalents. While some are regarded as more tax-efficient, others are not.

Offshore funds that seek to market into the UK may do so if the FCA is satisfied they meet the FCA's criteria for authorised funds, in which case they are known as 'recognised schemes'.

4.2.4 Offshore Funds

Offshore funds are funds that are established outside the UK and usually provided by non-UK resident companies. Although offshore funds may be based in any overseas jurisdiction, most funds marketed in the UK are based in the Channel Islands (Jersey and Guernsey), the Isle of Man, Ireland and Luxembourg. Other jurisdictions include the Cayman Islands and the British Virgin Islands.

For tax purposes, offshore funds fall into one of two categories:

* Reporting funds.
* Non-reporting funds.

Reporting Funds

* A reporting fund does not have to distribute all of its income, but must report its income to Her Majesty's Revenue & Customs (HMRC).
* The income need not be physically distributed, as the regime allows for deemed distributions or a combination of physical and deemed distributions.
* Offshore reporting funds are generally taxed in the same way as unit trusts and OEICs and a UK investor will be taxed on their share of the income of the fund, even if an actual distribution is not received.
* The main difference is that the investor receives the income without deduction of tax at source, because the fund that pays it is based outside the UK. These distributions are then subject to tax as dividends, i.e. at 0%, 10%, 32.5% or 42.5%, and have the benefit of a notional 10% tax credit.

- If the underlying fund has more than 60% of assets invested in cash deposits or fixed interest securities, then the distribution is treated as an interest payment and taxed in the same way as any other interest receipt.
- The investor's gains on encashment or disposal are subject to CGT.

Non-reporting Funds

- If an offshore fund has not been certified as a reporting fund, it is treated as a non-reporting fund and may roll up investment income within the fund and so they are often called 'gross roll-up funds'.
- Income and gains accruing to an offshore non-reporting fund can roll up within the fund free of tax.
- On disposal by a UK resident investor, all the gains are subject to income tax. As a result, capital gains and rolled up dividends and interest are subject to income tax rather than capital gains tax.
- As this 'income' has arisen outside of the UK, it is not deemed to be dividend income, and a basic rate income taxpayer therefore suffers tax at the basic rate, higher or additional rate.

4.2.5 The Alternative Investment Fund Managers Directive (AIFMD)

In April 2009, the European Commission (EC) introduced proposals for a Directive which would require alternative investment fund managers (AIFMs) established within the EU to be authorised and subject to ongoing supervision. For the purpose of the Directive, an alternative investment fund is any fund which is not regulated at EU level by the UCITS Directive and includes a variety of funds including hedge funds, private equity and property funds. The aim of the Directive is to:

- increase transparency for investors, supervisors and employees of investee companies (private equity)
- provide supervisors, the European Securities Markets Agency (ESMA) and the European Systemic Risk Board (ESRB) with information necessary to monitor and respond to any build-up of systemic risk caused by the operations of AIFMs
- protect investors
- increase investor choice and competition within the EU
- increase accountability of AIFMs holding controlling stakes in private equity companies.

The AIFMD was finalised in July 2011 and was implemented into national law in July 2013.

4.3 Track Record

Funds usually choose an index to be their performance benchmark. The index will match the region or sector the fund invests in. A British technology fund might choose one of the Techmark indices, whereas an emerging markets fund may choose one of the MSCI indices.

The use of indices as benchmarks is one of the reasons why so many different indices exist: they need to match the variety of funds. Even so, some funds and portfolios are better served by using a composite of several indices.

One danger this brings is that it tempts managers to track their benchmark index (and thus avoid the risk of under-performing) rather than genuinely trying to beat it: supposedly actively managed funds thus become closet trackers.

Indices are not perfect benchmarks for performance measurement. Limitations include the range available (although this can be overcome by using synthetic indices specially calculated for a specific portfolio). Another problem is that changes in composition introduce a form of survivorship bias.

This is the tendency for failed companies to be excluded from performance studies because they no longer exist. It often causes the results of studies to skew higher, because only companies which were successful enough to survive until the end of the period are included.

For example, a fund company's roster of funds today will include only those that are successful now. Many losing funds are closed and merged into other funds to hide poor performance.

4.4   Asset Cover and Redemption Yield

A split capital investment trust (split) is a type of investment trust which issues different classes of share to give the investor a choice of shares to match their needs. Most splits have a limited life determined at launch, known as the **wind-up date**. Typically the life of a split capital trust is five to ten years.

Split capital trusts will have at least two classes of share and other varieties include:

- Zero dividend preference shares – no dividends, only capital growth at a pre-established redemption price (assuming sufficient assets).
- Income shares – entitled to most (or all) of the income generated from the assets of a trust until the wind-up date, with some capital protection.
- Annuity income shares – very high and rising yield, but virtually no capital protection.
- Ordinary income shares (income and residual capital shares) – a high income and a share of the remaining assets of the trust after prior ranking shares.
- Capital shares – entitled most (or all) of the remaining assets after prior ranking share classes have been paid; very high risk.

Capital shares, if issued by a split capital trust, are the most risky, whereas zero dividend preference shares have conventionally been the most popular, although in recent years their popularity has been declining, relative to newer collective investment schemes.

Zeros are the lowest risk class of share issued by split capital trusts because, as preference shares, they have a higher priority over the assets of the underlying trust than other types of shareholder. Zeros have no right to receive a dividend, but, instead, are paid a predetermined maturity price at a specified redemption date, providing that the trust has sufficient assets to fund this.

Providing a trust has sufficient assets to meet the redemption price payable to zero shareholders, the return is predictable, as is the timing of when an investor will realise their gain. As all the return comes in the form of capital, zeros are also very tax efficient for those investors who are unlikely to exceed their annual capital gains tax allowance. For these reasons, zeros were once a popular tool for school fees and retirement planning.

The question that should be first and foremost in any investor's mind is: *'what is the potential for this zero not to pay out its stated redemption price?'* There are a number of financial ratios that can be used to analyse zeros but essentially each stock should be assessed on three criteria: portfolio quality, gearing and hurdle rate/asset cover.

- First, a trust which already has sufficient assets to fully fund the redemption price to the zero shareholders is lower risk than one which still needs to appreciate in the remaining time before maturity.
- Secondly, gearing is an important factor to consider, since financial institutions who have loaned money to the trust have a higher priority over the assets in the event of a wind-up than all types of shareholder.
- Thirdly, the quality of the underlying portfolio will be important. A trust may have sufficient asset cover to meet the full redemption price of the zero shareholders, but if the underlying portfolio is volatile or comprises specialist types of investments, this undoubtedly puts the zeros more at risk than a trust invested in a portfolio of mainstream shares that will be easy to sell in the event of a wind-up.

There can be potential to make relatively high returns at the more speculative end of the zero market, where trusts may not yet have sufficient asset cover to meet their zero redemption prices. Returns from the higher quality zeros which have sufficient asset care are still sufficiently attractive for much less risk. GRYs on quality zero funds are currently higher than prevailing gilt yields, and also attractive compared to yields on UK equities, which are riskier.

4.5 Fund Rating Agencies

Investment funds are usually promoted on the basis of their past performance and level of charges. One of the most frequently asked questions in the investment world is *'is past performance a reliable guide to future performance?'*

Another way of phrasing this question is to ask what is the probability of this year's above-average-performing fund still being an above-average performer next year? One of the greatest myths perpetuated by many product providers is, the better a fund's past performance and the higher its level of charges, the greater its chances of outperforming the peer group in the future.

Although past performance provides prima facie evidence of a portfolio manager's skill and investment style, as well as evidence of the risks taken to generate this performance, against this must be weighed the possibility of:

- **Chance** – the chance that good performance could be the result of luck not skill.
- **Change** – even if good performance is attributable to skill, very few portfolio managers manage the same portfolio for any considerable length of time. Moreover, manager skill, especially an ability to exploit a particular investment style or rotate between styles, is rarely consistent in changing market conditions.

Unsurprisingly, therefore, this leads to a significant amount of research being undertaken. There are a number of independent ratings agencies that provide ratings for investment funds, most of whom provide this data free of charge to financial advisers. The majority of these ratings are based on risk-adjusted past performance, though some place considerable weight on qualitative factors, such as how a portfolio manager runs their fund. However, even the evaluation of qualitative factors only provides an indication of how a certain portfolio manager is likely to perform, when adopting a particular investment style, under specified market conditions.

A simple conclusion can be reached: past performance should never be used as the sole basis on which to judge the suitability of a fund or, indeed, be relied upon as a guide to future performance. Moreover, it goes without saying that funds that impose high charges will put the investor at an immediate disadvantage and prove to be a significant drag on subsequent fund performance.

Although there is no failsafe way of ensuring that a particular fund will consistently achieve above-average performance, the following factors improve the chances of selecting an above-average performing fund.

4.5.1 Independent Fund Ratings

There are a number of independent ratings agencies that provide ratings for investment funds, some of whom have a fee structure but most of whom provide this data free of charge to financial advisers. Some of the main ratings agencies and the differing approaches they adopt are considered next.

Lipper is a fund-rating system that provides a simple, clear description of a fund's success in meeting certain investment objectives, such as preserving capital, lowering expenses or building wealth.

Lipper ratings are derived from formulae that analyse funds against a set of clearly defined metrics. Funds are compared to their peers and only those that truly stand out are awarded **Lipper Leader** status. Each fund is ranked against its peers, based on metrics such as total return or total expense. Funds are ranked against their Lipper peer group classifications each month and also for three-year, five-year, ten-year and overall periods. These ratings are based on an equal-weighted average of percentile ranks of the five Lipper Leaders metrics.

For each metric:

- the top 20% of funds receive a rating of 5 and are named Lipper Leaders
- the next 20% of funds receive a rating of 4
- the middle 20% of funds receive a rating of 3
- the next 20% of funds receive a rating of 2
- the lowest 20% of funds receive a rating of 1.

FE Trust net uses FE Crown Fund Ratings which are a quantitative measure covering the hundreds of thousands of investment instruments collected worldwide. A tiered distribution is used with the top 10% achieving a five FE Crown Fund Rating reflecting the highest tier.

The rating system is as follows:

- the top 10% – five FE Crowns
- the next 15% – four FE Crowns
- the next 25% – three FE Crowns
- the next 25% – two FE Crowns
- the bottom 25% – one FE Crown.

Morningstar's qualitative rating system gives an assessment of a fund's investment merits. The rating scale is used by Morningstar analysts with three positive ratings of gold, silver and bronze, a neutral rating and a negative rating. The rating is based on their analysts' convictions in a fund's ability to outperform its peer group and/or relevant benchmark on a risk-adjusted basis over the long term.

Morningstar evaluates funds based on five key pillars.

- **Process** – what is the fund's strategy and does management have a competitive advantage enabling it to execute the process well and consistently over time?
- **Performance** – is the fund's performance pattern logical given its process? Has the fund earned its keep with strong risk-adjusted returns over relevant time periods?
- **People** – what is Morningstar's assessment of the manager's talent, tenure, and resources?
- **Parent** – what priorities prevail at the firm? Stewardship or salesmanship?
- **Price** – is the fund a good value proposition compared with similar funds sold through similar channels?

The ratings should be interpreted as follows:

- **Gold** – these funds are Morningstar's highest-conviction recommendations and stand out as best of breed for their investment mandate.
- **Silver** – funds that fall in this category are high-conviction recommendations. They have notable advantages across several, but perhaps not all, of the five pillars.
- **Bronze** – these funds have advantages that clearly outweigh any disadvantages across the pillars, giving Morningstar the conviction to award them a positive rating.
- **Neutral** – these are funds in which Morningstar doesn't have a strong positive or negative conviction. In their judgment, they are not likely to deliver standout returns, but they are not likely to seriously underperform their relevant performance benchmark and/or peer group either.
- **Negative** – these funds possess at least one flaw that Morningstar believes is likely to significantly hamper future performance, such as high fees or an unstable management team.

Morningstar uses the above procedure to assign scores for Morningstar Return and Morningstar Risk for three, five, and 10 years. Funds are scored from one to five and these scores are typically expressed as word labels in Morningstar products.

Though some place considerable weight on qualitative factors, such as how a portfolio manager runs their fund. However, even the evaluation of qualitative factors only provides an indication of how a certain portfolio manager is likely to perform, when adopting a particular investment style under specified market conditions.

Although none of these ratings agencies claim to have predictive power, they seek to provide a valuable tool for financial advisers, to filter out those funds that consistently under perform. Indeed, research tends to suggest that funds awarded a top rating by one of these ratings agencies improves upon the 50:50 chance of that fund being an above-average performer in the future.

4.5.2 Fund Fact Sheets

With so many funds available, the ratings agencies provide a valuable way of filtering them down to a manageable number that an adviser can review and decide whether they are suitable for recommendation to a client. The adviser will then need to drill down into the detail of these particular funds, and this can be achieved using the readily available fund fact sheets. The typical content of a fund fact sheet includes:

- investment objective
- fund profile and its asset allocation
- portfolio composition
- portfolio turnover
- fund performance
- risk measures.

The section on risk measures assesses the fund using a variety of industry-standard measures, with a history of at least three years. These measures assess a fund's volatility as well as looking at its risk against a given benchmark and typically include:

- **Standard deviation** – this measures the dispersion of the fund's returns over a period of years. Funds with a higher standard deviation are generally considered to be riskier.
- **R-squared** – this measures the degree to which the fund's performance can be attributed to the index against which it is benchmarked. For example, if a fund is benchmarked against the S&P 500 and has an R-squared of 80%, this indicates that 80% of its returns can be attributed to movements in the index itself.
- **Information ratio** – this is a measure of the risk-adjusted return achieved by a fund. A high information ratio indicates that when the fund takes on higher risks (so that its standard deviation rises), it increases the amount by which its returns exceed those of the benchmark index. It is therefore a sign of a successful fund manager.
- **Sharpe ratio** – this is simpler, and measures the fund's return over and above the risk-free rate. The higher the Sharpe ratio, the better the risk-adjusted performance of the portfolio and the greater the implied level of active management skill. But the Sharpe ratio makes no allowance for the extra risk incurred in achieving those higher returns.

4.5.3 Fund Manager Ratings

As well as assessing the fund itself, many advisers believe it is also important to consider individual fund manager ratings. Fund managers regularly switch funds and jobs, so the top-performing funds are not necessarily being run by the managers who were responsible for their high performance levels.

One organisation that evaluates fund managers' performance is **Citywire**, which covers fund managers from across Europe. It produces fund manager ratings to identify the individual managers who have the best risk-adjusted personal performance track records over three years. Its rating approach uses a version of the information ratio to identify which fund managers are adding value to their funds in terms of outperformance against their benchmark. A figure of more than 1 is regarded as unusual and impressive, as it indicates the fund manager delivers more than 1% outperformance of the index for each 1% deviation from the index. A figure of 0.5 is 'impressive'. A positive figure is good, but a negative one is clearly is not.

Citywire's approach filters fund managers to identify a top pool, which is then grouped into three classifications rated AAA, AA or A. Within each country, fewer than 1% of managers receive an AAA rating, and fewer than 10% receive any rating at all.

4.5.4 Fund Group Publications

Many fund management groups now exploit the internet to provide greater levels of detail about the funds they are managing and prospects for different market sectors. They now regularly schedule web-based presentations about new funds and markets or arrange online conferences where a fund manager is questioned about their investment strategy and plans.

4.5.5 Fund Size

As an actively managed fund becomes larger, its performance may suffer. The portfolio manager has less time to conduct in-depth research and monitor each of the fund's holdings, and may move the market against the fund if they were to trade a sizeable amount of stock.

However, large funds can spread their costs over a wider base. By contrast, size works in favour of passively managed funds, especially those that employ full replication, solely for this latter reason.

Data on fund size can be obtained from a range of inexpensive sources, such as independent financial adviser (IFA) monthly publications.

4.5.6 Fund Charges

High charges put a fund's potential performance at an immediate disadvantage.

Investment fund charges typically comprise an initial charge and an AMC. If an initial charge is not levied, the fund usually makes an exit charge that decreases the longer the period over which the fund is held. Increased competition and price transparency in the UK investment funds market has led to initial charges in particular falling quite considerably, though AMCs have yet to feel the full force of competition.

Other charges levied against a fund's assets that are not as transparent as initial and management charges are collectively known as the fund's **total expense ratio (TER)**. The TER typically includes brokers' commission and auditors' and custodian fees.

Active funds generally have higher initial and AMCs and TERs than passive funds, whilst open-ended funds generally have higher charges than closed-ended funds.

The fact that many index tracker funds do not have either an initial or exit charge puts their future performance prospects at an immediate advantage. By contrast, those trackers that closely tie their stock selection to the index they seek to outperform, without adjusting their charges almost certainly guarantee underperformance against the index they seek to outperform.

Fund charges are usually detailed in the same IFA data sources as those which publish fund sizes.

See also Section 1.1.3.

4.6   Liquidity, Trading Access and Price Stability

A final factor to be aware of is the impact of liquidity and price volatility for investment funds.

Trading in investment trust shares raises the potential issue of liquidity and whether there will be sufficient buyers and sellers to enable the shares to be readily traded. This issue becomes more acute with smaller and more specialist trusts, such as those that target specialist investment strategies, such as infrastructure or woodlands.

With open-ended funds it is also important to be aware of the impact of dual pricing and single pricing for unit trusts and OEICs.

Unit trusts will typically use dual pricing and may move their pricing to an offer or bid basis.

- **Offer basis**
  - A fund may switch to an offer basis if the market is moving upwards or the fund is attracting investors.
  - In these circumstances, managers can move the spread to the top of the range.
  - This effectively means that the offer price being paid will be the creation price plus initial charges and so increases the price for buyers.
  - However, it also increases the price for sellers of units, who will get a price of 5–7% below the creation price and considerably higher than normal.
- **Bid basis**
  - When the market is moving downwards or more money is leaving the fund than is coming in the fund may switch to a bid basis.
  - In these circumstances, managers can move the spread to the bottom of the range.
  - This effectively means that the buying price being paid will be the cancellation price and reduces the price for sellers.
  - However, it also reduces the price for buyers of units who will get a price of 5–7% above the cancellation price and considerably lower than normal.

OEICs will typically be single priced and so need a mechanism to ensure the fund is not disadvantaged by large inflows and outflows. It can do this in a number of ways:

- Applying a dilution levy to all deals above a certain size to make an allowance for the costs of dealing in the underlying fund.
- Switching to a so-called 'swinging price basis' when there are large flows. This effectively means switching to a dual price basis for a temporary period.
- Offering in specie settlement for very large deals. This involves the fund returning a portion of the underlying assets to the investor, leaving them to realise the investments in the market.

Whilst open-ended funds are typically valued and dealt daily, it is important to be aware that this can break down in the event of severe market falls. This was seen with property funds during the credit crisis, when the number of redemptions was such that funds could not sell property quickly enough to raise the funds needed to meet the amounts due to selling investors. Many imposed moratoriums of up to 12 months during which the investor was unable to realise their investment.

See also Section 4.2.5 on AIFMD.

End of Chapter Questions

Think of an answer for each question and refer to the appropriate workbook section for confirmation.

1. What is an alternative and more commonly used name for an ICVC?
    Answer reference: Section 1.1.2

2. How and when are the units within a unit trust valued and priced?
    Answer reference: Section 1.1.4

3. Describe the main characteristics of an investment trust and how are they accessible to the single investor.
    Answer reference: Section 1.2.1

4. What is the difference between an open-ended fund and a closed-ended fund?
    Answer reference: Sections 1.1 and 1.2.1

5. What is the total expense ratio as used in regard to collective investment vehicles?
    Answer reference: Section 1.1.3

6. At what times of the day can one purchase an exchange-traded fund (ETF)?
    Answer reference: Section 2.1

7. What is an inverse ETF and why would one decide to invest in such an instrument?
    Answer reference: Section 2.1.2

8. Explain the relevance of reporting and non-reporting status.
    Answer reference: Section 4.2.4

Chapter Five
Derivatives

This syllabus area will provide approximately 6 of the 80 examination questions

1. General

Mention derivatives and people tend to think of high-risk instruments that are impenetrably complex.

Derivatives can be high-risk; after all, it was mainly trading in derivatives that brought about the collapse of Lehman Brothers and massive monetary losses at many other organisations during the recent credit crisis. However, it is not necessarily true that these instruments are inherently dangerous. In fact, many of these derivatives are not particularly complex either.

They are chiefly designed to be used to reduce the risk faced by organisations and individuals; an approach technically referred to as hedging.

1.1 Uses of Derivatives

Learning Objective

5.1.1 Understand the purpose, risks and rewards associated with derivatives: uses of derivatives: hedging, speculation and arbitrage; counterparty, market and liquidity risk; specific risks to buyers, writers and sellers

Derivatives are not a new concept – they have been around for hundreds of years.

Their origins can be traced back to agricultural markets, where farmers needed a mechanism to guard against price fluctuations, caused by gluts of produce and drought. In order to fix the price of agricultural produce in advance of harvest time, farmers and merchants entered into forward contracts.

These set the price at which a stated amount of a commodity would be delivered between a farmer and a merchant (termed the **counterparties**) at a pre-specified future time. A forward is, therefore, a derivatives contract that creates a legally binding obligation between two parties for one to buy and the other to sell a pre-specified amount of an asset at a pre-specified price on a pre-specified future date. As individually negotiated contracts, forwards are not traded on a derivatives exchange.

These early derivative contracts introduced an element of certainty into commerce and gained immense popularity; they led to the opening of the world's first derivatives exchange in 1848, the Chicago Board of Trade (CBOT).

The exchange soon developed a futures contract that enabled standardised qualities and quantities of grain to be traded for a fixed future price on a stated delivery date. Unlike the forward contracts that preceded it, the futures contract could itself be traded. These futures contracts were subsequently extended to a wide variety of commodities and offered by an ever-increasing number of derivatives exchanges.

It was not until 1975 that CBOT introduced the world's first **financial futures** contract. This set the scene for the exponential growth in product innovation and the volume of futures trading that soon followed.

1.2 Types of Derivatives

Learning Objective

5.1.2 Understand the differences between forwards, futures and options: obligations; default risk; margin; contract specification flexibility; establishment of price and term

---

Forwards, futures and options will be considered in more detail in the following sections but for now, the essential difference between them is shown below.

A forward contract is an OTC transaction in which delivery of the commodity/asset is deferred until a date in the future that is specified in the contract. Although the delivery is made in the future, the price is determined on the initial trade date.

A future is a contract between two parties to make or take delivery of a specific quantity and quality of a specified asset on a fixed future date at a price agreed today. The contract is standardised and traded on an exchange.

An option is a contract that allows the holder to choose whether to buy or sell an asset at a price that is agreed today in return for payment of a premium. The contract is standardised and traded on an exchange.

The **European Market Infrastructure Regulation (EMIR)** came in to effect in March 2013 and includes requirements for the reporting of derivative contracts. The main purpose of the regulation is to reduce counterparty and operational risk.

Among the requirements are the reporting of all derivatives and compulsory clearing of certain derivatives via a central counterparty (CCP). It is expected that some trading volumes will move from OTC trading to exchange-traded to improve cost and efficiency.

2. Futures

Learning Objective

5.2.1 Understand the core concepts and key characteristics of futures: obligations; fixed price; fixed exercise date; closing out; physical delivery

---

A future is an agreement between a buyer and a seller. The buyer agrees to pay a pre-specified amount for the delivery of a particular quantity of an asset at a future date. The seller agrees to deliver the asset at the future date, in exchange for the pre-specified amount of money. It is a legal agreement between two parties to make or take delivery of a specific quantity and quality of a specified asset on a fixed future date at a price agreed today.

2.1   Key Characteristics

Futures are often described as futures contracts because they are traded on organised exchanges, such as NYSE Liffe London, or the Chicago Mercantile Exchange (CME) Group in the US, and the Dubai Mercantile Exchange in the United Arab Emirates (UAE).

The terms of each contract are standardised in a legal document called the **contract specification**. This is because it is not financially viable for an exchange precisely to satisfy every single trader's requirements regarding particular underlying assets. The aim of the contract specifications is to allow participants to take positions on general price movements in any given market.

The price is agreed between buyer and seller. In fact, it is the sole element of the futures contract that is open to negotiation. However, the exchange does specify the minimum permitted movement in price and the method of quotation.

Example

The Chicago Board of Trade (CBOT), now part of the CME Group, trades wheat futures, where the contract is based on a set of specific grades of wheat and the specific quantity is 5,000 bushels; in other words each individual contract represents 5,000 bushels of wheat.

The specified asset is obviously wheat, but of what quality? The contract specification goes to great lengths to detail precisely what is acceptable under the terms of each contract. For example, the CBOT's wheat future specifies that the grain must be a specific deliverable grade, a list of which is set out by the exchange. It also specifies what form of delivery is acceptable, by listing the names of storage/warehouses to which delivery must be made.

For a wheat future contract the quote is on a per bushel basis and the minimum movement is 0.25 of a cent ($0.0025) per bushel (known as the 'tick size') and, because each contract represents 5,000 bushels, the value of the minimum price movement per contract (the 'tick value') is $12.50 per contract.

The fixed future date is also laid down by the exchange. Although it is a set day within the month, the fixed future date is often referred to as the 'contract month', and for the CBOT wheat future there are delivery months in March, May, July, September and December each year.

For all futures contracts, the contract specification standardises the futures product and, as long as the contracts have a common underlying asset and a common delivery date, the contract is said to be **fungible**; in other words it is identical to, and substitutable with, others traded on the same exchange.

The term fungible derives from medieval Latin and refers to where goods are replaceable by another identical item; in other words they are mutually interchangeable.

Futures contracts and options are fungible since they are highly standardised contracts. To be interchangeable, they need to be for the same underlying asset and delivery date. For example:

* all March long gilt futures on NYSE Liffe London are fungible
* a March long gilt future on NYSE Liffe London is not fungible with a June Long Gilt future on the same exchange, because the delivery dates are different.

Forwards and swaps are not fungible since they are customised contracts.

The consequences of standardisation and fungibility are:

- traders know what they are trading.
- traders know what their delivery obligations are; buyers know the cost of the asset they have bought, and sellers know the amount they will receive and the quality of the asset they have sold
- contracts are easy to trade because activity is concentrated in a single contract.
- it is possible to trade large volumes.
- the concentration of activity provides liquidity and therefore efficiency to the market.

The fungible nature of contracts also means that a trader can remove any delivery obligations by taking an equal and opposite position. The trader is described as having **closed out** his position. For example, a trader who has bought a future and is required to buy a specified quantity of the underlying asset can simply sell a fungible future. The result is that they have agreed to both buy and sell the same item at the same future date.

Futures positions are opened by going long (buying) or short (selling).

- By opening either a long or short futures position, the trader becomes exposed to changes in the futures price and the position will incur profits or losses as a result of the movement in price.
- Holding the contract to expiry will oblige the trader to meet the delivery obligations. If the price of the asset rises, the futures buyer will have made a profit. The trader will take delivery at the lower price and be able to sell the asset in the cash market at the higher price.
- Conversely, if the price is lower than the agreed price, the trader's counterparty (the futures seller) will make a profit.

2.2 Terminology

Futures have their own specialised terminology and some of the key terms that are regularly encountered are:

- **Futures Contract** – an exchange-traded contract that is a firm agreement to make/take delivery of a standard quantity of a specified asset on a fixed future date at a price agreed today.
- **Contract specification**.
- **Tick size** – the smallest permitted variation between prices quoted to buy and sell on derivatives exchanges. For example, the tick for gold is 10 cents so prices of $390.00, $390.10, $390.20 can be quoted, but not $390.13.
- **Tick value** – the profit or loss that arises when prices move by one tick.
- **Delivery** – the settlement of a contract by delivery of the asset by the seller to the exchange clearing house. The long position holder takes delivery from the clearing house against payment.

2.3 Contracts for Difference

Some futures contracts are based on tangible goods such as grain and oil. If the contract is carried through to expiry there will be an exchange of the underlying for the pre-agreed cash sum. These contracts are described as being **physically deliverable**.

However, many people trade in futures contracts where the underlying is intangible such as a stock market index. At the end of the contract, physical delivery of the underlying is either impossible or impractical. Contracts where the underlying is intangible are known as **contracts for differences (CFDs)** and are cash-settled.

Example

An investor buys a FTSE 100 future at an agreed 'price' of 5100 points and at expiry the index stands at 5215 points. The investor has made a profit, not by buying or selling a tangible asset, such as grain or a bond, but by receiving a set amount of cash for each point gained.

The amount of money for each point is specified in the futures contract. In the case of NYSE Liffe London's traded FTSE 100 futures, that amount is £10, so the seller of the future simply pays the buyer 115 points multiplied by £10, in other words £1,150.

An alternative way of entering into a contract for difference is to place a bet with a spread betting firm.

2.4   Futures Pricing

Learning Objective

5.1.3   Understand the mechanisms for futures and options pricing and the relationship with the underlying cash prices: a contract for difference; contango; backwardation; in-the-money; at-the-money; out-of-the money

Whilst it is tempting to think that the futures price is the market's perception of what the price of the underlying asset will be at the time of delivery, this is not the case.

Although prices in both markets are set by the interaction of buyers and sellers, there is a mathematical relationship that binds them together.

Fair value of the future = cash price + cost of carry

The cost of carry can be understood by comparing buying an asset today in the cash market or a future for delivery in three months' time:

*   By buying the asset today, the investor is forgoing the interest which could be earned on the funds for the coming three months.
*   There might be costs associated with storing the asset until it is needed, such as in the case of a commodity.
*   The result is that anyone wanting delivery of the asset in three months' time will be willing to pay a higher price, because they are earning interest on their funds, in the meantime, and not incurring any storage costs.
*   Similarly, the person holding the asset will require a higher price for future delivery to compensate for the costs involved.

These are referred to as **costs of carry**. The main components of costs of carry are:

- Finance costs (interest) over the period.
- Storage costs.
- Insurance.

Knowing what the cash price of an asset is, and knowing how much it will cost to carry the asset up to the moment of delivery, it is possible to calculate a futures price that will be fair to both the buyer and seller of the contract. This is known as the **fair value of the future**.

- If the differential between the cash price and futures price is less than the cost of carry, the investor is better off buying the future, rather than buying the asset and holding it.
- If the differential is greater than the cost of carry, an investor is better off buying the asset and holding it.
- It is only when the differential exactly reflects the cost of carry that the buyer is indifferent as to whether to buy in the cash market or the futures market.

When the futures price is higher than that of the underlying asset, the market is said to be in **contango**. This is usual for a financial future and is the normal situation for equity markets. Interest rates are higher than dividend yields, therefore there is a net cost of carry.

However, when the futures price is lower than that of the underlying asset, the market is in **backwardation**. Backwardation can occur within both bond and short-term interest rate (STIR) markets when long-term interest rates are higher than short-term rates. Backwardation is also common within commodities markets when there is a very steep premium for material available for immediate delivery, indicating a perception of a current shortage in the underlying commodity.

Basis measures the difference between cash and futures prices.

- Basis is negative in contango markets. In contango markets the futures price is greater than the cash price, so the basis will be a negative number.
- Basis is positive in backwardation markets. In backwardation markets, the futures price is less than the cash price, so the basis will be a positive number.

Because of convergence, in both types of market the basis must narrow to zero, as the contract moves towards expiry. As the cost of carry determines the differential between cash and futures prices and is the cost associated with holding the asset from now until expiry, it follows that as the point of expiry approaches, the costs of carry diminish and the differential must narrow. At expiry, the cost of carry is zero, so the cash and futures prices must converge over the life of the future until they meet at expiry.

In a perfect market, the basis should reflect the cost of carry and the future would always trade at its fair value. However, as markets are not perfect, the actual difference between two prices will be influenced by short-term supply-and-demand pressures. It is unlikely that the future will be trading exactly at its fair value at any moment in time.

Basis can change as a result of:

- Changes in supply and demand.
- Changes to the cost of carry, eg, interest rates, insurance costs, dividend yields.
- Changes in time remaining to expiry (convergence).

Movements in basis can adversely impact hedging strategies and correctly anticipating the changes in basis can provide trading opportunities.

2.5   Risk/Reward Profile of Futures

There are three ways futures can be used.

- **Speculation**
  - Speculators seek to make a profit from price movements, by buying or selling futures contracts. Speculative investments involve a high degree of risk and usually have short holding periods.
  - If an investor feels the price of the underlying is going to go up, he can speculate by buying the underlying asset itself or, alternatively, by buying futures contracts on that underlying.
  - Futures are often seen to be more attractive than the underlying asset itself because they are highly geared. Put simply, this means that a small expenditure/initial investment gives the holder a big exposure to a market, ie, the potential for large profits or losses.
- **Hedging**
  - People who want to guard themselves against adverse price movements hedge using futures.
  - A hedger seeks to protect a position, or anticipated position, in the spot market by taking an opposite position in the futures market. A perfect hedge is a risk-free position.
  - For example, a fund manager can remove his exposure to a stock market fall that will affect the portfolio of shares he manages. He does this by taking a temporary short position in futures in an equity index. It will deliver profits to offset the impact a fall in the stock market would have.
  - Fund managers often use these hedging strategies as temporary shields against market movements.
- **Arbitrage**
  - An arbitrageur observes that the same underlying asset or financial instrument is selling at two different prices in two different markets.
  - He undertakes a transaction whereby he buys the asset or instrument at the lower price in one market and sells it at the higher price in the other market.
  - Arbitrage gives him a risk-free profit that will be realised when the prices in the two markets come back into line and the arbitrageur closes out the position.

The buyer of the future is described as going long. In other words, the buyer is agreeing to take delivery of the underlying asset and hopes that the price of the underlying asset will rise.

As the following diagram shows, the long futures position makes money in a rising market and loses money in a falling market.

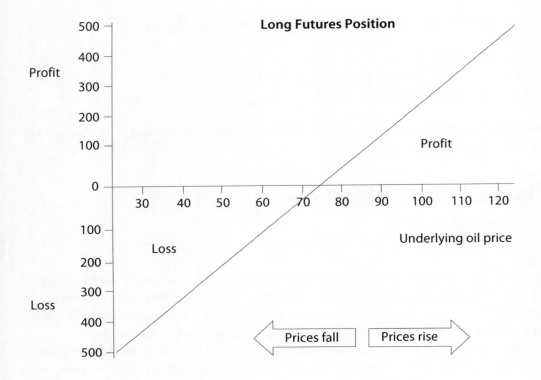

The seller of the future is taking a short position. In other words, the seller is undertaking to make delivery of the underlying asset and hopes that the price of the underlying asset will fall.

As the diagram below shows, the short futures position hopes to make money in a falling market and loses money in a rising market.

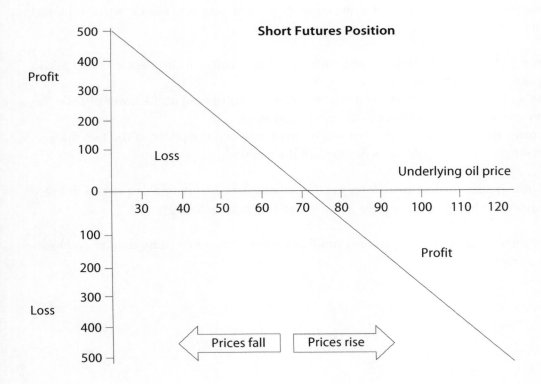

As you can see, the long and short positions are mirror images of each other, so that if the long position gains then the short position loses. For this reason, futures contracts are often referred to as a zero sum game.

Given that futures are highly geared instruments, if the market moves against the speculator, then losses can mount up very quickly. Indeed, following several high profile disasters involving derivatives, most non-practitioners tend to think of futures solely as speculative instruments, used in the pursuit of making quick profits, despite evidence to the contrary.

Whatever the perception, speculation per se should not be discouraged as, apart from adding to market liquidity, or brisk two-way trade, in futures contracts, without speculators those wishing to use futures to hedge risk would be unable to do so.

2.6 LIFFE Futures Contracts

The main financial futures contracts traded on Liffe include:

- FTSE 100 index future.
- Long gilt futures.
- STIR futures.
- Universal stock futures.

2.6.1 FTSE 100 Index Future

Futures such as the FTSE 100 future can be used to hedge portfolios of UK equities against adverse market movements. Before looking at how this operates, it is useful to consider why they would be used in preference to selling the underlying portfolio.

There are four reasons for this:

- The portfolio manager's mandate may require equities to be held within the portfolio regardless of market conditions.
- Selling a large portfolio will:
  - move the price of the shares against the portfolio manager
  - take time
  - result in significant dealing costs.
- Futures markets, being more liquid than securities markets, will not move the price of the transaction against the fund manager and will be completed more swiftly.
- Futures incur lower dealing costs.

The FTSE 100 index future is based upon the FTSE 100 index, which derives its value from the share price performance of the UK's top 100 companies. In this section, we will look at its key features and consider how it can be used to hedge a portfolio.

The number of contracts required to hedge a portfolio is known as the hedging ratio and the future is priced in index points with a tick value of £10 per index point.

Example

A portfolio manager has a portfolio of major UK equities valued at £1.5 million and believes that the FTSE will fall. They could take out protection against the fall by selling FTSE 100 futures.

Let us assume that the portfolio manager wants to hedge the portfolio over the next month against a market fall with the FTSE 100 at 6,000 and the future priced at 6,042. The number of contracts that the fund manager will need to sell is calculated as follows:

$$\frac{\text{Portfolio value}}{\text{FTSE 100 futures contract value x £10}} \quad \text{or} \quad \frac{£1,500,000}{6,042 \times £10} = 24.82 \text{ contracts}$$

Since futures can only be dealt in whole contracts, this is rounded up to 25 contracts.

The effect of the hedge can be seen by looking at what will happen if the FTSE 100 index falls to 5,900 taking the futures price to, say, 5,940. The effect of the hedge can be seen by looking at what will happen if the FTSE 100 index falls to 5,900 taking the futures price to, say, 5,940.

Example

Assuming that the portfolio tracks the FTSE 100, it will fall in value to:

$$£1,500,000 \quad \times \quad \frac{5,900}{6,000} = £1,475,000 \text{ giving a loss of £25,000}$$

This loss will, however, be covered by the gain on the future. The future has fallen by 102 points which at £10 per index point is £1,020 and we have sold 25 contracts, so the profit on the future is £25,500 as shown below.

$$6,042 - 5,940 = 102 \text{ points x £10} = £1,020 \text{ per contract x 25 contracts} = £25,500$$

If the futures contract were to rise then the hedge can, of course, be closed out at any time before expiry, by buying 25 FTSE 100 index futures, with the same delivery date, to offset the original short position. In so doing the portfolio manager will then crystallise a loss.

2.6.2 Long Gilt Futures

Long gilt futures contracts can be used within the portfolio management process in exactly the same way as FTSE 100 index futures contracts.

These contracts differ from the FTSE 100 index contract, however, in that they are:

- based on a notional gilt with a £100,000 nominal value and a 3% coupon. Each contract has a tick value of £10 per 0.01 movement in the contract price. 0.01 is known as one basis point (1bp);
- physically settled, rather than cash settled, if held until the delivery month and the seller, or short position, has given notice to Liffe of its intention to deliver. The short position will then deliver gilts with a nominal value of £100,000 for each contract sold, from an approved list, to the buyer of the contract, in exchange for a cash sum calculated by Liffe, known as the **invoicing amount**.

The most likely gilt to be delivered by the seller to the buyer from the approved list in each case is known as the cheapest to deliver (CTD) gilt. The price of the CTD gilt determines the price of the gilt future and ultimately the invoicing amount.

If, however, the short position does not wish to go to delivery, they have until the last trading day in the delivery month to close out the contract.

Although the long position also has the option of closing out their position on or before the last trading day, if they have no intention of taking delivery of the CTD gilt, their position must be closed out three business days before the start of the delivery month, to eliminate any possibility of being required to take delivery of the CTD gilt.

2.6.3 STIR Futures

STIR futures are based on the British Bankers' Association (BBA) LIBOR for three-month sterling deposits. Each contract has a notional value of £500,000 with a tick value of £12.50 per 0.01 movement in the contract price.

The contract can be used for both speculation and hedging:

- If a speculator believes that short-term interest rates are heading higher, then they will sell the contract as higher interest rates will cause the price of the contract to fall, in the same way that higher bond yields result in lower bond prices.
- If a hedger, however, having deposited cash at a short-term money market rate, fears that interest rates may fall, then they will buy the contract to guard against receiving a lower interest income. Once again, the activities of hedgers and speculators create a liquid two-way market in risk, the former transferring risk to the latter.

2.6.4 Universal Stock Futures

Rather than hedging the risk of an entire portfolio, universal stock futures allow a fund manager to hedge the price risk associated with individual stocks held within a portfolio.

However, they are currently limited to a selection of larger multinational companies.

Each position taken in a contract is for 1,000 UK company shares or 100 US or European company shares. Universal stock futures are cash settled.

3. Options

The growth of options can be traced to the work of two US academics – Fischer Black and Myron Scholes – who produced the Black Scholes option pricing model in 1973.

Until then, options contracts could not easily be priced, which prevented them from being traded. This model, however, paved the way for the creation of standardised options contracts and for the opening of the Chicago Board Options Exchange (CBOE) in the same year.

This in turn led to an explosion in product innovation and the creation of other options exchanges, such as Liffe.

Options can still be traded off-exchange, or over-the-counter (OTC), however, in much the same way as forward contracts, where the contract specification determined by the parties is bespoke.

3.1 Key Characteristics

Learning Objective

5.3.1 Understand the core concepts and key characteristics of options: calls and puts; writing and buying; exercise price; European style; American style

5.1.3 Understand the mechanisms for futures and options pricing and the relationship with the underlying cash prices: a contract for difference; contango; backwardation; in-the-money; at-the-money; out-of-the money

An option gives a buyer the right, but not the obligation, to buy or sell a specified quantity of an underlying asset at a pre-agreed exercise price, on or before a pre-specified future date or between two specified dates. The seller, in exchange for the payment of a premium, grants the option to the buyer.

- A call option gives the right to buy a specified quantity of an asset at a pre-agreed price.
- A put option gives the right to sell a specified quantity of an asset at an agreed price.

The two parties to an options contract are the holder and the writer. The writer confers the right, rather than the obligation, to the holder to either buy or sell an asset, at a pre-specified price, in exchange for the holder paying a premium for this right. This premium represents a fraction of the cost of the asset or the notional value of the contract. Options, therefore, differ from futures in that a right is conferred in exchange for the payment of a premium.

As the holder is in possession of a right, rather than an obligation, they do not have to exercise this right if the transaction ultimately proves not to work in their favour. The option can simply be abandoned with the loss of the premium paid. The writer, however, is obliged to satisfy this right if taken up, or exercised, against them by the holder.

Potentially the writer has an obligation to deliver the asset to the holder of a call option at the exercise price if the option is exercised. Alternatively, the writer could be required to take delivery from the holder of a put option if exercised. All the holder can lose is the premium paid. As a result, only the writer is required to make initial and variation margin payments to the clearing house.

Most exchange-traded financial options are cash settled rather than physically settled. Therefore, if exercised, the cash difference between the exercise price of the option and that of the underlying asset, rather than the asset itself, passes from the writer to the holder.

3.2   At-the-money, In-the-money and Out-of the-money

Assume an investor buys a call option on ABC shares at a premium of 10p and an exercise price of 100p.

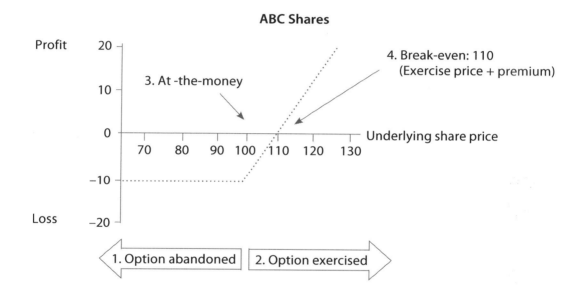

The diagram shows:

1.   Out-of-the-money – If the underlying share price is below 100p, the holder will abandon the option and lose the 10p premium.
2.   In-the-money – If the underlying share price is above 100p, the holder will exercise the option.
3.   At-the-money – the underlying share price is the same as the exercise price.
4.   Break-even – If at expiry the underlying share price is 110p, the holder will break even as it costs 100p to buy shares plus the premium of 10p.

Now we can see how this looks for a put option. Assume an investor buys a put option on ABC shares for a premium of 60 which can be exercised at 200. The position will instead look as follows:

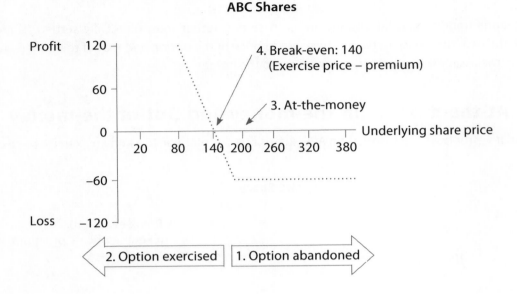

The diagram shows:

1. Out-of-the-money – if the underlying share price is above 200, then the holder will abandon the option.
2. In-the-money – if the underlying share price is less than 140, the holder can exercise option to sell at 200.
3. At-the-money – the underlying share price is the same as the exercise price.
4. Break-even – if at expiry, the underlying share price is 140, the holder could buy the shares in the open market and exercise the option to sell at 200. Profit of 60 is offset by premium of 60.

3.3   Exercise Style

The exercise style of an option describes how it may be exercised. The three most popular exercise styles are:

*   **European option** – with a European option, the holder can exercise the option only on the expiry date. With a three-month option, for example, he can choose only at the end of three months whether or not to exercise.
*   **American option** – an American option, however, allows the holder to choose to exercise at any time between the purchase of the option and expiry. The premium is normally higher for American options, if all other specifications of the option are the same.
*   **Bermudan option** – Bermudan options lie between European and American. A Bermudan option can be exercised on any of various specified dates between original purchase of the option and expiry.

European and American options are both available everywhere; the terms are technical, not geographical.

What happens at expiry depends on the price of the underlying shares on the expiry day.

- **Call Option**
  - If the share price is below exercise price, the option is worthless and the holder will abandon the option.
  - If the prevailing share price is above the exercise price, the holder has the right to buy the shares at a lower price than in the cash market. He will, therefore, exercise the option, paying the exercise price for the share and then may sell it in the market for the higher price.
  - Even if the market price is not above the breakeven price, the option is worth exercising as the holder will make a profit of, say, 1p per contract which can then be used to offset the up-front cost of the premium.
- **Put Option**
  - If the share price is above the exercise price, the holder will abandon the option. The option is worthless.
  - If the share price is below the exercise price, the holder can buy the share in the cash market at the lower price, then exercise the option at the strike price, thus selling the share at the higher price to make a profit.

3.4 Terminology

As with futures, options have their own specialised terminology. The terms have been explained above but are summarised here for ease of reference.

- **Call option** – an option that gives the buyer the right to buy an underlying asset.
- **Put option** – an option that gives the buyer the right to sell an underlying asset.
- **Holder** – the term used to describe the buyer of the option, ie, the person who has bought it. It is also referred to as the **long** position.
- **Writer** – the term used to describe the seller of an option. It is also referred to as the **short** position.
- **Premium** – the term used to describe the price paid for an option.
- **Strike price** – the price at which the underlying asset may be bought or sold. Also referred to as the **exercise price**.
- **At-the-money** – a call option whose strike price is the same as the current price of the underlying asset.
- **In-the-money** – a call option whose strike price is below the current price of the underlying asset and which could therefore be exercised for a profit, hence the term in-the-money.
- **Out-of-the-money** – a call option whose strike price is above the current price of the underlying asset and so, if exercised, would result in a loss; hence it is out-of-the-money.
- **Expiry date** – the last day of the option's life.
- **European style** – options that may be exercised on their expiry date only.
- **American style** – options that may be exercised at any time during their lives up to and including the expiry date.

3.5 Option Strategies

Learning Objective

5.3.2 Be able to calculate and understand the purpose and construction of option strategies and the potential risks, rewards and costs of each: buying calls; buying puts; selling calls; selling puts; caps; floors; collars

In this section, we will consider four basic option strategies by looking at a call and put option from the perspective of the holder and the writer (seller).

3.5.1 Call Options

Buyers of a call option take a long call position, while the writer of the same option takes the opposite short call position.

Using the same example as before, the buyer of a call pays a premium of 10 for the right to buy the underlying shares at expiry.

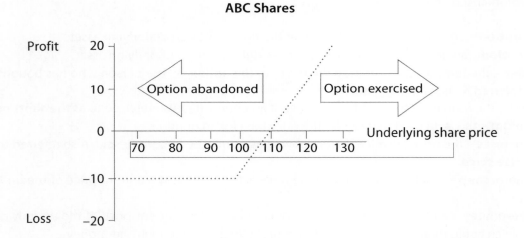

The higher the price of the underlying shares, the more profit the buyer will make and vice versa. The potential risks and rewards for the long call position are:

- The maximum profit is unlimited.
- The maximum loss for the buyer is limited to the premium paid, as they can simply abandon the option.

The writer of the option clearly has a different perspective on the transaction. In return for writing the option, the seller of the option receives the premium and is hoping that the underlying share price will not rise and so the holder will not exercise the option but instead abandon it, leaving the writer with the premium.

The higher the price of the underlying asset, the more loss the writer of the option will make. As a result, potential risks and rewards for the short call position are:

- The maximum profit is the premium.
- The maximum loss for the writer is unlimited.

3.5.2   Put Options

Buyers of a put option take a long put position, while the writer of the same option takes the opposite short put position.

With a put option, the buyer pays a premium for the right to sell the underlying asset on expiry if they wish. The more the price of the underlying asset falls, the more profit the buyer will make.

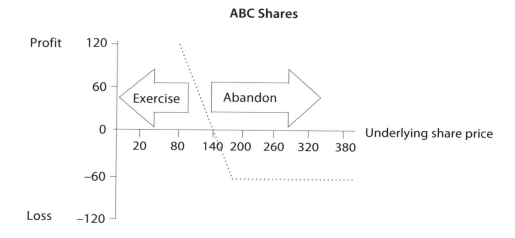

The potential risks and rewards for the long put position are:

- The maximum profit is the strike price less the premium paid.
- The maximum loss for the buyer is limited to the premium paid as they can simply abandon the option.

The seller of the put option will receive the premium but takes on the obligation to buy the underlying asset at expiry. From the perspective of the writer, therefore, they are hoping that the share price will not fall as expected and so the buyer will abandon the option, leaving them with the premium.

As a result, potential risks and rewards for the short put position are:

- The maximum profit is the premium.
- The maximum loss for the writer is the strike price less the premium.

3.5.3 Caps, Floors and Collars

Various OTC option-based products are offered by banks to their customers, some of which can be constructed from straightforward options. Caps, floors and collars are commonly employed with regard to interest rates.

Caps

A cap is an option product which can be used to protect the cost of a floating-rate borrowing over a series of settlement periods.

Example

Suppose that a borrower has a five-year loan which he rolls over every three months at the three-month LIBOR then current. He can buy a five-year cap which will put a maximum cost on each of the rollovers. Whenever the rollover rate exceeds the cap strike rate, he receives the difference.

Suppose the strike rate on the cap is 1% and LIBOR is set at 0.5%. Then, at the end of the three-month interest rate period, the purchaser of the cap will receive 0.5% accrued over the three-month period.

Whenever the rollover rate is lower than the cap strike rate, nothing is paid or received.

The settlement for a cap is paid at the end of the interest period, exactly as for a swap.

Floors

Floors are options that enable the buyer to demand a minimum rate of interest paid on a deposit, regardless of a fall in the prevailing rate of interest.

Floors can be used to protect the income on a floating-rate investment by putting a minimum return on each rollover. Whenever the rollover rate is lower than the floor strike rate, the buyer receives the difference. Whenever the rollover rate is higher than the floor strike rate, nothing is paid or received.

The settlement mechanics for a floor are analogous to those for a cap.

Collars

Collars are contracts that incorporate both a cap and a floor. For a borrower, a cap provides a fixed worst-case level of interest but allows the customer to pay the market rate if this turns out better.

A collar allows the customer to pay a better market rate in the same way, but only down to a certain level. Beyond that level the customer must pay interest at another fixed best-case level. In return for this reduced opportunity, the customer pays a lower premium for the option. Indeed, the premium can be zero (a zero-cost option) or even negative.

3.6 Intrinsic and Time Value

Learning Objective

5.3.3 Be able to calculate the intrinsic and time value of an option and understand the factors determining option premiums and pricing including: influences on intrinsic value and time value; volatility; time to expiry; strike or exercise price; underlying asset price; interest rates; dividends/coupons

The premium for an option is made up of its intrinsic value and its time value:

- Intrinsic value – this is simply the value of the option if it were to be exercised now.
- Time value – an option with a long time to expiry will have a greater amount of time value incorporated into its price, so that the longer the period, the greater will be the time value.

We can consider this by looking at a simple example.

Example

A call option with the right to buy at 90 is trading at 30 when the underlying is trading at 100. The intrinsic value is ten and the time value is the remaining 20.

From this example you can see that: intrinsic value + time value = premium.

In practice, the option premium will be affected by many factors including:

- The underlying asset price – the higher the asset price, the more valuable are call options and the less valuable are put options.
- The exercise price – the higher the exercise price, the less valuable are call options and the more valuable are put options.
- Time to maturity – the longer the term of the option, the greater the chance of the option expiring in-the-money; therefore, the higher the time value and the higher the premium.
- Volatility of the underlying asset price – the more volatile the price of the underlying asset, the greater the chance of the option expiring in-the-money; therefore, the higher the premium.

There are two other factors that will affect the option premium: the income yield on the underlying asset and short-term interest rates. It should be noted that their effects on option prices are fairly minor in relation to the other factors.

- Income yield of the underlying asset – the greater the income yield of the underlying asset, the greater the sacrifice being made by the call option holder by not holding this asset, but the greater the benefit to the put option holder. Therefore, the higher the income yield, the more valuable the put option and the less valuable the call option.
- Short-term interest rates – the higher the short-term rate of interest, the greater the interest income received by the call option holder on the cash not committed to buying the underlying asset. This makes call options more valuable. However, the outlay on a put option not earning this higher rate of interest makes put options less valuable.

265

4. The London Clearing House (LCH)

A clearing house is fundamental to the integrity, efficiency and credibility of a derivatives exchange. LCH.Clearnet acts as the clearing house and central counterparty for Euronext.Liffe and for SETS as well as a number of other exchanges.

Its role is to provide an efficient and cost effective clearing service to the clearing members of its member exchanges. An exchange clearing member is one who has authority to process, or clear, a derivatives trade once executed. Most clearing members also have the authority to execute derivatives trades but must hold an exchange-trading permit to do so.

It will also act as the central counterparty to all trades registered on a member exchange. In its capacity as central counterparty, LCH.Clearnet becomes the counterparty to each and every trade registered on a member exchange. It achieves this through a process known as **novation**.

Novation is the cancelling of the original contractual relationship between the counterparties to the trade at the point at which the trade is registered on the exchange and replacing this with a new contractual relationship between each counterparty and LCH.Clearnet. By being the counterparty to each registered trade, anonymity is preserved between the original counterparties.

As a central counterparty, LCH.Clearnet ultimately acts as the guarantor to each registered trade executed on the exchange in the event of a counterparty defaulting.

To minimise the risk of default it:

- Sets stringent clearing member admission and continuing obligation requirements.
- Requires collateral, or margin, to be deposited by exchange clearing members when futures positions are initially registered and then throughout the term of the contract on any losses accumulated whilst this position remains open.
- This margin takes two forms: initial margin and variation margin.
- Initial margin is payable by both exchange clearing members to LCH, upon a futures contract being registered and usually represents between 2% and 5% of the transaction's notional value, depending on prevailing market conditions. This sum covers LCH against the most probable adverse one-day price movement in the contract. Initial margin can be paid either in cash or in securities that are acceptable to LCH.Clearnet and is returned once the contract has been settled between the parties or upon the contract being closing out. Cash deposited with LCH earns interest daily.
- As initial margin only potentially covers LCH.Clearnet for a one day price movement in the contract, the profit and loss position of each party is calculated on a daily basis for the previous trading day and settled between the exchange clearing members in cash each morning. This is known as variation margin.
- In addition, the existence of a central counterparty enables margin payments and receipts from multiple trades to be netted out.

5. Warrants

5.1 Characteristics of Warrants

Learning Objective

5.4.1 Be able to analyse the key investment characteristics and differences between equity warrants and equity options: purpose and issuers; benefits to an investor or speculator; time to expiry; where traded; strike prices; effect of exercise; settlement; gearing against the underlying; effect of corporate actions on equity warrants

Warrants are negotiable securities issued by companies which confer a right on the holder to buy a certain number of the company's ordinary shares at a preset price on or before a predetermined date.

Warrants are issued on a stand-alone basis and so, unlike convertible loan stock or preference shares, the conversion right contained within the warrant is traded separately.

Although these are essentially long-dated call options, they are traded on the London Stock Exchange and, if exercised, result in the company issuing additional equity shares. The warrants market is relatively small.

Given the terms of the warrant issue, the conversion premium or discount can be calculated.

The basis for calculating the conversion premium follows similar principles as were considered for convertible preference share and convertible bonds, depending on the terms of the warrant.

5.2 Covered Warrants

Learning Objective

5.4.2 Be able to analyse the main purposes, characteristics, behaviours and relative risk and return of warrants and covered warrants: benefit to the issuing company; right to subscribe for capital; effect on price of maturity and the underlying security; exercise and expiry; calculation of the conversion premium on a warrant

A covered warrant is similar to an option, but, unlike a traditional option, is traded on the LSE. Covered warrants are well established in most international markets but have only been available in the UK since 2002.

A covered warrant is a securitised derivative, issued by someone other than the company whose shares it relates to. It gets its name from the fact that, when it is issued, the issuer will usually buy the underlying asset in the market (ie, he/she is **covered** if he/she should need to deliver the underlying shares and is not exposed to the risk of having to buy them in the market at a much higher price than might otherwise have been the case).

Covered warrants are issued by a number of leading investment banks and can be based on individual stocks, indices, currencies or commodities. They can be either leveraged, as with individual stock options, or unleveraged, as with commodities.

As with an option, a covered warrant gives the holder the right to buy or sell an underlying asset at a specified price, on or before a predetermined date. There are both call and put warrants available.

A covered warrant does not carry an obligation to buy or sell, so that an investor's maximum loss is restricted to their initial investment. Investors can buy and sell either call or put warrants daily on the LSE.

The calculation of a warrant's conversion premium is simply:

$$\text{market price} - \text{warrant exercise price} = \text{premium}$$

The premium is made up largely of the intrinsic value although market supply and demand of the warrant may make the warrant price slightly larger or smaller than the intrinsic value.

6. Swaps

Learning Objective

5.5.1   Be able to analyse the purpose, key characteristics, benefits, costs and valuation of: interest rate swaps and swaptions; types of swap agreements: vanilla, basis, coupon, index and currency; interest calculations (compared to bond markets); foreign exchange forwards and swaps; equity forwards, swaps and swaptions (volatility; bullet; variance)

So far the focus has been on exchange-traded derivatives (ETDs) rather than OTC or off-exchange derivatives. The OTC derivatives market is by far the larger in terms of notional value of contracts traded.

OTC derivatives are heavily used for risk management, speculation and arbitrage, principally because they are not standardised but constructed around the unique needs of users. The most significant growth in OTC derivatives has been experienced in the swaps market, which is mainly populated by investment banks, securities houses, portfolio managers, supranationals and multinational companies.

As seen earlier, exchange-traded futures and options are standardised contracts. By contrast, in the OTC market, the terms of each contract are agreed individually between the parties to each transaction. There is considerably less visibility in the terms of OTC derivatives as a result, as these will change from contract to contract.

6.1   Interest Rate Swaps (IRSs)

An interest rate swap (IRS) is an agreement between two parties to periodically exchange a series of interest payments in the same currency to collectively reduce the cost of borrowing.

Being cash-settled CFDs, at no stage in the transaction is the notional loan principal, upon which the swap is based, exchanged. IRSs can be used for both new and existing borrowing for terms up to about 25 years.

Interest rate swaps take two forms:

*   Fixed rate into floating rate. This is commonly known as a coupon or vanilla swap.
*   One type of floating rate into another type of floating rate. This is termed a basis swap.

Example

Company A is embarking on a three-year project to build and equip a new manufacturing plant and borrows funds to finance the cost. Because of its size and credit status, it has to borrow at variable rates.

It can reasonably estimate what additional returns its new plant will generate but, because the interest it is paying will be variable, it is exposed to the risk that the project may turn out to be uneconomic if interest rates rise unexpectedly.

If the company could secure fixed-rate finance, it could remove the risk of interest rate variations and more accurately predict the returns it can make from its investment. To do this, Company A could enter into an interest rate swap with an investment bank.

As part of the swap, it pays a fixed rate to the investment bank and in exchange receives an amount of interest calculated on a variable rate. With the amount it receives from the investment bank, it then has the funds to settle its variable rate lending.

In this way, it has hedged its interest rate exposure risk.

The two exchanges of cash flow are known as the legs of the swap, and the amounts to be exchanged are calculated by reference to a notional amount. The notional amount in the above example is the amount that Company A has borrowed to fund its project.

Typically, one party will pay an amount based on a fixed rate to the other party, who will pay back an amount of interest that is variable and usually based on LIBOR. The variable rate will usually be set as LIBOR plus, say, 0.5% and will be reset quarterly.

A swaption is an arrangement where a buyer pays an upfront sum for the right to enter into a swap agreement by a pre-agreed date in the future. In other words, the buyer of a swaption has the option to enter into a swap. The concept is the same as we saw for options earlier.

6.2   Currency Swaps

Currency swaps are simply interest rate swaps made in two different currencies that require an exchange of the loan principal at the beginning and at the end of the swap period.

The exchange rate at which the loan principal is swapped is agreed at the outset. As a result of this exchanging of principal, the credit risks between the parties are higher than for a single currency interest rate swap.

Currency swaps are mainly used as a hedging, or risk management, tool rather than for speculation and arbitrage.

6.3   Equity Swaps

Volatility or equity swaps are an agreement between two parties, an institutional investor and a bank for instance, to exchange a series of periodic payments between one another, based on a notional principal amount.

One set of payments is linked to the total return on an equity index, the other usually to a fixed or floating rate of interest, though this can be the return on another equity index.

The swap may be a vanilla swap based in a single currency or a cross-currency swap based in two different currencies. Being cash settled, no principal is exchanged between the counterparties, only payments representing the servicing costs of the two sides of the transaction.

An example of a vanilla equity swap, based on a single currency, may be between the FTSE 100 index and a rate of interest based on LIBOR. This is equivalent to the party receiving the return on the FTSE 100 simply funding this equity exposure by drawing on a cash deposit.

The advantages to a portfolio manager being in receipt of the cash flows from the equity exposure include:

- Gaining equity exposure without the costs associated with buying and holding equities.
- Facilitating index tracking.
- Facilitating access to illiquid markets that may be inaccessible to foreigners.
- Permitting a longer-term exposure than would be possible using ETDs.

However, if the return on the equity index is negative in any period, then the portfolio manager will be required to make both an interest payment and an additional payment in respect of this negative return.

Alternatively, by using a cross-currency swap, exposure can be gained to an overseas equity market, again by swapping this return for a fixed or floating rate of interest.

6.4   FX Forwards and Swaps

Foreign exchange is covered in Chapter 7 but for now it is sufficient to note that there are two main types of FX transaction:

- The FX spot market involves the exchange of two currencies very soon after the date of transaction. For most currency transactions in the wholesale market this is T+2.
- All other transactions are forwards where the exchange rate is agreed today but which settle at some future agreed time.

A forward contract is simply a deal between two participants to agree now the rate at which a certain amount of foreign currency will be exchanged at some pre-agreed date in the future. These forward contract rates are quoted over-the-counter by banks. The quotation is based on applying a margin to the spot quotes to arrive at a forward rate.

Any FX contract that matures one day beyond the normal spot date (T+2) is considered a forward deal. For the major currencies forwards, or outright forwards as they are known, can have maturities out to five or ten years. But note that the longer the maturity, the less liquid the market.

The key advantage of forward contracts is certainty.

As well as commercial users, the forward market is used extensively by speculators, for example, hedge funds and the proprietary trading desks at investment banks. Since forward rates are based on the interest rate differential between the two currencies, the FX forward market is used to speculate on expected changes in the difference between these two interest rates.

This is done using FX swaps which entail buying one currency spot and selling it at a future/forward date at the same time. Therefore, any movements in the forward points, which are based on the interest rate differential between the two currencies, will be the basis for any profits or losses on such a trade.

Speculators on the movements in spot rate mainly take spot or outright forward positions.

End of Chapter Questions

Think of an answer for each question and refer to the appropriate workbook section for confirmation.

1. How can a speculator avoid taking delivery of an underlying asset in their long futures position?
    Answer reference: Section 2.1

2. Explain the difference between European and American style options.
    Answer reference: Section 3.4

3. Explain the difference between a call and a put option.
    Answer reference: Section 3.1

4. An investor buys a January £5 call option at 25p. At the expiry, the stock is at £4.75. How much will the investor lose per share?
    Answer reference: Section 3.5.1

5. If you were to sell a 240 put option for 17, what would be your maximum profit?
    Answer reference: Section 3.5.2

6. An increase in which factors would cause all option premiums to increase?
    Answer reference: Section 3.6

7. What is the difference between intrinsic value and time value?
    Answer reference: Section 3.6

8. A call option has a strike price of £3.85. If the share is currently trading at £4.00 what is the intrinsic value of this option today?
    Answer reference: Section 3.6

Chapter Six
Other Investments

This syllabus area will provide approximately 4 of the 80 examination questions

1.   Property

As an asset class, property has at times provided positive real long-term returns, allied to low volatility and a reliable stream of income.

An exposure to property can provide diversification benefits, owing to its low correlation with both traditional and alternative asset classes. However, property can be subject to prolonged downturns and, if invested in directly, its lack of liquidity and high transaction costs on transfer only really make it suitable as an investment medium for the long term.

The availability of indirect investment, however, makes property a more accessible asset class to those portfolio managers running smaller diversified portfolios.

1.1   Types of Property

Learning Objective

6.1.1   Understand and analyse the differences between the residential and commercial property markets

Over the past decade, investment in property has proliferated as people saw the value of properties rise and has led to greater interest in this asset class.

Property has a role to play in a well diversified portfolio and an investment manager needs to consider whether exposure to the residential or commercial sector is appropriate for the portfolio they are managing. It is therefore important to understand the differences between the two.

Some of the key differences are shown in the table below.

	Residential Property	**Commercial Property**
Direct Investment	Range of investment opportunities including second homes, holiday homes and buy to let	Size of investment required means direct investment in commercial property is limited to property companies and institutional investors
Tenancies	Typically short renewable leases	Long-term contracts with periods commonly in excess of ten years
Repairs	Landlord is responsible	Tenant is usually responsible
Returns	Largely linked to increase in house prices	Significant component is income return from rental income

Although property has a place in a well diversified portfolio, its volatility and lack of liquidity should not be forgotten. The recent financial crisis saw the values of both residential and commercial property fall significantly and they have yet to fully recover. Investors were unable readily to sell their properties, and property funds imposed redemption moratoriums, so that investors had to wait up to 12 months to realise their holdings, as fund managers tried to restrict the damage that flooding the market with forced sales would have caused.

1.2 The Role of Commercial Property in a Portfolio

Learning Objective

6.1.2 Understand and apply the rationale for investing in commercial property within a portfolio: cash flow; investment returns; lower volatility; diversification

Commercial property as an asset class offers a number of portfolio benefits including stable cash flows, performance, low volatility and diversification.

A significant part of the return from commercial property comes as rental income, so the length of leases and the income yield are important factors. On average, commercial property leases provide a contracted income stream of 7.1 years, based on the period to the expiry of the lease, but ignoring break options. Although the length of new leases has been shortening over the last ten years, the average is over ten years for retail property, more than seven years for offices and slightly less than seven years for industrials. The income yield from commercial property is relatively high and has been one of its attractions.

Capital growth has, however, fluctuated considerably. Property outperformed UK bonds and UK equities between 2000 and the end of 2006. In the second half of 2007, the commercial property market fell sharply. Despite significant falls experienced between 2007–2009, during the 10 years to 2013 the UK commercial property delivered a return of over 80% – compared to the equity market returns of around 65%.

These fluctuations demonstrate the point that returns from different asset classes vary with economic conditions and emphasise the importance of diversification and asset allocation.

Commercial property's volatility has tended to be lower than that of other asset classes and offers diversification benefits as the real estate market in the UK does not follow the same pattern as the two other main asset classes, equities and gilts. In contrast, the performance of equities and gilts is strongly correlated.

Residential Property

Over the 30 years to 2015, investors in shares enjoyed the best overall returns. However, since 2000 property prices have risen significantly and, in that time, the performance is better for property market investors.

UK equities have returned more than a 1433% return in the last 30 years, assuming that all income was reinvested.

Ignoring dividend reinvestment, a basic return would still have yielded over 433% with a very similar return in interest on cash deposits at 438%.

During that period, returns on property investments have yielded only 402% overall but it is important to realise the more recent advancement in the property markets. It is true that it is possible to select any period in history and see one class of investment outperform another, depending on the period selected.

1.3 The Commercial Property Market

Learning Objective

6.1.3 Understand how the direct commercial property market operates: ownership and lease structures; buying and selling; costs – transactional and management; property valuation; use of gearing; investment performance measurement and the role of Investment Property Databank

In England and Wales, an interest in property can either take the form of a freehold or a leasehold interest.

- **Freehold** – the freeholder of a property has the right to use or dispose of the property as they wish, albeit subject to legislation, local planning laws and any covenants that specifically apply to the property.
- **Leasehold** – the freeholder can create a lesser interest in the property known as a leasehold interest. The leaseholder, or tenant, to whom this interest is conferred, has the right to use the property for a specific period, subject to the terms of the lease and the payment of rent. Unless prevented from doing so under the terms of the lease, the leaseholder can also create a sublease and act as the head lessee to a subtenant.

Commercial property is divided into three main sectors: retail, offices and industrial. The types of underlying property contained in each sector are:

- **Retail** – shopping centres, retail warehouses, standard shops, supermarkets and department stores.
- **Offices** – standard offices and business parks.
- **Industrial** – standard industrial estates and distribution warehousing, or logistics facilities.

A breakdown of the UK investment market based on mainstream institutional property is monitored by the Investment Property Databank (IPD). It covers only the three main sectors and its reports show:

- London and the South East have the lion's share of commercial property investments.
- Retail property is more evenly distributed across regions than offices or industrial. Shopping centres, retail warehouses, department stores, supermarkets and standard shops are found in most towns throughout the country and, with the exception of standard shops, come in large lot sizes.

- The office market is heavily skewed towards London and the South East. London alone accounts for more than 66%, with concentrations in the City, West End, Canary Wharf and Docklands.
- Industrial property is also concentrated in London and the South East.

Some leases include break clauses that can significantly impact on the investment value of a property, as they can give the landlord and the tenant the option to end the lease before its expiry date. The standard convention is to assume that a tenant's break option will be exercised and that it will negatively impact, as the income from the property can change or even disappear at this point. On the other hand, landlords' break options can have a positive impact, as they give the opportunity to re-let at a higher rent, find a better tenant or refurbish the property.

When a commercial property is rented out, a rent review period is agreed between the landlord and the tenant and set out in the terms of the lease. Typically, commercial rents in the UK are reviewed every five years and the revised rent is based on what rents can be achieved in the open market for comparable properties. Leases often provide for upwards-only reviews where the new rent cannot be lower than the rent that the tenant is currently paying.

With the exception of auctions, there is obviously no formal public market in commercial property and transactions are agreed between buyers and sellers, often using the services of specialised agents. There has been a steady growth in the number of commercial properties offered at auction, and research published by the IPD found that the average holding period for a commercial property investment is seven years, suggesting growing liquidity in this sector.

This lack of a formal exchange means that valuers are used to estimate the likely selling price of a commercial property. This process combines financial information about the property with market data to come to a balanced, evidence-supported assessment of its value using the RICS Appraisal and Valuation Standards (known colloquially as the Red Book).

As with other types of property, sales and purchases are both time-consuming and expensive. The costs of buying a property are significant when compared with other assets and average 1.7625% for agents fees and legal costs plus stamp duty land tax.

Commercial property investors need a standard benchmark to measure the returns they achieve on their real estate and compare its performance. This is provided by the IPD, which produces objective, reliable property benchmarks and indices for around 20 countries.

1.4   Indirect Property Investment

Learning Objectives

6.1.4   Understand the routes to indirect property investment: unit-linked life and pension funds; life bonds; limited partnerships; derivatives

6.1.5   Be able to compare and contrast the key features, accessibility, risks, tax treatment, charges, valuation and yield characteristics of real estate investment trusts (REITs) with property authorised investment funds (PAIFs)

Commercial property has traditionally been the domain of institutional and professional investors, although the increasing number of indirect investment vehicles has made it more widely available to individual investors.

The IPD collects data on the distribution of commercial property among different types of investors. Some of the principal investors are:

- **Financial institutions** – UK insurance companies and pension funds are the largest investors in commercial property and are estimated to own 40% of commercial property, through direct holdings and through indirect investment vehicles.
- **UK property companies and REITs** – there are over 100 quoted property companies and REITs in the UK along with over 3,300 private property companies, which between them account for 29% of the commercial property market.
- **Offshore property trusts** – limited partnerships and property unit trusts offer tax efficiency as well as access to a pool of assets in a particular market and have become the indirect vehicle of choice for many investors. The Channel Islands, and Guernsey in particular, are the main domicile for these funds.
- **Traditional estates and charities** – traditional estates such as Grosvenor, Portland, Cadogan, the Crown and Church Commissioners, together with charities and charitable trusts, account for 5% of the market.
- **Private investors** – interest in the commercial property sector by private investors has been on the increase, but because direct investment requires relatively large amounts of capital, investment is made through indirect investment vehicles.
- **Overseas investors** – foreign investors account for a significant 15% proportion of the commercial property market and utilise the UK market to diversify their risk by investing outside of their domestic property market.

Indirect exposure to property can be obtained through the following investment media:

- **Unit-Linked Life and Pension Funds** – life insurance companies have unit-linked life and/or pension funds that invest directly in property. They are typically part of a range on offer to investors in occupational or personal pension schemes and their longer-term nature usually allows them to operate with less cash reserves than authorised unit trusts.
- **Life Bonds** – these are typically single premium bonds that invest in either a with-profits fund or unit-linked life fund.

- **Limited Partnerships** – until the Finance Act 2004, limited partnerships were popular with institutional investors as they are tax transparent and can be leveraged. The imposition of stamp duty land tax (SDLT) on the transfer of partnership interests has, however, reduced their attractions.

- **Derivatives** – real estate derivatives are financial instruments which give investors a return that reflects the performance of the direct property market. They are a relatively new area but include property income certificates, structured products based on the IPD index and IPD index swaps.

1.4.1 Real Estate Investment Trusts (REITs)

UK property companies and REITs – the shares of property developers – can be a useful way of gaining exposure to the fortunes of the property market. However, they can be difficult to value and tend to mirror the fortunes of the equity market rather than the property market. Many REITs invest in commercial developments which may leave them vulnerable to a downturn in this sector.

REITs were introduced in the UK in January 2007. They can invest in both residential and commercial property but the latter is more common. They are required to distribute 90% of taxable profits and have 12 months in which to make the distribution to shareholders. This income is treated as rental income rather than dividend income, with the REIT being exempt from both capital gains tax and corporation tax. The June 2010 budget proposed changes to allow REITs to pay stock dividends and still retain their tax treatment as rental income. REITs can provide investors with tax-efficient and diversified exposure to rental properties, as they are tax-transparent property investment vehicles.

There are over 100 quoted property companies and REITs in the UK along with over 3,300 private property companies, which between them account for 29% of the commercial property market. UK-REITs can be listed on the main market or the AIM market of the LSE, thus providing liquidity with ease of buying and selling along with transparency of pricing. Transaction costs are usually much cheaper than purchasing property directly with the main charges being 0.5% stamp duty and dealing commission.

REITs can prove to be a high-yielding investment if the UK economy is in generally good shape. REITs' performance is closely linked to the performance of the economy, with many securing rental income from retailers and making gains on the underlying value of the property within the trust.

1.4.2 Property Authorised Investment Funds (PAIFs)

PAIFs are a UK tax-efficient, regulated property fund structure and are open-ended investment companies (OEICs), or OEIC sub-funds. They are required to have at least 60% of their net asset value and income from property investment business. PAIFs are established as either as non-UCITS retail schemes (NURSs) or as qualified investor schemes (QISs) under the rules of the FCA. Historically, any rental income distributed by property funds was taxed within the fund itself, which made them unattractive to investors who were unable to claim the tax back. Thus, PAIFs were introduced to allow tax-exempt investors a much more tax-efficient way of investing in collective property investments.

A PAIF's net income must be either distributed to, or accumulated for, its shareholders each year and the income is split into property income, interest and dividends. For tax-exempt investors, all income and interest is paid (or reinvested) gross. For tax-paying investors, 20% tax on property income and interest applies. Dividends are assessed as regular company dividends.

Investing in and the valuation of PAIFs, as open-ended funds, are generally made in the same way as other types of OEIC with the involvement of the fund managers in the subscription, redemption and pricing of units process as well as the collection of management fees. A PAIF is often widely marketed to most investors, particularly to retail investors, that may not be able to access other property investment vehicles. Although regulated under the FCA, PAIFs carry similar market risks to other property vehicles.

1.5   Risks Associated with Property Investment

Learning Objective

6.1.6   Understand the risks associated with property investment, both direct and indirect: individual property risk (heterogeneous and indivisible assets); valuation compared with price; market risk; sector risk; liquidity

Property as an asset class is unique in its distinguishing features:

- It is heterogeneous in nature. Given that each individual property is unique in terms of location, structure and design, the property market can be segmented into an infinite number of individual markets.
- Valuation is subjective, as property, due to its heterogeneity, is not traded in a centralised market place and continuous and reliable price data is not available.
- It is subject to complex legal considerations and high transaction costs upon transfer.
- It is highly illiquid as a result of not being instantly tradeable.
- It is not easily divisible. Since property can only be purchased in discrete units, diversification is made difficult.
- The supply of land is finite and its availability can be further restricted by legislation and local planning regulations. Therefore, price is predominantly determined by changes in demand.

The risks associated with property investment include:

- **Property risk**
  - location of the property.
  - the effect of the use of the property on its value.
  - the credit quality of the tenants.
  - the length of the lease
  - liquidity
- **Market risk**
  - the effect of changes in interest rates on valuations.
  - the performance of individual property sectors.
  - the prospects for rental income growth.
- **Investment vehicle risk**
  - liquidity of indirect investment vehicles.
  - diversification of the underlying portfolios.
  - level of gearing.

It is difficult to track property fund performance and measure the risk of property funds, due to non-daily revaluation of the underlying asset, even if the fund is daily priced. This means volatility measures like standard deviation are less credible.

2. Alternative Investments

Learning Objective

6.2.1 Understand and be able to explain the main purpose and basic characteristics of the following alternative investments: private equity; structured products; commodities (eg, timber); collectables (eg, fine wine, art, autographs, stamps, coins); hedge funds (single hedge funds, fund of funds); currencies; absolute return

2.1 Hedge Funds

Hedge funds seek to eliminate or reduce market risk and capture returns through manager stock selection skill, regardless of market conditions. They do this by combining long and short positions taken in a portfolio of carefully selected securities, without predicting or relying on the direction of the broader market. That is, they hedge market risk. The concept of profiting regardless of directional market movements is core to the hedge fund concept.

There are, however, a wide range of complex hedge fund structures, many of which place a greater emphasis on producing highly geared returns than the control of market risk.

Some other features of hedge funds are:

*   **Structure** – most hedge funds are set up either as private partnerships in the US or as unauthorised collective investment schemes in offshore financial centres. An investment bank, known as a prime broker, typically provides the fund with trading and credit facilities as well as administrative support, while the fund management is usually conducted in a major financial centre such as New York or London.
*   **High investment entry levels** – the minimum initial investment into a hedge fund ranges somewhere between US$100,000 and US$1 million. Most hedge funds also impose a limit on the size to which they can grow, so as to keep the fund nimble.
*   **Investment flexibility** – hedge funds have complete investment flexibility in terms of where, how and in what assets they decide to invest. In addition to being able to take long and short positions in securities, hedge funds also take positions in commodities, currencies and mortgage-backed securities.
*   **Gearing** – hedge funds borrow and employ derivatives to potentially enhance returns through gearing.
*   **Low correlation to world securities markets** – despite the greater concentration of their portfolio holdings, hedge funds, when combined with conventional portfolios, usually provide additional diversification, owing to their low correlation with world equity and bond market movements. However, the extent to which the inclusion of a hedge fund diversifies the risk of a portfolio containing traditional assets is wholly dependent upon the hedge fund's chosen investment strategy.

- **Performance related fees** – hedge funds typically levy an annual management fee of 2% in addition to a performance related fee of about 20% if an absolute performance target in excess of the risk-free rate of return is met or exceeded and previous losses have been made good.
- **Manager investment** – hedge fund managers are further incentivised by being expected to invest some of their own wealth into the fund. This reinforces the alignment of manager and investor interests.
- **Dealing** – many hedge funds impose an initial lock-in period of between one and three years before investors may deal in the hedge fund's shares. Any dealing that subsequently takes place is then usually only permitted at the end of each month or quarter.
- **Regulation** – hedge funds are usually domiciled in an offshore financial centre such as the Cayman Islands or Dublin and are usually subject to a light-touch regulatory regime.

Hedge funds are largely unregulated and are able to undertake a wider range of deals than would be allowed for a regulated product. As a result, hedge funds can have a higher level of risk than traditional assets, but they also have the potential for higher returns. Their performance can be largely uncorrelated to other asset classes for long periods of time.

However, when a major event or shock occurs in the financial markets the correlation returns to other asset classes and can increase markedly.

Hedge funds typically make use of gearing (or leverage) to enhance returns and they may also use more sophisticated investment strategies, such as derivatives. They are generally used by wealthy individuals or entities such as pension funds or insurance companies and are included in benchmark indices such as the Association of Private Client Investment managers and Stockbrokers (APCIMS) private client indices. Hedge funds can be a single fund or a fund that invests in other hedge funds.

Specific risks include:

- gearing is used widely
- settlement is OTC
- currency risk
- dealing delays
- illiquid investments
- lack of visibility on portfolios
- fraud
- lack of independent trustee boards.

To overcome some of these risks and so that funds can be designed that can have wider appeal, some fund management groups are choosing to launch hedge funds as UCITS-compliant funds.

2.2   Absolute Return Funds

Absolute return funds aim to deliver a positive return for investors regardless of market conditions. Their design builds on the attractiveness of the concept of absolute return, rather than relative return (ie, most unit trusts and OEICs aim to produce a return that exceeds a benchmark, hence the term 'relative').

They are, however, structured in the same way as mainstream funds, are often FCA-authorised and are usually established as UCITS funds.

It is important to recognise that this is an investment strategy and that absolute return funds deploy different ways to achieve this. Some focus on equities, some on bonds and some multi-asset. The fund strategy may then target a specific market such as the UK, Europe, emerging markets or global markets. It will then look to deliver positive returns by utilising uncorrelated assets to provide diversification, by using synthetic short selling or a combination of both.

2.3 Private Equity

Private equity is another alternative investment class that has gained increased popularity among institutional investors, notably because of its low correlation to broad equity market movements and the higher than average returns it has historically delivered.

Private equity is a key source of funding for many companies and can take the form of equity, bond or mezzanine finance, the latter combining the characteristics of the former two.

Private equity or venture capital can be sourced from either wealthy individuals or institutions. Deals can generate very large returns in a short period of time for investors. There are generally two types of private equity deals:

- small start-up companies, or
- taking over existing businesses that have the potential to be transformed.

Private equity is different to obtaining business loans (from a bank, for example). If a company runs into difficulty, a bank will generally foreclose and demand immediate repayment. Private equity is more committed to their investment.

Start-up finance and development capital is provided to small but potentially fast-growing unquoted companies, with private capital investors reaping their reward from realising the often significant equity stake they take in the business through either a trade sale or upon the company floating its equity in the new issue market. Private equity is also used to finance management buyouts.

Given the specialist nature of each type of transaction, it is imperative that such investments are well diversified geographically, between industries and across differing stages of company development.

Recently, private equity firms have been accused of secrecy in their dealings and the ruthless pursuit of profit at any cost. Massive job losses have been the result of several high-profile companies being taken over by private equity firms. Before the recession, the sector had experienced explosive growth, fuelled by cheap debt. The credit crisis made debt too expensive, leading to large falls in the value of their investments. The sector is now starting to recover, but it demonstrates that private equity is a high risk and long-term investment.

Types of private equity include venture capital, distressed, leveraged and mezzanine.

2.4   Currencies

The global currency market is the largest market in the world by volume and has no central trading or central regularity mechanism. The market is quite unique as, unlike other markets (because of its geographical diversity) it is open 24 hours per day during weekdays. For individuals, it is common for the investor to access the market through a broker or bank. The market offers significant leverage and the possibility to make substantial profits (or indeed losses).

As well as trading currencies directly, investors can access the market though investment vehicles such as exchange-traded funds (ETFs) or exchange-traded notes (ETNs), futures, options, currency denominated bonds and notes and currency funds. Investing in currencies can involve a great deal of risk during times of economic uncertainty or activity when they can be extremely volatile. However, an advantage of the currency market is that it operates on quite a level playing field. It is a global market with world events that affect currency pricing being communicated through global media and other communication channels around the clock with an open transparency.

Currencies also provide an opportunity to diversify a portfolio or to hedge investments that are purchased and/or priced in foreign currencies as well as assisting global companies actively using foreign exchange to hedge the impact of currency risk on profits and supplies.

2.5   Other Types of Alternative Investment

Other examples of alternative investments include:

- jewellery
- antiques
- books
- art
- classic cars
- autographs
- posters
- coins
- stamps (rare stamps were rated in the top four investments for the 20th century with annual returns of around 10% per annum)
- comic books
- toys (worth four to five times more if in the original packaging)
- racehorses (although more money is made from stud breeders)
- fine wine
- memorabilia.

2.6   Risks Associated with Alternative Investments

Learning Objective

6.2.2   Understand the main risks inherent in alternative investments

6.2.3   Understand the role of alternative investment strategies in a portfolio

Alternative investments are those which fall outside the traditional asset classes of equities, property, fixed interest, cash and money market instruments. Alternative investments are often physical assets which tend to be popular with collectors. However, they also have the potential to appreciate substantially in value.

An advantage is that they are not exclusive to wealthy clients and, owing to the wide variety of options available, even modest investments are possible. The disadvantage is that they often suffer from illiquidity and can be difficult to sell quickly if funds are required for other purposes. They can also be difficult to value due to the size of the different markets. Prices can change rapidly as markets are subject to trends and fashions.

Alternative investments have always been popular with wealthy individuals. They provide an additional level of diversification for a portfolio and have the potential for significantly higher returns.

Many investors will also use gearing (or leverage) to enhance the returns of their portfolio. An example is margin lending for equities, which has become increasingly popular over the last few years. This involves investors obtaining a loan to invest in equities. Gearing has the potential to magnify both gains and losses. It should really only be used by sophisticated investors due to the higher levels of risk involved.

3.   Pensions

Learning Objective

6.3.1   Understand the benefits and options of pension planning: tax relief; capital gains; lifetime allowance; annuity verses income drawdowns; self-invested personal pensions (SSIPs); small self-administered schemes (SSAPs)

It is generally recognised that people are living longer than ever due to medical advances and general improvements in health and that most people's life expectancy has increased significantly over the last few decades.

The bad news, however, is that to enjoy those extra years means having a level of income that will be enough to fund the lifestyle that people would like to enjoy. Being able to enjoy rather than endure retirement requires individuals to plan and take action to achieve that objective.

Before looking at aspects of pension planning, it is important to understand why planning for retirement is so important:

- Worldwide, state pension benefits account for only about 40% of net average earnings.
- Changing demographics and the increasing cost of state pension provision will see this source of retirement income decline and become, at best, a modestly adequate source of income.
- Increasing costs of providing state pensions are forcing governments to reassess how much they pay.
- Relying on the state, therefore, to provide a comfortable retirement is clearly not going to work.
- Existing pension plans may also fall short of providing the funds needed in retirement.
- Defined benefit pension schemes, which were supposed to offer employees a secure retirement income, have been withdrawn by many companies, and for those remaining in such schemes, their companies are reducing the benefits payable and deferring the retirement age at which they are payable.

3.1 Pension Products

Pension schemes tend to receive favourable tax treatment from governments, so that they can encourage individuals to make their own retirement provision and thus relieve the state of the need to fund it. The tax benefits tend to be twofold: tax relief on contributions made into the scheme and either exemption or additional allowances against tax on gains and dividend income.

For this reason, pension arrangements will often provide a better investment vehicle for meeting clients' needs.

We will now consider briefly the major types of pension products.

3.1.1 Occupational Pension Schemes

Occupational pension schemes are, as the name implies, pension schemes provided by an employer, usually as part of their employees' remuneration and benefits package.

The main features of such schemes are:

- It is the employer that sets up the scheme.
- The employer contributes to the overall cost, providing a significant extra benefit to the employee.
- The scheme usually benefits from very attractive tax treatment.
- The scheme can provide a very efficient vehicle for meeting the retirement needs of an individual.

The amount of contribution will be for the employer to decide, as will any eligibility conditions for joining such as who the scheme is open to, and any minimum age and service conditions. The schemes will also usually require the employees to contribute a proportion of their earnings; these are known as contributory pension schemes. In some cases, the employer funds the whole cost and these are known as non-contributory schemes.

The benefits payable under a company pension scheme will depend upon whether it is a defined benefit scheme or a defined contribution scheme.

3.1.2 Defined Benefit Schemes

An occupational pension scheme that takes the form of a defined benefit scheme, also known as a 'final salary scheme', is where the pension received is related to the number of years of service and the individual's final salary.

A defined benefit scheme essentially promises a given level of income at retirement, usually expressed as a proportion of final earnings. Contributions to the fund will normally be made by both the employer and the employee, although who contributes what will vary from scheme to scheme.

For the employee, this has the advantage of allowing retirement plans to be made in the knowledge of what income will be received. Its potential disadvantages are that, in the final years of working, the employee may not be earning as much as when they were at their peak earning power. In assessing such a scheme, consideration also needs to be given to the funding position of the scheme and whether it can afford to pay out the promised benefits.

If it is a defined benefit scheme, then a client can have some reasonable certainty about the amount of income that will be received in retirement and so the main concerns will be whether this is sufficient, how any annual increases are calculated, and the long-term security of the pension fund.

3.1.3 Defined Contribution Schemes

Alternatively, it could take the form of a defined contribution scheme, where the pension provided is related to the contributions made and investment performance achieved.

In a defined contribution scheme the approach is different. Contributions will be made to the scheme by both the employer and the employee and these are invested to build up a fund that can be used to purchase benefits at retirement. These funds will usually be held in a designated account for the employee and this gives certainty that the funds will be available at retirement. The disadvantage, however, is that the actual income that the employee will receive in retirement will not be known until the funds can be invested, and this makes effective planning significantly more difficult.

In a defined contribution scheme, the eventual size of the pension fund will depend upon its investment performance. At retirement, the client will be looking to use this fund to generate the pension, possibly by purchasing an annuity. The amount of pension that the client will be able to generate will therefore depend upon the size of the fund at that time and the prevailing rates of interest at the time of retirement.

3.1.4 Personal Pensions

A company scheme is not available to everyone and, in this case, personal pensions are available for an individual to provide a vehicle for providing retirement benefits. These will usually also benefit from the same generous tax treatment, making them an effective alternative. A personal scheme has the benefit that the individual can choose the provider and the funds that they are invested in, but is clearly at a disadvantage as there are no employer contributions.

3.1.5 Self-Invested Personal Pensions (SIPPs)

A SIPP is basically a personal pension plan with wider investment opportunities. The contribution limits, tax rules and retirement options are the same as other pension schemes.

There are broadly three types of SIPP available in the market.

- **Full SIPP** – these offer the widest range of investment opportunities, including direct investment in commercial property and individual listed securities, in the UK and overseas.
- **Hybrid SIPP** – these are insurance company products, typically offering a choice of the provider's insured funds and non-insured investments, with many providers stipulating a minimum investment to the insured element.
- **Deferred SIPP** – this is a personal pension written under a SIPP trust. It therefore allows the opportunity to use SIPP investments on request.

A further difference between SIPPs and personal pension plans is the charging structure. SIPP providers generally have far higher charges than personal pensions, justifying them by the extra administration required to invest in non-insured funds. This is understandable when the investment mix is genuinely diverse, as evidenced in full SIPPs. However, many hybrid SIPPs have investments wholly or largely in insured funds, making them look very similar to personal pensions, and it is questionable whether they are SIPPs at all. Deferred SIPPs generally only make extra charges above the standard personal pension rates, if and when the plan is switched to SIPP mode.

SIPPs are able to invest in commercial property, and another feature that facilitates this is that they are able to borrow funds. In fact, a SIPP can borrow 50% of the net scheme assets.

So a SIPP with assets of £200,000 can to borrow a further £100,000 potentially to buy a commercial property and make it an asset of the SIPP. This property is frequently the one out of which the business operates and so future rental payments are paid to the SIPP. The SIPP itself will have to pay a commercial rate of interest on the borrowing.

SIPPs can also be used to help finance an individual's business, by using SIPP assets to purchase private company shares.

3.1.6 Small Self-Administered Schemes (SSASs)

SSASs originally started as a derivation of executive pension plans and were popular with company directors of small and medium-sized businesses. SSASs were marketed at the same type of companies, but with the added extras of the self-investment options and borrowing facility.

The small nature of SSAS is defined as having a maximum of 11 members. All members have to be trustees with an equal say in the running of the SSAS and so, in reality, most SSASs have a maximum of three to four people. They are generally family-run businesses that may offer a separate type of pension plan for the employees, and keep the SSAS element for the directors.

Just as with SIPPs, SSASs are able to borrow up to 50% of the net scheme assets. Often this may be used for the same purpose of bringing a company's commercial property under the ownership of a pension scheme, with the tax benefits (ie, no CGT) that attracts.

Unlike SIPPs, SSASs are also able to loan money from the scheme to the sponsoring employer and not face unattractive tax penalties. There are certain conditions which these loans must meet:

- Not more than 50% of the scheme assets can be lent.
- The SSAS must charge interest at a minimum rate of 1% over the average base rate.
- The maximum term of the loan is five years, which may be rolled over once.

If any conditions aren't met, the loan will be an unauthorised payment, which could, ultimately, result in the SSAS being deregistered.

SSASs can invest in the sponsoring employer, although the extent of this investment is limited and a SSAS can only invest up to 5% of scheme assets in any one sponsoring employer and under 20% of scheme assets where the shareholdings relate to more than one sponsoring employer.

3.2 Tax Treatment

The tax rules surrounding pensions changed significantly in 2006. Prior to then there were eight different pension regimes operating and these disparate rules were consolidated into one. The change is referred to as **A-day**.

Some of the key features of the tax regime are noted below.

- **Annual Allowance**
  - A limit is now placed on the total amount of benefit that can build up from contributions into registered pension schemes each tax year without incurring a tax charge.
  - Any pension input above this, will be subject to a tax charge on the excess of 40% payable by the member.
  - Since April 2016, a new measure restricts pensions tax relief by introducing a tapered reduction in the amount of the annual allowance for individuals with income (including the value of any pension contributions) of over £150,000 and who have an income (excluding pension contributions) in excess of £110,000.
- **Lifetime Allowance**
  - A limit is now also placed on the total value an individual can accrue within registered pension funds without incurring tax charges.
  - The amount started at £1.5 million in 2006/07 and was subsequently increased. Since 2010, there have been a number of pension reforms which have led to the lifetime allowance being reduced. Its current level in the 2016/17 tax year is £1 million, having been reduced from £1.25 million.
  - The lifetime allowance can be exceeded, but tax charges will apply. This will only be tested following a benefit crystallisation event (BCE), which, simplistically, is the time an individual decides to take some or all of their pension fund.
  - It is quite conceivable for one individual to have a number of BCEs throughout their lifetime.
  - The tax charge applicable following a BCE where the lifetime allowance is exceeded depends on the way the excess benefits are taken:
    - If they are all taken as income, the excess is taxed at 25%.
    - If they are all taken as a lump sum, the excess is taxed at 55%.
- **Tax Relief on Contributions**
  - For an individual to be eligible for tax relief on their pension contributions they must:
    - have relevant UK earnings (ie, earned income), and

- be resident in the UK during the tax year, or
- have been resident in the UK at some time in the last five tax years and paid contributions to an approved/registered pension scheme, or
- be an individual (or spouse or civil partner of that individual) with earnings from overseas Crown employment that is subject to UK tax.
  - Contributions from both individuals and employers qualify for tax relief.
- **Tax Treatment of the Pension Investments**
  - A pension scheme requires approval by HMRC.
  - Once approved, no capital gains tax arises on gains arising within the portfolio.
  - Any income arising in the portfolio is not subject to tax but the tax credit on dividends cannot be reclaimed.

3.3　Pension Benefits

The main purpose of pension planning of course, particularly from the view of HMRC, is to provide an income in later life.

With effect from April 2015, the UK government has made some radical changes to pensions and how individuals can benefit. They now have much more choice and flexibility.

The new rules apply to individuals with a defined contribution pension – eg, individual or group personal or stakeholder pensions, SIPPs and some additional voluntary contribution (AVC) schemes.

Most pension investors can now make some key choices. The most common are detailed below:

- Take the whole fund as cash in one go – 25% tax free and the rest taxed at the individual's higher rate
- Take small cash sums when required and leave the balance, with 25% of each withdrawal tax free and the rest taxed as income
- Take up to 25% tax free and secure a regular taxable income from the balance. An individual may re-invest the rest into funds designed to provide a regular taxable income which can be adjusted periodically according to income needs and performance, or buy a lifetime annuity
- Leave the pension untouched and delay taking a pension till a later date. The funds can continue to grow tax-free
- Use the entire fund to buy a lifetime annuity
- Use the pension to provide an income for life for a dependent or other beneficiary after the individual dies.

The other common pension type is a defined benefit scheme, where the following applies:

- For final salary schemes a pension will be paid that is based on the number of years pensionable service and the final pensionable salary received by the individual and the scheme's accrual rate.
- The accrual rate is the proportion of salary that is received in pension for each year of service. For example, if the accrual rate is 60ths, an individual will receive 1/60th of pensionable salary for each year of completed pensionable service.
- It may also be possible to choose a tax-free lump sum. The amount of the lump sum will depend upon the scheme's rules and, in any event, will be limited to 25% of the capital value of the pension.

End of Chapter Questions

Think of an answer for each question and refer to the appropriate workbook section for confirmation.

1. How do tenancies of residential and commercial property differ?
    Answer reference: Section 1.1

2. What three sectors is the commercial property market divided into?
    Answer reference: Section 1.3

3. How would you expect a tenant's break clause to impact the investment value of a property?
    Answer reference: Section 1.3

4. Describe the risks associated with property investment.
    Answer reference: Section 1.5

5. What is the core investment concept at the heart of hedge funds?
    Answer reference: Section 2.1

6. How do absolute return funds differ from hedge funds?
    Answer reference: Section 2.2

7. How do defined benefit and defined contributions differ from each other in terms of the pension payable?
    Answer reference: Sections 3.1.2 and 3.1.3

8. What is a SIPP and what are the main types encountered?
    Answer reference: Section 3.1.5

Chapter Seven
Financial Markets

This syllabus area will provide approximately 6 of the 80 examination questions

7

1. Exchanges

1.1 The Role of Exchanges

Learning Objective

7.1.1 Understand the role of the exchanges for trading: shares; bonds; derivatives

Financial markets are best described by the functions they perform.

The main functions of financial markets are to:

- Raise capital for companies. This function is performed by stock exchanges.
- Provide maturity transformation, by channelling short-term savings into longer-term business investment.
- Bring buyers and sellers together in highly organised marketplaces to reduce search and transaction costs and facilitate price discovery, so that securities and other assets can be valued objectively. This function is performed by stock and derivatives exchanges and other marketplaces.
- Allocate capital efficiently from low-growth to high-growth areas.
- Transfer risk from risk-averse to risk-seeking investors. This was considered in this manual when looking at the activities of hedgers and speculators in derivatives markets. This role is equally well performed by the insurance market, which underwrites the risk from a large number of insurance policies. It is not, however, a function of stock markets or stock exchanges.
- Provide borrowing and lending facilities to match surplus funds with investment opportunities. This function is performed by banks and stock exchanges.

1.2 Stock Market Listings

Learning Objective

7.1.2 Understand why companies obtain listings on overseas stock exchanges: liquidity; marketability; sources of capital/capital requirements

A stock exchange is an organised marketplace for issuing and trading securities by members of that exchange. Each exchange has its own rules and regulations for companies seeking a listing and continuing obligations for those already listed.

Historically, stock exchanges have operated as national monopolies from a central location, or physical marketplace, mainly catering for the needs of domestic investors and domestic issuers. As mainly mutually owned, or not-for-profit, organisations, many stock exchanges had become bureaucratic, parochial and resistant to change and, ironically, had restricted access to new capital for fund development, investment in new trading and settlement technology and facilitation of expansion into new markets.

Recently, however, in an attempt to meet the challenges posed by competing trading systems and the globalisation of financial market, in an increasingly price-sensitive and competitive global marketplace, many have sought to become more dynamic and cost-efficient and have striven to create new markets. Indeed, stock exchanges have been taking their lead from the radical changes recently undertaken in the derivatives markets. These have included abandoning restrictive mutual ownership by exchange members to become shareholder-owned listed companies, operating as electronic trading networks as the move to electronic trading has gathered pace, and creating new markets through strategic mergers and alliances with other exchanges.

The motivation behind many of these mergers and alliances has been a realisation that financial markets have become integrated to such a degree that the shares of most multinational companies, rather than just being listed on their domestic stock exchange, are instead listed on those stock exchanges that best reflect the global distribution and capital requirements of their business. Listing on an overseas stock exchange also enhances the liquidity and marketability of companies' shares and can also build the company's brand. In effect, a global capital market has been created through the globalisation of markets and economies.

1.3 The Role of the London Stock Exchange (LSE)

Learning Objective

7.1.3 Understand the role and responsibilities of the London Stock Exchange (LSE): member firm supervision; market regulation; provision of a primary securities market; provision of a secondary securities market; dissemination of market information

The LSE began life in 1773 when traders who regularly met to buy and sell the shares of joint stock companies in Jonathan's Coffee House voted to change the name of the coffee house to that of the London Stock Exchange. The LSE is Europe's largest stock exchange, accounting for over 35% of European stock market capitalisation, about 10% of world stock market value and over 50% of foreign equity trading on world stock exchanges. Despite this, the LSE continues to evolve in a very competitive global marketplace.

The LSE is a recognised investment exchange (RIE) and, as such, is responsible for:

* Providing a primary and secondary market for equities and fixed interest securities.
* Supervising its member firms.
* Regulating the markets it operates.
* Recording all transactions, or bargains, executed on the exchange.
* Disseminating price-sensitive company information received by its regulatory news service (RNS) and distributed through commercial quote vendors, also known as secondary information providers (SIPs).

The LSE operates both a primary and secondary market for:

- Domestic PLCs including:
  - companies with a full listing
  - smaller UK PLCs admitted to the Alternative Investment Market (AIM).
- Exchange-traded funds (ETFs) and other innovative investments on its extraMARK exchange.
- International equities.
- Domestic bonds:
  - Gilts.
  - Local authority fixed-interest securities.
  - Corporate bonds.

2. Dealing and Settlement

2.1 Bond Trading

Learning Objective

7.2.1 Understand the differences between a primary market and a secondary market in respect of gilts, UK corporate bonds and eurobonds: two-way trading; new issues; market prices

Primary markets exist to raise capital and enable surplus funds to be matched with investment opportunities while secondary markets allow the primary market to function efficiently by facilitating two-way trade in issued securities.

A primary market is the market for new issues or initial public offerings (IPOs). New equity issues can be made via an offer for sale, offer for subscription, placing, or, if no new capital is to be raised, via an introduction. New equity issues have also started to be offered directly to investors via online investment banks.

Secondary markets, by injecting liquidity into what would otherwise be deemed illiquid long-term investments, also reduce the cost of issuing securities in the primary, or new issue, market. However, these roles can only be performed efficiently if markets are provided with accurate and transparent information, so that securities may be valued objectively and investors can make informed decisions. This is particularly important if capital is to be allocated efficiently from what are perceived to be low-growth to high-growth areas to the overall benefit of the economy.

2.1.1 Gilts

The primary market for gilts is managed by the Debt Management Office (DMO), which acts on behalf of the UK government. Most gilt issues are used to finance the Public Sector Net Cash Requirement (PSNCR) and are made via auctions and tranches.

Auctions

This new issue method was adopted by the UK government in 1987, in preference to the previous method of issuing gilts on a tender basis which required setting a strike price.

The DMO invites applications to be submitted on either a competitive or non-competitive basis.

*   Competitive bids must be for a minimum of £500,000 and require the bidder to pay the price tendered.
*   Non-competitive bids can be submitted for amounts between £1,000 and £500,000 and are satisfied at the weighted average price of all successful competitive bids.

Tranches

Rather than make a completely new gilt issue, the DMO can add to the issue of an existing stock on exactly the same terms as before, thereby adding to the liquidity of the issue.

The DMO usually drip-feeds these tranches into the market, through what are known as tap stock issues. This mechanism is also used to feed those stocks that remain unsold from an unsuccessful auction into the market.

Once issued, gilts are traded on the LSE which exercises day-to-day control of this secondary market, while the Bank of England has responsibility for its stability and liquidity.

Gilts are traded either directly between market participants or by using the LSE's SEAQ system. It is via a quote-driven trading system where gilt-edged market makers (GEMMs) indicate the prices they are prepared to trade at. As a condition of remaining a GEMM, they are required to make a two-way market in all conditions. The London Stock Exchange requires a minimum of two market makers for any stock traded on SEAQ.

Gilt bargains are settled in exactly the same way as equities through CREST, except that they settle one business day after the trade, known as T+1.

2.1.2   UK Corporate Bonds

UK corporate bonds are also traded through GEMMs, though prices in this relatively illiquid secondary market are disseminated through SEAQ.

Since 2001, private investors have been able to trade investment grade corporate bonds through a stockbroker via Bondscape, a trading facility that permits small deals to be executed inexpensively. More recently, the LSE has launched a retail bond service, the Order book for Retail Bonds (ORB) in response to increasing retail demand for access to the bond market. The ORB is an electronic trading platform offering investors a cost-effective, transparent and efficient mechanism for concentrating on screen liquidity and facilitating price discovery in a range of corporate bonds and gilts.

All UK corporate bond deals are settled on a T+2 basis.

2.1.3 Eurobonds

Most new eurobond issues are placed by an international securities house, appointed by the issuer to act as the lead manager to the issue. This lead manager will then form a syndicate of other securities houses through which the bonds will be marketed and sold to their respective clients.

Once issued, trading takes place over-the-counter between ICMA dealers, rather than being conducted on a physical exchange. ICMA dealers will, upon request, quote a two-way price for a specific transaction in a particular issue, although, as most issues tend to be held until maturity, the secondary market is relatively illiquid.

2.2 Equity Trading

Learning Objective

7.2.2 Understand the following order types and their differences: limit; at best; fill or kill; execute and eliminate; multiple fills

Equity trading is conducted through trading systems broadly categorised as either:

* quote-driven, or
* order-driven.

Quote-driven trading systems employ market makers to provide continuous two-way, or bid and offer, prices during the trading day, in particular securities, regardless of market conditions. Market makers make a profit, or turn, through this price spread. Although outdated in many respects, many practitioners argue that quote-driven systems provide liquidity to the market when trading would otherwise dry up. The NASDAQ and the LSE's SEAQ trading systems are two of the last remaining examples of quote-driven equity trading systems.

An order-driven market, however, is one that employs either an electronic order book such as the LSE's SETS or an auction process such as that on the NYSE floor to match buyers with sellers. In both cases, buyers and sellers are matched in strict chronological order by price and the quantity of shares being traded and do not require market makers.

2.2.1 London Stock Exchange (LSE) Systems

The LSE has been operating for over 300 years and, throughout its history, its trading methods have evolved.

Until the mid-1980s, trading was face-to-face on the trading floor of the exchange (an open-outcry market). In 1986, the LSE moved to screen-based trading, with market makers (firms that undertake to quote both buying and selling prices, continuously, for the companies in which they are market makers) quoting prices and handling telephone responses from interested buyers/sellers. Nowadays, market makers are still used for less liquid stocks, with larger companies' shares traded on an electronic order-based system that automatically matches buyers and sellers.

The LSE has undertaken major development of its trading platforms in response to the introduction of the Markets in Financial Instruments Directive (MiFID). Its underlying trading system is known as Millennium Exchange and there are a number of trading platforms that serve different sectors of the market.

The main trading system is SETS, which is used to trade the nearly 1,000 shares that are contained within the FTSE All-Share Index. It combines electronic order-driven trading with integrated market maker liquidity provision, delivering guaranteed two-way prices for the most liquid and international securities.

In this system, LSE member firms (investment banks and brokers) input orders via computer terminals. These orders may be for the member firms themselves, or for their clients.

Very simply, the way the system operates is that these orders will be added to the **buy queue** or the **sell queue**, or executed immediately. Investors who add their order to the relevant queue are prepared to hold out for the price they want. Those seeking immediate execution will trade against the queue of buyers (if they are selling) or against the sellers' queue (if they are buying).

Example

For a liquid stock, like Vodafone for example, there will be a 'deep' order book – the term 'deep' implies that there are lots of orders waiting to be dealt on either side. The top of the queues might look like this:

Buy Queue		Sell Queue	
We will buy for at least		We will sell for at least	
7,000 shares	£1.24	3,550 shares	£1.25
5,150 shares	£1.23	1,984 shares (2)	£1.26
19,250 shares (1)	£1.22	75,397 shares (2)	£1.26
44,000 shares (1)	£1.22	17,300 shares	£1.27

Queue priority is given on the basis of price, and then time.

So, for the orders noted (1), the order to buy 19,250 shares must have been placed before the 44,000 order – hence its position higher up the queue. Similarly, for the orders noted (2), the order to sell 1,984 shares must have been input before the order to sell 75,397 shares.

Less liquid securities that are not traded on the SETS order book are traded on the Stock Exchange Electronic Trading Service – quotes and crosses (SETSqx), which supports electronic auctions along with continuous stand-alone quote-driven market making.

Its key features are:

- It combines market maker quotes with periodic auctions.
- Market makers provide continuous liquidity throughout the trading day.
- It provides order book execution through periodic auctions with four uncrossings designed to concentrate liquidity.

- Both market makers and non-market makers can participate in auctions.
- The order book will support named and anonymous limit orders, and any member firm has the option to phone the counterparty behind a named order and fill this before the next uncrossing if terms are agreed.

SEAQ is the LSE's service for the fixed interest market and AIM securities that are not traded on either SETS or SETSqx. It is a quote-driven market.

2.2.2 ISDX

'ISDX is an independent UK stock exchange regulated by the Financial Conduct Authority and is a member of the ICAP Group. (See Chapter 3, Section 2.3.3)

2.3 Trade Reporting

Details of trades once executed need to be reported to both the regulator and to the market.

Transaction reporting is done to facilitate settlement of the transaction and provide information to the regulator, enabling review of transactions after the fact – a measure of market completeness. Trade reporting is a mechanism to feedback to the marketplace on market depth and liquidity – a measure of market transparency. Trade reports must include a variety of details, including the identity of the reporting member firm, the date and time of the transaction, the security traded and the type of trade.

Trade reporting is automatic for all those trades that are executed on the LSE's electronic order books – embracing UK equities traded on SETS, depository receipts and international equities. Since the trades are executed automatically on the order books, they will generate automatic trade reports and there is no need for participants to manually report the trades.

'Off order book' transactions are trades executed by one or more member firms in securities away from the order book, often over the telephone. Such trades need to be reported by the member firm to the exchange within three minutes of execution.

Trades in gilt-edged securities need to be reported to the LSE within the same timetable as trades in equity securities (normally within three minutes of the trade) by reference to the trade reporting period.

The responsibility for trade reporting rests with the more senior party to the trade, ie, the market maker member firm, followed by the broker-dealer member firm, followed by the non-member. If the two parties to the trade are of the same seniority, it is the selling member firm that trade reports.

2.4 Order Types

All orders input to SETS must be firm and not indicative orders as, once displayed, an order must be capable of immediate execution.

Some of the order types that can be entered:

- **Limit orders** – these require the investor to specify both the quantity of a particular security to be traded and a minimum price at which to sell or a maximum price at which to buy. A limit order does not have to be executed immediately, and can remain displayed on the SETS system for up to 90 calendar days.
- **At best** – this specifies the number of shares to be bought or sold and is executed immediately at the best possible price(s). Placing an order at best can be precarious when two-way trade in a particular stock is thin as prices can lose touch with reality, especially at the very beginning and very end of the trading day.
- **Fill or kill** – if the entire order cannot be filled immediately, at a price no worse than that stipulated by the investor, it is automatically deleted.
- **Execute and eliminate** – these orders are filled in whole or in part at, or better than, the stipulated price with any unfilled portion of the order being automatically deleted from the system.

Some but not all trades can be executed immediately using the SETS order book. Others, however, are too large and the trade has to be executed in tranches. When this is done it is referred to as **multiple fills**.

2.5   Equity Dealing Costs

Dealing in UK equities incurs the following costs:

- **Dealing spread** – the size of the dealing spread, or the difference between bid and offer prices, will depend on how liquid the market for a particular share is. Trades executed on SETS typically have low dealing spreads.
- **Commission** – although negotiable, a typically institutional bargain will attract commission at 0.2% of the value of the transaction.
- **Panel on Takeovers and Mergers (POTAM) levy** – £1 is charged on all transactions over £10,000.
- **Stamp duty** –– SDRT is due at 0.5% of the transaction value for purchase of:

  ◦ Shares in a UK company
  ◦ Shares in a foreign company with a share register in the UK
  ◦ An option to buy shares
  ◦ Rights arising from shares already owned
  ◦ An interest in shares, like an interest in the money made from selling them.

All of these fees – excluding the statutory taxes – will vary from one broker to the next.

2.6   Settlement

CREST is operated by Euroclear UK & Ireland, and is a commercially run electronic book entry transfer and settlement system used for all LSE-traded UK equity and preference shares, warrants, gilts and corporate bonds.

By enabling securities to be held, transferred and settled electronically, CREST seeks to reduce the flow of paper in the settlement and registration process. Shares held in electronic form are referred to as being dematerialised. CREST does, however, permit certificated shareholdings to be held and settled through the system. Dematerialised holdings can also be transferred into certificated holdings and vice versa.

Shares in CREST are held in an uncertificated form and can be held in the following three ways:

- **Direct member** – involves the member's name appearing on the issuing company's register. Each member has a stock account containing records of its securities and each appoints a CREST payment bank to pay out and receive monies in respect of CREST transactions. Direct members are permitted to hold more than one account, to facilitate designation of accounts (for example, for different underlying clients).
- **Sponsored member** – are generally private investors and their name will appear on the issuing company's register. A direct member will act as their sponsor to provide the link to CREST and is typically a broker, fund manager or custodian who charges a fee for the service. A sponsored member is also required to appoint a CREST payment bank.
- **Custodian** – where the beneficial shareholder appoints a nominee who is a direct member of CREST. The nominee holds the securities on behalf of the shareholder, through a specially designated stock account. The nominee company's name appears on the issuing company's share register as opposed to the shareholder's name. The nominee company is typically operated by a broker, fund manager or custodian.

The diagram below illustrates how a sterling sale of UK-registered shares between two counterparties on a recognised exchange is input, matched and settled in CREST.

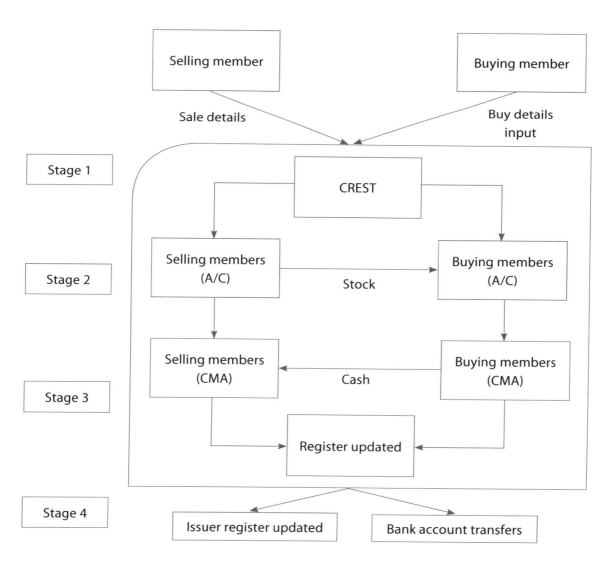

Stage 1 – Trade Matching

- The buying and selling members input instructions in CREST detailing the terms of the agreed trade.
- CREST authenticates these instructions to check that they conform to the authentication procedures stipulated by CREST. If the input data from both members is identical, CREST creates a matching transaction.

Stage 2 – Stock Settlement

- On the intended settlement date, CREST checks that the buying member has the funds, the selling member has sufficient stock in its stock account, and the buyer's CREST settlement bank has sufficient liquidity at the Bank of England to proceed to settlement of the transaction.
- If so, CREST moves the stock from the selling member's account to the buying member's account.

Stage 3 – Cash Settlement

- CREST also credits the cash memorandum account (CMA) of the selling member and debits the CMA of the buying member which simultaneously generates a settlement bank payment obligation of the buying member's settlement bank in favour of the Bank of England.
- The selling member's settlement bank receives that payment in Bank of England funds immediately upon the debit of the purchase price to the buying member's CMA.

Stage 4 – Register Update

- CREST then automatically updates its operator register of securities to effect the transfer of shares to the buying member.
- Legal title to the shares passes at this point – electronic transfer of title (ETT), as described earlier.
- This prompts the simultaneous generation by the CREST system of an register update request (RUR) requiring the issuer to amend its record of uncertificated shares.

In practice, stages 2, 3 and 4 occur simultaneously.

The function of the CMA and the difference between the operator register and issuer register are explained below.

CREST members are required to appoint a CREST payment bank to receive and pay out monies in respect of settlements in CREST. It maintains one or more CMAs for each member in one or more CREST settlements currencies (eg, euro, sterling or US dollars) as required by the member. A CMA is an electronic transaction ledger which shows the net balance of payments made and received at any time during the course of the settlement day. Settlement is instantaneous and payments are made between settlement banks on the central accounts at the Bank of England as they occur.

Under the CREST system, the register of securities comprises two parts:

- CREST maintains the uncertificated part of the register – the operator register of securities.
- The relevant issuer maintains the certificated part of the register – the issuer register of securities.

When any transfer of title occurs in CREST, the CREST system will generate an RUR requiring the issuer to amend the relevant record of uncertificated shares.

The issuer register of uncertificated securities is simply a duplicate of the CREST register, but the combination of this and the issuer's register of certificated securities means that the issuer is aware of, and can communicate with all, the holders of its securities.

2.7   Operational Risks

Learning Objective

7.2.3   Understand the main operational risks in dealing internationally

The Basel Committee defines operational risk as: *'The risk of loss resulting from inadequate or failed internal processes, people and systems or from external events.'*

Some of the operational risks that may affect international deals include:

- system failure, eg, stock exchange IT system failure
- fraud
- vandalism or political unrest (resulting in offices/equipment for trading being damaged or staff being unable to work)
- people (eg, making mistakes due to not understanding international rules).

Beyond that, other operational risks that will arise in the execution of trades and their settlement include:

- Need for authorisation to trade in certain markets or the establishment of legal arrangements with a local broker-dealer.
- Legal restrictions that may be in place for certain types of trades such as short selling.
- Delays between placing of the order and its execution, due to time differences which may lead to the trade taking place at widely different prices, due to market volatility.
- Need to undertake due diligence on a local custodian to hold and settle trades in that market.
- Delays in transmitting details of executed orders due to timing differences.
- Delays in the asset manager issuing trade settlement instructions to a local custodian, due to timing differences.
- Different rules and penalties for settlement delays and possibly compulsory buy-ins.
- Legal and physical arrangements for the safeguarding of assets.
- Communication, understanding and subsequent processing of any corporate actions.

2.8   Settlement of Collective Funds

Learning Objective

7.2.4   Understand how the settlement cycle operates for collectives: UK alternative funds; exchange-traded funds; investment trusts

The process for settlement of purchases and sales of collectives depends upon whether they are exchange-traded or dealt direct with fund managers.

Exchange-traded funds and investment trusts are exchange-traded and the settlement process follows the same pattern for equity trades. Holdings are dematerialised in CREST, and settlement takes place at T+2.

Dealings in UK authorised and unauthorised funds take place directly with the fund manager. The fund will retain the shareholder register and settle each trade directly with the unitholder.

For purchases, once the investment has been made and the amount invested has been received, the fund group will record ownership of the relevant number of units or shares in the fund's share register.

When the investor decides to sell, he/she needs to instruct the fund manager (or ask his/her adviser or the fund supermarket to instruct the fund manager) who then has four days, from receipt of the instruction, in which to settle the sale and remit the proceeds to the investor.

Traditionally, this instruction used to have to be in writing, but from 2009 managers, supermarkets and advisers are able to accept instruction via the internet or over the telephone, using appropriate security checks.

3. International Markets

3.1 Characteristics and Risks of Established Markets

Learning Objective

7.3.1   Understand the characteristics and risks of an established market: UK; USA; Japan; China; Europe

3.1.1 United States

Since over 40% of global GDP is accounted for by the US, it is no surprise that two of its many exchanges, the NYSE and the NASDAQ, comprise almost half of the world's total stock exchange activity. As well as trading domestic US stocks, these exchanges are also involved in the trading of shares in major international companies.

The NYSE, operated by NYSE Euronext, is the largest stock exchange in the world, as measured by its domestic market capitalisation and is significantly larger than any other exchange worldwide. Although it trails NASDAQ for the number of companies quoted on it, it is still larger in terms of the value of shares traded.

The NYSE trades in a continuous auction format, that is, member firms act as auctioneers in an open-outcry auction market environment, in order to bring buyers and sellers together and to manage the actual auction. This makes it unique in world stock markets but, as more than 50% of its order flow is now delivered to the floor electronically, it is effectively a hybrid structure combining elements of open outcry and electronic markets.

NYSE merged with Euronext in 2007 to create the world's largest and most liquid exchange. Both are more correctly referred to as NYSE Euronext.

NASDAQ is an electronic stock exchange with 3,200 companies listed on it. It is the third-largest stock exchange by market capitalisation and has the second-largest trading volume.

There are a variety of companies traded on the exchange, but it is well known for being a high-tech exchange – that is, many of the companies listed on it are telecoms, media and technology companies; it is typically home to many new, high-growth, and volatile stocks.

Although it is an electronic exchange, trades are still undertaken through market makers who make a book in specific stocks so that, when a broker wants to purchase shares, it does so directly from the market maker.

The main depository in the US is the Depository Trust Company (DTC) which is responsible for corporate stocks and bonds, municipal bonds and money market instruments. The Federal Reserve Bank is still the depositary for most US government bonds and securities.

Transfer of securities held by the DTC is by book entry, although shareholders have the right to request a physical certificate in many cases. However, about 85% of all shares are immobilised at DTC, and efforts are under way in the US to eliminate the requirement to issue physical certificates at the state level.

Equities settle at T+3, while US government fixed-income stocks settle at T+1. Corporate, municipal and other fixed income trades settle at T+3.

3.1.2   Japan

The Tokyo Stock Exchange (TSE) is one of five exchanges in Japan but is, undoubtedly, one of the more important world exchanges.

The TSE uses an electronic, continuous auction system of trading. This means that brokers place orders online and when a buy and sell price match, the trade is automatically executed. Deals are made directly between buyer and seller, rather than through a market maker. The TSE uses price controls so that the price of a stock cannot rise above or fall below a certain point throughout the day. These controls are used to prevent dramatic swings in prices that may lead to market uncertainty or stock crashes. If a major swing in price occurs, the exchange can stop trading on that stock for a specified period of time.

Settlement in Japan takes place at T+3 for both equities and fixed-income trades.

The Japan Securities Depository Centre (JASDEC) acts as the CSD for equities. The Bank of Japan (BOJ) provides the central clearing system and depository for JGBs and treasury bills.

Settlement within JASDEC is by book entry transfer, but without the simultaneous transfer of cash. However, these movements are co-ordinated through the TSE.

3.1.3   China

The Shanghai Stock Exchange is the largest exchange in China and is the fifth largest in the world – with a market capitalisation of around $3.5 trillion (US). The exchange in Shenzhen is ranked eighth largest in the world – with a market capitalisation of around $2.3 trillion (US).

There are some restrictions on foreign investment imposed by the Chinese authorities.

The China Securities Depository and Clearing Corporation Ltd (CSDCC) acts as the central counterparty for both equities and bonds. At the end of the day, the CSDCC reconciles its positions with the stock exchange and settles obligations with the custodian banks. A and B shares are registered automatically by the CSDCC in the name of the beneficial owner on settlement. Nominee registration is permitted only for B shares. Short selling is prohibited in the A share market by the China Securities Regulatory Commission (CSRC) since 1 December 2001.

Equity A share trades settle on the same day as dealt (T+0) with equity B shares settling on T+3. Bonds generally settle on T+0.

In July 2015, China's stock exchange regulator imposed limits on stock market selling, after extreme volatility in the market led to major companies' shares falling by the daily limit of 10%. About 1,400 companies (over half of those listed) called for a trading halt in an attempt to prevent further losses.

In the weeks before this, Shanghai stocks had seen falls of 30% having gained more than 150% in the previous year.

3.1.4 Europe

Europe is now home to more than 70 regulated markets/stock exchanges with the oldest being the Amsterdam Stock Exchange founded in 1602 (now part of Euronext: Euronext Amsterdam).

The London Stock Exchange (LSE) was founded in 1801, although a market had existed previously (with records beginning in 1698) at Jonathan's Coffee House, also in London. The LSE is the only true global exchange in Europe with a market capitalisation of around $6 trillion (US dollars), making it the world's third largest.

Euronext is one of two major Pan-European exchanges which is based in Amsterdam and incorporates other exchanges in Belgium, Portugal and France. The other Pan-European exchange group is OMX, which incorporates both Baltic and Scandinavian exchanges: Nordic (Denmark, Finland and Iceland with activity in Norway and the Faroe Islands), Baltic Market (Estonia, Latvia and Lithuania) and there is also First North, which is an alternative exchange in Sweden.

Another large exchange group in Europe is Deutsche Börse Group, which operates in Germany and incorporates exchanges in Berlin, Hamburg, Munich, Stuttgart, Frankfurt and also the Eurex exchange, as well as sponsorship of the Budapest Stock Exchange in Hungary.

LCH.Clearnet Ltd and SIX x-clear are the CCPs for the LSE while LCH.Clearnet SA acts as clearer for the Euronext markets. Deutche Börse has Eurex Clearing which acts as CCP for the German exchanges and also includes the Irish Stock Exchange. EuroCCP, the DTCC-owned clearing house, acts for some of Europe's multilateral trading facilities (MTFs).

There are also a number of central securities depositaries (CSDs) that facilitate settlement. The CREST system (owned by Euroclear UK & Ireland) is the CSD for UK and Ireland (and some other foreign securities) while Clearstream provides CSD services for Germany. For the Euronext markets there are Euroclear Nederland, Euroclear France and Euroclear Belgium (Portugal is serviced by Interbolsa).

The European trading, clearing and settlement structure is remarkably fragmented when compared to countries like the USA, with its sole equities CSD and one currency structure.

T2S (TARGET2-Securities) is an ECB-led project to introduce a European securities settlement engine which offers real time delivery versus payment (DVP) settlement in central bank money. The main objective of the T2S initiative is to start to integrate and harmonise the fragmented securities settlement infrastructure in Europe, which in time should also reduce cost.

Another initiative for improving and harmonsing securities settlement in the EU was first adopted on 7 March 2012 by European regulation. The Central Securities Depositary Regulation (CSDR) aims to improve the securities settlement process in Europe and introduces a number of legal obligations to the market including:

1. Dematerialisation of securities so that holdings are represented electronically and transferred in book entry form. This is likely to be introduced over a few years, in stages.
2. To settle security trades on a rolling settlement basis on T+2. This was implemented across most of Europe in October 2015, changing from the previous T+3 environments. A major benefit of this is a reduction in credit risk.

3.2   Characteristics and risks of Developing Markets

Learning Objective

7.3.2   Understand the characteristics and risks of a developing market: economic liberalisation; foreign ownership restrictions; currency restrictions; liquidity; ownership recognition

There are many benefits to investing overseas. At a general level, these benefits arise from the fact that the world economy is not totally synchronised, most investment themes are global, many industries are either over- or under-represented in the UK and the UK equity market accounts for less than 10% of world stock market capitalisation. To be effectively diversified, then, a portfolio should be adequately spread with no one geographical region or asset class monopolising it – although that does depend entirely on the client mandate and what they are seeking.

Although most overseas investment held by UK investors is in developed equity markets, emerging markets represent a rapidly increasing proportion of UK overseas investment. The term **emerging market** can be defined in various ways:

*   markets in countries classified by the World Bank as low or middle income, and
*   markets with a stock market capitalisation of less than 2% of the total world market capitalisation.

The attractions of investing in emerging markets comprise:

*   **Rapid economic growth** – developing nations tend to grow at faster rates of economic growth than developed nations, as they attempt to catch up with rich country living standards, by developing their infrastructure and financial systems. This process is assisted by domestic saving rates being generally higher than in developed nations and the embracing of world trade and foreign direct investment (FDI). Rapid economic growth tends to translate into rapid profits growth.

- **Low correlation of returns** – emerging markets offer significant diversification benefits when held with developed market investments, owing to the historically low correlation of returns between emerging and developed markets. However, it should be noted that when a major financial shock occurs, such as the credit crunch, the correlation of returns between developed and emerging markets can increase suddenly.
- **Attractive valuations** – emerging markets have historically traded at a discount to developed market valuations.
- **Industry representation** – investors are able to gain exposure to industries not represented in developed nations.
- **Inefficient pricing** – as emerging markets are not as well researched as their developed counterparts, pricing anomalies often appear.

However, there are also significant drawbacks:

- **Lack of transparency** – the quality and transparency of information is generally lower than for developed nations while accounting and other standards are generally not as comprehensive or as rigorously applied.
- **Regulation** –regulation is generally more lax in emerging than in developed markets and incidents of insider trading and fraud by local investors more prevalent. Corporate governance also tends to be lacking.
- **Volatility** – emerging market performances have been more volatile than those of developed markets owing to factors such as developing nations being less politically stable and more susceptible to banking and other financial crises.
- **Settlement and custodial problems** – the logistics of settling transactions and then arranging for custody of the securities purchased can be fraught with difficulty. In addition, property rights are not as well defined as in developed nations. However, these problems can be mitigated by using global depositary receipts (GDRs).
- **Liquidity** – as emerging markets are less liquid, or more concentrated, than their developed counterparts, investments in these markets tend not to be as readily marketable and, therefore, tend to trade on wider spreads.
- **Currencies** – emerging market currencies tend to be less stable than those of developed nations and periodically succumb to crises, resulting from sudden significant outflows of overseas investor capital.
- **Controls on foreign ownership** – some developing nations impose restrictions on foreign ownership of particular industries and use taxation to limit foreign investment in certain sectors.
- **Taxation** – emerging market returns may be subject to local taxes that may not be reclaimable under double taxation treaties.
- **Repatriation** – there may be severe problems in repatriating capital and/or income from investments made in some emerging markets. Moreover, new rules governing the repatriation of capital can be suddenly introduced – for example, due to a run on the domestic currency.

4. Foreign Exchange (FX)

4.1 Structure of the Foreign Exchange (FX) Market

Learning Objective

7.4.1 Understand the basic structure and operation of the foreign exchange market: market place; OTC market; cross rates; settlement system; interest rates; effect of demand for goods; effect of exchange rate changes

The foreign exchange, or forex, market exists to serve a variety of needs from companies and institutions purchasing overseas assets denominated in currencies different to their own, to satisfying the foreign currency needs of business travellers and holidaymakers.

The increasing globalisation of financial markets has seen explosive growth in the movement of international capital. Over $3 trillion a day flows through world foreign exchange centres, with over a third of this turnover passing through London alone. Despite the introduction of the euro, the world's most heavily traded currency remains the US dollar, the world's premier reserve, or safe haven, currency.

The forex market does not have a centralised marketplace. Instead, it comprises an international network of major banks, each making a market in a range of currencies in a truly internationalised 24-hour market.

Each bank advertises its latest prices, or rates of exchange, through commercial quote vendors and conducts deals on either Reuters 2002, an automated broking system, or via an electronic broking system (EBS).

4.1.1 Quotes, Spreads and Exchange Rate Information

All foreign exchange quotations involve specifying an exchange rate/relationship between two currencies.

When one currency is quoted in terms of another, the former is known as the base currency (X) and the latter, the quoted currency (Y). The exchange rate given by X/Y represents the value of one unit of the base currency in terms of the quoted currency.

In the spot market, the base currency is usually the US dollar. However, when sterling is quoted against the US dollar, sterling is the base currency and the US dollar is the quoted currency. So, £1 is quoted in terms of its value in dollars rather than $1 being quoted in terms of its value in pounds. This same approach is used for the euro.

As a general rule of thumb, exchange rates around the world are often quoted against the US dollar. However a great amount of trading takes place between currencies which do not include the US dollar. Technically speaking, a cross rate is any foreign currency rate that does not include the US dollar. For example, the GBP/JPY (Great Britain pound/Japanese yen) is a cross rate.

A currency pair is the quotation of the relative value of a currency unit against the unit of another currency in the foreign exchange market. The currency that is used as the reference is called the counter currency or quote currency and the currency that is quoted in relation is called the base currency or transaction currency.

Currency pairs are written by concatenating currency codes, which are formalised in ISO 4217, of the base currency and the counter currency, separating them with a slash character.

A widely traded currency pair is the euro against the US dollar which is designated as EUR/USD. The quotation EUR/USD 1.2500 means that one euro is exchanged for 1.2500 US dollars.

The most traded currency pairs in the world are called the **Majors**. They involve the euro, US dollar, Japanese yen, pound sterling, Australian dollar, Canadian dollar, and the Swiss franc.

The convention in the spot market is for the exchange rate to be quoted as a mid-rate and then a bid-offer spread around this mid-rate. The mid-rate is the mid-point between the bid and offer prices. The bid price is the rate at which the quoted currency can be purchased with the base currency and the offer price the rate at which the quoted currency can be sold in exchange for the base currency.

Example

If the quotation of EUR/USD is 1.3607/1.3609, then the spread is USD 0.0002, or 2 pips. In general, markets with high liquidity exhibit smaller spreads than less frequently traded markets.

Currencies are traded in fixed contract sizes, specifically called lot sizes, or multiples thereof. The standard lot size is 100,000 units of the base currency. Retail brokerage firms also offer 10,000 units or mini-lots. Leverage is widely employed in forex trading and it is not uncommon for brokerage accounts to offer leverage of up to 200:1, which can be quite dangerous for the retail investor considering the volatility of many currency pairs.

4.2   Spot and Forward Rates

Learning Objective

7.4.2   Understand the difference between spot and forward exchange rates: settlement periods; effect of interest rates

There are two types of transaction conducted on the foreign exchange market:

*   Spot transactions.
*   Forward transactions.

The spot rate is the rate quoted by a bank for the exchange of one currency for another immediately. Deals struck in the spot market are for delivery and settlement two business days after the date of the transaction, that is, on a T+2 basis.

The forward rate is the rate quoted by a bank for the exchange of one currency for another at some agreed future date. This allows companies or individuals entering into forward transactions to know how much an overseas currency will cost or generate in advance. This will enable them to plan and budget more accurately.

4.3   Spot Rates

Learning Objective

7.4.3   Understand the determinants of spot foreign exchange prices: currency demand – transactional and speculative; economic variables; cross-border trading of financial assets; interest rates; free and pegged rates

The users of the foreign exchange market fall into two broad camps:

*   **Transactional** – settling accounts for international trade.
*   **Speculative** – including arbitrageurs and financial engineers using derivatives.

4.3.1   Currency Demand

Foreign exchange transactions are partly driven by international trade. Trade can be in either goods or services. Using the wider definition of trade, to include financial services and financial instruments such as bonds, helps to explain the bulk of the transactional component to the movements in exchange rates.

From a traditional product perspective, if, for example, a Japanese company sells goods to a US customer, they might invoice the transaction in US dollars. These dollars will need to be exchanged for Japanese yen by the Japanese company and this will require a foreign exchange transaction. The Japanese company may not be expecting to receive the dollars for a month after submission of the invoice. This gives them two choices:

- they can wait until they receive the dollars and then execute a spot transaction, or
- they can enter into a forward transaction to sell the dollars for yen in a month's time. This will provide them with certainty as to the number of yen they will receive and assist in their budgeting efforts.

Spot foreign exchange dealings are those which occur with immediate effect, if the transaction is settled with reference to the actual or real-time pricing of foreign currencies in the highly liquid foreign exchange market.

Another major factor which accounts for foreign exchange transactions is speculative transactions. If an investor felt that the US dollar was likely to weaken against the euro, he or she could buy the euro from the proceeds of selling dollars in either the spot or forward market to profit if he or she is right.

Other ways in which the foreign exchange market provides speculative opportunities are in relation to very small arbitrage opportunities related to interest rate differentials between two or more countries.

Other speculative activities in foreign exchange are related to complex derivative products and swaps created through financial engineering, and even those will be more focused on the forward market in foreign exchange, these will impact the spot market.

In the spot market, the base currency is usually the US dollar. However, when sterling is quoted against the US dollar, sterling is the base currency and the US dollar is the quoted currency. So, £1 is quoted in terms of its value in dollars rather than $1 being quoted in terms of its value in pounds.

Generally, exchange rates around the world are quoted against the US dollar. A s stated in Section 4.1.1, a cross rate is technically any foreign currency rate that does not include the US dollar, however the term has become more loosely used to describe the exchange rate between any currency pair.

Speculators and traders in currencies can participate in the forex market by opening accounts with brokers who will enable them to do one or more of the following:

- Trade in the spot market with or without leverage.
- Trade in the futures markets for currencies which are listed on some futures exchanges, eg, the Chicago Mercantile Exchange (CME).
- Trade via a derivative such as an exchange traded fund or via a spread betting instrument.

4.3.2 Economic Variables and Global Capital Flows

When looking at the fundamental factors which help to determine exchange rates, the demand and supply considerations which arise through international trade and, to some extent, speculation, will be much influenced by macro-economic factors within both the world economy and the economies of the two countries for which a particular exchange rate is being determined.

The key factors are as follows.

- **World Demand and Global GDP**
  - During recessions and periods of slow economic growth, there will be less international trade, as was the experience in 2009 in the aftermath of the 2008 banking crisis. This will tend to affect all countries and thus not greatly influence any specific currency.
- **Safe-Haven Currencies**
  - During times of economic and financial stress, the US dollar, Swiss franc and Japanese yen have proven to be the most sought-after currencies. It is also fair to say that the so-called commodity currencies, such as the Australian and Canadian dollar, will tend to fall in value against the US dollar especially as the demand for commodities falls and as these currencies are seen as less 'safe'.
- **Debt/GDP Ratios**
  - Global capital flows for the purchase of government debt are increasingly affecting global exchange rates.
  - Those countries or currency unions, in the case of the Eurozone, where the public debt/GDP is relatively high will, on the whole, attract less capital for their respective bond markets and the currencies will under-perform those countries with lower debt/GDP ratios.
  - This is more complex than it appears as a country like the UK which has a high debt/GDP ratio also has a separate currency which it can manage internally, whereas a country like Germany which has a lower debt/GDP ratio is part of the Eurozone and has seen the value of its currency – the euro – fall more with respect to the dollar, as a result of the high debt/GDP ratios of its other Eurozone partners.
- **Interest Rates and the Carry Trade**
  - One of the principal driving factors for speculative capital flows is to exploit interest rate differentials between countries. This has given rise to what is called the forex 'carry trade'.
  - In essence, large institutional investors will borrow funds in a currency if there is a relatively low borrowing rate, eg, the yen, and will invest those funds, after converting to another currency such as Australian dollars if there is a higher rate of interest available for short-term deposits.
  - The spread between the borrowing cost and the interest earning rates motivates the trades but this will also affect the cross rates.
- **Economic Growth and Outlook**
  - Capital flows are a primary determinant of exchange rates. If an individual economy reveals positive economic fundamentals, such as a relatively high rate of annual GDP growth, low inflation and stable monetary policy this will prove more attractive to foreign investors than those economies which are stagnating and where there is a much more uncertain economic outlook.
- **Capital Account Flows**
  - There are considerable imbalances in the global trade of goods and services with many nations running large deficits on their visible trade accounts (ie, visible trade refers to the trade in products) and having to export more invisibles (eg, financial services) and also to attract capital flows from the large surplus nations.

4.3.3 Fixed and Floating Exchange Rates

The foreign exchange system which has emerged, for much of the global economy, in recent years has some elements of management of rates by central banks and governments, but is largely a system which is described as **free-floating**.

- Pure free float is where no government intervention takes place and only market forces' rates determine rates.
- The present-day system is largely based upon the activities of the large banks and other institutions which are conducting transactions between themselves in the forex market.
- The central banks can issue policy statements and from time to time may intervene directly into the market to buy or sell their currency or another currency from their reserves.
- Central banks will attempt to guide the markets with respect to determining factors such as interest rates, trade policies and other capital market incentives.

In contrast to (more or less) freely floating exchange rates there are alternative models which have been used historically.

- **Managed Floating** – if market forces are interspersed with intervention by government via central banks the term used is **managed floating**.
- **Fixed Exchange Rates** – the post-1945 era saw a period of rigid fixed exchange rates in which no floating was permitted. There was a rigid regulation of the market forces to ensure that currencies were pegged. This was less arduous in that era as there was nothing like the free movement of capital around the globe as seen today.

4.4 Forward Rates

Learning Objective

7.4.4 Be able to calculate forward exchange rates using: premiums and discounts; interest rate parity

The value of a currency can be described as a country's share price, as its value tends to reflect most aspects of a country's fortunes. This makes currencies probably the most unpredictable of all the asset classes and exchange rates one of the most difficult macroeconomic variables to forecast.

Although currencies very rarely go into terminal decline, they can under- and over-shoot their long-term fundamental values, often for significant periods of time, for a variety of economic and political reasons and in response to fickle changes in market sentiment. Currency forecasting can, therefore, be extremely hazardous.

4.4.1 Premiums and Discounts

Where interest rates are higher in the base currency (£) than the quoted currency ($), a premium between the spot and forward exchange rate is said to arise. When the opposite is true, a discount arises.

As a result of three-month interest rates in the UK being higher than those in the US, a premium might arise. This premium is given by the difference between the spot and forward rates of $1.5220 – $1.5157 = $0.0063 – (note: $ premiums and discounts are usually quoted in cents. Premiums are identified by the letters 'pm' and discounts 'dis').

As premiums imply that the quoted currency will strengthen over time, premiums are deducted from the spot exchange rate to derive the forward exchange rate while discounts, for the opposite reason, are added.

Market convention is for the spot rate to be quoted with the premium or discount, rather than for the forward rate to be quoted.

So, if the spot rate is $1.5220–$1.5226 and a three-month premium of 0.63c–0.57c is quoted then the three-month forward exchange rate will be:

Spot exchange rate	$1.5220–$1.5226
Three-months forward	0.63c–0.57c pm
Three-month forward exchange rate	$1.5157–$1.5169

4.4.2 Interest Rate Parity

The only unbiased estimate of a currency's future spot exchange rate can be obtained by establishing the forward exchange rate.

A forward exchange contract is an agreement between two parties to either buy or sell foreign currency at a fixed exchange rate for settlement at a future date. The forward exchange rate is the exchange rate set today even though the transaction will not settle until some agreed point in the future, such as in three months' time.

The relationship between the spot exchange rate and forward exchange rate for two currencies is simply given by the differential between their respective nominal interest rates over the term being considered. The relationship is purely mathematical and has nothing to do with market expectations.

The idea behind this relationship is embodied in the principle of interest rate parity and is expressed as follows.

$$\text{Forward rate for £: \$} = S_£ \times \left[\frac{(1 + R_\$)}{(1 + R_£)} \right]$$

or

$$\text{Forward rate for £: \$} = \text{Sterling Spot Rate} \times \left[\frac{(1 + \text{Dollar interest rate})}{(1 + \text{Sterling interest rate})} \right]$$

This principle is best illustrated by an example.

Example

The £:$ spot exchange rate = 1.5220. If the interest rate for the UK is 4.88% and for the US, 3.20%, what will the three-month forward exchange rate be?

As the interest rates are quoted on a per annum basis, they must be divided by four to obtain the rate of interest that will be payable (%) over three months:

Sterling: 4.88%/4 = 1.22%. Dollar: 3.20%/4 = 0.8%. Applying the interest rate parity formula:

$$\text{Forward rate for £:\$} = 1.5220 \times \left[\frac{(1 + 0.8\%)}{(1 + 1.22\%)} \right] = 1.5220 \times \frac{1.008}{1.0122} = \$1.5157$$

The forward exchange rate of $1.5157 in the example is lower than the spot exchange rate of $1.5220. That is, in three months' time, £1 will buy $1.5220 minus $1.5157 = $0.0063 fewer dollars. The dollar will strengthen against sterling. The reason for this is due to three-month interest rates in the UK being higher than those in the US.

If this relationship did not exist, then an arbitrage opportunity would arise between the spot and forward rates. Therefore, in order to prevent these arbitrage opportunities arising, the spot and forward exchange rates must be linked by the interest rate parity principle or by arbitrage pricing.

This is not to say, however, that the spot rate in three months' time will be the same as the three-month forward rate quoted today. The three-month forward rate in this example is simply an unbiased, or mathematically based, estimate, or the best guess, of the spot rate in three months' time.

4.5   Hedging Foreign Currency Exposure

There are many benefits to investing in overseas assets, particularly overseas equities, owing to the positive diversification effects that can result.

Currency risk can, however, either augment or detract from the return generated by the asset.

Foreign currency risk can be reduced, though not completely eliminated, by employing the following hedging instruments or strategies:

- Forward contracts.
- Back-to-back loans.
- Foreign currency options.
- Foreign currency futures.
- Currency swaps.

Exchange rate forecasting is an inexact science despite the existence of parity relationships and advances in forecasting techniques. Although when investing overseas currency hedging should be considered, like any other form of hedging the result is usually imperfect.

Depending on the method adopted, hedging strategies can also be costly to devise, time-consuming and sometimes inflexible. Indeed, research suggests that, on balance, hedging should be used when investing in overseas bonds but generally avoided when investing in a diversified portfolio of overseas equities denominated in a variety of currencies.

End of Chapter Questions

Think of an answer for each question and refer to the appropriate workbook section for confirmation.

1. Describe six key features of financial markets.
   Answer reference: Section 1.1

2. What are the UK settlement conventions for gilts and corporate bonds?
   Answer reference: Sections 2.1.1, 2.2.2 and 2.2

3. How do order-driven and quote-driven markets differ?
   Answer reference: Section 2.2

4. The order book for ABC shares is as follows:

Buy Queue		Sell Queue	
We will buy for at least		We will sell for at least	
7,000 shares	£1.24	3,550 shares	£1.25
5,150 shares	£1.23	1,984 shares	£1.26
19,250 shares	£1.22	75,397 shares	£1.26
44,000 shares	£1.22	17,300 shares	£1.27

   If an investor places a fill or kill order to buy 5000 shares with a limit of 125, what will happen to the order?
   Answer reference: Section 2.4

5. When is SDRT charged?
   Answer reference: Section 2.5

6. What does the term 'cross rate' in the foreign exchange market, when used in its precise sense, mean?
   Answer reference: Section 4.1.1

7. If the spot rate for sterling against the US dollar is $1.5420 – $1.5426 and a three-month premium of 0.63c – 0.57c is quoted, then what would be the quotation for the three-month forward exchange rate?
   Answer reference: Section 4.4.1

8. If the sterling/US dollar spot exchange rate is $1.5500 and the three-month interest rate for the UK is 1.35% and for the US, 0.65%, what will the three-month forward exchange rate be?
   Answer reference: Section 4.4.2

Chapter Eight
Accounting

This syllabus area will provide approximately 10 of the 80 examination questions

1. Basic Principles

Financial statements summarise all transactions entered into by a company during its accounting period.

Companies are subject to strict time limits within which their report and accounts must be published. The Companies Acts specifically require private limited companies to publish their financial accounts within nine months of the relevant accounting reference period, and within six months for public companies.

These statements must be presented at the company's AGM and filed with the Registrar of Companies. Small and medium-sized companies may file abbreviated accounts.

1.1 The Legal Requirement to Prepare Accounts

Learning Objective

8.1.1 Understand and be able to apply the legal requirements to prepare accounts and the differences between private and public company requirements: responsibility for preparation; accounting standards board; required information in accounts

Under the Companies Acts, the directors of a company are legally required to prepare financial statements and make other disclosures within an annual report and accounts.

The format of those statements and disclosures is based on standards issued by the Accounting Standards Board (ASB).

These set out the results of the company's activities during its most recent accounting period and its financial position as at the end of the period. An accounting period typically spans a 12-month period.

The amount of information contained in the company's report and accounts and the requirement for its independent verification, or audit, depends upon whether the company is categorised by the Companies Acts as being:

- a small, medium or larger private limited company (Ltd), or
- a public limited company (PLC).

To qualify as either a small or medium-sized private limited company, at least two of the following three size criteria must not have been exceeded in the current and preceding accounting period:

	Small	Medium
Turnover	£6.5m	£25.9m
Total assets	£3.26m	£12.9m
Average number of employees	50	250

If a company qualifies as either a small or medium-sized company over two successive accounting periods, then it will automatically qualify as such in the accounting period that immediately follows.

Small Companies

Small companies are not subject to an independent audit of their accounting information or required to publish an accompanying auditors' report. Under certain conditions they may also be exempt from producing a director's report.

Medium-Sized Companies

Medium-sized companies must, in addition to the other information detailed above, also publish a cash flow statement within their annual report and accounts. This financial statement identifies how a company's financial resources have been generated over the accounting period and how they have been applied, or expended. The Companies Acts also require explanatory notes to the cash flow statement to appear in the company's accounts.

Medium-sized private limited companies and those small private limited companies that are subject to an audit are required to publish an abridged auditors' report, termed a **special auditors' report**.

Public Limited Companies (PLCs)

In addition to the above requirements, public listed companies with a full stock market listing must also incorporate the following within their annual report and accounts:

- A statement of changes in equity. This financial statement details all profits made and losses incurred by the equity holders of the company over the accounting period, whether realised or not. It also reflects any dividends paid to the shareholders during the period. Since dividends paid to shareholders are an appropriation of profit rather than an expense against profit, dividends paid are not reflected in the income statement, but in the statement of changes in equity. Accounting standards allow the details to be presented as a 'statement of recognised income and expenses' instead of a full statement of changes in equity.
- An operating and financial review (OFR) which provides a narrative on the company's performance and prospects, consistent with the company's accounts.
- Additional disclosures required under the UKLA's listing rules including whether the company has complied with the UK corporate governance code in discharging its corporate governance responsibilities and whether the company has issued shares or warrants to investors, other than its ordinary shareholders, following the passing of a special resolution.

Many listed companies voluntarily provide additional information about their strategy, business performance and financial management. These are encapsulated in a chairman's statement, a chief executive's review and a finance director's report, respectively. Some now also provide a detailed environmental report of their activities.

Listed companies must also publish a half yearly, or interim, set of report and accounts. Apart from not being subject to a full independent audit, they do not contain as much information about the company's activities as the annual report and accounts.

1.2 The Framework for Financial Statements

Learning Objective

8.1.2 Understand the objectives and qualitative characteristics of accounts: decision-useful information; relevance; faithful representation; comparability; verifiability; understandability; timeliness; materiality

The International Accounting Standards Board (IASB) has issued guidance on financial statements in a document known as the *Framework for the Preparation and Presentation of Financial Statements*.

The framework describes the basic concepts by which financial statements are prepared and it:

- defines the objectives of financial statements
- identifies the qualitative characteristics that make information in financial statements useful, and
- defines the basic elements of financial statements and the concepts for recognising and measuring them.

1.2.1 The Objectives of Financial Statements

The management of a business has the primary responsibility for preparing and presenting its financial statements and the objective of these is to provide information about the financial position, performance and changes in financial position of a business that is useful to a wide range of users in making economic decisions.

- **Financial position** – is affected by the economic resources it controls, its financial structure, its liquidity and solvency, and its capacity to adapt to changes in the environment in which it operates. This information is contained in the balance sheet.
- **Performance** – is the ability of an entity to earn a profit on the resources that have been invested in it. Information about this is provided in the income statement and in a further financial statement, the statement showing changes in equity.
- **Changes in financial position** – information about the investing, financing and operating activities that a business has undertaken during the reporting period is contained in the cash flow statement. This information helps in assessing how well the entity is able to generate cash and cash equivalents and how it uses those cash flows. Notes and supplementary schedules – should be used to:
  - Explain items in the balance sheet and income statement.
  - Disclose the risks and uncertainties affecting the business.
  - Explain any resources and obligations not recognised in the balance sheet.

The framework also sets out the underlying assumptions of financial statements:

- **Accrual basis** – the effects of transactions and other events are recognised when they occur, rather than when cash or its equivalent is received or paid, and they are reported in the financial statements of the periods to which they relate.
- **Going concern** – the financial statements presume that an entity will continue in operation indefinitely or, if that presumption is not valid, disclosure and a different basis of reporting are required.

The accruals concept requires revenue and the associated costs to be shown in the period they are earned or incurred, not in the period they are received.

For example, a company has a financial year end of 30 June. It invoices £5,000 for work undertaken in early June but the invoice is not paid until July, in other words in the next financial year. The revenue from this work is accounted for in the current year, even though the money is not received until the next one.

1.2.2 The Qualitative Characteristics of Financial Statements

The framework addresses general purpose financial statements that a business prepares and presents at least annually, to meet the common information needs of a wide range of external users.

The principal classes of users are present and potential investors, employees, lenders, suppliers and other trade creditors, customers, governments and their agencies and the general public. All of these categories of users rely on financial statements to help them in decision-making.

As investors are providers of risk capital, financial statements that meet their needs will also meet most of the general financial information needs of other users.

The framework provides that information should be presented in a way that is readily understandable by users who have a reasonable knowledge of business and economic activities and accounting and who are willing to study the information with reasonable diligence.

The principles that should be followed in the presentation of the financial statements should address:

- Relevance of the information.
- Reliability of the information.
- Comparability with earlier periods.

Relevant information enables users to make economic decisions and the financial statements assist, both by helping them evaluate past, present and future events and by confirming or correcting past evaluations they have made. To be relevant, information should also be material and timely. Information is material if its omission or mis-statement could influence the economic decisions of users. To be useful, information must be provided to users within the time period in which it is most likely to bear on their decisions.

Information in financial statements is reliable if it is free from material error and bias and can be depended upon by users to represent events and transactions faithfully. Financial statements, however, have to use estimates, and the uncertainty surrounding these is dealt with by disclosure and by exercising prudence. Prudence is the inclusion of a degree of caution, in the exercise of the judgements needed, in making the estimates required under conditions of uncertainty, such that assets or income are not overstated and liabilities or expenses are not understated.

Users must also be able to compare the financial statements of a business over time, so that they can identify trends in its financial position and performance. They will also want to be able to compare the financial statements of different businesses, so disclosure of accounting policies is important for comparability.

1.2.3 The Elements of Financial Statements

Financial statements portray the financial effects of transactions and other events by grouping them into broad classes, according to their economic characteristics. These broad classes are termed the elements of financial statements.

The elements directly related to financial position are contained in the statement of financial position and are:

- **Assets** – a resource controlled by the business and from which future economic benefits are expected to flow.
- **Liabilities** – a present obligation of the entity, the settlement of which is expected to result in an outflow from the business.
- **Equity** – the residual interest in the assets of the business after deducting all its liabilities.

The elements directly related to performance (income statement) are:

- **Income** – increases in economic benefits during the accounting period, in the form of inflows or enhancements of assets or decreases of liabilities that result in increases in equity. It includes both revenue and gains. It excludes contributions from equity participants.
- **Expenses** – decreases in economic benefits during the accounting period in the form of outflows, depletion of assets or liabilities that result in decreases in equity. It includes losses as well as those expenses that arise in the ordinary course of business. Again it excludes distributions to equity participants.

The cash flow statement reflects both income statement elements and some changes in balance sheet elements.

Having defined what the content of financial statements should be, the framework defines when they should be recognised in the financial statements. Recognition is the process of incorporating in the balance sheet or income statement an item that meets the definition of an element and satisfies the following criteria for recognition:

- it is probable that any future economic benefit associated with the item will flow to or from the business, and
- the item's cost or value can be measured with reliability.

Measurement involves assigning monetary amounts at which the elements of the financial statements are to be recognised and reported. The framework acknowledges that a variety of measurement bases are used today to different degrees and in varying combinations in financial statements, including:

- Historical cost.
- Current cost.
- Net realisable (settlement) value.
- Present value (discounted).

Historical cost is the measurement basis most commonly used today, but it is usually combined with other measurement bases. The framework does not include concepts or principles for selecting which measurement basis should be used for particular elements of financial statements or in particular circumstances. Individual standards and interpretations do provide this guidance.

1.3 Accounting Standards

Learning Objective

8.1.3 Understand the function and purpose of: The Accounting Standards Board (ASB); International Accounting Standards Board (IASB); International Financial Reporting Standards (ifrss)

The form and content of all UK company financial statements and their respective disclosures are prescribed by the Companies Acts and mandatory accounting standards are set by the UK Accounting Standards Board (ASB).

The objectives of the ASB include establishing and improving standards of financial accounting and reporting, issuing new accounting standards as business practices evolve, and addressing urgent accounting issues. These objectives are designed to support investor, market and public confidence in the financial and governance stewardship of listed entities. It also works with the international accounting standards board (IASB), with national standard-setters and relevant EU institutions on the development and adoption of IASB standards.

The IASB aims to harmonise the way that accounts are presented, regardless of international boundaries. International accounting standards (IASs) comprise international financial reporting standards (IFRSs), which are issued by the IASB, together with an earlier set of IASs which were set by an earlier organisation from 1973 onwards.

All companies listed on EU stock exchanges are required to prepare their financial statements in conformity with these international accounting standards. IAS 1 'Presentation of Financial Statements' sets out the overall framework for presenting financial statements.

The objective of IAS 1 (2007) is to prescribe the basis for presentation of general purpose financial statements, to ensure comparability both with the entity's financial statements of previous periods and with the financial statements of other entities. IAS 1 sets out the overall requirements for the presentation of financial statements, guidelines for their structure and minimum requirements for their content. Measures for recognising, measuring, and disclosing specific transactions are addressed in other standards and interpretations.

In addition to accounting standards, there is a guiding principle that overrides every other in the preparation of UK company accounts. This is the legal requirement under the Companies Acts that the accounts must provide a 'true and fair view' of the company's results and financial position. Financial reporting Standard (FRS) 18 contains a provision that allows directors to depart from mandatory disclosure requirements and accounting regulations, if failure to do so prevents a true and fair view being given.

1.4　The Auditors' Report

Learning Objective

8.1.4　Understand the purpose of the auditors' report and the reasons why reports are modified: independent assessment; modified reports

Companies whose accounts are subject to a statutory independent audit must appoint, or reappoint, an auditor at the company's AGM to carry out an independent assessment of the company's accounts prepared by the directors.

The audit report must:

- Identify to whom the report is addressed.
- Identify the financial statements being audited.
- Contain a section covering the responsibilities of the:
  - auditor – to express an opinion;
  - directors – to prepare the accounts and accept responsibility for their truth, fairness and compliance with the Companies Act.
- Indicate the basis of the auditor's opinion, ie, the adherence to auditing standards, description of the audit process such as audit testing done and consideration of the appropriateness of accounting policies used.
- State that the auditor has planned and performed the audit in such a way as to obtain reasonable assurance that the financial statements are free from material error or mis-statement, however arising.
- Contain an audit opinion on the statement of financial position at the period end and the profit or loss and cash flows for the period.

The audit report gives an opinion on whether or not the accounts give a true and fair view of the company's activities and financial position and whether they have been prepared in accordance with the Companies Acts and mandatory accounting standards. If so, then an unqualified audit report is issued. If not, then the auditor must modify the report.

These modified reports fall into two categories:

- **Limitation of scope of the audit** – where there has been a limitation on the scope of the auditor's work, that prevents him from obtaining sufficient evidence to give an unqualified opinion.
- **Adverse opinion** – where the auditor disagrees with an accounting treatment or a view made in the statements, which the directors refuse to amend.

The importance of the qualification also falls into two categories:

- **Material**
  - Where the auditor has material disagreement with the treatment adopted by the directors or a material uncertainty that limits the scope of the audit opinion. The effect of the disagreement or limit in scope is not so material to require an adverse or disclaimer of opinion.

○ The reader's view of the accounts in specifically stated parts would be altered by this limitation or disagreement.

- **Fundamental**
  ○ The limitation or disagreement is so material as to render the whole accounts meaningless.

As a result, there are four possible styles of qualification, each of which will attract a slightly different wording in the auditor's report. The table below shows the form of wording that will be used when the auditor is stating his opinion.

	Limitation of Scope	Disagreement
Material	Give a true and fair view except for	Give a true and fair view except for
Fundamental	Unable to express an opinion (disclaimer of opinion)	Do not give a true and fair view (adverse opinion)

In all cases, the auditor will state what he/she is uncertain about or disagrees with.

1.5 Summary of Reporting Requirements

Reporting requirement	Private limited companies			Plcs
	Small	Medium	Large	All
Balance sheet	Yes	Yes	Yes	Yes
Income statement	Yes	Yes	Yes	Yes
Directors' report	No	Yes	Yes	Yes
Cash flow statement	No	Yes	Yes	Yes
Auditors' report	Special auditors' report if above certain size and turnover	Special auditors' report	Yes	Yes
Disclosure of accounting policies	Yes	Yes	Yes	Yes
Explanatory notes	Yes	Yes	Yes	Yes
Comparative figures	Yes	Yes	Yes	Yes
Statement of changes in equity	No	No	No	Listed PLCs only
Disclosures required by UKLA Listing Rules	No	No	No	Listed PLCs only

2. The Statement of Financial Position

As mentioned earlier, IAS 1 'Presentation of Financial Statements' sets out the overall framework for presenting financial statements. The International Accounting Standards Board (IASB) has reissued IAS 1 and made changes to the presentation and the terminology used. The revised IAS standard is effective for annual periods beginning on or after 1 January 2009 and has changed the name of the balance sheet to a 'statement of financial position'.

2.1 Purpose and Main Content

Learning Objective

8.2.1   Understand the purpose and main contents of the balance sheet: company's financial position; fixed assets; current assets; current liabilities; long-term borrowing; issued share capital; capital reserves; revenue reserves

The statement of financial position (also known as the balance sheet) provides a snapshot of a company's financial position, as at its accounting year end, by summarising the assets it owns and how these are financed. It is often described as being a photograph of the company's financial position in that it doesn't tell the user anything about the company either immediately before or immediately after its date, only at this one point in time.

The purpose of the financial statements is described in the ASB Statement of Principles for Financial Reporting as follows:

- The objective of financial statements is to provide information about the reporting entity's financial performance and financial position that is useful to a wide range of users for assessing the stewardship of the entity's management and for making economic decisions.
- The objective of financial statements can usually be met by focusing exclusively on the needs of present and potential investors. Such investors need information about financial performance and financial position that is useful to them in evaluating the reporting entity's ability to generate cash and in assessing the entity's financial adaptability.
- Financial statements do not provide all the information needed by users; they do, however, provide a frame of reference against which users can evaluate the more specific information they obtain from other sources.

The statement of the financial position of a PLC is shown next in a format prescribed by the Companies Acts.

Although not shown in the example, the format requires the previous year's comparative statement of financial position numbers to be set out alongside those of the current year and for a numerical reference to be inserted in the notes column, to support explanatory notes to the various balance sheet items.

The top half of the statement which records the total net assets owned by the company is as folllows.

ABC plc			
Consolidated Statement of Financial Position			
		As at 31 December	
	Notes	2011 (£m)	2010 (£m)
Assets			
Non-current assets			
Property, plant and equipment		8900	
Intangible assets		1800	
Investments in associates		300	
Assets available for sale		300	
		11300	
Current Assets			
Inventories		3600	
Trade and other receivables		2600	
Investments held for trading		120	
Cash		860	
		7180	
Total Assets		18480	

The bottom half of the statement which reflects shareholders' funds and liabilities is shown below.

		As at 31 December	
	Notes	2011 (£m)	2010 (£m)
Equity			
Capital and reserves			
Share capital – 50p ordinary shares		5000	
Share capital – preference shares		100	
Share premium account		120	
Revaluation reserve		100	
Capital redemption reserve		80	
Retained earnings		6880	
Total Equity		12280	
Liabilities			
Non-Current Liabilities			
Bank loans		2000	
		2000	
Current Liabilities			
Trade and other payables		4200	
		4200	
Total Liabilities		6200	
Total Equity and Liabilities		18480	

As you can see from the example statement, the construction of the statement of financial position is underpinned by the accounting equation:

Assets = Liabilities + Equity

In other words, the balance sheet 'balances'.

Other versions on this equation are:

- Net assets (total assets less liabilities) = Shareholders funds
- Assets – Liabilities = Share capital + Reserves
- Assets = Liabilities + Share capital + Reserves

2.2 Assets

Learning Objective

8.2.2   Understand how assets are classified and valued: investments/long term investments; tangibles; intangibles; pre-payments; stocks/work in progress; trade receivables; directors loans; land/buildings; machinery

8.2.3   Be able to apply the difference between capitalising costs and expensing costs

An asset is anything that is owned and controlled by the company and confers the right to future economic benefits. Assets are categorised as either **non-current assets** or **current assets**.

2.2.1   Non-Current Assets

Non-current assets are alternatively called fixed assets or 'long-lived assets'. They are those assets used within the business to generate revenue on a continuing basis, rather than being purchased for immediate resale. They, therefore, represent capital expenditure made by the company. Fixed assets are categorised as either:

- Tangible.
- Intangible.
- Investments.

As shown on the example statement, fixed assets can also be classified as assets held for sale. This is where their value is to be realised principally through a sale transaction and a sale is considered highly probable.

Tangible Fixed Assets

A company's tangible fixed assets are those that have physical substance, such as land and buildings and plant and machinery. Tangible fixed assets are alternatively referred to as 'property, plant and equipment'.

Property, Plant and Equipment are physical assets that are used within the business over a number of years with a view to deriving some benefit from their use, eg, through their use in the manufacture of goods for resale.

It includes such items as

- freehold land and buildings
- leasehold land and buildings
- plant and machinery
- motor vehicles
- fixtures and fittings.

In accordance with IAS 16 Property, Plant and Equipment and the historic cost convention, tangible fixed assets are initially recorded in the statement of financial position at their actual cost.

This actual cost includes any additional costs directly attributable in bringing the asset into its working condition, such as the delivery costs, installation costs, and other costs associated with financing the purchase of the asset. Since these costs are not expenses to the income statement in the accounting period in which they were incurred, but are included on the balance sheet as assets, they are known as **capitalised costs**.

IAS 16 allows a choice of accounting. Under the **cost model**, the asset continues to be carried at cost. Under the alternative **revaluation model** the asset can be carried at a revalued amount, with revaluation required to be carried out at regular intervals.

Intangible Fixed Assets

Intangible fixed assets are those assets which, although without physical substance, can be separately identified and are capable of being realised.

Intangibles are literally assets without physical form. They frequently represent intellectual property rights of the company that enable it to operate and generate profits in a way that competitors cannot.

The types of intangible assets that most frequently appear on the statement of financial position are:

- Development expenditure.
- Patents, licences and trademarks.
- Publishing rights and titles.
- Goodwill.
- Brands.

Ownership of an intangible fixed asset confers certain rights. These rights give a company a competitive advantage over its peers and commonly include brand names, patents, trademarks and purchased goodwill.

Investments

Fixed asset investments are typically long term investments held in other companies.

They are initially recorded in the balance sheet at cost, and then subsequently revalued to their fair value at each period end. Any gains or losses are reflected directly in the equity section of the balance sheet and disclosed in the statement of changes in equity. However, if they suffer an impairment in value, then such a fall is charged to the income statement.

If the shareholding represents at least 20% of the issued share capital of the company in which the investment is held, or if the investing company exercises significant influence over the management policies of the other, then the investing company is subject to additional reporting requirements.

2.2.2 Current Assets

Current assets are those assets purchased with the intention of resale or conversion into cash, usually within a 12-month period.

They are therefore known as revenue items and include stocks of goods, the debtor balances that arise from the company providing its customers with credit and any short-term investments held.

Current assets also include cash balances held by the company and pre-payments.

Current assets are listed in the statement of financial position in descending order of liquidity and typically appear at the lower of cost or net realisable value (NRV).

Strictly speaking, current assets are all assets other than non-current assets. They are probably better thought of as those assets held for conversion into cash in the ordinary course of business.

Current assets are categorised into the following:

*   **Inventory** – goods held available for sale.
*   **Accounts receivable** – amounts owed to the company, perhaps as a result of selling goods on credit (often referred to as trade receivables).
*   **Investments** – shares held in the short term with the intention of reselling, eg, short-term speculative investments.
*   **Cash** – either held physically or by a financial institution such as a bank.

Accounting for Stock

NRV is defined as the estimated selling price of each stock item, less any further costs to be incurred in both bringing the stock, work in progress or raw materials into a saleable condition, including any associated selling and marketing costs.

Therefore, if for reasons such as obsolescence, the NRV of the stock has fallen below cost, the item must be written down to this NRV for statement reporting purposes.

Determining what constitutes cost should be relatively straightforward unless the company purchases vast quantities of stock in different batches throughout its accounting period, making the identification of individual items or lines of stock particularly difficult when attempting to match sales against purchases.

In such instances, cost can be determined by making an assumption about the way stock flows through the business. Companies can account for their stock on one of three ways:

- **First in first out (FIFO)** – FIFO assumes that the stock first purchased by the business is the first to be sold. Therefore, the value of the closing stock at the end of the accounting period is given by the cost of the most recent stock purchased. This produces a closing stock figure in the balance sheet that closely resembles the current market value of the stock. It also results in the highest reported profit figure of the three bases, in times of rising prices.
- **Last in first out (LIFO)** – LIFO assumes that the most recent stock purchased by the company is the first to be sold. IAS 2 does not permit the use of LIFO since, in times of rising prices, the statement of financial position value of closing stock will be that of the stock first purchased and will, therefore, not resemble current prices. It also produces the lowest reported profit figure of the three bases.
- **Weighted average cost (AVCO)** – AVCO values closing stock at the weighted average cost of stock purchased throughout the accounting period. This method produces a closing stock figure and a reported profit between that of the FIFO and LIFO methods.

2.3 Impairment and Amortisation

Learning Objective

8.2.4   Understand how goodwill and other intangible assets arise and are treated: types of intangibility (eg, trademarks, patents, client relations); calculation upon acquisition; amortisation; impairment; capitalisation

The accounting treatment of goodwill is detailed in IFRS 3 'Business Combinations' and for other intangible fixed assets is prescribed by IAS 38 Intangible Assets.

The main provisions of these standards are as follows:

- Intangible fixed assets that have been purchased separately, such as brand names, are capitalised in the statement of financial position at their cost of purchase.
- If purchased as the result of taking over another company, however, they can only be capitalised as a separately identifiable intangible fixed asset if their value can be reliably measured.
- Otherwise their value is subsumed within purchased goodwill.
- If capitalised, intangible fixed assets are accounted for like tangible fixed assets – either under the 'cost model' or the 'revaluation model'.
- The equivalent of depreciation of tangible fixed assets is the 'amortisation' of intangible fixed assets.
- Purchased goodwill arises when the consideration, or price, paid by the acquiring company for the target exceeds the fair value of the target's separable, or individually identifiable, net assets.
- Purchased goodwill = price paid for company – fair value of separable net tangible and intangible assets.
- Purchased goodwill is capitalised in the statement of financial position and IFRS 3 then requires it to be held on the statement of financial position and not subjected to regular amortisation charges.

- Instead, goodwill should be subjected to impairment reviews at least annually.
- Separately acquired trademarks and licences are shown at historical cost. They have a finite useful life and are carried at cost less accumulated amortisation. Amortisation is calculated using the straight-line method to allocate the cost of trademarks and licences over their estimated useful lives of 15 to 20 years.
- Intangible fixed assets that have been created internally by the company rather than being acquired, such as brand names, customer lists and the like, tend not to be capitalised in the balance sheet because their cost cannot be distinguished from the cost of developing the business as a whole.

However, certain costs incurred by the company, rather than being written off against the company's revenue in the income statement in the period in which they were incurred, can instead be capitalised as intangible fixed assets, if it can be shown that a future benefit will arise from the expenditure.

So as to meet with the accruals concept, this capitalised cost is then matched against the company's revenue in subsequent accounting periods, in line with the estimated flow of the expected future benefits to arise from the capitalised asset.

Most notable amongst these is the capitalisation of development expenditure. Development expenditure is that made on the application of technical know-how that is expected to result in improved products or processes and ultimately increased profits for the company.

Although any expenditure devoted to research must be written off in the accounting period in which it is incurred, IAS 38 permits development expenditure to be capitalised after technical and commercial feasibility of the resulting product or service have been established.

2.4 Depreciation

Learning Objective

8.2.5   Understand and be able to apply the different methods of depreciation and amortisation: straight line; reducing balance

The Companies Acts and IAS 16 require all tangible fixed assets with a limited economic life to be depreciated over this term. An annual depreciation charge is made to the income statement against the carrying value of the asset over the asset's useful economic life.

To calculate the annual depreciation charge to be applied to a tangible fixed asset, the difference between its carrying or 'book' value and estimated disposal value, termed the 'depreciable amount', must first be established. This value is then written off over the asset's remaining useful economic life, by employing the most appropriate depreciation method.

The two most common depreciation methods comprise:

- The straight line method, and
- The reducing balance method.

The **straight line method** is the simpler of the two methods, as it simply spreads the depreciable amount equally over the useful economic life of the asset. The straight line method is given by the following formula:

$$\text{Straight Line Depreciation} = \frac{(\text{Cost} - \text{Disposal Value})}{\text{Remaining Useful Economic Life (Years)}}$$

The **reducing balance method,** however, employs a more complex formula:

$$\text{Annual Depreciation} = 1 - \sqrt[n]{\frac{\text{Expected Residual Value}}{\text{Original Cost}}}$$

This method produces a depreciation percentage rate which, rather than being applied to the depreciable amount, is instead applied to book value of the asset. This results in a higher depreciation charge than the straight line method in the early years of the asset's life, but a lower charge in the later years. The total amount written off over the asset's useful economic life will be the same in both cases.

Which of the depreciation methods is the more appropriate depends on the type of asset being depreciated and its use in the business. The argument in favour of using the reducing balance method over the straight line method, is that, as tangible fixed assets tend to confer the greatest benefits in the earliest years of their use, these should be matched by a higher depreciation charge.

Once a depreciation method has been chosen, it must be consistently applied to similar assets and between successive accounting periods. The method may only be changed in order to present a fairer view of the company's results and financial position. A note to this effect must be disclosed in the company's accounts.

Example

A machine purchased for £24,500 has an estimated useful economic life of six years and an estimated disposal value after six years of £1,000. Calculate the depreciation that should be charged to this asset and its net book value (NBV) in years one to six, using:

1. The straight line depreciation method.
2. The reducing balance depreciation method.

Straight Line Depreciation

$$\frac{(24,500 - £1,000)}{6} = £3,916.67 \text{ per annum}$$

The depreciation charge will be the same in years one to six.

Reducing Balance Depreciation

$$1 - \sqrt[6]{\frac{£1,000}{£24,500}} = 41.32\%$$

The results can be seen in the following table:

Year	Straight Line Method		Reducing Balance Method	
	Depreciation charge (£)	NBV (£)	Depreciation charge (£)	NBV (£)
1	3,916.67	20,583.33	10,123.40	14,376.60
2	3,916.67	16,666.66	5,940.41	8,436.19
3	3,916.67	12,749.99	3,485.83	4,950.36
4	3,916.67	8,833.32	2,045.49	2,904.87
5	3,916.67	4,916.65	1,200.29	1,704.58
6	3,916.67	998.98	704.33	1,000.25
Total	23,500.02	–	23,499.75	–

On occasion, tangible fixed assets, such as land, are not depreciated because they are accounted for under the **revaluation model** allowed under IAS 16. The standard requires revaluations to be carried out with sufficient regularity so that the carrying amount does not differ materially from that which would be determined using fair value at the statement of financial position date. This provides the user of the accounts with a truer and fairer view of the assets, or capital, employed by the company. Any increase in the asset's value arising on revaluation is transferred to a revaluation reserve, which forms part of the equity section on the statement of financial position.

Investment properties are covered by separate provisions contained within IAS 40 Investment Properties. Investment properties are properties that are not owner-occupied and are held to earn rentals or for capital appreciation, or both. When properties are classified as investment properties, they are measured at fair value instead of being subjected to depreciation charges.

2.5 Liabilities

Learning Objective

8.2.6 Understand how liabilities are categorised: due in less than or more than one year; current liabilities; trade payables; bank overdraft; dividends due; tax due; non-current liabilities; debenture stock; long term loans

There are three broad categories of liabilities:

- **Creditors or payables** – these are known amounts owed by the company, eg, invoices received, bank overdrafts, and so on.
- **Accruals** – these are liabilities for which the timing of payment is generally known, but the amount to be paid is uncertain. Accruals normally arise from routine transactions of the business, either of an operating or financing nature.
- **Provisions** – a provision represents either an amount to account for the reduction in the value of an asset (eg, depreciation) or an estimate of a known but not exactly quantified liability, arising from something outside of the normal trading activities of a company.

Liabilities are categorised according to whether they are to fall due within or more than one year.

Current Liabilities

This balance includes the amount the company owes to its suppliers, or trade creditors, as a result of buying goods and/or services on credit, any bank overdraft and any dividends and/or tax payable within 12 months of the balance sheet date.

Current liabilities should fully reflect all liabilities payable within 12 months of the period end. They include bank overdrafts and taxation payable within one year, as well as amounts owed to suppliers known as trade payables.

Non-current Liabilities or Long-term Liabilities

This comprises the company's borrowing not repayable within the next 12 months. This could include debentures and/or loan stock issues as well as longer-term bank borrowing:

Non-current liabilities typically include such items as

- Long-term bank loans.
- Loan stock and debentures issued by the company.

Both must be repaid long term. It also includes any other known liabilities, such as trade payables that do not require settlement within the year.

A proposed dividend is not recognised as a liability in the statement of financial position at the year-end although it will be disclosed within the report and accounts. IAS 10 requires that proposed dividends are treated as non-adjusting events, arising after the statement of financial position date; they are not liabilities until declared by a resolution approved by shareholders at a general meeting.

2.6   Equity

Learning Objective

8.2.7   Understand the difference between authorised and issued share capital and capital reserves
and revenue reserves

As we saw above, the items shown on the statement of financial position under equity or shareholders' funds can include:

- Share capital.
- Share premium account.
- Revaluation reserve.
- Capital redemption reserve.
- Retained earnings.

Authorised and Issued Share Capital

When a company is created, the memorandum of association must state the amount of the share capital with which the company proposes to be registered and the division of that share capital into shares of a fixed amount. This capital amount is known as the authorised share capital and acts as a ceiling on the amount of shares that can be issued, although it can subsequently be increased by the passing of an ordinary resolution at a company meeting.

The issued share capital is the actual number of shares that are in issue at any point in time.

Under the Companies Act 2006, the requirement to have an authorised share capital has been removed. Instead, directors can be authorised by the articles or by a resolution to allot shares up to a maximum amount and for a limited period.

Capital Reserves

Capital reserves include the revaluation reserve, share premium reserve and capital redemption reserve.

- The revaluation reserve arises from the upward revaluation of fixed assets, both tangible and intangible.
- The share premium reserve arises from issuing shares at a price above their nominal value.
- The capital redemption reserve is created when a company redeems, or buys back, its shares and makes a transfer from its revenue reserves to its capital reserves, equal to the nominal value of the shares redeemed.

Capital reserves are not distributable to the company's shareholders as, apart from forming part of the company's capital base, they represent unrealised profits, though they can be converted into a bonus issue of ordinary shares.

Companies can issue shares at greater than their nominal value, in other words at a premium.

An example of this is a rights issue. For example, a company might raise £100 million by issuing new ordinary £1 shares at a price of £2.50 each. The premium is the difference between the nominal value of the ordinary shares and the price they are issued at which in this case is £1.50.

Under the Companies Act, the company must record the issue of these shares by increasing the ordinary share capital by only the nominal value of the shares issued, ie, £100 million. The premium of £150 million must be added to the share premium account.

Retained Earnings

Retained earnings is a revenue reserve and represents the accumulation of the company's distributable profits that have not been distributed to the company's shareholders as dividends, or transferred to a capital reserve, but have been retained in the business. You should not confuse this balance with the amount of cash the company holds or with the income statement that shows how the retained, or undistributed, profit in a single accounting period was arrived at.

2.7 Contingent Liabilities and Post Balance Sheet Events

Learning Objective

8.2.8 Understand contingent liabilities and post balance sheet events

The rules on provisions are set out in IAS 37 'Provisions, Contingent Liabilities and Contingent Assets'.

This creates a separate heading for provisions that have resulted from past events or transactions and for which there is an obligation to make a payment, but the exact amount or timing of the expenditure has yet to be established. Such provisions may arise as a result of the company undergoing a restructuring, for example.

Given the uncertainty surrounding the extent of such liabilities, IAS 37 requires the company to create a realistic and prudent estimate of the monetary amount of the obligation, once it is committed to taking a certain course of action.

Provisions cannot, however, be made in respect of possible but not probable future obligations that may arise on the occurrence of a future event: customers making claims on goods sold with warranties for instance. Given the unpredictable nature of these so-called contingent liabilities, the company's potential liability and the uncertainties surrounding this, where quantifiable, are instead disclosed by way of a note in the accounts.

IAS 10 sets out the procedures that are to be followed if there have been significant developments in the company's fortunes between the statement of financial position date and the directors approving and signing the accounts.

If the development materially affects an item already recorded in the statement, this is termed an adjusting event, as the item in question must be adjusted to reflect this development: the impact of the liquidation of a major debtor on the debtor's balance at the statement date, for example.

However, when a significant development does not directly impact the pre-existing statement, this is known as a non-adjusting event, as only a note outlining the nature and impact of the event on the post statement of financial position of the company is required to be disclosed in the accounts.

3. The Income Statement

The IASB has reissued IAS 1 and made changes to the presentation and the terminology used. The revised IAS standard is effective for annual periods beginning on or after 1 January 2009 and has changed the required presentation of the income statement.

3.1 The Purpose and Content of the Income Statement

Learning Objective

8.3.1 Understand the purpose and main contents of the income statement: company's performance; turnover; cost of sales; depreciation charge; interest income/expenditure; investment income; taxation; Profit; extraordinary items and exceptional items

The income statement summarises the company's revenue transactions over the accounting period to produce a profit or a loss. As a result, the income statement is often referred to as the profit and loss account. However, being constructed on an accruals basis, rather than a cash basis, profit must not be confused with the company's cash position.

The two specific functions of this financial statement are to:

- detail how the company's reported profit was arrived at, and
- state how much profit has been earned and how it has been distributed. The amount of profit earned over the accounting period will impact the company's ability to pay dividends and its ability to finance the growth of the business from internal resources.

Like the statement of financial position, the format of the income statement is governed by the Companies Acts and its construction underpinned by accounting standards.

Additionally, IAS 1 has brought about changes to the income statement. The amendment requires companies to present other comprehensive income items such as revaluation gains and losses, and actuarial gains and losses, as well as the usual income statement items, on the face of the primary financial statements. IAS 1 allows this information to be presented in one 'statement of comprehensive income' or in two separate statements; an **income statement** and a **statement of comprehensive income**.

An example income statement for ABC PLC is shown below. As with the statement of financial position, comparative numbers and explanatory notes must be provided.

ABC plc			
Income Statement			
		As at 31 December	
	Notes	2011 (£m)	2010 (£m)
Continuing Operations			
Revenue		9,500	
Cost of sales		(7,000)	
Gross Profit		2,500	
Distribution costs		(110)	
Administrative expenses		(30)	
Other income		–	
Operating Profit		2,360	
Exceptional loss		(260)	
		2,100	
Income from fixed asset investments		30	
Interest receivable		90	
Interest payable		(230)	
Profit before Taxation		1,990	
Taxation		(555)	
Net Income		1,435	
Earnings per share (pence)		14.3p	

The next example shows the Statement of Comprehensive Income for ABC plc. As before, comparative numbers and explanatory notes must be provided.

The statement of comprehensive income records items such as foreign exchange translation differences, gains or losses on revaluation of property and actuarial gains or losses on pension scheme plans. The net income from the income statement is added to this to generate a total comprehensive income for the financial year.

ABC plc			
Statement of Comprehensive Income			
		As at 31 December	
	Notes	2011 (£'000)	2010 (£'000)
Other Comprehensive Income			
Exchange differences on translating foreign operations		100	
Available-for-sale financial assets		–	
Cash flow hedges		–	
Gains on property revaluation			
Actuarial gains (losses) on defined benefit pension plans		(75)	
Taxation on components of other comprehensive income		(25)	
Other Comprehensive Income for the Year		0	
Net Income		1,435	
Total Comprehensive Income		1,435	
Earnings per share (pence)		14.3p	

The net income is then taken to the statement of changes in equity for the year and shown as retained earnings as shown in the following example.

ABC plc						
Statement of Changes in Equity for the Year Ended 31 December 2010						
	Ord Share Capital	Pref Share Capital	Share Premium Account	Revaluation Reserve	Capital Redemption Reserve	Retained Earnings	Total
As at 1 January 2009	4,470	100	0	0	80	5,880	10,530
Gain on revaluation				100			100
Issue of shares	530		120				650
Net income for the year						1,435	1,435
Preference dividends paid						−5	−5
Ordinary dividends paid						−430	−430
As at 31 December 2009	5,000	100	120	100	80	6,880	12,280

3.2 Revenue Recognition

Learning Objective

8.3.2 Be able to apply the basic concepts underlying revenue recognition

Revenue is calculated on an accruals basis and represents sales generated over the accounting period regardless of whether cash has been received. However, since there are no prescriptive rules as to when revenue should be recognised in the profit and loss account, this leaves scope for subjective judgement.

IAS 18 'Revenue' prescribes the accounting treatment for revenue arising from certain types of transactions and events, essentially only allowing recognition of revenues when appropriate. Revenue is recognised in the income statement when it meets the following criteria:

- It is probable that any future economic benefit associated with the item of revenue will flow to the company.
- The amount of revenue can be measured with reliability.

The IASB has published guidance on when revenue from the sale of goods, rendering of services and interest, royalties and dividends should be recognised as noted below.

Revenue arising from the sale of goods should be recognised when all of the following criteria have been satisfied:

- The seller has transferred to the buyer the significant risks and rewards of ownership.
- The seller retains neither continuing managerial involvement, to the degree usually associated with ownership, nor effective control over the goods sold.
- The amount of revenue can be measured reliably.
- It is probable that the economic benefits associated with the transaction will flow to the seller.
- The costs incurred or to be incurred in respect of the transaction can be measured reliably.

Revenue arising from the rendering of services should be recognised based on the stage of completion of the transaction, providing that all of the following criteria are met:

- The amount of revenue can be measured reliably.
- It is probable that the economic benefits will flow to the seller.
- The stage of completion at the balance sheet date can be measured reliably.
- The costs incurred, or to be incurred, in respect of the transaction can be measured reliably.

When the criteria are not met, revenue should be recognised only to the extent of the expenses that are recoverable.

For interest, royalties and dividends, revenue should be recognised as follows:

- **Interest** – on a time-proportion basis that takes into account the effective yield.
- **Royalties** – on an accruals basis.
- **Dividends** – when the shareholder's right to receive payment is established.

3.3   Accounting for Costs

Learning Objective

8.3.3   Understand how expenses, provisions and dividends are accounted for

The cost of sales is arrived at by adding purchases of stock made during the accounting period, again by applying accruals rather than cash accounting, to the opening stock for the period and deducting from this the value of the stock that remains in the business at the end of the accounting period.

$$\text{Cost of sales} = [\text{opening stock (if any)} + \text{purchases} - \text{closing stock}]$$

The opening stock figure used in this calculation will necessarily be the same as the closing stock figure that appears in the current assets section of the balance sheet from the previous accounting period.

IAS 37 details how provisions should be recognised and measured and that sufficient information is disclosed in the notes to the financial statements to enable users to understand their nature, timing and amount. The key principle is that a provision should be recognised only when there is a liability resulting from past events where payment is probable and the amount can be estimated reliably.

IAS 1 does not actually use the term **exceptional item**; however, the term is widely used in accounting. Essentially, the idea behind classifying an item as exceptional is to remove the distorting influence of any large one-off items on reported profit, so that users of the accounts may establish trends in profitability between successive accounting periods and derive a true and fair view of the company's results.

IAS 1 acknowledges that, owing to the effects of a company's various activities, transactions and other events that differ in frequency, potential for gain or loss and predictability, disclosing the components of financial performance assists in understanding that performance and making future projections. In other words, if an item is exceptional, it should be separately disclosed.

An exceptional item could be the profit made on selling a significant fixed asset or the loss on selling an unprofitable operation. These profits and losses only represent book profits and losses rather than actual cash profits and losses. We will return to this point when considering cash flow statements later in this chapter.

Exceptional profits are added to, and exceptional losses deducted from, operating profit in arriving at the company's profit before taxation.

The income statement does not record the payment of dividends, as profit is struck before payment of dividends. Instead these are shown in the statement of changes in equity and as a cash outflow in the cash flow statement. You can see an example of how dividend payments are treated in the Statement of changes in equity in Section 3.1 and how they are shown in the cash flow statement in Section 4.1.

3.4 Calculating Profit

Learning Objective

8.3.4 Be able to calculate the different levels of profit given revenue and different categories of cost: gross profit; profit before tax; net profit; profit excluding exceptionals

Gross Profit

Gross profit is calculated by deducting the cost of goods sold from revenue:

$$\text{Gross profit} = \text{revenue} - \text{cost of sales}$$

Operating Profit

Operating profit is stated after deducting distribution costs and administration expenses. Administration expenses usually include depreciation charges.

Although not shown in the above income statement, IFRS 5 'Non-current Assets Held for Sale and Discontinued Operations' requires the company's revenue and all items leading to and including the operating profit for the accounting period to be shown in respect of the company's continuing, or ongoing operations, and separately for operations discontinued during the period.

Profit Before and After Taxation

In addition to exceptional items, net dividend income from long-term investments made in other companies, gross interest receivable as well as gross interest payable must all be accounted for on an accruals rather than a cash paid and received basis, when moving between operating profit and profit before taxation.

A provisional estimate of the company's corporation tax liability is deducted from profit before taxation to give profit after taxation.

Net Income

Net income is the company's total earnings or profit. In the UK it is also referred to as profit after tax.

It is calculated by taking the total revenues adjusted for the cost of business, interest, taxes, depreciation and other expenses. The net income is the profit that is attributable to the shareholders of the company and is stated before the deduction of any dividends because dividends are an appropriation of profit and are at the discretion of the company directors.

The net income is added to the retained earnings in the balance sheet and disclosed within the statement of changes in equity. It is also within this statement that the dividends paid during the year are deducted from the retained earnings. As we will see later in the chapter, dividends paid are also disclosed in the cash flow statement.

Earnings per Share (EPS)

The EPS is calculated as follows:

$$EPS = \frac{\text{Profit available to equity shareholders}}{\text{Number of issued ordinary shares}}$$

IAS 33 Earnings per Share standardises the calculation of EPS and is considered in Chapter 9.

Exceptional Items

Extraordinary items still appear on some companies' income statements, but it is far less common than it used to be. This is because accountancy standards boards have set increasingly restrictive criteria as to which item can be classified as extraordinary.

Extraordinary items are reported at the bottom of the income statement, net of their tax effects. To be classified as extraordinary, an event or transaction must be both unusual and infrequent.

What is unusual will depend upon the typical activities of a company and so should be outside of the normal type and scope of its operations, its lines of business and operating policies.

An infrequent event or transaction is one that is not reasonably expected to recur in the foreseeable future. Because this determination also depends on the environment in which a company operates, what is extraordinary for one company may not be for another. The past occurrence of an event or transaction provides some evidence of the probability of recurrence of that type of event or transaction in the foreseeable future.

From what we have already considered, therefore, it is possible to identify that the following gains and losses are not considered extraordinary:

- Gains or losses from exchange or translation of foreign currencies.
- Gains or losses arising from the sale or abandonment of property, plant and equipment used in the business.
- Write-downs or write-offs of receivables, inventories and equipment leased to others, deferred research and development costs, or other intangible assets.

The reason for this approach is that analysts and other users of financial statements focus on the net income generated by a business before any gains or losses on disposal of a part of the business or extraordinary gains or losses. As unusual and infrequent items are not expected to recur, these can generally be ignored when projecting future profits and cash flows. It also reduces the opportunity for earnings manipulation that might mislead investors by preventing companies from classifying items as extraordinary in order to report stable and predictable profit trends.

4. The Cash Flow Statement

The IASB has reissued IAS 1 and made changes to the presentation and the terminology used. The revised IAS standard is effective for annual periods beginning on or after 1 January 2009 and has changed the name of the cash flow statement to a 'statement of cash flows'.

4.1 The Purpose of the Cash Flow Statement

Learning Objective

8.4.1 Understand the purpose and main contents of the cash flow statement: generation and use of cash; ignore accruals; ignore movements in balance sheet items; remove depreciation and book profits; cash from customers/operations; cash to suppliers/employees; dividends/interest paid/received; purchase fixed assets; tax paid; loans drawn/repaid; share issue/redemption

Cash flow statements seek to identify how a company's cash has been generated over the accounting period and how it has been expended.

Not all income statement items result in an immediate cash flow or even any cash flow at all. For example:

- **Depreciation** – a cash flow occurs when the asset is purchased and when it is sold, but not when it is depreciated.
- **Accrued expenses/purchases on credit** – cash flows in relation to these items are when these amounts are actually paid, which is after they have been charged against profits.
- **Sales on credit/prepaid expenses** – cash flows are when these debts are settled which, again, differs from when they are taken into the income statement.

Since cash is such an important figure in determining the continuing existence of a company, we need a statement showing how the company's financial resources have been generated and have been used in order to highlight the liquidity position and trends of the company.

It is constructed by:

- Removing accruals, or amounts payable and receivable, from the income statement, so that these amounts may be accounted for on a cash paid and received basis.
- Adjusting for balance sheet items such as an increase in the value a company's stock or debtors or a decrease in creditors, all of which increase reported profit but do not impact cash.
- Adding back non-cash items, such as depreciation charges, amortisation and book losses from the sale of fixed assets, whilst deducting book profits from fixed asset disposals recorded in the income statement, which impact recorded profit but not the company's cash position.
- Bringing in changes in balance sheet items that impact the company's cash position, such as finance raised and repaid over the accounting period and fixed assets bought and sold.

As not all of the effects of accruals accounting can be stripped out from a company's operating profit, the cash flow statement is a bit of a misnomer in that it contains a mixture of accruals, cash and credit, or fund, flows.

Analysis of the cash flow statement shows that it is important that a company generates positive cash flow at the operating level, otherwise it will become reliant upon fixed asset sales and borrowing facilities to finance its day-to-day operations.

A company's survival and future prosperity is also dependent upon it replacing its fixed assets to remain competitive. However, these assets must be financed with capital of a similar duration to the economic life and payback pattern of the asset; otherwise the company will have insufficient funds to finance its operating activities. The cash flow statement will also identify this.

The statement of cash flows for ABC plc, based on the IAS 7 format, is given next. Although not shown, explanatory notes to the cash flow statement and comparatives are also required.

ABC plc			
Consolidated Balance Sheet			
		As at 31 December	
	Notes	2011 (£m)	2010 (£m)
Operating Activities			
Cash receipts from customers		4,528	
Cash paid to suppliers and employees		(2,001)	
Cash generated from operations		2,527	
Tax paid		(440)	
Interest paid		(150)	
Net Cash from Operating Activities		4,464	
Investing Activities			
Interest received		80	
Dividends received		40	
Purchase of fixed assets		(1,890)	
Proceeds on sale of investments		120	
Net Cash Used in Investing Activities		(1,650)	
Financing Activities			
Dividends paid		(435)	
Repayments of borrowings		(200)	
Proceeds on issue of shares		650	
Net cash generated from financing activities		15	
Net increase in cash and cash equivalents		2,829	
Cash and cash equivalents at the beginning of the year		425	
Cash and Cash Equivalents at the End of the Year		3,254	

As you can see from the statement, cash flows are broken down into the following areas:

* Net cash flow as a result of activities.
* Operating activities are the main revenue-producing activities of the company that are not investing or financing activities, so operating cash flows include cash received from customers and cash paid to suppliers and employees.
* Investing activities are the acquisition and disposal of long-term assets and other investments.
* Financing activities alter the equity capital and borrowing structure of the company.
* Cash and cash equivalents show the overall movements in cash and cash equivalents during the period. Cash and cash equivalents comprise cash in hand and demand deposits, together with short-term, highly liquid investments that are readily convertible to a known amount of cash and that are subject to an insignificant risk of changes in value.

4.2 Calculating Net Cash Flow

Learning Objective

8.4.2   Be able to calculate net cash flow from operations from operating profit

In order to establish the cash generated from operating activities figure in the cash flow statement – essentially the company's operating cash flow – IAS 7 allows one of two alternative presentations on the face of the cash flow statement.

The preferred method is the direct method, where the cash received from customers and paid to suppliers and employees is shown. Alternatively, the indirect method is where reconciliation is shown between the company's income statement's operating profit and the cash generated from operations in the cash flow statement.

This reconciliation requires the following adjustments to be made to the operating profit figure:

• Non-cash charges, such as the depreciation of tangible fixed assets and the amortisation of intangible assets must be added back as these do not represent an outflow of cash.
• Any increase in debtors or stock or decrease in short-term creditors over the accounting period must be subtracted, as these all increase reported profit but do not increase cash.
• Any decrease in debtors or stock or increase in short-term creditors over the accounting period must be added, as these all decrease reported profit but do not decrease cash.

Example

Given the income statement and balance sheet items below, how can the cash generated from operations figure of £2,527,000 in ABC plc's cash flow statement be reconciled with ABC plc's operating profit of £2,360,000?

ABC plc	£000
Depreciation	62
Goodwill amortisation	17
Increase in stock	12
Decrease in debtors	77
Increase in creditors	23

Solution:

ABC plc	£000
Operating profit	2360
Add: Depreciation	62
Add: Goodwill amortisation	17
Subtract: Increase in stock	(12)
Add: Decrease in debtors	77
Add: Increase in creditors	23
Net cash inflow from operating activities	2527

5.   Consolidated Company Report and Accounts

Learning Objective

8.5.1   Understand the basic principles of accounting for: associated companies; subsidiaries

5.1   Investments

If company A has less than a 20% holding in the voting share capital of company B and does not exercise any significant influence over the operating policies of company B, then this investment is recognised in company A's statement of financial position as either:

- a fixed asset investment at cost, less any impairment to its value, or
- a current asset at the lower of cost or NRV. In this instance NRV is the current market value.

In both cases, any dividends received will be taken to the income statement in arriving at profit on ordinary activities before taxation.

If, however, this shareholding represents at least 20% of company B's voting capital or company A is in a position to exert considerable influence over company B's management, then company A is required to show the position of the combined entity in its statement of financial position and income statement.

5.2   Subsidiaries

When a company controls another company, it is known as a parent company with a subsidiary. The controlled entity is called the subsidiary company, and the controlling entity is called its parent (or the parent company).

The most common way that control of a subsidiary is achieved is through the ownership of shares in the subsidiary by the parent. These shares give the parent the necessary votes to determine the composition of the board of the subsidiary and so exercise control. This gives rise to the common presumption that owning more than 50% of the shares is enough to create a subsidiary.

A subsidiary may itself have subsidiaries, and these, in turn, may have subsidiaries of their own. A parent and all its subsidiaries together are called a group of companies.

5.3   Group Accounts

To account for its control, a parent company is required to present **group accounts** that amalgamate the assets and liabilities of the parent with those of its subsidiary companies.

These accounts are alternatively termed **consolidated accounts**, and by amalgamating the assets and liabilities the shareholders of the parent are clearly able to see all of the resources the group controls, and the liabilities the group owe to others.

The vast majority of listed companies are parent companies that control one or more subsidiary companies. As a result, listed companies present group accounts to their shareholders.

As stated above, a subsidiary is established when the parent company controls more than 50%. In instances where the parent has greater than 50% but less than 100% of the shares of the subsidiary, the remaining shares are owned by persons other than the parent and are known as the **minority interests**.

The percentage of the net income that is owned by the minority shareholders are shown as a deduction at the foot of the group income statement. A similar adjustment is also made at the base of the group statement of financial position as a separate entry within equity for the minority interests.

5.4   The Equity Method of Accounting

IAS 28 'Investments in Associates' prescribes the accounting treatment for fixed asset investments held in other companies if there is a 20% to 50% shareholding or the investing company participates in, or exercises, a significant influence over the management of the other company.

The company in which the shareholding is held is known as an associate company and the method employed to account for the investment is termed the equity method of accounting.

The equity method of accounting requires that if A has a 30% shareholding in B, for instance, then:

- 30% of company B's post-acquisition operating profit, interest payable, interest receivable and tax is added to company A's respective income statement items in the consolidated income statement. Any dividends received by A from B do not, however, enter the consolidated income statement. Company B's post-acquisition profits are those that arise after A has taken a stake in B as an associated company.
- 30% of the value of company B's net assets and the value of any purchased goodwill that arose on making this investment in company B will appear in the consolidated statement of financial position.

End of Chapter Questions

Think of an answer for each question and refer to the appropriate workbook section for confirmation.

1. Explain what the accruals concept is.
    Answer reference: Section 1.2.1

2. A German company is listed on the Frankfurt stock exchange and has issued its financial report and accounts. What standards will it have utilised in preparing the accounts?
    Answer reference: Section 1.3

3. What types of modified audit report might be produced?
    Answer reference: Section 1.4

4. What is the relationship between a company's income statement and its statement of financial position?
    Answer reference: Section 2.1 and 3.1

5. What are the three categories of non-current assets of a company?
    Answer reference: Section 2.1

6. How is property accounted for in the statement of financial position under IAS 16?
    Answer reference: Section 2.2.1

7. Machinery has been purchased for £50,000 and has a useful economic life of 7 years after which its estimated disposal value will be £15,000. What depreciation charge would be applied if the straight line method is used?
    Answer reference: Section 2.4

8. What are capital reserves and are they distributable to shareholders?
    Answer reference: Section 2.6

9. A company has the following:

    *   Sales of £1m
    *   Cost of sales of £450k
    *   Administrative expenses of £75k
    *   Interest payable of £25k

    What is its gross profit, operating profit and profit before tax?
    Answer reference: Section 3.4

10. Company A has a 15% stake in company B and exercises considerable influence over its management. How should the investment be accounted for?
    Answer reference: Section 5

Chapter Nine
Investment Analysis

This syllabus area will provide approximately 6 of the 80 examination questions

1. Fundamental and Technical Analysis

Learning Objective

9.1.1   Know the characteristics and examples of fundamental and technical analysis: primary objectives; quantitative techniques; charts; primary movements; secondary movements; tertiary movements

The methods used to analyse securities in order to make investment decisions can be broadly categorised into:

- fundamental analysis, and
- technical analysis.

We will consider the key features and the main differences below.

1.1   Fundamental Analysis

Fundamental analysis involves the financial analysis of a company's published accounts, along with an analysis of its management, markets and competitive position. It is a technique that is used to determine the value of a security by focusing on the underlying factors that affect a company's business.

Fundamental analysis looks at both quantitative factors, such as the numerical results of the analysis of a company and the market it operates in, and qualitative factors such as the quality of the company's management, the value of its brand and areas such as patents and proprietary technology.

The assumption behind fundamental analysis is that the market does not always value securities correctly in the short term, but that, by identifying the intrinsic value of a company, securities can be bought at a discount and the investment will pay off over time, once the market realises the fundamental value of a company.

Companies generate a significant amount of financial data and fundamental analysis seeks to extract meaningful data about a company. Many of the key ratios that can be derived from this are considered later in this chapter.

In addition to this quantitative data, fundamental analysis also assesses a wide range of other qualitative factors such as:

- a company's business model
- its competitive position
- the quality and experience of its management team
- how the company is managed, the transparency of available financial data and its approach to corporate governance
- the industry in which it operates, its market share and its competitive position relative to its peers.

1.2   Technical Analysis

Technical analysis also seeks to evaluate a company but, instead of analysing a company's intrinsic value and prospects, it uses historical price and volume data to assess where the price of a security or market will move in the future.

The assumptions underlying technical analysis are that:

*   The market discounts everything.
*   Prices move in trends.
*   History tends to repeat itself.

Technical analysis uses charts of price movements along with technical indicators and oscillators to identify patterns that can suggest future price movements. **Indicators** are calculations that are used to confirm a price movement and to form buy and sell signals. **Oscillators** are another type of calculation that indicates whether a security is over-bought or over-sold. It is, therefore, unconcerned whether a security is undervalued and simply concerns itself with future price movements.

One of the most important concepts in technical analysis is, therefore, **trend**.

Trends can, however, be difficult to identify, as prices do not move in a straight line and so technical analysis identifies series of highs or lows that take place to identify the direction of movements. These are classified as uptrend, downtrend and sideways movements.

The following diagram seeks to explain this by describing a simple uptrend.

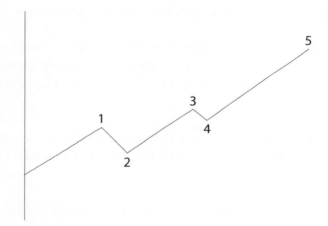

Figure 1: A Simple Upward Trend

Point 1 on the chart reflects the first high and point 2 the subsequent low and so on. For it to be an uptrend, each successive low must be higher than the previous low point, otherwise it is referred to as a reversal. The same principle applies for downtrends.

Along with direction, technical analysis will also classify trends based on time.

Primary movements are long-term price trends, which can last a number of years. Primary movements in the broader market are known as bull and bear markets: a bull market is a rising market and a bear market is a falling market. Primary movements consist of a number of secondary movements, each of which can last for up to a couple of months, which in turn comprise a number of tertiary or day-to-day movements.

The results of technical analysis are displayed on charts that graphically represent price movements. After plotting historical price movements, a trendline is added to clearly show the direction of the trend and to show reversals.

The trendline can then be analysed to provide further indicators of potential price movement. The diagram below shows an upward trend line which is drawn at the lows of the upward trend and which represents the support line for a stock as it moves from progressive highs to lows.

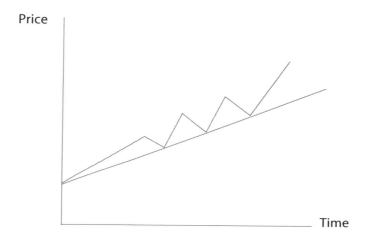

Figure 2: Upward Trendline

This type of trendline helps traders to anticipate the point at which a stock's price will begin moving upwards again. Similarly, a downward trendline is drawn at the highs of the downward trend. This line represents the resistance level that a stock faces every time the price moves from a low to a high.

There are a variety of different charts that can be used to depict price movements and some of the main types of chart are:

- **Line charts** – line charts are where the price of an asset, or security, over time is simply plotted using a single line. Each point on the line represents the security's closing price. However, in order to establish an underlying trend, chartists often employ what are known as **moving averages** so as to smooth out extreme price movements. Rather than plot each closing price on the chart, each point on the chart instead represents the arithmetic mean of the security's price over a specific number of days. Ten, 50, 100 and 200 moving-day averages are commonly used.
- **Point and figure charts** – these record significant price movements in vertical columns, by using a series of Xs to denote significant up moves and Os to represent significant down moves, without employing a uniform timescale. Whenever there is a change in the direction of the security's price, a new column is started.

- **Bar charts** – bar charts join the highest and lowest price levels attained by a security over a specified time period by a vertical line. This time scale can range from a single day to a few months. When the chosen time period is one trading day, a horizontal line representing the closing price on the day intersects this vertical line.
- **Candlestick charts** – these are closely linked to bar charts. Again, they link the security's highest and lowest prices by a vertical line, but they employ horizontal lines to mark both the opening and closing prices for each trading day. If the closing price exceeds the opening price on the day, then the body of the candle is left clear, while if the opposite is true, it is shaded.

Technical analysis also contain channel lines, which is where two parallel lines are added to indicate the areas of support and resistance which respectively connect the series of highs and lows. Users of technical analysis will expect a security to trade between these two levels until it breaks out, when it can be expected to make a sharp move in the direction of the break. If a support level is subsequently broken, this provides a sell signal, while the breaking of a resistance level, as the price of the asset gathers momentum, indicates a buying opportunity.

These are known as **breakouts**.

An example of such a breakout pattern is the triangle which is shown below. Here price movements become progressively less volatile but often break out in either direction in quite a spectacular fashion.

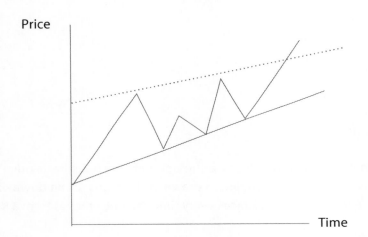

Figure 3: Breakout Pattern

Other continuation patterns include the rectangle and the flag.

Chartists typically use what are known as relative strength charts to confirm breakouts from continuation patterns. Relative strength charts simply depict the price performance of a security, relative to the broader market. If the relative performance of the security improves against the broader market, this may confirm that a suspected breakout on the upside has or is about to occur.

However, acknowledging that prices do not always move in the same direction and trends eventually cease, technical analysts also look to identify what are known as reversal patterns, or sell signals. Probably the most famous of these is the head and shoulders reversal pattern, as the following example shows.

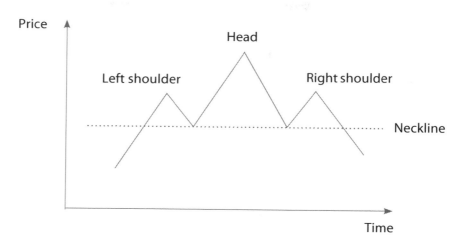

Figure 4: Head and Shoulders Reversal Pattern

A head and shoulders reversal pattern arises when a price movement causes the right shoulder to breach the neckline, the resistance level, indicating the prospect of a sustained fall in the price of the security.

1.3   The Difference between Fundamental and Technical Analysis

Fundamental and technical analysis are the two main methodologies used for investment analysis and, as you can see from comparing their key characteristics, they differ widely in their approaches.

The principal differences between them can be summarised as follows:

- **Analysing financial statements versus charts**
  - At a basic level, fundamental analysis involves the analysis of the company's balance sheet, cash flow statement and income statement.
  - Technical analysis considers that there is no need to do this, as a company's fundamentals are all accounted for in the price, and the information needed can be found in the company's charts.
- **Time horizon**
  - Fundamental analysis takes a relatively long-term approach to investment.
  - Technical analysis uses chart data over a much shorter timeframe of weeks, days and even minutes.
- **Investing versus trading**
  - Fundamental analysis is often used to make long-term investment decisions.
  - Technical analysis is often used to determine short-term trading decisions.

Although the approaches adopted by technical and fundamental analysis differ markedly, they should not be seen as being mutually exclusive techniques. Indeed, their differences make them complementary. Used collectively, they can enhance the portfolio management decision-making process.

2. Yields and Ratios

The financial statements and associated explanatory notes issued by a company contain a significant amount of data that needs to be turned into meaningful numbers. These can then be used for assessing the profitability of a company, the risks attached to those earnings and its ability to meet its liabilities as they fall due and to identify trends.

We now turn, therefore, to look at the range of yields and ratios that can be used as part of fundamental analysis.

These ratios can be grouped under four headings.

- Profitability – measures to assess the trading or operating performance of the company, ie, levels of trading profits generated and the effectiveness of the use of trading assets.
- Liquidity – measures to assess the trading risk of the company. This is the risk that, as a result of trading activities, the company may be unable to pay its suppliers, as debts fall due and cease to exist.
- Investors' ratios – measures to assess the returns to providers of finance, who may be either shareholders or lenders.
- Gearing – measures to assess the risks to providers of finance, due to the company's level of borrowing.

2.1 Profitability Ratios

Learning Objective

9.2.1 Understand and be able to analyse securities using the following profitability ratios: return on capital employed (ROCE); asset turnover; net profit margin; gross profit margin; equity multiplier

9.2.2 Be able to calculate the following profitability ratios: return on capital employed; asset turnover; net profit margin; gross profit margin; equity multiplier

Profitability ratios are used to assess the effectiveness of a company's management in employing the company's assets to generate profit and shareholder value. A wide range of ratios is used but in this section we will just consider return on capital employed (ROCE), asset turnover, profit margins and the equity multiplier.

2.1.1 Return on Capital Employed (ROCE)

Firstly, we will look at return on capital employed (ROCE). ROCE is a key measure of a company's profitability and looks at the returns that have been generated from the total capital employed in a company that is debt as well as equity.

It expresses the income generated by the company's activities as a percentage of its total capital. This percentage result can then be used to compare the returns generated to the cost of borrowing, establish trends across accounting periods and make comparisons with other companies.

ROCE is calculated as follows:

$$ROCE = \frac{\text{Profit before interest and tax}}{\text{Capital employed}} \times 100 \ = x\%$$

This profit figure can be viewed as operating profit plus interest receivable and income from other investments, ie, the profits that management has generated from the resources it has available. It is specifically before interest payable, since that will clearly be dependent on the financing of the business; the larger the loans, the larger the interest payable.

The component parts of **capital employed** are shown below in an expanded version of the formula:

$$ROCE = \frac{\text{Profit before interest and tax}}{\text{(Total assets – Current liabilities + Short-term borrowing)}} \times 100 = x\%$$

Capital employed is total assets less current liabilities (but excluding borrowings in current liabilities, such as overdrafts and finance lease obligations).

Alternatively, capital employed can be calculated from the financing side of the statement of financial position as:

Shareholders' funds + Non-current liabilities + Borrowings in current liabilities

It should be noted that the result can be distorted in the following circumstances:

- The raising of new finance at the end of the accounting period, as this will increase the capital employed but will not affect the profit figure used in the equation.
- The revaluation of fixed assets during the accounting period, as this will increase the amount of capital employed while also reducing the reported profit by increasing the depreciation charge.
- The acquisition of a subsidiary at the end of the accounting period, as the capital employed will increase but there will not be any post-acquisition profits from the subsidiary to bring into the consolidated profit and loss account.

2.1.2   Asset Turnover and Profit Margin

Having established the ROCE, we now need to consider what may have caused any change from one year to the next. This is caused by one of two factors.

- Changes in profit margin.
- Changes in turnover volumes.

This can be undertaken by breaking ROCE down further into two secondary ratios: asset turnover and profit margin.

Asset turnover looks at the relationship between sales and the capital employed in a business. It describes how efficiently a company is generating sales by looking at how hard a company's assets are working.

The formula for calculating asset turnover is:

$$\text{Asset turnover} = \frac{\text{Sales}}{\text{Capital employed}}$$

Profit margin looks at how much profit is being made for each pound's worth of sales. Clearly the higher the profit margin the better.

The formula for calculating profit margin is:

$$\text{Profit margin} = \frac{\text{Profit before interest and tax}}{\text{Sales}}$$

In both cases, sales refers to revenue or turnover.

The relationship between ROCE and each of these can be shown as follows.

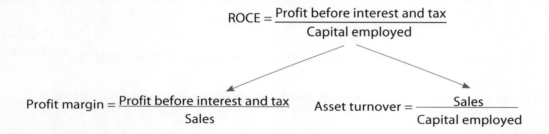

$$\text{ROCE} = \frac{\text{Profit before interest and tax}}{\text{Capital employed}}$$

$$\text{Profit margin} = \frac{\text{Profit before interest and tax}}{\text{Sales}} \qquad \text{Asset turnover} = \frac{\text{Sales}}{\text{Capital employed}}$$

You can see that if we multiply the profit margin by the asset turnover, we will get back to the return on capital employed since the revenue figures will cancel.

Example

Assume ABC ltd has sales of £5m, a trading profit of £1.5m and the following items on its statement of financial position:

- Share capital   £1.0m
- Reserves   £5.0m
- Loans   £1.0m
- Overdraft   £0.5m

So its ROCE, profit margin and asset turnover can be calculated as follows:

Return on Capital Employed:

$$\frac{\text{Profit before interest and tax}}{\text{Capital employed}} \quad \text{or} \quad \frac{£1.5m}{(£1.0m + 5.0m + £1.0m + £0.5m)} \times 100 = 20\%$$

Profit Margin:

$$\frac{\text{Profit before interest and tax}}{\text{Sales}} = \frac{£1.5m}{£5m} \times 100 = 30\%$$

Asset Turnover:

$$\frac{\text{Sales}}{\text{Capital employed}} = \frac{£5m}{£7.5m} = 0.67 \text{ times}$$

Profit margin and asset turnover can therefore be used in conjunction with ROCE to gain a more comprehensive picture of how a company is performing. The results of the calculations will then need interpreting to determine whether they represent a positive picture, which will depend upon the returns being achieved by comparative firms operating in the same or similar industries.

Asset turnover measures how efficiently the company's assets have been utilised over the accounting period, while the company's profit margin measures how effective its price and cost management has been in the face of industry competition. High or improving profit margins may, of course, attract other firms into the industry, depending on the existence of industry barriers to entry, thereby driving down margins in the long run.

The asset turnover ratio tends to be inversely related to the net profit margin ie, the higher the net profit margin, the lower the asset turnover. The result is that investors can compare companies using different models (low-profit, high-volume versus high-profit, low-volume) and determine which one is the more attractive business.

2.1.3   Gross, Operating and Net Profit Margin

Various profit margins can be looked at to analyse the profitability of a company in order to determine if it is both liquid and being run efficiently.

The gross profit margin shows the profit a company makes after paying for the cost of goods sold. It shows how efficient the management is in using its labour and raw materials in the process of production.

The formula for gross profit margin is:

$$\text{Gross profit margin (\%)} = \frac{\text{Gross profit}}{\text{Revenues}} \times 100$$

Firms that have a high gross profit margin are more liquid and so have more cash flow to spend on research and development expenses, marketing and investing. Gross profit margins need to be compared with industry standards to provide context and should be analysed over a number of accounting periods.

The operating profit margin shows how efficiently management is using business operations to generate profit.

Operating profit margin is calculated using the formula:

$$\text{Operating profit margin (\%)} = \frac{\text{Operating profit}}{\text{Revenues}} \times 100$$

The higher the margin the better, as this shows that the company can keep its costs under control and can mean that sales are increasing faster than costs and the firm is in a relatively liquid position.

The difference between gross and operating profit margin is that the gross profit margin accounts for just the cost of goods sold, whereas the operating profit margin accounts for the cost of goods sold and administration/selling expenses.

The net profit margin analyses profitability further by taking into account interest and taxation. Again it needs to be compared to industry standards to provide context.

The formula for calculating net profit margin is:

$$\text{Net profit margin (\%)} = \frac{\text{Net income}}{\text{Revenues}} \times 100$$

With net profit margin ratio, all costs are included to find the final benefit of the income of a business and so measures how successful a company has been at the business of making a profit on each sale. It is one of the most essential financial ratios, as it includes all the factors that influence profitability whether under management control or not. The higher the ratio, the more effective a company is at cost control. Compared with industry average, it tells investors how well the management and operations of a company are performing against its competitors. Compared with different industries, it tells investors which industries are relatively more profitable than others.

2.1.4 Equity Multiplier

The equity multiplier is a financial leverage ratio that evaluates a company's use of debt to purchase assets.

The formula for equity multiplier is total assets divided by shareholders' funds:

$$\text{Equity multiplier} = \frac{\text{Total assets}}{\text{Shareholders' funds}}$$

It is possible for a company with terrible sales and margins to take on excessive debt and artificially increase its return on equity. The equity multiplier allows the investor to see what portion of the return on equity is the result of debt.

The equity multiplier is a component part of the DuPont system of financial analysis, which was created in 1919 and is still used around the world today. It uses the net profit margin, asset turnover and the equity multiplier to determine return on equity.

The formula for calculating return on equity is:

$$\text{Return on equity} = \text{Net profit margin} \times \text{Asset turnover} \times \text{Equity multiplier}$$

If return on equity is unsatisfactory, the Du Pont identity helps locate the part of the business that is underperforming by showing that return on equity is affected by three things:

- Operating efficiency, which is measured by profit margin.
- Asset use efficiency, which is measured by total asset turnover.
- Financial leverage, which is measured by the equity multiplier.

2.2   Liquidity Ratios

Learning Objective

9.2.5   Understand and be able to analyse securities using the following liquidity ratios: working capital (current) ratio; liquidity ratio (acid test); z-score analysis;

9.2.6   Be able to calculate the following liquidity ratios: working capital (current) ratio; liquidity ratio (acid test)

A company's survival is dependent upon both its profitability and its ability to generate sufficient cash to support its day-to-day operations. This ability to pay its liabilities as they become due is known as **liquidity** and can be assessed by using the current ratio and the acid test.

2.2.1   Current Ratio

The working capital ratio is more commonly referred to as the current ratio.

The current ratio is simply calculated by dividing a company's current assets by its current liabilities as follows:

$$\text{Current ratio} = \frac{\text{Current assets}}{\text{Current liabilities}}$$

Although a company will want to hold sufficient stock to meet anticipated demand, it must also ensure that it doesn't tie up so many resources as to compromise its profitability or its ability to meet its liabilities. The higher the result, therefore, the more readily a company should be able to meet its liabilities that are becoming due and still fund its ongoing operations.

2.2.2　Liquidity (Acid Test) Ratio

The liquidity ratio is also known as the quick ratio and the acid test.

It excludes stock from the calculation of current assets, as stock is potentially not liquid, in order to give a tighter measure of a company's ability to meet a sudden cash call.

The formula for liquidity ratio is:

$$\text{Liquidity ratio} = \frac{\text{Current assets} - \text{Stock}}{\text{Current liabilities}}$$

For most industries a ratio of more than one will indicate that a company has sufficient short-term assets to cover its short-term liabilities. If it is less than one it may indicate the need to raise new finance.

2.2.3　Z-Score Analysis

A z-score analysis is generally considered to be a more detailed way of establishing whether a company is dangerously close to becoming insolvent.

A z-score analysis is undertaken to determine the probability of a company going into liquidation by analysing such factors as the company's gearing and sales mix and distilling these into a statistical z-score. If negative, this implies that a company's insolvency is imminent.

Other danger signals include an increased use of leased assets and an overdependence on one customer.

2.3　Investor Ratios

Learning Objectives

9.2.7　Understand and be able to analyse securities using the following investors' ratios: earnings per share (EPS); earnings before interest, tax, depreciation, and amortisation (EBITDA); earnings before interest and tax (EBIT); historic and prospective price earnings ratios (PERs); dividend yields; dividend cover; price to book

9.2.8　Be able to calculate the following investors' ratios: earnings per share (EPS); earnings before interest, tax, depreciation, and amortisation (EBITDA); historic and prospective price earnings ratios (PERs); dividend yields; dividend cover; price to book

In the following section we will consider some of the ratios that are used to assess potential investments.

2.3.1　Earnings per Share (EPS)

Earnings per share is a measure of the profitability of a company that is expressed in an amount per share in order that meaningful comparisons can be made from year to year and with other companies.

The quality of a company's earnings stream and its ability to grow its EPS in a consistent manner are probably the most important factors affecting the price of a company's shares, not least because earnings provide the ability to finance future operations and the means to pay dividends to shareholders.

There are three principal measures we need to consider:

*   Earnings per share (EPS).
*   Earnings before interest and tax (EBIT).
*   Earnings before interest, tax, depreciation and amortisation (EBITDA).

The earnings per share ratio measures the profit available to ordinary shareholders and is taken as the profit after all other expenses and payments have been made by the company.

EPS is calculated as follows:

$$EPS = \frac{(\text{Net income} - \text{Preference dividends})}{\text{Number of ordinary shares in issue}}$$

The resulting figure is known as basic EPS.

Earnings Before Interest and Tax (EBIT)

Earnings per share can also be calculated before the impact of interest payments and taxation. EBIT is, therefore, operating income or operating profit.

Earnings Before Interest, Tax, Depreciation and Amortisation (EBITDA)

Earnings can also be analysed before making any financial, taxation and accounting charges through an EPS measure known as EBITDA. EBITDA provides a way for company earnings to be compared internationally, as the earnings picture is not clouded by differences in accounting standards worldwide.

2.3.2   Price Earnings Ratio (PER)

The price earnings ratio (PER) measures how highly investors value a company in its ability to grow its income stream.

The PER ratio is calculated by dividing the market price by the EPS as follows:

$$PE\ ratio = \frac{\text{Share price}}{\text{EPS}}$$

A company with a high PER ratio relative to its sector average reflects investors' expectations that the company will achieve above-average growth. By contrast, a low PER ratio indicates that investors expect the company to achieve below average growth in its future earnings.

Although PERs ratios differ significantly between markets and industries, there could be several reasons why a company has a higher PER ratio than its industry peers, apart from its shares simply being overpriced.

These may include:

- A greater perceived ability to grow its EPS more rapidly than its competitors.
- Producing higher quality or more reliable earnings than its peers.
- Being a potential takeover target.
- Experiencing a temporary fall in profits.

One way of establishing whether a company's PER is justified is to divide it by a realistic estimate of the company's average earnings growth rate for the next five years. A number of less than one indicates that the shares are potentially attractive. This is sometimes referred to as the price earnings to growth (PEG) rate.

2.3.3   Dividend Yields and Cover

Dividend yields give investors an indication of the expected return on a share so that it can be compared to other shares and other investments.

Dividend yields are calculated by dividing the net dividend by the share price as follows:

$$\text{Dividend yield} = \frac{\text{Net dividend per share}}{\text{Share price}} \times 100 = x\%$$

A dividend yield also provides an indication of a company's perceived ability to grow its dividends. A low dividend yield implies high dividend growth, whereas the opposite is true of a high dividend yield.

As well as looking at the dividend yield, investors will also consider the ability of the company to continue paying such a level of dividend. They do this by calculating dividend cover which looks at how many times a company could have paid out its dividend based on the profit for the year.

$$\text{Dividend cover} = \frac{\text{EPS}}{\text{Net dividend per share}}$$

The higher the dividend cover, the less likely it is that a company will have to reduce dividends if profits fall.

2.3.4   Price to Book Ratio

The price to book (P/B) ratio measures the relationship between the company's share price and the net book, or asset value per share attributable to its ordinary shareholders.

The P/B ratio divides the share price by the net asset value per share and is expressed as a multiple to indicate how much shareholders are paying for the net assets of a company.

The formula is:

$$\text{P/B ratio} = \frac{\text{Share price}}{\text{NAV per share}}$$

If the ratio shows that the share price is lower than its book value, it can indicate that it is undervalued or simply that the market perceives that it will remain a stagnant investment. If the share price is higher than its book value, this suggests that investors view it as a company which has above-average growth potential.

2.4　Gearing Ratios

Learning Objectives

9.2.3　Understand and be able to analyse securities using the following gearing ratios: financial gearing; interest cover

9.2.4　Be able to calculate interest cover

Gearing or debt ratios are used to determine the overall financial risk that a company and its shareholders face. In general, the greater amount of debt that a company has, then the greater the risk of bankruptcy.

2.4.1　Financial Gearing

Investors prefer consistent earnings growth, or high quality earnings streams, to volatile and unpredictable earnings. The quality of this earnings stream is dependent upon whether the company's business is closely tied to the fortunes of the economic cycle. It also depends on the level of a company's financial gearing, or capital structure.

A company's financial gearing (alternatively termed 'leverage') describes its capital structure, or the ratio of debt to equity capital it employs.

Financial gearing is also known as the debt to equity ratio and is calculated as follows:

Debt to Equity Ratio is calculated by dividing the market price by the EPS as follows:

$$\text{Debt to equity ratio} = \frac{\text{Interest bearing debt} + \text{Preference shares}}{\text{Ordinary shareholders equity}} \times 100$$

Preference shares are included in the 'debt' part of the calculation as their dividends take priority over the payment of equity dividends.

A company's financial gearing can also be expressed in net terms by taking into account any cash held by the company, as this may potentially be available to repay some of the company's debt.

Debt finance can enhance a company's earnings growth as it is a more tax-efficient and generally less expensive means of financing than equity capital. If it is excessive, however, it can also lead to an extremely volatile earnings stream, given that debt interest must be paid regardless of the company's profitability.

2.4.2   Interest Cover

Shareholders and prospective lenders to the company will also be interested in the company's ability to service, or pay the interest on, its interest-bearing debt. The effect of a company's financial gearing policy on the profit and loss account is reflected in its interest cover which is calculated as follows:

$$\text{Interest cover} = \frac{\text{Profit before interest and tax}}{\text{Interest payable}}$$

The higher interest cover that a company has, the greater the safety margin for its ordinary shareholders and the more scope it will have to raise additional loan finance without dramatically impacting its ability to service the required interest payments or compromise the quality of its earnings stream. An interest cover of 1.5 or less indicates that its ability to meet interest expenses may be questionable. This ratio, however, requires careful interpretation, as it is susceptible to changes in the company's capital structure and general interest rate movements, unless fixed-rate finance or interest rate hedging is employed.

2.5   Limitations of Investment Ratios

Learning Objective

9.2.9   Understand the difficulties in interpreting the above ratios for: companies in different industries; different companies within the same industry; the same company over successive accounting periods

The three principal financial statements – the statement of financial position, income statement and cash flow statement – and associated explanatory notes published by companies in their annual report give a considerable amount of information. However, ratio analysis on this information has its limitations, but does prompt further investigation and allows investors or potential investors to ask questions.

- As financial statements contain historic data, ratios are not predictive. Past performance may give no indication of future performance, particularly for research and development companies which may, for example, make a major discovery in medicine or technology.
- Despite accounting regulations, accounting data can be window-dressed.
- Ratios do not provide all the answers and are of limited value in isolation, but do prompt further investigation.
- Different companies within the same industry may be at different stages of building their business. For example, a new technology company may have very high levels of debt and limited cash flow. It may have ratios which are poor compared with more established companies in the same industry. However, because of a culture of innovation and enterprise, it may actually perform better and ultimately give a higher return on investment.
- Industry averages can also be misleading as they may be based on different accounting policies. This can be a problem when comparing industries in different countries that have different accounting standards.

3. Valuation

The final strand of fundamental analysis to be considered is that of equity valuation. Equities can be valued on four bases:

- Dividend flows.
- Earnings growth.
- Net asset value (NAV).
- Shareholder value added.

3.1 Gordon Growth Model

Learning Objective

9.3.1   Understand equity valuations based on Dividends: Gordon Growth Model

The dividend valuation model applies a theoretical price to a company's shares, by discounting the company's expected flow of future dividends into infinity.

In other words, it uses the same formula that we considered earlier in this workbook to calculate the present value of a perpetuity and instead uses it to calculate the value of a share. The required rate for the formula is derived by adjusting the risk-free rate given by a treasury bill or stock for the relative risk of the investment.

Example

ABC PLC is expected to pay a dividend of 10p next year. Assuming the required return to equity holders is 11% and the dividend is expected to continue at this level, the share price should be:

$$\text{Share price} = \frac{\text{Next year's dividend}}{\text{Required return to equity holders}} = \frac{10\text{p}}{0.11} = 91\text{p}$$

This, however, takes no account of the potential for rising dividends. This gives rise to Gordon's growth model, which assumes that future dividends will grow at a constant rate.

The formula for calculating it is:

$$\text{Share price} = \frac{\text{Dividend in one year's time}}{\text{Required return to equity holders} - \text{growth rate of dividends}}$$

Example

Continuing with the example above, if ABC PLC's dividends are expected to grow at a constant rate of 5%, the share price should be:

$$\text{Share price} = \frac{(10p)}{(0.11 - 0.05)} = 166.67p$$

3.2 Earnings and Asset Valuation Models

Learning Objective

9.3.2   Be able to calculate equity valuations based on Earnings and assets: price earnings ratios (PERs); net asset value

As we saw earlier, a PER ratio provides an indication of how highly rated a company is in its ability to grow its earnings stream.

Very simply, a PER, therefore, indicates the number of years that it would take at the current EPS to repay the share price, ignoring the time value of money. It, therefore, can simply be turned around to provide an indication of the value of an equity.

Example

XYZ PLC is operating in a sector where the average prospective PER is currently eight times. If XYZ's earnings per share are expected to be 30p, the implied value of an XYZ PLC share is:

PER x expected EPS = 8 x 30p = 240p

NAV represents the net asset value per share attributable to ordinary shareholders and is calculated as follows:

$$NAV = \frac{(\text{Total Assets} - \text{Liabilities} - \text{Preference shares})}{\text{Number of shares in issue}}$$

As a measure of the value of a share, it does not take account of the fact that the ordinary shares of a company will normally be expected to trade at premium to their NAV.

An example of this is the internally generated goodwill attributable to the company's management, market positioning and reputation that is not capitalised in the company's balance sheet under the historic cost convention. The latter underpins the preparation of financial statements.

However, the NAV per share is useful for assessing the following:

- The minimum price at which a company's shares should theoretically trade.
- The underlying value of a property company.

- The underlying value of an investment trust; a PLC that invests in other company and government securities.

NAV per share is not useful for assessing the value of service or people oriented businesses that are driven by intellectual, rather than physical, capital because the former cannot be capitalised in the balance sheet.

3.3 Shareholder Valuation Models

Learning Objective

9.3.3   Understand and be able to apply the basic concept behind shareholder value models: economic value added (EVA); market value added (MVA)

The approach taken by shareholder value models is to establish whether a company has the ability to add value for its ordinary shareholders, by earning returns on its assets in excess of the cost of financing these assets.

Economic value added (EVA) is the most popular of these shareholder value approaches.

The EVA for any single accounting period is calculated by adjusting the operating profit in the company's income statement, mainly by adding back non-cash items, and subtracting from this the company's weighted average cost of capital (WACC) multiplied by an adjusted net assets figure from the company's balance sheet, termed invested capital.

If the result is positive, then value is being added. If negative, however, value is being destroyed.

It should be noted that EVA:

- is based on accounting profits and accounting measures of capital employed
- only measures value creation or destruction over one accounting period, and
- in isolation cannot establish whether a company's shares are overvalued or undervalued.

In order to determine whether a company's shares are correctly valued, the concept of market value added (MVA) needs to be employed.

A company's MVA is the market's assessment of the present value of the company's future annual EVAs.

Quite simply, if the present value of the company's future annual EVAs discounted at the company's WACC is greater than that implied by the MVA, this implies that the company's shares are undervalued and vice versa if less than the MVA.

Like EVA, MVA also relies on accounting values to establish the invested capital figure and in addition requires analysts to forecast EVAs several years into the future to determine whether the resultant MVA is reasonable.

End of Chapter Questions

Think of an answer for each question and refer to the appropriate workbook section for confirmation.

1. In technical analysis, what is a primary movement?
    Answer reference: Section 1.2

2. What is the relationship between breakouts from continuation patterns and relative strength charts?
    Answer reference: Section 1.2

3. A company has the following:

    *   Total assets of £100m
    *   Current liabilities of £35m
    *   Short term borrowings of £5m
    *   Profit before interest and tax of £8m

    What is its return on capital employed?
    Answer reference: Section 2.1.1

4. What is asset turnover and what does it measure?
    Answer reference: Section 2.1.2

5. What is asset turnover and profit margin and how are they related?
    Answer reference: Section 2.1.2

6. A Z-score analysis on a company has produced a negative result. What is a Z-score and what would the result indicate?
    Answer reference: Section 2.2.3

7. What is the PE ratio used for?
    Answer reference: Section 2.3.2

8. A company has profit before interest and tax of £1m and has interest payable of £750k. What is its interest cover and what would the result indicate?
    Answer reference: Section 2.4.2

9. What are the limitations of ratio analysis?
    Answer reference: Section 2.5

10. A company paid a dividend last year of 5p per share. It will increase by 5% this year and in forthcoming years. Using Gordon's Growth Model what would you expect its share price to be if the required return to equity holders is 7%?
    Answer reference: Section 3.1

Chapter Ten
Taxation

This syllabus area will provide approximately 4 of the 80 examination questions

An understanding of tax is essential in investment management.

The interaction of taxes needs to be fully understood so that the client's assets are suitably invested to minimise the impact that tax will have on either growth or income. This can make a substantial difference to the returns from an investment and at the same time complicate the investment decision-making process.

Although it is important to maximise the use of tax allowances, exemptions and reliefs, investment decisions should never be based solely on the tax considerations. With certain exceptions, tax breaks are usually only given in exchange for accepting a higher level of risk.

When managing tax implications for a client, it is important to appreciate the difference between tax evasion and tax avoidance. Tax evasion is a financial crime and is illegal; tax avoidance is organising your affairs within the rules so that you pay the least tax possible. The latter is a responsibility of the adviser when they are undertaking financial planning.

In this chapter, we will consider the taxes that affect companies, in order to understand the impact that this can have in the selection of investment opportunities and then the taxes that affect individuals.

1. UK Corporation Tax

If a company is resident in the UK, its total profits are generally chargeable to corporation tax. Total profits include both the profits from its activities and any chargeable gains.

Non-UK resident companies are only liable to pay corporation tax on profits generated in the UK.

As with personal taxes, Her Majesty's Revenue and Customs (HMRC) is responsible for the administration, assessment and collection of corporation tax.

1.1 Basics of Corporation Tax

Learning Objective

10.1.1 Understand what corporation tax is and the circumstances in which trading companies are taxed and the payment timetable: taxable profits; franked investment income; capital losses; depreciation; when due

Companies are subject to corporation tax in respect of their taxable profit for their chargeable accounting period (CAP).

Accounting Periods

Unlike individuals who pay tax for a set fiscal year, companies pay tax for what is known as an accounting period.

If a company is resident in the UK, it is liable to corporation tax on the profits arising for an accounting period which is normally the period covered by its accounts. An accounting period for tax purposes can never be longer than 12 months.

An accounting period starts when:

*   a company first becomes chargeable to corporation tax, or
*   the previous accounting period ends.

An accounting period ends when the earliest of the following takes place:

*   the company reaches its accounting date.
*   it is 12 months since the start of the accounting period.
*   the company starts or stops trading.

A number of adjustments are made to a company's profit to calculate the profit on which corporation tax is due in accordance with HMRC rules. This taxable profit is termed the 'profits chargeable to corporation tax'.

The main adjustments comprise:

*   **Including book losses and book profits in respect of asset sales.**
    *   As the depreciation charge can be subjective, depreciation is removed from reported pre-tax profit and replaced by capital allowances.
    *   Capital allowances are standardised rates of depreciation that are applied to tangible fixed assets, on a reducing balance basis.
    *   Capital allowance rates are set by HMRC; they differ according to the size of the company and the type of fixed asset to which they are applied.
*   **Removing dividend income received from other UK companies.**
    *   Dividend income received from other UK companies is known as franked investment income (FII).
    *   As FII is received net of UK corporation tax, no further tax is due from the recipient company. Therefore, it should not be included in the calculation of taxable profit.
    *   Unfranked investment income (UFII), such as interest income, however, being received gross, is subject to corporation tax.
*   **Adding back any provisions made.**
    *   Provisions are by their very nature subjective, so should not be allowed to reduce taxable profit.
*   **Adding back any book losses and deducting any book profits in respect of asset sales.**
    *   As UK companies are subject to corporation tax on any capital gains made during the accounting period and are given relief for capital losses, any book gains and losses recorded in the income statement should be replaced by the appropriate capital gains or losses figure.

Once a company's taxable profit has been calculated for the CAP, the appropriate corporation tax rate is then applied to this figure to determine the corporation tax liability. If as a result of making the necessary adjustments to the reported pre-tax profit a loss is arrived at, this may be carried back three financial years so that a corporation tax rebate may be received, or carried forward indefinitely to be offset against future taxable profits.

Corporation Tax Rates

Since 1 April 2015 there has been a single corporation tax rate of 20% for non-ringfenced profits.

In its 2015 budget, the government announced legislation setting the corporation tax main rate (for all profits except ringfenced profits) at 19% for the years starting 1 April 2017, 2018 and 2019 and at 18% for the year starting 1 April 2020. In 2016 budget, the government announced a further reduction to the corporation tax main rate (for all profits except ringfenced profits) for the year starting 1 April 2020, setting the rate at 17%.

There is a special rate for unit trusts and OEICs of 20%.

If the company's accounting period does not coincide with the financial year but instead straddles two financial years, each with different corporation tax rates, the rate applied to the taxable profit figure will be a weighted average of the two rates.

HMRC issues companies with a notice to deliver its company tax return, known as form CT 603, usually between three and seven weeks after the end of the company's accounting period. The company can then send in its company tax return at any time after the end of its accounting period, but must do so no later than the statutory filing date. This is normally the later of:

- 12 months after the end of the accounting period, or
- three months after the company receives the notice to deliver.

HMRC will then review the company tax return to determine how much tax is payable and issue a corporation tax assessment to the company showing the amount of tax due.

Corporation tax is then normally due to be paid exactly nine months and one day after the company's last day of their accounting period. Large companies, that is ones whose profits are greater than £1.5 million and so are liable to the main rate of corporation tax, have to pay their tax by quarterly instalments.

1.2 Franked Investment Income

Learning Objective

10.1.2 Be able to apply the differences between franked and unfranked investment income: payment from net profits; sources of franked income; corporation tax payable on unfranked income

Investment income is treated differently from trading profits on the corporation tax return and the following types of investment income must be disclosed separately:

- Bank interest.
- Dividends.
- Other investment income.
- Annuities.
- Income from UK land and buildings.
- Certain types of overseas income and expenses.

The corporation tax treatment of investment income depends upon whether it is treated as franked investment income or unfranked investment income.

It is common for one company to hold shares in another, and therefore to receive dividends from that company. If this happens, tax will in effect already have been paid out on that dividend, because the investee company has paid it out of its post-tax profits. For this reason, the dividend will be paid up to the investor company with a tax credit attached, reflecting the fact that the company which has paid the dividend has done so out of post-tax profits. This is called franked income. Franked income is free of further tax to the receiving company.

Until 30 June 2009 franked investment income was restricted to qualifying distributions from UK resident companies, but dividends from foreign companies are now also included.

All other investment income is treated as unfranked investment income and is taxed at the same rate as trading profits. However, if you make any losses in these areas, you can only offset them against trading profits from the same accounting period. If these are insufficient to absorb such losses, they can only be offset against gains in other accounting periods arising from non-trading activities.

2. UK Personal Taxes

Individuals in the UK are potentially liable to three types of taxation:

- Income tax.
- Capital gains tax (CGT).
- Inheritance tax (IHT).

Each of these is considered below along with the principle of domicile and its impact on private client management.

2.1 Income Tax

Learning Objective

10.2.1 Understand the application of income tax on earnings, dividend and interest income

Income tax is the tax that is charged on individuals who are classed as resident in the UK and who are liable to tax on virtually all income received.

Individuals who are defined as being resident and ordinarily resident in the UK are liable to UK income tax. Although residency rules are applied on a case-by-case basis, a UK resident is generally one who is physically present in the UK for at least 183 days in any tax year while ordinary residence is judged by the time an individual spends in the UK on a regular basis.

If an individual is based overseas and spends more than an average of 91 days per annum over four consecutive years or more than eight months in any one year visiting the UK, they are likely to be deemed ordinarily resident.

For individuals, the tax year runs from 6 April to 5 April and is known as the fiscal year.

2.1.1 Taxable Income

As mentioned above, income tax is chargeable on virtually all income, so it is important to understand what income is charged to tax and what is not.

Income tax is chargeable on what HMRC terms taxable income which includes:

*   Earnings from employment.
*   Earnings from self-employment.
*   Pension income including state, company and personal pensions.
*   Interest on savings.
*   Income from shares.
*   Rental income.
*   Income paid from a trust.

Income that is exempt from tax includes:

*   State benefits.
*   Working tax credit and child tax credit.
*   Income from tax exempt accounts such as Individual Savings Accounts (ISAs) and savings certificates.
*   Premium bond wins.

2.1.2 Tax Allowances

Having considered what income is taxable, the next step is to look at what allowances are available as everyone is entitled to receive a certain amount of income tax-free during the tax year.

This is known as an income tax personal allowance and the amount depends on age. Personal allowances are announced each year by the Chancellor of the Exchequer as part of the pre-budget report which normally takes place in November and December. They are set for the following fiscal year which runs from 6 April in one year to 5 April of the following year.

Personal Allowances

Personal Allowance	2016/17	Income Limit
Basic rate	£11,000	£100,000
Age 65–74	£11,000	£27,700
Age 75 and over	£11,000	£27,700

- The personal allowance reduces if the income is above £100,000 – by £1 for every £2 of income above the £100,000 limit. It can go down to zero.
- For individuals born before 6 April 1938 the allowance reduces by £1 for every £2 above the income limit.
- The married couple's allowance is intended for circumstances where one party does not have sufficient income to utilise the personal allowance. It only applies where one party was born before 6 April 1935. It is an allowance that is taken off a tax bill and so only applies if an individual pays tax, but any unused allowance can be transferred to the other partner.
- Depending on an individual's circumstances, they may also be able to claim certain other allowances.

2.2   Tax Rates

So far, we have looked at what income is chargeable to income tax and what tax-free allowance can be deducted from that. The next step is to look at what rates of tax are payable on the resulting taxable income.

The Chancellor announces the taxable bands and the rates of tax at the budget report which normally takes place in March.

Tax is paid on the amount of taxable income remaining after allowances have been deducted.

Band	Rate	Income after allowances 2016 to 2017	Income after allowances 2015 to 2016	Income after allowances 2014 to 2015	Income after allowances 2013 to 2014
Starting rate for savings	10% (0% from 2015 to 2016)	Up to £5,000	Up to £5,000	Up to £2,880	Up to £2,790
Basic rate	20%	Up to £32,000	Up to £31,785	Up to £31,865	Up to £32,010
Higher rate	40%	£32,001 to £150,000	£31,786 to £150,000	£31,866 to £150,000	£32,011 to £150,000
Additional rate	45%	Over £150,000	Over £150,000	Over £150,000	Over £150,000

2.3   Tax Treatment of Savings Income and Dividends

The tax treatment of income arising from investments depends upon whether it is interest or dividends. The amount of tax that is due will depend upon the tax position of the individual:

Band	Dividend Tax Rates
Basic rate (and non-taxpayers)	10%
Higher rate	32.5%
Additional rate (from 6 April 2013)	37.5%
Additional rate (dividends paid before 6 April 2013)	42.5%

Since April 2016 there has been new dividend allowance.

Tax on dividends from April 2016

From 6 April 2016, tax is not due on the first £5,000 of dividends in the tax year.

Above this allowance the tax due depends on which income tax band the individual is in. Income from dividends is added to other taxable income when calculating this. Therefore tax pay may be at more than one rate.

Tax Band	Tax Rate on Dividends over £5,000
Basic rate	7.5%
Higher rate	32.5%
Additional rate	38.1%

Tax on Savings Interest

From 6 April 2016, most people can earn some income from their savings without paying tax. This is known as a personal savings allowance. It applies to each tax year, from 6 April to 5 April the following year.

Personal Savings Allowance

If an individual's taxable income is £17,000 or less, no tax is due on the savings income.

Otherwise the savings allowance depends on the individual's income tax band.

Income Tax Band	Tax-Free Savings Income
Basic rate	£1,000
Higher rate	£500
Additional rate	£0

Any income above this is paid at the individual's usual rate of income tax.

2.4 Tax Wrappers

Learning Objective

10.2.2 Understand which types of company can be held within and the tax advantages of investing in: ISAs; Enterprise Investment Schemes (EISs); Venture Capital Trusts (VCTs)

As mentioned above, there are certain sources of income which are not liable to income tax or where the individual receives a tax reduction.

The key features of some of these are considered below.

2.4.1 Individual Savings Account (ISA)

An individual savings account (ISA) is often referred to as an investment wrapper because it is essentially an account that holds other investments, such as deposits, shares and unit trusts and allows them to be invested in a tax-efficient manner.

ISAs were introduced in 1999 as a replacement for personal equity plans (PEPs). Following changes to the tax regime covering both ISAs and PEPs, all PEP accounts automatically became stocks and shares ISAs from 6 April 2008.

Investors and savers are able to contribute to two components of an ISA; cash and stocks and shares. ISAs are generally available to any individual who is UK-resident and ordinarily resident. A cash ISA can be opened for 16- or 17-year-olds but a stocks and shares ISA can only be opened once someone reaches 18.

The June 2010 Budget announced that from 6 April 2011 the annual allowance would be increased in line with changes in the RPI. The 2011 budget amended this approach and from the 2012–13 tax year, the CPI was to be used instead.

The new limits are calculated by reference to the RPI for the September before the start of the following tax year and the government announces the new limits each year, in advance of the start of the new tax year, in which they apply. In the event that the RPI is negative, the ISA limits remain unchanged.

Using this approach, HMRC announced that the maximum overall subscription limit for 2016–17 is £15,240 and that within the overall limit, no more than 50% may be placed in the cash component.

ISAs receive both income tax and capital gains tax advantages:

- Any interest income received in an ISA is not liable to income tax.
- The tax credit on a dividend cannot be reclaimed, but there is no further liability to income tax for a higher rate taxpayer.
- Any gains on investments are not liable to CGT.

HMRC sets the rules for ISAs and places restrictions on the type of investments that can be held within an ISA. The types of investment that can be held include:

- Qualifying shares and certain investment trusts.
- Depositary interests.
- Qualifying securities.
- Government securities.
- UCITS funds and qualifying authorised funds and non-UCITS funds.
- Cash.

The rules are complex, however, and so reference needs to be made to the HMRC rules whenever a new security is to be added to a portfolio.

2.4.2 Enterprise Investment Scheme (EIS)

The enterprise investment scheme (EIS) is designed to help smaller, higher-risk trading companies to raise finance by offering a range of tax reliefs to investors who purchase new shares in these companies.

Companies who wish to issue shares under the scheme have to meet a certain number of rules regarding the kind of company it is, the amount of money it can raise, how and when that money must be employed for the purposes of the trade, and the trading activities carried on.

An investor receives tax advantages when investing in EIS companies providing that they invest in fully paid ordinary shares that carry the full risk of ordinary shares and carry no preferential rights that protect the investor from the normal risks of investing in shares.

Income tax relief is given on investments in an EIS-qualifying company subject to a minimum of £500 and a maximum of £1 million. For shares issued after 6 April 2011, the relief is 30% of the cost of the shares that can be set against the individual's income tax liability for the year in which the investment was made. The shares must then be held for a minimum period of three years otherwise the income tax relief is withdrawn.

From 2009–10, an investor may carry back part or all of the amount invested and claim tax relief for the previous year subject to the limits for relief for that year.

EIS shares can also qualify for CGT relief providing that they have qualified for income tax relief and that has not been withdrawn. If they have qualified for relief, any disposals after the minimum three-year period are free from capital gains tax.

If a gain is made, the payment of tax can be deferred if the gain is invested in shares of another EIS-qualifying company, within a period of one year before, or three years after, the gain arose.

If a loss is made instead, the amount of the loss less any income tax relief can be set against income of the year in which they were disposed of or the previous year instead of being set off against any capital gains.

2.4.3 Venture Capital Trusts (VCTs)

Venture capital trusts (VCTs) are companies listed on the LSE and are similar to investment trusts. They are designed to enable individuals to invest indirectly in a range of small higher-risk trading companies, whose shares and securities are not listed on a recognised stock exchange, by investing through VCTs.

Investment in VCTs attracts special tax advantages and so needs to gain HMRC approval to be treated as such. Once approved, VCTs are exempt from corporation tax on any gains arising on the disposal of their investments.

Investors may also be entitled to various income tax and CGT reliefs. These include:

- Exemption from income tax on dividends from ordinary shares in VCTs.
- Income tax relief at 30% of the amount subscribed up to a maximum of £200,000 and providing they are held for at least five years.
- Any gain made on disposal is free of CGT if held for five years.

The relief for dividend income and gains applies whether the shares were acquired at issue or subsequently via a stock exchange trade. The income tax relief is only available for initial subscriptions.

2.5 Capital Gains Tax (CGT)

Learning Objective

10.2.3 Understand capital gains tax (CGT) and the assets that are subject to or exempt from CGT: sale of shares/convertible loan stock; sale of gilts/corporate bonds; losses carried forward; principal residence/second homes

Capital Gains tax (CGT) is a tax on capital gains made when an asset is disposed of.

Individuals that are resident and ordinarily resident in the UK are known as chargeable persons for CGT purposes. Chargeable persons are potentially liable to CGT on capital gains made on the disposal of chargeable assets regardless of where in the world the capital gain arose.

Most assets are chargeable to CGT including:

- Shares in a company.
- Units in a unit trust.
- Land and buildings.
- Higher-value jewellery, paintings, antiques and other personal effects.
- Assets used in a business, such as goodwill.

There are some exceptions to this, and the following assets are exempt.

- An individual's nominated main or principal private residence (PPR).
- Gilts and qualifying corporate bonds. (A qualifying corporate bond is one that meets certain qualifying conditions set by HMRC. Any profit on its sale or disposal is exempt from Capital Gains Tax and any loss is not an allowable loss. Most sterling bonds, securities, debentures, loan notes and loan stock are qualifying corporate bonds.)
- Jewellery, paintings, antiques and other personal effects that are individually worth £6,000 or less.
- Savings certificates and premium bonds.
- Assets held in an ISA.
- EIS and VCT investments subject to being held for a qualifying period.

- Betting, lottery or pools winnings.
- Personal injury compensation.

CGT arises when a chargeable asset is disposed of. A disposal arises as a result of a transfer of ownership, the making of a gift, the receipt of a capital sum from an asset and even the destruction of an asset.

However, a disposal is not potentially chargeable to CGT, or allowable as a capital loss, if made between spouses, made upon death or if the asset is exempt.

The Finance Act 2008 simplified CGT calculations considerably and introduced the concept of a Section 104 holding.

- From 6 April 2008 all shares of the same class in the same company are treated as part of a section 104 holding.
- The costs of all purchases are added together and each share is treated as if they were acquired at the same average cost.
- There is therefore a single pool of expenditure usually representing the actual cost of the shares.
- The exception is any shares held on 31 March 1982. Any investments held at that date are revalued at market value as at 31 March 1982 to create a single pool of shares. The section 104 holding then consists of assets valued at 1982, plus actual costs for subsequent purchases.
- The pool then adjusted every time there is an operative event.

The basic steps for working out a gain (or loss) on a disposal of shares in a Section 104 holding are as follows:

- If all the shares in the holding are disposed of, the allowable expenditure is all of the pool of cost.
- If only some of the shares are disposed of, the allowable expenditure is an appropriate fraction of the pool of actual cost.
- The remaining cost in the holding, to be identified against future disposals, is reduced accordingly.

Example

An investor has a holding of 10,000 ABC ordinary shares. The Section 104 holding therefore has a pool of 10,000 shares and a total pool cost £9,000 which is equivalent to 90p per share.

If a sale of 5,000 shares is made then the acquisition cost of the 5,000 shares that are sold is simply £9,000 x 5,000/10,000 = £4,500.

The pool cost of the remaining holding is £4,500.

When you dispose of shares you cannot work out your capital gain or loss until you have matched the shares disposed of with shares you acquired. You are treated as disposing of shares in the following order:

- First, shares acquired on the same day as the disposal (the **same day** rule).
- Second, shares acquired in the 30 days following the day of disposal (the **bed and breakfasting** rule) provided the person making the disposal was resident in the United Kingdom at the time of the acquisition, if the relevant acquisition was on or after 22 March 2007.
- Third, shares in the Section 104 holding.
- If the above rules fail to exhaust the shares disposed of, the remaining shares are matched with later acquisitions, taking the earliest one first.

You can then calculate whether the disposal results in a chargeable gain or loss.

Calculating CGT

The basic layout for calculating CGT is as follows:

ABC Holdings ordinary shares
Proceeds of sale on --/--/--
Less: Incidental disposal costs
Chargeable gain
Less: Allowable expenditure
Chargeable gain or loss

- Proceeds of sale – consideration for the sale of the holding
- Incidental disposal costs – broker's commission
- Allowable expenditure – cost of acquiring the asset including brokers commission, SDRT and any POTAM levy.

In order to calculate the total CGT position, it is necessary to repeat the exercise for each disposal. Once you've worked out all of the individual gains and losses for each asset sold or disposed of, you can then work out the overall gain or loss to see the tax due.

Calculating CGT Due

Total gains	Add together all of the gains for the year
Less – Allowable losses	Add together all of the allowable losses for the year
Overall gain or loss	Deduct losses from gains to work out overall gain or loss
Less – Annual exempt amount	Deduct annual exemption – if overall gain is below then there is no CGT to pay
Less – Unused allowable losses	If gain is above annual exempt amount, deduct unused allowable losses from previous tax years
Net gain	Net gain is taxable at either 10% or 20%

If an overall gain is made, individuals have an annual allowance and any gains within this are exempt from tax.

- The annual exempt amount (AEA) for 2016–17 is £11,100. Gains that are in excess of the AEA are taxable at either 10% or 20%.
- For individuals, if their total taxable income and gains after all allowable deductions are less than the upper limit of the basic rate income tax band, the rate of CGT will be 10%. For gains and any parts of gains above that limit, the rate will be 20%.
- For trustees and personal representatives of deceased persons, the rate will be 20%. The annual exempt amount for most trustees is half of the amount available to individuals.

Unused allowable losses are ones carried forward from previous tax years. To carry unused losses forward to the next tax year, you have to inform HMRC before you are allowed to deduct the losses from gains. There are time limits for making a claim namely, five years from 31 January after the end of the tax year in which the loss was made

2.6   Inheritance Tax

Learning Objective

10.2.4   Understand what inheritance tax (IHT) is and the assets subject to or exempt from IHT: potentially exempt transfers; lifetime transfers; transfers to a spouse; business property relief

Inheritance tax (IHT) is the tax that is due when someone dies or makes a gift of assets during their lifetime.

IHT is charged on the value of an individual's assets, or estate, at death and on certain lifetime transfers of assets. IHT is chargeable on all worldwide assets of a UK-domiciled individual.

IHT is payable at 40% on the net value of someone's estate that is in excess of the nil rate band. For the 2012–13 tax year this amount is £325,000. It should be noted that for deaths on or after 9 October 2007 it is possible for spouses and civil partners to transfer their unused inheritance tax nil rate band allowances to the surviving partner.

There are certain exemptions from IHT that allow an individual to legally pass their estate on to others, both before and after your death, without its being subject to IHT.

Gifts to certain beneficiaries are exempt including:

- Gifts to a spouse or civil partner.
- Gifts to UK charities.
- Gifts to certain national institutions such as the National Trust.
- Gifts to political parties.

Equally, certain gifts are exempt from IHT including:

- Wedding gifts by parents up to £5,000, by grandparents up to £2,500 and £1,000 for anyone else.
- Small gifts up to £250 per annum to as many people as the individual wishes.
- Annual exemption for other gifts of £3,000 per tax year, which can be carried forward to the next year if not used but no further.
- Gifts that can be made out of normal expenditure; that is, out of after-tax income.
- Maintenance payments to a spouse, an ex-spouse, dependent relatives and children.

Gifts can be made in excess of these exemption, during an individual's life and are known as potentially exempt transfers. These gifts are free of IHT providing that the individual making the gift survives for seven years after making the gift.

Business Property Relief (BPR) is a very important and valuable relief from IHT. It reduces the value upon a transfer of certain types of business or business property by a specified percentage. The current BPR rates are 100% and 50% respectively. The actual rate of relief depends on the type of business property. It is available for lifetime transfers and for relevant business property included in an individual's estate on death.

From January 2017, new inheritance tax measures will apply.

As published by HMRC, these will include:

Individuals with direct descendants who have an estate (including a main residence) with total assets above the Inheritance Tax (IHT) threshold (or nil-rate band) of £325,000 and personal representatives of deceased persons.

An additional nil-rate band when a residence is passed on death to a direct descendant of:

- *£100,000 in 2017 to 2018*
- *£125,000 in 2018 to 2019*
- *£150,000 in 2019 to 2020*
- *£175,000 in 2020 to 2021*

It will then increase in line with Consumer Prices Index (CPI) from 2021 to 2022 onwards. Any unused nil-rate band will be able to be transferred to a surviving spouse or civil partner.

The additional nil-rate band will also be available when a person downsizes or ceases to own a home on or after 8 July 2015 and assets of an equivalent value, up to the value of the additional nil-rate band, are passed on death to direct descendants.

There will be a tapered withdrawal of the additional nil-rate band for estates with a net value of more than £2 million. This will be at a withdrawal rate of £1 for every £2 over this threshold.

The existing nil-rate band will remain at £325,000 from 2018 to 2019 until the end of 2020 to 2021.

2.7 Domicile and Residence

Learning Objective

10.2.5 Understand the principle of domicile and its implication on private client management

The residence and domicile of an individual will determine how any income or gains are taxed in the UK. Residence and domicile are complex subjects and can have a significant bearing on the tax treatment of a private client and therefore how an adviser recommends they structure their affairs.

2.7.1   Domicile

In very simplistic terms, domicile is where you have your permanent home but is different than nationality or residence.

- In general domicile will be in a country as a whole.
  - You cannot be domiciled in the UK but in England and Wales, Scotland or Northern Ireland.
  - In countries with a federal system, domicile will relate to the individual state, province or canton, eg, Texas, Ontario, and Zurich.
- Domicile is separate from other connecting factors such as nationality or residence. So, it is possible to be a national of the UK, resident (say) in Spain but domiciled (say) in Jersey. However, nationality and place(s) of residence are relevant facts to consider when ascertaining your permanent home.
- The mechanics of domicile ensure that you have one, and only one, domicile.

When a person is born, they acquire a domicile of origin, which is the country in which they are born or the domicile of their father if that is different. Once a person reaches the age of 16, they can change their domicile but this requires a deliberate breaking of all ties with the previous country, combined with an intention to live there permanently. The new country is termed a domicile of choice.

2.7.2   Residence

Broadly, an individual who is resident and ordinarily resident in the UK will pay tax on their worldwide income. For others, special rules apply depending upon where they are resident or domiciled.

There are three types of residence status:

- ordinarily resident
- resident but not ordinarily resident
- ordinarily resident but not resident.

Residence Status

- Ordinarily resident/ordinary residence
  - If you are resident here your ordinary residence position in the UK generally matters only if you have income from outside the UK.
  - In exceptional circumstances you may be not resident but still ordinarily resident in the UK. This is very rare but if it does apply, you also pay UK tax on your capital gains.
- Resident but not ordinarily resident
  - You can be resident in the UK but not ordinarily resident here.
  - It means that, although they are resident in the UK for a particular tax year, they normally live somewhere else.
  - For example, if you are resident in a tax year, because you have been in the country for more than 183 days but you normally live outside the UK, it is likely that you are not ordinarily resident.
- Ordinarily resident but not resident
  - You can be ordinarily resident in the UK but not resident.
  - If you normally live in the UK but, during a tax year, you have gone abroad for a long holiday and you do not set foot in the UK in the tax year, you are ordinarily resident but not resident.
  - It is very rare.

If you are ordinarily resident in the UK you are normally treated as being on the 'arising basis of taxation'. This means that you will pay UK tax on all of your income as it arises and on your gains as they accrue, wherever that income and those gains are in the world.

Individuals who are resident in the UK but not domiciled here, or resident in the UK but not ordinarily resident, receive special tax treatment in respect of income and gains arising outside the UK.

If either applies, the individual can use the remittance basis of taxation. Under this, individuals still pay UK tax on any income arising in the UK, but income and gains that arise overseas are treated differently. Instead they only account for UK tax on these to the extent they are brought into the UK; in other words, the amount remitted into the UK.

- **Resident but not domiciled in the UK** – can use the remittance basis for both foreign income and foreign capital gains.
- **Resident and domiciled in the UK but not ordinarily resident** – can only use the remittance basis for foreign income. Does not apply to their foreign capital gains which will be taxed on the arising basis.

As a result of the Finance Act 2008, limitations were introduced on how and when this can be claimed. These meant that some people using the remittance basis lost their entitlement to personal allowances and had to pay a remittance basis charge of £30,000. From April 2015, a new charge was introduced. The £30,000 charge remains the same for those resident in the UK for seven of the past nine years. The 12 out of 14 year charge increased form £50,000 to £60,000, with the seven out of 20 year charge of £90,000.

Remittance Basis Charge (RBC)

People with less than £2,000 unremitted foreign income or gains in a tax year:

- Are not affected by these changes. They will still be able to use the remittance basis and will keep their entitlement to UK personal tax allowances. They will not need to pay the RBC.
- They will still have to pay UK tax on any foreign income and gains which they remit to the UK.

People with £2,000 or more unremitted foreign income and/or gains in a tax year:

- If they wish to use the remittance basis they must make a claim for this on a self-assessment return.
- People who are over 18 years old in the tax year they make the claim but who have not been resident in the UK for at least seven of the last nine tax years, do not need to pay the £30,000 RBC. They will still have to pay UK tax on any income or gains they remit to the UK and they will lose their entitlement to UK personal tax allowances and to the AEA for capital gains.
- People claiming the remittance basis who have £2,000 or more in unremitted foreign income and gains and have been resident in the UK for at least seven of the previous nine tax years, will have to pay the RBC.

People entitled to the remittance basis may choose not to claim it. They will then be taxed in the same way as other UK residents on the arising basis. Tax will become due on worldwide income and gains for that tax year. But the RBC will not apply and they will be entitled to UK personal tax allowances and to the AEA for capital gains. They will need to complete a UK self-assessment return if they have any foreign income or gains for that year.

People entitled to claim the remittance basis are able to decide on a year-by-year basis whether they want to do so. In one year, a person might opt to pay the RBC and lose their allowances, while in the next year they might choose to pay tax on all of their worldwide income and gains.

3. Overseas Taxation

Learning Objective

10.3.1 Know the principles of withholding tax (WHT): types of income subject to WHT; relief through double taxation agreements; deducted at source

10.3.2 Know the principles of double taxation relief (DTR): purpose

If investors hold shares in overseas companies, they will receive dividends that may be subject to the tax of that country. The tax that is deducted is known as withholding tax (WHT).

In many countries, local tax regulations require that any income payments that are made to non-residents should be taxed at source before payment. WHT is usually deducted at source by the issuer or their paying agent and has to be reclaimed by investors from the tax authorities in that country.

Where an investor receives a dividend from an overseas company that has had WHT deducted, it will still remain liable to UK income tax, and that raises the risk of the double taxation of the dividend or interest income. To address this issue, governments enter into what are known as double taxation treaties to agree how any payments will be handled.

In very simple terms, the way that a double taxation agreement operates is that the two governments agree what rate of tax will be withheld on any interest or dividend payment. The rate of tax will usually be less than the rate that the investor is due to pay in the UK, so that the UK tax authorities can collect the balance. This prevents double taxation and shares the tax revenue between the two countries.

End of Chapter Questions

Think of an answer for each question and refer to the appropriate workbook section for confirmation.

1. What adjustments are made to a company's profit to calculate the profit on which corporation tax is due in accordance with HMRC rules?
   Answer reference: Section 1.1

2. When determining the profits chargeable to corporation tax, dividend income from other companies is removed. Why is this the case?
   Answer reference: Sections 1.1 and 1.2

3. When determining the profits chargeable to corporation tax, depreciation is removed. Why is this the case?
   Answer reference: Section 1.1

4. In 2016/17, what is the personal allowance for an individual aged 62 and how is it reduced for income over £100,000.
   Answer reference: Sections 2.1.2

5. In 2014/15, an investor has received £900 of dividend income. What tax would be payable on this by a basic rate taxpayer, a higher rate taxpayer and an additional tax rate payer?
   Answer reference: Section 2.3

6. How is a venture trust shareholding income distribution treated for income tax purposes?
   Answer reference: Section 2.4.3

7. A higher rate taxpayer has £100,000 of taxable income and invests £50,000 into a qualifying EIS company. How would this affect his tax position?
   Answer reference: Section 2.4.2

Chapter Eleven
Portfolio Management

This syllabus area will provide approximately 10 of the 80 examination questions

1. Risk and Return

This section looks at the financial theory, which, over the past 50 years, has had a pronounced effect on the construction of investment portfolios.

Risk arises from the uncertainty of outcomes. As investors, each time we decide to invest, the outcome is uncertain in the same way that any future event is. We are concerned that we may incur a loss if we have miscalculated the opportunity, or that we may not realise, fully or even partially, the expected return. At the macro level we may be concerned about the risks of market crashes, terrorist incidents that cause markets to plunge and other critical events. All of this contributes to the potential for profit from investment and speculation and the accompanying uneasiness that we all feel about the possibility of losses or adverse consequences from our investment or speculation activities. This is our general notion of risk.

The most general kind of risk is market or systematic risk, which is primarily influenced by macro-economic conditions and the state of the financial system. To a large extent this risk cannot be avoided, but for the typical investor there are some precautionary measures which will help to alleviate one's exposure to non-systematic risk. By spreading the total investments made in a portfolio over several different securities, from different asset classes, it is possible to get more or less the same returns that any one of them can offer, but with a much lower risk since, though one may become worthless, it is unlikely that they will all do so simultaneously. Diversification reduces risk without necessarily reducing returns. However, not all risk can be diversified away.

Risks and reward are important aspects of investment decisions. Risk and potential reward are generally positively correlated: investments with a higher potential return generally carry a higher risk of loss. High-risk investments generally have potential for a higher reward, plus a greater possibility of loss. Low-risk investments generally have a lower reward, with a lower possibility of loss.

1.1 Correlation

Learning Objective

11.1.1 Understand the concept of correlation of performance between asset classes

From an investment perspective the statistical notion of correlation is fundamental to portfolio theory.

The very simplest idea is that, if one is seeking diversification in the holdings of a portfolio, one would like to have, say, two assets where there is a low degree of association between the movements in price and returns of each asset. The degree of association can also be expressed in terms of the extent to which directional changes in each asset's returns, or their co-movement, are related.

Example

If assets A and B have a tendency to react to the same kinds of business conditions in a very similar and predictable manner they could be said to be strongly correlated. Let us assume that a certain kind of regular release of economic data (for example the monthly CPI data) is announced and company A's shares move up by 3% and company B's shares move up by 2.5% when the data is below expectations, and that the inverse pattern of price movement is seen when the data is above expectations. In such a case there is a strong correlation between the movements (or changes) in the performance returns of A and B, and this is expressed as strong positive correlation.

It is possible to measure the degree of co-movement in asset prices and determine the coefficient of correlation between changes in the prices of two assets such as share prices. The limiting cases for the coefficient of correlation are –1, which is perfect negative correlation, and +1, which is perfect positive correlation.

- In the example above, both companies' shares will tend to move up and down together, although the magnitude of the change may not be the same. The two company's shares will have a very high degree of positive correlation.
- If on the other hand the prices of two assets tend to move in opposite directions, so that when one is moving upwards the other is moving downwards and vice versa then there will be a strong negative correlation between the two assets.

Example

There are not many obvious cases in the financial world where strong negative correlation is observed, but a recently observed example involves the strength of the US dollar in its exchange rate with many other currencies.

Increasingly, strength in the US dollar appears to be negatively correlated with the movements in global equities. The reason for the negative correlation that is cited is the tendency of investors to either seek out riskier assets such as global equities or to turn to the safe haven of the dollar when equity prices are sinking.

If price changes in two assets are strongly correlated and they are combined together in a simple small portfolio, there are relatively minimal benefits to the diversification of the portfolio, as the two assets will tend to move in harmony with each other.

The benefits of diversification are to be found in having a more heterogeneous collection of assets, some of which may move upwards in respect to economic developments and some of which may move sideways or downwards. From a diversification perspective, it can be demonstrated that the weaker the correlation between the two assets, the greater the degree of diversification. It should be remembered, however, that correlation does not remain constant.

1.2 Modern Portfolio Theory (MPT)

Learning Objective

11.1.2 Understand the main principles of Modern Portfolio Theory (MPT) and the need for diversification: purpose; correlation; diversification; future returns; efficient frontier

Modern portfolio theory (MPT) is commonly attributed to an article entitled *Portfolio Selection* by Harry Markowitz which appeared in 1952 in the Journal of Finance. The principles that were proposed in this highly influential paper now seem to be unremarkable, but at the time the emphasis on diversification, and the mathematical model that enabled a portfolio manager to assemble positions which provide the best level of expected return for a given risk tolerance, helped to usher in a period of great innovation in investment theory.

Prior to the MPT, the received wisdom on the manner of combining securities in a portfolio was to screen securities that offered the most attractive opportunities for gain with the least risk and then add these together in a portfolio. Bringing individual securities together in such a fashion would often lead to exposing the portfolio to too many securities from the same sector, where the correlations between the returns amongst the securities selected was imprudently high. In other words, the portfolio lacked the benefits of diversification.

Markowitz's major contribution was to outline a framework for deriving the benefits of diversification for a portfolio manager. They focused attention on the manner in which the overall volatility of a portfolio (which is considered to be the suitable proxy for its degree of risk) is calculated from the covariance matrix of the returns of its constituents.

MPT provided the asset manager with a systematic procedure for evaluating different combinations of securities and selecting those combinations which provided the optimal reward for a given level of risk. The optimal allocations will be a trade-off between the risks the client is willing to tolerate and the anticipated returns.

MPT states that by combining securities into a diversified portfolio, the overall risk is less than the risk inherent in holding any one individual stock and so reduces the combined variability of their future returns.

MPT states the risk for individual stocks consists of:

- Systematic risk – these are market risks that cannot be diversified away.
- Unsystematic risk – this is the risk associated with a specific stock and can be diversified away by increasing the number of stocks in a portfolio.

So a well diversified portfolio will reduce the risk that its actual returns will be lower than expected.

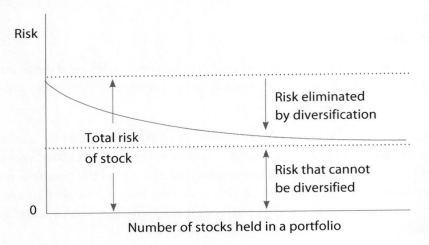

The process advocated by Markowitz enabled a fund manager to calculate the correlated portfolio volatility and the expected returns for numerous combination scenarios. From the range of possible portfolio combinations, there are a series of combinations that will optimally balance the risk and reward.

The optimal combinations that maximise the reward for the different possible levels of risk lie on what Markowitz termed the efficient frontier.

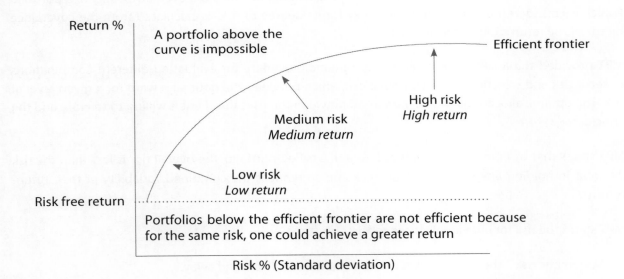

The efficient frontier shows that it is possible for different portfolios to have different levels of risk and return. Each investor decides how much risk they can tolerate and diversifies their portfolio accordingly. The optimal risk portfolio is usually determined to be somewhere in the middle of the curve because as you go up the curve, you take on proportionately higher risk for lower incremental returns. Equally, positioning a portfolio at the low end of the curve is pointless as you can achieve a similar return by investing in risk-free assets.

So a fundamental part of MPT is that constructing a portfolio with multiple securities, and guided by correlations between those securities, will lead to greater diversification, which will in turn reduce the risk of holding that portfolio.

Although since its origins in the early 1950s this basic portfolio selection model has been developed into more sophisticated models, such as the capital asset pricing model (CAPM) in the mid-1960s and arbitrage pricing theory (APT) in the late 1970s, it remains the backbone of finance theory and practice.

1.3 The Efficient Markets Hypothesis (EMH)

Learning Objective

11.1.3 Know the main propositions and limitations of the efficient markets hypothesis (EMH): strong form; semi-strong form; weak form

The efficient markets hypothesis (EMH) states that it is impossible to beat the market, as prices already incorporate and reflect all relevant information. It is also a highly controversial and often disputed theory.

Behind the EMH lie a number of key assumptions that underpin most finance theory models. Aside from investors being rational and risk averse, they are also assumed to possess a limitless capacity to source and process freely available information accurately.

Under EMH, market efficiency can be analysed at three levels, each of which have different implications for how markets work.

- **Weak form** – one in which security prices fully reflect past share price and trading volume data. As a consequence, successive future share prices should move independently of this past data in a random fashion, thereby nullifying any perceived informational advantage from adopting technical analysis to analyse trends.
- **Semi-strong form** – one in which share prices reflect all publicly available information and react instantaneously to the release of new information. As a consequence, no excess return can be earned by trading on that information and neither fundamental nor technical analysis will be able to produce excess returns reliably.
- **Strong form** – one in which share prices reflect all available information and no-one can earn excess returns. Insider dealing laws should make strong form efficiency impossible, except where they are universally ignored.

Generally speaking, most established Western equity markets are relatively price-efficient. Although testing for strong form efficiency is impossible, as inside information is required, the most conclusive evidence supporting the semi-strong efficient form of the EMH is that very few active portfolio managers produce excess returns consistently.

However, pricing anomalies and trends do occasionally arise as a result of markets and individual securities under- and over-shooting their fundamental values. As a consequence, some active managers do outperform their respective benchmarks and often do so in quite a spectacular fashion.

The limitations of the theory can, therefore, be seen to include the following:

*   Investors do not always invest in a rational fashion, thereby providing others with pricing anomalies to exploit.
*   Investors frequently use past share price data, especially recent highs and lows and the price they may have paid for a share, as anchors against which to judge the attractiveness of a particular share price, which in turn influences their decision-making.
*   The inability for all market participants to absorb and interpret information correctly, given varying abilities and the way in which the information is presented.
*   Stockmarket bubbles develop and eventually burst, which is a phenomenon which stands at odds with the EMH.
*   Investors frequently deal in securities for reasons completely unrelated to investment considerations, such as to raise cash or following a trend.

1.4 The Capital Asset Pricing Model (CAPM)

Learning Objective

11.1.4   Understand the assumptions underlying the construction of the capital asset pricing model (CAPM) and its limitations

One of the consequences of Markowitz's work on MPT is the realisation that through using quantitative techniques in portfolio construction, diversification of holdings of assets reduces risk. However there is a residual risk element that cannot be completely diversified away. This residual element is known as systematic risk.

The total risk of an investment can be divided into two subcategories:

*   **Systematic** or **Market Risk** – the variability of returns from an investment can be influenced by many macro-economic or market-wide factors:
    *   Changes in economic and monetary policy, eg, higher interest rates.
    *   Changes in the rate of inflation.
    *   Fiscal changes, eg, changes to corporation or income taxes.
    *   Systemic (as opposed to systematic risk) from contagion in the financial markets.
    *   General economic conditions and the influence of the business cycle.
*   **Unsystematic Risk** or **Specific Risk** – the kinds of influences which will lead to specific or unsystematic variability in the returns to an investment can be summarised briefly as follows:
    *   The quality of top management and their effectiveness in operating the business.
    *   Changes in the specific market place for the products or services of the business.
    *   Competitive factors and industry-specific cost-dislocations.

Unsystematic risk or specific risk can be eliminated through diversification. For an investor who has exposure to various sectors of the economy in his or her portfolio there has been a **spreading** of one's risk. Systematic or market risk is something that impacts on the economy in general and this is the type of risk that cannot be eliminated.

An undiversified investor, for example, would be one who has invested largely in the shares of a single company and will face the full risk of that investment. The investor should, therefore, look for a return commensurate with this undiversified risk.

A diversified investor will have eliminated, through diversification, the unsystematic risk inherent in the individual securities in his portfolio and face just the systematic risk. For this diversified investor a return should be sought which is commensurate with the level of systematic risk only.

The CAPM says that the expected return on a security or portfolio equals the rate on a risk-free security plus a risk premium and that if the expected return does not meet or beat this required return, then the investment should not be undertaken.

CAPM has some built-in assumptions:

- All market participants borrow and lend at the same risk-free rate.
- All market participants are well-diversified investors and specific risk has been diversified away.
- There are no tax or transaction costs to consider.
- All investors want to achieve a maximum return for minimum risk.
- Market participants have the same expectations about the returns and standard deviations of all assets.

Using these assumptions, CAPM is used to predict the expected or required returns to a security by using its systematic risks, in other words, its beta.

Systematic risk is assessed by measuring beta, which is the sensitivity of a stock's returns to the return on a market portfolio and so provides a measure of a stock's risk relative to the market as a whole.

Beta is calculated by constructing a scattergram of returns achieved by the stock against the market as a whole. By using regression analysis, a line of best fit is then drawn and the gradient of the line represents the stock's beta:

- If the stock's beta is 1, then the stock has the same volatility as the market as a whole.
- If it has a beta of greater than 1, then the stock is more volatile than the market as a whole.
- If a stock has a beta of 1.5, then it has 50% greater volatility than the market portfolio.
- If it has a beta of less than 1, the stock is less volatile than the market as a whole, so a stock with a beta of 0.7 has 30% less volatility.

We can use a stock's beta in conjunction with rate of return on a risk-free asset and the expected return from the market to calculate the return we should expect from a stock.

The CAPM formula is usually expressed as:

$$\text{Return} = r_f + \beta \times (r_m - r_f)$$

where:

r_m = the return expected from the market portfolio.

r_f = the return offered by a risk-free security.

β = the risk of the investment opportunity relative to that of the market portfolio (systematic risk only).

This can be expressed more clearly as:

Required return = Risk-Free Rate + Beta x (market rate – risk-free rate)

That is, the investor can expect to achieve the risk-free return (r_f) plus a proportion of the market risk premium ($r_m - r_f$) based on the levels of relative risk (β) he/she is willing to face.

By using the CAPM equation, it enables what is termed the **security market line** to be presented graphically. If a graph is plotted depicting the expected return from a security against its beta, then the relationship is revealed as a straight line.

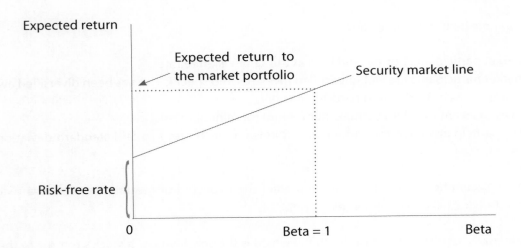

The security market line shows that the higher the risk of an asset, the higher the expected return. The market risk premium is the return an investor would expect over and above the risk-free rate (such as the return on a gilt) as a reward for taking on the additional market risk.

Example

We can use the CAPM formula to calculate the return we should expect from a stock. For example, if the current risk-free rate is 5% and the expected return from the market is 10%, what return should we expect from a security that has a beta of 1.5?

The beta of the individual stock tells us that it carries more risk than the market as a whole and the CAPM formula tells us that we should expect a return of?

Expected return = 5% + (10% – 5%) x 1.5 = 12.5%

CAPM, by providing a precise prediction of the relationship between a security's risk and return, therefore provides a benchmark rate of return for evaluating investments against their forecasted return.

CAPM is the tool which enables us to create portfolios where we have determined the degree of risk that the client is willing to face.

- An individual seeking a high return will need to take on high risk in order to have the chance of a higher return.
- To achieve a higher return we need to construct a portfolio with a high β. A portfolio with a β greater than 1 could be expected to give a return greater than that of the market, but at a correspondingly enhanced level of risk.
- An investor with a long time horizon, who is not overly risk-averse, might seek out adventurous investments and be willing to take additional risks in the promise of higher returns.
- A more risk-averse individual, such as someone reaching retirement, is liable to be seeking a more secure and less risky portfolio and will, therefore, prefer a portfolio with a β less than 1.
- As the proportion of risk-free investments is increased in the portfolio, and the proportion of riskier assets reduced, the portfolio β reduces towards 0.

CAPM does however have its limitations. Some of its assumptions appear to be inapplicable in modern capital markets but it has certain specific limitations:

- The required rate of return derived from the model is only valid as long as the inputs (market return, risk free rate and beta) are valid. As a result of changing economic and fiscal circumstances we can expect that one or more of these factors will change over a year.
- The model assumes that the overall portfolio held is diversified and equates to the market as a whole.
- To calculate a β factor for an investment we are relying on historical data and the observed co-movements in the returns of different assets and the market in general. Several studies have shown that the results of analysing historical data over many different time periods reveal that beta is, itself, subject to large fluctuations. Therefore, when applying the results of historical analysis and determining a beta value there is good reason to be sceptical that the future beta of a portfolio will resemble the past beta of a portfolio.
- An investment portfolio is said to be positioned on the efficient frontier if it is expected to produce returns greater than other portfolios with different asset mixes of the same or lesser risk. In practice, investments are often not able to locate on the outer edge of this theoretical position and are instead located within, rather than on, the efficient frontier.

1.5   Arbitrage Pricing Theory (APT)

Learning Objective

11.1.5   Understand the main principles behind arbitrage pricing theory (APT): risk-free rate; market rates; diversification; uncorrelated; risk premium; beta; differences between CAPM and APT

Arbitrage pricing theory (APT) was developed in the late 1970s in response to CAPM's main limitation that a single market beta is assumed to capture all factors that determine a security's risk and expected return.

APT, rather than relying on a single beta, adopts a more complex multi-factor approach by:

- seeking to capture exactly what factors determine security price movements by conducting regression analysis
- applying a separate risk premium to each identified factor
- applying a separate beta to each of these risk premiums, depending on a security's sensitivity to each of these factors.

Examples of factors that are employed by advocates of the APT approach include both industry-related and more general macroeconomic variables, such as anticipated changes in inflation, industrial production and the yield spread between investment grade and non-investment grade bonds.

The underlying assumptions of APT include the following:

- Securities markets are price efficient.
- Investors seek to maximise their wealth, though do not necessarily select portfolios on the basis of mean variance analysis.
- Investors can sell securities short. Short selling is selling securities you don't own, with the intention of buying them back at a lower price in order to settle and profit from the transaction.
- Identified factors are uncorrelated with each other.

APT is attractive in that it:

- explains security performance more accurately than CAPM, by using more than one beta factor
- uses fewer assumptions than CAPM
- enables portfolios to be constructed that either eliminate or gear their exposure to a particular factor.

However, APT's shortcomings include a reliance on:

- identified factors being uncorrelated with each other
- stable relationships being established between security returns and these identified factors.

1.6 Foreign Currency Risk

Learning Objective

11.1.6 Understand the implications of foreign currency risk on an investor investing in domestic/ overseas assets

Investing in overseas assets is considered to be a good way of diversifying a portfolio and also gaining exposure to potentially higher returns, by investing in countries that have higher economic growth. However, there is an additional layer of risk for the investment in that the exchange rate may fall significantly during the period the asset is held. This is called **foreign currency risk** and a fall in value may wipe out any of the gains the asset has made in the overseas market. Conversely, it can enhance returns if the exchange rate rises relative to the domestic currency.

For example, a UK investor may directly buy NYSE-listed equities. At the time of purchase they are required to convert GBP into USD. After one year, the UK investor is delighted to discover their investment has risen by 15% in the US. They decide to sell and convert the USD proceeds into GBP. However, during the year the pound has appreciated significantly against the USD (by 30%). To their dismay, they discover that they have actually lost money on their investment.

Example

Scenario A

A UK-based investor decides to invest $15,550,000 into a portfolio of US equities when the exchange rate is $1.55/£1.

Scenario B

Following a major change in investor sentiment towards the US dollar, the exchange rate changes some 12 months later to $1.85/£1.

Consider the impact on the sterling-based investor on a 'weakened dollar'.

Scenario A

$15,550,000 ÷ $1.55 = £10,032,258

Scenario B

$15,550,000 ÷ $1.85 = £8,405,405

Change in pound sterling value for the UK investor = a loss of £1,626,853

2. The Role of the Portfolio Manager

As a portfolio manager, it is important to understand the distinction between investment and speculation.

Investment can be differentiated from speculation by the timeframe adopted and the level of risk assumed by the investor. Investment is generally undertaken via a diversified portfolio of assets for the medium to long term whereas speculation is based on profiting from the short-term price movements of individual securities or assets.

Wealth management can be further differentiated by its structured approach to identifying client needs and developing holistic plans that address the complete range of a client's needs.

2.1 The Investment Advice Process

Learning Objective

11.2.1 Understand the establishment of: relationships with clients; client investment objectives; risk profile; income and/or growth; time horizons; restrictions; liquidity; discretionary and non-discretionary portfolio management

Portfolio management is the management of an investment portfolio on behalf of a private client or institution with a primary focus on meeting the client's investment objectives.

Portfolio management can be conducted on either a:

- **discretionary basis** – the portfolio manager makes investment decisions within the parameters laid down by the client, or
- **non-discretionary** or **advisory basis** – the client makes all of the investment decisions with or without seeking advice from the portfolio manager.

In both cases, the portfolio manager usually has the choice of investing directly in a range of asset classes and indirectly via investment funds.

2.1.1 Relationships with Clients

Individuals and institutions have varying objectives and expectations. Clearly, before advising the client an adviser must be aware of these various needs, preferences, expectations and the financial situation of the client; the adviser must know the client before being able to provide appropriate advice. Indeed, regulators make this an essential requirement in many countries – the know your customer (KYC) process.

The information that needs to be captured can be broken down into the following:

- Personal and financial details.
- Objectives.
- Risk tolerance.
- Liquidity and time horizons.
- Tax status.
- Investment preferences.

Below, we will consider some of the key client information that an adviser needs to establish.

2.1.2 Investment Objectives

Given the wide range of available investment opportunities that may be suitable for a client, an adviser needs to start with understanding what the client's investment or financial objectives are.

This requires the client to consider what they are trying to achieve. The answer will determine the overall investment strategy that will be driving the investment planning process.

Typical financial objectives include:

- maximising future growth
- protecting the real value of capital
- generating an essential level of income
- protecting against future events.

It is also important to remember that a client may have more than one financial objective, such as funding school fees, while at the same time maximising the growth of their investments to provide the funds needed in retirement.

Having determined the client's overall financial objectives, the adviser also needs to know how this will affect the choice of investments. Investment objectives are often categorised into:

- **Income** – investors seek a higher level of current income at the expense of potential future growth of capital.
- **Income and growth** – investors need a certain amount of current income but also invest to achieve potential future growth in income and capital.
- **Growth** – investors do not seek income and their primary objective is capital appreciation.
- **Outright growth** – the investor is seeking maximum return through a broad range of investment strategies, which generally involve a high level of risk.

2.1.3 Risk Tolerance

Volatility in the prices of investments or the overall value of an investment portfolio is inevitable. At a personal level this translates into the risk that prices may be depressed at the time when an investor needs funds and will mean that they will not achieve their investment goals.

A client needs to have a very clear understanding of their tolerance to risk as it is essential to choosing the right investment objectives. Risk tolerance is a very personal subject and is very dependent upon the emotional make-up of a person. It is also objective as well, in that age will affect how much risk a client can assume. As you get older, there is less time to recover from poor investment decisions or market falls and so appetite to take risk may change.

Although risk is an emotive subject, establishing a client's tolerance towards risk need not be subjective. Indeed, an objective measure of a client's risk tolerance is provided by the risks that will need to be taken if the client's stated investment objective is to be met. If the client believes these risks are too great, then the client's objective will need to be revised.

Attitude to risk will affect the investment policy that is implemented. If we look at three simple definitions of risk tolerance – cautious, moderate and adventurous – we can see how this might influence the choice of investments contained within each of the investment objectives considered above.

Investment Objective	Risk Tolerance	Attitude to Risk and Possible Investments
Income	Cautious	• Willing to accept a lower level of income for lower risk • Exposure to high yield bonds and equities will be low
	Moderate	• Seek to balance potential risk with potential for income growth • Exposure to high yield bonds and equities will be higher
	Adventurous	• Willing to adopt more aggressive strategies that offer potential for higher income • Exposure to high yield bonds and equities may be substantial
Income and Growth	Cautious	• Seeking maximum growth and income consistent with relatively modest degree of risk • Equities will form a relatively small percentage of the portfolio
	Moderate	• Seeking to balance potential risk with growth of both capital and income • Equities will form a significant percentage of the portfolio
	Adventurous	• Able to adopt a long-term view that allows them to pursue a more aggressive strategy • Equities will form the principal part of the portfolio
Growth	Cautious	• Seeking maximum growth consistent with relatively modest degree of risk • Equities will form a significant percentage of the portfolio
	Moderate	• Seeking to balance potential risk with growth of capital • Equities will form the principal part of the portfolio
	Adventurous	• Able to adopt a long-term view that allows them to pursue a more aggressive strategy • Equities may form the whole of the portfolio

2.1.4 Liquidity and Time Horizons

It is also essential to understand a client's liquidity requirements and the time horizons over which they can invest, as these will also have a clear impact on the selection and construction of any investments.

Liquidity refers to the amount of funds a client may need both in the short and long term. When constructing an investment portfolio, it is essential that an emergency cash reserve is put to one side which the client can access without having to disturb longer-term investments.

If there are known liabilities that may arise in future years, consideration should also be given as to how funds will be realised at that time. Consideration needs to be given as to whether it is sensible to plan on realising profits from equities, as market conditions may be such as to require losses to be established unnecessarily. Instead, conservative standards suggest investing an appropriate amount in bonds that are due to mature near the time needed so that there is certainty of the availability of funds.

Time horizon refers to the period over which a client can consider investing their funds. Definitions of time horizons vary, but short term is usually considered to be from one to four years, while medium term refers to a period from five to ten years and long term is considered to be for a period of ten years or more.

Time horizon is very relevant when selecting the types of investment that may be suitable for a client. It is generally stated that an investor should only invest in equities if they can do so for a minimum period of five years. This is to make the point that growth from equities comes about from long-term investment and the need to have the time perspective that can allow an investor to ride out periods of market volatility.

The lower the client's liquidity requirements and the longer their timescale, the greater will be the choice of assets available to meet the client's investment objective.

The need for high liquidity allied to a short timescale, demands that the client should invest in lower-risk assets such as cash and short-dated bonds, which offer a potentially lower return than equities; if the opposite is true, the portfolio can be more proportionately weighted towards equities.

Whatever their requirements, it is important, however, that the client maintains sufficient liquidity to meet both known commitments and possible contingencies.

2.1.5 Tax Status

Establishing the client's tax position is essential so that their investments can be organised in such a way that the returns attract the least tax possible.

This requires the investment manager to be aware of what taxes may affect the investor, such as taxes on any income arising or on any capital gains, how these are calculated and what allowances may be available.

An adviser will also need to establish the client's residence and domicile status as these may impact how any investments are structured.

2.1.6 Investment Preferences

Some investors prefer to either exclude certain areas of the investment spectrum from their portfolios or concentrate solely on a particular investment theme, such as socially responsible investment (SRI) or require the portfolio to be constructed in accordance with Islamic principles.

2.2 Establishing an Investment Strategy

Learning Objective

11.2.2 Understand the establishment of the investment strategy: the importance of asset allocation; the difference between active and passive management; top-down versus bottom-up active management; implications of the various investment styles on portfolio risk and return; ethical, environmental and socially responsible investment

We saw earlier the need to diversify and having regard to the client's objectives, it is unlikely that a single investment fund or security will meet the client's requirements. Therefore, the portfolio manager needs to decide how to approach selecting suitable investments for inclusion in the client's portfolio.

Developing an investment strategy involves an understanding of asset allocation and the choices available between different investment styles. These are covered briefly here and then in more depth later in this chapter.

2.2.1 Asset Allocation

Asset allocation involves considering the big picture first, by assessing the prospects for each of the main asset classes within each of the world's major investment regions, against the backdrop of the world economic, political and social environment.

Once asset allocation has been decided upon, the next step is to consider the prospects for those sectors within their favoured bond and equity markets. Sector selection decisions in equity markets are usually made with reference to the weighting each sector assumes within the index against which the performance in that market is to be assessed.

The final stage of the process is deciding upon which stocks should be selected within the favoured sectors. A combination of fundamental and technical analysis will typically be used in arriving at the final decision.

The investment strategy adopted will need to determine whether this asset allocation is achieved using passive or active investment management.

2.2.2 Passive Investment Management

Passive management will be seen in those collective investment funds that are described as index tracker funds.

Index tracking, or indexation, necessitates the construction of an equity portfolio to track, or mimic, the performance of a recognised equity index. Indexation is undertaken on the assumption that securities markets are efficiently priced and cannot, therefore, be consistently outperformed. Consequently, no attempt is made to forecast future events or outperform the broader market.

416

There are two main methods in use; physical and synthetic replication. The traditional method used is physical replication and is the approach that has been used by index trackers and the first ETFs. Physical replication can be achieved using either full replication, or optimised sampling. The alternative to physical replication is synthetic replication which involves the portfolio entering into a total return swap with an investment bank, which undertakes to provide the return on the index that is being tracked.

The advantages of employing indexation are that:

- relatively few active portfolio managers consistently outperform benchmark equity indices;
- once set up, passive portfolios are generally less expensive to run than active portfolios, given a lower ratio of staff to funds managed and lower portfolio turnover.

The disadvantages of adopting indexation, however, include the following:

- Performance is affected by the need to manage cash flows, rebalance the portfolio to replicate changes in index-constituent weightings and adjust the portfolio for index promotions and demotions.
- Most indices assume that dividends from constituent equities are reinvested on the ex-dividend (xd) date, whereas a passive fund can only invest dividends when received, usually six weeks after the share has been declared xd.
- Indexed portfolios cannot meet all investor objectives.
- Indexed portfolios follow the index down in bear markets.

2.2.3 Active Investment Management

In contrast to passive equity management, active equity management seeks to outperform a predetermined benchmark over a specified time period, by employing fundamental and technical analysis to assist in the forecasting of future events and the timing of purchases and sales of securities.

Actively managed portfolios can be constructed on either a top-down or a bottom-up basis.

- Top down active investment management involves portfolio managers considering the big picture first by assessing the prospects for each of the main asset classes within each of the world's major investment regions against the backdrop of the world economic, political and social environment. This output then drives the asset allocation decision.
- A bottom up approach to active management describes one that focuses solely on the unique attractions of individual stocks. Managers applying the 'bottom-up' method of portfolio construction pay no attention to index benchmarks. Bottom-up methods are usually dependent on the style or approach of the individual fund manager or team of managers.

The advantage of employing active investment management is that it can generate greater returns than the market. It will involve taking greater risk than a passive approach and so its suitability will depend on the risk profile of the client. Its other main drawback is finding investment managers who can consistently outperform the market; many actively managed fund fail to do so.

2.2.4   Ethical and Socially Responsible Investment (SRI)

Ethical funds were launched in the 1980s but to a muted response. After a slow start, however, the popularity of ethical investing soon gathered pace, as public awareness of environmental issues grew and governments began to respond with a combination of environmental legislation and taxes.

The growing popularity of ethical funds can be seen by looking at the market statistics produced by a UK organisation, Ethical Investment Research Services (EIRIS), which shows that funds under management in UK-based collective investment schemes grew from £199 million in 1989 to over £9.5 billion by the end of 2009.

The growing interest in actively encouraging corporate social responsibility is central to what has become known as socially responsible investment (SRI); the phrase designed to describe the inclusion of social and environmental criteria in investment fund stock selection.

Indeed, SRI funds have been at the forefront of an industry-wide move to include the analysis of the non-financial aspects of corporate performance, business risk and value creation into the investment process.

There are two principal SRI approaches: ethical investing and sustainability investing, both of which are considered below.

Ethical funds, occasionally referred to as dark-green funds, are constructed to avoid those areas of investment that are considered to have significant adverse effects on people, animals or the environment. They do this by screening potential investments against negative, or avoidance, criteria.

As a screening exercise combined with conventional portfolio management techniques, the strong ethical beliefs that underpin these funds typically results in a concentration of smaller company holdings and volatile performance, though much depends on the criteria applied by individual funds.

Sustainability funds are those that focus on the concept of sustainable development, concentrating on those companies that tackle or pre-empt environmental issues head-on. Unlike ethical investing funds, sustainability funds, sometimes known as light-green funds, are flexible in their approach to selecting investments.

Sustainability investors focus on those risks which most mainstream investors ignore. For instance, while most scientists and governments agree that the world's carbon dioxide absorption capacity is fast reaching critical levels, this risk appears not to have been factored into the share valuations of fossil fuel businesses. Factors such as these are critical in selecting stocks for sustainability funds.

Sustainability fund managers can implement this approach in two ways:

- Positive sector selection – is selecting those companies that operate in sectors likely to benefit from the global shift to more socially and environmentally sustainable forms of economic activity, such as renewable energy sources. This approach is known as investing in industries of the future and gives a strong bias towards growth-oriented sectors.
- Choosing the best of sector – companies are often selected for the environmental leadership they demonstrate in their sector, regardless of whether they fail the negative criteria applied by ethical investing funds. For instance, an oil company which is repositioning itself as an energy business focusing on renewable energy opportunities will probably be considered for inclusion in a sustainability fund but will be excluded from an ethical fund.

With the growing trend among institutional investors of encouraging companies to focus on their social responsibilities, sustainability-investing research teams enter into constructive dialogue with companies to encourage the adoption of social and environmental policies and practices, so that they may be considered for inclusion in a sustainability investment portfolio.

Integrating social and environmental analysis into the stock selection process is necessarily more research-intensive than that employed by ethical investing funds and dictates the need for a substantial research capability. Moreover, in addition to adopting this more pragmatic approach to stock selection, which results in the construction of better-diversified portfolios, sustainability funds also require each of their holdings to meet certain financial criteria, principally the ability to generate an acceptable level of investment return.

Typically, financial, environmental and social criteria are given equal prominence in company performance ratings by sustainability-investing research teams. This is known as the triple bottom line.

A common misconception with ethical and SRI is that it will involve accepting poorer investment returns compared to mainstream investments. EIRIS has undertaken research which shows that ethical investing need not necessarily involve accepting lower performance. Several of their studies undertaken over the last decade have indicated that investing according to ethical criteria may make little difference to overall financial performance, depending on the ethical policy applied. Five ethical indices created by them produced financial returns roughly equivalent to the returns from the FTSE All-Share Index.

There are a range of indices that can be used to track performance, such as the FTSE4Good indices, which cover most sizeable companies around the world and set three global benchmarks, against which companies are judged for inclusion.

2.3 The Role of Benchmarks and Performance Reporting

Learning Objectives

11.2.3 Understand deciding on the benchmark and the basis for review: portfolio's asset allocation; risk/return profile; alternative investments; taxation; maintenance of capital value

11.2.4 Understand the measurement and evaluation of performance and the purpose and requirements of annual and periodic reviews

When constructing a client's portfolio, it is essential to understand their investment objectives, risk tolerance and tax position, to ensure that the investments chosen are suitable and meet their expectations of how the portfolio is to be run.

An important part of determining the risk tolerance is how a client will react to the volatility of their returns. The more a client is concerned about maintaining capital values, the more orientated their portfolio will be to lower risk assets, such as bonds and cash deposits. If this is a lesser concern, portfolios will be more orientated to stocks and other risk assets.

When reviewing a portfolio, a client will be interested in the after-tax return. Given the different tax rates in force for income and capital taxes, this has become an important factor in portfolio construction. Even within asset classes, this may influence whether the manager should invest in direct or collective vehicles.

The risk return/profile also helps to determine the allocation of stocks versus bonds and other asset classes. Alternative assets may be included in a portfolio if they can provide diversification opportunities, as returns may be uncorrelated with the classic asset classes, and a client is comfortable with their relative illiquidity.

Once the portfolio has been constructed, the portfolio manager and client need to agree on a realistic benchmark against which the performance of the portfolio can be judged. The choice of benchmark will depend on the precise asset split adopted and should be compatible with the risk and expected return profile of the portfolio. If an index is used, this should represent a feasible investment alternative to the portfolio constructed.

Portfolio performance is rarely measured in absolute terms but in relative terms against the predetermined benchmark and against the peer group.

In addition, indexed portfolios are also evaluated against the size of their tracking error, or how closely the portfolio has tracked the chosen index. Tracking error arises from both under-performance and outperformance of the index being tracked.

It is essential that the portfolio manager and client agree on the frequency with which the portfolio is reviewed, not only to monitor the portfolio's performance but also to ensure that it still meets with the client's objectives and is correctly positioned given prevailing market conditions.

Benchmarks and portfolio performance are considered in more detail in Chapter 12.

2.4   Conflicts of Interest

Learning Objective

11.2.5   Understand the issues associated with conflicts of interest and the duty to clients

The FCA has strict regulations regarding the fair treatment of clients, and all policies and procedures must be followed by law. Portfolio managers, along with other involved parties, have a legal duty to disclose any material interest or conflict of interest when dealing on behalf of a client. They are also required to act honestly, fairly and in the best interests of their clients.

Companies that are subject to MiFID are required to establish and maintain a written policy for the handling of conflicts of interest. The policy must identify both actual and potential conflicts of interest for all types of clients.

---

3. Market Information and Research

3.1 Sources of Market Information and Research

Learning Objective

11.3.1 Understand how to access and use regulatory, economic and financial communications: news services; government resources and statistics; broker research and distributor information; regulatory resources

Financial communications and reports from numerous bodies, both in the private and public sector, are a vital part of the tools required for the research and analysis functions that are crucial to decision making about investment strategies and asset allocation. The data needed by an investment manager can be sourced from the following broad categories:

- News services – eg, Bloomberg, Reuters, CNBC.
- Government resources and statistics – the Office for National Statistics (ONS) and the Bank of England.
- Broker research and distributor information – eg, market commentary and analysis from major investment banks such as Goldman Sachs and Barcap.
- Desk research – secondary source research and analysis by an investment fund management team.
- Regulatory resources where relevant – eg, communications from the FCA.

3.1.1 News Services

The major providers of financial news would include the following companies:

Bloomberg

Bloomberg L.P. is a privately held financial software, news and data company. According to a recent market survey by the *New York Times*, it has a one-third share of the market for financial information services. Bloomberg L.P. was founded by Michael Bloomberg in 1981 with a 30% ownership investment by Merrill Lynch. The company provides financial software tools such as analytics and equity trading platforms, data services and news to financial companies and organisations around the world through the Bloomberg Terminal, its core money-generating product. Bloomberg L.P. has grown to include a global news service, including television, radio, the Internet and printed publications.

Thomson Reuters (TR)

Thomson Reuters (TR) is an information company created by the Canadian company Thomson Corporation's purchase of Reuters in April 2008. TR shares are listed on the Toronto Stock Exchange and the NYSE. According to the New York Times survey cited above. TR also has approximately one-third of the market for financial information services. The company has recently launched a television service called Insider and is very visible on the internet as a major source of financial and non-financial news coverage.

Business News Channels

CNBC is a satellite and cable television business news channel in the US, owned and operated by NBC Universal. The network and its international spinoffs cover business headlines and provide live coverage of financial markets. The combined reach of CNBC and its siblings is 390 million viewers around the world. It is headquartered in New Jersey and has a European headquarters in London.

Fox News is a competitor of CNBC in rolling business news coverage. The Fox Business News Network is part of News Corporation, owned partly by the Murdoch family, which also owns the Wall Street Journal.

Business Newspapers

Two print publications are also widely followed by global investors and there are of course many other newspapers which provide detailed coverage of financial matters both in the UK and around the world.

The Financial Times reports business, and features share – and financial – product listings. About 110 of its 475 journalists are outside the UK. The FT is usually in two sections. The first section covers national and international news, the second company and markets news.

The Wall Street Journal is an English-language international daily newspaper, published by Dow Jones & Company, a division of News Corporation, in New York, with Asian and European editions. The Wall Street Journal is the largest newspaper in the US by circulation. According to the Audit Bureau of Circulations, it has a circulation of over two million copies including over 500,000 online paid subscriptions as at March 2012.

3.1.2   Government Sources

Authoritative in-depth analysis of financial, economic and social trends is produced by government statistical departments, central banks, international agencies such as the World Bank, the International Monetary Fund (IMF) and the Organisation for Economic Cooperation and Development (OECD), and by business schools and other academic research organisations.

In the UK, two key sources of economic data on the UK economy come from the Office for National Statistics (ONS) and the Bank of England.

ONS produces and publishes a wide range of information about Britain that can be used for social and economic policy-making. Importantly, it also produces a wide range of widely followed economic data including GDP, inflation, employment data, balance of trade data and other personal finance data.

Its economic publications are grouped by theme and include:

- **Personal finance**
  - personal income and wealth
  - consumers and customers
  - personal debt and insolvencies
  - pensions.
- **National accounts**
  - balance of payments
  - national income, expenditure and output
  - regional accounts
  - satellite accounts
  - UK sector accounts
  - supply and use tables.
- **Prices, output and productivity**
  - price indices and inflation
  - productivity measures
  - output.
- **Government receipts and expenditure**
  - public sector finance
  - taxes and revenue
  - public spending
  - local government finance.

The Bank of England publishes a series of detailed reports about the UK financial system. Some of the key reports that are widely followed include:

- **Financial Stability Report** – covers the Committee's assessment of the outlook for the stability and resilience of the financial sector at the time of preparation of the Report, and the policy actions it advises to reduce and mitigate risks to stability.
- **Inflation Report** – sets out the detailed economic analysis and inflation projections on which the Bank's monetary policy committee bases its interest rate decisions, and presents an assessment of the prospects for UK inflation
- **Minutes of the Monetary Policy Committee** – published two weeks after the interest rate decision. The minutes give a full account of the policy discussion, including differences of view. They also record the votes of the individual members of the committee.
- **Quarterly Bulletin** – provides regular commentary on market developments and UK monetary policy operations. It also contains research and analysis and reports on a wide range of topical economic and financial issues, both domestic and international. It carries a broad range of material, particularly in relation to the formulation and conduct of monetary policy.

The Financial Stability Report is published half-yearly by bank staff under the guidance of the Bank's Financial Stability Executive Board. It aims to identify the major downside risks to the UK financial system and thereby help financial firms, authorities and the wider public in managing and preparing for these risks.

Extracts from the July 2016 Report are shown below to provide an example of the key nature of the information that is provided.

Risks around the EU referendum

Consistent with its remit, the FPC identified in March the risks around the referendum on the United Kingdom's membership of the European Union as the most significant near-term domestic risks to financial stability. It set out its assessment of those risks in the Statement following, and the Record of, its March meeting. The financing of the United Kingdom's large current account deficit, which is high by historical and international standards. The financing of the deficit is reliant on continuing material inflows of portfolio and foreign direct investment, which have been used to finance the public sector deficit and corporate investment, including in commercial real estate. A sudden shift in the supply of foreign capital and in the current account deficit would be associated with a sharp increase in risk premia and adjustment in sterling.

- *__The UK commercial real estate market__ – The UK commercial real estate market, which had experienced particularly strong inflows of capital from overseas over recent years. Foreign investors accounted for around 45% of the value of total transactions since 2009. Valuations in some segments of the market, notably the prime London market, had become stretched. Foreign inflows of capital to the UK CRE market fell by almost 50% in the first quarter of 2016. More recently, share prices of real estate investment trusts have fallen sharply, reflecting the risk of future marked adjustments in commercial real estate prices.*

- *__Fragilities in financial market functioning__ – Fragilities in financial market functioning, including reductions in the provision of market liquidity services in a number of core financial markets, such as government and corporate bond markets. These fragilities could be tested during a period of elevated market activity and volatility. Following the referendum, the foreign exchange market experienced particularly high volumes of transactions relative to normal levels with no apparent impairment of price discovery. Activity in some fixed-income markets has been subdued but largely orderly. This means that the capacity of these markets has not to date been tested materially by market adjustments.*

Challenges to the outlook for financial stability

The FPC judges that the current outlook for financial stability is challenging. It is monitoring closely the risks of:

- *__Further deterioration in investor appetite for UK assets__ – During a prolonged period of heightened uncertainty, the risk premium on UK assets could rise further and overseas investors could continue to be deterred from investing in the United Kingdom. Persistent falls in capital inflows would be associated with further downward pressure on the exchange rate and tighter funding conditions for UK borrowers.*

- *__Adjustments in commercial real estate markets tightening credit conditions__ – Any adjustment in CRE markets could potentially be amplified by the behaviour of leveraged investors and investors in open-ended commercial property funds. Although they have a range of measures to manage stressed levels of redemptions, these open-ended funds could be forced to sell illiquid assets to meet redemptions if conditions persist beyond funds' notice periods. Any such amplification of market adjustments could affect economic activity by reducing the ability of companies that use commercial real estate as collateral to access finance.*

- ***Increasing numbers of vulnerable households and procyclical behaviour of buy-to-let investors** – Since their implementation in 2014, the FPC's recommendations on owner-occupier mortgage underwriting standards have guarded against a sharp increase in the proportion of households that are very highly indebted. However, the ability of some households to service their debts would be challenged by a period of weaker employment and income growth. These vulnerable households could affect broader economic activity by cutting back sharply on expenditure in order to continue to service debts. In March, the FPC welcomed the PRA's Supervisory Statement on underwriting standards in the buy-to-let market. The Committee is monitoring the behaviour of buy-to-let investors, which has the potential to amplify movements in the housing market.*

3.1.3 Broker Research

Securities research is a discipline within the financial services industry.

Securities research professionals are known most generally as analysts, research analysts, or securities analysts.

- They are commonly divided between the two basic kinds of securities: equity analysts (researching stocks and their issuers) and fixed-income analysts (researching bond issuers). However, there are some analysts who cover all of the securities of a particular issuer, stocks and bonds alike.
- Securities analysts are usually further subdivided by industry specialisation (or sectors) – among the industries with the most analyst coverage are technology, financial services, energy, software and retailing. Fixed-income analysts are also often subdivided with specialised analyst coverage for convertible bonds, high-yield bonds, distressed securities and other financial products.

Securities analysts communicate to investors, through research reports and commentary, insights regarding the value, risk and volatility of a covered security, and thus assist investors to decide whether to buy, hold, sell, sell short or simply avoid the security in question or derivative securities.

Those analysts who are engaged by a brokerage firm are usually referred to as **sell-side analysts**. This differentiates them from **buy-side analysts**, who are engaged by asset management firms as part of their research efforts before they **buy** securities rather than **sell** them.

Securities analysts review periodic financial disclosures of the issuers (as required by the LSE and UKLA in the UK and the SEC in the US) and other relevant companies, read industry news, use trading history and industry information databases and interview managers and customers of the companies which they follow.

3.1.4 Regulatory Resources

The main sources of information which reflect changes in financial regulations that need to be complied with in the financial services industry in the UK are those that originate within the FCA. These can start out as consultation papers but may then become official rule changes and appear in the rulebook.

In addition it is worth monitoring the FCA website for general regulatory developments, disciplinary actions, money laundering issues and other developments regarding the transition of its responsibilities to the PRA.

Other areas where potential changes in regulations may be relevant arise from changes in listing requirements from the UKLA, changes affecting takeover regulation from the POTAM and changes in legislation affecting companies in general which will eventually be incorporated into updates of the Companies Acts.

3.2 Key Factors Influencing Markets

Learning Objective

11.3.2 Be able to assess key factors that influence markets and sectors: responses to change and uncertainty; volume, liquidity, and nature of trading activity in domestic and overseas markets; market abuse regime – enforcement and effectiveness; publication of announcements, research and ratings

3.2.1 Change and Uncertainty

It is an adage amongst investment professionals that markets hate uncertainty. Uncertainty is effectively a synonym for risk as risk arises from the uncertainty of outcomes. As investors, each time we decide to purchase a security or invest in an opportunity, the outcome is uncertain in the same way that any future event is. We are concerned that we might incur a loss if we have miscalculated the opportunity or that we may not realise, fully or even partially, the expected return.

However, some traders welcome uncertainty. A well-known hedge fund manager has described the procedures which are followed, so that his fund can actually seize the opportunities presented by the uncertainty in markets.

'Every morning traders assemble for a 30 minute premarket meeting where everyone at the firm works closely together to outline the various potential scenarios for the market that day and then place specific odds on what they think is most likely to occur and why. One trader every day is in charge of diagramming out the different market scenarios on a whiteboard which resembles a flow chart so that the firm has a structured and easy to follow game plan...By having the plan in place with various market scenarios outlined and positions to profit from those scenarios, uncertainty is no longer a factor. In fact, traders learn to love uncertainty because uncertain market conditions tend to favour those who are the most prepared to handle anything and everything the markets throw their way.'

3.2.2 Volume and Liquidity

The presence or absence of **liquidity** in financial markets is one of the most important conditions for transactions to take place.

It is worth looking at the different motives of the investor and the speculator or trader.

- The investor, such as a pension fund or unit trust manager may be purchasing (or selling) securities as part of a long-term portfolio management exercise.
- By contrast, the speculator or trader may be interested in trying to profit from short-term movements in the prices of securities, without the intention of holding the securities for an extended period.

- Speculators and traders help to provide liquidity to a market which would see less activity if it was just long-term investors that were conducting the activity.
- Trading activities create larger volumes in the markets, and thereby enhance the ability of the long-term investors and allocators of capital to buy and sell without moving the market excessively.

This is a somewhat controversial topic as there are some who would argue that the activity of speculators, rather than providing greater liquidity and acting as a way of smoothing price fluctuations, may actually lead to larger moves in prices or volatility, which has the consequence of de-stabilising markets.

Economists have really not provided a satisfactory account of liquidity, but rather assume that it will be present in markets. The term refers to the depth of interest from both buyers and sellers for a security and if, as occurs from time to time – as in Q4, 2008 – there is an absence of interest from buyers in many securities, a market will become lopsided and the desire by many to sell their shares and bonds at the same time causes disorderly market behaviour and results in rather sudden and abrupt drops in prices of securities.

In its more extreme form this can be referred to as a **market crash**. The classic example of such an event took place in October 1987, when global markets dropped precipitously and the NYSE fell by more than 20% in a single session on Monday 19 October of that year, with other indices such as the LSE registering similar falls.

There is growing evidence that the highly inter-connected nature of markets today and the global investment strategies followed by large investment banks and asset managers reveal a high degree of co-movement or correlation between major global asset classes. The consequences can be seen each day in the manner in which certain asset classes will move together, depending on the degree of risk that the short-term trading desks are willing to take.

For example, and to engage in simplification, following the 2008 banking crisis and the sovereign debt problems within the eurozone, it is possible to discern a clear pattern whereby when markets become more anxious there is a movement towards the US dollar and away from the euro and the so-called commodity currencies such as the Australian and Canadian dollar. Investors/traders will also purchase US treasury instruments and shun the emerging markets and commodities.

When there is more of an appetite for buying riskier assets the converse will tend to be the case. Capital will move away from the safe harbour of the US dollar and US Treasuries, global equity indices will tend to move higher, the commodity currencies will often move up sharply against the dollar and the emerging markets will see capital inflows.

A lot of these movements will be of short-term duration but it is also possible to discern similar dynamics at work with respect to global asset allocation decision making.

3.2.3   Market Abuse Regime

Market abuse is a serious offence that damages investor confidence and the integrity of financial markets.

On 1 July 2005, the FSMA 2000 (Market Abuse) Regulation 2005 came into force in order to implement the EC Directive on Insider Dealing and Market Manipulation (Market Abuse).

The market abuse directive (MAD), a key element of the EU Financial Services Action Plan, introduces a common EU approach for preventing and detecting market abuse and ensuring a proper flow of information to the market. The Regulations amend the market abuse provisions in Part 8 of the FSMA 2000.

The market abuse regime applies to the public at large, not just to the regulated sector. The amendments to the FSMA market abuse regime introduced important changes for publicly traded issuers, their advisors and senior management, those authorised under FSMA, those who recommend investments or investment strategies and those who participate in the investment markets.

The sanctions which may be imposed following a finding of market abuse are severe. Offenders may face unlimited financial penalties and, if they work in the financial services industry, they may have their livelihood removed by having their authorisation/approval withdrawn or a prohibition order made against them.

The Directive also introduced into the UK a new requirement for firms to report transactions giving rise to suspicions of market abuse. Transaction reports, as they are called, play a key role in the FCA's market abuse monitoring work. The FCA takes a serious view of firms which fail to report transactions in line with FCA rules or which do not have in place adequate internal transaction reporting procedures and systems.

Even in cases of market misconduct which do not necessarily fall within the definition of civil market abuse, the FCA can still take action against a firm or individual (if they are authorised to conduct investment business) based on a breach of its Principles in the FCA Handbook.

Market abuse relates to behaviour by a person, or a group of persons working together, which occurs in relation to qualifying investments on a prescribed market that satisfies one or more of the following three conditions. The behaviour as it is currently defined is:

- based on information that is not generally available to those using the market and, if it were available, it would have an impact on the price, and
- likely to give a false or misleading impression of the supply, demand or value of the investments concerned, and
- likely to distort the market in the investments.

Prescribed UK Markets
- The LSE (including the AIM market).
- PLUS Stock Exchange.
- EDX London.
- LIFFE Administration and Management.
- NYMEX Europe.
- ICE Futures.
- The LME.

Qualifying Investments

Article 5 of the 2001 Order defines qualifying investments as all financial instruments within the meaning of the Directive, that is:

- Transferable securities – for example, shares and other securities equivalent to shares in companies, bonds and other forms of securitised debt, which are negotiable on the capital market and any other securities normally dealt in giving the right to acquire any such transferable securities by subscription or exchange or giving rise to a cash settlement, excluding instruments of payment.
- Derivatives on commodities.
- Financial futures contracts, including equivalent cash-settled instruments.
- Forward interest-rate agreements.
- Interest rate, currency and equity swaps.
- Money-market instruments.
- Options to acquire or dispose of any instrument falling into these categories.
- Options on currency and on interest rates.
- Units in collective investment undertakings.
- Any other instrument admitted to trading on a regulatory market in a member state or for which a request for admission to trading on such a market has been made.

The FCA is required to prepare and issue guidance on what behaviour does and does not amount to market abuse. This is called the **Code of Market Conduct** and includes aspects of insider dealing as well as expanding on behaviours that constitute market abuse. They extend to seven circumstances which are covered below.

- **Insider Dealing** – the first type of behaviour categorised as market abuse is insider dealing, which occurs if an insider deals or attempts to deal on the basis of inside information. This sits alongside the existing criminal offence of insider dealing under the Criminal Justice Act.

  There is a separate definition of inside information for persons charged with the execution of orders, ie, traders and market makers. For such persons, inside information includes information conveyed by a client and related to the client's pending orders. The purpose behind this provision is to expressly ensure that the practice of front running is classified as market abuse. Front running is purchasing shares for a trader's own benefit on the basis of, and ahead of, orders from investors in order to benefit from an anticipated impact on prices.
- **Improper Disclosure.**
- **Misuse of Information** – market abuse can also arise from the misuse of information. An example of this behaviour is where an employee of a company informs a friend over lunch that the company has received a takeover offer and the friend then places a spread bet with a bookmaker that the same company will be the subject of a bid within a week. The person making the bet is not guilty of insider dealing as he is not dealing in qualifying investments, which is a requirement of the insider dealing behaviour.
- **Manipulating Transactions** – market abuse can arise from manipulating transactions, which occurs where a false or misleading impression is given as to the supply or demand for investments. An example of this behaviour is an abusive squeeze which is where, for example, a trader with a long position in bond futures buys or borrows a large amount of the cheapest-to-deliver bonds and either refuses to re-lend those bonds or will only lend them to parties he believes will not re-lend to the market. His purpose is to position the price at which those with short positions have to deliver to satisfy their obligations at a materially higher level, making him a profit from his original position.

- **Manipulating Devices** – this consists of trades which employ fictitious devices or any other form of deception or contrivance. An example is taking advantage of occasional or regular access to the traditional or electronic media, by voicing an opinion about qualifying investments, whilst having previously taken positions on the investments and profiting subsequently from the impact of the opinions voiced on the price of that instrument, without having simultaneously disclosed that conflict of interest to the public in a proper and effective way. Other examples include 'pump and dump' which is taking a long position in an investment and then disseminating misleading positive information about that investment, with a view to increasing its price, and 'trash and cash' which is taking a short position in an investment and then disseminating misleading negative information about it with a view to driving down its price.
- **Dissemination** – this consists of the dissemination of information by any means which gives, or is likely to give, a false or misleading impression. An example is the posting of information which contains false or misleading statements about a qualifying investment on an internet bulletin board or in a chat room in circumstances where the person knows that the information is false or misleading.
- **Misleading Behaviour or Distortion** – the final type of behaviour amounting to market abuse is 'misleading behaviour' or 'distortion', which is any behaviour not covered under the previous headings. An example could be an empty cargo ship that is used to transport a particular commodity is moved. This could create a false impression of changes in the supply of, or demand for, that commodity or the related futures contract. It could also artificially change the price of that commodity or the futures contract, and lead to people making the wrong investment decisions.

An FCA-authorised firm which arranges or executes a transaction with or for a client in a qualifying investment admitted to trading on a prescribed market and which has reasonable grounds to suspect that the transaction may constitute market abuse, is required to notify the FCA without delay. If the FCA is satisfied that a person is engaging in, or has engaged in market abuse, or has required or encouraged another person to do so, it may:

- Impose an unlimited civil fine.
- Make a public statement that the person has engaged in market abuse.
- Apply to the court for an injunction to restrain threatened or continued market abuse.
- Require a person to disgorge profits made or losses avoided as a result of market abuse.
- Require the payment of compensation to victims.

3.2.4 Publication of Announcements, Research and Ratings

Capital markets, from a short-term perspective, are highly sensitive to the publication of certain information. Amongst the announcements that are most likely to have an impact on market behaviour and settlement are the following.

Takeovers

The POTAM is an independent body, established in 1968, whose main functions are to issue and administer the City Code on Takeovers and Mergers and to supervise and regulate takeovers and other matters to which the Code applies. Its central objective is to ensure fair treatment for all shareholders in takeover bids.

Stringent regulations are laid down concerning the manner in which announcements must be made, the accuracy of the information and disclosure of dealings.

The following is a brief summary of some of the most important rules of the Code.

- When a person or group acquires interests in shares carrying 30% or more of the voting rights of a company, they must make a cash offer to all other shareholders at the highest price paid in the 12 months before the offer was announced (30% of the voting rights of a company is treated by the Code as the level at which effective control is obtained).
- When interests in shares carrying 10% or more of the voting rights of a class have been acquired by an offeror in the offer period and the previous 12 months, the offer must include a cash alternative for all shareholders of that class, at the highest price paid by the offeror in that period. Further, if an offeror acquires for cash any interest in shares during the offer period, a cash alternative must be made available at that price at least.
- If the offeror acquires an interest in shares in a target company at a price higher than the value of the offer, the offer must be increased accordingly.
- The target company must appoint a competent independent adviser whose advice on the offer must be made known to all the shareholders, together with the opinion of the board.
- Favourable deals for selected shareholders are banned.
- All shareholders must be given the same information.
- Those issuing takeover circulars must include statements taking responsibility for the contents.
- Profit forecasts and asset valuations must be made to specified standards and must be reported on by professional advisers.
- Misleading, inaccurate or unsubstantiated statements made in documents or to the media must be publicly corrected immediately.
- Actions during the course of an offer by the target company, which might frustrate the offer, are generally prohibited, unless shareholders approve these plans.
- Stringent requirements are laid down for the disclosure of dealings in relevant securities during an offer.
- Employees of both the offeror and the offeree must be informed about an offer and the employee representatives of the offeree have the right to have a separate opinion on the effects of the offer on employment appended to the offeree board's circular.

Economic Data

The UK ONS publishes key economic reports regarding the labour market, inflation (CPI and RPI data) and the rate of growth (decline) in the GDP.

All of these reports will be subjected to detailed scrutiny and the markets will often react to the data. The key issue with respect to such data releases is the degree to which the published data has already been discounted by market participants. In other words, traders and investors will form opinions about the level of inflation before the actual release of the monthly CPI data and only if the numbers presented are notably out of alignment with the expectations, will the market react strongly.

In the US, the monthly report from the Department of Labour on non-farm payrolls is one of the most widely followed by market participants across the globe, as it provides one of the best indicators of the state of the US economy. Traders and investors use the data to make forward forecasts about the prospects for GDP growth and inflation and how this might affect the interest rate decisions by the Federal Reserve.

Central Bank Policy Announcements

Each month the Federal Open Market Committee (FOMC) in the US, the European Central Bank (ECB) in the eurozone and the Bank of England MPC meet to review their short-term interest rate policy.

Market participants watch the announcements about rates very closely. Unexpected moves in interest rates, both up and downwards, have a large impact across all major asset classes. Bond prices respond well to reductions in short-term rates, sterling may suffer as the rate available for short-term sterling deposits is reduced and the FTSE 100 tends to move upwards on rate reductions. The opposite reactions tend to be seen on a rate increase, and more so if the rate hike was unexpected or more than had been expected.

Also of interest to the markets is the release of the minutes of each meeting, which are usually published a few weeks after the actual meeting. The comments expressed by the committee members are analysed carefully for any indications that monetary policy may be about to change.

Very similar issues arise in the case of the deliberations of the Chinese government on its monetary policy, as well as the Chinese participation in the US treasury market.

Credit Ratings Announcements

During recent times, global capital markets have become increasingly anxious about sovereign debt and this is reflected in the enormous increase in the use of credit default swaps (CDS) on individual sovereign borrowers.

The decisions made by the major credit ratings agencies to downgrade the debt of a particular sovereign issuer such as happened to Greece, Ireland and Spain can cause a 'flight to safety' as investors dump bonds from such issuers and seek out the safe haven of US treasury bonds, and to some extent gilts.

The announcement that a country is being put on credit watch by an agency can have a large impact in a market which is anxious about the levels of public debt in many nations.

Research Reports

The reports issued by brokerage firms and investment banks may have large macro implications for markets in general, but will more often involve a particular sector or even a particular company's securities. The downgrade of a company's earnings outlook, which may itself have been triggered by the company's own announcements and forward-looking statements, or even an unexpected comment on a conference call with investors, can often see a company's shares tumble.

If Goldman Sachs or JP Morgan tips a particular share for whatever reason, the price of that share is likely to rise. Once again this may be caused by buying or simply by the market makers pushing up the price in anticipation of likely buying.

Political Announcements

Some political announcements, especially relating to fiscal policy also have the capacity to cause significant movements in markets. The recent series of announcements from governments regarding financial regulations and policies toward the banking system have introduced uncertainty into the future prospects for the banking sector.

3.3 The Relationship between Securities and Derivatives Markets

Learning Objective

11.3.3 Be able to assess the interactive relationship between the securities and derivatives markets, and the impact of related events on markets

The financial markets have seen a constant stream of innovations in recent years and many of these are based on derivatives. In its simplest form a derivative is a security which is based upon, or derived from another asset such as an individual equity, an equity index, a commodity or a financial instrument such as a gilt (or in the US, a Treasury bond) or a foreign exchange rate.

By its nature a derivative is a contractual asset, which is traded actively, some more than others, and where the valuation of the derivative is largely, if not completely, influenced by price movements in the underlying asset. In addition to price changes of the underlying, other variables, such as interest rates and price volatility, (ie, variability in the price behaviour) will also be factored into the pricing and valuation of derivatives.

The value and therefore the price of all derivatives is based on and has a close relationship with the price of its underlying security. If this were not true, the markets would be full of arbitrage opportunities. While these opportunities do exist in certain conditions, they do so for only a short period and are relatively small, since the markets are efficient.

Securities and derivatives respond in the same way to change and uncertainty. In many cases, derivatives might seem to be the first to react, for example to increased uncertainty, which results in higher volatility in their price; however, any difference will be small and short-lived.

All of the key factors that influence a security's price, such as trading volume, liquidity, news announcements and market sentiments, will have the same effect on the related derivatives price. The recent advances in communication and inter-market dealing have ensured that both markets move together.

3.4 The Relationship between Fixed-Interest Securities

Learning Objective

11.3.4 Be able to assess the interactive relationship between different forms of fixed-interest securities and the impact of related events on markets

There are numerous forms of fixed-interest securities, and these cover a wide range including sovereign issues, eurobonds and corporate bonds.

Fund managers will almost invariably want to have a sizeable portion of their portfolio allocated to fixed-income securities, and they could include government bonds as well as both investment grade corporate bonds and high yield bonds.

Much attention is placed by asset managers on the relationships which exist between the different kinds of fixed-income securities, and much of this analysis is based upon what are commonly called **spread** relationships.

Spreads can exist between the same type of fixed income security, for example, between different maturities of that security, the most obvious example being the relationship between government bonds of different maturities. On the other hand there are many kinds of spreads, involving different securities from different issuers with contrasting credit qualities, and these are analysed and followed closely by asset allocators.

The broad kinds of spreads which are most relevant to asset managers fall into the following categories:

- Term spreads.
- Default spreads.
- Credit quality spreads.
- Sovereign spreads.

3.4.1   Term Spreads

The term **spread** is the difference between the yields of long- and short-dated bonds. Often used for this purpose for UK investors is the yield spread between a two-year note or gilt and a ten-year gilt. The key value which is used for calculating the spreads is the GRY or the YTM.

The GRY of a two-year note can be expressed in basis points. For example, a two-year note which has a GRY of 1.5% can be quoted as being a yield of 150 basis points. Let us say that the GRY on a ten-year gilt is quoted at 3.5% or 350 basis points; then the 2/10 spread can be stated simply as the difference between the two yields, in this case simply as 200 basis points.

There are many reasons why following this particular spread can be important for investment managers.

Example

Some reasons have to do with the ability to trade the spread. For example, if one believes that the spread is going to widen to say, 250 basis points then the asset manager could decide to have long positions in the two-year note and short positions in the ten-year gilt. Most likely the widening of the spread will be based upon an increase in yield in the ten-year leg of the spread, and an increase in yield will result from a decrease in the price, which will benefit someone who has taken a short position in the ten-year leg of the spread.

All that matters is that the differential or spread moves in accordance with the anticipation of a widening of the spread and the trade can be profitable.

In general terms, the term structure of interest rates, or yield curve, is often regarded as a leading indicator of economic activity, or at least captures the market's perception of the future rate of economic activity.

- In the growth part of an economic cycle, 2/10 spread measure tends to be more positive, with an upward-sloping yield curve with long-bond yields exceeding short-bond yields. This spread will often exceed 200 basis points and could go much higher depending on the overall level of interest rates.
- At the onset of a recession, the 2/10 measure tends to flatten and can even become negative if the yield curve inverts.

The 2/10 spread can, with some allowance for other factors relating to the role of the public finances, therefore be used to predict the position in the economic cycle and so what kind of interest rate environment lies ahead.

Careful analysis of the term spread could also be used to determine when a yield curve ride may be most beneficial and to undertake spread trades or engage in a form of trading activity known as **riding the yield curve**.

3.4.2   Default Spread

The default spread is the difference between the yields of investment grade corporate bonds and gilts.

In assessing the overall investment risk from a credit perspective of fixed income securities in general, it is customary to compare the GRY on a ten-year investment grade bond – perhaps limited to those of A– and above – with the GRY of a ten-year gilt. For a US-based investor, the comparison will be between an investment grade corporate bond and the YTM on a ten-year US Treasury note.

As seen above, it is customary to quote this spread in basis points, and the prevailing level of this spread can provide a good barometer of the market's perceptions regarding the overall creditworthiness of the corporate sector.

Government bonds are assumed in most financial theory to be risk-free, and, if the spread between the yield on a ten-year government bond and the equivalent yield for a ten-year corporate bond is relatively speaking rather low or narrow, then this low spread will reflect the perception that the corporate fixed income sector is not considered to be at much risk.

In other words, in a buoyant economy the default spread tends to narrow, whereas in a recession, the spread tends to widen. This widening can be especially acute during times of financial crisis such as were seen in Q4 2008.

As before, the default spread can, if used judiciously, be helpful in predicting the position in the economic cycle for market timing purposes.

3.4.3   Credit Quality Spreads

Another variation on this theme is to consider the spread between high-yield bonds and investment grade corporate bonds, or the spread between so called 'junk bonds' and gilts.

As an example, let us suppose that the typical GRY for a AAA corporate bond is quoted at 5% and the average GRY for a high-yield corporate is quoted at 8%; then the yield spread for investment grade to junk can be quoted as 300 basis points.

As an alternative approach, the spread can be quoted between the GRY for high-yield corporates and government bonds of similar maturities.

During the financial crisis of 2008 there were two factors at work which caused the spread between high-yield and government bonds to widen rather dramatically. At the height of the banking crisis in 2008 there was considerable anxiety amongst asset managers about the possibility of bankruptcies and economic dislocation in general. This anxiety produced a flight to safety in which asset managers sold many assets which were perceived to be of inferior quality and invested the proceeds from such liquidations into government securities.

For example, at the end of 2008 the GRY on the US ten-year Treasury note was barely 2% or 200 basis points (similarly, extremely low yields were seen on gilts, bunds and in most government bond markets), while the typical yield on a junk bond reached up into the mid-teens. In such circumstances, the spread between government and junk widened substantially from a more typical value of 200/300 basis points to as high as 1,500 basis points.

Admittedly, there were some very extreme spreads between many kinds of fixed-income securities during the 2008 crisis, and many astute investors and traders decided to purchase those securities which were very much out of favour, as they anticipated that, given an eventual return to more normal circumstances, the spreads would revert back to their more typical levels. By purchasing out-of-favour speculative and non-investment grade corporate bonds during the early part of 2009, many fund managers were able to make huge profits when the liquidity of corporate bond markets returned to more normal conditions.

Another feature of this spread relationship is to observe that the yields on government bonds will tend to increase when there is less anxiety about systematic (and systemic) risk and less desire to seek out the safe haven of gilts and treasury securities.

3.4.4 Sovereign Spreads

There is one further type of spread which is becoming increasingly important for investment managers to follow, and this one relates to the difference between the yields available on the government bonds of different sovereigns.

Historically, several governments have defaulted on their debt obligations, with Argentina and Russia being two of the most notable. More recently, the issue of potential default has become especially significant with the much-publicised difficulties for peripheral states in the eurozone in terms of their creditworthiness.

The Eurozone Crisis

In the summer of 2011, the Greek government was subject to emergency funding by the IMF and the EU, as it was unable to raise any capital from private investors in the capital markets and had to rely on continual funding provided by the ECB.

The GRY on ten-year Greek government bonds climbed to almost 30% during June 2011, indicating that the market believed that there was a very high likelihood that the Greek government would have to restructure its debt or possibly experience an outright default. By the summer of 2015, Greece's national debt was €320 billion.

Historically, several governments have defaulted on their debt obligations, with Argentina and Russia being two of the most notable.

Although Greece's troubles are the most extreme, they highlight the problems that also apply to some other countries in the eurozone. Before the credit crisis, these countries ran up huge debts and are now facing the reality that they are going to be very hard to repay. Because they are in the euro they do not have the option of devaluing their currencies to regain a competitive edge and instead are having to pursue austerity programmes that are increasingly unpopular with their people.

Concerns about further defaults remain very high. These debt levels have raised serious concerns about the sustainability of fiscal policy in the industrial world and heightened worries about sovereign risk.

During the sovereign debt crisis in Europe, the most commonly quoted spread was between the ten-year yield on Greek, Irish, Portuguese and Spanish debt and the yield on the ten-year bund from Germany, which is considered to be the safest government issue in the eurozone and globally one of the safest credits available.

Bond Spreads

The following table shows the yield on 10-year bonds from a range of sovereign governments as at July 2016.

Country	Latest yield	Spread versus bund	Spread versus T-notes
Australia	1.94%	+1.94	+0.36
Austria	0.22%	+0.22	-1.36
Belgium	0.27%	+0.26	-1.31
Canada	1.14%	+0.41	-0.44
France	0.24%	+0.23	-1.34
Germany	0.00%	–	-1.58
Greece	8.05%	+8.05	+6.47
Ireland	0.53%	+0.53	-1.05
Italy	1.25%	+1.25	-0.33
Japan	-0.23%	-0.23	-1.80
Portugal	3.06%	+3.06	+1.48
Spain	1.15%	+1.14	-0.43
Switzerland	-0.53%	-0.53	-2.10
UK	0.85%	+0.85	-0.73
US	1.58%	+1.58	–

Source: FT

Factors which affect sovereign spreads are clearly related to macro-economic circumstances in the various economies and, specifically, the differences in such factors as GDP growth rates, the level of public finance deficits and the competitiveness of the two economies for which the spread is quoted.

Central Government Debt

One way to get a picture of the level of borrowing of a country is through external debt. External debt is a measure of a total debt in a country that is owed to creditors outside that country; foreign liabilities, capital plus interest that the government, institutions and people within a nation's borders must eventually pay. In short, this number extends beyond simply government debt, but also debt owed by corporations and individuals.

A useful measure of a country's debt position is by comparing gross external debt to gross domestic product. By comparing a nation's total debt to what it produces, this ratio can be used to help determine the likelihood that a country as a whole will be able to repay its debt.

The following table shows data from the OECD on GDP as a % of central government debt for a selection of countries as at the end of 2010.

	Debt as a % of GDP
Austria	102.2
Belgium	129.5
Canada	107.7
France	118.8
Germany	82.2
Greece	178.8
Ireland	125.4
Italy	156.4
Netherlands	81.2
Portugal	150.6
Spain	117.9
United Kingdom	113.6
United States	123.2

The credit ratings agencies (CRAs) have been very active during the crisis in the eurozone in monitoring the creditworthiness of sovereign borrowers. Many states have suffered serious downgrades as the CRAs have become incresingly focused on the high levels of public sector debt, weak tax revenues and very slow economic growth.

Also troubling is the fact that many other European governments have been placed on alert by the CRAs with negative outlooks. In 2011, Spain, Italy and Belgium have either been downgraded or put on a negative outlook. In June 2015, Standard & Poor's downgraded Greece's long-term ratings from CCC to CCC-. As of July 2016, the UK's rating for Standard & Poor's is AA, as is Belgium's and France's. Italy remains on BBB-, while Spain is BBB+.

As a consequence of these factors, large private sector investors – mainly the large banks, insurance companies and pension funds – have either decided not to buy the debt of those sovereigns which are seen to be at risk, or are demanding very substantial yields to compensate them for the possibility of restructurings or default. This makes the debt correspondingly more difficult to service for the sovereign borrower.

In addition, the market for sovereign CDSs has been extremely active, with many fund managers deciding to either hedge or insure against default on existing exposure to sovereign credit risk, or to speculate on widening or narrowing of spreads even if they have no actual cash positions in the underlying sovereign debt market to protect.

3.4.5   The Impact of Events

For a fund manager, the impact of many kinds of events will lead to asset re-allocations amongst different securities in general, and more specifically to the mix they hold of different fixed income securities. Such reallocations are often referred to as **policy switching**.

Some of the factors which will instigate policy switches can be summarised as follows.

*   **Changes in Interest Rates.**
    *   Intuitions about the future direction of interest rates, and market timing in general, is one of the primary factors that will encourage fund managers to switch between different bonds. Switching from low-duration to high-duration bonds if interest rates are expected to fall is an example of a policy switch which will cause spreads to change.
*   **Changes in the Structure of the Yield Curve.**
    *   Normally, the yield curve is a smooth relationship between yield and maturity. Occasionally, however, there may be humps or dips in the curve. If the humps or dips are expected to disappear, then the prices of the bonds on the hump can be expected to rise (and their yield fall correspondingly), and the prices of the bonds in the dips can be expected to fall (and their yields correspondingly rise). A policy switch involves the purchase of the high-yield bond and the sale of the low-yield bond.
*   **Changes in Bond Quality Ratings.**
    *   A bond whose credit quality rating as, for example, rated by Standard & Poor's or Moodys is expected to fall, will drop in price. To prevent a capital loss, it can be switched for a bond whose quality rating is expected to rise or remain unchanged. This is an uncertain process and often there are no advance warnings of the re-rating of credit by the major rating agencies.
*   **Changes in Sector Relationships.**
    *   An example of a change in sector relationships is a change in taxes between two sectors. For example, one sector may have withholding taxes on coupon payments, eg, domestic bonds, whereas another, eg, eurobonds, may not.

- **Expectations about the Future Shape of the Yield Curve**
  - A downward-sloping or inverted curve suggests that markets believe that rates will fall. In the inverse pattern to that when expectations are for higher rates in the future, if the expectation is for lower rates in the future, bond purchases will be keen to lock in higher coupons now as the expectation is that coupons will decline in the future. A flat yield curve suggests that the market thinks that rates will not materially change in the future.
- **Anticipation of Monetary Policy**
  - If short-term interest rates are deliberately being moved higher by the bank, the market's expectation may well be that eventually this will lead to a downward sloping yield curve, referred to as an 'inverted' curve. This reflects the market's expectations that the bank may be trying to arrest inflationary pressures in the economy.
  - If the market believes that inflation will rise in the future, then the yields on longer-dated gilts will have to rise in order to compensate investors for the fall in the real value of their money. The expectation of inflation is more of a problem with the long-end, rather than the short-end, owing to the greater sensitivity to interest rates of longer-duration fixed income instruments. Once again, this will be reflected in the 2/10 spread referred to earlier.

3.4.6 Summary

The financial markets have become very sophisticated in analysing the co-movements of yields and interest rates across a wide spectrum of fixed-income instruments. Many spreads are quoted in real time in the money markets, and the manner in which other sectors of capital markets respond to these changes in spreads has led to increasingly co-ordinated movements across multiple asset classes.

Many market observers and sophisticated investors have observed that the manner in which many assets behave in reactions to changing financial spreads has introduced a new kind of risk dynamic into asset management.

As with many other kinds of relationships, the influence is best seen as a two-way feedback loop in which changed circumstances in one sector of the market – for example a ratings downgrade for a sovereign state – will lead to a widening of spreads in many other parts of the market. As governments have undertaken to protect their banking systems from critical points of failure, there has been a blurring of the distinction between the creditworthiness of sovereigns, banks and private sector.

4 . Portfolio Construction

4.1 Portfolio Risk

Learning Objective

11.4.1 Understand the main types of portfolio risk and their implications for investors: systemic risk; market risk – asset price volatility, currency, interest rates, commodity price volatility; investment horizon; liquidity, credit risk and default; counterparty risk

---

4.1.1 Investors' Risks

There are a number of types of risk faced by investors that are difficult to avoid, and the main categories can be identified in overview under the following headings.

- **Market or Systematic Risk** – this is the risk that the overall market in general, or the relevant part of the capital markets for investors wanting exposure to specific sectors, will rise or fall, as economic conditions and other market factors change. This may affect returns over a period of time or it may have a more immediate impact if an investor buys at the top of the market or sells at the bottom.
- **Inflation Risk** – inflation will erode returns or purchasing power and, even if the investor has taken account of inflation in his or her analysis, the actual and expected inflation may be different from that assumed in calculating expected returns.
- **Interest Rate Risk** – changes in interest rates will affect prices; this is possibly a subcategory of market risk. In addition, there are a number of risks specific to particular companies or sectors, which can be reduced by diversification or by ignoring an investment altogether.
- **Exchange Rate Risk** – any investor who purchases securities which are denominated in a foreign currency may suffer (or benefit) from changes in the exchange rates between the home or base currency and the other currency. In addition, one has to consider the risk that one's base or home currency may fall against other currencies, thereby diminishing one's purchasing power for global assets.
- **Default Risk** – an investor may find that a company from which he/she has purchased a security could become insolvent due to a harsh operating environment, high levels of borrowing, poor management or other financial miscalculations. Fixed-income investors, who purchase the bonds of companies, have some access to alerts of possible credit defaults through credit ratings agencies such as Moody's.
- **Liquidity Risk** – the assumption usually made is that large capital markets such as the LSE provide liquidity for investors to sell a security easily with a narrow spread between the ask and the bid prices. During stressful periods this liquidity can diminish and it can become much harder to sell a security readily. In extreme cases, the price quoted by the market-makers or investment bank may be for a relatively small amount of shares.

4.1.2 Investment Horizon

In considering the risk to an investor from purchasing and holding certain assets, it is vital also to consider the time frame of the holding period and whether the investor has resources sufficient to follow through on a long-term investment strategy.

- Equities are volatile and, over the short to medium term, can and have delivered negative returns.
- An investor whose goal is to meet some liabilities in, say, two years' time, may find that the appropriate investment vehicle is a two-year low-coupon gilt. This will be the case especially if the client is a high rate taxpayer as he/she will be able to benefit from a tax-free capital gain on these gilts at redemption. For other taxpayers, a high rate savings account is likely to be more attractive.
- For an investor that has liabilities to meet in 20 years' time, equities may be appropriate as there is scope to protect the investor against the effects of inflation.

Time horizon will also influence the level of risk that can be taken in order to achieve the objectives. An investor with a long-term time horizon may be able to tolerate a higher risk, as any poor returns in one year will be cancelled by high returns in subsequent years before the fund is required to deliver its required outcome.

4.1.3 Counterparty Risk

Counterparty risk is the risk that the party to a transaction will fail to meet their obligations.

- For exchange-traded instrument there are clearing and settlement processes for each trade which ensure that the risk that the other party has to a trade is transferred to a clearing house entity which stands behind the trade.
- The use of a central counterparty, such as the LCH, reduces the uncertainty and risk associated with counterparty risk. The risk that the other side of the transaction will default is reduced because they are replaced by one of the central counterparties, both of which are well capitalised and have insurance policies in place lessening the risk of default.
- Counterparty risk is especially an issue in the OTC market as with the assets which are created and traded in the OTC market, there is always a risk that one of the parties will not be able to rely on the credit-worthiness of the counterparty.

There are global initiatives to move the trading and settlement of OTC transactions on exchange in order to reduce the risk of systemic collapse of the financial system.

4.1.4 Systemic Risk

Systemic risk is the risk of collapse of the entire financial system or entire market, as opposed to risk associated with any one individual entity, group or component of the financial system.

To say that the entire financial system might collapse may have appeared fanciful until the credit crisis. Central bankers, including the Governor of the Bank of England, Mervyn King, have gone on record since to describe how close the world's financial system came to a total collapse.

One of the characteristics and vulnerabilities of the financial system which was exposed as a result of the crisis in asset-backed finance in 2007/8 were the interdependencies in the credit markets and banking system, where the failure of a single entity or cluster of entities had the potential to cause a cascading failure, which could potentially have bankrupted or brought down the entire system, causing widespread panic and chaos in the capital markets.

Insurance is often difficult to obtain against systemic risks because of the inability of any counterparty to accept the risk or militate against it, because, by definition, there is likely to be no (or very few) solvent counterparties in the event of a systemic crisis.

The essence of systemic risk is that it is highly dependent on the correlation of losses. Under normal market conditions, many asset classes and individual securities will show a significant degree of independence of co-movement. In other words their price action will be weakly correlated. When, however, markets become subject to financial contagion and panic there is a tendency for most assets and securities to become much more highly correlated. In fact, the correlation can approach unity as their price behaviour will tend towards a uniform direction, ie, downwards, and because of the interdependencies between market participants, an event triggering systemic risk is much more difficult to evaluate than specific risk.

For instance, while econometric estimates and expectation proxies in business-cycle research led to a considerable improvement in forecasting recessions, good analysis on 'systemic risk' protection is often hard to obtain, since interdependencies and counterparty risk in financial markets play a crucial role in times of systemic stress, and the interaction between interdependent market players is extremely difficult (or impossible) to model accurately. If one bank goes bankrupt and sells all its assets, the drop in asset prices may induce liquidity problems in other banks, leading to a general banking panic.

One concern is the potential fragility of liquidity – the ability to raise cash through selling securities – in highly leveraged financial markets. If major market participants, including investment banks, hedge funds and other institutions, are trading with high degrees of leverage, in other words, at levels far in excess of their actual capital bases, then the failure of one participant to settle trades (as in the case of AIG) may deprive others of liquidity, and through a domino effect expose the whole market to systemic risk.

One of the functions of a central bank is to act as the lender of last resort in times of financial panic and to ensure that the money markets can still function when there is a systemic risk to the market. The Bank of England acted as lender of last resort to Northern Rock, when it got into difficulties during 2007, and there was effectively a run on the bank with depositors queuing to withdraw deposits from branches of the bank. The Bank of England has since provided even more extensive support to the money markets since the financial crisis of Q4, 2008 and has undertaken massive injections of liquidity and quantitative easing to facilitate the functioning of the banking system and credit market.

4.2 Mitigating Portfolio Risk

Learning Objective

11.4.2 Understand the core principles used to mitigate portfolio risk: correlation; diversification; active and passive strategies; hedging and immunisation

4.2.1 Correlation and Diversification

From an investment perspective the statistical notion of correlation is fundamental to portfolio theory.

The very simplest idea is that, if one is seeking diversification in the holdings of a portfolio, one would like to have, say, two assets where there is a low degree of association between the movements in price and returns of each asset. The degree of association can also be expressed in terms of the extent to which directional changes in each asset's returns, or their co-movement, are related.

The benefits of diversification are to be found in having a more heterogeneous collection of assets, some of which may move upwards in respect to economic developments and some of which may move sideways or downwards. From a diversification perspective, it can be demonstrated that the weaker the correlation between the two assets, the greater the degree of diversification.

4.2.2 Active and Passive Management Strategies

Active fund managers are those that use discretion as to the timing of investments and asset allocation decisions and may change the composition of a portfolio on a regular basis. The underlying assumption is that the fund manager's expertise will enhance the overall return of the fund.

Active fund management rests on the notion that markets are not correctly explained by the EMH and that mispricing of securities not only exists but that it can be identified and exploited.

- A skilful fund manager will be able to identify such opportunities and purchase or sell the mispriced security and derive a profit when the mispricing is eliminated.
- A less skilful manager may suffer from not recognising such mis-pricing or be poor at timing the asset allocation decisions.
- As a matter of fact, which is somewhat awkward for active fund managers, research has shown that the average fund manager will often under-perform a simple index-tracking strategy.

Passive investment management aims to provide an appropriate level of return for a fund that is commensurate with a simple buy and hold strategy for a broad cross-section of the market.

- Passive management often takes the form of index tracking in which the funds are simply used to replicate the constituents of a broad market index such as the FTSE 100 Index or the Standard & Poors 500 Index in the US.
- More specialised tracker funds can also be linked to the performance of securities in emerging markets, and specific industry sectors.

- Increasingly, the proliferation of exchange-traded funds allows investors to purchase shares in a fund which trades actively on a major exchange and which provides exposure to certain kinds of securities and where the minimal management fees are incorporated into the actual price of the shares of the ETF.
- The benefit to an investor purchasing such ETFs is that there is usually a high degree of liquidity, the asset values of the fund constituents as well as the price of the ETF shares is updated on a real-time basis and the costs for the packaging of the securities is minimal.

Passive fund management is consistent with the idea that markets are efficient and that no mispricing exists. If the EMH is an accurate account of the way that capital markets work, then there is no benefit to be had from active trading. Such trading will simply incur dealing and management costs for no benefit. Investors who do not believe that they can identify active fund managers whom they are confident can produce returns above the level of charges for active management will often elect to invest in passive funds or index trackers.

4.2.3 Hedging

The risks that are inevitable when investing in shares, bonds and money market instruments can be mitigated, but not entirely, removed by entering into **hedging**.

An example of hedging using futures was shown in the Chapter 5.

Hedging can be difficult to implement and becomes mathematically intensive especially if the investment portfolio contains complex instruments.

Also hedging strategies will have a cost that inevitably impacts investment performance.

Hedging is usually achieved by using derivatives such as options, futures and forwards.

- Buying put options on investments held will enable the investor to remove the risk of a fall in value, but the investor will have to pay a premium to buy the options.
- Futures, such as stock index futures, as seen below, can be used to hedge against equity prices falling – but the future will remove any upside as well as downside.
- Forwards, such as currency forwards, can be used to eliminate exchange-rate risk – but, like futures, the upside potential will be lost in order to hedge against the downside risk.

4.2.4 Immunisation

Passive bond strategies are employed either when the market is believed to be efficient, in which case a buy-and-hold strategy is used, or when a bond portfolio is constructed around meeting a future liability fixed in nominal terms.

Immunisation is a passive management technique employed by those bond portfolio managers with a known future liability to meet. An immunised bond portfolio is one that is insulated from the effect of future interest rate changes.

Immunisation can be performed by using either of two techniques: cash matching or duration-based immunisation.

- Cash matching involves constructing a bond portfolio, whose coupon and redemption payment cash flows are synchronised to match those of the liabilities to be met.
- Duration-based immunisation involves constructing a bond portfolio with the same initial value as the present value of the liability it is designed to meet and the same duration as this liability.

A portfolio that contains bonds that are closely aligned in this way is known as a bullet portfolio. Alternatively, a barbell strategy can be adopted. If a bullet portfolio holds bonds with durations as close as possible to ten years to match a liability with a ten-year duration, a barbell strategy may be to hold bonds with a durations of five and 15 years. Barbell portfolios necessarily require more frequent rebalancing than bullet portfolios.

4.3 Investment Allocation

Learning Objective

11.4.3 Understand the key approaches to investment allocation for bond, equity and balanced portfolios: asset class; geographical area; currency; issuer; sector; maturity

4.3.1 Asset Classes and Sectors

Asset allocation involves considering the big picture first, by assessing the prospects for each of the main asset classes within each of the world's major investment regions against the backdrop of the world economic, political and social environment.

Once asset allocation has been decided upon, the next step is to consider the prospects for those sectors within the various asset classes, eg, equities, bonds, commodities and derivatives. Sector selection decisions in equity markets are usually made with reference to the weighting each sector assumes within the index against which the performance in that market is to be assessed. The final stage of the process is deciding upon which specific issuers should be selected within the favoured sectors. A combination of fundamental and technical analysis will typically be used in arriving at the final decision.

The investment strategy adopted will need to determine whether this asset allocation is achieved using passive or active investment management.

Within larger portfolio management organisations, asset allocation and top-down strategy are usually determined on a monthly basis by an asset-allocation committee. The committee draws upon forecasts of risk and return for each asset class and correlations between these returns. It is at this stage of the top-down process that quantitative models are often used, in conjunction with more conventional fundamental analysis, to assist in determining which geographical areas and asset classes are most likely to produce the most attractive risk-adjusted returns, taking full account of the client's mandate.

Most asset allocation decisions, whether for institutional or retail portfolios, are made with reference to the peer group median asset allocation. This is known as asset allocation by consensus and is undertaken to minimise the risk of underperforming the peer group.

When deciding if and to what extent certain markets and asset classes should be over or under weighted, most portfolio managers set tracking error, or standard deviation of return, parameters against peer group median asset allocations.

Finally, a decision on whether to hedge market and/or currency risks must be taken. Over the long term, academic studies have concluded that the skills in decision-making with regard to asset allocation can account for over 90% of the variation in returns for pension fund managers.

4.3.2 Geographical Area

Many investors wish to seek out opportunities in international markets and there are now available many investment products, including a wide range of ETFs, which enable professional and retail investors to have exposure to specific geographical regions and even specific country funds.

A primary reason to invest in overseas markets is for diversification. More specifically, it is prudent to own assets in countries whose economies have different attributes than the domestic market of the investor.

- A service-based economy has different attributes to a commodity-based economy.
- Exporting surplus nations differ from importing surplus nations.
- Economies with large public deficits (eg, US, UK and Japan) can be contrasted with those with large surpluses (eg, China).

These different attributes can help to alleviate the coincidence of the timing of the economic cycles in these respective countries. In turn this might result in the fact that the respective stock market cycles are unlikely to be largely correlated with the business cycle in the investor's domestic market.

Whatever countries are selected for inclusion in a portfolio strategy should be blended in consistently with the required attributes.

- If one favours commodity-based economies one will want exposure to such countries as Australia, Canada, Russia and South Africa.
- Another investor, who may want exposure to the semiconductor industry or computer hardware, might want to own a fund which specialises in South Korea or Taiwan or Asia, possibly excluding Japan.
- Some funds are structured in such a manner that one can have exposure to most of the Asian markets but not Japan, because its economy is considered by many investors to be a special case based upon the massive decline in Japanese equities since 1990.

Many enthusiasts for investing in emerging markets such as the BRIC nations (Brazil, Russia, India and China) like to point to the much greater rate of economic growth in such nations compared to the rates currently seen in the US and most of Europe. This has also given rise to the notion that the emerging markets have become de-coupled from the economic cycles which manifest themselves in the developed world.

While it is certainly the case that China and India, especially, have rates of GDP growth that western countries are unlikely to see in the foreseeable future, it must also be recalled that when the banking crisis occurred in 2008 some of the hardest hit markets were the emerging markets.

One barometer to use for this is to consider the Hong Kong market, which is part of the emerging world but which has well established and very liquid capital markets. From the onset of the financial crisis in the summer of 2007 the Hang Seng Index (as well as the Shanghai index) experienced a drop of more than 60% which was considerably in excess of the decline seen in the US and Europe.

One other statistic is worth contemplating with regard to the notion that China in particular may be able to lead the world out of its current anaemic growth rates because of the dynamism of its economy.

- The IMF has estimated that the People's Republic of China is now the second largest economy in the world (if the EU is not considered as a bloc) and has an annual GDP of about $2.5 trillion. However, to keep things in perspective, in 2010 this is about 4% of the total world GDP.
- By comparison, if one takes the US and all of the EU countries together, they account for about 50% of world GDP.

Undoubtedly, exposure to the emerging markets should be a part of most investment strategies, except for the risk averse, and in general terms a good spread of assets across many geographical regions will provide a degree of diversification. But even this last comment needs to be qualified, as the degree of diversification appears, from some correlation studies by quant funds, to be diminishing.

4.3.3 Currency

Foreign currencies are an asset class in their own right and not just as a medium of exchange for purchasing other assets.

The following chart reveals the exchange rate tracked historically for the Australian dollar versus the US dollar during the period from early 2008 until mid-2016.

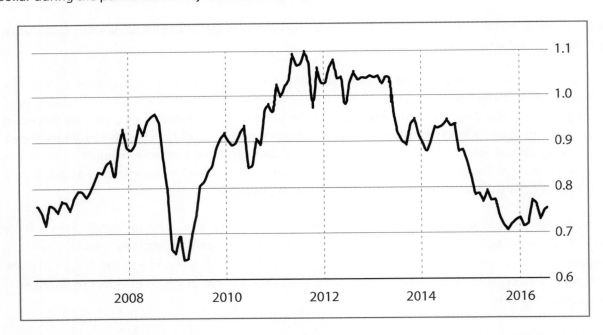

As can be seen from the chart above, the Australian dollar dropped by about 40% from having almost reached parity (ie, $1USD = $1AUD) in July 2008 to about 60 cents against the US dollar at the end of 2008.

What is also interesting about the chart is that it very closely resembles the chart for many global equity indices, including the S&P 500 and the FTSE 100. In fact, the S&P 500 lost almost exactly 40% during the comparable period to that shown on the above chart.

The more traditional explanations that are given when discussing currencies relate to the importance of hedging. Some fund managers will hedge their foreign currency exposure by using forward currency contracts to limit risk and reduce volatility. However, this will depend on their mandate and investors need to be aware that not all funds are automatically hedged.

Foreign currency risk can be reduced, though not completely eliminated, by employing hedging instruments or strategies such as:

- Forward contracts
- Back-to-back loans
- Foreign currency options
- Foreign currency futures
- Currency swaps.

4.3.4   Issuer Selection

A bottom-up approach to asset allocation is one which focuses on the unique attractions of individual securities and the characteristics of the issuer.

The considerations in the case of an equity investment are the Price/Earnings (P/E) multiple for the issuer, the P/E multiples for competitors, the rate of earnings-growth and other financial ratios relating to profitability and gearing.

In the case of considering a bond purchase the investor will want to examine the credit ratings reported by the major credit ratings agencies, the spreads between the issuer's bonds and other benchmarks such as government issues of similar maturity.

In addition, there are opportunistic factors to consider in evaluating the attractiveness of an individual issuer of securities. Although the health and prospects for the world economy and markets in general are taken into account, these are secondary to factors such as whether a particular company is a possible takeover target or is about to launch an innovative product, for instance.

4.3.5   Sector Selection

A 'top-down' approach to portfolio management is one where the major asset-allocation decisions are based on first selecting asset classes which are in accordance with the objectives and constraints of the fund, as stated in the mandate or prospectus. Thereafter, individual securities are selected to fit within this very structured approach.

Where a top-down approach is adopted, investment management involves the following three activities in the sequence below:

- Asset allocation.
- Market timing or tactical asset allocation.
- Stock selection.

Once asset allocation has been decided upon, top-down managers then consider the prospects for those sectors within their favoured equity markets. Sector-selection decisions in equity markets are usually made with reference to the weighting each sector assumes within the index against which the performance in that market is to be assessed.

Given the strong interrelationship between economics and investment, however, the sector selection process is also heavily influenced by economic factors, notably where in the economic cycle the economy is currently positioned.

The investment clock below describes the interrelationship between the economic cycle and various sectors.

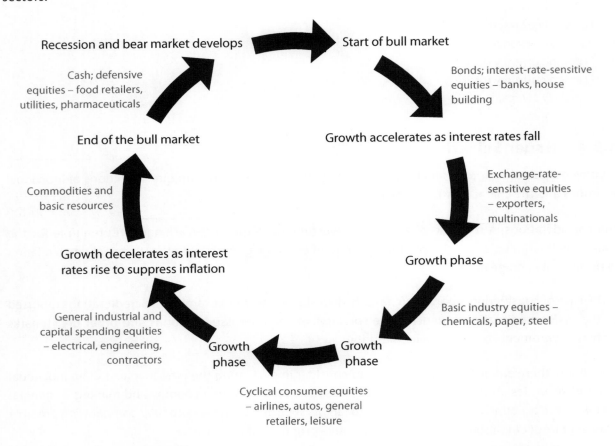

However, the clock assumes that the portfolio manager knows exactly where in the economic cycle the economy is positioned and the extent to which each market sector is operationally geared to the cycle.

Moreover, the investment clock doesn't provide any latitude for unanticipated events that may, through a change in the risk appetite of investors, spark a sudden flight from equities to government bond markets, for example, or change the course that the economic cycle takes.

4.3.6 Maturity

The ongoing fluctuation of interest rates poses a particular problem for fund managers with a portfolio of bonds because of re-investment risk. However, by using an approach based upon bond duration matching or immunisation, it is possible to maintain a steady return over a specific time horizon, irrespective of any changes in the interest rate.

In the case where there is a need to match a set of cash outflows, a bond portfolio with the same duration as the liabilities should be constructed.

Example

Suppose that a bond is purchased with a yield of 10% and interest rates fall to 7%. The current price of the bond will rise but the overall return on the bond will fall, as it is now only possible to reinvest the coupons received at the rate of 7%. As the bond approaches maturity, this fall in the return will become greater as the reinvestment loss outweighs the gain (which will fall as the bond moves to redemption and the price pulls to redemption at its face value). Under this scenario, the overall return from the investment will fail to have realised the quoted yield of 10%.

The same is true of the opposite situation where interest rates rise and bond prices fall. The downward adjustment in the bond's current price will diminish as the bond approaches maturity and the bond pulls to redemption. The coupons, however, will have been reinvested at a higher rate, therefore generating greater returns. Under this scenario, the overall return from the investment will have outperformed the quoted yield of 10%.

Yield is not an effective measure of the anticipated return on a bond if it is held to maturity precisely because it assumes reinvestment at the same rate as the yield.

Duration matching or immunisation relies on the fact that these two effects (price and reinvestment) are balanced at the point of duration, the weighted average life of the bond. This is illustrated in the diagram below. If a bond is held to its duration and not its maturity, the return can be guaranteed.

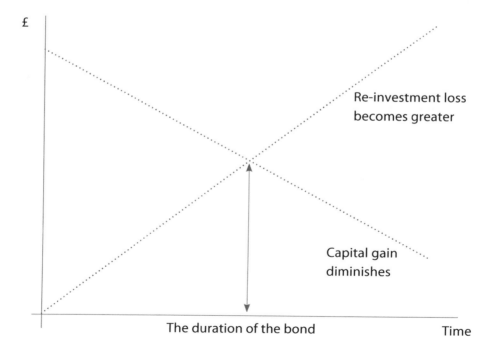

The process of immunisation requires the fund manager to purchase a portfolio of bonds with a duration equal to the liabilities that need to be matched. Through immunisation the fund manager can guarantee that the bond portfolio will earn the GRY, since any alteration in capital value of the bonds will be balanced by the reinvestment gain or loss.

4.4   Investment Strategies and Styles

Learning Objective

11.4.4   Understand the main aims and investment characteristics of the main cash, bond and equity portfolio management strategies and styles: indexing/passive management; active/market timing; passive-active combinations; growth versus income; market capitalisation; liability-driven; immunisation; long, short and leveraged; issuer and sector-specific; contrarian; quantitative

4.4.1   Active Equity Selection Strategies

Stock selection, or stock picking, is important whenever the fund managers are prepared to accept the overall consensus for the market as a whole, but believe that certain individual securities are mis-priced.

- An overpriced security is one that has an expected return that is less than should be expected on a risk-adjusted basis.
- An underpriced security has an expected return that is more on a risk-adjusted basis than would be expected.

Active stock selection can involve the application of various fundamental, technical or quantitative techniques. In terms of the capital asset pricing model (CAPM), which is a methodology for valuing securities in reference to the overall market or what can be called the securities market line (SML), a security is said to be mispriced if it has a non-zero alpha value. Such a security has a return above what might otherwise be expected and is therefore undervalued.

The objective of a stock picker is to pick portfolios of securities with positive alpha. In terms of active stock selection the manager will try to construct portfolios of securities that will have a more than proportionate weighting of the underpriced or positive alpha securities, and correspondingly less than proportionate weighting of the overpriced securities which are exhibiting negative alpha.

Bottom-up methods are usually dependent on the style or approach of the individual fund manager or team of managers. A fund management style is an approach to stock selection and management based on a limited set of principles and methods. The most widely recognised pure styles are:

- Value – the oldest style, based on the premise that deep and rigorous analysis can identify businesses whose value is greater than the price placed on them by the market. By buying and holding such shares often for long periods. a higher return can be achieved than the market average. Managers of equity income or income and growth funds often adopt this style, since out of fashion stocks often have high dividend yields.
- Growth at a Reasonable Price (GAARP) – based on finding companies with long-term sustainable advantages, in terms of their business franchise, quality of management, technology or other specific factors. Proponents argue that it is worth paying a premium price for a business with premium quality characteristics. The style is used mainly by active growth managers.
- Momentum – an investment strategy that aims to capitalise on the continuance of existing trends in the market. The momentum investor believes that large increases in the price of a security will be followed by additional gains and vice versa for declining values. This is the strategy most widely adopted by middle-of-the-road fund managers.

- Contrarianism – the concept behind contrarian investing is that high returns can be achieved by going against the trend. Correctly judging the point where a trend has reached an extreme of optimism or pessimism is difficult and risky. This style is found most often in hedge fund managers.

Other investment styles include the following.

Quantitative Funds

A quantitative (quant) fund is an actively managed fund where the stock-selection process is driven by computer models. A pure quant fund relies solely on computer models to make this stock selection.

In a quant fund there is no place for manager's judgement based on fundamental analysis. Instead, the fund manager uses pre-determined or pre-set models to undertake this stock selection process. Such models sometimes rely on ideas such as portfolio theory, CAPM, the dividend valuation model and options pricing techniques – ie, fundamental evaluation tools – in order to determine which stocks to hold and in what proportions. Sometimes the models are more based on the identification of patterns as discussed in conjunction with technical analysis.

Typical strategies of quant funds:

- Growth strategies.
- Value strategies.
- Statistical arbitrage strategies.
- Correlation strategies.
- Long/short equity strategies.
- Dispersion strategies.

It used to be observed that quant funds tend to perform better in market downturns whereas more fundamental funds perform better in upswings. Quant funds, based on correlations and exploiting convergence or mean reversion strategies assume that the historical statistical relationships between stocks will continue into the future, which clearly may not hold true. Their experience in the recent market downturns are leading many to question whether this still holds.

Income Investing

Income investing aims to identify companies that provide a steady stream of income.

Income investing may focus on mature companies that have reached a certain size and are no longer able to sustain high levels of growth. Instead of retaining earnings to invest for future growth, mature firms tend to pay out retained earnings as dividends as a way to provide a return to their shareholders. High dividend levels are prominent in certain industries such as utility companies.

The driving principle behind this strategy is to identify good companies with sustainable high dividend yields to receive a steady and predictable stream of income over the long term.

Because high yields are only worth something if they are sustainable, income investors will also analyse the fundamentals of a company to ensure that the business model of the company can sustain a rising dividend policy.

Absolute Return

An absolute return strategy seeks to make positive returns in all market conditions by employing a wide range of techniques, including short selling, futures options, derivatives, arbitrage, leverage and unconventional assets.

Alfred Winslow Jones is credited with forming the first absolute return fund in New York in 1949. In recent years, the use of an absolute return approach has grown dramatically with the growth of hedge funds and the launch of numerous open-ended funds following the same strategy.

Combined Approach

In practice, successful managers usually develop their own personal styles over a period of years, usually based on one or other of the major styles outlined above.

Many houses use a combined approach with fundamental analysis and quantitative analysis dictating the markets and stocks which they wish to buy, and technical analysis being used to determine the timing of entry into the market place.

As already noted, increasing numbers of fund managers are becoming familiar with technical analysis since if sufficient numbers do believe the technical analysts, then the markets will have a tendency to move in line with the anticipations of technically focused traders.

When evaluating the style that is being followed it is also important to understand whether the fund manager is operating within the restrictions imposed by a house style or is free to follow their own convictions. Centralised versus decentralised refers to this approach:

- **Centralised approach** – a firm decides that it will have an agreed investment policy that all of its investment managers will follow.
- **Decentralised approach** – a firm will give discretion to its investment managers to operate freely or within general constraints.

The approach adopted can often be important in the analysis of a fund. Large fund groups often have the organisational infrastructure that can support extensive research and are likely to have several people involved in the management of a fund, so that the departure of one individual will not necessarily have a great impact on performance.

By contrast, a smaller fund can allow a talented fund manager to demonstrate his or her skills and deliver exceptional returns without the bureaucracy and constraints that might exist in a larger organisation. Many boutique fund management operations have been set up to exploit this very edge. However, these types of fund can present a risk through their dependence on one key individual. The potential for superior investment returns needs to be balanced against the absence of organisational support and the potential impact that can have on the consistency of returns.

4.4.2 Passive Management

Buy and Hold

A buy and hold strategy involves buying a portfolio of securities and holding them for a long period of time, with only minor and infrequent adjustments to the portfolio over time.

Under this strategy, investments bought now are held indefinitely, or if they have fixed maturities, held until maturity and then replaced with similar ones.

The following is taken from an article which appeared in the New York Times in February 2009 and reflects the relatively dire performance of equities during the 1998–2008 period and the dangers of this strategy.

In the last 82 years – the history of the Standard & Poor's 500 – the stock market has been through one Great Depression and numerous recessions. It has experienced bubbles and busts, bull markets and bear markets.

But it has never seen a ten-year stretch as bad as the one that ended last month.

Over the ten years through January, an investor holding the stocks in the S&P's 500 Stock Index, and reinvesting the dividends, would have lost about 5.1% a year after adjusting for inflation, as is shown in the following chart.

A Poor Decade

Annual total return of Standard & Poor's 500 Stock Index, adjusted for inflation, over ten-year periods on date shown.

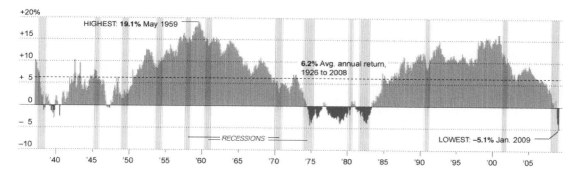

Figures are based on the total return of the S&P 500, with dividends reinvested, adjusted for the change in the Consumer Price Index (CPI). Figures are not reduced for either transaction costs or taxes, and thus overstate what the average investor would be likely to receive. Figures assume the CPI will be unchanged for January.

Sources: *Standard & Poor's, Bloomberg, Bureau of Labor Statistics via Haver Analytics*

What lessons are there for investors seeking exposure to equities? One point is that spreading investment over a period can reduce some of the effects of market volatility. If, instead of a single investment of say £10,000 made in 1999, when the US and UK stock markets were at their peak, an investor had invested perhaps £2,000 per year over the next ten years, the principle of cost averaging would have lessened the impact of poor returns for equities over the financial crisis. However, it is worth noting that equity markets have seen significant growth since the crisis with the Dow Jones Industrial Average 30 Index seeing returns of well over 60% since 2011 up to the start of 2016.

The question of buying and holding equities or even index-tracker products such as one based on the FTSE 100 is being questioned by more financial analysts in the light of the more recent data.

Indexation

There is a variant to the buy and hold strategy that eliminates the diversifiable risk and effectively replicates the performance of a market index, and this is known as index matching or indexation.

There are several different ways of proceeding with respect to indexation, but the most fundamental one is to decide on the appropriate index for the client, as there are many different market indices available.

- An investor may want exposure to large cap UK stocks, in which case the FTSE 100 is the obvious index to select.
- Alternatively the investor may be more interested in the large cap stocks which are primarily US based and for this area the Standard & Poor's 500 Index is one of the most appropriate indices.
- As the name suggests, the UK index consists of around 100 large cap stocks whereas its most closely matched US counterpart comprises 500 different companies.

The duplication of an index by holding all of its constituents is also known as complete indexation. The requirement is to match exactly the underlying components of the relevant index and as such it can often be complex and expensive. For example, the FTSE All-Shares Index contains several hundred securities weighted according to their relative market proportions. To construct a portfolio of all these securities with the same proportions as the index would involve extremely high commissions and dealing costs.

Although the large world indices are relatively stable in terms of their constituents there is a need from time to time to make changes and modify the components. In the case of the US index, the S&P 500, the company Standard & Poor's will make periodic adjustments to the constituents in the light of changes of ownership of certain companies, eg, a company may have been taken over by another. Also, the custodians of indices will periodically have to remove some stocks from an index if the market capitalisation falls below a certain threshold level and then they will substitute another company which has grown in stature and market capitalisation to qualify for entry to the index.

If a fund manager is replicating such an index, where modifications are being made from time to time, then all of the changes and re-balancing will need to be made to the replica and this will involve dealing costs and commissions as well as dealing spreads. The manner of re-balancing is more critical in the case of an index like the S&P 500, which is market cap weighted rather than in the case of the Dow Jones Industrial Average which is a simple average of the 30 constituent stocks and where there is not a balancing in the composition of the index based on market capitalisation.

A bond index fund will be more complex and expensive to replicate. With the passage of time the average maturity of a bond index will decline and to replace those bonds which are reaching redemption with suitable alternatives and preserve the duration characteristics of the bond fund is a particularly challenging undertaking.

In general terms duplication or complete indexation is often not practical, and therefore alternative strategies designed to emulate the index's performance are used.

Stratified Sampling

- As in statistical theory, the use of stratified sampling involves the selection of a sample of securities from the total population comprising the index.
- The sample should be stratified so that it is representative of the primary characteristics of the whole population, eg, the total population of the index constituents can be divided into sectors in the case of equities and into different maturities in the case of bonds.
- A cross-section of securities is then selected from each sector with the intention that the sample exhibits the highest correlation to the sector's overall return and likewise that there is a strongly correlated fit between the returns from the sample and those from the entire populations of the assets in the index.
- This procedure limits the initial transaction costs and subsequent rebalancing costs, but increases the risks of tracking errors, ie, the difference between the fund's return and the return on the market index.

Factor Matching

- Factor matching involves the construction of an index fund using securities selected on the basis of specifically chosen factors or risk characteristics.
- If the first risk factor required is that the sample matches the level of systematic risk, then the selected portfolio will need to be chosen to have the same level of beta as the market.
- Other factors may be sector breakdown, dividend pattern, firm size, financial structure, eg, gearing ratio.
- The selected index fund will be a subset of the available securities within the whole index that matched the market in terms of the required factor(s) and have the highest overall correlation with the market.

Co-mingling

- Co-mingling involves the use of co-mingled funds, such as unit trusts or investment trusts, rather than the explicit formation of an index fund. Co-mingling may be especially suitable for clients with relatively small portfolios and may provide an acceptable compromise between the transaction costs of complete indexation and the tracking error of stratified sampling.

Tracking Error

The desire to replicate the performance of an index with a subset or sample is prone to tracking errors.

- In other words, when the index is changed in some fashion, for example to remove certain securities which may have been taken over or which have fallen below the market capitalisation threshold and then to include some new entrants, the replication format used may no longer be suitable.

- If the sample was based upon stratification and reflection of the sector composition of the index, the removal of one or two key securities from a sector could have quite a pronounced effect on the sample which was set up to emulate the previous composition of the index by sector.
- The replication may need to be quite significant in terms of changing the constituents of the sample or replica to reflect again the stratification of the whole index.

Another problem arises when the constituents of an index are changed.

- When the announcement of a change is made, the price of the security being deleted tends to fall, while the price of the security being added tends to rise.
- Fund managers are then forced to take a loss on some of their holdings as they eject them from their surrogate portfolio and to have to pay over the odds for the additions, where the prices will fall back over time after the index has settled down again.
- These effects can cause major tracking errors between index funds and the index itself.

Apart from the transaction costs involved in setting up and rebalancing, there are other problems associated with running an index fund.

- The most important of these concerns income payments on the securities.
- The total return on an index may include not only capital gains but also income in the form of dividend or coupon payments.
- In order to match the performance of the index in terms of income, the index fund needs to have the same pattern of income payments as the index.
- It will also have to make the same reinvestment assumptions.

Unless complete indexation had been undertaken, it is unlikely that an index fund will exactly replicate the income pattern of the index.

In addition, the index may assume that gross income payments are reinvested without cost back into the index on the day each security becomes ex-div. In practice, however, this assumption can be violated for the following reasons:

- The dividend or coupon payment is not made until an average of six weeks after the ex-div date.
- The payment is received net of tax.
- There are dealing costs of reinvesting income payments.
- The income payments on different securities may be fairly small and it may not be worthwhile investing such small sums on the days they are received.

In general terms, over the longer term there is an expectation that the fund will underperform the index, ie, suffer a tracking error.

Despite these issues, indexation is a popular form of fund management. It attempts to avoid, as far as possible, decisions about selection and timing of investment yet it is not purely passive. At the very least, the choice of index and the reinvestment of income involve active intervention.

4.4.3 Active Bond Selection Strategies

As with an equities portfolio, a bond portfolio will be actively managed whenever there are mis-priced bonds available.

Active bond portfolio management operates around the activities of security selection and market timing. However, there is a difference between active share selection and active bond selection. Most equity managers engage in security selection, whereas most bond managers engage in market timing.

- A bond picker will construct a portfolio of bonds that, in comparison with the market portfolio, has less than proportionate weightings in the overpriced bonds and more than proportionate weightings in the underpriced bonds.
- A market timer engages in active management when he/she does not accept the consensus market portfolio and is either more bullish or more bearish than the market. Expectations of interest rate changes are therefore a crucial input into successful market timing.

A bond market timer is interested in adjusting the relative duration of his portfolio over time.

- Market timing with bonds is sometimes called duration switching.
- If the fund manager is expecting a bull market because he/she is expecting a fall in the general level of interest rates, he/she wants to increase the duration of their portfolio by replacing low-duration bonds with high-duration bonds.
- If the fund manager is expecting a bear market because he/she is expecting a rise in the level of interest rates, he/she wants to reduce the duration of their portfolio.

Active bond portfolio management is generally not as profitable as active share portfolio management. There are several reasons for this.

- There are more shares than bonds traded in the UK.
- The most liquid bonds are UK government bonds that have only certain maturities.
- The volatility of bond prices is generally much lower than that of shares, hence fewer opportunities for substantial mis-pricing of bonds exists.
- With only a few bonds suitable for active trading, the portfolio consisting of these bonds will be relatively undiversified.
- The cost of active bond portfolio management can be reduced using futures and options.

Riding the Yield Curve

Riding the yield curve is a valid strategy when the yield curve is upward sloping.

- If this is the case, then an investment manager can buy bonds with maturities in excess of their investment horizon.
- He/she proceeds to hold the bonds until the end of his investment period and then sells them.
- If the yield curve has not shifted during that period, the investment manager will have generated higher returns than if he/she had bought bonds with the same maturity as their investment horizon.
- This follows because as the time to maturity declines, the yield to maturity falls and the price of the bond rises, thereby generating a capital gain (hence, the term yield curve ride).
- These gains will be higher than those available if bonds with the same maturity as the investment horizon are used, because the maturity value of the latter bonds is fixed.

Example

The following example shows an opportunity to ride the yield curve where the term structure of interest rates is upward sloping showing that longer-dated instruments are yielding more than shorter-dated ones.

To keep the example simple we shall assume that the two instruments are zero coupon treasury notes with one and two years remaining to maturity. The current yield curve reveals that a one-year note will have a yield to maturity of 0.8%, whereas a two-year note will have a yield to maturity of 0.9%. Since there are no coupons all of this is effected in the current price of the bond.

Zero Coupon Treasury Bond	Time Left to Maturity	Yield to Maturity as per the Yield Curve	Formula	Price of Bond
A	1	0.8%	(100/1008)^1	99.21
B	2	0.9%	(100/1009)^2	98.23

If the fund manager buys the one-year zero coupon bond and holds it for one year until redemption the return will be exactly as provided for by the yield curve, ie, 0.8%.

$$r = \frac{(100 - 99.21)}{99.21} = 8\%$$

Since this is a zero coupon held to maturity, the risk is zero.

The alternative scenario is to buy the two-year note and hold it for one year and sell it then as a zero coupon with one year remaining. The return available then is as follows:

$$r = \frac{(99.21 - 98.23)}{98.23} = 10.00\%$$

The return can again be determined from the holding period return calculation, though an assumption is required regarding the selling price in one year. The risk this time is not zero as the fund manager is exposed to movements in the yield curve.

In conclusion, the yield curve ride is a strategy by which investors take on some risk in order to enhance returns.

Bond Switching

There are valid reasons for bond portfolio adjustments involving the purchase and sale of bonds, in other words bond switching or swapping. There are two main classes of bond switches:

- **Anomaly switches** – an anomaly switch is a switch between two bonds with very similar characteristics, but whose prices or yields are out of line with each other.
- **Policy switches** – a policy switch is a switch between two dissimilar bonds, which is designed to take advantage of an anticipated change in interest rates, the yield curve, possible changes in the bond credit rating from the major ratings agencies and sector relationships.

Anomaly Switching

- Substitution Switching
  - This involves switching between two bonds that are similar in terms of maturity, coupon and quality rating and every other characteristic, but which differ in terms of price and yield. Since two similar bonds should trade at the same price and yield, this circumstance results in an arbitrage between the dear bond being sold and the cheap bond being purchased.
  - If the coupon and maturity of the two bonds are similar, then a substitution swap involves a one-for-one exchange of bonds.
  - However, if there are substantial differences in coupon or maturity, then the duration of the two bonds will differ. This will lead to different responses if the general level of interest rates changes during the life of the switch. It will therefore be necessary to weight the switch in such a way that it is hedged from changes in the level of interest rates.
- Pure Yield Pickup Switch
  - A pure yield pickup switch involves the sale of a bond that has a given yield to maturity and the purchase of a similar bond with a greater yield to maturity.
  - With this switch, there is no expectation of any yield or price correction, so no reverse transaction will need to take place at a later date, which may be the case with a substitution switch.

Policy Switches

Policy switches are expected to lead to a change in the relative prices and yields of the two bonds and involve greater expected returns, but also greater potential risks, than anomaly switches.

- **Changes in interest rates**
  - Intuitions about the future direction of interest rates, and market timing in general, is one of the primary factors that will encourage fund managers to switch between different bonds.
  - Switching from low-duration to high-duration bonds if interest rates are expected to fall is an example of a policy switch.
- **Changes in the structure of the yield curve**
  - Normally, the yield curve is a smooth relationship between yield and maturity. Occasionally, however, this will not be the case.
  - A policy switch involves the purchase of the high-yield bond and the sale of the low-yield bond.
  - Another example of a policy switch resulting from changes in the structure of the yield curve is the bridge swap. As a result of an abnormal distortion in the yield curve, perhaps due to very high demand for bonds of a specific maturity there may be exploitable opportunities from a form of arbitrage between different sections of the yield curve. As an example, suppose that eight- and ten-year bonds are selling at lower yields and higher prices than the nine-year bond. A bridge swap involves selling the eight and ten-year bonds and buying nine-year bonds.
- **Changes in bond credit ratings**
  - A bond whose credit rating is expected to fall will fall in price. To prevent a capital loss, it can be switched for a bond whose quality rating is expected to rise or remain unchanged. This is an uncertain process and often there are no advance warnings of the re-rating of credits by the major rating agencies.
- **Changes in sector relationships**
  - A change in sector relationships is a change in taxes between two sectors: one sector may have withholding taxes on coupon payments, eg, domestic bonds whereas another, eg, eurobonds may not.

4.4.4 Passive Bond Management

There are three types of passive bond selection strategy suitable for the management of the bond element of the portfolios.

- Duration matching or immunisation.
- Cash flow matching.
- Horizon matching or combination matching.

Duration Matching or Immunisation

The ongoing fluctuation of interest rates poses a particular problem for fund managers with a portfolio of bonds because of re-investment risk. By using an approach based upon bond duration, matching or immunisation, it is possible to maintain a steady return over a specific time horizon, irrespective of any changes in the interest rate.

The primary factor which can introduce risk into the approach to immunisation outlined in Section 4.2.4 will be caused by non-parallel shifts in the yield curve. If this happens matching the duration of the investment to the liability horizon no longer guarantees immunisation.

Cash Flow Matching

Cash flow matching is a much simpler approach to portfolio management. The approach is simply to purchase bonds whose redemption proceeds will meet a liability of the fund as they fall due.

Starting with the final liability, a bond is purchased whose final coupon and redemption proceeds will extinguish the liability. Turning next to the penultimate liability, this may be satisfied in part by the coupon flows arising from bond one and any remaining liability is matched against the final coupon and redemption value of a second bond. This process is continued for each liability, ensuring that bonds are purchased whose final coupon and redemption values extinguish the net liabilities of the fund as and when they occur.

The approach outlined is a simple buy and hold strategy and as such does not require a regular rebalancing. In practice, it is unlikely that bonds exist with exactly appropriate maturity dates and coupons but, intuitively, it is easier to understand.

Horizon Matching

Horizon matching or combination matching is a mixture of the above two approaches to managed bonds. It is possible to construct a portfolio where, for example, the cash flow matches the liabilities for the next four quarters but is then immunised for the remaining investment horizon. At the end of the four quarters, the portfolio is rebalanced to cash flow match over the subsequent four quarters and is again immunised for the remaining period.

4.4.5   Core Satellite Management

Having considered both active and passive management, it should be noted that active and passive investment strategies are not mutually exclusive.

Index trackers and actively managed funds can be combined in what is known as core-satellite management. This is achieved by indexing, say, 70% to 80% of the portfolio's value so as to minimise the risk of underperformance, and then fine-tuning this by investing the remainder in a number of specialist actively managed funds or individual securities. These are known as the satellites.

This concept is illustrated in the diagram below.

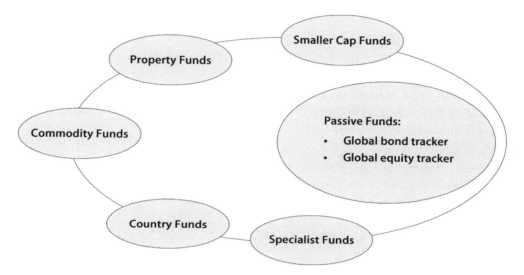

The core can also be run on an enhanced index basis, whereby specialist investment management techniques are employed to add value. These include stock lending and anticipating the entry and exit of constituents from the index being tracked.

In addition, indexation and active management can be combined within index tilts. Rather than hold each index constituent in strict accordance with its index weighting, each is instead marginally overweighted or underweighted relative to the index based on their perceived prospects.

4.5 Measuring Portfolio Risk and Return

Learning Objective

11.4.5 Understand how portfolio risk and return are evaluated using the following measures: holding period return; total return and its components; standard deviation; volatility; covariance and correlation; risk-adjusted returns; benchmarking

As we have seen earlier, risk arises from the uncertainty of outcomes and so it is essential that we understand how it can be evaluated.

- **Holding Period and Total Return**
  - In its simplest form, the performance of a portfolio of investments can be measured by regarding all of the incoming cash flows in the form of dividends or coupon payments and also factor in capital growth (final market value less initial value) and express these items which could be called the total return as a percentage of the initial amount invested. This gives rise to the core concept of the holding period return.
  - By calculation of the percentage holding period return for any investment it becomes possible to compare the relative performance of a variety of investments of different sizes and with different objectives and characteristics.
  - Holding period return is covered in Chapter 12.
- **Standard Deviation**
  - To measure the degree of variability of an investment, we can use either standard deviation or variance.
  - Standard deviation has the advantage that it is expressed in the same units as the returns, whereas variance is in the original units squared.
  - For some calculations in portfolio theory it is necessary to use the variance rather than standard deviation, but in discussions of risk in financial theory it is more common to use standard deviation.
  - Standard deviation was covered in Chapter two.
- **Volatility**
  - There are many different opinions on what constitutes the best measurement of volatility, ranging from the simplest which is the variance in the returns of an asset, or more commonly the standard deviation in returns.
- **Covariance and Correlation**
  - Standard deviation has been shown to be one of the key metrics in portfolio theory to measure risk but there is another important notion which provides a different view of the risk of holding an asset.
  - Covariance is a statistical measure of the relationship between two variables such as share prices and was covered in Chapter two.
  - Correlation is the degree of association to which directional changes in each asset's returns, or their co-movement, are related and was covered in Chapter 2.
- **Risk-Adjusted Returns and Benchmarking**
  - Once one has calculated the returns from a portfolio it is very useful in assessing the amount of risk borne by the investor or fund manager to compare the portfolio's performance against the market as a whole or against other portfolios. This requires the use of risk adjusted performance measurements such as the Sharpe ratio, Jensen measure, and the information ratio. These ratios are covered in Chapter 12.

5. Investment Selection

5.1 Client Information

Learning Objective

11.5.1 Be able to apply a range of essential information and factors to form the basis of appropriate financial planning and advice for clients: financial needs, preferences and expectations; income and lifestyle – current and anticipated; attitude to risk; level of knowledge about investments; existing debts and investments

---

5.1.1 Client Investment Profiles

Any individual is likely to have a number of objectives, for which some financial provision may be required. Having a particular view of risk does not imply that the same attitude to risk should be applied to all of the individual's objectives.

An individual may have investments that they wish to use for specific purposes or objectives and which they cannot easily afford to bear a great degree of shortfall risk. In such cases, the individual may wish to choose low-risk investments, so that they can be reasonably certain that their objective will be achievable by the desired date.

An individual might have other discretionary possibilities in mind for which the person is prepared to tolerate a higher level of risk. The objective may be seen as less essential to the individual, and may be something that the person accepts that they will have to do without if investment returns are not sufficient.

Of course, every investor is different, and the ways in which people rank their objectives and their risk tolerance in relation to different objectives vary. For one person, having enough money to spend on a comfortable home may take a higher priority than having the funds to travel widely. Another person may treat travelling as a higher priority than spending on a home. In general, the objectives that an individual sees as having the highest priority are those for which they will want to take the lowest risk if they are investing to achieve those objectives. Lower priority objectives can generally be more easily foregone if investments suffer losses.

5.1.2 Wealth and Investment Exposure

When considering a client's investment profile, their existing wealth is clearly an important consideration. If there is an excess of capital to invest, then clearly it is sensible for the individual to take steps to make the best use of that capital.

It is possible, although not generally advisable, for someone with little wealth to gain exposure to investment markets, for example by borrowing money to invest, or by using investments such as derivatives or spread betting to gain a greater exposure than the individual's free resources.

When investing in risky assets such as equities, a good principle is the often-stated one that someone should only invest what they can afford to lose. Someone who borrows to invest without having other capital to back it up if things go wrong has the problem that they may end up with liabilities in excess of their assets.

An investor who uses instruments such as derivatives to increase their exposure should maintain other accessible resources (eg, cash on deposit) that can be used to meet losses that may arise. Clearly, it is also important that they understand the risks they are undertaking.

5.1.3 Life Cycle, Age and Commitments

Some of the most vital characteristics in defining the client profile are as follows:

- The age of an investor.
- Number of dependents.
- The stage of their life cycle.
- Other financial commitments.

Adventurous risk-taking may be unwise for someone with heavy financial commitments. Another aspect of an investor's commitments is that of how much time he/she has available: if he/she works full-time and has a family, there may be little time left for them to manage their own investments even if he/she has an interest and knowledge to do so, and their commitments may mean that he/she is more likely to wish to seek professional financial advice.

5.1.4 Timescale and Risk

The effect of the investment timescale is particularly important for equity or equity-backed investments.

Over short-term horizons, ie, less than five years the returns from equities has often been negative but over very long-term horizons, equities have usually shown a relatively high return, which exceeds that of most other asset classes.

One of the most important issues to clarify within an investor's profile is their holding period or, in other words, the period for which they are committed to a particular investment programme. If an individual is only seeking to invest over a period of a few months, at the end of which they wish to redeem their investment, then it is inadvisable to invest the money in higher-risk investments such as equities. Given the volatility of equity returns there is an uncomfortably high probability that any investments made in equities for a short timescale might have to be liquidated at a loss.

5.1.5 Existing Portfolios

The issues which an investment adviser faces when taking over an existing portfolio and reconstructing it are similar to those involved when constructing an entirely new portfolio. A full profiling of the client's needs will be required to determine the need for accessibility and liquidity, income needs, attitude to risk, timescale, tax position and any ethical preferences.

From the point of view of professional ethics for fund managers, it is deemed to be part of their code of conduct that they do not engage in churning a client's investments: churning is excessive trading or switching investments on behalf of clients often with a view to generating fee income for the fund manager or associated brokerage firms.

There may be tax penalties if investments are disposed of. For property, shares and collective investments not sheltered within an ISA, there may be a capital gains tax charge. Encashment of a life assurance investment bond may create a chargeable event, resulting in a possible higher rate tax liability.

5.1.6   Liquidity

There are several meanings attributed to liquidity but specifically for many clients the key issue is how readily the asset can be converted into cash. Another liquidity requirement, which is particularly important for large funds which have a need to trade in large deal sizes, has to do with whether the asset can be traded in substantial quantities without the transaction causing disproportionately large changes in the price at which the trades occur.

With the need for liquidity in mind, it is wise for an investor to have sufficient funds held on deposit at any time to meet likely cash needs. Keeping funds liquid brings the benefit of accessibility but there is a trade-off in terms of returns: the most liquid investments, such as cash or instant access accounts, will have relatively lower returns than for other assets.

5.1.7   Affordability and Accessibility

In addition to liquidity issues, some investments are constrained in their accessibility and require long-term commitments by the investor. In some cases, the investment cannot be realised early even if the investor wishes it. Also, early redemption may be possible, but at the expense of a penalty or a significant reduction in returns.

It is sometimes possible to sell an investment before maturity on the open market, as for example with traded endowment policies. Although this should achieve a higher price than surrendering the policy to the insurance company, there is still likely to be a loss in the rate of return compared with retaining the investment until maturity. As a rule of thumb it is prudent to avoid the premature redemption, or in a worse-case scenario, distressed selling of investments and good planning should seek to alleviate the need for this.

5.1.8   Clients' Ethical Preferences

Some investors wish to support ethical and environmental issues and they can accomplish their objectives by selecting ethical investments or following the principles of SRI.

There are funds referred to generically as **ethical funds** that screen investments on ethical, social or environmental criteria and an investment adviser's task is to present the relevant information on such funds being considered to the client. Certain funds focus on a particular theme, such as renewable energy or public transport.

It may be that an investor wishes to concentrate on including positive ethical or SRI criteria, or alternatively that one wishes to exclude certain investments based upon the application of exclusion or negative criteria, or, as is often the case, a mixture of both (positive and negative screening).

5.1.9 Assessment of Attitude to Risk

Amongst the methods of assessment which can be developed by firms in order to evaluate an individual's risk profile, the questionnaire is common and useful.

Questions asked to assess an individual's risk profile will include the following:

1. How long do you expect to leave your investment in place until you sell it?

2. Which outcome is most important to you from an investment portfolio? (Choose one);

    - Preserving capital.
    - Generating income.
    - Long-term growth and capital gains.

3. Which of the following asset classes have you owned previously or do you now own?

    - Bank or building society deposit account.
    - Government stocks (gilts).
    - Unit trusts or OEICs.
    - Investment trusts.
    - Individual company shares.

4. Which of the following best describes your main objective in investing? (Choose one.)

    - The education of my children.
    - Savings.
    - Capital growth and returns.
    - My retirement.
    - To leave money in my will.

5. How large is your investment plan in proportion to your total savings?

    - Less than 10%.
    - Between 10% and 20%.
    - Between 20% and 30%.
    - Between 30% and 40%.
    - Above 40%.

5.2   Selecting Suitable Strategies and Investments

Learning Objectives

11.5.2   Be able to analyse and select strategies suitable for the client's aims and objectives in terms of: investment horizon; current and future potential for capital protection, growth and yield; protection against inflation; risk tolerance; liquidity, trading and ongoing management; mandatory or voluntary investment restrictions; impact of tax; impact of fees and charges

11.5.3   Be able to analyse and select investments suitable for a particular portfolio strategy: direct holdings, indirect holdings and combinations; role of derivatives; impact on client objectives and priorities; balance of investments

Selecting a suitable investment strategy will be driven by the client's investment objectives and their risk profile. The circumstances of every individual are unique and it is essential therefore that the investment strategy is appropriate to meet the needs of a client.

As we saw in Section 2, typical financial objectives include:

- Maximising future capital growth.
- Protecting the real value (ie, inflation-adjusted) of capital.
- Generating an essential level of income.
- Protecting against future events.

Once the client's investment objectives have been agreed, the next step is to develop an investment strategy that can be used to achieve these objectives. In developing an investment strategy, the following will need to be incorporated:

- Risk tolerance.
- Investment preferences.
- Liquidity requirements.
- Time horizons.
- Tax status.

The investment strategy should be summarised in an investment policy statement which is based on the client's risk profile and investment goals. The policy statement should set out:

- The purpose of the investments.
- The income or growth objectives.
- The timescale.
- A statement about the client's risk profile – in detail or outline.
- A statement about asset allocation in detail or outline.
- Other issues – such as ethical or SRI.

The investment policy statement therefore represents the distillation of all of the factors that have been considered so far into a strategy that meets the needs of the client.

Investment recommendations are usually presented in the form of a report. This will usually contain an outline of the client's circumstances and needs with a summary of the recommendations, followed by more detailed sections on risk profile, asset allocation and investment and wrapper selection.

End of Chapter Questions

Think of an answer for each question and refer to the appropriate workbook section for confirmation.

1. Two assets have a correlation coefficient of -1. What does this indicate?
   Answer reference: Section 1.1

2. What factors influence unsystematic risk?
   Answer reference: Section 1.4

3. What are six areas of personal information needed from clients?
   Answer reference: Section 2.1.1

4. What are the advantages and disadvantages of using passive management?
   Answer reference: Section 2.2.2

5. Why is the Financial Stability Report issued by the Bank of England closely scrutinised?
   Answer reference: Section 3.1.2

6. What is the default spread and what does it indicate?
   Answer reference: Section 3.4.2

7. What type of investment management technique is immunisation?
   Answer reference: Section 4.2.4

8. What type of investment management technique is core-satellite management?
   Answer reference: Section 4.4.5

9. How might the age of an investor affect their attitude to risk?
   Answer reference: Section 5.1.3

10. When selecting a suitable investment strategy for a client, how are an investor's recommendations normally presented?
    Answer reference: Section 5.2

Chapter Twelve
Performance Management

This syllabus area will provide approximately 5 of the 80 examination questions

12

472

1. Administration and Maintenance

1.1 Portfolio Monitoring and Reporting

Learning Objective

12.1.1 Be able to apply key elements involved in managing a client portfolio: systematic and compliant approach to client portfolio monitoring, review, reporting and management; selection of appropriate benchmarks to include market and specialist indices, total return and maximum drawdown; arrangements for client communication

A key requirement for an investment fund management team is the provision of current, reliable and useful reporting on the current state of a client's portfolio. Issuance of statements showing the deployment of funds and the returns currently achieved as well as historical summaries is just the basic requirement.

Given the complex nature of the investment possibilities available in the capital markets, the fact that clients may have exposure to different currencies, derivatives, hedge instruments and diverse asset classes then the task of presenting this information to a client becomes a major challenge for good investment managers.

Clearly the fund manager should be using state-of-the-art information technology and reporting software to generate timely information to a client and this may often have to be available in real time and accessible via the internet or distributed electronically. The issuance of hard copy statements is often a formality, as the client will require more immediate information than something which is out of date as soon as it is printed.

IT systems are a part of the systematic nature of portfolio reporting and in addition the fund manager will need to ensure that other relevant contextual information is provided to assist the client in making the best use of the information being provided. References to standard portfolio metrics should be included in the reports issued to clients including key ratios such as the Sharpe Ratio which will inform the client as to the risk/reward ratio of the portfolio. The investment skills and judgments of fund managers are in fact largely determined by the manner in which their performance is calibrated by such ratios.

Portfolio management should address issues of compliance. The actual execution of the portfolio management strategy should be monitored regularly to ensure satisfactory progress against stated objectives, costs/charges and performance criteria. Part of the investment management function is to regularly review the appropriateness and effectiveness of measures to manage risks.

Relevant documentation, registrations and other matters of compliance with legislation, reporting and taxation-related matters should be considered as vital to the portfolio monitoring process. In addition the portfolio manager and his/her team need to keep abreast of all relevant changes in legislation and rules from financial regulators in order to ensure that they are complying with the most current methods of reporting and following industry best practice.

- **Assessing portfolio performance**
  - From portfolio construction theory it is generally accepted that a time-weighted measure of returns is the most suitable for determining the returns achieved from an investment.
  - The next challenge is to find a way of deciding how good a return that actually is. In other words, a benchmark should be referenced to which comparisons of the returns achieved can be referenced.
  - Benchmarks and performance evaluation are considered in Section 2 of this chapter.
- **Total return and maximum drawdown**
  - Total return is a measure of investment performance that includes the change in price of the asset plus any other income (including dividends, interest and capital gains distributions). It is assumed that all income is reinvested over the period. The calculation of total return is expressed as a percentage of the initial asset value and is covered in Section 3 of this chapter.
  - Maximum drawdown is the distance from the highest value of a portfolio ('the high-water mark') to the lowest trough. Maximum drawdown is a key variable used by portfolio managers and is not adequately addressed by some measures of risk/return and portfolio theory.

Client Communication

The most appropriate method for client communication is for information to be made available to clients on a current, probably real-time, basis via the internet. Many fund managers will provide clients with a monitoring facility which enables them to inspect their portfolio performance, at least in summary form, via web-based portals.

In addition clients will need to receive periodic hard copy documents outlining portfolio performance as well as other material relating to compliance and taxation-related matters. Professional advisers of the client may often be the recipients of this information so that other financial management matters can be co-ordinated with investment management.

Meetings with clients should also be held periodically and at the specific request of the client.

1.2   Changes that can Affect a Client Portfolio

Learning Objective

12.1.2   Understand how changes can affect the management of a client portfolio: client circumstances; financial environment; new products and services available administrative changes or difficulties; investment-related changes (eg, credit rating, corporate actions); portfolio rebalancing; benchmark review

1.2.1   Client Circumstances

Individual investors and institutional investors have varying objectives and expectations.

Clearly, before advising any client an adviser or fund manager must be aware of these various needs, preferences, expectations and the financial situation of the client. The financial circumstances of the client are of course subject to change over time. Sometimes these changes can be anticipated and sometimes they will be almost completely unexpected.

The basic information about a client's circumstance that need to be captured can be broken down into the following:

- Personal and financial details.
- Objectives.
- Risk tolerance.
- Liquidity and time horizons.
- Tax status.
- Investment preferences.

There are changes which can take place in any one of these items. It may happen that if a client loses a regular source of income, even temporarily, there may be a need to liquidate a part of the client's holdings in order to raise cash.

- If the current portfolio has an adequate allocation of cash and short-term money market instruments available, this may not present any immediate issues.
- Alternatively, if part of a portfolio has to be liquidated this will alter the balance of the remaining assets and will require a re-balancing exercise to be performed at some future point in time.
- The redemption of certain instruments may attract penalties and charges; the need to liquidate equities at a time when the overall market is performing poorly could lead to capital losses and loss of future dividend income and, if there are derivatives in a portfolio, which have been used for tactical asset allocation, the timing of the exit from derivatives contracts can be very sensitive and could trigger premature losses, which would not have arisen if the instruments were held to maturity.

1.2.2 The Financial Environment

The changes which can take place in the overall financial environment and which will effect the current asset allocation strategy can be quite drastic, as was evidenced by the market developments we have seen since the start of the credit crisis.

The impact of large scale macro-economic factors such as the abrupt drop in GDP and employment which followed the banking crisis of 2008 or the austerity measures that have followed will have an impact on many clients' individual circumstances.

- There will be some clients who will be faced with the loss of employment income but the largest capacity for damage is to overall investor sentiment and the general appetite for risk.
- It is fair to say that many investors are now more risk averse than at any time in the last 30 years and perhaps a case could be made that one would need to return to the 1930s to find a parallel era.
- On the one hand this has meant that many investors have altered their attitude towards holding assets which they perceive to be too risky.
- On the other hand there are many who think more opportunistically and see the drop in asset prices as an excellent buying opportunity.

1.2.3   Availability of New Products and Services

Financial innovation over the last twenty years has been extraordinary. This has been especially the case in terms of the products which are now available to investors such as CFDs, ETFs, new kinds of collective investment vehicles and the proliferation of derivatives including credit default swaps and other asset-backed securities.

Amongst the different kinds of services available now to investors are many kinds of hedge funds and alternative asset management companies which provide non-traditional ways of investing. The availability of such a diversified offering of products and services is transforming the whole nature of the securities industry.

These changes question some of the underlying theories of investment and asset allocation and certainly require of professionals working in financial services that they constantly re-educate themselves on the conditions and products of their business.

The need for prudence and skill in investment decision making is perhaps more than ever at a premium and this is also leading to new attitudes towards allocation, the need for greater flexibility and pragmatism and also the possibility of fundamental changes in the regulation of the domestic and global financial environment.

1.2.4   Administrative Changes

The innovations just discussed as well as the changes in the operational side of the securities industry including new multilateral trading facilities and other regulatory changes including the dismantling of the FSA by the end of 2012 and the removal of the banking supervision function to the Bank of England will continue to impose a severe burden on the compliance and fund administration functions within investment management.

At the same time there are pressures on fund managers from competitors and from poor performance by many fund managers to cut fees and charges. The expectation is that there will need to be quite radical 'back office' changes at many investment firms.

1.2.5   Investment-Related Changes

Credit ratings for corporate borrowers are regularly reviewed and are often revised in the light of changed economic conditions and/or changes in the outlook for an industry or the issuer's specific circumstances.

Rating agencies will signal they are considering a rating change by placing the security on CreditWatch (S&P), Under Review (Moody's) or on Rating Watch (Fitch Ratings).

Most revisions result in credit downgrades rather than upgrades. The price change resulting from a credit downgrade is usually much greater than for an upgrade, given that the price of a bond can fall all the way to zero, whereas there is a limit to how high a bond's price can rise.

Corporate Actions such as a rights issue will impact the pricing of securities and under certain circumstances the decision by a company to engage in a secondary offering or proposal to alter its capital structure might trigger a major response from the markets. Under these circumstances a decision may be made to change a portfolio holding in the wake of the proposed corporate action.

1.2.6 Portfolio Re-Balancing

Earlier in this section the issue of making changes to the composition of a portfolio, as a result of the need to liquidate certain holdings, was discussed and how this will then require a re-balancing of the portfolio to reflect the changed circumstances.

If a portfolio has to be re-balanced following an expected development either in relation to client circumstances or to changes in the financial environment, the proper approach for an investment manager is to re-think the entire asset allocation strategy. Rather than making piecemeal changes and attempting to re-implement a revised version of the previous allocation strategy, it is preferable to devise a new strategic allocation, which takes into account the new circumstances. This could lead to a re-classification of the investor's profile and risk tolerance characteristics.

There are other circumstances of a more routine nature where a portfolio manager will re-balance a portfolio and to some extent the reasons why a portfolio manager may wish to re-balance are closely related to market timing and active management strategies.

1.2.7 Benchmark Review

Once a portfolio has been constructed, the portfolio manager and client need to agree on a realistic benchmark, against which the performance of the portfolio can be judged. The choice of benchmark will depend on the precise asset split adopted and should be compatible with the risk and expected return profile of the portfolio.

It is essential that the portfolio manager and client agree on the frequency with which the portfolio is reviewed, not only to monitor the portfolio's performance, but also to ensure that it still meets with the client's objectives and is correctly positioned given prevailing market conditions.

12

2. Performance Benchmarks

It is important that investors and other interested parties are able to monitor the performance of a fund in order to assess the results that the investment manager has produced. In this section, we consider the use of performance benchmarks and look at how performance can be measured and the results analysed.

2.1 Benchmarking

Learning Objective

12.2.1 Understand the purpose and concept of benchmarking

If the performance of an investment fund or investment manager is to be assessed, then the first issue to address is how to measure that performance.

Investment performance is usually monitored by comparing it to a relevant benchmark. To be useful, a benchmark should align with the style and risk adopted by the investment manager and should be:

- Specified in advance.
- Appropriate to the manager's investment approach and style.
- Measurable so that its value can be calculated on a frequent basis.
- Unambiguous in its construction.
- Reflective of the manager's current investment opinions and knowledge and experience of the securities included within the benchmark.
- Accepted by the investment manager who will be accountable for deviations in construction of the portfolio due to active management.
- Investable so that it is possible to replicate the benchmark.

The ways in which portfolio performance is assessed can be grouped into three main categories:

- **Comparison with a relevant bond or stock market index**
  - An index comparison provides a clear indication of whether the portfolio's returns exceed that of the bond or stock market index that is being used as the benchmark return.
  - As well as the main stock market indices that are generally seen, many sub-indices have been created over the years which allow a precise comparison to be made.
- **Comparison to similar funds or a relevant universe comparison**
  - Investment returns can also be measured against the performance of other fund managers or portfolios which have similar investment objectives and constraints.
  - A group of similar portfolios is referred to as an investment universe.
- **Comparison to a custom benchmark**
  - Customised benchmarks are often developed for funds with unique investment objectives or constraints.
  - If a portfolio spans several asset classes, then a composite index may need to be constructed, by selecting several relevant indices and then multiplying each asset class weighting to arrive at a composite return.

2.2 Indices and Weighting Methods

Learning Objective

12.2.2 Understand the weighting methods, uses and market in respect of: FTSE 100; FTSE All-share index; FTSE Actuaries Government Securities indices; MSCI World index; Dow Jones Industrial Average index; S&P 500 index; Nikkei 225; WMA benchmarks; Hang Seng

Stock market indices have the following uses:

- To act as a market barometer. Most equity indices provide a comprehensive record of historic price movements, thereby facilitating the assessment of trends. Plotted graphically, these price movements may be of particular interest to technical analysts, or chartists, and momentum investors, by assisting the timing of security purchases and sales, or market timing.
- To assist in performance measurement. Most equity indices can be used as performance benchmarks against which portfolio performance can be judged.
- To act as the basis for index tracker funds, ETFs, index derivatives and other index-related products.
- To support portfolio management research and asset allocation decisions.

There are three main types of market index:

- **Price-weighted index** – these are constructed on the assumption that an equal number of shares are held in each of the underlying index constituents. However, as these equal holdings are weighted according to each constituent's share price, those constituents with a high share price, relative to that of other constituents, have a greater influence on the index value. The index is calculated by summing the total of each constituent's share price and comparing this total to that of the base period. Although such indices are difficult to justify and interpret, the most famous of these is the Dow Jones Industrial Average (DJIA).
- **Market-value weighted index** – in these indices, larger companies account for proportionately more of the index, as they are weighted according to each company's market capitalisation. The FTSE 100 is constructed on a market capitalisation weighted basis.
- **Equal-weighted index** – in certain markets, the largest companies can comprise a disproportionately large weighting in the index and, therefore, an index constructed on a market capitalisation basis can give a misleading impression. An equal-weighted index assumes that equal amounts are invested in each share in the index. The Nikkei 225 is an example of an equal-weighted index.

Most of the major indices used in performance measurement are market-value weighted indices such as: the S&P 500 and other S&P indices; the Morgan Stanley Capital International index; and the FTSE 100 and FTSE All Share indices.

The following table shows some of the world's leading indices, their basis of construction and some of their uses.

FTSE 100	The FTSE 100 is a market-capitalisation weighted index representing the performance of the 100 largest UK-domiciled blue chip companies. It is free-float weighted to ensure that a true investable opportunity is represented within the index and screened for liquidity to ensure that the index is tradeable. Capital and total return versions are available. It is reviewed and its components rebalanced every quarter in March, June, September and December. The index represents approximately 80% of the UK's market capitalisation and is used as the basis for investment products, such as funds, derivatives and ETFs.
FTSE All-Share Index	The FTSE All-Share measures the performance of companies listed on the LSE's main market. It covers close to 700 companies, representing approximately 98% of the UK's market capitalisation. It is a market-capitalisation weighted index and screened for size and liquidity. It is considered to be the best performance measure for the overall London equity market and is the basis for a wide range of investment tracking products.
FTSE Actuaries Government Securities Index	FTSE also produces indices based on British government securities. The indices are divided into conventional gilts and index-linked gilts and are also available in maturity bands. There is also a yield index that provides the term structure of the gilt market from one year up to 50 years.
MSCI World Index	The MSCI World index is a free-float-adjusted market-capitalisation weighted index that is designed to measure the equity market performance of developed markets. The index includes securities from 24 countries and is calculated on a capital or total return basis and in both dollars and other currencies. It is the common benchmark index used for global funds.
Dow Jones Industrial Average (DJIA)	The DJIA was introduced over 100 years ago in 1896 and was the first convenient benchmark for comparing individual stocks to the performance of the market or for comparing the market with other indicators of economic conditions. It is the best known index in the world and its 30 stocks account for close to 25% of the total US equity market. It was obviously designed in pre-computer days and it is based on a simple price-weighted arithmetic calculation making it less suitable for index products.
S&P 500 Index	The S&P 500 is regarded as the best indicator of the US equity markets. It focuses on the large cap segment of the US market and provides coverage of approximately 75% of US equities that trade on the NYSE and NASDAQ. It is a market-capitalisation weighted index that requires a free float of at least 50% and a minimum market capitalisation of US$4 billion. It is widely used as the basis for index products.

Nikkei 225	The Nikkei 225 or Nikkei Stock Average is Japan's most widely watched index of stockmarket activity and is the oldest and most-watched Asian index.
	As mentioned above, it is an equal weighting index, which is based on each constituent having an equal weighting based on a par value of 50 yen per share. Because it is an equal weighting index it needs to be rebalanced periodically.
	The Nikkei 225 is designed to reflect the overall market, so there is no specific weighting of industries. The 225 components of the Nikkei Stock Average are among the most actively traded issues on the first section of the TSE.
Hang Seng Index	The Hang Seng Index (HIS) is comprised of 50 companies of the Hong Kong stock market and is the main index in Hong Kong. The 50 companies represent about 58% of the capitalisation of the market.
	It is a freefloat-adjusted, market capitalisation-weighted stock market index and is calculated and maintained by Hang Seng Indexes Company Limited.

Note: WMA benchmarks are considered later in Section 2.4 on the differences between single and composite benchmarks.

In October 2013, the APCIMS membership voted in favour of re-branding their association as the Wealth Management Association (WMA).

2.3 Free-Float Indices

Learning Objective

12.2.4 Know why free float indices were introduced and understand the benefits they bring

Under market-capitalisation weighted indices, the total market capitalisation of a company is included, irrespective of who is actually holding the shares and whether they are freely available for trading.

The free-float methodology includes only that proportion of a company's issued shares that are available for trading in the market. It generally excludes promoters' holdings, government holdings, strategic holdings and other locked-in shares, which will not come to the market in the normal course of trading. Their introduction was driven by investors who wanted to remove the distortion that 'unavailable to trade' holdings brought to global indices and the impact that had on resulting asset allocation decisions.

For example, a number of Dow Jones Euro STOXX indices were changed in October 2008 to reflect changes in the shareholder structure of Volkswagen and which resulted in a lower weighting of Volkswagen in the indices.

The free-float method is seen as a better way of calculating market capitalisation, because it provides a more accurate reflection of market movements. When using a free-float methodology, the resulting market capitalisation is smaller than what would result from a full-market capitalisation method. This is useful for performance measurement as it provides a benchmark more closely related to what money managers can actually buy.

2.4 Single and Composite Benchmarks

Learning Objective

12.2.3 Understand the differences between a single and a composite (synthetic) benchmark

There are various types of benchmarks in use but the primary types are shown in the following table.

Absolute	These have an objective of aiming to exceed a minimum target return. For example, some absolute return funds have an objective to deliver positive returns over a rolling one-, two- or three-year period of a specified margin over LIBOR.
Manager universes	This uses peer group averages to determine the benchmark by taking the performance of the median manager as the benchmark. As a result, it cannot be specified in advance and has been criticised as creating a herd mentality rather than a focus on the need of the portfolio.
Broad Market indices	There are several broad market indices that can be used such as the MSCI World Index, the S&P 500 or the FTSE All Share. They have the advantage that they are well recognised, easy to understand and readily measurable. Their drawback is that the manager's investment style may be different.
Style indices	These represent a proportion of the available securities within an asset category that can be effectively grouped together such as large capitalisation stocks or small cap stocks.
Factor models	This is a benchmark that is created by relating one or more systematic sources of returns (factors or exposures) to returns of the benchmark. The factors that make up the benchmark might be areas such as performance of the market, the sector or company size. Whilst they can help explain how performance is achieved, they are not easy to understand, are not specified in advance, can be ambiguous and expensive to use.
Returns based	These compare a manager's return to the returns of several style indices that best explains the manager's return. They are generally easy to use and measurable but the mix of underlying styles may not reflect the manager's investment process.
Custom based	These use a selection of securities that best reflects the investment manager's approach to produce a composite or synthetic benchmark.

482

Customised benchmarks are often developed for funds with unique investment objectives or constraints.

Where a portfolio spans several asset classes, then a composite index may need to be constructed, by selecting several relevant indices and then multiplying each asset class by a weighting to arrive at a composite return.

An example is the private investor indices produced by FTSE and the WMA. There are five private investor indices, which each have different asset allocations and are composed of related indices to reflect the differing aims of investors.

The current allocations and respective indices within the WMA indices are as follows:

Asset Class	Conservative Index	Income Index	Balanced Index	Growth Index	Underlying Asset Index
UK Equities	19.0	35.0	35.0	40.0	FTSE All-Share Index
International Equities	13.5	17.5	30.0	37.5	FTSE All-World Ex-UK Index (calculated in sterling)
Bonds	40.0	27.5	17.5	7.5	FTSE Gilts All-Stocks Index
Cash	5.0	5.0	5.0	2.5	7-Day LIBOR −1% (London Interbank Offered Rate)
Commercial Property	5.0	5.0	5.0	5.0	FTSE All-UK Property Index
Hedge Funds/ Alternatives	7.5	10.0	7.5	7.5	WMA Custom Hedge Index
Total	100.0	100.0	100.0	100.0	

Source: WMA

The final index is the WMA Customised Index comprised of hedge funds/alternatives.

2.5 Global Investment Performance Standards (GIPS)

Learning Objective

12.2.5 Understand global investment performance standards (GIPS) as a method of benchmarking:

Global investment performance standards (GIPS) are not a way of benchmarking performance, but are global standards for calculating and presenting performance figures. As such, they represent a great leap forward for the performance measurement industry.

Originally established in 1999 by the Chartered Financial Analyst (CFA) Institute, GIPS were significantly enhanced in 2005 and have been voluntarily adopted by industry representative organisations in over 20 countries in order to help promote best standards.

Key features of the GIPS include the following:

- They are ethical standards for investment performance presentation to ensure fair representation and full disclosure of investment performance.
- In order to claim compliance, firms must adhere to the requirements included in the GIPS standards.
- Firms are expected to adhere to the recommendations to achieve best practice in the calculation and presentation of performance.
- Firms should include all actual, discretionary, fee-paying portfolios, in at least one composite, defined by investment mandate, objective, or strategy, in order to prevent firms from cherry-picking their best performance.
- The GIPS standards require firms to adhere to certain calculation methodologies and to make specific disclosures along with the firm's performance to ensure accuracy of data.

3. Performance Evaluation

Performance evaluation attempts to explain why a portfolio produced a certain return. It does so by breaking down the performance and attributing the results based on the decisions made by the fund manager on asset allocation, sector choice and security selection.

This involves three elements:

- **Performance measurement** – calculating the performance of the fund based on changes in its value over specified time periods.
- **Performance attribution** – assessing how the investment manager attained that performance by undertaking performance attribution to identify the sources of the portfolio's performance.
- **Performance appraisal** – evaluating the performance to determine whether it was due to investment decisions, market movements or chance.

3.1 Performance Measurement

The rate of return on a portfolio is the percentage change in the value of the portfolio over the period being considered. This requires us to consider firstly what constitutes the portfolio's return and then how that return can be calculated in such a way that accounts for the distorting effect of external cash flows into and out of the portfolio

There are three different methods used to measure portfolio performance:

- Holding period return – sometimes referred to as total return.
- Money weighted rate of return.
- Time weighted rate of return.

3.1.1 Total Return

Learning Objective

12.3.1   Understand total return and its components

Total return is a measure of investment performance that includes the change in price of the asset plus any other income (including dividends, interest and capital gains distributions). It is assumed that all income is reinvested over the period.

The calculation of total return is expressed as a percentage of the initial asset value. The formula for calculating total return if there have been no external cash flows during the period is:

$$R_{TR} = \frac{(EMV - BMV)}{BMV}$$

where:

R_{TR} = total return
EMV = end market value
BMV = beginning market value

As a result, calculating total return is straightforward.

Example

If an investor's portfolio is valued at £250,000 at the beginning of the year and by the end, it is worth £262,500 and dividends of £5,000 have been received what is the total return on the portfolio?

$$R_{TR} = \frac{((£262,500 + £5,000) - £250,000)}{£250,000} = \frac{£17,500}{£250,000} = 7\%$$

So the total return is the growth plus the dividends totalling £17,500 as a percentage of the starting value. In percentage terms the total return was 7%.

Was that a good return? Total return alone cannot answer that question as it cannot make any allowance for whether funds were added to the portfolio or withdrawn.

So, for example, a 7% return may seem attractive but what if £7,500 in cash had been added to the portfolio on the last day of the year? That would reduce the return to just 4%. What would happen if funds were regularly added and withdrawn during the year? Simply using total return will not provide a useable rate of return and so we need to look at calculation methods that can adjust for this.

3.1.2   Money Weighted Rate of Return (MWRR)

Learning Objective

12.4.1   Be able to calculate the money weighted rate of return (MWRR) and the time weighted rate of return (TWRR)

The money weighted rate of return (MWRR) is used to measure the performance of a fund that has had deposits and withdrawals during the period being measured. It is also referred to as the internal rate of return of the fund.

The MWRR formula is the rate of return that solves the following:

$$MV_1 = (MV_0 \times (1+r)^m) + \{\text{Sum of } (CF_i \times 1+r^{Li})\}$$

where:

MV_1 = End portfolio value
MV_0 = Beginning portfolio value
m = the number of days in the period
CF_i = cash flows
Li = number of days the cash inflow is included in the portfolio or the number of days that a cash outflow is absent

The money weighted rate of return therefore calculates the return on a portfolio as being equal to the sum of:

- the difference in the value of the portfolio at the end of the period and the value of the portfolio at the start of the period, plus
- any income or capital distributions made from the portfolio during that period.

The difference is then expressed as a percentage, the money weighted rate of return.

One of the main drawbacks of this method is that it cannot be solved algebraically as was seen earlier in Chapter 2 when we considered internal rate of return (IRR). To calculate the return is an iterative process and the return must be found through trial and error or interpolation as it is necessary to use a discount factor in a DCF tabular calculation, which causes the NPV of all the cash flows to be equal to zero. At this point the discount factor will then provide the MWRR.

As a result, it is a more time-consuming calculation than other methods. Due to the trial and error nature of the calculation, it is unlikely that you will see a problem in the exam that requires this method to be used. Instead we need to consider a simpler way to calculate this, which is shown below.

In simple terms, the money weighted return equals:

$$\frac{\text{Value at the end of the period} - \text{Value at the beginning of the period} \pm \text{Cash outflows}}{\text{Value at the start of the period} \pm \text{Cash flows adjusted for the number of months}}$$

So the formula is:

$$MWRR = \frac{(V_1 - V_0) \pm C_f}{V_0 + \left(C_f \times \dfrac{n}{12}\right)}$$

where:

V_0 = value at the start of the period.
V_1 = value at the end of the period.
C_f = net out cashflows.
$\dfrac{n}{12}$ = number of months.

If cash is added to the portfolio, it is a positive figure and will be subtracted from the returns in the numerator; if it is a withdrawal, it is a negative figure and has to be added back in to get the return. On the bottom line of the equation this logic is reversed, as the fund had use of any capital injected for the balance of the year and lost the use of withdrawals for the remainder of the year.

Example

So, using this formula, let's assume that a portfolio is worth £100,000 (V_0) at the beginning of the year and £110,000 (V_1) at the end of December of that year. The transactions that took place during the year were a cash injection of £5,000 at the end of March and a cash withdrawal of £7,000 at the end of September to give a net cash outflow of £2,000.

The money weighted return can be seen to be:

$$MWRR = \frac{((£110,000 - £100,000) + £2,000)}{\left[£100,000 + \left(£5,000 \times \dfrac{9}{12}\right) + \left(-£7,000 \times \dfrac{3}{12}\right)\right]}$$

So, on the top line £2,000 has been added as there has been a net cash outflow and on the bottom line, the cash injection is included for the nine months it was held and a proportion of the cash outflow of £7,000 is subtracted as it was lost for the final three months of the year.

So, the money weighted return equals:

$$\frac{((£110,000 - £100,000) + £2,000)}{(£100,000 + £3,750 - £1,750)} = \frac{£12,000}{£102,000} = 0.11765 \text{ multiplied by } 100 = 11.77\%$$

3.1.3 Time Weighted Rate of Return (TWRR)

Learning Objective

12.4.1 Be able to calculate the money weighted rates of return (MWRR) and the time weighted rates of return (TWRR)

The TWRR removes the impact of cash flows on the rate of return calculation.

The TWRR is established by breaking the investment period into a series of sub-periods. A sub-period is created whenever there is a movement of capital into or out of the fund. Immediately prior to this point, a portfolio valuation must be obtained to ensure that the rate of return is not distorted by the size and timing of the cash flow.

The TWRR is calculated by compounding the rate of return for each of these individual sub-periods, applying an equal weight to each sub-period in the process. This is known as unitised fund performance.

The formula for time weighted rate of return is:

$$TWRR = \{(1 + R_{SP1})(1 + R_{SP2})\ldots\ldots(1 + R_{SPn})\} - 1$$

Where SPn equals the percentage return during a sub-period.

This can be seen in the following example.

Example

A portfolio is valued at £1,000 at the beginning of October and grows in value to £1,100 by 15 October. It receives a cash inflow of £215 on 16 October and at 31 October is valued at £1,500.

Using TWRR, a percentage return is calculated for each separate period as follows:

$$\text{Sub-period 1: } r = \frac{(£1,100 - £1,000)}{£1,000} = 0.1 = 10\%$$

$$\text{Sub-period 2: } r = \frac{£1,500 - (£1,100 + £215)}{£1,315} = \frac{£185}{£1,315} = 0.141 = 14.1\%$$

The returns for each sub-period are then linked to produce the TWRR.

$$TWRR = (1 + 0.10) \times (1 + 0.141) = 1.2551 - 1 = 25.51\%$$

3.1.4 TWRR versus MWRR

The primary difference between these two calculation methods is that MWRR assumes that exactly the same rate of return is earned during each sub-period, whilst TWRR on the other hand considers the number of days invested when each potentially different sub-period return is calculated.

	TWRR	MWRR
Advantages	It is unaffected by external cash flow activity and so correctly reflects the return that an investor receives if they invested at the start of the period. Most investment managers have little control over the size and timings of cash flows and so using a rate of return that is not influenced by them is more appropriate.	It is appropriate where the investment manager has control over the timing and size of cash inflows and outflows. It only requires a valuation at the start and end of the period.
Disadvantages	Valuations are required on every day when an external cash flow takes place meaning practically that daily valuations are required. Daily valuations are administratively more expensive and prone to errors.	It can be distorted by the size and timing of external cash flows. If a manager has little or no control over cash flows it is not a suitable measure to evaluate portfolio performance.

In many cases, the differences between MWRR and TWRR will be relatively small, but in certain circumstances wide variations can occur. For example, the MWRR will change dramatically if a large cash flow is received or paid near the beginning as opposed to near the end of the measurement period, whilst TWRR rectifies this by defining periods according to cash flows.

As a result, the time weighted rate of return is more widely used. GIPS requires the use of a TWRR to calculate returns.

3.2   Performance Attribution

Learning Objective

12.3.2   Be able to calculate the deviations from a performance benchmark attributable to: actual versus relative performance; asset allocation; stock selection

Investors, trustees and plan sponsors will want to assess the returns achieved by a fund manager to determine which elements of the strategy were responsible for results and why.

Performance attribution is a set of techniques that analysts use to explain why a portfolio's performance differed from the benchmark. This difference between the portfolio return and the benchmark return is known as the active return.

The process is known as performance attribution and attributes the performance to:

- Asset allocation.
- Sector choice.
- Security selection.

This can be best seen by looking at an example.

The first stage in the process is to determine the performance of the fund and of its external benchmarks.

Example

We will assume that the investment fund we are analysing had a fund value of £10 million at the start of the period we are considering and was valued a £10.5 million at the end.

The benchmark used for the fund assumed an asset allocation of 50% in equities and 50% in bonds. Over the period equities produced a negative return of 10% and gilts a positive return of 5%.

The asset allocation of the fund, however, was 80% in bonds and 20% in equities.

Following this, the next step is to use the fund and benchmark statistics above to determine the absolute outperformance or underperformance of the fund so that it can be compared to that of the benchmark.

For simplicity, we will assume that there were no cash inflows or outflows during the period. The absolute performance of the fund can be calculated, therefore, by using the holding period return formula to assess the absolute performance of the fund.

The holding period return formula is:

$$R_{TR} = \frac{(EMV - BMV)}{BMV}$$

So, the absolute performance of the fund is:

$$R_{TR} = \frac{(£10.5m - £10m)}{£10m} = \frac{£0.5m}{£10m} = 5\%$$

Next, the benchmark performance can be calculated.

The benchmark used for the fund assumed an asset allocation of 50% in equities and 50% in bonds. Over the period equities produced a negative return of 10% and gilts a positive return of 5%.

The benchmark performance is therefore:

	Asset Allocation	Value at Start of the Period	Return	Value at End of Period
Equities	50%	£5m	−10%	£4.5m
Bonds	50%	£5m	+5%	£5.25m
Total		£10m		£9.75m

The weighted average returns from the benchmarks are therefore:

R = (−10% x 0.5) + (5% x 0.5) = −2.5%

The next step is to calculate the absolute outperformance or underperformance of the fund relative to the benchmark that is attributable to asset allocation.

The performance that is attributable to asset allocation can therefore be seen to be:

	Asset Allocation	Value at Start of the Period	Return	Value at End of Period
Equities	20%	£2m	−10%	£1.8m
Bonds	80%	£8m	+5%	£8.4m
Total		£10m		£10.2m

The fund has, therefore, outperformed the benchmark by £475k.

From this example, we can observe that the fund has delivered a positive return of 2% which exceeds the returns available from adopting a purely passive approach of having a 50:50 allocation to the two benchmarks.

The active approach taken by the investment manager has enabled them to outperform the benchmarks by 4.5% as a result of the asset allocation decision.

Finally, the returns can be decomposed further by looking at the impact of stock selection. To determine a portfolio manager's stock selection skill, you need to subtract the fund value resulting from asset allocation from the actual fund value at the end of the period.

Performance Attributable to Stock Selection

The fund value at the end of the period is £10.5 million whilst the fund value attributable to asset allocation is £10.2 million. The outperformance attributable to stock selection is therefore £300k.

To decompose this further, we will need a breakdown of the fund's value at the end of the period. Let's assume that the equities were valued at £1.8 million and the bonds at £8.7 million. The performance that is attributable to stock selection can therefore seen to be:

	Value at Start of the Period	End Value – Asset Allocation	Value at End of Period	Value Added
Equities	£2m	£1.8m	£1.8m	£0
Bonds	£8m	£8.4m	£8.7m	£300k
Total	£10m	£10.2m	£10.5m	£300k

Good stock selection within the bond segment of the portfolio has therefore added £300k to the fund's performance.

4. Performance Measures

Learning Objective

12.4.2 Understand the concepts of: alpha; beta; Sharpe ratio; Treynor ratio; Jensen ratio; information ratio

---

Performance evaluation attempts to explain why a portfolio produced a certain return and involves three elements – performance measurement, performance attribution and performance appraisal.

The final stage of performance evaluation, performance appraisal, uses measures to evaluate returns on a risk adjusted basis to determine whether they were due to investment decisions, market movements or chance.

4.1 Alpha and Beta

Alpha is usually defined as the degree to which a particular portfolio manager is able to outperform a benchmark index such as the FTSE 100 or the S&P 500.

Alpha is eagerly sought-after by fund managers, as it is often the basis that is used for ranking asset management performance. Fairly obviously, passive index-tracking funds will (if they are doing their job correctly) not exhibit alpha with respect to their chosen benchmark.

Being able to quantify alpha is important if we want to assess the performance of a fund manager and separate out the degree to which the portfolio was affected by market movements and the degree to which fund management skill has influenced returns.

Beta provides the systematic risk element of the portfolio, in other words that part of the total risk that is related to movements in the market portfolio. It is not equivalent to the volatility of a security but rather provides an answer to the question – if the overall market moves up (or down) by (say) 3%, what movement should one expect to see in the security in question?

Beta tells us how closely an asset performs in relation to a benchmark or market index. The simple rule of thumb is that:

- If beta is equal to a value of 1, then the fund is performing exactly in accordance with the market. In other words, if the market shows a return of 10% (after deducting the risk-free rate), then the portfolio with a beta of one will also have delivered a 10% return (after deducting the risk-free rate).
- A beta of 1.5% means that the fund has moved by an average of 1.5% for every 1% market movement.
- A beta of less than 1 indicates that the fund has generally acted defensively to general market moves.

To be able to calculate alpha or the extent of any outperformance or underperformance, we need to know what the expected rate of return is. This can be identified by calculating the total risk of the portfolio.

The total risk for a portfolio is found by adding the variances (the square of the standard deviation) of the systematic risk and the unsystematic or specific risk of the investment. The result is the variance of the total risk.

$$\text{Expected return} = R_F + \frac{\sigma_A}{\sigma_M} \times (R_M - R_F)$$

where:

R_F = Average risk free return.
R_M = Expected return on a market index.
σ_A = Standard deviation of account returns.
σ_M = Standard deviation of market returns.

The alpha value is simply the actual return on a portfolio minus the expected return on the portfolio, as determined in the formula above. This can be seen in the following example.

Example

We want to compare the performance of four different funds where the risk free return is 4%, the expected market return is 10% and the market standard deviation is 14%. The standard deviation of account returns or portfolio risk for each fund is: Fund A – 14%; Fund B – 15%; Fund C – 13%; Fund D – 17%.

Firstly we can calculate the expected return as follows:

Fund	Total Portfolio Risk (σ_A)	$\dfrac{\sigma_A}{\sigma_M}$	Return Required	Expected Return
A	14%	$\dfrac{14}{14} = 1.00$	4% + 1.00 × (10% − 4%) = 10%	10.0%
B	15%	$\dfrac{15}{14} = 1.07$	4% + 1.07 × (10% − 4%) = 10.4%	10.4%
C	13%	$\dfrac{13}{14} = 0.93$	4% + 0.93 × (10% − 4%) = 9.6%	9.6%
D	17%	$\dfrac{17}{14} = 1.21$	4% + 1.21 × (10% − 4%) = 11.3%	11.3%

If we then add some actual returns, the alpha for each fund can then be readily seen.

Fund	Expected Return	Actual Return	Alpha
A	10.0%	10%	0%
B	10.4%	14%	3.6%
C	9.6%	11%	1.4%
D	11.3%	15%	3.7%

From this we can then observe that:

- The performance of Fund A is exactly in line with the market, suggesting that it is an index tracker.
- Fund D has the highest level of alpha with a 3.7% greater return than the expected value for the risk/ return profile.

If we are assessing the performance of a fund and it has an alpha value of 1%, this means that asset selection skills have led to an outperformance of the fund in reference to the market returns of one percent.

- If a portfolio moves up and down completely in unison with the overall market it will have zero alpha.
- If it underperforms the overall market it can be said to have negative alpha.
- If it outperforms the overall market it has positive alpha.

If a fund is not delivering the required investment performance, the fund manager will be keen to improve the alpha of the fund, that is, improve performance or achieve some outperformance, by changing the composition of the fund. If this occurs, it is critical to understand the additional risk that is being taken on, or beta, so that a judgement can be made on whether the portfolio remains suitable for a client.

4.2 Sharpe Ratio

The Sharpe ratio measures the return over and above the risk-free interest rate from an undiversified equity portfolio for each unit of risk assumed by the portfolio: risk being measured by the standard deviation of the portfolio's returns.

The ratio is expressed as follows.

$$\text{Sharpe ratio} = \frac{(R_A - R_F)}{\sigma_A}$$

where:

R_A = Average return on the account.
R_F = Average risk free return.
σ_A = Standard deviation of account returns.

The higher the Sharpe ratio, the better the risk-adjusted performance of the portfolio and the greater the implied level of active management skill. The Sharpe ratio provides an objective measure of the relative performance of two similarly undiversified portfolios.

The ratio was first proposed by the Nobel Laureate, William F. Sharpe who is emeritus professor of finance at Stanford University. The assumption behind the calculation, and the reason why the standard deviation is used as the denominator to the equation, is that, since investors prefer a smooth ride to a bumpy one, the higher the standard deviation, the lower will be the Sharpe ratio. Accordingly, high Sharpe ratios are to be preferred and positive values are obviously better than negative values.

4.3   Treynor Ratio

The Treynor ratio is a measurement of the returns earned in excess of that which could have been earned on a riskless investment such as a Treasury bill.

The Treynor ratio is sometimes called reward-to-volatility ratio, as it relates the excess return over the risk-free rate to the additional risk taken as measured by the beta of the fund or portfolio. As the portfolio's return would have been generated only by the systematic risk it had assumed, the Treynor ratio, therefore, divides the portfolio's return over and above the risk free interest rate by its CAPM beta.

The ratio is expressed as follows.

$$\text{Treynor ratio} = \frac{(R_A - R_F)}{\beta_A}$$

where:

R_A = Average return on the account.
R_F = Average risk free return.
β_A = Standard deviation of account returns (the portfolio's beta).

The Treynor ratio takes a similar approach to the Sharpe ratio but is calculated for a well diversified equity portfolio and is used to compare performance to other portfolios.

Once again, the higher the ratio, the greater the implied level of active management skill.

4.4   Jensen Measure

The Jensen measure of risk-adjusted equity portfolio returns is employed to evaluate the performance of a well-diversified portfolio against a CAPM benchmark with the same level of systematic risk as that assumed by the portfolio.

The ratio is expressed as follows:

Jensen measure: $R_A - \{R_F + \beta_A \times (R_M - R_F)\}$

where:

R_A =   Average return on the account.
R_F =   Average risk free return.
β_A =   Standard deviation of account returns (the portfolio's beta).
R_M =   Average market return.

It can also be more simply expressed as – (Return on the Portfolio – Return predicted by CAPM).

The extent of any outperformance or underperformance is known as Jensen's alpha.

The Jensen measure establishes whether the portfolio has performed in line with its CAPM benchmark and, therefore, lies on the security market line (SML) or whether it has outperformed or underperformed the benchmark and is, therefore, positioned above or below the SML.

- A portfolio that generates a positive alpha will plot above the SML.
- A portfolio that generates a zero alpha will plot on the SML.
- A portfolio that generates a negative alpha will plot below the SML.

4.5   Information Ratio

The information ratio is often used to gauge the skill of a fund manager, as it measures the expected active return of the manager's portfolio divided by the amount of risk that the manager takes relative to the benchmark.

So, the information ratio compares the excess return achieved by a fund over a benchmark portfolio to the fund's tracking error.

Its tracking error is calculated as the standard deviation of excess returns from the benchmark. The tracking error gives us an estimate of the risks that the fund manager takes in deviating from the benchmark.

The ratio is expressed as follows.

$$\text{Information ratio} = \frac{R_A - R_B}{\sigma_{A-B}} \text{ or } \frac{\text{Expected value of excess returns}}{\text{Standard deviation of excess returns}}$$

where:

R_A = Average return on the account.

R_B = Benchmark return.

σ_{A-B} = Standard deviation of excess returns as measured by the difference between account and benchmark returns.

A fund's performance may deviate from the benchmark due to the investment manager's decisions concerning asset weighting. If the fund outperforms, the ratio will be positive and if it underperforms it will be negative. A high information ratio is, therefore, a sign of a successful fund manager.

End of Chapter Questions

Think of an answer for each question and refer to the appropriate workbook section for confirmation.

1. Explain maximum drawdown.
   Answer reference: Section 1.1

2. What is total return?
   Answer reference: Section 1.1

3. What are the key characteristics of a relevant benchmark?
   Answer reference: Section 2.1

4. What are the three main ways in which indices are constructed and which approach is most commonly used as a benchmark?
   Answer reference: Section 2.2

5. What are factor benchmarks and what are the drawbacks in their use?
   Answer reference: Section 2.4

6. A portfolio was valued at £100,000 at the beginning of the year and at the end was valued at £103,500. If income was received in addition of £2,000, what was the total return?
   Answer reference: Section 3.1.1

7. A portfolio was worth £100,000 at the beginning of the year and £106,000 at the end of December of that year. The transactions that took place during the year were a cash injection of £2,000 at the end of March and a cash withdrawal of £3,000 at the end of September. What was the money weighted rate of return?
   Answer reference: Section 3.1.2

8. What does the Sharpe ratio of a fund indicate?
   Answer reference: Section 4.2

Glossary and Abbreviations

Active Management

An investment approach employed to exploit pricing anomalies in those securities markets that are believed to be subject to mispricing by utilising Fundamental Analysts and/or Technical Analysis to assist in the forecasting of future events and the timing of purchases and sales of securities. Also known as *Market Timing*.

Active Risk

The risk that arises from holding securities in an actively managed portfolio in different proportions from their weighting in a benchmark index. Also known as *Tracking Error*.

Aggregate Demand

The total demand for goods and services within an economy.

Aggregate Supply

The amount of output firms are prepared to supply in aggregate at each general price level in an economy, assuming the price of inputs to the production process are fixed, in order to meet Aggregate Demand.

Alpha

The return from a security or a portfolio in excess of a risk-adjusted benchmark return. Also known as *Jensen's Alpha*.

Alternative Investments

Alternative investments are those which fall outside the traditional asset classes of equities, property, fixed interest, cash and money market instruments.

Alternative Investment Market (AIM)

The London Stock Exchange's (LSE) market for smaller UK public limited companies (PLCs). AIM has less demanding admission requirements and places less onerous continuing obligation requirements upon those companies admitted to the market than those applying for a full list on the LSE.

Amortisation

The depreciation charge applied in company accounts against capitalised intangible assets.

Annual Equivalent Rate (AER)

See *Effective Rate*.

Annual General Meeting (AGM)

The annual meeting of directors and ordinary shareholders of a company. All companies are obliged to hold an AGM at which the shareholders receive the company's report and accounts and have the opportunity to vote on the appointment of the company's directors and auditors and the payment of a final dividend recommended by the directors.

Annuity

An investment that provides a series of prespecified periodic payments over a specific term or until the occurrence of a prespecified event, eg, death.

Arbitrage

The process of deriving a risk-free profit by simultaneously buying and selling the same asset in two related markets where a pricing anomaly exists.

Arithmetic Mean

A measure of central tendency established by summing the observed values in a data distribution and dividing this sum by the number of observations. The arithmetic mean takes account of every value in the distribution.

Articles of Association

The legal document which sets out the internal constitution of a UK company. Details of shareholder voting rights and company borrowing powers are included.

Asset Allocation

The process of investing an international portfolio's assets geographically and between asset classes before deciding upon sector and stock selection.

Association of Private Client Investment Managers and Stockbrokers (APCIMS)

The trade association that represents stockbrokers' interests.

Backwardation

When the futures price stands at a discount to the price of the underlying asset.

Balance of Payments

A summary of all economic transactions between one country and the rest of the world, typically conducted over a calendar year.

Base Currency

The currency against which the value of a quoted currency is expressed. The base currency is currency X for the X/Y exchange rate.

Basis

The difference between the futures price and the price of the underlying asset.

Bear Market

Conventionally defined as a 20%+ decline in a securities market. The duration of the market move is immaterial.

Bearer Securities

Those whose ownership is evidenced by the mere possession of a certificate. Ownership can, therefore, pass from hand to hand without any formalities.

Beneficiaries

The beneficial owners of trust property.

Beta

The covariance between the returns from a security and those of the market relative to the variance of returns from the market.

Bonus Issue

The free issue of new ordinary shares to a company's ordinary shareholders, in proportion to their existing shareholdings through the conversion, or capitalisation, of the company's reserves. By proportionately reducing the market value of each existing share, a bonus issue makes the shares more marketable. Also known as a *capitalisation issue* or *scrip issue*.

Broker Dealer

A London Stock Exchange (LSE) member firm that can act in a dual capacity both as a broker acting on behalf of clients and as a dealer dealing in securities on their own account.

Bull Market

A rising securities market. The duration of the market move is immaterial.

Business Cycle

See *Economic Cycle*.

Call Option

An option that confers a right (but not an obligation) on the holder to buy a specified amount of an asset at a prespecified price on or sometimes before a prespecified date.

Capitalisation Issue

See *Bonus Issue*.

Central Bank

Those public institutions that operate at the heart of a nation's financial system. Central banks typically have responsibility for setting a nation's or a region's short-term interest rate, controlling the money supply, acting as banker and lender of last resort to the banking system and managing the national debt. They increasingly implement policies independently of government control. The Bank of England is the UK's central bank.

Certificate of Deposit (CD)

Negotiable bearer securities issued by commercial banks in exchange for fixed-term deposits.

Ceteris Paribus

Other things being equal. In economics, the ceteris paribus caveat is used when considering the impact of a change in one factor or variable on another variable, market or the economy as a whole, holding all other factors constant.

Clean Price

The quoted price of a bond. The clean price excludes accrued interest or interest to be deducted, as appropriate.

Closing Out

The process of terminating an open position in a derivatives contract by entering into an equal and opposite transaction to that originally undertaken.

Code of Best Practice

See *UK Corporate Governance Code*.

Combinations

A strategy requiring the simultaneous purchase or sale of both a call option and a put option on the same underlying asset, sometimes with different exercise prices but always with the same expiry dates. Combinations include straddles and strangles.

Commercial Paper (CP)

Unsecured bearer securities issued at a discount to par by public limited companies (PLCs) with high credit ratings. Commercial paper is a money market instrument with maturities up to 270 days and does not pay coupons but is redeemed at par.

UK Competition Commission

The body to which a merger or takeover is referred for investigation by the UK Business Secretary in order to establish whether the combined entity will work against the public interest or will prove to be anti-competitive.

Complement

A good is a complement for another if a rise in the price of one results in a decrease in demand for the other. Complementary goods are typically purchased in conjunction with one another.

Consumer Prices Index (CPI)

Geometrically weighted inflation index targeted by the Monetary Policy Committee.

Contango

When the futures price stands at a premium to the price of the underlying asset.

Continuous Data

Where numbers in a data series can assume any value.

Convertible Bonds

Bonds issued with a right to convert into either another of the issuer's bonds or, if issued by a company, the company's equity, both on prespecified terms.

Convertible Loan Stock

Bonds issued with a right to convert into the issuing company's equity on prespecified terms.

Convertible Preference Shares

Preference shares issued with a right to convert into the issuing company's equity on prespecified terms.

Convexity

The non-symmetrical relationship that exists between a bond's price and its yield. The more convex the bond, the greater the price rise for a fall in its yield and the smaller the price fall for a rise in its yield. Also see *Modified Duration*.

Corporate Governance

The mechanism that seeks to ensure that companies are run in the best long-term interests of their shareholders.

Correlation

The degree of co-movement between two variables determined through regression analysis and quantified by the correlation coefficient. Correlation does not prove that a cause-and-effect or, indeed, a steady relationship exists between two variables, as correlations can arise from pure chance.

Coupon

The predetermined rate of interest applying to a bond over its term expressed as a percentage of the bond's nominal value or par value. The coupon is usually a fixed rate of interest.

Covariance

The correlation coefficient between two variables multiplied by their individual standard deviations.

Cross Elasticity of Demand (XED)

The effect of a small percentage change in the price of a complement or substitute good on a complement or substitute.

Deadweight Loss

A measure of the inefficient allocation of resources that results from a monopoly, restricting output and raising price to maximise profit.

Debenture

A corporate bond issued in the domestic bond market and secured on the issuing company's assets by way of a fixed or a floating charge.

Demand Curve

The depiction of the quantity of a particular good or service consumers will buy at a given price. Plotted against price on the vertical axis and quantity on the horizontal axis, a demand curve slopes downwards from left to right.

Depreciation

The charge applied in a company's accounts against its tangible fixed assets to reflect the usage of these assets over the accounting period.

Derivative

An instrument whose value is based on the price of an underlying asset. Derivatives can be based on both financial and commodity assets.

Dirty Price

The price of a bond inclusive of accrued interest or exclusive of interest to be deducted, as appropriate.

Discount

The difference in the spot and forward exchange rate that arises when interest rates in the quoted currency are higher than those in the base currency.

Discount Rate

The rate of interest used to establish the present value of a sum of money receivable in the future.

Discounted Cash Flow (DCF) Yield

See *Internal Rate of Return (IRR)*.

Discrete Data

Where numbers in a data series are restricted to specific values.

Dividend

The distribution of a proportion of a company's distributable profit to its shareholders. Dividends are usually paid twice a year and are expressed in pence per share.

Dow Jones Industrial Average (DJIA)

A price-weighted arithmetic index of 30 actively traded US stocks.

Duration

The weighted average time, expressed in years, for the present value of a bond's cash flows to be received. Also known as *Macaulay Duration*.

Economic Cycle

The course an economy conventionally takes as economic growth fluctuates over time. Also known as the *Business Cycle*.

Economic Growth

The growth of Gross Domestic Product (GDP) or Gross National Product (GNP) expressed in real terms usually over the course of a calendar year. Often used as a barometer of an economy's health.

Economies of Scale

The resulting reduction in a firm's unit costs as the firm's productive capacity and output increases. Economies of scale are maximised and unit costs minimised at the minimum efficient scale (MES) on a firm's long-term average total cost (LTATC) curve. Beyond this point, diseconomies of scale set in.

Effective Rate

The annualised compound rate of interest applied to a cash deposit. Also known as the *Annual Equivalent Rate (AER)*.

Efficient Frontier

A convex curve used in modern portfolio theory that represents those efficient portfolios that offer the maximum expected return for any given level of risk.

Efficient Markets Hypothesis (EMH)

The proposition that everything that is publicly known about a particular stock or market should be instantaneously reflected in its price. As a result of active portfolio managers and other investment professionals exhaustively researching those securities traded in developed markets, the EMH argues that share prices move randomly and independently of past trends, in response to fresh information, which itself is released at random.

Equilibrium

A condition that describes a market in perfect balance, where demand is equal to supply.

Equity

That which confers a direct stake in a company's fortunes. Also known as a company's *ordinary share capital*.

Eurobond

International bond issues denominated in a currency different from that of the financial centre(s) in which they are issued. Most eurobonds are issued in bearer form through bank syndicates.

Euronext

The Paris, Amsterdam, Brussels and Lisbon stock and derivatives exchange which is now part of NYSE Euronext.

Exchange Rate

The price of one currency in terms of another.

Ex-dividend (xd)

The period during which the purchase of shares or bonds (on which a dividend or coupon payment has been declared) does not entitle the new holder to the next dividend or interest payment.

Exercise Price

The price at which the right conferred by an option can be exercised by the holder against the writer.

Expectations Theory

The proposition that the difference between short- and long-term interest rates can be explained by the course short-term interest rates are expected to take over time.

Ex-Rights (xr)

The period during which the purchase of a company's shares does not entitle the new shareholder to participate in a rights issue announced by the issuing company. Shares are usually traded ex-rights (xr) on or within a few days of the company making a rights issue announcement.

Fair Value

The theoretical price of a futures contract.

Financial Gearing

The ratio of debt to equity employed by a company within its capital structure.

Financial Conduct Authority (FCA)

The Financial Conduct Authority (FCA) replaced the Financial Services Authority (FSA) on 1 April 2013 as the body responsible for regulating conduct in retail and wholesale markets; supervising the trading infrastructure that supports those markets; and for the prudential regulation of firms not prudentially regulated by the Prudential Regulation Authority (PRA).

Financial Services Authority (FSA)

The former UK regulator for financial services created by FSMA 2000.

Fiscal Policy

The use of government spending, taxation and borrowing policies to either boost or restrain domestic demand in the economy so as to maintain full employment and price stability. Also known as *Stabilisation Policy* and *Monetary Policy*.

Fixed Interest Security

A tradeable negotiable instrument, issued by a borrower for a fixed term, during which a regular and predetermined fixed rate of interest based upon a nominal value is paid to the holder until it is redeemed and the principal is repaid.

Flat Rate

The annual simple rate of interest applied to a cash deposit.

Flight to Quality

The movement of capital to a safe haven during periods of market turmoil to avoid capital loss.

Floating-Rate Notes (FRNs)

Debt securities issued with a coupon periodically referenced to a benchmark interest rate.

Forward

A derivatives contract that creates a legally binding obligation between two parties for one to buy and the other to sell a prespecified amount of an asset at a prespecified price on a prespecified future date. As individually negotiated contracts, forwards are not traded on a derivatives exchange.

Forward Exchange Rate

An exchange rate set today, embodied in a forward contract, that will apply to a foreign exchange transaction at some prespecified point in the future.

Forward Rate

The implied annual compound rate of interest that links one spot rate to another assuming no interest payments are made over the investment period.

Frequency Distribution

Data either presented in tabulated form or diagrammatically, whether in ascending or descending order, where the observed frequency of occurrence is assigned to either individual values or groups of values within the distribution.

Full Employment Level of Output

See *Potential Level Output*.

Listing

Those public limited companies (Plcs) admitted to the London Stock Exchange's (LSE) official list. Companies seeking a full listing on the LSE must satisfy the UK Listing Authority's (UKLA) stringent listing requirements and continuing obligations once listed.

Fund of Funds

A fund of funds is a multi-manager fund. It has one overall manager that invests in a portfolio of other existing investment funds and seeks to harness the best investment manager talent available within a diversified portfolio.

Fundamental Analysis

The calculation and interpretation of yields, ratios and discounted cash flows (DCFs) that seek to establish the intrinsic value of a security or the correct valuation of the broader market. The use of fundamental analysis is nullified by the semi-strong form of the Efficient Markets Hypothesis (EMH).

Future

A derivatives contract that creates a legally binding obligation between two parties for one to buy and the other to sell a prespecified amount of an asset at a prespecified price on a prespecified future date. Futures contracts differ from forward contracts in that their contract specification is standardised so that they may be traded on a derivatives exchange.

Future Value

The accumulated value of a sum of money invested today at a known rate of interest over a specific term.

Geometric Mean

A measure of central tendency established by taking the nth root of the product (multiplication) of n values.

Geometric Progression

The product (multiplication) of n values.

Gilts

UK government securities issued primarily to finance government borrowing. See also *Public Sector Net Cash Requirement (PSNCR)*.

Gross Domestic Product (GDP)

A measure of the level of activity within an economy. More precisely, GDP is the total market value of all final goods and services produced domestically in an economy typically during a calendar year.

Gross National Product (GNP)

Gross Domestic Product (GDP) at market prices plus net property income generated from overseas economies by UK factors of production.

Gross Redemption Yield (GRY)

The annual compound return from holding a bond to maturity taking into account both interest payments and any capital gain or loss at maturity. Also known as the *Yield to Maturity (YTM)*.

Hedging

A technique employed to reduce the impact of adverse price movements in financial assets held.

Immunisation

Passive bond management techniques that comprise cash matching and duration-based immunisation.

Income Elasticity of Demand (YED)

The effect of a small percentage change in income on the quantity of a good demanded.

Index

A single number that summarises the collective movement of certain variables at a point in time in relation to their average value on a base date or a single variable in relation to its base date value.

Index-Linked Gilts

Gilts whose principal and interest payments are linked to the Retail Prices Index (RPI) with an eight-month time lag.

Inflation

The rate of change in the general price level or the erosion in the purchasing power of money.

Inflation Risk Premium (IRP)

The additional return demanded by bond investors based on the volatility of inflation in the recent past.

Initial Margin

The collateral deposited by exchange clearing members with the clearing house when opening certain derivatives transactions.

Initial Public Offering

See *New Issue*.

Interest Rate Parity

The mathematical relationship that exists between the spot rate and forward exchange rate for two currencies. This is given by the differential between their respective nominal interest rates over the term being considered.

Internal Rate of Return (IRR)

The discount rate that when applied to a series of cash flows produces a net present value (NPV) of zero. Also known as the *Discounted Cash Flow (DCF) Yield*.

International Fisher Effect

The proposition that, in a world of perfect capital mobility, nominal interest rates should take full account of expected inflation rates so that real interest rates are equal worldwide.

Interpolation

A method by which to establish an approximate Internal Rate of Return (IRR).

Irredeemable Security

A security issued without a prespecified redemption, or maturity, date.

Issuing House

An institution that facilitates the issue of securities.

Jensen's Alpha

See *Alpha*.

Keynesians

Those economists who believe that markets are slow to self-correct and who therefore advocate the use of fiscal policy to return the economy back to a full employment level of output.

Kondratieff Cycles

Long-term economic cycles of 50 years+ duration that result from innovation and investment in new technology.

Liquidity

The ease with which a security can be converted into cash, is often referred to as how easy it is to deal in and out of a security based on volume and a narrow spread. Liquidity also describes that amount of an investor's financial resources held in cash.

Liquidity Preference Theory

The proposition that investors have a natural preference for short-term investments and therefore demand a liquidity premium in the form of a higher return the longer the term of the investment.

Loan Stock

A corporate bond issued in the domestic bond market without any underlying collateral, or security.

London Clearing House (LCH)

The institution that clears and acts as central counterparty to all trades executed on member exchanges.

London Interbank Offered Rate (LIBOR)

A benchmark money market interest rate.

London International Financial Futures and Options Exchange (Liffe)

The UK's principal derivatives exchange for trading financial and soft commodity derivatives products. It is owned by the New York Stock Exchange and is called NYSE Liffe but is more commonly referred to as Liffe.

London Stock Exchange (LSE)

The UK market for listing and trading domestic and international securities.

Long Position

The position following the purchase of a security or buying of a derivative.

MacCaulay Duration

See *Duration*.

Macroeconomics

The study of how the aggregation of decisions taken in individual markets determines variables such as national income, employment and inflation. Macroeconomics is also concerned with explaining the relationship between these variables, their rates of change over time and the impact of monetary policy and fiscal policy on the general level of economic activity.

Manager of Managers Fund (MoM)

A multi-manager fund. It does not invest in other existing retail collective investment schemes. Instead it entails the MoM fund arranging segregated mandates with individually chosen fund managers.

Marginal Cost (MC)

The change in a firm's total cost resulting from producing one additional unit of output.

Marginal Revenue (MR)

The change in the total revenue generated by a firm from the sale of one additional unit of output.

Markets in Financial Instruments Directive (MiFID)

MiFID came into effect on 1 November 2007. It replaced the Investment Services Directive (ISD) and covers the regulation of certain financial services for the 30 member states of the European Economic Area.

Market Capitalisation

The total market value of a company's shares or other securities in issue. Market capitalisation is calculated by multiplying the number of shares or other securities a company has in issue by the market price of those shares or securities.

Market Segmentation

The proposition that each bond market can be divided up into distinct segments based upon term to maturity, with each segment operating as if it is a separate bond market operating independently of interest rate expectations.

Market Timing

See *Active Management*.

Marking to Market

The process of valuing a position taken in a securities or a derivatives market.

Mean-Variance Analysis

The use of past investment returns to predict the investment's most likely future return and to quantify the risk attached to this expected return. Mean Variance Analysis underpins Modern Portfolio Theory (MPT).

Median

A measure of central tendency established by the middle value within an ordered distribution containing an odd number of observed values or the arithmetic mean of the middle two values in an ordered distribution containing an even number of values.

Member Firm

A firm that is a member of a stock exchange or clearing house.

Microeconomics

Microeconomics is principally concerned with analysing the allocation of scarce resources within an economic system. It is the study of the decisions made by individuals and firms in particular markets and how these interactions determine the relative prices and quantities of factors of production, goods and services demanded and supplied.

Minimum Efficient Scale (MES)

The level of production at which a firm's long-run average production costs are minimised and its economies of scale are maximised.

Mode

A measure of central tendency established by the value or values that occur most frequently within a data distribution.

Modern Portfolio Theory (MPT)

The proposition that investors will only choose to hold those diversified, or efficient, portfolios that lie on the Efficient Frontier.

Modified Duration (MD)

A measure of the sensitivity of a bond's price to changes in its yield. Modified duration approximates a bond's convexity.

Monetarists

Those economists who believe that markets are self-correcting, that the level of economic activity can be regulated by controlling the money supply and that fiscal policy is ineffective and possibly harmful as a macroeconomic policy tool. Also known as New Classical Economists.

Monetary Policy

The setting of short-term interest rates by a central bank in order to manage domestic demand and achieve price stability in the economy. Monetary policy is also known as Stabilisation Policy.

Money

Anything that is generally acceptable as a means of settling a debt.

Money Weighted Rate of Return (MWRR)

The internal rate of return (IRR) that equates the value of a portfolio at the start of an investment period plus the net new capital invested during the investment period with the value of the portfolio at the end of this period. The MWRR, therefore, measures the fund growth resulting from both the underlying performance of the portfolio and the size and timing of cash flows to and from the fund over this period.

Multi-Manager Funds

A fund that offers a portfolio of separately managed funds. There are two main types: Fund of Funds and Manager of Managers.

Multiplier

The factor by which national income changes as a result of a unit change in Aggregate Demand.

National Association of Securities Dealers Automated Quotations (NASDAQ)

The second-largest stock exchange in the US. NASDAQ lists certain US and international stocks and provides a screen-based quote-driven secondary market that links buyers and sellers worldwide. NASDAQ also operates a stock exchange in Europe (NASDAQ OMX Europe).

National Debt

A government's total outstanding borrowing resulting from financing successive budget deficits, mainly through the issue of government-backed securities.

Negotiable Security

A security whose ownership can pass freely from one party to another. Negotiable securities are, therefore, tradeable.

Net Present Value (NPV)

The result of subtracting the discounted, or present, value of a project's expected cash outflows from the present value of its expected cash inflows.

Net Redemption Yield (NRY)

The annual compound return from holding a bond to maturity, taking account of both the coupon payments net of income tax and the capital gain or loss to maturity.

New Classical Economists

See *Monetarists*.

New Issue

A new issue of ordinary shares whether made by an offer for sale, an offer for subscription or a placing. Also known as an *Initial Public Offering (IPO)*.

New Paradigm

The term applied to an economy that can produce robust economic growth without accompanying inflation through the employment of productivity-enhancing new technology.

Nominal Value

The face or par value of a security. The nominal value is the price at which a bond is issued and usually redeemed and the price below which a company's ordinary shares cannot be issued.

Normal Distribution

A distribution whose values are evenly, or symmetrically, distributed about the arithmetic mean. Depicted graphically, a normal distribution is plotted as a symmetrical, continuous, bell-shaped curve.

Normal Profit

The required rate of return for a firm to remain in business taking account of all opportunity costs.

Opportunity Cost

The cost of forgoing the next best alternative course of action. In economics, costs are defined not as financial but as opportunity costs.

Option

A derivatives contract that confers the right from one party (the writer) to another (the holder) to either buy (call option) or sell (put option) an asset at a prespecified price on, and sometimes before, a prespecified future date, in exchange for the payment of a premium.

Ordinary Share Capital

See *Equity*.

Over-the-Counter (OTC) Derivatives

Derivatives that are not traded on a derivatives exchange owing to their non-standardised contract specifications.

Pari Passu

Of equal ranking. New ordinary shares issued under a rights issue, for instance, rank pari passu with the company's existing ordinary shares.

Par Value

See *Nominal Value*.

Passive Management

An investment approach employed in those securities markets that are believed to be price-efficient. The term also extends to passive bond management techniques collectively known as Immunisation.

Permanent Interest Bearing Securities (PIBS)

Irredeemable fixed interest securities issued by mutual building societies. Known as perpetual subordinated bonds (PSBs) if the building society demutualises.

Perpetuities

An investment that provides an indefinite stream of equal prespecified periodic payments.

PLUS Markets

A stock exchange competitor to the London Stock Exchange.

Population

A statistical term applied to a particular group where every member or constituent of the group is included.

Potential Output Level

The sustainable level of output produced by an economy when all of its resources are productively employed. Also known as the Full Employment Level of Output.

Pre-Emption Rights

The rights accorded to ordinary shareholders under company law to subscribe for new ordinary shares issued by the company, in which they have the shareholding, for cash before the shares are offered to outside investors.

Preference Shares

Those shares issued by a company that rank ahead of ordinary shares for the payment of dividends and for capital repayment in the event of the company going into liquidation.

Premium

The amount of cash paid by the holder of an option to the writer in exchange for conferring a right. Also, the difference in the spot and forward exchange rate that arises when interest rates in the base currency are higher than those in the quoted currency.

Present Value

The value of a sum of money receivable at a known future date expressed in terms of its value today.   A present value is obtained by discounting the future sum by a known rate of interest.

Price Elasticity of Demand (PED)

The effect of a small percentage change in the price of a good on the quantity of the good demanded. PED is expressed as a figure between zero and infinity.

Prima Facie

At first sight. For instance, a portfolio's past performance provides prima facie evidence of a portfolio manager's skill and investment style.

Primary Data

Data commissioned for a specific purpose.

Primary Market

The market for new issues or Initial Public Offerings (IPOs).

Production Possibility Frontier (PPF)

The PPF depicts all feasible combinations of output that can be produced within an economy given the limit of its resources and production techniques.

Provisional Allotment Letter

A document sent to those shareholders who have certificated holdings and are entitled to participate in a rights issue. The letter details the shareholder's existing shareholding, their rights over the new shares allotted and the date(s) by which they must act.

Prudential Regulation Authority (PRA)

The UK body responsible for prudential regulation of all deposit-taking institutions, insurers and investment banks.

Public Sector Net Cash Requirement (PSNCR)

The extent to which the UK government needs to borrow, mainly through the issue of government backed securities, to finance a budget deficit as a result of its spending exceeding tax revenue for the fiscal year. See also Gilts.

Pull to Maturity

A term used to explain why the price of short-dated bonds is less affected by interest rate changes than that of long-dated bonds.

Purchasing Power Parity (PPP)

The nominal exchange rate between two countries that reflects the difference in their respective rates of inflation.

Put Option

An option that confers a right (but not an obligation) on the holder to sell a specified amount of an asset at a prespecified price on or sometimes before a prespecified date.

Qualifying Corporate Bonds (QCBs)

UK corporate bonds issued in sterling without conversion rights. QCBs are free of UK capital gains tax (CGT).

Quantity Theory of Money

A truism that formalises the relationship between the domestic money supply and the general price level.

Quoted Currency

The currency whose value is expressed in terms of one unit of the base currency. The quoted currency is currency Y for the X/Y exchange rate.

Redeemable Security

A security issued with a known maturity, or redemption, date.

Redemption

The repayment of principal to the holder of a Redeemable Security.

Regression Analysis

A statistical technique used to establish the degree of correlation that exists between two variables.

Reinvestment Risk

The inability to reinvest coupons at the same rate of interest as the gross redemption yield (GRY). This in turn makes the GRY conceptually flawed.

Repo

The sale and repurchase of bonds between two parties: the repurchase being made at a price and date fixed in advance. Repos are categorised into general repos and specific repos.

Reserve Ratio

The proportion of deposits held by banks as reserves to meet depositor withdrawals and Bank of England credit control requirements.

Resistance Level

A term used in technical analysis to describe the ceiling put on the price of a security resulting from persistent investor selling at that price level.

Retail Prices Index (RPI)

An expenditure-weighted measure of UK inflation based on a representative basket of goods and services purchased by an average UK household.

Rights Issue

The issue of new ordinary shares to a company's shareholders in proportion to each shareholder's existing shareholding, usually at a price deeply discounted to that prevailing in the market. Also see Pre-emption Rights.

Running Yield

The return from a bond calculated by expressing the coupon as a percentage of the clean price. Also known as the flat yield or interest yield.

Sample

A statistical term applied to a representative subset of a particular population. Samples enable inferences to be made about the population.

Scrip Issue

See *Bonus Issue*.

Secondary Data

Pre-existing data.

Secondary Market

The market for trading securities already in issue.

Securitisation

The packaging of rights to the future revenue stream from a collection of assets into a bond issue.

Separate Trading of Registered Interest and Principal (STRIPS)

The principal and interest payments of those designated gilts that can be separately traded as zero coupon bonds (ZCBs).

Settlor

The creator of a trust.

Share Buyback

The redemption and cancellation by a company of a proportion of its irredeemable ordinary shares subject to the permission of the High Court and agreement from HMRC.

Share Capital

The nominal value of a company's equity or ordinary shares. A company's authorised share capital is the nominal value of equity the company may issue while issued share capital is that which the company has issued. The term 'share capital' is often extended to include a company's preference shares.

Share Split

A method by which a company can reduce the market price of its shares to make them more marketable without capitalising its reserves. A share split simply entails the company reducing the nominal value of each of its shares in issue while maintaining the overall nominal value of its share capital. A share split should have the same impact on a company's share price as a Bonus Issue.

Short Position

The position following the sale of a security not owned or selling a derivative.

Spot Rate

A compound annual fixed rate of interest that applies to an investment over a specific time period. Also see *Forward Rate*.

Spreads

A strategy requiring the simultaneous purchase of one or more options and the sale of another or several others on the same underlying asset with either different exercise prices and the same expiry date or the same exercise prices and different expiry dates. Spreads include bull spreads, bear spreads and butterfly spreads.

Stabilisation Policy

See *Fiscal Policy* and *Monetary Policy*.

Standard Deviation

A measure of dispersion. In relation to the values within a distribution, the standard deviation is the square root of the distribution's variance.

Stock Exchange

An organised marketplace for issuing and trading securities by members of that exchange.

Stock Exchange Automated Quotation (SEAQ)

The London Stock Exchange's (LSE) quote-driven screen-based trading system that displays firm bid and offer prices quoted by competing market makers during the mandatory quote period.

Stock Exchange Electronic Trading Service (SETS)

The London Stock Exchange's (LSE) screen-based order-driven trading system that electronically matches buy and sell orders input to the system. Only the most liquid securities in the UK equity market can be traded through SETS and all orders must be firm and not indicative, as, once displayed, an order must be capable of immediate execution.

Subordinated Loan Stock

Loan stock issued by a company that ranks above its preference shares but below its unsecured creditors in the event of the company's liquidation.

Substitute

A good is a substitute for another if a rise in the price of one results in an increase in demand for the other. As substitute goods perform a similar function to each other, they typically have a high price elasticity of demand (PED).

Supply Curve

The depiction of the quantity of a particular good or service firms are willing to supply at a given price. Plotted against price on the vertical axis and quantity on the horizontal axis, a supply curve slopes upward from left to right.

Swap

An over-the-counter (OTC) derivative whereby two parties exchange a series of periodic payments based on a notional principal amount over an agreed term. Swaps can take the form of interest rate swaps, currency swaps and equity swaps.

T+3

The three-day rolling settlement period over which all equity deals executed on the London Stock Exchange's (LSE) SETS are settled. This is also a standard settlement period for most international equity markets.

TechMARK

The London Stock Exchange (LSE) sub-market for those public limited companies (PLCs) committed to technological innovation.

Technical Analysis

The analysis of charts depicting past price and volume movements to determine the future course of a particular market or the price of an individual security. Technical analysis is nullified by the weak form of the Efficient Markets Hypothesis (EMH).

Tick

The minimum price movement of an instrument or a derivatives contract as specified by the exchange on which it is traded.

Tick Value

The monetary value of one tick.

Time Value

That element of an option premium that is not intrinsic value. Time value also relates to a sum of money which, by taking account of a prevailing rate of interest and the term over which the sum is to be invested or received, can be expressed as either a future value or as a present value, respectively.

Time Weighted Rate of Return (TWRR)

The unitised performance of a portfolio over an investment period that eliminates the distorting effect of cash flows. The TWRR is calculated by compounding the rates of return from each investment sub-period, a sub-period being created whenever there is a movement of capital into or out of the portfolio.

Tracking Error

See *Active Risk*.

Treasury Bills

Short-term government-backed securities issued at a discount to par via a weekly Bank of England auction. Treasury bills do not pay coupons but are redeemed at par. Treasury bills are also issued in a similar fashion in the US.

Trustees

The legal owners of trust property who owe a duty of skill and care to the trust's beneficiaries.

UK Listing Authority (UKLA)

Under European Union (EU) regulations each member state must appoint a competent authority for the purpose of listing securities. The competent authority for listing in the UK is the Financial Conduct Authority (FCA); in this capacity, the FCA is called the UK Listing Authority.

UK Corporate Governance Code

The code that embodies best corporate governance practice for all public limited companies (PLCs) quoted on the London Stock Exchange (LSE). Also known as the Code of Best Practice.

Undertakings for Collective Investments in Transferable Securities (UCITS) Directive

An EU directive originally introduced in 1985 but since revised to enable collective investment schemes (CISs) authorised in one EU member state to be freely marketed throughout the EU, subject to the marketing rules of the host state(s) and certain fund structure rules being complied with.

Unemployment

The percentage of the labour force registered as available to work at the current wage rate.

Variance

A measure of dispersion. In relation to the values within a distribution, the variance is the mean of the sum of the squared deviations from the distribution's arithmetic mean.

Variation Margin

The cash that passes between the exchange clearing members daily via the clearing house in settlement of the previous day's price movement in an open derivatives contract.

Volatility

A measure of the extent to which investment returns, asset prices and economic variables fluctuate. Volatility is measured by the standard deviation of these returns, prices and values.

Warrants

Negotiable securities issued by public limited companies (PLCs) that confer a right on the holder to buy a certain number of the company's ordinary shares on prespecified terms. Warrants are essentially long-dated call options but are traded on a stock exchange rather than on a derivatives exchange.

Weighted Average Cost of Capital (WACC)

The average post-tax cost of servicing a company's long-term sources of finance. The WACC acts as the discount rate for establishing the net present value (NPV) of investment projects of equivalent risk to those currently undertaken by the company.

Yield Curve

The depiction of the relationship between the gross redemption yields (GRYs) and the maturity of bonds of the same type.

Yield to Maturity

See *Gross Redemption Yield*.

Zero Coupon Bonds (ZCBs)

Bonds issued at a discount to their nominal value that do not pay a coupon but which are redeemed at par on a prespecified future date.

3G

Third Generation

ACD

Authorised Corporate Director

AD

Aggregate Demand

ADR

American Depositary Receipt

AEA

Annual Exempt Allowance

AER

Annual Equivalent Rate

AGM

Annual General Meeting

AIFM

Alternate Investment Fund Manager

AIFMD

Alternate Investment Fund Managers Directive

AIM

Alternative Investment Market

AMC

Annual Management Charge

AMEX

American (Stock) Exchange

APCIMS

Association of Private Client Investment Managers and Stockbrokers

APT

Arbitrage Pricing Theory

AR

Average Revenue

ASB

Accounting Standards Board

ASX

Australian Securities Exchange

ATC

Average Total Cost

AVC

Average Variable Cost

AVCO

Average Cost (but AC is more frequent usage)

B2B

Business to Business

BAI

Banking Administration Institute

BBA

British Bankers' Association

BCE

Benefit Crystalisation Event

BM&F

Bolsa de Mercadorias e Futuros (Brazilian Mercantile & Futures Exchange)

BMV

Beginning Market Value

BOISL

Bank Of India Shareholding Limited

BOJ

Bank Of Japan

Bovespa

Bolsa de Valores de São Paulo (São Paulo Stock Exchange)

bp

basis point

BPR

Business Property Relief

BRIC

Brazil, Russia, India, China

BSE

Bombay Stock Exchange

BT

British Telecom

CAC

Cotation Assistée en Continu

CAP

Chargeable Accounting Period

CAPM

Capital Asset Pricing Model

CAPS

Combined Actuarial Performance Services

CASE

Cairo and Alexandria Stock Exchange

CBF

Clearstream Banking Frankfurt

CBOE

Chicago Board Options Exchange

CBOT

Chicago Board of Trade

CCASS

Central Clearing Automated Settlement System

CCP

Central Clearing Counterparty

CD

Certificate of Deposit

CDO

Collateralised Debt Obligation

CDS

Credit Default Swap

CFA

Chartered Financial Analyst

CFD

Contract For Difference

CGT

Capital Gains Tax

CIF

Common Investment Fund

CLO

Collateralised Loan Obligation

CMA

Cash Memorandum Account

CME

Chicago Mercantile Exchange

CMBS

Commercial Mortgage-Backed Security

CoCo

Conditional/Contingent Convertible Bond

CP

Commercial Paper

CPI

Consumer Prices Index

CRA

Credit Rating Agency

CSCCRC

China Securities Central Clearing and Registration Corporation

CSD

Central Securities Depository

CSDCC

China Securities Depository and Clearing Corporation

CSDR

Central Securities Depository Regulation

CSRC

China Securities Regulatory Commission

CTD

Cheapest To Deliver

DAX

Deutscher Aktien IndeX

DB

Defined Benefit

DC

Defined Contribution

DCF

Discounted Cash Flow

DIE

Designated Investment Exchange

DIFC

Dubai International Financial Centre

DIFX

Dubai International Financial Exchange

dis

Discount

DJIA

Dow Jones Industrial Average

DMO

Debt Management Office

DPS

Dividend Per Share

DRIP

Dividend Reinvestment Plan

DTC

Depository Trust Company

DTCC

Depository Trust and Clearing Corporation

DTR

Double Taxation Relief

DVP

Delivery Versus Payment

EBIT

Earnings Before Interest and Tax

EBITDA

Earnings Before Interest, Tax, Depreciation and Amortisation

EBS

Electronic Broking System

EC

European Commission

ECB

European Central Bank

EEA

European Economic Area

EFA

European Finance Association

EIC

Earned Income Credit

EIRIS

Ethical Investment Research Services

EIS

Enterprise Investment Scheme

EMH

Efficient Market Hypothesis

EMIR

European Market Infrastructure Regulation

EMV

End Market Value

EPS

Earnings Per Share

ESMA

European Securities and Markets Authority

ESRB

European Systemic Risk Board

ETC

i.   Exchange-Traded Commodity
ii. Exchange-Traded Currency

ETD

Exchange-Traded Derivative

ETF

Exchange-Traded Fund

ETN

Exchange-Traded Note

ETP

Exchange-Traded Product

ETT

Electronic Transfer of Tille

EU

European Union

EUR

Euro

EVA

Economic Value Added

FCA

Financial Conduct Authority

FDI

Foreign Direct Investment

FHLB

Federal Home Loan Bank

FHLMC

Fedaral Home Loan Mortgage Company (Freddie Mac)

FNMA

Federal National Mortgage Association (Fannie Mae)

FIFO

First In First Out

FII

Fixed Investment Income

FOMC

Federal Open Market Committee

FRN

Floating Rate Note

FRS

Financial Reporting Standard

FSA

Financial Services Authority

FSCS

Financial Services Compensation Scheme

FSMA

Financial Services and Markets Act

FTSE

Financial Times Stock Exchange

FX

Foreign Exchange

GAARP

Growth At A Reasonable Price

GATT

General Agreement on Trades and Tariffs

GDP

Gross Domestic Product

GDR

Global Depositary Receipt

GEMM

Gilt-Edged Market Makers

GIPS

Global Investment Performance Standard

GNI

Gross National Income

GNP

Gross National Product

GRY

Gross Redemption Yield

GST

Goods and Services Tax

HSI

Hang Seng Index

HICP

Harmonised Index of Consumer Prices

HKFE

Hong Kong Futures Exchange

HKSCC

Hong Kong Securities Clearing Corporation

HMRC

Her Majesty's Revenue and Customs

IA

Investment Association

IAS

International Accounting Standard

IASB

International Accounting Standards Board

ICMA

International Capital Markets Association

ICVC

Investment Company with Variable Capital

IDR

Initial Deposit Receipt

IFA

Independent Financial Adviser

IFRS

International Financial Reporting Standard

IHT

Inheritance Tax

IMA

Investment Management Association

IMF

International Monetary Fund

IOSCO

International Organisation of Securities Commissions

IPD
Investment Property Databank

IPE
International Petroleum Exchange

IPO
Initial Public Offering

IRR
Internal Rate of Return

IRS
Interest Rate Swap

ISA
Individual Savings Account

JASDEC
Japan Securities Depository Center

JFSA
Japan Financial Services Authority

JGB
Japanese Government Bond

KMR
Key Man Risk

KYC
Know Your Customer

LCH
London Clearing House

LIBID
London InterBank Bid Rate

LIBOR
London InterBank Offered Rate

LIFO
Last In First Out

LRAC
Long Run Average Cost

LRAS
Long Run Aggregate Supply

LRATC
Long Run Average Total Costs

LRMC
Long Run Marginal Cost

LSE
London Stock Exchange

MBS
Mortgage-Backed Security

MC
Marginal Cost

MCDR
Misr (Egypt) for Central Clearing, Depository and Registry

MEI
Marginal Efficiency of Investment

MES
Minimum Efficient Scale

MiFID
Markets in Financial Instruments Directive

MPC
i   Marginal Propensity to Consume
ii. Monetary Policy Committee

MPM
Monetary Policy Meeting

MPT
Modern Portfolio Theory

MR

Marginal Revenue

MSCI

Morgan Stanley Capital International

MTF

Multilateral Trading Facility

MTS

Mercato Telematico Secondario

MUICP

Monetary Union Index of Commercial Prices

MVA

Market Value Added

MWRR

Money Weighted Rate of Return

NAIRU

Non-Accelerating Inflation Rate of Unemployment

NASDAQ

National Association of Securities Dealers Automated Quotations

NAV

Net Asset Value

NBV

Net Book Value

NED

Non-Executive Director

NOMAD

Nominated Adviser

NPV

Net Present Value

NRV

Net Realisable Value

NRY

Net Redemption Yield

NSCC

National Securities Clearing Corporation

NURS

Non-UCITS Retail Scheme

NYMEX

New York Mercantile Exchange

NYSE

New York Stock Exchange

OAD

Option Adjusted Duration

OCF

Ongoing Charges Figure

OECD

Organisation for Economic Co-operation and Development

OEIC

Open Ended Investment Company

OFEX

Off Exchange

OFR

Operating and Financial Review

ONS

Office for National Statistics

OPEC

Organisation of Petroleum Exporting Companies

OTC

Over The Counter

PAIF

Property Authorised Investment Fund

PB

Price to Book

PCE

Personal Consumption Expenditure

P/E

Price/Earnings

PED

Price Elasticity of Demand

PEG

Price Earnings to Growth

PEP

Personal Equity Plan

PER

Price Earnings Ratio

PIBS

Permanent Interest Bearing Share

PIK

Payment in Kind

PIP

Primary Information Provider

PLC

Public Limited Company

PM

Premium

POTAM

Panel On Takeovers And Mergers

PPI

Producer Price Index

PPP

Purchasing Power Parity

PRA

Prudential Regulation Authority

PSNCR

Public Sector Net Cash Requirement

QE

Quantitive Easing

QFII

Qualified Foreign Institutional Investor

QIS

Quantified Investor Scheme

REIT

Real Estate Investment Trust

RGV

Relit Grande Vitesse

RIE

Recognised Investment Exchange

RNS

Regulatory News Service

ROCE

Return On Capital Employed

ROCH

Recognised Overseas Clearing House

ROIE

Recognised Overseas Investment Exchange

RPI

Retail Prices Index

RUR

Register Update Request

S&P

Standard & Poor's

SCARP

Structured Capital At Risk Product

SD

Stamp Duty

SDLT

Stamp Duty Land Tax

SDCC

Shenzhen Depository and Clearing Corporation

SDRT

Stamp Duty Reserve Tax

SEAQ

Stock Exchange Automated Quotation

SEC

Securities and Exchange Commission

SEHK

Stock Exchange of Hong Kong

SETS

Stock Exchange Electronic Trading Service

SETSqx

Stock Exchange Electronic Trading Service – Quotes and Crosses

SIP

Secondary Information Provider

SIPP

Self-Invested Pension Plan

SME

Small and Medium Enterprises

SML

Security Market Line

SPV

Special Purpose Vehicle

SRAS

Short Run Aggregate Supply

SRATC

Short Run Average Total Cost

SRAVC

Short Run Average Variable Cost

SRI

Socially Responsible Investment

SRMC

Short Run Marginal Costs

SSAS

Small Self-Administered Scheme

SSE

Shanghai Stock Exchange

STIR

Short Term Interest Rate

STRIP

Separate Trading of Registered Interest and Principal

SZSE

Shenzhen Stock Exchange

TARP

Troubled Asset Relief Programme

TEF

Tax-Elected Fund

TER

Total Expense Ratio

TIPS

Treasury Inflation-Protected Security

TMX
Toronto Montreal Exchange

TSE
Tokyo Stock Exchange

TWRR
Time Weighted Rate of Return

UCITS
Undertakings for Collective Investment in Transferable Securities

UAE
United Arab Emirates

UKLA
United Kingdom Listing Authority

VAT
Value Added Tax

VCT
Venture Capital Trust

WACC
Weighted Average Cost of Capital

WEF
World Economic Fund

WHT
Withholding Tax

WMA
Wealth Management Association

WTO
World Trade Organisation

VRN
Variable Rate Note

X
Base Currency

XD
Ex Dividend

XED
Cross Elasticity of Demand

Y
Quoted Currency

YED
Income Elasticity of Demand

YTM
Yield to Maturity

ZCB
Zero Coupon Bond

Multiple Choice
Questions

The following additional questions have been compiled to reflect as closely as possible the examination standard that you will experience in your examination. Please note, however, they are not the CISI examination questions themselves.

1. ABC is a relatively large company. Why did it breach the required protocols in the operation of its audit committee?

    A. The company appointed a total of six members to the committee

    B. The company arranged for the committee to approve the remuneration of its external auditors

    C. The committee's sole independent director has a non-financial background

    D. The committee's chairperson is over the age of 70

2. Which of the following statement concerning CIS charges is correct?

    A. Unit trusts are dual-priced and purchases incur an additional initial charge

    B. ETFs are single-priced and dealing incurs a dilution levy

    C. Investment trust pricing depends on demand and supply and incurs initial commission

    D. OEICs are single-priced and may charge a dilution levy

3. Under the 'accrual concept' of accounting:

    A. Revenue is based on income when received and expenses when paid

    B. Revenue is based on income when earned and expenses when paid

    C. Revenue is based on income when received and expenses when incurred

    D. Revenue is based on income when earned and expenses when incurred

4. Under the Capital Asset Pricing Model, if a stock has a beta of 1.2 this means that:

    A. It has outperformed its sector average by 20%

    B. It is 20% more volatile than the market

    C. Its profits grew by 20% over the last 12 months

    D. Its dividend level is likely to fall by 20%

5. A lump sum is to be invested for a five-year period at a fixed rate of interest of 6% p.a. compound, with interest credited annually. What initial sum should be invested if the end amount is to be £20,000?

    A. £14,099

    B. £14,945

    C. £15,671

    D. £15,842

6. If you were to buy a 100 put for a premium of 13, what would be your maximum potential profit?

    A. 13
    B. 87
    C. 100
    D. Unlimited

7. If a company's share price is £1.10 and its net asset value per share is £1.00, then 1.1 will represent the company's:

    A. Price/earnings ratio
    B. Price to book ratio
    C. Earnings per share
    D. Z-score analysis

8. Which ratio compares the excess return achieved by a fund over a benchmark portfolio to the fund's tracking error?

    A. Information ratio
    B. Jensen ratio
    C. Sharpe ratio
    D. Treynor ratio

9. A portfolio of shares has experienced the following annual returns recently: 2015: 3.22%; 2014: (6.74%) (negative); 2013: 11.56%. What is the variance (assume a population)?

    A. 0.5596
    B. 0.8394
    C. 0.3487
    D. 0.6206

10. What factor would be least important when assessing a defined benefit pension?

    A. Age at which benefits can be taken
    B. Expected amount payable
    C. Investment performance of the fund
    D. Lump sum available at retirement

11. A parallel shift in the demand curve to the left for a particular good might be caused by which of the following?

    A. Rising price of a complement
    B. Falling consumer income
    C. The good becomes fashionable
    D. Increasing disposable income

12. A lack of liquidity, high management costs and void periods are characteristics associated with investment in which of the following assets?

    A. Commercial property

    B. Depository interests

    C. Eurobonds

    D. Hedge funds

13. The order book for a stock is shown below.

Buy Queue		Sell Queue	
7,000 shares	£1.24	3,550 shares	£1.25
5,150 shares	£1.23	1,984 shares	£1.26
19,250 shares	£1.22	75,397 shares	£1.26
44,000 shares	£1.22	17,300 shares	£1.27

    An investor has placed an execute and eliminate order to buy 5,000 shares at 1.25. Which statement correctly describes what action will take place with this order?

    A. As the entire order cannot be filled, the whole order will be eliminated from the order book

    B. It will automatically execute against the order to sell 3,550 shares at a limit of 125p and the balance of the order will be cancelled

    C. It will automatically execute against the order to sell 3,550 shares and the balance of the order will remain on the order book as a limit order

    D. It will automatically execute against the order to sell 3,550 shares and the balance of the order will be executed against the second order to sell 1,984 shares

14. The following extracts have been taken from Z plc's income statement for the period ending 31 December 2015:

Income Statement Item	£000
Turnover	15,410
Cost of sales	11,375
Net operating expenses	1,675
Exceptional loss	1,308
Interest receivable	989
Tax	602

With reference to the above profit and loss items, what is Z plc's operating profit and profit attributable to its shareholders, respectively?

A. £4,035,000 and £1,439,000

B. £2,360,000 and £1,439,000

C. £4,035,000 and £646,000

D. £2,360,000 and £646,000

15. Bond 1 has a Standard & Poor's rating of B and Bond 2 has a Standard & Poor's rating of BBB. This usually means that Bond 1:

A. Has a higher yield than Bond 2

B. Is lower risk than Bond 2

C. Has a smaller coupon than Bond 2

D. Is cheaper than Bond 2

16. If a company's z-score analysis is negative, this is likely to indicate that the company:

A. Has a volatile profit performance

B. Is heading for imminent insolvency

C. Has a low level of gearing

D. Is relying too heavily on a limited customer base

17. Company A's operating profit is £255,000. Given the following information, calculate Company A's net cash flow from operations.

Items to reconcile operating profit with net cash flow from operations	£000
Depreciation	65
Goodwill amortisation	11
Increase in debtors	49
Increase in creditors	38
Profit on sale of fixed asset	15

Company A's net cash flow from operations is:

A. £433,000

B. £357,000

C. £327,000

D. £305,000

18. Diversification is best achieved by combining securities whose returns:

    A. Are as positively correlated as possible
    B. Are as negatively correlated as possible
    C. Have similar standard deviations
    D. Have widely different standard deviations

19. Under the efficient market hypothesis, a market is unlikely to operate as a 'strong form efficient market' due to the existence of:

    A. Insider dealing laws
    B. Money laundering regulations
    C. Best execution procedures
    D. Data protection rules

20. As part of the rebalancing of a portfolio, a portfolio manager decides to sell and buy similar bonds in all respects apart from the yield on which both trade. The result is that the underlying client moves out of the more to the less highly priced bond. This process is known as which one of the following?

    A. Bond switching
    B. Anomaly switching
    C. Redemption switching
    D .Price switching

21. If a government decides to deal with a current account deficit by allowing the value of its currency to decline against other currencies, what will be the impact on a company?

    A. It will reduce its costs for importing raw materials
    B. The cost of services it obtains from abroad will be cheaper
    C. Profits earned in other currencies will be worth less when translated into sterling
    D. Its goods will be more competitive in overseas markets

22. What is the running total of each member's payment obligations within CREST known as?

    A. Cash Memorandum Account
    B. Debit Cap
    C. Net Settlement Limit
    D. Real Time Gross Settlement

23. Total expense ratio is used in conjunction with which of the following?

    A. Analysis of company accounts

    B. Collective investment schemes

    C. Discretionary investment management

    D. Performance measurement

24. A company's shares are currently trading at £5. If it implements a 1 for 4 rights issue at a discounted market price of £4, what will be the theoretical post-issue share price?

    A. £4.50

    B. £4.70

    C. £4.75

    D. £4.80

25. A machine was purchased by a company for £32,000, has a useful economic life of five years and is estimated to have a disposal value at this point of £2,000. What is the annual depreciation using the straight line method?

    A. £4,400

    B. £5,667

    C. £6,000

    D. £6,400

26. One of the key differences between fundamental analysis (FA) and technical analysis (TA), when evaluating companies, is that:

    A. FA tends to use a longer time horizon

    B. TA tends to use a longer time horizon

    C. FA ignores untypical poor or healthy periods

    D. TA ignores untypical poor or healthy periods

27. Which of the following removes the impact of cash flows in and out of a portfolio when measuring performance?

    A. Total return

    B. Time-weighted rate of return

    C. Holding period return

    D. Money-weighted rate of return

28. If a government increases its spending and finances this through the issue of gilts, this would indicate it is adopting what type of fiscal stance?

    A. Contractionary

    B. Expansionary

    C. Neutral

    D. Recessionary

29. Which one of the following is an example of backwardation?

    A. Futures price at fair value, slightly higher than the cash value of the underlying

    B. Futures price below fair value, but above cash value

    C. Futures price below cash value

    D. Futures price has risen out of the arbitrage channel

30. A company successfully applied for listing on the London Stock Exchange, but deliberately raised no capital as part of this process. What listing method was used?

    A. Placing

    B. Introduction

    C. Order for sale

    D. Order for subscription

31. Withholding tax is tax deducted:

    A. Against revenues from safekeeping activities conducted by custodians on behalf of foreign investor clients

    B. In respect of capital gains generated by investors on their investment activity

    C. As a deposit by a jurisdiction's tax authorities against potential non-payment of tax by a foreign investor

    D. In the issuer's country of residence on income paid by issuers to investors

32. A portfolio was worth £500,000 at the beginning of the year and £550,000 at the end of December of that year. The transactions that took place during the year were a cash injection of £15,000 at the end of March and a cash withdrawal of £7,000 at the end of September. What is its money-weighted rate of return?

    A. 8.24%

    B. 8.43%

    C. 11.38%

    D. 11.63%

33. Bonds have differing sensitivities to changes in yields. Which of the following statements correctly places the bonds mentioned in the order of most to least sensitive?

    A. $1^7/_8$% Index-linked Treasury Gilt 2022; 4% Treasury Gilt 2022; Gilt strip repayable 2022; 3½% War Loan

    B. 3½% War Loan; Gilt strip repayable 2022; $1^7/_8$% Index-linked Treasury Gilt 2022; 4% Treasury Gilt 2022

    C. 4% Treasury Gilt 2022; $1^7/_8$% Index-linked Treasury Gilt 2022; Gilt strip repayable 2022; 3½% War Loan

    D. Gilt strip repayable 2022; $1^7/_8$% Index-linked Treasury Gilt 2022; 4% Treasury Gilt 2022; 3½% War Loan

34. Which of the following characteristics is TRUE of hedge funds? Hedge funds usually:

    A. Only use derivatives for efficient portfolio management (EPM)

    B. Focus on relative investment returns typically against a sector average

    C. Adopt an unauthorised collective investment scheme (CIS) structure

    D. Have a high correlation with world equity and bond markets

35. If you buy an option, what is the effect, if any, of gearing for a given price change in the underlying asset?

    A. A similar proportionate change in the option value

    B. A greater proportionate change in the option value

    C. A smaller proportionate change in the option value

    D. None

36. As part of a review, the value of a company's patents was significantly reduced. This directly caused a fall in the value of which section of the company's balance sheet?

    A. Current assets – inventory

    B. Current assets – trade and other receivables

    C. Tangible fixed assets

    D. Intangible fixed assets

37. A company issued 6% cumulative redeemable preference shares at 125p. They are currently priced at 150p and can be converted into ordinary shares at the rate of 4 to 1. If the ordinary shares are priced at 500p, what is the conversion premium?

    A. 5%

    B. 10%

    C. 15%

    D. 20%

38. A multilateral trading facility is:

    A. A regulated stock exchange that supports trading from broker members from multiple jurisdictions

    B. A registered non-exchange trading venue that brings together buyers and sellers of securities

    C. A share-trading market established to support trading of small cap equities

    D. An order-driven market where investors can route orders to the platform electronically or via a floor broker

39. If a share price falls, which of the following is TRUE?

    A. P/E ratio rises; dividend yield falls

    B. P/E ratio falls; dividend yield rises

    C. P/E ratio rises; dividend yield rises

    D. P/E ratio falls; dividend yield falls

40. Following a liquidation there are sufficient funds to pay preference shareholders. Consequently, they will receive:

    A. The pre-liquidation market price

    B. The nominal value

    C. The equitable value decided by the liquidator

    D. The unpaid net dividends only

41. An investor buys a January £5 call option at 25p. At expiry, the stock is at £4.75. How much will the investor lose per share?

    A. 25p

    B. 50p

    C. £4.75

    D. £5.00

42. A company pays the main rate of corporation tax. How will profits chargeable to corporation tax be calculated?

    A. Profit before tax less depreciation and dividends from other companies and plus provisions

    B. Profit before tax less depreciation and provisions and plus dividends from other companies

    C. Profit before tax plus depreciation and dividends from other companies and less provisions

    D. Profit before tax plus depreciation and provisions and less dividends from other companies

43. Which of these correlation coefficients indicates the weakest relationship between two assets?

    A. +1
    B. +0.2
    C. −0.5
    D. −1

44. Which of these statements most accurately describes arbitrage?

    A. The purchase and sale of substantially identical assets in order to profit from a price difference between the two assets
    B. The simultaneous purchase and sale of substantially identical assets in order to profit from a price difference between the two assets
    C. The process of converting a convertible bond into its underlying equity
    D. The simultaneous purchase and sale of a convertible bond and its underlying equity in order to profit from a price difference between the two assets

45. What would an American Depositary Receipt (ADR) holder expect to receive when the issuing company makes a rights issue?

    A. Shares in the underlying security
    B. New shares in ADR form
    C. Proceeds of the sale of the rights
    D. Revaluation of the ADR

46. The current exchange rate is US$1.65 = £1 and the interest rates in the US and UK for the next year are 3% and 4% respectively. What is the one-year forward rate of exchange using interest rate parity?

    A. US$1.6341 = £1
    B. US$1.6540 = £1
    C. US$1.6995 = £1
    D. US$1.7165 = £1

47. A company's balance sheet shows share capital of £2 million, reserves of £8 million, loans of £1.5 million, overdraft of £0.5 million and sales of £6 million. What is its asset turnover?

    A. 0.10
    B. 0.20
    C. 0.25
    D. 0.50

48. Which one of the following is compared to the current price to determine whether an investment trust share is trading at a discount or premium?

   A. Bid price

   B. Mid-market price

   C. Net asset value

   D. Offer price

49. What event will cause Permanent Interest-Bearing Securities to be reclassified as Perpetual Subordinated Bonds?

   A. A fall in their value below a threshold level

   B. A series of missed interest payments

   C. Completion of the prescribed investment holding period

   D. Demutualisation of the issuer

50. Annual returns for a particular equity asset in each of the last six years were: 1.6%, −2.6%, 4.9%, 12.2%, 6.1% and 4.3%. What is the median return?

   A. 3.9%

   B. 4.4%

   C. 4.6%

   D. 5.1%

51. A key assumption when performing technical analysis is that:

   A. Prices move in silos

   B. The market discounts everything

   C. Volatility is cyclical

   D. Marketing aids profitability

52. Which one of the following best describes an investment in an Exchange-Traded Product?

   A. Speculative

   B. Passive

   C. Long-Term

   D. Hedge-based

53. You have an investment that generates an annual income of £10,000 in perpetuity. At an interest rate of 10%, what is its value?

    A. £100

    B. £1,000

    C. £10,000

    D. £100,000

54. How does a listed PLC know in what format they must produce a statement of financial positions?

    A. It is composed on a best accounting endeavours basis under the direction of the Accountancy Standards Board

    B. The format is devised and set out according to the UK Companies Acts

    C. As directed by the head of finance in accordance with European accountancy law

    D. There is no standard model and it is very much individualised according to sector

55. Which one of the following is true if, when analysing a company, its future annual EVA value discounted at the company's WACC, is less than the Market Value Added value?

    A. The company needs to effect a capitalisation

    B. The share price is too high

    C. The forecast yield is ahead of market expectations

    D. The company is facing financial difficulty in the short term

56. Which one of the following is often cited as a benefit of a quote-driven market over an order-driven market?

    A. It can provide liquidity within a market where eg, some smaller companies' shares trade and where liquidity may otherwise not exist

    B. Two-way spreads are much narrower so the end consumer obtains a more advantageous price

    C. In a quote-driven market dominated by market makers, all buyers are exempt from transfer tax because of the HMRC intermediary exemption status

    D. The technology involved in a market-supplied by market makers quoting pricing and size performs much faster than legacy order-driven platforms

57. Within a market of perfect competition, which one of the following best describes why firms make only a normal profit in the long term on a single homogeneous product?

    A. Because the price is set by the interaction of consumer demand for the industry's total supply

    B. Because the typical supply and demand ratios will always show a tail-off in demand after an initial buoyancy for any consumer product

    C. Because, on a single product offering, supply will ultimately always exceed demand, leading to the falling away of around 30% of competitors with the first two years of product production

    D. Because economic prosperity is cyclical in nature, leaving firms with both a volatile profit history and predicted profit forecast charts

58. Which one of the following is the correct description of the term optimisation in relation to ETFs?

    A. The fund manager uses instruments such as boost ETFs to increase the leverage of the fund and to attain a performance over its usual benchmark

    B. The fund creates its own index by careful selection of components from the world's major indices, focussing on stable and less volatile pricing histories

    C. The fund composition and performance is based on a computer-based modelling technique for the purpose of achieving parallel performance without buying all of the basket's components

    D. A simple fund of funds model based on the traditional premise that a weighted average of all major indices should provide a performance, when compounded, in excess of any of the individual baskets

59. Which of the following is the formula to calculate interest cover?

    A. Profit before interest and tax / interest payable

    B. Profit before tax – interest receivable

    C. Profit after interest and tax / interest receivable

    D. Profit after interest / interest payable

60. How is the initial cost of subscribing for shares in a company represented in the shares held?

    A. As a percentage of NPV

    B. In the nominal value

    C. From the initial deposit receipt

    D. By the number of shares x 25p

61. If an investor trading in a derivative finds himself with a position where the share price is higher than the exercise price, the option has no value and he feels he has no choice but to abandon the option, what was the initiating trade?

    A. A call option sale

    B. A put option purchase

    C. A call option purchase

    D. A put option sale

62. How is legal title evidenced if you hold UK shares as a direct member of CREST?

    A. A direct membership sees the member's legal name appearing on the issuing company's register

    B. Through use of a nominee company which offers custody of the assets to its clients

    C. Through the company secretary who periodically makes enquiries on the percentages of shares held by beneficial owners

    D. From the share certificate which is always registered in a legal and direct holder's name

63. What is the standard formula for presenting straight line depreciation?

A. (Cost - Disposal Value) / Remaining Useful Economic Life (Years)

B. (Weighted Cost – Discounted Value) / Time to Worthlessness (days/360)

C. (Appreciation + Cost) x (Standard Depreciative Formula – Shelf Life)

D. (Marketing Value + Projected Usage, in Years) – (Pro-rata Cost – Actual Value)

64. What fact does the efficient markets hypothesis (EMH) state, that is regarded as somewhat controversial?

A. Returns on stock markets historically do not outperform deposit returns

B. It is not possible to beat the market

C. Gold is never a safe haven in turbulent markets

D. To guarantee a return, do not use public markets

65. Which one of the following best describes what is termed as marginal propensity to consume (MPC)?

A. The amount of a person's spending on consumer durables, taking into account their overall wealth, income, capital and savings

B. The proportion of disposable income a person spends, rather than saves, on consumer goods and services (after taxation)

C. Within a company's profit and loss account, it is the percentage of expenditure versus pre-tax profit on items consumed by the business in its day-to day-activity

D. In evaluating the marketability and profitability of a single homogeneous product, it is the likelihood of a successful launch at retail level

66. In what way do deferred shares differ from non-voting shares?

A. Deferred shares always have normal voting rights

B. The dividends for deferred shares will not be paid for a period of time

C. Non-voting shares never carry an entitlement to rights issues

D. Deferred shares cannot be dematerialised

67. What is the main feature of a Bermudan-style option that differentiates it from a European or American option?

A. It can only be dealt in US dollars

B. It can be exercised on a number of dates until expiry

C. They are not regarded as derivatives

D. A position always contains both a put and a call

68. How can a sovereign spread assist investors and investment managers in assessing the comparative values of the global government bond market?

   A. It shows the differences in the yields of different term-groupings of government bonds

   B. It is a direct comparison between the yields of government debt and money market rates

   C. It provides the difference in the yields of government bonds between countries

   D. It portrays the real value difference between the yields of government bonds and gold instruments

69. A company's accounting period started on 1st January. It went into administration on 31st March, stopped trading on 31st May and was wound up on 30th November. When does its accounting period end?

   A. End of March

   B. End of May

   C. End of November

   D. End of December

70. Under US company law, shareholders have limited liability and have no individual liability for any of the company's debts. How is this reflected in the classification of the shares?

   A. They are scripless

   B. They have no par value

   C. They are always in bearer form

   D. Each certificate has its own notation

71. When setting up a PAIF, what are two modes of establishment under the rules of the FCA?

   A. NURS, QIS

   B. QAIF, UCITS

   C. AIF, TEF

   D. FAIF, QFA

72. What is regarded as the most important method of client communication in order for clients to keep track of their portfolio performance?

   A. Through the prescribed frequency and mode of client reporting and the issuance of portfolio statements under MiFID

   B. Via a web-based portal, secured with password access

   C. By proactive liaison by telephone at least once daily between the investment manager and the client

   D. Through media data, provided to provide real-time or near real time (delayed) pricing data

73. How are key components of effective board practice imposed among companies seeking a listing of shares on the London Stock Exchange?

   A. Through compliance with the UK Corporate Governance Code

   B. Through the FCA's Principles of Governance

   C. Through the Association of Company Directors', Establishing a Corporate regime

   D. By following the guidance of the European Bankers' Association

74. Within the CREST system, how does a deliverer of a UK security receive real-time funds for a sale of shares to a buyer?

   A. The seller's nominated settlement bank will receive the credit of good-value funds from Bank of England funds immediately as the trade settles

   B. The seller's cash memorandum account (CMA) in CREST is credited and the total CMA balance is posted to the seller's settlement bank at end of day

   C. The seller receives a credit of real-time funds after settlement after the Register Update Request (RUR) has been accepted by the register

   D. Settlement happens when the overnight sweep is enacted at the CREST processing centre with all settlement banks remaining open to accept debits and credits for CREST deliveries

75. Which one of the following best describes the abusive behaviour of dissemination?

   A. The act of alerting another to information gained from a company insider

   B. Passing on information which gives a misleading impression

   C. Bribing a company director to divulge price-sensitive information

   D. Creating false liquidity to create an illusion of high trading volume

76. The recognition of revenue in an income statement applies when it meets which one of the following criterion?

   A. The amount can be reliably measured

   B. The source is from intended and deliberate index-linked investment

   C. The amount will be constant for the next three accounting periods

   D. It is likely that shareholders will eventually benefit

77. By using what type of financial instrument do issuers from emerging and other markets usually enable their shares to be traded outside of their jurisdictions?

   A. Credit depository interests

   B. Exchange-traded funds

   C. Global depositary receipts

   D. Eurobonds

78. If the payment of an operating-related liability is expected on a certain date but there is no certainty of the actual amount, how is this categorised for accounting purposes?

    A. Payable

    B. Provision

    C. Current liability

    D. Accrual

79. In what way does the market abuse regime help to apply to, what is considered to be, the appropriate population of possible offenders?

    A. It applies to the public at large

    B. It is one of the FCA's core principles

    C. It applies to all investors

    D. It is included in the PRA's code of conduct

80. You are an investment manager assessing the performance of an ETF index tracking fund. Which of the following would you generally expect to see when using alpha as the basis of tracking performance?

    A. A small negative alpha

    B. A small positive alpha

    C. An alpha of zero or near zero

    D. A large positive alpha

Answers to Multiple Choice Questions

1.   **C**   **Chapter 8, Section 1.4**

A company's audit committee is expected to have a minimum number of independent non-executive directors who have recent and relevant financial experience.

2.   **D**   **Chapter 4, Section 1.1.2**

OEICs are single-priced and may impose dilution levies as this method of pricing does not provide the ability to recoup dealing expenses and commissions within the spread.

3.   **D**   **Chapter 8, Section 1.2.1**

The accrual concept requires accounts to reflect revenue and expenses as they are earned and incurred.

4.   **B**   **Chapter 11, Section 1.4**

Beta is a measure of the sensitivity of a stock's return to the returns of the market as a whole.

5.   **B**   **Chapter 2, Section 2.2.1**

The present value = £20,000 ÷ $(1.06)^5$ = £20,000 ÷ 1.33823 = £14,945.

6.   **B**   **Chapter 5, Section 3.5.2**

The maximum gain on a long put = strike price – premium (100 – 13 = 87).

7.   **B**   **Chapter 9, Section 2.3.4**

Price to book ratio = share price divided by net asset value per share.

8.   **A**   **Chapter 12, Section 4.5**

The information ratio compares the excess return achieved by a fund over a benchmark portfolio to the fund's tracking error. The higher the information ratio, the more consistent a manager is.

9.   **A**   **Chapter 2, Section 1.4.2**

Variance = $[(3.22\% - 2.68\%)^2 + (-6.74\% - 2.68\%)^2 + (11.56 - 2.68)^2] \div 3 = 0.5596\%$

10. **C** **Chapter 6, Section 3.1.2**

Under a defined benefit scheme, the pension payable is related to the length of service and usually expressed as a proportion of final earnings. The investment performance of the fund would therefore be the least important factor to consider, although, in assessing such a scheme, consideration needs to be given to the funding position of the scheme and whether it can afford to pay out the promised benefits.

11. **B** **Chapter 1, Section 1.1.1**

A parallel shift in the demand curve would occur where demand for a product falls. A fall in consumer income should lead to a fall in demand for normal goods and cause the demand curve to move to the left.

12. **A** **Chapter 6, Section 1.3**

Distinguishing features of property investment are its lack of liquidity, costs associated with its management, and void periods when the property is not rented.

13. **B** **Chapter 7, Section 2.4**

Execute and eliminate orders are filled in whole or in part at, or better than, the stipulated price with any unfilled portion of the order being automatically deleted from the system.

14. **B** **Chapter 8, Section 3.1**

Operating profit = 15,410 – 11,375 – 1,675 = 2,360

Profit attributable to shareholders = operating profit 2,360 + 989 – 1,308 – 602 = 1,439

15. **A** **Chapter 3, Section 10.2.4**

Securities with a rating of BB and below (which includes B but not BBB) are considered non-investment grade and so will have a higher yield to compensate for the risk.

16. **B** **Chapter 9, Section 2.2.3**

Z-score analysis establishes whether a company is dangerously close to insolvency.

17. **D** **Chapter 8, Section 4.2**

£255,000 + £65,000 + £11,000 – £49,000 + £38,000 – £15,000 = £305,000

18. **B** **Chapter 11, Section 1.1**

Diversification is best achieved by combining securities whose returns ideally move in the opposite direction to one another.

19.   **A**   **Chapter 11, Section 1.3**

Insider dealing laws should prevent all available information appearing in the public domain.

20.   **B**   **Chapter 11, Section 4.4.3**

Anomaly switching involves moving between two bonds similar in all respects apart from the yield and price on which each trades. This pricing anomaly is exploited by switching away from the more to the less highly priced bond.

21.   **D**   **Chapter 1, Section 2.3.3**

If a country's currency falls in value against other countries, then imports will be more expensive and exports cheaper.

22.   **A**   **Chapter 7, Section 2.6**

A CMA is an electronic transaction ledger which shows the net balance of payments made and received at any time during the course of the settlement day.

23.   **B**   **Chapter 4, Section 1.1.3**

TERs are used to compare costs between collective investment schemes.

24.   **D**   **Chapter 3, Section 4.2.3**

If, for example, 20 shares are held, the post-issue share price will be $((20 \times 5) + (5 \times 4)) \div 25 = £4.80$.

25.   **C**   **Chapter 8, Section 2.4**

It is $(32,000 - 2,000) \div 5 = £6,000$.

26.   **A**   **Chapter 9, Sections 1.1 and 1.2**

Fundamental analysis tends to take a long-term approach to investment, whereas technical analysis takes a shorter-term approach.

27.   **B**   **Chapter 12, Section 3.1.3**

The holding period yield or return simply measures how much the portfolio's value has increased over a period of time and expresses it as a percentage. It suffers from the limitation of not taking into account the timing of cash flows into and out of the fund.

The money-weighted rate of return is used to measure the performance of a portfolio that has had deposits and withdrawals during the period being measured. One of the main drawbacks of this method is that to calculate the return is an iterative process and so is time-consuming.

28.   **B**   **Chapter 1, Section 2.6.1**

Spending more money and financing this through borrowing is an example of an expansionary fiscal stance.

29.   **C**   **Chapter 5, Section 2.4**

The market is said to be in backwardation when the futures prices are lower than the cash prices. Where the futures prices are higher than cash prices, the market is said to be in contango.

30.   **D**   **Chapter 3, Section 3**

$P = £1,000 \div (1 + 0.0935)^{10} = £1,000 \div 2.4445 = £409.08$

31.   **B**   **Chapter 3, Section 4.1.6**

No capital is raised under this listing method.

32.   **A**   **Chapter 12, Section 3.1.2**

The MWRR is:

$$\frac{£550,000 - £500,000 - £8,000}{\left[£500,000 + \left(£15,000 \times \frac{9}{12} \right) + \left(-£7,000 \times \frac{3}{12} \right) \right]} =$$

$$\frac{£42,000}{£500,000 + £11,250 - £1,750} =$$

$$\frac{£42,000}{£509,500} = 8.24\%$$

33.   **B**   **Chapter 3, Section 10.6.5**

A bond's sensitivity to changes in interest rates depends on a number of factors including its coupon and period to redemption. 3½% War Loan is irredeemable and will be the most sensitive to changes in interest rates, followed by the gilt strip which carries no income. The index-linked gilt carries a lower flat yield than the conventional gilt.

34.   **C**   **Chapter 6, Section 2.1**

Hedge funds are typically structured as unauthorised funds as regulators do not permit them to be marketed to retail investors.

35.   **B**   **Chapter 5, Section 3.1**

The option value, or premium, is much smaller than the price of the underlying so a change in the value of the underlying will tend to produce a much greater proportionate change in the value of the option.

36.   **D**   **Chapter 8, Section 2.2.1**

Ownership of intangible fixed assets confers certain rights; they commonly include brand names, patents, trademarks and purchased goodwill.

37.   **D**   **Chapter 3, Section 1.1.2**

The premium = (4 x 150 ÷ 500) – 1 x 100 = 20%

38.   **B**   **Chapter 3, Section 3.2.3**

MTFs are alternative trading systems which enable securities to be bought and sold.

39.   **B**   **Chapter 9, Section 2.3.2 and 2.3.3**

The PE ratio is calculated as price/earnings per share and the dividend yield is calculated as dividend/price, so a fall in the price will lower the PE ratio and raise the dividend yield.

40.   **A**   **Chapter 3, Section 1.1.6**

Following liquidation, preference shares are repaid at their nominal value if there are sufficient funds available.

41.   **A**   **Chapter 5, Section 3.5.1**

Rather than exercise the option, the investor abandons it and loses his premium – 25 pence.

42.   **D**   **Chapter 10, Section 1.1**

Profit chargeable to corporation tax is calculated by adding back depreciation and provisions but deducting any dividends from other companies as they are classed as franked income.

43.   **B**   **Chapter 11, Section 1.1**

High correlation between two assets gives a coefficient of +1.0 (perfect positive correlation) or –1.0 (perfect negative correlation). Assets with a high level of positive correlation (close to +1) tend to move in the same direction at the same time. Assets with strong negative correlations (close to –1) tend to move in opposite directions but are still strongly related to one another. Assets with a low correlation (close to 0) tend to move independently of each other and have the weakest relationships.

44.   **B**   **Chapter 11, Section 1.5**

Arbitrage is the simultaneous purchase and sale of substantially identical assets in order to profit from a price difference between the two assets.

45.   **C**   **Chapter 3, Section 1.2.5**

ADR shareholders receive the proceeds of the sale of any rights.

46.   **A**   **Chapter 7, Section 4.4.2**

The forward rate on one year's time will be based on the spot rate adjusted by the relative interest rates. So US$1.65 x 1.03 will be equivalent to £1 x 1.04. The one-year forward rate will be based on US$1.6995 = £1.04. Dividing both sides by 1.04 = US$1.6995/1.04 = £1.04/1.04. The one-year forward rate = US$1.6341 = £1.

47.   **D**   **Chapter 9, Section 2.1.2**

Asset turnover = 6 ÷ (2 + 8 + 1.5 + 0.5) = 6 ÷ 12 = 0.5

48.   **C**   **Chapter 4, Section 1.2.1**

The net asset value of an investment trust is reported daily to the stock exchange and its price will then be at either a discount or premium to that figure.

49.   **D**   **Chapter 3, Section 6.1.1**

PIBS are issued by mutual building societies. If the society demutualises, the PIBS are reclassified as PSBs.

50.   **C**   **Chapter 2, Section 1.3.2**

The two mid-range values (3rd and 4th) are 4.3% and 4.9%, so the average of the two is the median, ie, 4.6%.

51.   **B**   **Chapter 9, Section 1.2**

The assumptions underlying technical analysis are that:
- The market discounts everything.
- Prices move in trends.
- History tends to repeat itself.

52. **B** **Chapter 4, Section 2**

Exchange traded products (ETPs) are open-ended investments that are listed on an exchange and traded and settled like shares. The main types are:

- Exchange-traded funds (ETFs).
- Exchange-traded commodities (ETCs).
- Exchange-traded notes (ETNs).

They are passive investments aiming to replicate the performance of a given market, generally by tracking an underlying benchmark index.

53. **D** **Chapter 2, Section 2.2.3**

Present value of a perpetuity = annuity x 1

54. **B** **Chapter 8, Section 2.1**

The statement of the financial position of a PLC is shown in a format prescribed by the Companies Acts.

55. **B** **Chapter 9, Section 3.3**

If the present value of the company's future annual EVAs discounted at the company's WACC is greater than that implied by the MVA, this implies that the company's shares are undervalued and vice versa if less than the MVA.

56. **A** **Chapter 7, Section 2.2**

Although outdated in many respects, many practitioners argue that quote-driven systems provide liquidity to the market when trading would otherwise dry up. The NASDAQ and the LSE's SEAQ trading systems are two of the last remaining examples of quote-driven equity trading systems.

57. **A** **Chapter 1, Section 1.3.1**

A perfectly competitive firm is one that operates within an industry containing an infinite number of firms, each of which accepts the market price for a homogeneous product set by the interaction of consumer demand for the industry's total supply. In the long run, perfectly competitive firms only generate normal profits.

58. **C** **Chapter 4, Section 2.1.1**

Optimisation is a computer-based modelling technique which aims to approximate to the index through a complex statistical analysis based on past performance.

59. **A** **Chapter 9, Section 2.4.2**

Interest cover = Profit before interest and tax/interest payable.

60.   B   Chapter 3, Section 1.1.1

When a company is first created, individuals come together and subscribe funds to form the company. They may subscribe equal amounts or different ones but they will obviously have a share in the company. This ownership or part share in the company is represented by the number of shares they have in the business. For example, if the nominal value of the shares is £1 at the outset of the company this would be the amount per share of the initial subscription.

61.   B   Chapter 5, Section 3.3

With a put option, if the share price is above the exercise price, the holder (or buyer of the option) will abandon the option. The option is worthless.

62.   A   Chapter 7, Section 2.6

Direct membership involves the member's name appearing on the issuing company's register. Each member has a stock account containing records of its securities and each appoints a CREST payment bank to pay out and receive monies in respect of CREST transactions. Direct members are permitted to hold more than one account, to facilitate designation of accounts (for example, for different underlying clients).

63.   A   Chapter 8, Section 2.4

$$\text{Straight Line Depreciation} = \frac{(\text{Cost} - \text{Disposal Value})}{\text{Remaining Useful Economic Life (Years)}}$$

64.   B   Chapter 11, Section 1.3

The efficient markets hypothesis (EMH) states that it is impossible to beat the market, as prices already incorporate and reflect all relevant information. It is also a highly controversial and often disputed theory.

65.   B   Chapter 1, Section 2.1.1

The consumption function shows the planned level of consumer spending at each level of national income or GDP. It comprises a fixed amount of spending that is independent of the national income level, representing spending on necessities and an amount that varies directly with GDP.

This planned or fixed amount of spending at each level of GDP output is known as the marginal propensity to consume (MPC) and determines what proportion of consumers' post-tax, or disposable, income is spent, rather than saved, on goods and services.

66.   **B**   **Chapter 3, Section 1.1.1**

In order to retain an element of control, a company's original promoters may have deferred, or founders', shares that confer enhanced voting rights in exchange for their right to a dividend being deferred for a set period.

67.   **B**   **Chapter 5, Section**

Bermudan options lie between European and American. A Bermudan option can be exercised on any of various specified dates between original purchase of the option and expiry.

68.   **C**   **Chapter 11, Section 3.4.4**

A sovereign spread relates to the difference between the yields available on the government bonds of different sovereigns.

69.   **B**   **Chapter 10, Section 1.1**

An accounting period ends when the earliest of the following takes place:
* the company reaches its accounting date.
* it is 12 months since the start of the accounting period.
* the company starts or stops trading.

70.   **B**   **Chapter 3, Section 1.1.1**

Under company law, a company's shareholders have what is known as limited liability. This means that they have no personal liability for the payment of the company's debts and their liability extends only to any outstanding payment on the nominal value of the company's shares held if issued partly paid.

71.   **A**   **Chapter 6, 1.4.2**

PAIFs are established as either as non-UCITS retail schemes (NURSs) or as qualified investor schemes (QISs) under the rules of the FCA.

72.   **B**   **Chapter 12, 1.1**

The most appropriate method for client communication is for information to be made available to clients on a current, probably real-time, basis via the internet. Many fund managers will provide clients with a monitoring facility which enables them to inspect their portfolio performance, at least in summary form, via web-based portals.

73.   **A**   **Chapter 3, Section 2.2.2**

All listed companies are expected to abide by the UK Corporate Governance Code as a condition of their listing on the LSE, and report on how they have applied the code in their annual report and accounts.

74. **A** **Chapter 7, Section 2.6**

CREST credits the cash memorandum account (CMA) of the selling member and debits the CMA of the buying member which simultaneously generates a settlement bank payment obligation of the buying member's settlement bank in favour of the Bank of England. The selling member's settlement bank receives that payment in Bank of England funds immediately upon the debit of the purchase price to the buying member's CMA.

75. **B** **Chapter 11, 3.2.3**

Dissemination is the dissemination of information by any means which gives, or is likely to give, a false or misleading impression.

76. **A** **Chapter 8, Section 3.2**

Revenue is recognised in the income statement when it meets the following criteria:
* It is probable that any future economic benefit associated with the item of revenue will flow to the company.
* The amount of revenue can be measured with reliability.

77. **C** **Chapter 3, Section 1.2.2**

Depository receipts are increasingly issued by Asian and emerging market issuers. For example, more than 400 GDRs from 37 countries are quoted and traded on a section of the London Stock Exchange. GDRs are also listed and traded in Luxembourg, Singapore and Dubai.

78. **D** **Chapter 8, Section 2.5**

Accruals are liabilities for which the timing of payment is generally known, but the amount to be paid is uncertain. Accruals normally arise from routine transactions of the business, either of an operating or financing nature.

79. **A** **Chapter 11, Section 3.2.3**

The market abuse regime applies to the public at large, not just to the regulated sector.

80. **C** **Chapter 12, Section 4.1**

Alpha is usually defined as the degree to which a particular portfolio manager is able to outperform a benchmark index such as the FTSE 100 or the S&P 500. If a portfolio moves up and down completely in unison with the overall market it will have a zero alpha.

Syllabus Learning Map

Syllabus Unit/ Element		Chapter/ Section
Element 1	**Economics**	**Chapter 1**
1.1	**Microeconomic Theory** On completion, the candidate should:	
1.1.1	understand and be able to assess how price is determined and the interaction of supply and demand • supply curve • demand curve • reasons for shifts in curves • elasticities of demand and supply • change in price • change in demand	1.1
1.1.2	understand and be able to apply the theory of the firm: • profit maximisation • normal, supernormal and sub-normal profits • all types of costs relating to the firm • associated cost curves • explicit and opportunity costs • increasing and diminishing returns to factors • economies and diseconomies of scale • relationship between the different types of revenue	1.2
1.1.3	understand firm and industry behaviour under: • perfect competition • price discrimination • perfect free market • monopoly • oligopoly	1.3

Syllabus Unit/ Element		Chapter/ Section
1.2	**Macroeconomic Analysis** On completion, the candidate should:	
1.2.1	understand how national income is determined, composed and measured in both an open and closed economy • gross domestic product • gross national product	2.1
1.2.2	understand the stages of the economic cycle	2.2
1.2.3	understand the composition of the balance of payments and the factors behind and benefits of international trade and capital flows • current account • imports • exports • effect of low opportunity cost producers	2.3
1.2.4	understand the nature, determination and measurement of the money supply and the factors that affect it • reserve requirements • discount rate • government bond issues	2.4
1.2.5	understand the macroeconomic tools and mechanisms that the central banks and supranational organisations use and how they have been applied during recent economic cycles • qualitative easing • lenders of last resort • other mechanisms	2.5
1.2.6	understand the role, basis and framework within which monetary and fiscal policies operate; • government spending • government borrowing • private sector investment • private sector spending • taxation • interest rates • inflation • currency revaluation/exchange rates/purchasing power parity • Monetary Policy Committee	2.6
1.2.7	understand how inflation, deflation and unemployment are determined, measured and their inter-relationship	2.7
1.2.8	be able to apply the concept of nominal and real returns	2.7

Syllabus Unit/ Element		Chapter/ Section
Element 2	**Financial Mathematics and Statistics**	**Chapter 2**
2.1	**Statistics** On completion, the candidate should:	
2.1.1	Understand the different types, uses and availability of research and reports: • fundamental analysis • technical analysis • fund analysis • fund rating agencies and screening software • broker and distributor reports • sector-specific reports	1.1
2.1.2	be able to calculate the measures of central tendency: • arithmetic mean • geometric mean • median • mode	1.3
2.1.3	be able to calculate and distinguish between the different types of measures of dispersion: • variance (sample/population) • standard deviation (sample/population) • range	1.4
2.1.4	be able to calculate the correlation and covariance between two variables and analyse the data	1.5.2/1.5.3
2.1.5	understand the use of regression analysis to quantify the relationship between two variables and the interpretation of the data	1.5.1
2.2	**Financial Mathematics** On completion, the candidate should:	
2.2.1	be able to calculate and explain the present value of: • lump sums • regular payments • annuities • perpetuities	2.2
2.2.2	be able to calculate and explain the future value of • lump sums • regular payments	2.3
2.2.3	be able to calculate and interpret the data for • compound interest • simple interest • net present values (NPV) • internal rates of return (IRR)	2.1
2.2.4	understand the importance of selecting an appropriate discount rate for discounting cash flows	2.4.4

Syllabus Unit/ Element		Chapter/ Section
Element 3	**Asset Classes and Investment Strategies**	**Chapter 3**
3.1	**Characteristics of Equities** On completion, the candidate should:	
3.1.1	understand the main investment characteristics, behaviours and risks of different classes of equity: • ordinary, cumulative, participating, redeemable and convertible preference shares • bearer and registered shares • voting rights, voting and non-voting shares • ranking for dividends • ranking in liquidation • tax treatment of dividend income	1.1
3.1.2	understand the purpose, main investment characteristics, behaviours and risks of Depositary Receipts: • American Depositary Receipts • Global Depositary Receipts • beneficial ownership rights • structure • unsponsored and sponsored programmes • transferability	1.2
3.2	**Issuing Equity Securities** On completion, the candidate should:	
3.2.1	understand the purpose, key features and differences between the following • primary issues • secondary issues • issuing, listing and quotation • dual listings	2.1
3.2.2	understand the main regulatory, supervisory and trade body framework supporting UK financial markets • Companies Acts • The Financial Conduct Authority (FCA) • The Prudential Regulation Authority (PRA) • UK Listing Authority (UKLA) • HM Treasury • the Panel on Takeovers and Mergers (POTAM) • exchange membership and rules • relevant trade associations and professional bodies	2.2

Syllabus Unit/ Element		Chapter/ Section
3.2.3	understand the structure of the London Stock Exchange, the types of securities traded on its markets and the criteria and processes for companies seeking admission: • Main Market • AIM • PLUS markets • Market participants • Implications for investors	2.3
3.3	**Equity Markets and Trade Execution** On completion, the candidate should:	
3.3.1	be able to apply fundamental UK regulatory requirements with regard to trade execution and reporting • best execution • aggregation and allocation • prohibition of conflicts of interests and front running	3.1
3.3.2	understand the key features of the main trading venues: • regulated and designated investment exchanges • recognised overseas investment exchanges • structure and size of markets • whether quote or order driven • main types of order – limit, market, iceberg, named • liquidity and transparency	3.2
3.3.3	understand the concepts of trading cum, ex, special cum and special ex: • the meaning of 'books closed', 'ex-div' and 'cum div', cum, special ex, special cum, and ex rights • effect of late registration	3.3
3.3.4	assess how the following factors influence equity markets and equity valuation: • trading volume and liquidity of domestic and international securities markets • relationship between cash and derivatives markets, and the effect of timed events • market consensus and analyst opinion • changes to key pricing determinants such as credit ratings and economic outlook	3.4
3.3.5	understand the purpose, construction, application and influence of indices on equity markets: • developed and emerging market regional and country sectors • market capitalisation sub-sectors • free float and full market capitalisation indices	3.5

Syllabus Unit/ Element		Chapter/ Section
3.4	**Corporate Actions** On completion, the candidate should:	
3.4.1	understand the purpose and structure of corporate actions and their implications for investors: • stock capitalisation or consolidation • stock and cash dividends • rights issues • open offers, offers for subscription and offers for sale • placings	4.1
3.4.2	calculate the theoretical effect on the issuer's share price of the following mandatory and optional corporate actions: • bonus/scrip • consolidation • rights issues	4.2
3.4.3	understand and be able to assess the following in respect of corporate actions: • rationale offered by the company • the dilution effect on profitability and reported financials	4.3
3.5	**Fixed-Income Securities** On completion, the candidate should:	
3.5.1	understand the main issuers of government debt and the main investment characteristics, behaviours and risks of the major government bond classes: • supranationals • sovereign governments • public authorities: local government/municipalities • short-, medium- and long-dated • dual-dated • undated • floating rate • zero coupon	5.1
3.5.2	understand the relationship between interest rates and government bond prices: • yield • interest payable • accrued interest (clean and dirty prices) • effect of changes in interest rates	5.2
3.5.3	understand the main investment characteristics, behaviours and risks of index-linked debt: • retail prices index as a measure of inflation • process of index linking • indexing effects on price, interest and redemption • return during a period of zero inflation	5.1.7

Syllabus Unit/ Element		Chapter/ Section
3.6	**Characteristics of Corporate Debt** On completion, the candidate should:	
3.6.1	understand the main issuers of corporate debt and the main investment characteristics, behaviours and risks of secured debt • corporates • financial institutions and special purpose vehicles • fixed and floating charges • debentures • types of asset backed securities • mortgage-backed securities • securitisation process • yield to maturity • roles of participants	6.1
3.6.2	Understand the main investment characteristics, behaviours and risks of the main types of unsecured debt • income bonds • subordinated • high yield • convertible bonds • conditional convertible bonds • rating	6.2
3.7	**Characteristics of Eurobonds** On completion, the candidate should:	
3.7.1	understand the main investment characteristics, behaviours and risks of Eurobonds: • types of issuer: sovereign, supranational and corporate • types of eurobond: straight, FRN/VRN, subordinated, asset-backed • convertible • international bank syndicate issuance • immobilisation in depositories • continuous pure bearer instrument: implications for interest & capital repayment • taxation of interest and capital gains • accrued interest, ex-interest date	7.1
3.8	**Bond Issues** On completion, the candidate should:	
3.8.1	Understand the main bond pricing benchmarks and how they are applied to new bond issues: • spread over government bond benchmark • spread over/under LIBOR • spread over/under swap	9.2

Syllabus Unit/ Element		Chapter/ Section
3.8.2	Understand and be able to explain the characteristics and uses of strips and repos • use in packaged products • which gilts strippable • resulting number of securities • coupon and redemption payments • as zero coupon bond • payment dates	8
3.9	**Fixed Income Markets and Trade Execution** On completion, the candidate should:	
3.9.1	understand the role, structure and characteristics of global corporate bond markets: • decentralised dealer markets and dealer provision of liquidity • impact of default risk on prices • relationship between bond and equity markets • bond pools of liquidity versus centralised equity exchanges • access considerations • regulatory/ supervisory environment • ICMA and other relevant trade associations	9.1
3.9.2	understand the differences in yield, spread and price quotation methods, and the circumstances in which they are used	9.2
3.10	**Valuation of Fixed-Income Securities** On completion, the candidate should:	
3.10.1	understand the purpose, influence and limitations of global credit rating agencies, debt seniority and ranking in cases of default/ bankruptcy: • senior • subordinated • mezzanine • PIK (Payment in Kind)	10.1
3.10.2	be able to analyse sovereign, government and corporate credit ratings from an investment perspective: • main rating agencies • country rating factors • debt instrument rating factors • investment & sub-investment grades • use of credit enhancements • impact of grading changes	10.2

Syllabus Unit/ Element		Chapter/ Section
3.10.3	understand the role of ratings agencies; their impact on the market and the structure of their credit ratings • agencies • rating effect on the cost of raising funds • use as a risk identification tool • types of securities rated • rating securitised products • implications of the conflicts in the rating process	10.3
3.10.4	be able to analyse the factors that influence bond pricing: • yield to maturity • credit rating • impact of interest rates • market liquidity • clean and dirty prices	10.4
3.10.5	understand the characteristics of the yield curve: • normal • inverted	10.5
3.10.6	be able to analyse fixed income securities using the following valuation measures, and understand the benefits and limitations of using them: • flat yield • nominal and real return • gross redemption yield (using internal rate of return) • net redemption yield • modified duration	10.6
3.10.7	be able to analyse the specific features of bonds from an investment perspective: • coupon and payment date • maturity date • embedded put or call options • convertible bonds • exchangeable bonds	10.7
3.10.8	calculate and interpret: • simple interest income on corporate debt • conversion premiums on convertible bonds • flat yield • accrued interest (given details of the day count conventions)	10.7
3.10.9	understand and be able to apply the main bond strategies: • bond switching • riding the yield curve • immunisation • rate anticipation • horizon analysis • barbell/bullet/ladder portfolios	10.8

Syllabus Unit/ Element		Chapter/ Section
3.10.10	understand the role of fixed interest in a portfolio • stable cash flow • lower volatility • standard investment vehicles	10.9
3.11	**Cash and Money Market Instruments** On completion, the candidate should:	
3.11.1	be able to analyse the main investment characteristics, behaviours and risks of cash deposit accounts • deposit taking institutions and credit risk assessment • term, notice, liquidity and access • fixed and variable rates of interest • inflation • statutory protection • foreign currency deposits	11.1
3.11.2	be able to analyse the main investment characteristics, behaviours and risks of Treasury Bills and Commercial paper • purpose and method of issue • minimum denomination • normal life • zero coupon and redemption at par • redemption • market access, trading and settlement • maturity • discounted security • unsecured and secured • asset backing	11.2
3.11.3	be able to analyse the main investment characteristics, behaviours and risks of repurchase agreements • purpose • sale and repurchase at agreed price, rate and date • reverse repo – purchase and resale at agreed price and date • documentation	11.3
3.11.4	be able to analyse the main characteristics, risks and returns of money market funds • cash assets only • near cash assets • pricing, liquidity and fair value • market access, trading and settlement	11.4
3.11.5	be able to analyse the factors to take into account when selecting between different types of cash deposits, accounts and money market funds	11.5

Syllabus Unit/ Element		Chapter/ Section
Element 4	**Collective Investments**	**Chapter 4**
4.1	**Characteristics of Collective Investment Funds and Companies** On completion, the candidate should:	
4.1.1	be able to analyse the key features, accessibility, risks, tax treatment, charges, valuation and yield characteristics of open-ended investment companies (OEICs)/investment companies with variable capital (ICVCs)	1.1
4.1.2	be able to analyse the key features, accessibility, risks, tax treatment, charges, valuation and yield characteristics of unit trusts	1.1
4.1.3	be able to analyse the key features, accessibility, risks, tax treatment, charges, valuation and yield characteristics of investment trusts	1.2
4.2	**Exchange-Traded Products** On completion, the candidate should:	
4.2.1	Be able to analyse the key features, accessibility, risks, tax treatment, charges, valuation and yield characteristics of the main types of exchange-traded products	2
4.3	**Structured Products** On completion, the candidate should:	
4.3.1	be able to analyse the key features, accessibility, risks, valuation and yield characteristics of the main types of retail structured products and investment notes, compared with other forms of direct and indirect investment: • structure • income and capital growth • investment risk and return • counterparty risk • expenses • capital protection • tax efficiency	3

Syllabus Unit/ Element		Chapter/ Section
4.4	**Analysis of Collective Investments** On completion, the candidate should:	
4.4.1	be able to analyse the factors to take into account when selecting collective investments: • quality of firm, management team, product track record and administration • investment mandate – scope, controls, restrictions and review process • investment strategy • exposure, allocation, valuation and quality of holdings • asset cover and redemption yield • track record compared with appropriate peer universe and market indices • key man risk (KMR) and how this is managed by a firm • measures to prevent price exploitation by dominant investors • total expense and turnover ratios • liquidity, trading access and price stability	4

Element 5	Derivatives	Chapter 5
5.1	**General** On completion, the candidate should:	
5.1.1	understand the purpose, risks and rewards associated with derivatives: • uses of derivatives: hedging, speculation and arbitrage • counterparty, market and liquidity risk • specific risks to buyers, writers and sellers	1.1
5.1.2	understand the differences between forwards, futures and options: • obligations • default risk • margin • contract specification flexibility • establishment of price and term	1.3
5.1.3	understand the mechanisms for futures and options pricing and the relationship with the underlying cash prices: • a contract for difference • contango • backwardation • in-the-money • at-the-money • out-of-the money	2.4/3.1

Syllabus Unit/ Element		Chapter/ Section
5.2	**Futures** On completion, the candidate should:	
5.2.1	understand the core concepts and key characteristics of futures: • obligations • fixed price • fixed exercise date • closing out • physical delivery	2
5.3	**Options** On completion, the candidate should:	
5.3.1	understand the core concepts and key characteristics of options: • calls and puts • writing and buying • exercise price • European style • American style	3.1
5.3.2	be able to calculate and understand the purpose and construction of option strategies and the potential risks, rewards and costs of each: • buying calls • buying puts • selling calls • selling puts • caps • floors • collars	3.5
5.3.3	be able to calculate the intrinsic and time value of an option and understand the factors determining option premiums and pricing including: • influences on intrinsic value and time value • volatility • time to expiry • strike or exercise price • underlying asset price • interest rates • dividends/coupons	3.6

Syllabus Unit/ Element		Chapter/ Section
5.4	**Warrants** On completion, the candidate should:	
5.4.1	be able to analyse the key investment characteristics and differences between equity warrants and equity options: • purpose and issuers • benefits to an investor or speculator • time to expiry • where traded • strike prices • effect of exercise • settlement • gearing against the underlying • effect of corporate actions on equity warrants	5.1
5.4.2	be able to analyse the main purposes, characteristics, behaviours and relative risk and return of warrants and covered warrants • benefit to the issuing company • right to subscribe for capital • effect on price of maturity and the underlying security • exercise and expiry • calculation of the conversion premium on a warrant	5.2
5.5	**Swaps** On completion, the candidate should:	
5.5.1	be able to analyse the purpose, key characteristics, benefits, costs and valuation of: • interest rate swaps and swaptions • types of swap agreements: vanilla, basis, coupon, index and currency • interest calculations (compared to bond markets) • foreign exchange forwards and swaps • equity forwards, swaps and swaptions: • volatility • bullet • Variance	6

Syllabus Unit/ Element		Chapter/ Section
Element 6	**Other Investments**	**Chapter 6**
6.1	**Property** On completion, the candidate should:	
6.1.1	understand and analyse the differences between the residential and commercial property markets	1.1
6.1.2	understand and apply the rationale for investing in commercial property within a portfolio: • cash flow • investment returns • lower volatility • diversification	1.2
6.1.3	understand how the direct commercial property market operates • ownership and lease structures • buying and selling • costs – transactional and management • property valuation • use of gearing • investment performance measurement and role of the Investment Property Databank • Databank	1.3
6.1.4	understand the routes to indirect property investment • unit linked life and pension funds • life bonds • limited partnerships • derivatives	1.4
6.1.5	• be able to compare and contrast the key features, accessibility, risks, tax treatment, charges, valuation and yield characteristics of real estate investment trusts (REITs) with property authorised investment funds (PAIFs)	1.4
6.1.6	understand the risks associated with property investment, both direct and indirect: • individual property risk (heterogeneous and indivisible asset) • valuation compared with price • market risk • sector risk • liquidity	1.5

Syllabus Unit/ Element		Chapter/ Section
6.2	**Alternative Investments** On completion, the candidate should:	
6.2.1	understand and be able to explain the main purpose and basic characteristics of the following alternative investments: • private equity • structured products • commodities (eg, timber) • collectables (eg, fine wine, art, autographs, stamps, coins) • hedge funds (single hedge funds, fund of funds) • currencies • absolute return	2
6.2.2	understand the main risks inherent in alternative investments	2.6
6.2.3	understand the role of alternative investment strategies in a portfolio	2.6
6.3	**Pensions** On completion, the candidate should:	
6.3.1	Understand the benefits and options of pension planning: • tax relief • capital gains • lifetime allowance • annuity versus income drawdowns • self-invested personal pensions • small self-administered schemes	3

Element 7	Financial Markets	Chapter 7
7.1	**Exchanges** On completion, the candidate should:	
7.1.1	understand the role of the exchanges for trading: • shares • bonds • derivatives	1.1
7.1.2	understand why companies obtain listings on overseas stock exchanges: • liquidity • marketability • sources of capital/capital requirements	1.2
7.1.3	understand the role and responsibilities of the London Stock Exchange (LSE) • member firm supervision • market regulation • provision of a primary securities market • provision of a secondary securities market • dissemination of market information	1.3

Syllabus Unit/ Element		Chapter/ Section
7.2	**Dealing and Settlement** On completion, the candidate should:	
7.2.1	understand the differences between a primary market and a secondary market in respect of gilts, UK corporate bonds and eurobonds: • two way trading • new issues • market prices	2.1
7.2.2	understand the following order types and their differences: • limit • at best • fill or kill • execute and eliminate • multiple fills	2.2
7.2.3	understand the main operational risks in dealing internationally	2.7
7.2.4	understand how the settlement cycle operates for collectives: • UK alternative funds • exchange-traded funds • investment trusts	2.8
7.3	**International Markets** On completion, the candidate should:	
7.3.1	understand the characteristics and risks of an established market: • UK • USA • Japan • China • Europe	3.1
7.3.2	understand the characteristics and risks of a developing market: • economic liberalisation • foreign ownership restrictions • currency restrictions • liquidity • ownership recognition	3.2
7.4	**Foreign Exchange** On completion, the candidate should:	
7.4.1	understand the basic structure and operation of the foreign exchange market: • market place • OTC market • cross rates • settlement system • interest rates • effect of demand for goods • effect of exchange rate changes	4.1

Syllabus Unit/ Element		Chapter/ Section
7.4.2	understand the difference between spot and forward exchange rates: • settlement periods • effect of interest rates	4.2
7.4.3	understand the determinants of spot foreign exchange prices: • currency demand – transactional and speculative • economic variables • cross border trading of financial assets • interest rates • free and pegged rates	4.3
7.4.4	be able to calculate forward exchange rates using: • premiums and discounts • interest rate parity	4.4

Element 8	Accounting	Chapter 8
8.1	**Basic Principles** On completion, the candidate should:	
8.1.1	understand and be able to apply the legal requirements to prepare accounts and the differences between private and public company requirements • responsibility for preparation • Accounting Standards Board • required information in accounts	1.1
8.1.2	understand the objectives and qualitative characteristics of accounts: • decision useful information • relevance • faithful representation • comparability • verifiability • understandability • timeliness • materiality	1.2
8.1.3	understand the function and purpose of: • the Accounting Standards Board (ASB) • International Accounting Standards Board (IASB) • International Financial Reporting Standards (IFRSs)	1.3
8.1.4	understand the purpose of the auditors' report and the reasons why reports are modified: • independent assessment • modified reports	1.4

Syllabus Unit/ Element		Chapter/ Section
8.2	**Statement of Financial Position** On completion, the candidate should:	
8.2.1	understand the purpose and main contents of the balance sheet: • company's financial position • fixed assets • current assets • current liabilities • long term borrowing • issued share capital • capital reserves • revenue reserves	2.1
8.2.2	understand how assets are classified and valued: • investments/long-term investments • tangibles • intangibles • pre-payments • stocks/work in progress • trade receivables • directors' loans • land/buildings • machinery	2.2
8.2.3	be able to apply the difference between capitalising costs and expensing costs	2.2
8.2.4	understand how goodwill and other intangible assets arise and are treated: • types of intangibility (eg, trademarks, patents, client relations) • calculation upon acquisition • amortisation • impairment • capitalisation	2.3
8.2.5	understand and be able to apply the different methods of depreciation and amortisation: • straight line • reducing balance	2.4
8.2.6	understand how liabilities are categorised: • due in less than or more than one year • current liabilities • trade payables • bank overdraft • dividends due • tax due • non-current liabilities • debenture stock • long-term loans	2.5

Syllabus Unit/ Element		Chapter/ Section
8.2.7	understand the difference between authorised and issued share capital and capital reserves and revenue reserves	2.6
8.2.8	understand contingent liabilities and post-balance sheet events	2.7
8.3	**Income Statement** On completion, the candidate should:	
8.3.1	understand the purpose and main contents of the income statement: • company's performance • turnover • cost of sales • depreciation charge • interest income / expenditure • investment income • taxation • profit • extraordinary items and exceptional items	3.1
8.3.2	be able to apply the basic concepts underlying revenue recognition	3.2
8.3.3	understand how expenses, provisions and dividends are accounted for	3.3
8.3.4	be able to calculate the different levels of profit given revenue and different categories of cost: • gross profit • profit before tax • net profit • profit excluding exceptionals	3.4
8.4	**Cash Flow Statement** On completion, the candidate should:	
8.4.1	understand the purpose and main contents of the cash flow statement: • generation and use of cash • ignore accruals • ignore movements in balance sheet items • remove depreciation and book profits • cash from customers / operations • cash to suppliers / employees • dividends / interest paid / received • purchase fixed assets • tax paid • loans drawn/repaid • share issue/redemption	4.1
8.4.2	be able to calculate net cash flow from operations from operating profit	4.2
8.5	**Consolidated Company Report and Accounts** On completion, the candidate should:	
8.5.1	understand the basic principles of accounting for: • associated companies • subsidiaries	5

Syllabus Unit/ Element		Chapter/ Section
Element 9	**Minority Interests**	**Chapter 9**
9.1	**Fundamental and Technical Analysis** On completion, the candidate should:	
9.1.1	understand the characteristics and examples of fundamental and technical analysis: • primary objectives • quantitative techniques • charts • primary movements • secondary movements • tertiary movements	1
9.2	**Yields and Ratios** On completion, the candidate should:	
9.2.1	understand and be able to analyse securities using the following profitability ratios: • return on capital employed (ROCE) • asset turnover • net profit margin • gross profit margin • equity multiplier	2.1
9.2.2	be able to calculate the following profitability ratios • return on capital employed • asset turnover • net profit margin • gross profit margin • equity multiplier	2.1
9.2.3	understand and be able to analyse securities using the following gearing ratios: • financial gearing • interest cover	2.4
9.2.4	be able to calculate interest cover	2.4
9.2.5	understand and be able to analyse securities using the following liquidity ratios: • working capital (current) ratio • liquidity ratio (acid test) • z-score analysis	2.2
9.2.6	be able to calculate the following liquidity ratios: • working capital (current) ratio • liquidity ratio (acid test)	2.2

Syllabus Unit/ Element		Chapter/ Section
9.2.7	understand and be able to analyse securities using the following investors' ratios: • earnings per share (EPS) • earnings before interest, tax, depreciation, and amortisation (EBITDA) • earnings before interest and tax (EBIT) • historic and prospective price earnings ratios (PERs) • dividend yields • dividend cover • price to book	2.3
9.2.8	be able to calculate the following investors' ratios: • earnings per share (EPS) • earnings before interest, tax, depreciation, and amortisation (EBITDA) • historic and prospective price earnings ratios (PERs) • dividend yields • dividend cover • Price to book	2.3
9.2.9	understand the difficulties in interpreting the above ratios for: • companies in different industries • different companies within the same industry • the same company over successive accounting periods	2.5
9.3	**Valuation** On completion, the candidate should:	
9.3.1	understand equity valuations based on dividends: • Gordon Growth Model	3.1
9.3.2	be able to calculate equity valuations based on earnings and assets: • price earnings ratios (PERs) • net asset value	3.2
9.3.3	understand and be able to apply the basic concept behind shareholder value models: • economic value added (EVA) • market value added (MVA)	3.3

Element 10	Taxation	Chapter 10
10.1	**UK Corporation Tax** On completion, the candidate should:	
10.1.1	understand what corporation tax is and the circumstances in which trading companies are taxed and the payment timetable: • taxable profits • franked investment income • capital losses • depreciation • when due	1.1

Syllabus Unit/ Element		Chapter/ Section
10.1.2	be able to apply the differences between franked and unfranked investment income: • payment from net profits • sources of franked income • corporation tax payable on unfranked income	1.2
10.2	**UK Personal Taxes** On completion, the candidate should:	
10.2.1	understand the application of income tax on earnings, dividend and interest income	2.1
10.2.2	understand which types of company can be held within and the tax advantages of investing in: • ISAs • Enterprise Investment Schemes (EIS) • Venture Capital Trusts (VCTs)	2.4
10.2.3	understand capital gains tax (CGT) and the assets that are subject to or exempt from CGT: • sale of shares/convertible loan stock • sale of gilts/corporate bonds • losses carried forward • principal residence/second homes	2.5
10.2.4	understand what inheritance tax (IHT) is and the assets subject to or exempt from IHT • potentially exempt transfers • lifetime transfers • transfers to a spouse • business property relief	2.6
10.2.5	understand the principle of domicile and its implication on private client management	2.7
10.3	**Overseas Taxation** On completion, the candidate should:	
10.3.1	understand the principles of withholding tax (WHT): • types of income subject to WHT • relief through double taxation agreements • deducted at source	3
10.3.2	understand the principles of double taxation relief (DTR) • purpose	3

Syllabus Unit/ Element		Chapter/ Section
Element 11	**Portfolio Management**	**Chapter 11**
11.1	**Risk and Return** On completion, the candidate should:	
11.1.1	understand the concept of correlation of performance between asset classes	1.1
11.1.2	understand the main principles of modern portfolio theory (MPT) and the need for diversification: • purpose • correlation • diversification • future returns • efficient frontier	1.2
11.1.3	understand the main propositions and limitations of the Efficient Markets Hypothesis (EMH) • strong form • semi-strong form • weak form	1.3
11.1.4	understand the assumptions underlying the construction of the capital asset pricing model (CAPM) and its limitations	1.4
11.1.5	understand the main principles behind Arbitrage Pricing Theory (APT) • risk free rate • market rates • diversification • uncorrelated • risk premium • beta • differences between CAPM and APT	1.5
11.1.6	understand the implications of foreign currency risk on an investor investing in domestic/overseas assets	1.6
11.2	**The Role of the Portfolio Manager** On completion, the candidate should:	
11.2.1	understand the establishment of: • relationships with clients • client investment objectives • risk profile • income and/or growth • time horizons • restrictions • liquidity • discretionary and non-discretionary portfolio management	2.1 2.2

Syllabus Unit/ Element		Chapter/ Section
11.2.2	understand the establishment of the investment strategy: • the importance of asset allocation • the difference between active and passive management • top down versus bottom up active management • implications of the various investment styles on portfolio risk and return • ethical, environmental and socially responsible investment	
11.2.3	understand deciding on the benchmark and the basis for review: • portfolio's asset allocation • risk/return profile • alternative investments • taxation • maintenance of capital value	2.3
11.2.4	understand the measurement and evaluation of performance and the purpose and requirements of annual and periodic reviews	2.3
11.2.5	understand the issues associated with conflicts of interest and the duty to clients	2.5
11.3	**Market Information and Research** On completion, the candidate should:	
11.3.1	understand how to access and use regulatory, economic and financial communications: • news services • government resources and statistics • broker research and distributor information • regulatory resources	3.1
11.3.2	be able to assess key factors that influence markets and sectors: • responses to change and uncertainty • volume, liquidity, and nature of trading activity in domestic and overseas markets • market abuse regime – enforcement and effectiveness • publication of announcements, research and ratings	3.2
11.3.3	be able to assess the interactive relationship between the securities and derivatives markets, and the impact of related events on markets	3.3
11.3.4	be able to assess the interactive relationship between different forms of fixed-interest securities and the impact of related events on markets	3.4

Syllabus Unit/ Element		Chapter/ Section
11.4	**Portfolio Construction** On completion, the candidate should:	
11.4.1	understand the main types of portfolio risk and their implications for investors: • systemic risk • market risk – asset price volatility, currency, interest rates, commodity price volatility • investment horizon • liquidity, credit risk and default • counterparty risk	4.1
11.4.2	understand the core principles used to mitigate portfolio risk: • correlation • diversification • active and passive strategies • hedging and immunisation	4.2
11.4.3	understand the key approaches to investment allocation for bond, equity and balanced portfolios: • asset class • geographical area • currency • issuer • sector • maturity	4.3
11.4.4	understand the main aims and investment characteristics of the main cash, bond and equity portfolio management strategies and styles: • indexing/passive management • active/market timing • passive-active combinations • growth versus Income • market capitalisation • liability-driven • immunisation • long, short and leveraged • issuer and sector-specific • contrarian • quantitative	4.4
11.4.5	understand how portfolio risk and return are evaluated using the following measures: • holding period return • total return and its components • standard deviation • volatility • covariance and correlation • risk-adjusted returns • benchmarking	4.5

Syllabus Unit/ Element		Chapter/ Section
11.5	**Investment Selection** On completion, the candidate should:	
11.5.1	be able to apply a range of essential information and factors to form the basis of appropriate financial planning and advice for clients: • financial needs, preferences and expectations • income and lifestyle – current and anticipated • attitude to risk • level of knowledge about investments • existing debts and investments	5.1
11.5.2	be able to analyse and select strategies suitable for the client's aims and objectives in terms of: • investment horizon • current and future potential for capital protection, growth and yield • protection against inflation • risk tolerance • liquidity, trading and ongoing management • mandatory or voluntary investment restrictions • impact of tax • impact of fees and charges	5.2
11.5.3	be able to analyse and select investments suitable for a particular portfolio strategy: • direct holdings, indirect holdings and combinations • role of derivatives • impact on client objectives and priorities • balance of investments	5.2

Element 12	Performance Management	Chapter 12
12.1	**Administration and Maintenance** On completion, the candidate should:	
12.1.1	be able to apply key elements involved in managing a client portfolio: • systematic and compliant approach to client portfolio monitoring, review, reporting and management • selection of appropriate benchmarks to include market and specialist indices, total return and maximum drawdown • arrangements for client communication	1.1
12.1.2	understand how changes can affect the management of a client portfolio: • client circumstances • financial environment • new products and services available • administrative changes or difficulties • investment-related changes (eg, credit rating, corporate actions) • portfolio rebalancing • benchmark review	1.2

Syllabus Unit/ Element		Chapter/ Section
12.2	**Performance Benchmarks** On completion, the candidate should:	
12.2.1	understand the purpose and concept of benchmarking	2.1
12.2.2	understand the weighting methods, uses and market in respect of: • FTSE 100 • FTSE All-share index • FTSE Actuaries Government Securities indices • MSCI World index • Dow Jones Industrial Average index • S&P 500 index • Nikkei 225 • WMA benchmarks • Hang Seng	2.2
12.2.3	understand the differences between a single and a composite (synthetic) benchmark	2.4
12.2.4	understand why free-float indices were introduced and understand the benefits they bring	2.3
12.2.5	understand Global Investment Performance Standards (GIPS) as a method of benchmarking:	2.5
12.3	**Performance Attribution** On completion, the candidate should:	
12.3.1	understand total return and its components	3.1.1
12.3.2	be able to calculate the deviations from a performance benchmark attributable to: • actual versus relative performance • asset allocation • stock selection	3.2
12.4	**Performance Measures** On completion, the candidate should:	
12.4.1	be able to calculate the money weighted rates of return (MWRR) and the time weighted rates of return (TWRR)	3.1.2/3.1.3
12.4.2	understand the concepts of: • alpha • beta • Sharpe ratio • Treynor ratio • Jensen ratio • information ratio	4

Examination Specification

Each examination paper is constructed from a specification that determines the weightings that will be given to each element. The specification is given below.

It is important to note that the numbers quoted may vary slightly from examination to examination as there is some flexibility to ensure that each examination has a consistent level of difficulty. However, the number of questions tested in each element should not change by more than plus or minus 2.

Element Number	Element	Questions
1	Economics	5
2	Financial Mathematics and Statistics	4
3	Asset Classes and Investment Strategies	15
4	Collective Investments	5
5	Derivatives	6
6	Other Investments	4
7	Financial Markets	6
8	Accounting	10
9	Investment Analysis	6
10	Taxation	4
11	Portfolio Management	10
12	Performance Management	5
Total		**80**

CISI Chartered MCSI Membership can work for you...

Studying for a CISI qualification is hard work and we're sure you're putting in plenty of hours, but don't lose sight of your goal!

This is just the first step in your career; there is much more to achieve!

The securities and investments industry attracts ambitious and driven individuals. You're probably one yourself and that's great, but on the other hand you're almost certainly surrounded by lots of other people with similar ambitions.

So how can you stay one step ahead during these uncertain times?

Entry Criteria for Chartered MCSI Membership

As an ACSI and MCSI candidate, you can upgrade your membership status to Chartered MCSI. There are a number of ways of gaining the CISI Chartered MCSI membership.

A straightforward route requires candidates to have:
- a minimum of one year's ACSI or MCSI membership;
- passed a full Diploma; Certificate in Private Client Investment Advice & Management or Masters in Wealth Management award;
- passed the IntegrityMatters with an A grade; and
- successfully logged and certified 12 months' CPD under the CISI's CPD Scheme.

Alternatively, experienced-based candidates are required to have:
- a minimum of one year's ACSI membership;
- passed the IntegrityMatters with an A grade; and
- successfully logged and certified six years' CPD under the CISI's CPD Scheme.

Joining Fee:	Current Grade of Membership	Grade of Chartership	Upgrade Cost
	ACSI	Chartered MCSI	£75.00
	MCSI	Chartered MCSI	£30.00

By belonging to a Chartered professional body, members will benefit from enhanced status in the industry and the wider community. Members will be part of an organisation which holds the respect of government and industry, and can communicate with the public on a whole new level. There will be little doubt in consumers' minds that chartered members of the CISI are highly regarded and qualified professionals and as a consequence will be required to act as such.

The Chartered MCSI designation will provide you with full access to all member benefits, including Professional Refresher where there are currently over 60 modules available on subjects including Behavioural Finance, Cybercrime and Conduct Risk. CISI TV is also available to members, allowing you to catch up on the latest CISI events, whilst earning valuable CPD hours.

Revision Express Interactive

You've bought the workbook... now test your knowledge before your exam.

Revision Express Interactive is an engaging online study tool to be used in conjunction with CISI workbooks. It contains exercises and revision questions.

Key Features of Revision Express Interactive:

- Examination-focused – the content of Revision Express Interactive covers the key points of the syllabus
- Questions throughout to reaffirm understanding of the subject
- Special end-of-module practice exam to reflect as closely as possible the standard you will experience in your exam (please note, however, they are not the CISI exam questions themselves)
- Interactive exercises throughout
- Extensive glossary of terms
- Useful associated website links
- Allows you to study whenever you like

IMPORTANT: The questions contained in Revision Express Interactive elearning products are designed as aids to revision, and should not be seen in any way as mock exams.

Price per elearning module: £35
Price when purchased with the CISI workbook: £100 (normal price: £110)

To purchase Revision Express Interactive:

call our Customer Support Centre on:
+44 20 7645 0777

or visit CISI Online Bookshop at:
cisi.org/bookshop

For more information on our elearning products, contact our Customer Support Centre on +44 20 7645 0777, or visit our website at cisi.org/study

Professional Refresher

Self-testing elearning modules to refresh your knowledge, meet regulatory and firm requirements, and earn CPD.

Professional Refresher is a training solution to help you remain up-to-date with industry developments, maintain regulatory compliance and demonstrate continuing learning.

This popular online learning tool allows self-administered refresher testing on a variety of topics, including the latest regulatory changes.

There are over 120 modules available which address UK and international issues. Modules are reviewed by practitioners frequently and new ones are added to the suite on a regular basis.

Benefits to firms:
- Learning and testing can form part of business T&C programme
- Learning and testing kept up-to-date and accurate by the CISI
- Relevant and useful – devised by industry practitioners
- Access to individual results available as part of management overview facility, 'Super User'
- Records of staff training can be produced for internal use and external audits
- Cost-effective – no additional charge for CISI members
- Available for non-members to purchase

Benefits to individuals:
- Comprehensive selection of topics across sectors
- Modules are regularly refreshed and updated by industry experts
- New modules added regularly
- Free for members
- Successfully passed modules are recorded in your CPD log as active learning
- Counts as structured learning for RDR purposes
- On completion of a module, a certificate can be printed out for your own records

The full suite of Professional Refresher modules is free to CISI members, or £250 for non-members. Modules are also available individually. To view a full list of Professional Refresher modules visit:

cisi.org/refresher

If you or your firm would like to find out more, contact our Client Relationship Management team:

+ 44 20 7645 0670
crm@cisi.org

For more information on our elearning products, contact our Customer Support Centre on +44 20 7645 0777, or visit our website at cisi.org/refresher

Professional Refresher

Top 5

SCORM COMPLIANT

Integrity & Ethics
- High-Level View
- Ethical Behaviour
- An Ethical Approach
- Compliance vs Ethics

Anti-Money Laundering
- Introduction to Money Laundering
- UK Legislation and Regulation
- Money Laundering Regulations 2017
- Proceeds of Crime Act 2002
- Terrorist Financing
- Suspicious Activity Reporting
- Money Laundering Reporting Officer
- Sanctions

General Data Protection Regulation (GDPR)
- Understanding the Terminology
- The Six Data Protection Principles
- Data Subject Rights
- Technical and Organisational Measures

Information Security and Data Protection
- Cyber-Security
- The Regulators

UK Bribery Act
- Background to the Act
- The Offences
- What the Offences Cover
- When Has an Offence Been Committed?
- The Defences Against Charges of Bribery
- The Penalties

Latest

Cryptocurrencies
- Bitcoin
- Altcoins
- Central Bank Digital Currency and Cryptofiat
- Trading Cryptocurrencies
- The Impact of Cryptocurrencies

Change Management
- Types of Change
- Change Theories
- The Complexities of Change
- Leading Change
- Key Skills and Competencies

Regulatory Update
- General Regulatory Changes
- Sector Changes

Common Reporting Standard (CRS)
- What is the CRS?
- Implementation and Compliance
- Practical Issues
- The Global Perspective

Cross-Border Investment Services
- The UK System
- Overseas Regulation
- Applicability
- Face-to-Face Meetings
- Distance Communications
- Brexit Implications
- Gifts and Entertainment
- Tax Evasion, Money Laundering, and Terrorist Financing

Operations

Best Execution
- What Is Best Execution?
- Achieving Best Execution
- Order Execution Policies
- Information to Clients & Client Consent
- Monitoring, the Rules, and Instructions
- Best Execution for Specific Types of Firms

Approved Persons Regime
- The Basis of the Regime
- Fitness and Propriety
- The Controlled Functions
- Principles for Approved Persons
- The Code of Practice for Approved Persons

Corporate Actions
- Corporate Structure and Finance
- Life Cycle of an Event
- Mandatory Events
- Voluntary Events

Wealth

Client Assets and Client Money
- Protecting Client Assets and Client Money
- Segregation and Holding
- Due Diligence of Custodians and Banks
- Reconciliations
- Records and Accounts
- CASS Oversight

Investment Principles and Risk
- Diversification
- Factfind and Risk Profiling
- Investment Management
- Modern Portfolio Theory and Investing Styles
- Direct and Indirect Investments
- Socially Responsible Investment
- Collective Investments
- Investment Trusts
- Dealing in Debt Securities and Equities

Banking Standards
- Introduction and Background
- Strengthening Individual Accountability
- Reforming Corporate Governance
- Securing Better Outcomes for Consumers
- Enhancing Financial Stability

Suitability of Client Investments
- Assessing Suitability
- Risk Profiling
- Establishing Risk Appetite
- Obtaining Customer Information
- Suitable Questions and Answers
- Making Suitable Investment Selections
- Guidance, Reports and Record Keeping

International

Foreign Account Tax Compliance Act (FATCA)
- Foreign Financial Institutions
- Due Diligence Requirements
- Reporting
- Compliance

MiFID II
- The Organisations Covered by MiFID II
- The Products Subject to MiFID II
- The Origins of MiFID II
- The Impact of MiFID II
- The Products Covered by MiFID II
- Cross-Border Business Under MiFID II

UCITS
- The Original UCITS Directive
- UCITS III
- UCITS IV
- Non-UCITS Funds
- Latest Developments

cisi.org/refresher

Feedback to the CISI

Have you found this workbook to be a valuable aid to your studies? We would like your views, so please email us at learningresources@cisi.org with any thoughts, ideas or comments.

Accredited Training Partners

Support for examination students studying for the Chartered Institute for Securities & Investment (CISI) Qualifications is provided by several Accredited Training Partners (ATPs), including Fitch Learning and BPP. The CISI's ATPs offer a range of face-to-face training courses, distance learning programmes, their own learning resources and study packs which have been accredited by the CISI. The CISI works in close collaboration with its ATPs to ensure they are kept informed of changes to CISI examinations so they can build them into their own courses and study packs.

CISI Workbook Specialists Wanted

Workbook Authors

Experienced freelance authors with finance experience, and who have published work in their area of specialism, are sought. Responsibilities include:
- Updating workbooks in line with new syllabuses and any industry developments
- Ensuring that the syllabus is fully covered

Workbook Reviewers

Individuals with a high-level knowledge of the subject area are sought. Responsibilities include:
- Highlighting any inconsistencies against the syllabus
- Assessing the author's interpretation of the workbook

Workbook Technical Reviewers

Technical reviewers provide a detailed review of the workbook and bring the review comments to the panel. Responsibilities include:
- Cross-checking the workbook against the syllabus
- Ensuring sufficient coverage of each learning objective

Workbook Proofreaders

Proofreaders are needed to proof workbooks both grammatically and also in terms of the format and layout. Responsibilities include:
- Checking for spelling and grammar mistakes
- Checking for formatting inconsistencies

If you are interested in becoming a CISI external specialist call:
+44 20 7645 0609

or email:
externalspecialists@cisi.org

For bookings, orders, membership and general enquiries please contact our Customer Support Centre on +44 20 7645 0777, or visit our website at cisi.org